RedH Enterprise Linux 9 for Beginners

A comprehensive guide for learning, administration, and deployment

Vishesh Kumar

Geetanjali Mehra

www.bpbonline.com

First Edition 2024

ISBN: 978-93-55516-626

LIMITS OF LIABILITY AND DISCLAIMER OF WARRANTY

www.bpbonline.com

Dedicated to

My mother ***Ibha Jha***
and
My father ***Vijay Kant Jha***

– Vishesh Kumar

My mother ***Indu Mehra***
and
My father ***Mohan Lal Mehra***

– Geetanjali Mehra

About the Authors

- **Vishesh Kumar** is a seasoned Linux professional and technical writer with over 20 years of extensive experience in Linux, system administration, networking, cyber security and cloud technologies. His journey commenced in 2002 with Red Hat Linux 3, and since then, he has been actively involved in professional work across multiple Linux, Unix, and Cloud platforms. Additionally, Vishesh holds multiple certifications in Red Hat Enterprise Linux and IT Security. As the founder of "Linux Mantra IT Services," Vishesh leads a global team providing comprehensive Linux and Cloud-based services and solutions. Over the years, he has collaborated with numerous national and international organizations, including Yatra Ltd, Infoedge Ltd, Fortum, Ebix, Capgemini, Gilpin Travels, Radius Synergies, and many others, offering consultancy and services.

- **Geetanjali Mehra**, with over 17 years of experience in IT industry has played a key role in various organizations to manage various databases on multiple flavours of Linux. She has automated various server and database administration related routine tasks via the use of bash scripts. Her commitment to learn new technology and innovative problem-solving approach make her a valuable asset in the field. Geetanjali's dedication to sharing her knowledge is evident in her book.

About the Reviewers

- **Alberto Gonzalez** is a seasoned Principal Architect at Red Hat with two decades of professional experience in various roles. Currently specializing in infrastructure, cloud computing, and virtualization, he brings a wealth of expertise to the field. Alberto is also an accomplished author, having written three influential books. His works include a comprehensive guide on automation with Ansible, another on containers featuring Docker, and the latest publication titled *Linux Server Cookbook: Get Hands-on Recipes to Install, Configure, and Administer a Linux Server Effectively*, published by BPB Publications.

  Beyond his written contributions, Alberto has a rich history of creating engaging content and delivering effective teaching sessions. He frequently shares his insights at conferences, where he passionately discusses emerging technologies. Additionally, he actively contributes to the learning experience by designing and leading hands-on labs for participants, enhancing their practical understanding of the subject matter.

- **Sidhartha Rajak** is presently serving as a Technical Officer - 'A' in the Ministry of Defence, Government of India, accumulating over 6 years of valuable experience in Linux Server Administration and Virtual Machines. His array of certifications includes 'Cyber Security - Information Assurance Professional' from the esteemed DIAT (Defence Institute of Advanced Technology), 'Information Security' & 'Computer Networking and Security' from C-DAC (Centre for Development of Advanced Computing), and 'Virtualization & Cloud Computing' from NIELIT (National Institute of Electronics & Information Technology). Sidhartha has also undergone concise training in "Log Analysis Techniques and Management" from CERT-In (Indian Computer Emergency Response Team).

  His ongoing research endeavors focus on exploring Bare Metal Hypervisors, Cron Jobs, and optimizing Incremental Backup strategies within Linux Server Administration. In addition to his core competencies, Sidhartha is skilled in Dynamic Web Application Development, possesses proficiency in Hosting, Domain Configuration, and exhibits adept skills in Database Server Management.

Acknowledgements

We want to express our deepest gratitude to our family and friends, especially our parents, for their unwavering support and encouragement while writing this book.

We are also grateful to BPB Publications for allowing us to write this book and for their guidance and editorial expertise in bringing it to fruition. We are also deeply grateful to all the reviewers who gave their spare time to review the book's contents editorially and technically. The valuable participation and collaboration of all the reviewers, technical experts, and editors is remarkable.

We would also like to express our gratitude for the invaluable contributions of our clients and colleagues throughout our years in the tech industry. Their challenging assignments and projects have significantly enhanced our understanding and expertise in various technologies, enabling us to delve deeper into the subject matter.

We also extend our heartfelt gratitude to all the readers interested in this book. If this book proves helpful to you in any capacity, the months dedicated to its creation will have been incredibly meaningful to us. Thank you for your support and engagement.

Preface

RHEL is the widely used enterprise level Linux distribution and learning Linux is the demand of the hour. It is accepted as a de-facto standard worldwide to host several types of servers because it is scalable , reliable, and durable . Most of the IT-Industry software has Linux as its base, thus increasing the demand of specialists who can manage Linux Servers and thus drive the IT industry. This book will help you understand the Linux Operating System so that you will be the future Linux System Administrator.

In this book, you will learn the concepts of Linux/Unix from scratch easily and practically. It offers a comprehensive guide for effectively handling, managing, and administering one or multiple RHEL servers. It covers a wide spectrum of topics, including installation of RHEL, managing services and processes, various user-level and administrative-level commands, user management, managing filesystem and disk partitions, concepts of cloud and containers, package installation and management, database and web server setup, understanding shell scripts, strategies for enhancing server performance and much more.

After reading a wide array of topics given in this book, you will be able to install and handle not only Redhat Linux servers but many of the other Linux distributions. This book will allow you to become a competent Linux system specialist easily and practically.

This book is designed for System Engineers, Network Engineers, Linux Jr. Administrators, and Windows Administrators who want to gain knowledge in managing RHEL on a daily basis. This book also caters for the needs of Red Hat professionals who want to refresh their knowledge and get comfortable in using RHEL 9.

Chapter 1: The First Step to Linux – This book starts with a basic understanding of Linux Systems. In the first chapter, you will get acquainted with this open-source software and its application in today's world. This chapter will make you familiar with important Linux terminologies and its architecture to get you started. Then, this will guide you how to install/simulate RHEL 9 to get your system ready. Then it moves ahead to guiding how you get into your newly installed machine and how you can interact with your machine in the first place. Here you will try to get information about your machine

Chapter 2: Linux Filesystem and Administration – The second chapter will give you insight into the Linux Filesystem structure. Here you will know how the files in Linux are organized in the storage space of RHEL.

Chapter 3: Knowing Linux Commands – This chapter provides the essential content of the book. Here, you will master various basic and administrative-level commands to get the most out of the Linux box.

Chapter 4: Managing Processes and Services in RedHat Linux – The chapter discusses processes and services in Linux, and how are they managed.

Chapter 5: Handling and Managing Files – This chapter describes how you will handle files and directories and perform other operations on them.

Chapter 6: Managing Users and File Permissions – This chapter discusses user management and demonstrates the procedure to set permissions on files so that users can access them according to their roles.

Chapter 7: Interacting with Bash Shell and Scripting – This chapter will introduce you to an agent that is used to interact with Linux Systems . And that agent is a shell which makes it possible to do great things on Linux. Shell, actually , beautifies Linux. Here you will also learn how to interact with the shell and write shell scripts that can automate any task.

Chapter 8: Security and Networking in Linux – Chapter 8 will show how you can secure Linux Server and its network.

Chapter 9: Partitioning in Linux – Chapter 9 will show you how to create and manage disk partitions using the traditional vs LVM way.

Chapter 10: Containers – In this chapter, you will learn the fundamentals of containers. This chapter discusses various tools that you can use to build and manage containers. Containers allow you to host and run multiple applications independently on the same machine.

Chapter 11: Cloud Computing – Chapter 11 will give you highlights of Cloud computing in RHEL9.

Chapter 12: Graphical User Interface – Chapter 12 gives you highlights on the Desktop environment of RHEL machine. It shows how you can use and run various graphical applications on Linux environment.

Chapter 13: Software Updates and Patch Management – This chapter demonstrates how can you subscribe to RedHat Subscription Manager (RHSM), register your machines to RHSM and perform updates on them.

Chapter 14: Package Installation – Chapter 14 describes package installation and management in detail.

Chapter 15: Performance Monitoring and Tuning – Chapter 15 discusses various tools and utilities that are available to monitor the system's health and its current status. It will also give you hands-on performance monitoring and tuning of the Linux System.

Chapter 16: Backup and Troubleshooting in Linux – Chapter 16 deals with various utilities that can be used to take backup of the available data and how you can restore data and perform recovery when required.

Chapter 17: Web Server and Database Server Setup in Linux – This chapter demonstrates the webserver and database server setup in Linux.

Chapter 18: Miscellaneous – Miscellaneous topics are also covered in this book so that the readers can learn more and gain more.

Coloured Images

Please follow the link to download the
Coloured Images of the book:

https://rebrand.ly/460y2yk

We have code bundles from our rich catalogue of books and videos available at **https://github.com/bpbpublications**. Check them out!

Errata

We take immense pride in our work at BPB Publications and follow best practices to ensure the accuracy of our content to provide with an indulging reading experience to our subscribers. Our readers are our mirrors, and we use their inputs to reflect and improve upon human errors, if any, that may have occurred during the publishing processes involved. To let us maintain the quality and help us reach out to any readers who might be having difficulties due to any unforeseen errors, please write to us at :

errata@bpbonline.com

Your support, suggestions and feedbacks are highly appreciated by the BPB Publications' Family.

Piracy

If you come across any illegal copies of our works in any form on the internet, we would be grateful if you would provide us with the location address or website name. Please contact us at **business@bpbonline.com** with a link to the material.

If you are interested in becoming an author

If there is a topic that you have expertise in, and you are interested in either writing or contributing to a book, please visit **www.bpbonline.com**. We have worked with thousands of developers and tech professionals, just like you, to help them share their insights with the global tech community. You can make a general application, apply for a specific hot topic that we are recruiting an author for, or submit your own idea.

Reviews

Please leave a review. Once you have read and used this book, why not leave a review on the site that you purchased it from? Potential readers can then see and use your unbiased opinion to make purchase decisions. We at BPB can understand what you think about our products, and our authors can see your feedback on their book. Thank you!

For more information about BPB, please visit **www.bpbonline.com**.

Join our book's Discord space

Join the book's Discord Workspace for Latest updates, Offers, Tech happenings around the world, New Release and Sessions with the Authors:

https://discord.bpbonline.com

Table of Contents

CHAPTER 1

The First Step to Linux

Introduction

Today, Linux is used as the base operating system on almost all kinds of IT deployments and servers. It is used as a de-facto standard to host several types of applications and software, as it is scalable, reliable and durable. Linux is an open-source operating system released under GPL. Multiple distributions of Linux have been made available since its birth. RHEL is the widely used enterprise-level Linux distribution among them. It is an open-source operating system software backed by an organization named RedHat. This is why it is named RedHat Enterprise Linux System. This open-source software distribution is added with enhanced security features and support services so that it can readily be made available to big enterprises for their production use.

Structure

In this chapter, you will learn about the following topics:

- Open source software vs Enterprise solution
- Features of RedHat Enterprise Linux
- Linux architecture
- Installation of RHEL9
- Using RHEL machine

Objectives

The objective of this chapter is multifold. This chapter will help you understand the benefits of using RHEL over other open-source distributions. This chapter will help you learn the basic terminologies used in Linux systems. You will learn about the various ways to install RHEL9 and look at step-by-step instructions, along with screenshots, to make a RHEL9 machine ready. You will also learn various basic commands to get information about the system.

Open-source software vs Enterprise solution

When any open-source distribution is supported by an enterprise, organizations using that software distribution receive the benefits of enterprise support, reliability, scalability, and quality. Before delving into the key benefits of using RHEL, let us discuss why one should use open-source software and look at the benefits of using its enterprise counterpart.

Benefits of open-source software

Open-source software's source code is readily available for use. Anyone can read, modify, and then freely redistribute it or even sell copies of the modified code, and all this can be done under the same license. It is a collaborative effort without any vendor lock-in. The code is freely accessible and is also reviewed and modified by the community from time to time. So, it has transparency features, as one can view the code and know what is going on inside. **Open-Source software** (**OSS**) solutions provide reliability as they are constantly and actively updated by peers. It is not owned by a single organization or a person but is a collaborative effort. Since this is community-maintained, any bug fixes and changes are done at a faster pace and more efficiently than by the teams of any proprietary software. OSS has longevity as it is reviewed by a community of users and not by a single person or organization. You are free to use the source code anywhere, anytime, and for anything.

So far, we have seen many benefits of open-source solutions, but what are its limitations that motivate organizations to use enterprise solutions. Let us discuss.

Problems with open source

Open-source software is free, but you have to maintain it, secure it and make it production-ready for your business requirement yourself. This is not a complex task if you are a small / mid-sized organization, but organizations lined up for expansion and digital growth require backed-up support and security. They want a secure and reliable solution for their growing business needs. Bigger organizations have concerns for SSO, larger capacity data storage, security of their distributed growing information, etc. Their requirements are more complex than those of small and mid-sized businesses. This is where enterprise open-source software comes in; it provides support and service-level agreement. They provide support such that a company's production environment remains stable, irrespective of workloads.

Anybody can download and install an open-source project, but that can carry risk. It can have security vulnerabilities that organizations have to tackle with their own. Most of the time, they need expert advice to identify the security breaches and mitigate them. And this is where enterprise open-source software comes in. A company providing enterprise open-source software has a dedicated security team that helps in identifying the potential threats and dealing with them in customers' business scenario. Their team provides security bug fixes and patching of the software from time to time.

Open-source software provides varied options for a particular business requirement. If we want to deploy a web server, it has multiple options to choose from. If we want a database server, it again has multiple solutions to choose from. For distributed storage, data streaming, and so on, open source provides varied options. But what if you want to work with all these stacks together. Integrating all these technologies requires expert advice. Here, you will need an enterprise solution that has an expert team guiding you through the deployment of multiple technologies safely and efficiently.

Features of Enterprise open source

Any open-source product is said to be an enterprise open-source product if it has been produced after thorough testing and added security features, has been tuned for performance and retreated for security flaws, and it has a security team behind it and has processes in place for responding to new security vulnerabilities. They notify their customers about security issues and how to remediate them:

- **Added enterprise feature**: Big enterprises care about their growing information, its storage and complex IT infrastructure. Enterprise open-source software is software that is backed and supported by an organization so that enterprises receive more stable, reliable, secure and scalable solutions.
- **Support and service level agreement**: Enterprise open-source software provide a service level agreement that has concerns of running a production environment all the time. They provide a 24/7 support team that companies need during any unexpected downtimes. They also provide regular updates, security patches and bug fixes.
- **Integrating with multiple technology stacks**: At times, expanding organizations need to move into newer technology stacks. This decision requires several brainstorming sessions and expert guidance. Without proper steps and considerations, production can come to a halt while transitioning into the newer stack. Since a multitude of open-source software solutions are available, choosing

the best solution creates chaos among key decision makers without proper guidance. Any enterprise open-source software provides valuable consulting and guidance to the organizations in moving to newer technology stack.

- **Focused on customer requirement**: Enterprise open-source software is controlled and backed by a single entity responding to what the customer wants. New features are embedded into open-source software according to customers' needs.
- **Software life cycle**: Enterprise solution has longevity as it is maintained and updated by a single entity. When new releases are made, support for upgrading of the customer's system is immediately raised, thus supporting software up to a long life.
- **Auditing and compliance**: There are auditing and compliance concerns for bigger organizations. An enterprise open-source solution is valuable in this regard as well.
- **Delivers quality in IT infrastructure**: Companies providing enterprise open-source software test their software code with multiple hardware configurations before releases, ensuring quality software and solutions.
- **Enhanced quality of code**: Any open-source software lacks quality in code as it is reviewed by a community and not by a single person/organization. When an open-source software is backed up by experts inside an organization, companies gets enhanced quality of code.

Now, let's see what enterprise features are incorporated in RHEL by RedHat.

Features of RedHat Enterprise Linux

RedHat uses community-built code, added some security and other enterprise features on it and what is developed is more stable and reliable OS that is, RHEL. Most enterprises are using RHEL for their OS platform.

Licensing is a legal authorization of using a product or solution. Software is also a product, and like any other product, the software also has a licensing scheme. RedHat also comes with different software products, and RedHat Enterprise Linux Version 9 is one of them.

Commercial use of RedHat Linux is not allowed without purchasing the required license of RedHat Enterprise Linux. RedHat does not provide software updates for Enterprise Linux without purchasing the license. Software updates are must-haves for machines in production, as security bugs are patched only through software updates. In the absence of proper licensing, RedHat does not provide any kind of support and services over call or email.

Commercially using RedHat Enterprise Linux without proper licensing may be considered illegal and actionable as per local regulatory laws. There are other Linux-related products of RedHat that do not require a license, and they can be used if the user feels that they need RedHat Linux for some other purposes.

Other than licensing, RHEL is introducing new features with each new release. RHEL uses OpenSSL libraries for encryption and other security needs, with RHEL 9 OpenSSL version 3 being used in RHEL 9, and OpenSSL 3 supporting the Provider concept. OpenSSL 3 Provider module allows pluggable support for encryption/hashing and cipher algorithm. With the Provider module, new encryption algorithm support can be added without changing the OpenSSL Version of OS.

On the security front, RHEL 9 has disabled root login with password from SSH by default. So without changing configuration, remote login with the root account and password is discontinued now. Using a password increases the chances of brute force attacks, so key can be used for login with the root.

RHEL9 ships with control groups and Podman, a container Management utility. These days, containers are the backbone of cloud and serverless architecture, and building, deploying and running a container has become easy with control groups and Podman.

Previous RedHat Linux versions always had a common problem: not allowing the user to select a version before installing a particular software. RHEL 9 addresses that problem. The version selection helps the user to pick the right version for applications/software to install, as per business and technical requirements.

RedHat is enhancing its solution with each new release, providing a reliable and consistent solution to enterprises. We saw that many enhancements to the Linux Kernel have been made by RedHat and are still being made. These enhancements to Linux Kernel make RHEL a popular choice among enterprises.

Before looking at the installation of RHEL, let us study Linux core concepts. The next few sections will discuss Linux fundamentals briefly. Those who are already familiar with Linux internals and concepts can skip this section and move directly to the installation process.

Linux architecture

Linux Kernel and a set of software packages make up the Linux OS. Important components of the Linux OS are Kernel, system library, utility programs, hardware layer and shell.

Kernel

Any Linux OS distribution is based on Linux Kernel, which is the core part of Linux OS. It is fully developed in C language and interacts directly with the hardware. It performs all the fundamental operations of OS, such as hardware communication, memory management, process management, file management and service requests. It is the kernel that interacts with the hardware and the user processes. Linux kernel is a completely abstract layer, invisible to the user, working in its own kernel space. Kernel has full access to system resources such as CPU and memory. So, if kernel crashes, the entire Linux OS crashes. To interact with the hardware, a set of software called system libraries are implemented at the OS level.

System libraries

System libraries are used for implementing the operating system functionality, such as hardware communication. These system libraries are used to interact with the kernel to perform OS functionalities.

Utility programs/applications

Utility programs/applications are required to manage system at user level and let the users perform their daily duties. User programs run at their own space. They are the processes managed by kernel but do not have access to all the system resources. So, when a user program/process crashes, the OS is still running.

Shell

This is one of the pillars of Linux System. The beauty of Linux lies in shell, and Shell is what makes me love Linux. Seems silly? It's not. We hope you will feel the same after you learn about it in greater detail. Shell acts as an agent that sits between the user and the kernel. It take commands from the user and provides it to the kernel, and then the kernel preforms its functions, such as allocating memory and processor.

Linux FileSystem

Linux File System is a hierarchical data structure that organizes data in the storage system. Data is stored in the form of files, as in other OSes such as Windows. Files are grouped into directories. When multiple files share common properties and are stored together in a group, it is a filesystem. There can be different filesystems supported in different Linux Distributions. Some of the commonly used filesystems are **`ext2`**, **`ext3`** and **`ntfs`** . Each filesystem is stored in a separate disk partition. So, we can say that files on Linux systems are physically organized into multiple filesystems and disk partitions. Logically, Linux filesystems are organized into a tree-like structure in the form of files, directories and subdirectories.

Root (`/`), being the top-level directory, is the parent directory in the Linux Filesystem. It is denoted by '`/`' (a forward slash). Any other subdirectories or files are stored inside the root directory (`/`). Whether it is user-created files or system-generated default files, they will reside only under the '`/`' directory.

By default, any Linux distribution has, at most, these files/directories inside the root (`/`) filesystem:

- `/bin`
- `/boot`
- `/dev`
- `/etc`
- `/home`
- `/lib`
- `/media`
- `/mnt`
- `/misc`
- `/opt`
- `/usr`
- `/root`
- `/sbin`
- `/tmp`
- `/proc`
- `/sys`
- `/var`

Each of these directories has been provided with some specific purposes. Some of the directories are being used to store just the system data, while other directories are user specific. Users can create further levels of subdirectories inside `/` (root) or any of its sub-directories with appropriate permissions. Each or some of the mentioned sub-directories may or may not be kept under separate disk partitions. Each partition is characterized by a filesystem. Further details regarding the Linux filesystem, specifically in RHEL, will be discussed in *Chapter 2, Linux File System and Administration*. What we have discussed so far would be sufficient to proceed with the installation of RHEL.

SuperUser

Every Linux system has a top-level user known as root user. This is the default user created during installation. Root user is the powerful user who has all the access rights to the system and can view and do anything on the system. He is the super-user. Any process or applications running on the system should not be owned or run by root. If any application is running with the privileges of root, then it can modify any system files or damage the complete system. When you install any software, you may have noticed that the use of root user is completely discouraged. A specific software that you install on the Linux machine should be owned by a specific non-root user who should be given only the permissions that are required for that software to perform its tasks. Moreover, root user is known to all as it is the default admin user on any Linux machine. A hacker may break into the system as the root user and perform any malicious activity. So, it is beneficial to never use this user; instead, create a normal user that can be given privileged rights to perform admin duties. Further details on delegation of super-user rights will be discussed in *Chapter 6, Managing Users and File Permissions*. Hopefully, this short discussion on super-user may have provided you with the sufficient knowledge to install the product which is the part of our next section.

GUI

GUI gives you same experience with using Linux systems as you receive in Windows OS. Linux GUI provides you with an interface to interact with the system to perform some tasks. It gives you an experience of using desktop environments in Linux. Linux system provides multiple desktop environments, such as Gnome and KDE, but RHEL9 supports only Gnome. If you are more fascinated about GUI than about CLI, then *Chapter 12, Graphical User Interface*, is for you.

Now, we have enough knowledge about the Linux system to move on to the installation of RHEL 9.

Installation of RHEL9

Now that you know some basics of Linux Fundamentals, you are ready to perform the installation procedures. RHEL9 can be installed in multiple ways. But here, we will talk only about standard methods and not the advanced ones. This chapter will demonstrate the default GUI-based Linux installation. The following section will show you the step-by-step installation of RHEL9 software.

Getting the software

The first question that comes to your mind is to get the operating system. Here, we are talking about RedHat Enterprise Linux 9. It can be downloaded from the RedHat official website. The link to download RHEL9 software is **https://developers.RedHat.com/products/rhel/download**. With this link, you can download the trial version of the product or the subscription version.

Click on the **Download** button. It will ask you for your RedHat login credentials. If you don't have them, just register yourself and proceed with the login on the website.

After you log in, the software will begin to download automatically. After the download is complete, you will receive an iso image file **`rhel-baseos-9.0-x86_64-dvd`** of size 7.99 GB.

You can perform the installation on VMware or on a standalone machine. You also have the option to dual-boot your machine along with Windows or other operating systems. But the scope of this book is limited; we will only show the installation on a stand-alone machine or on a Windows machine. If you have a Windows machine, you can download and install VMware on it, and install and learn Linux inside VMware. In rest of the chapters, this book will be using standalone Linux installation box to demonstrate the concepts.

Hardware compatibility

Let's discuss the prerequisites of the machine you are going to install RHEL9 on. However, the installation is completed without any glitch in most modern machines. The prerequisites are as follows:

- **Processor architecture:**

  The CPU Architecture that is supported by RHEL9 are listed below:

  - AMD, Intel and ARM 64-bit Architectures
  - IBM Power Systems, Little Endian
  - 64-bit IBM Z

- **Disk space requirement:**

  You must have at least 10 GB of free disk space available to install RHEL9.

- **Memory requirement:**

  Recommended minimum RAM is 1.5GB.

Installation using VMware

This section assumes that you have Windows machine with 64-bit CPU architecture. We will use VMware Workstation Player 16 to install VMware and then RHEL9.

Download and install VMware

You can follow these steps to download and then install VMware:

1. You can download VMware using the following link:

   https://customerconnect.vmware.com/downloads/info/slug/desktop_end_user_computing/vmware_workstation_player/16_0

   Check whether the **Select Version** scroll button shows **16.0**. Click on **Go to Downloads**.

2. Scroll down and choose your platform. Click **Download Now** to start the VMware download.
3. You will receive an **.exe** file. Execute the file to install VMware software. This is GUI-based installation. Proceed to complete all the steps prompted, and your software will be ready to use.
4. The first screen asks, **Do you want to allow this app to make changes in your device** now? Click **Yes**.
5. Click **Next** on the **Welcome** screen.
6. On the next window, accept the license agreement and click **Next**.
7. Move to the following windows with all the default options set, and your installation will begin.
8. Click on **Finish** after it completes the installation.
9. Now, you can open your VMware from the **Start Menu**, as shown in *Figure 1.1*:

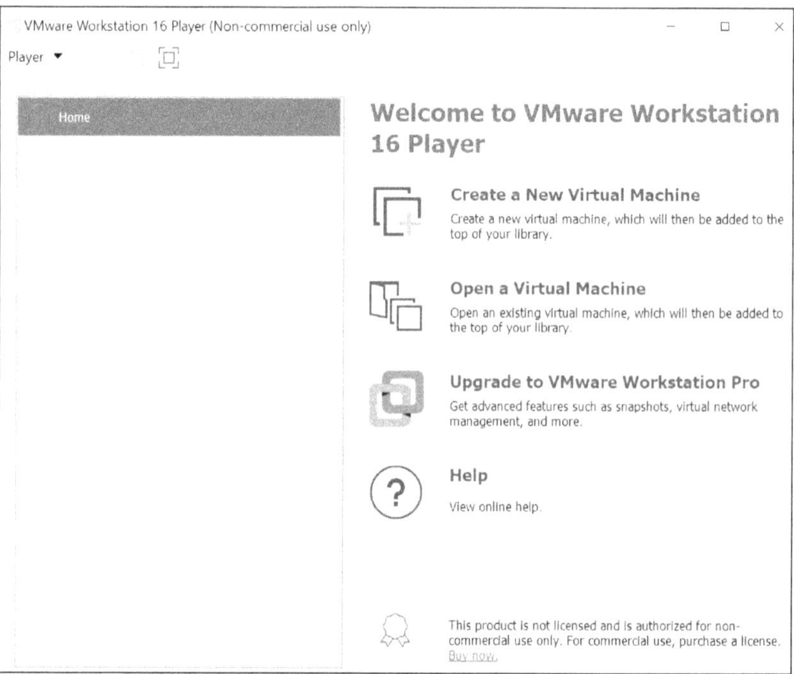

***Figure 1.1**: VMware Workstation Player*

Using VMware

Open VMware workstation from the **Start Menu**. You have to create a new Virtual Machine to install RHEL9 software. Following are the steps to create a new virtual machine:

1. Click on the **Create a New Virtual Machine** option to create a new virtual machine. **New Virtual Machine wizard** will open, as shown in *Figure 1.2*:

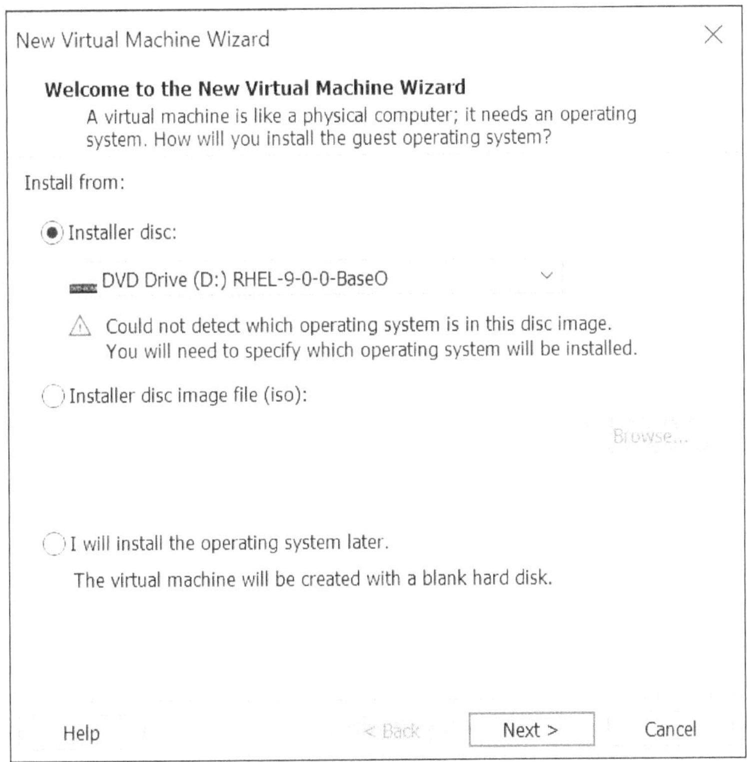

Figure 1.2*: New VM Wizard:choosing iso to install*

If you have already downloaded RHEL9 software's iso, the system will detect it automatically. Use the default **Installer disc:** option. Else, select your installer disc image **`.iso`** file by clicking on the **Browse** button for the **Installer disc image file (`iso`):** option. Click on **Next**.

2. The next window will ask you which OS you are going to install in this virtual machine. Select **Linux** for **Guest Operating System**. **Version** drop-down allows you to choose the version of the OS that you are going to install.

Note: The version of VMware that this book is using is VMware Workstation 16 and this does not support RHEL9 which can become visible in future releases of VMware Workstation Player.

So, choose **Other Linux 5.x kernel 64-bit** as RHEL9 is based on **kernel version 5.14.**

Refer to *Figure 1.3*:

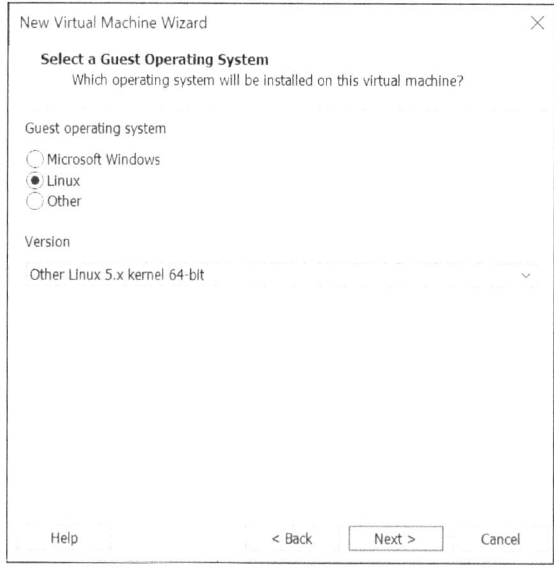

Figure 1.3: Selecting the type of OS that is being installed on VM

Click on **Next**.

3. Type the name of your new machine, using which you would like to identify it. We call it RHEL9Box. Choose the location where you want to keep your virtual machine. You can leave the default unchanged, as shown in *Figure 1.4*:

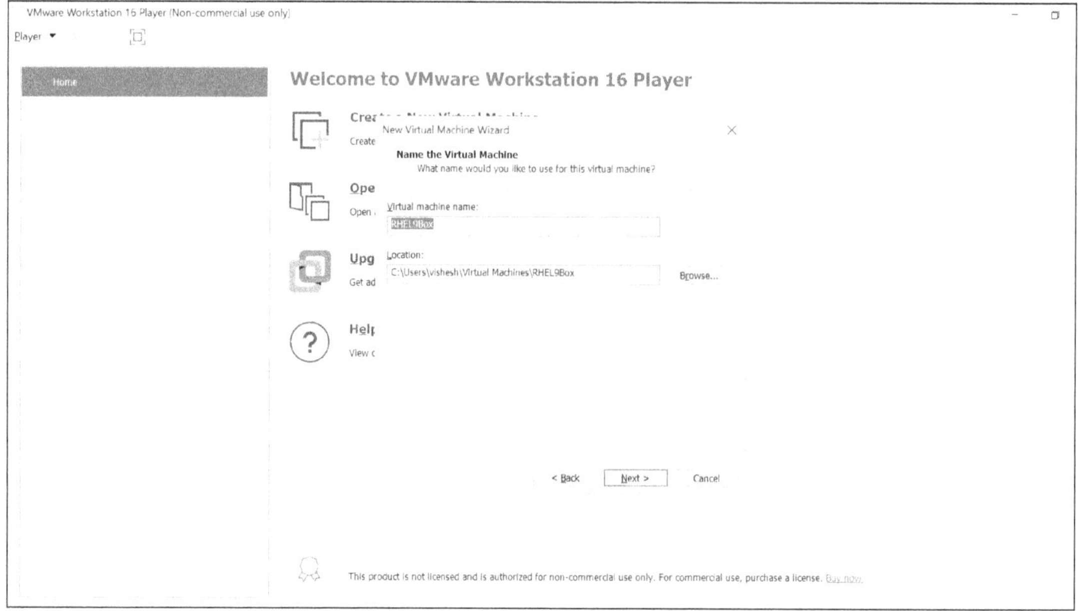

Figure 1.4: Choosing name and location of new VM

Click on the **Next** button.

4. It will ask you for the maximum disk size. Choose a value more than the required minimum. Let's choose **20 GB**. You can choose any number greater than 10 if your system free space allows you to do so, as shown in *Figure 1.5*:

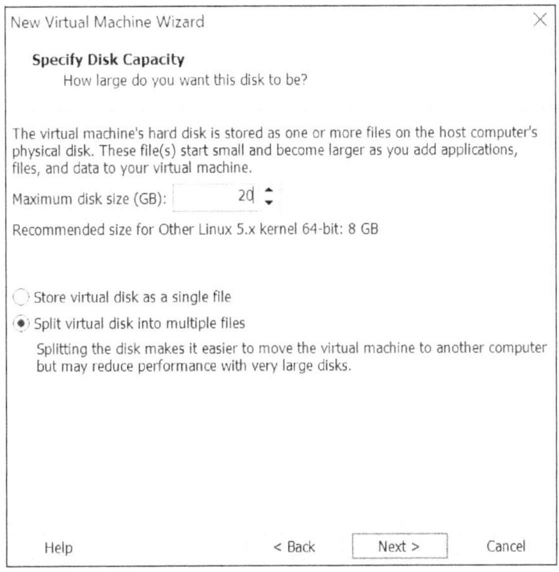

***Figure 1.5:** Choosing correct disk size to install RHEL9*

5. The next window (see *Figure 1.6*) will show you the configuration using which your newly virtual machine will be created.

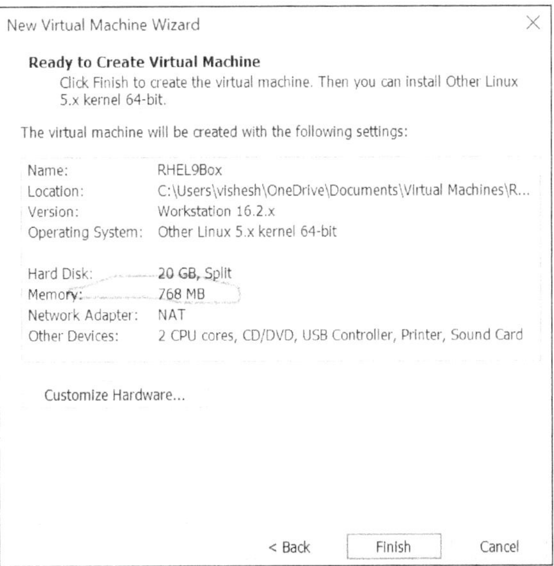

***Figure 1.6:** Summary configuration of virtual machine that is to be created; memory size is not optimal here and needs to increase*

We have read that the minimum required RAM is 1.5 GB, but it lists only 768 MB. So, let's click on the **Customize Hardware** button and set memory to **1.5 GB**. You can set more than the minimum required. Click on **Finish** after setting the required memory size.

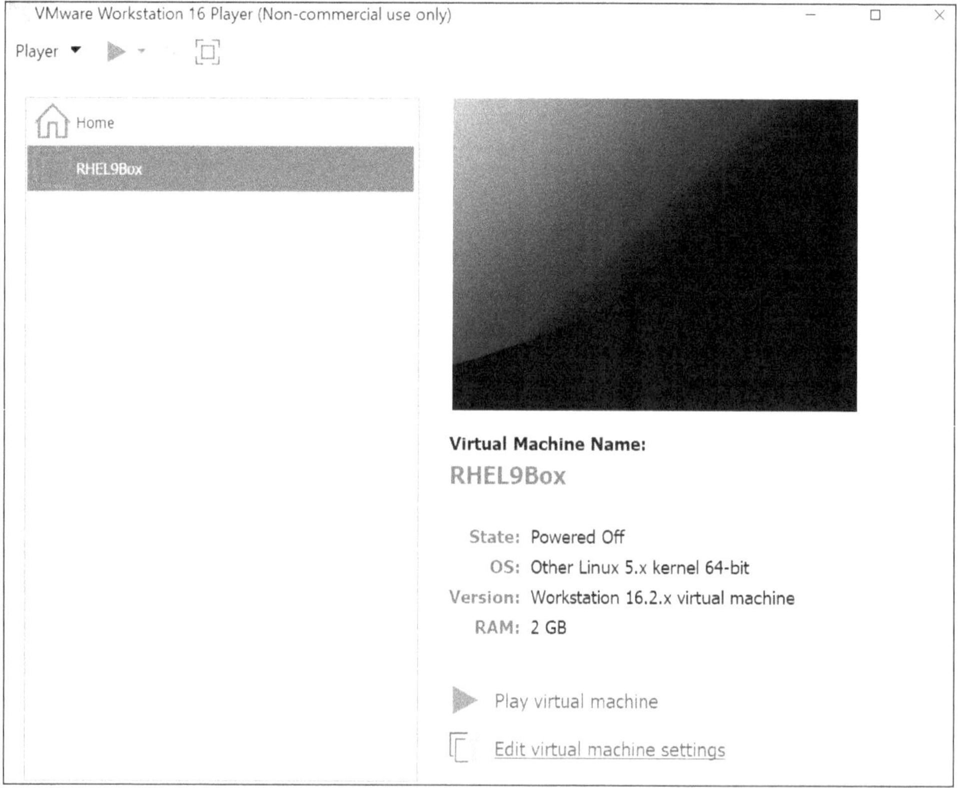

***Figure 1.7**: A blank VM with no OS installed on it*

6. After this step, your virtual machine will be ready to power on. But what we have created so far is a blank machine with no OS in it, as shown in *Figure 1.7*. We have already provided the RHEL9 software iso file path while creating this virtual machine so that your virtual box knows about it. This iso will be used to install the OS on this particular VM.

Installation of RHEL9 on Virtual Machine

By now, your virtual machine is ready to start with the installation procedures. These steps can be followed for the same:

1. Right now, your virtual machine is in the power off state. Let's power it on by clicking on the **Play Virtual Machine** option. Just ensure that the name of your newly created virtual machine is highlighted in the left pane.

2. Your virtual machine will automatically be booted using the DVD iso file that we specified while installing VMware.

3. *Figure 1.8* is the first screen that you will see when installing RHEL9. It will ask you to choose one option among these three:

   - **Install Red Hat Enterprise Linux 9.0**: This will immediately start RHEL Installer and the process to install RHEL 9.
   - **Test this media and install red hat Enterprise Linux 9.0**: This option is the default. It first verifies the integrity of your OS software and starts the installation.
   - **Troubleshooting**: This option only troubleshoots the existing installation.

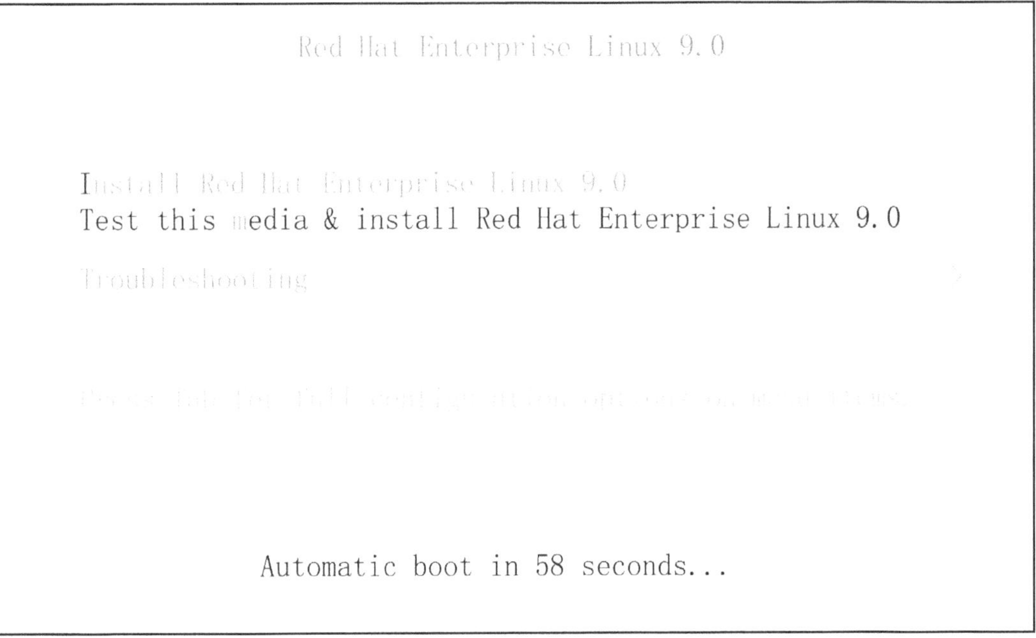

***Figure 1.8**: The first screen when RHEL9 installation starts*

Let us choose option 1, **Install Red Hat Enterprise Linux 9.0** using up and down arrow keys from the keyboard.

4. Then, it will show you a few lines of text. You should not worry about these lines at this stage of learning. These are just the logs or some testing that is being performed by the installer. After it displays enormous lines of logs on the screen, installation moves into GUI, which is supported by Anaconda.

5. In the next window, select your **Language** and click on **Continue**, as shown in *Figure 1.9*:

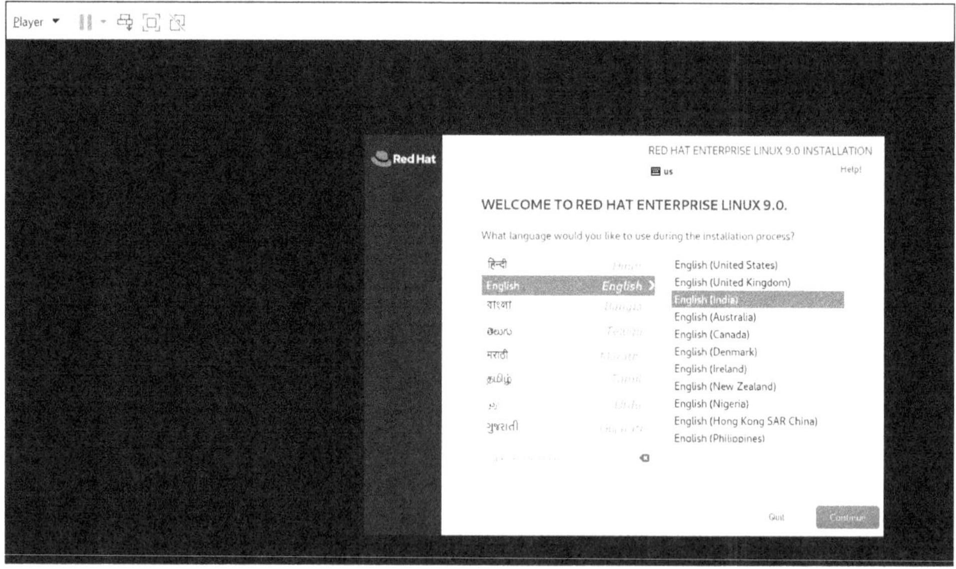

Figure 1.9: Anaconda installer asks to choose your language preference

6. Next, the installation summary is shown, as illustrated in *Figure 1.10*:

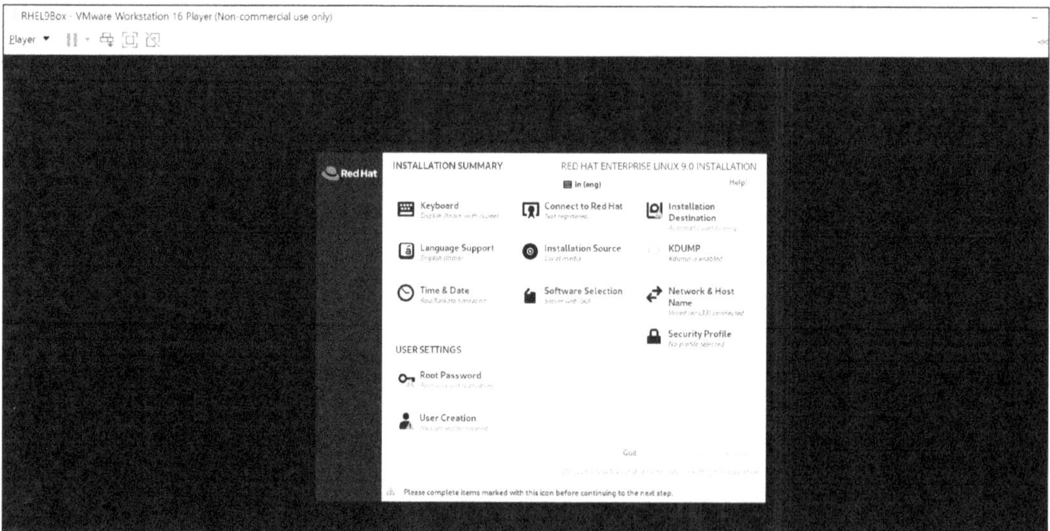

Figure 1.10: Anaconda Installer displaying installation summary and all the configuration using which RHEL9 will be installed.

Here, you must take action on marked items.

7. Let us click on **Installation destination** to verify the disk where the software will be installed and whether it is overwriting any useful data (*Figure 1.11*).

It will show you the virtual disk that you just created, while creating your virtual machine. See *Figure 1.11*; leave all the default values and click on **Done**.

*Figure **1.11**: Anaconda Installer: Storage disk verification*

8. It will jump to the previous installation summary window, as shown in *Figure 1.10*, to take action on other marked points. Another point to take action for is **Root Password**. So, click on **Root Password**. Here, the root account is locked. Let's unlock it and set the password. It will open a window that prompts for root password. Enter the root password and confirm it. You will notice that the password is not echoed on the screen. This is due to the security feature of Linux. Lock root account option is, by default, set to on. Turn it off as shown in *Figure 1.12* and click on **Done**.

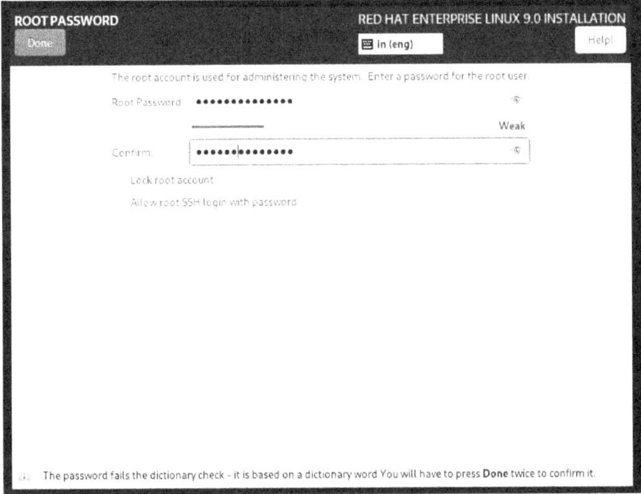

*Figure **1.12**: Setting root password*

9. Once again, you will receive the installation summary window, as shown in *Figure 1.10*. See whether any other points are left for certain action. You will see that **User Creation** requires an action. Click on **User Creation**.

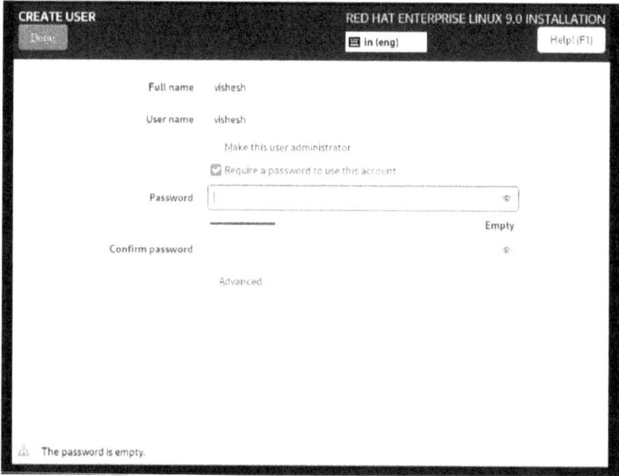

***Figure 1.13**: Creating a non-root user*

This window will allow you to create a normal or non-root user. Enter the **Full name**, **Username** and **password** of the new user and click on **Done**, as shown in *Figure 1.13*. When you enter the password, this window will also verify the password strength. This is, again, a security feature in Linux, as simple passwords can be guessed easily. It is recommended to never use dictionary-based or plain passwords. If you have used dictionary-based or plain password here, you must click the **Done** button twice. To make your password strong, use a combination of letters, digits, and special symbols.

10. Now, you will come back to the installation summary. After you have verified all the points listed here, the **Begin Installation** button is activated and can be clicked on, as shown in *Figure 1.14*:

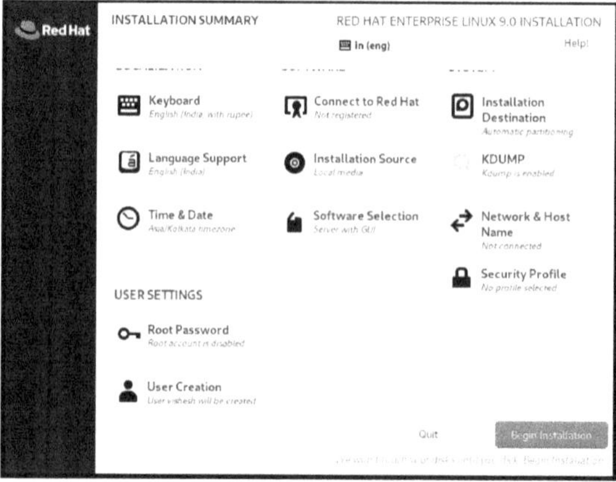

***Figure 1.14**: Final installation summary,*

After this the installation proceeds without any **`Back`** or **`Rewind`** button; used disk will be overwritten even if you press **`Quit`** in the middle of the installation

11. Now, your installation will begin. You will see the window shown in *Figure 1.15*:

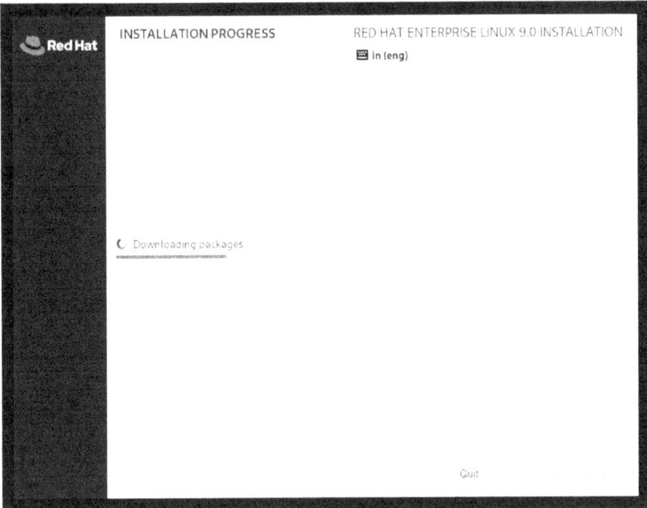

Figure 1.15*: rhel9.0 Installtion in progress*

12. In a few minutes, the installation will be completed. In the last screen of installation, as shown in *Figure 1.16*, it will prompt you to **Reboot** your system to explore your new RHEL box.

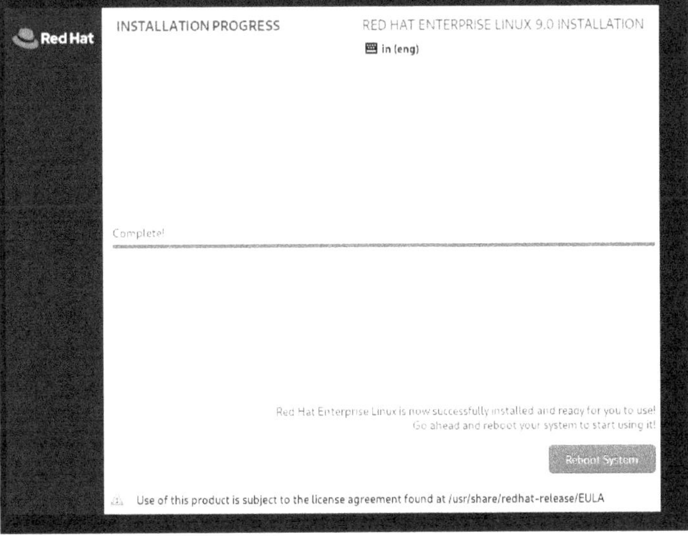

Figure 1.16*: Installation Complete Window*

13. Click on **Reboot System**.

Installation using bootable pendrive

In this section, we will see how we can install RHEL9 on an individual machine with no OS in it, or on one with an OS and data that can be safely deleted to reuse the space.

Preparing bootable USB

You can perform the installation on a standalone machine by using a pendrive that must be bootable. This section will demonstrate how you can prepare bootable USB media. There are various free tools available to prepare a bootable USB. Here, we will use **Fedora MediaWriter**. Follow these steps to write an iso file to a USB pendrive:

1. You can download **Fedora MediaWriter** using the following link:

   Releases FedoraQt/MediaWriter·GitHub

   Open the link and download the software for Windows.
2. Insert your USB drive into the correct port.
3. Double-click the exe file that is downloaded for *Fedora MediaWriter*.
4. Press **yes** when it asks for your permission to make changes to your device.
5. Then, accept the license agreement when it prompts.
6. It then opens *Fedora Media Writer Setup Window*, which will install Fedora Media Writer on your machine. The progress bar can be seen on this window.
7. At last, click on **Finish** to close the Fedora Media Writer Setup Window, and you can ensure that the **Run Fedora Media Writer** option is checked in this window, as shown in *Figure 1.17*.

***Figure 1.17**: Completing the setup of Fedora Media Writer*

8. Open Fedora Media Writer if it is not already open.
9. It will first prompt you to select the image source, as shown in *Figure 1.18*. Select the `.iso` file radio button since we have already downloaded the `.iso` file. Click on **Next**.

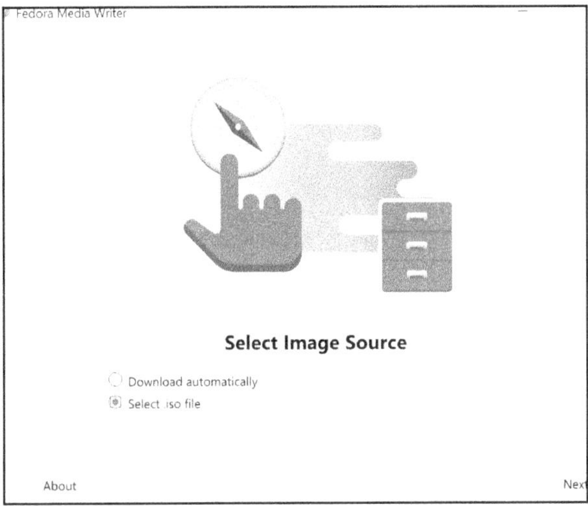

***Figure 1.18**: Fedora Media Writer: selecting the source iso file to write on USB pendrive*

10. Then, it will ask you to select a source and destination for writing. For source, click on the **Select...** button to select your downloaded iso file. The destination drive will automatically be detected if inserted, as shown in *Figure 1.19*. Here, you can see that Fedora Media Writer has automatically detected the USB drive for writing. Click on **Write**.

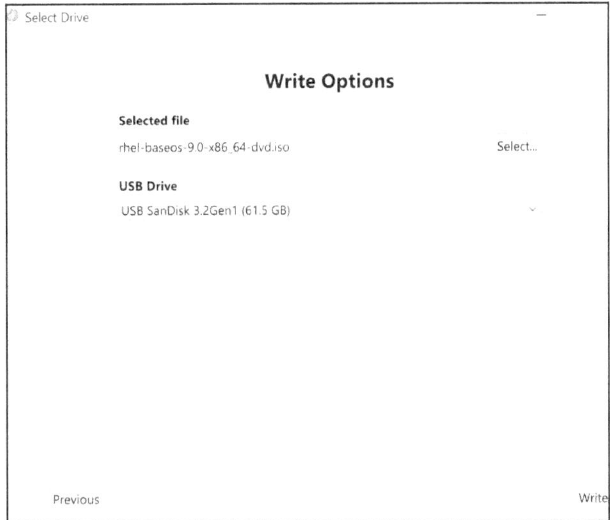

***Figure 1.19**: Fedora Media Writer: Verifying source and destination for writing image*

11. In the next window, as shown in *Figure 1.20*, the process to create a bootable USB drive starts.

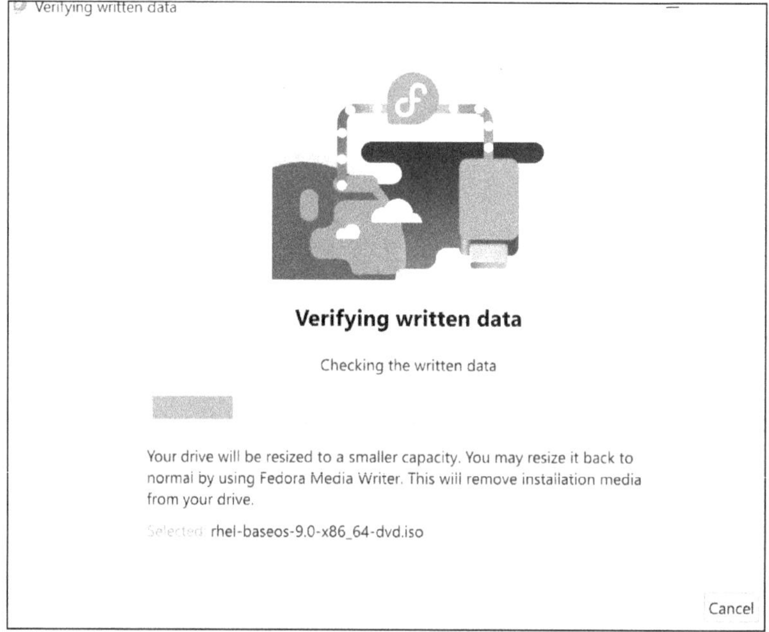

***Figure 1.20**: Fedora Media Writer: writing rhel9.0 iso to USB media*

It will take some time. So, be patient and let the process complete. After it completes successfully, click on finish and close the window.

Installing RHEL9 using bootable USB

We have just created a bootable media. Let's use this media to install RHEL9 on a new or old machine. You can follow these steps to install RHEL9 software:

1. Insert your bootable media in the machine where you want to install RHEL9 software.
2. Power on your machine with bootable media.
3. Your system should know that you want to boot using USB media and not from the hard disk. You have to set this priority by entering **BOOT Options**. To enter **BOOT Options**, you are required to press some keys when it is powered on. You have to check that key yourself according to your machine's model. In most machines, the machine boots into **BOOT Options** by pressing *F12*, but in some, the *Del* key works to do this.
4. After you enter **BOOT Options**, choose **USB media** and reboot the machine. Now, your machine boots from bootable USB.

5. The first screen that you receive is the same as *Figure 1.8*. Select **Install Red Hat Enterprise Linux 9.0** using the up and down arrow keys.
6. Some lines of logs will be displayed next.
7. Then, it will open Anaconda installer window. At first, it asks you to choose **Language**, as shown in *Figure 1.9*. After choosing your language preference, click on **Continue**.
8. Next, the installer will take you to the installation **Summary** window, as shown in *Figure 1.10*.
9. Click on the installation destination to verify this.

   Next, the **Installation Destination** window opens. It will show you disks that are available/attached to this machine. If this is a used machine, then you have to decide whether you want to overwrite all the disks' data and make all the used space available to your new installation, or you want to use only the available free space. If you choose to overwrite all the disk data, you cannot get your data back after the installation begins. If you only want to use the free space available, then you are on the safer side. Be very careful while selecting the options in the forthcoming windows, as any mistake here will delete all your existing data on the hard disk. This demo will choose to delete all the data and provide all the used disk space to the installation of RHEL9.0. Refer to *Figure 1.21*. Here, the system hard disk has almost no disk space available. Choose **Storage Configuration Automatic** here (this is the default option set), and click **Done**.

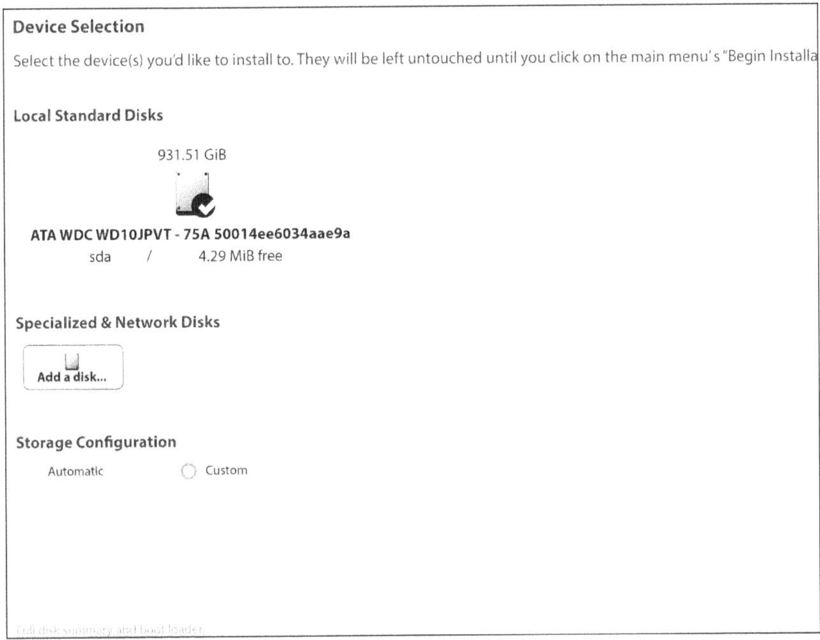

***Figure 1.21**: Anaconda Installer: Verifying storage disk for installation*

10. Click on **Done**; it show you a window as shown in *Figure 1.22*. It will describe to you the actions that you can take if you have very little amount of disk space available.

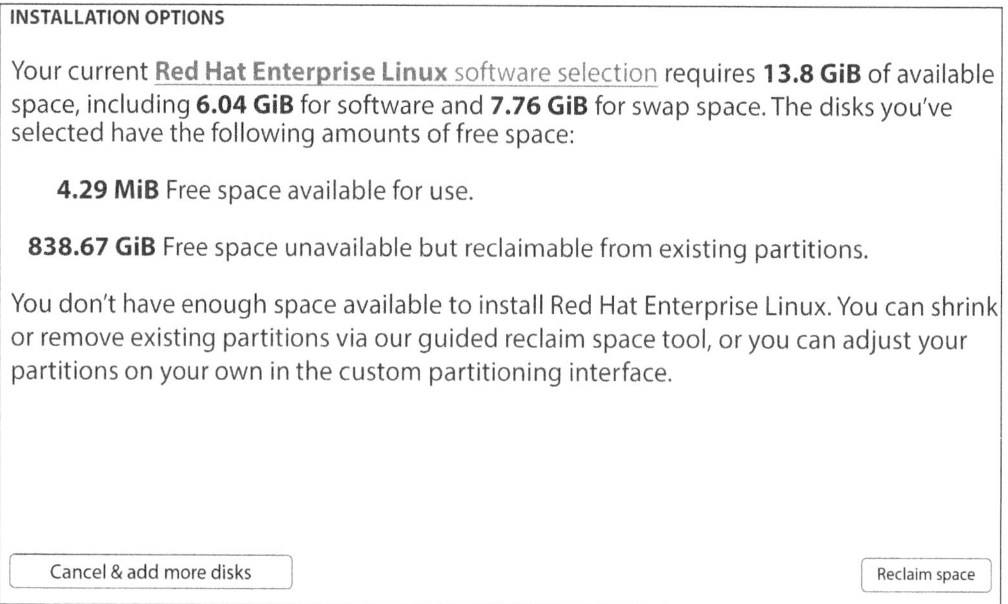

INSTALLATION OPTIONS
Your current Red Hat Enterprise Linux software selection requires 13.8 GiB of available space, including 6.04 GiB for software and 7.76 GiB for swap space. The disks you've selected have the following amounts of free space:
4.29 MiB Free space available for use.
838.67 GiB Free space unavailable but reclaimable from existing partitions.
You don't have enough space available to install Red Hat Enterprise Linux. You can shrink or remove existing partitions via our guided reclaim space tool, or you can adjust your partitions on your own in the custom partitioning interface.
Cancel & add more disks
Total selected space to reclaim: 0
Reclaim space

***Figure 1.22**: Anaconda Installer: Reclaim space if you want to use all the used disk data*

If you have decided to use all the used space as you do not need the data further, click on **Reclaim Space**.

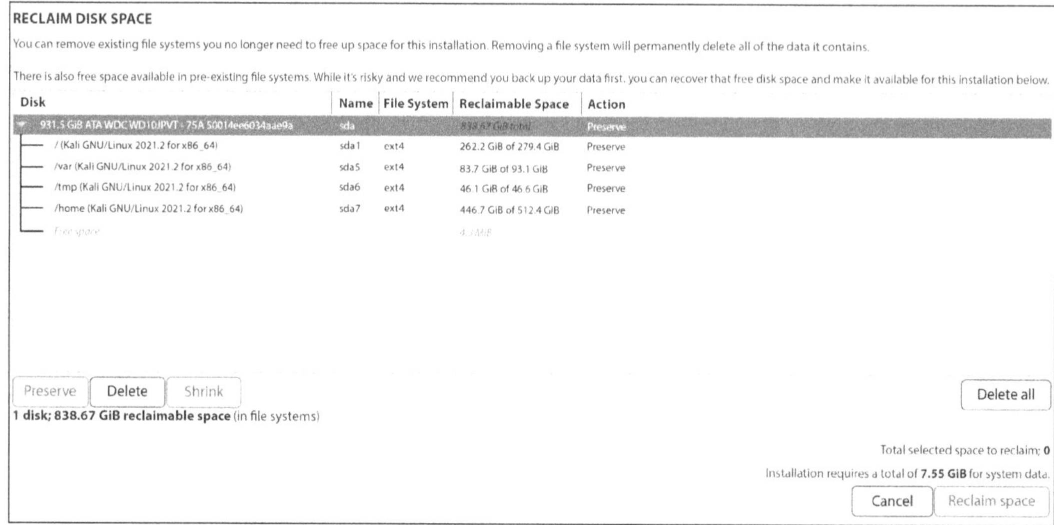

You can remove existing file systems you no longer need to free up space for this installation. Removing a file system will permanently delete all of the data it contains.
There is also free space available in pre-existing file systems. While it's risky and we recommend you back up your data first, you can recover that free disk space and make it available for this installation below.

/ (Kali GNU/Linux 2021.2 for x86_64)

262.2 GiB of 279.4 GiB

/var (Kali GNU/Linux 2021.2 for x86_64)

83.7 GiB of 93.1 GiB

/tmp (Kali GNU/Linux 2021.2 for x86_64)

46.1 GiB of 46.6 GiB

/home (Kali GNU/Linux 2021.2 for x86_64)

446.7 GiB of 512.4 GiB

***Figure 1.23**: Anaconda: Clicking on Delete or Delete all button marks selected disk or all the disks to be deleted during installation*

11. Then, it will show you the **Reclaim Disk Space** window, as shown in *Figure 1.23*, where you can select the disk partition that can be deleted. You have the option to either preserve the partition or delete it. Be careful here; if you want to delete all the partitions, select the disk and click on the **Delete all** button.

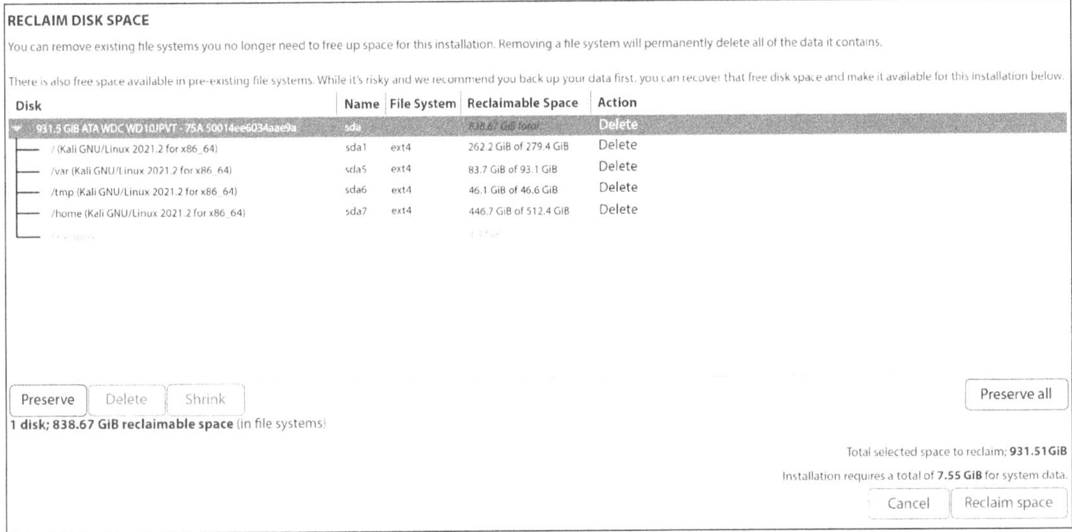

Figure 1.24: Anaconda: Reclaim Disk Space: Second chance to preserve any storage disk or its partition during installation

12. In *Figure 1.24*, you can see that the installer marked all the partitions of the disk to be deleted during installation. Here, you have the chance to preserve any partition if you want. Click on **Reclaim space**. The **Installation Destination** window opens again. Click on **Done** in this window.

13. Next, you will get the **Installation Summary** window once again. Here, you have to take actions on the remaining marked points. Follow steps 8 to 13 mentioned in the *Installation of RHEL9 on Virtual Machine* section.

Using RHEL machine

Now that you have the RHEL9 box ready, our next task is to get familiar with our new machine. This section will show you how will you can log in to the RHEL9 box and run various commands to fetch information about your machine.

Logging In

After you reboot the machine, you will get the login page, asking for the password of a normal user that you have created during the installation process. Type the password and press *Enter*.

Getting information about the machine

Now, you are looking at the first GUI screen of the newly installed OS. Click on **Activities** in the top-left corner of the screen. From the bottom menu that pops up, select **Terminal**. Terminal program will give you access to CLI, where you can interact with the shell, provide instructions to the kernel in the form of commands, and ask for the answers of the commands that you type. When you are typing into the terminal, you are actually giving instructions to the shell, which, in turn, interacts with the kernel to execute operations.

Using basic commands

Here, we will briefly discuss a few commands so that you can know about your machine. Type **`who`** in the terminal, as shown in *Figure 1.25*:

```
vkumar@192:~
[vkumar@192 ~]$ who
vkumar   tty2         2022-07-27 22:23 (tty2)
[vkumar@192 ~]$
```

***Figure 1.25**: who command*

You will get an output similar to *Figure 1.25*. The logged in user's name is **`vkumar`**, and they logged in from terminal **`tty2`** at 22:23 on 2022-07-27. This output shows that currently, only one user is logged in.

Let's see where in the filesystem you are placed. Type **`pwd`** as can be seen in the following figure:

vkumar@192:~
[vkumar@192 ~]$ pwd
/home/vkumar
[vkumar@192 ~]$

***Figure 1.26**: pwd command*

Your current working directory is **`/home/vkumar`**, as shown in *Figure 1.26*. As we read earlier, in Linux, all the file paths start with '**`/`**'. For all the users, a folder is created with their login name under **`/home`** which determines the home directory of the user. For example, here, **`/home/vkumar`** is the home directory of the user **`vkumar`**. But this does not apply to the root user; the home directory of the root user is **`/root`**.

Let us see what is inside your present working directory. Just type **`ls`**, as depicted in *Figure 1.27*:

vkumar@192:~
[vkumar@192 ~]$ pwd
/home/vkumar
[vkumar@192 ~]$ ls

Figure 1.27: ls command showing directories/files in the current working directory

It lists all the files and directories that are created upon installation by default. Files displayed in blue are actually directories and not regular files. Let's create a regular file. Just type the following:

```
cat > myfirstfile.txt
```

Here, the **cat** command is used to create a regular file; to write to a file named **myfirstfile**, we have used the **>** operator. This operator is standard input operatorm which means cat will take input from the keyboard as you type.

Type some text and press *Ctrl + D* to save the output to a **myfirstfile**. Type ls again to view the lists of all the files in your present working directory. You will now able to see the newly created file, along with directory listing, as shown in *Figure 1.28*.

```
[vkumar@192 ~]$ cat > myfirstfiel
this is myfirst file
[vkumar@192 ~]$
[vkumar@192 ~]$ ls
                    myfirstfiel
```

Figure 1.28: cat command creating a new file and taking file contents from the keyboard

To view the content of the file, use the following command:

```
cat <filename>
```

Note: Here, angle bracket (<>) is used just as a placeholder for filename. Throughout this book, <> will be used to denote the filename or any other entity whenever we will talk about the syntax of any command.

However, **cat** means concatenate. It can be used to concatenate the contents of two or more files and display it on the screen. Consider this example:

```
cat f1 f2 f3
```

The preceding command concatenates the contents of three files and displays them on screen.

Do it yourself

Let us create another file named file2 and add two lines of content in this file. Concatenate the content of myfirstfile and file2 together and display it on the screen.

You can change your current working directory by using the **cd** command. Let's create a directory using the **mkdir** command:

```
mkdir <dirname>
```

Then, use the following command to move to that directory:

```
cd <dirname>
```

Do it yourself

Let us create a directory named test in your home directory. Switch to that directory. Create a file named abc inside the test directory. List the files inside test.

To view the contents of a subdirectory under your current directory, use the following command:

```
ls <dirname>
```

The preceding command lists out the contents of the specified directory or specified path. You can create directories, subdirectories and files at many levels. To move one level back, use the following command:

```
cd ..
```

Let's see what directories/sub-directories are created by default under '/' referred as **root**, which is the top-level directory. Type the following command:

```
ls /
```

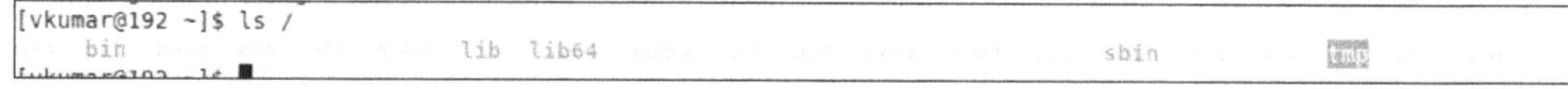

Figure 1.29: Default file/directories under root folder, which is denoted by '/'

Refer to *Figure 1.29*; the absolute path of all these files/subdirectories start with '**/**', such as /**home/** and **/bin** . The detailed discussion of these subdirectories will be done in the next chapter. Type **pwd** and see the absolute path of your current working directory.

Do it yourself

Enter the test subdirectory that you created inside your home directory and notice the absolute path.

To delete a file, say **myfirstfile1**, the **rm** command is used as follows:

```
rm myfirstfile1
```

To delete an empty directory, the **rmdir** command is used as follows:

```
rmdir <dirname>
```

rmdir deletes an empty directory. In *Chapter 5, Handling and Managing Files,* we will learn how to delete a non-empty directory.

The **tty** command is used to view the terminal name on which you are working. Just type the following command:

```
tty
```

Your output may look like this:

```
/dev/pts/1
```

Every user fetches their terminal name using the same command, but the output differs according to the terminal name on which they are working. Type **uname** to fetch system information.

```
[vkumar@192 ~]$ uname
Linux
[vkumar@192 ~]$ uname -r
5.14.0-70.13.1.el9_0.x86_64
```

***Figure 1.30**: Using uname command to get system infomation*

Using the **-r** option of **uname** provides you with information about your system configuration. See *Figure 1.30*; it says that your machine has 64-bit CPU architecture and has RHEL 9.0 installed, which is using kernel version 5.14.0.

You can take help on any command's usage any time by using the provided manual. Just type the following command:

```
man <any command >
```

It will open that command's manual page which will give vast amount of information on the command. Let us open the manual page of the **man** command and see how it looks. It looks as shown in *Figure 1.31*:

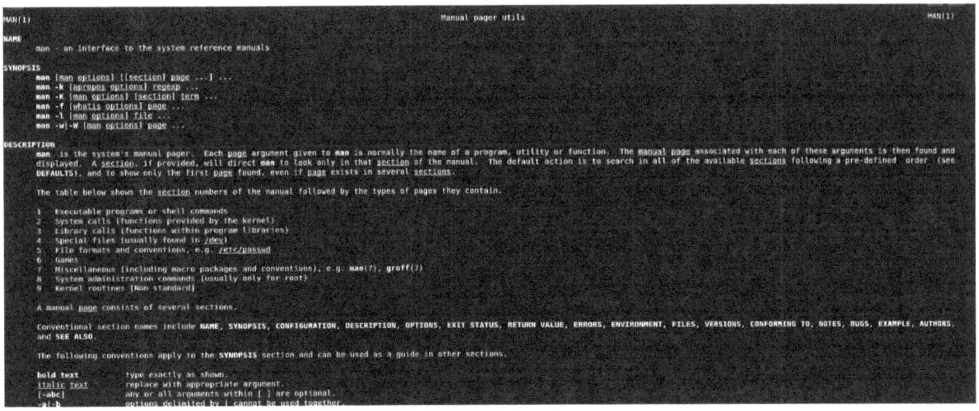

***Figure 1.31**: man command (Linux user manual)*

Press **q** to quit the **man** page. You can scroll down or up to move through the pages. Let's see your system date and time by typing date, as shown in *Figure 1.32*:

```
[vkumar@192 ~]$ date
Thursday 28 July 2022 03:27:01 PM IST
[vkumar@192 ~]$
```

***Figure 1.32**: Getting the current data and time*

You can also view the calendar of any specific month or year. Just type **`cal`** to view the calendar of the current month, as shown in *Figure 1.33*:

```
[vkumar@192 ~]$ cal
     July 2022
Su Mo Tu We Th Fr Sa
                1  2
 3  4  5  6  7  8  9
10 11 12 13 14 15 16
17 18 19 20 21 22 23
24 25 26 27 28 29 30
31
[vkumar@192 ~]$ cal Jun
     June 2022
Su Mo Tu We Th Fr Sa
          1  2  3  4
 5  6  7  8  9 10 11
12 13 14 15 16 17 18
19 20 21 22 23 24 25
26 27 28 29 30
```

***Figure 1.33**: Using the cal command to fetch the calendar*

To view the calendar of any specific month, type the following command:

`cal <name of the month>`

To view the calendar of a specific month and year, say June 2012, see *Figure 1.34*. The command to run is highlighted in yellow:

```
[vkumar@192 ~]$ cal Jun 2012
     June 2012
Su Mo Tu We Th Fr Sa
                1  2
 3  4  5  6  7  8  9
10 11 12 13 14 15 16
17 18 19 20 21 22 23
24 25 26 27 28 29 30

[vkumar@192 ~]$
```

***Figure 1.34**: Using cal to fetch the calendar of a specific month and year*

Try it yourself:

Try to find the calendar of a specific year, say 2013. You can take the help of man.

To take the any command's help, you can also use --**`help`** (two hyphens (`--`) before text help) switch of the command. Almost any command has this switch.

The **echo** command is used to print a message on the screen. Type the following command:

```
echo "hello to the linux world"
```

It just prints whatever text is displayed inside the double quotes. Besides, to fetch information about your system environment, you can use various built-in environment variables.

Any environment variables can be fetched using the **$** symbol before the name of the variable. And its value can be printed on the screen by using the **echo** command. Let's echo information about your present working directory and the home directory, as shown in *Figure 1.35*:

```
[vkumar@192 ~]$ echo $PWD
/home/vkumar
[vkumar@192 ~]$
[vkumar@192 ~]$ echo $HOME
/home/vkumar
```

***Figure 1.35**: Using environment variables*

The list of environment variables can be fetched using the **printenv** or **env** command. These variables could be of great use while writing shell scripts. In *Chapter 7, Interacting With Bash Shell and Scripting*, you will learn more about using environment and user-defined variables.

We have typed one screenful of commands on our terminal. Now, suppose we want to clear it. Use the **clear** command to clear the screen.

Do it yourself

Try to find your current shell and desktop session by using the $SHELL and $DESKTOP_SESSION environment variables, respectively.

Now, let's wrap up our discussion of initial command knowledge here; log out to move ahead to the second step and learn more.

Type **exit** and to close your terminal. The **exit** command will not close your session if you have logged in from GUI. To log out of the Desktop session, the system should receive a log out message. To log yourself out, click on the **Power** button in the top-right corner and select **Log Out** from the menu that pops up.

Clicking on the **Power** button also gives you an option to switch to another user without logging off your current session. Just click on the **Switch User...** button, and you can choose another user (if there are any) to log in.

Starting and stopping RHEL machine

When you power on your machine, it will give you a boot menu, as shown in *Figure 1.36*, to choose what you want to boot up.

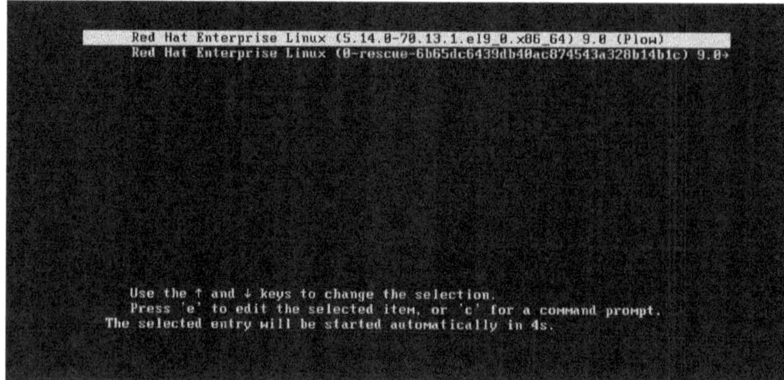

***Figure 1.36**: First boot screen of RHEL9 machine*

Choose the first option using up and down arrow keys to start RHEL9.0. The second option will take you to the rescue mode. Don't worry about understanding the **Rescue** option here as we have a dedicated chapter for system troubleshooting and rescue.

Press the **Power** button in the top-right corner of the screen to power off the machine. Alternatively, type the following command in the terminal:

```
init 0
```

Or

```
Poweroff
```

Both the commands immediately shut down the Linux machine in safe mode.

```
Shutdown
```

The `shutdown` command does not shut the machine immediately; it does so after 1 minute.

Conclusion

RedHat uses Linux Kernel, which is freely available. RedHat added supporting system libraries on Linux kernel to implement OS functionalities, enhanced security, added enterprise features and distributed this product as RHEL. Kernel and shell are the two pillars of Linux Systems. Shell actually beautifies Linux System; Linux is admired by all because it has shell. Opening a terminal gives you access to shell, which is actually responsible for interacting with the kernel, which, in turn, perform OS operations. You can type commands into the terminal; and Linux provides you with a vast user manual in the form of man to take command help. The upcoming chapters will take an in-depth look at all the concepts/terminologies that we have read about in this chapter.

In the next chapter, we will learn about the Linux files and filesystems in greater detail. We will see how the files are organized on the storage disks.

CHAPTER 2

Linux Filesystem and Administration

Introduction

Data in a computer is stored in its storage system in the form of files. They are organized in the storage devices using different filesystems. Without a filesystem, the storage device would contain just a huge pile of data, and the operating system wouldn't know how to store and read the data. The data would be just raw data that can't be interpreted to retrieve any information if there is no filesystem. Filesystem provides a way for the operating system to store, organize and fetch the data. You may have heard the name of FAT32, NTFS, ext2, and so on. These are actually the name of different filesystems that reside on different storage disks. Each of these filesystems follows specific properties that determine its purpose. NTFS is generally widely used in Windows machine, and ext2 is known to store data in Linux machines.

To store data in the storage device, the storage device must be partitioned first. Each partition should then beformatted using a filesystem. Each filesystem follows a specific property that decides how the files are named, stored and fetched. Multiple partitions can be created on a storage disk. Each attached storage disk must have at least one partition. After each partition is layered with a filesystem type, the storage disk must be attached to the main storage subsystem. This process is called mounting. In this chapter, you will learn how data is stored in a Linux system, look at its file structure and understand how can you access the data by mounting and unmounting it.

Structure

This chapter will cover the following topics:

- Linux filesystem
- Filesystem structure
- Mounting a filesystem
- Unmounting a filesystem
- Administering filesystem

Objectives

Upon completing this chapter, you will acquire the skills necessary to comprehend the Linux filesystem and its underlying structure, create disk partitions along with corresponding filesystems, manage diverse filesystem types, configure storage media for optimal data storage and retrieval, as well as proficiently mount and unmount various filesystems as needed.

Linux Filesystem

All files in the Linux system are organized in a tree-like structure, starting from the root directory (denoted by '/') and moving downwards through many branches. Here, branches refer to the various directories and sub-directories that store various system and user-related files. Many filesystems are stored under the hood of one root. Each storage device attached to a Linux machine may contain the same or different filesystem. The access path of files on all these storage devices always starts from '/'. '/' is known as the **root directory**. This is the **top-level directory** in the Linux filesystem.

To access the data stored in a storage device, the storage device must be partitioned first, and each partition should be formatted using the same or different filesystems. But this is not enough to access any data in the Linux system. Each filesystem has its own structure for storing files. To access the data in these formatted filesystems, the storage devices need to be made accessible to the root directory or top-level directory in the Linux system. Data on these formatted storage devices are made accessible by the use of mount points. A mount point is just like a new subtree in an already existing tree. It is a directory created under the main tree just to attach a filesystem lying on another partition of the same storage disk where the main tree resides or on a partition of another storage disk. Formatted storage disks must be attached to the top-level directory '/' of the Linux machine by a mount point so that they can be accessed using the absolute path starting with '/'. Thus, mounting refers to attaching a filesystem to the main tree. Before we delve further into filesystem, let's find out what partitions and filesystem are laid by default during installation. Type the following command to fetch the list of partitions and their mount points:

```
df -h
```

```
vkumar@localhost:~
[vkumar@localhost ~]$ df -h
Filesystem              Size  Used Avail Use% Mounted on
devtmpfs                3.7G     0  3.7G   0% /dev
tmpfs                   3.7G     0  3.7G   0% /dev/shm
tmpfs                   1.5G  9.5M  1.5G   1% /run
/dev/mapper/rhel-root    70G  4.5G   66G   7% /
/dev/sda1              1014M  271M  744M  27% /boot
/dev/mapper/rhel-home   853G  6.0G  847G   1% /home
tmpfs                   756M   96K  756M   1% /run/user/1000
[vkumar@localhost ~]$
```

Figure 2.1: *Default partition and filesystem in RHEL9.0*

In *Figure 2.1*, you can see a list of all the partitions and filesystem laid down on these partitions during installation. Here, **`/dev/mapper/rhel-root`** is a partition automatically created in RHEL9.0. This partition is mounted on '**/**'. This is called root partition. This creates the root of the tree. All other partitions of the same storage disk or other storage disks will reside in branches of this root.

Note: /dev/mapper/rhel-root is not the traditional or regular partition but is part of LVM. LVM is an alternate way of managing a storage system. Here, we are calling it a partition just for the sake of understanding. We will learn LVM in greater detail in Chapter 9, Partitioning in Linux.

`/dev/sda1` is another partition created and made accessible to Linux system by attaching it to the main directory tree '**/**' via **`/boot`** mount point. Note how **`/dev/sda1`** is attached to the top-level directory '**/**' of the Linux filesystem. This is known as boot partition.

Note: /dev/sda1 is the regular partition and not part of LVM.

We can say that **`/dev/sda1`** is attached to the root filesystem ('**/**') as a subtree via mount point, named **`/boot`**. Boot partition is not used by the user to store their data; just the boot information is used by the system. The third important partition is **`/dev/mapper/rhel-home`**, where the users' data is stored. This partition is made accessible by the **`/home`** mount point, which is said to be the home directory of all the non-root users. Three required partitions in any Linux system are root partition, boot partition and swap partition. Swap partition is used for swapping. There are other filesystems listed in the **`df`** command output: **`tmpfs`** and **`devtmpfs`**. In the next few sections, we will discuss filesystems supported by RHEL9.0 apart from the ones already mentioned.

Types of Filesystems

RedHat 9 ships with multiple filesystems. Each filesystem is used for different purposes and use cases. After you understand the basic features of each filesystem, you will be able to use the right filesystem in your scenario. The supported filesystems in RHEL9 can be broadly categorized into four groups:

- **Local filesystems**: These are the filesystems that run locally on a single server. They are directly attached to the local storage of the server and are the only choice for SATA and SAS disks. Available local filesystems are the following:
    - XFS
    - ext4
- **Network filesystems**: These filesystems are laid down on the storage device that is shared across the network. This is also called client/server filesystem. It allows clients to access the files from a shared server. This enables multiple users on multiple systems to share files and storage resources. Client machines do not have direct access to the storage block. Available network filesystems include the following:
    - NFS
    - CIFS
- **Shared storage filesystems**: This filesystem allows all the servers in a cluster to direct access files from a shared storage device, known as SAN. There is no client/server protocol followed. The available shared storage filesystem is GFS2.
- **Volume-managing filesystem**: Volume-managing filesystem integrates the entire storage stack for the purpose of simplicity. It includes Stratis.

Supported FileSystem in RHEL9.0

This section discusses some of the supported filesystem in RHEL9.0 along with pros and cons of each.

XFS FileSystem

High Performance Scalable File System (XFS) is the default filesystem in RHEL9. XFS is a highly scalable and high-performance driven filesystem. It supports very large files. This is a very old and mature journaling filesystem. In earlier days, it was widely used in very large servers.

It has been used as the default filesystem in Enterprise Linux versions of RedHat since RHEL7. It is a reliable filesystem as it provides metabase journaling. Matabase journaling keeps track of filesystem operations that can be replayed when the system is restarted after crash, and thus, it ensures filesystem integrity. It supports filesystem size up to 1024 TB.

EXT4 filesystem

In the earlier version of RHEL, ext4 (which stands for extended file system) was the default filesystem. It supports filesystem sizes upto 50TB. This is also a journaling fileysystem.

NFS Filesystem

This is a client/server model where **Network File System** (**NFS**) Client machines do not have direct access to the storage block. In this model, NFS server exports a local file system over the network, and NFS clients import these filesystems to access the files available.

CIFS Filesystem

Common Internet File System (**CIFS**) supports Microsoft's SMB protocol used to access Windows SMB share.

Tmpfs filesystem

It is a filesystem for virtual memory to store temporary files. In the output of the `df -h` command, you may see multiple `tmpfs` filesystems mounted. Mounting a filesystem as `tmpfs` ensures speed up in accessing the files. Their contents are automatically cleaned upon reboot.

- `devtmpfs`: This is mounted on `/dev`. Devtmpfs is also a `tmpfs`, which is specially created by kernel early in the boot process to keep the information of core devices.
- `/dev/shm`: This is used by the POSIX shared memory facilities.
- `/run`: This is used by running daemons or processes to keep its PID and locking information.
- `/run/user/1000`: 1000 is the UID of the first non-root user created by the system. This directory is used to store files used by running processes for that user. When another user logs in, you will see another temporary directory residing in the same path. If a user with UID 1001 logs in, you will get the `/run/user/1001` directory created, which holds the files used by the running processes of that user.

Choosing XFS or EXT4

Now, the question that comes to mind is which filesystem should be used for a server that runs locally. It depends on many factors. If you have very large servers with a large number of CPUs, large storage and high-concurrency workloads, XFS is the best choice. If you have a small server with limited I/O capability with little concurrency, ext4 is the best choice. If your workload is CPU bound with little concurrency, ext4 will perform best. RedHat recommends using ext4 if the application uses single threaded I/O and small files.

Another major difference between the two is that XFS can only extend the filesystem but cannot shrink it. If you would ever require shrinking a filesystem, stick to ext4.

FileSystem structure

RHEL follows the **Filesystem Hierarchy Structure** (**FHS**) filesystem structure. FHS is a standard that defines the name, location and purpose of many file types. This standard is followed by many other Linux variants so that FHS-complaint systems are compatible with each other. Let's look at the filesystem structure that is provided by RedHat in RHEL9. Go to the terminal and type the following command:

`ls /`

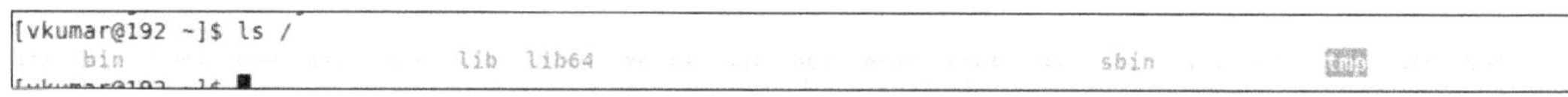

Figure 2.2: Files under root

You will get the output shown in *Figure 2.2*. This lists out the directories just beneath the top-level directory '**/**'.

Many of the files and directories residing here are symbolic links to others. What do you mean by symbolic links? These symbolic links are not the actual files and directories; they just point to another file or directory stored somewhere in the filesystem. To verify whether the file is a pointer or an actual file, use the **`ls -l`** command. **`ls -l`** displays multiple properties/attributes attached to each listed file. The last column in its output specifies whether the file is a just a pointer to another file or an actual file. More on this command will be discussed in *Chapter 5, Handling and Managing Files*.

For example, type **`ls -l /bin`**.

It will produce the following output:

```
lrwxrwxrwx. 1 root root 7 Aug 10 2021 /bin -> usr/bin
```

Where **`->`** refers to a pointer. Here, the **`/bin`** directory points to **`/usr/bin`**. **`/bin`** is a symbolic link to **`/usr/bin`**.

Let's discuss the role and purpose of all base subdirectories of '**/**':

- **`/bin`**: This directory is used to store executable files of most Linux shell commands. These executable files are actually binary files, and this directory contains the commands related to user tasks.
- **`/sbin`**: This directory stores the command files that are run by the root user for its administrative task.

- **/boot**: This is an essential directory that is required to boot the system properly. Note that you should not edit or remove this file.
- **/dev**: The **/dev** directory contains files related to all the devices attached to the system as well as virtual devices provided by the kernel. Devices in this directory can be broadly categorized into two types: character devices such as mouse, keyboard, etc., and block devices such as hard disks and optical disks. You may have noticed that whenever you attach a USB drive, the system automatically detects this device. This is the **udev** daemon, which performs the role of creating and removing device files as hardware is attached or detached. Devtmpfs filesystem is mounted on **/dev**. Devtmpfs is created early in the boot process by the kernel to keep the status of the core devices even before the **udev** demon is spawned. Let's drill down further and see what is inside the **/dev** directory. Type the following command:

  ```
  ls /dev
  ```

  You will see a high number of files, as shown in *Figure 2.3*. Watch carefully; there are multiple **tty** files. These are the device files related to the terminal. Obviously, the terminal in which you are looking when you type is also a device. In *Chapter 1, The First Step to Linux*, you have already verified the terminal in which you are working by using **who** command. **sda** is a file related to the attached hard disk. **lp0** is the first parallel port. **ttyS0** is the first serial port:

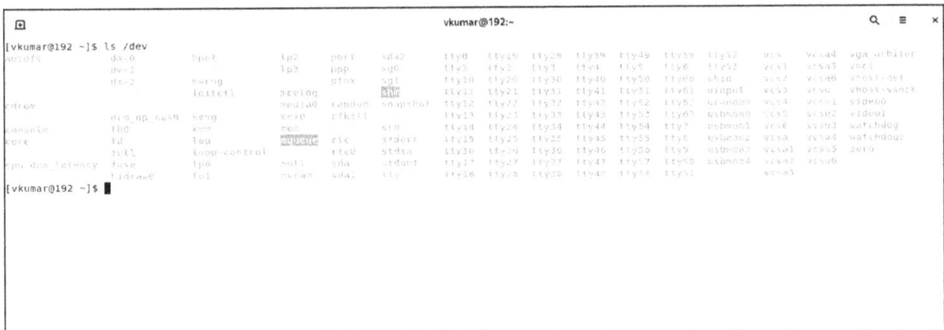

Figure 2.3: Files under /dev

- **/etc**: The **/etc** directory is used to keep all kinds of configuration files, whether it is application-related or system-related. This is a very important directory. You will use this directory most of the time in your role as system administrator. If you look inside **/etc**, you will find huge piles of files and subdirectories. Let's discuss some of them here.
  - **/etc/skel**: The **skel** directory determines the initial setting and configuration that is applied to a user's environment when it is first created. It contains some of the files that are copied over to the user's home directory when a new user is created.

Do it yourself:

Let's look inside the `/etc/skel` directory, which contains hidden files. Use the ls command to view the hidden files. You can take the help of man pages. Check whether you find these files inside your home directory too. Compare the contents of these files with whatever is present in the skel directory.

- o **`/etc/profile`: `/etc/profile`** is used to set system-wide environment variables for user's shell. For example, the PATH environment variable that is applied system-wide is set here. More on this is discussed in *Chapter 7, Interacting With Bash Shell and Scripting.*
- o **`/etc/bashrc`**: It is used to set system-wide functions and aliases for shell. This will be discussed in detail in *Chapter 7, Interacting With Bash Shell and Scripting.*

- **`/home`**: The **`/home`** directory is used to store user-specific files. When a user is created, a directory, named as the username, is created inside **`/home`**. Thus, **`/home`** is the place where all logged in users are placed. On user creation, various files are created automatically inside the home directory. Go to your home directory by typing the following command:

  ```
  cd ~
  ```

  And see what files there are by entering the **`ls -a`** command.

  ```
  ls -a
  ```

Note: ~ symbol refers to the home directory. -a switch of the ls command will also display hidden files in the directory. These hidden files are started with a dot (.)

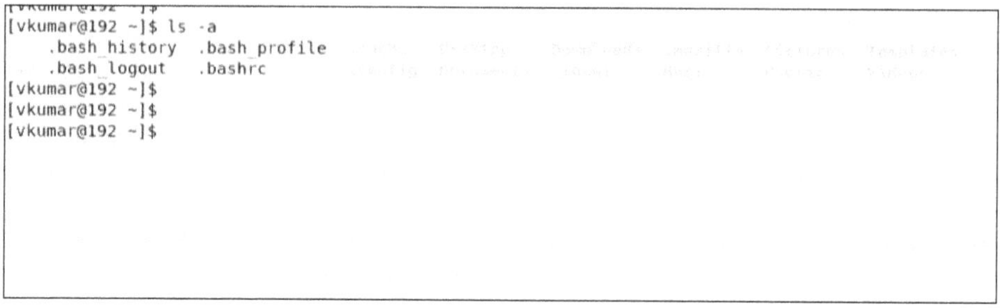

```
[vkumar@192 ~]$ ls -a
    .bash_history  .bash_profile
    .bash_logout   .bashrc
[vkumar@192 ~]$
[vkumar@192 ~]$
[vkumar@192 ~]$
```

Figure 2.4: Files under home directory of user

In *Figure 2.4*, you can see many hidden files as well as some regular files and directories. Let's discuss some of them:

- **`.bash_profile:`** The functioning of this file is same as that of **`/etc/profile`**. The difference is in the sense that it imports user-specific environment. When a new user is created, **`/etc/profile`** is copied over in its environment with this name. This is again a hidden file. You can access this file using **`~/.bash_profile`**. You can override any settings related to **`/etc/profile`** here, or you can add new environment variables here.

- **`.bashrc:`** The purpose and functioning of this file is the same as that of **`/etc/bashrc`**. The difference is in the sense that it imports user-specific functions and aliases. Any functions and aliases written in **`/etc/bashrc`** can be overridden here. Also, you can create new aliases here.
- **`/lib`**: This directory contains libraries that are needed by various commands in **`/bin`** and **`/sbin`**. These are very important libraries required to execute commands within the root filesystem.
- **`/lib64:`** This directory also contains libraries that are needed to execute commands inside **`/bin`** and **`/sbin`**. Its purpose may be to provide support for another variant of the same library that exists under **`/lib`**.
- **`/usr`**: It contains user-related programs, files and shareable data. It also contains many important subdirectories. It is often in its own partition and is mounted read-only. Here are some of files that reside under **`/usr`**:
  - `/usr/bin` contains programs for user-related tasks. **`/bin`** actually points to this directory. Type **`ls -l /bin`** to verify this.
  - `/usr/sbin` contains administration-related commands. **`/sbin`** actually points to this directory. Type **`ls -l /sbin`** to verify this.
  - `/usr/lib` and **`/usr/lib64`** contain user-related libraries. Again, **`/lib`** and **`/lib64`** are pointed to this directory.
  - `/usr/tmp` is used to store temporary files related to user tasks.
  - **`/usr/local`**: This directory is similar to the **`/usr`** directory with regard to structure. According to FSH, this directory is used by system administrator when installing the software locally, so any system software upgrades won't affect this software. According to RedHat, software upgrades can easily be performed with RPM packages. So, RedHat uses this directory for software that is downloaded local to machine.
- **`/media:`** It is used to provide mount points for removable media such as USB Pen drive.
- **`/mnt:`** It is used for temporarily mounted filesystems such as NFS mounts.
- **`/opt:`** It is used to store application software packages. There will be a subdirectory for each software package installed, and all the files related to that particular package will reside under the same subdirectory. The configuration file for the applications residing in /opt may reside under **`/etc/opt`**.

  `/proc`: This directory holds special files that hold the current system state and is also called the proc filesystem. It is also known as a virtual filesystem as it stores virtual files. It stores the real-time information of many system components. The **`/proc`** filesystem provides a file interface to the various system components, such as hard disks, CPU and memory. For example, to get information about **`cpu`**, type the following command:

```
cat /proc/cpuinfo
```

Let's look inside **`/proc`**, and you will find the following files:

- o **`/proc/devices`**: It displays various characters and block devices that are currently configured.
- o **`/proc/filesystems`**: It lists all the filesystem types currently supported by the kernel.
- o **`/proc/mounts`**: It stores information about all the current mounts on the system.
- o `/proc/partitions`: It contains information about block allocation of all the partitions.
- o **`/proc/meminfo`**: It contains the current memory usage information.

- **`/root`**: This is the home directory of root user. Note that root directory '**`/`**' is not the home directory of root user. Root user is never placed under **`/home`**.
- `/run`: This is a directory that stores volatile runtime data since the system was started. Data stored in this directory does not persist upon a reboot. **`/run`** is mounted as **`/tmpfs`**. It is meant for system daemons to store related temporary files.
- `/srv`: It keeps the data related to the services that run on the system, such as FTP and WWW.
- **`/sys`**: It is used to keep information about the devices and device drivers connected to the system. **`/sys`** uses another virtual filesystem: **`sysfs`**. This directory contains the same information as in **`/proc`** but displays a hierarchical view of a specific device's information. For example, **`/sys/block`** contains entries for each block device in the system. To view the device information from **`sysfs`**, type **`lsblk`** on terminal, and you will get an output similar to *Figure 2.5*. The output gives a hierarchical view of attached devices and its partitions.

```
[vkumar@192 ~]$ lsblk
NAME          MAJ:MIN RM   SIZE RO TYPE MOUNTPOINTS
sda             8:0    0 931.5G  0 disk
├─sda1          8:1    0     1G  0 part /boot
└─sda2          8:2    0 930.5G  0 part
  ├─rhel-root 253:0    0    70G  0 lvm  /
  ├─rhel-swap 253:1    0   7.8G  0 lvm  [SWAP]
  └─rhel-home 253:2    0 852.8G  0 lvm  /home
sr0            11:0    1  1024M  0 rom
[vkumar@192 ~]$
```

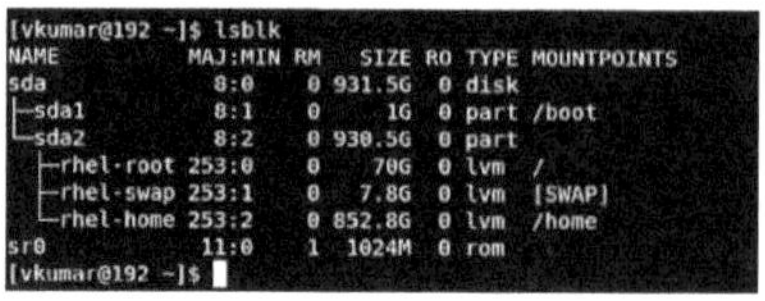

Figure 2.5: *lsblk displaying tree like structure of storage devices and its partitions*

- **`/tmp`**: This is the place where the system keeps temporary data. Any application program can create various temporary files during their execution, and they are deleted when they are no longer needed.

- **/var**: **/var** is used to store variable data files. For example, applications-related log files are stored inside the **/var/log** folder. Apache keeps its files in **/var/www**. FTP files are kept in **/var/ftp**. Spool files are stored in **/var/spool**.
- **/var/tmp**: It keeps temporary files that are preserved between system reboots. Temporary files kept in the **/tmp** folder are not preserved across the system reboots. **/usr/tmp** points to **/var/tmp**.
- **More on udev**: **udev** is introduced in kernel2.6 for dynamic device detection and management. It is based on some rules, which are written in **/lib/udev/rules**. It automatically creates device file nodes under **/dev** whenever it detects a new device and automatically removes device file node from **/dev** whenever a device is removed. To create a device node, **udev** must identify a device using its attributes, such as label and UUID. This information is exported by the **sysfs**. It receives several events whenever some device-related action is performed. For example, when a device is added to the system, it receives an **add** event. On removal of a device, it receives a **remove** event. Every device event is matched against a set of rules written in rule files, and **udev** executes those rules. This rule file determines how to identify devices and how to assign a name that persists across boots. To display **udev** events, run the following command on one terminal:

  ```
  udevadm monitor
  ```

  Now, connect a USB to your system and watch the generated kernel and **udev** events on the terminal where you have executed the preceding command.

Let's discuss symbolic link in further detail before moving on to the next section.

Symbolic link

A symbolic link, also known as a soft link, is a type of file that references or points to another file or directory in a filesystem. It allows you to create a shortcut to a file so that you can access that file from multiple locations without hovering around the filesystem. A symbolic link is created using the **ln** command as follows:

```
ln <source file name and path> <location of new reference file >
```

Suppose you want to create a symbolic link of the **/home/vishesh/RedHat/Chapter1** file; type this:

```
ln /home/vishesh/RedHat/Chapter1 /home/Chapter1
```

The preceding command creates a symbolic link named **Chapter1** under **/home.** Verify the symbolic link creation by typing the following command:

```
ls -l /home/Chapter1
```

You will see an arrow in the last field that points to the original file. Also, notice the small **l** character in the beginning of the output. Small **l** in the beginning means that the file is a symbolic link file.

Searching files in the filesystem

Your files may be scattered around the Linux filesystem. The **find** command is used to search a file within the filesystem according to given matching criteria. To search a file matching the given pattern, it starts recursively from the given path and moves downward until a match is found. If no file match is found, it silently exits. Let's find a file by its name. Let's find a file named **aa.gz** starting from the current directory:

```
find . -name aa.gz
```

It will show the relative path of all the files that match the name starting from the current location. If you want to find a particular file, say in the **/var/log** directory, specify the search path in the find command as follows:

```
find /var/log -name aa.gz
```

The preceding command searches for the file matching the name **aa.gz** starting from the given location. To perform a case-insensitive search, use the **-iname** option with the **find** command. **Find** command also takes multiple paths to find the files or directories, as follows:

```
find /tmp /home/vishesh -name foo
```

The preceding command will search for a file named **foo** in **/tmp** as well as in **/home/vishesh**. You have to be root if you want to perform your search starting from '**/**' as **find** performs its search recursively, starting from the given location. You cannot have access permission to navigate all the directories and subdirectories of **/**. If you do, you will see a *permission denied* error.

Mounting a Filesytem

We have studied that if we want to access a file from any filesystem, it needs to be mounted on a directory. Mounting means just to attach the filesystem to the root of the tree. Here, root of the tree is '**/**'. Mounting will create a new branch of that tree. To access this new branch, the path will start from **/**, then descend downward to the tree. Many of the filesystems can only be mounted by a root user. Some of the filesystems such as **/boot** must be mounted on boot. Some of the filesystems can be mounted by normal user because they are user-specific. Try to attach a USB pendrive to your system and see what happens. Have you successfully mounted it? Yes. Your system will show a pop-up as it automatically detects the removable media. Here, **udev** comes into the picture. On detecting a removable media, system will mount it on an appropriate location, and then you can read and write on this media.

Do it yourself:

Take a pendrive and attach it to your Linux Box. Use the df command to see whether it is mounted automatically.

/etc/mtab

What is in **/etc/mtab**? This directory holds the information of all the filesystem mounts currently held in the system. Let's explore this file. Type the following and you will get output similar to *Figure 2.6*:

```
cat /etc/mtab
```

```
vkumar@192:~
[vkumar@192 ~]$
[vkumar@192 ~]$ cat /etc/mtab
proc /proc proc rw,nosuid,nodev,noexec,relatime 0 0
sysfs /sys sysfs rw,seclabel,nosuid,nodev,noexec,relatime 0 0
devtmpfs /dev devtmpfs rw,seclabel,nosuid,size=3837168k,nr_inodes=959292,mode=755,inode64 0 0
securityfs /sys/kernel/security securityfs rw,nosuid,nodev,noexec,relatime 0 0
tmpfs /dev/shm tmpfs rw,seclabel,nosuid,nodev,inode64 0 0
devpts /dev/pts devpts rw,seclabel,nosuid,noexec,relatime,gid=5,mode=620,ptmxmode=000 0 0
tmpfs /run tmpfs rw,seclabel,nosuid,nodev,size=1548228k,nr_inodes=819200,mode=755,inode64 0 0
cgroup2 /sys/fs/cgroup cgroup2 rw,seclabel,nosuid,nodev,noexec,relatime,nsdelegate,memory_recursiveprot 0 0
pstore /sys/fs/pstore pstore rw,seclabel,nosuid,nodev,noexec,relatime 0 0
none /sys/fs/bpf bpf rw,nosuid,nodev,noexec,relatime,mode=700 0 0
/dev/mapper/rhel-root / xfs rw,seclabel,relatime,attr2,inode64,logbufs=8,logbsize=32k,noquota 0 0
selinuxfs /sys/fs/selinux selinuxfs rw,nosuid,noexec,relatime 0 0
systemd-1 /proc/sys/fs/binfmt_misc autofs rw,relatime,fd=31,pgrp=1,timeout=0,minproto=5,maxproto=5,direct,pipe_ino=23277 0 0
mqueue /dev/mqueue mqueue rw,seclabel,nosuid,nodev,noexec,relatime 0 0
debugfs /sys/kernel/debug debugfs rw,seclabel,nosuid,nodev,noexec,relatime 0 0
tracefs /sys/kernel/tracing tracefs rw,seclabel,nosuid,nodev,noexec,relatime 0 0
hugetlbfs /dev/hugepages hugetlbfs rw,seclabel,relatime,pagesize=2M 0 0
fusectl /sys/fs/fuse/connections fusectl rw,nosuid,nodev,noexec,relatime 0 0
configfs /sys/kernel/config configfs rw,nosuid,nodev,noexec,relatime 0 0
/dev/sda1 /boot xfs rw,seclabel,relatime,attr2,inode64,logbufs=8,logbsize=32k,noquota 0 0
/dev/mapper/rhel-home /home xfs rw,seclabel,relatime,attr2,inode64,logbufs=8,logbsize=32k,noquota 0 0
tmpfs /run/user/42 tmpfs rw,seclabel,nosuid,nodev,relatime,size=774112k,nr_inodes=193528,mode=700,uid=42,gid=42,inode64 0 0
tmpfs /run/user/1000 tmpfs rw,seclabel,nosuid,nodev,relatime,size=774112k,nr_inodes=193528,mode=700,uid=1000,gid=1000,inode64 0 0
gvfsd-fuse /run/user/1000/gvfs fuse.gvfsd-fuse rw,nosuid,nodev,relatime,user_id=1000,group_id=1000 0 0
[vkumar@192 ~]$
```

Figure 2.6: mtab stores information of all the currently held filesystem mounts

The output has many lines here. Each line represents a device partition/filesystem name, its mount point, filesystem type and attributes of the filesystem using which it is mounted. The first line says that proc filesystem is mounted on **/proc** directory as a proc filesystem using filesystem attributes listed at the end. These attributes are **rw**, **nosuid**, **noexec**, **relatime**, and so on. We will read about filesystem attributes later in this chapter.

Search for the line that belongs to **/boot**. *Figure 2.7* says that the **/dev/sda1** partition is mounted on the **/boot** directory as the **xfs** filesystem with the listed filesystem attributes:

```
/dev/sda1 /boot xfs rw,seclabel,relatime,attr2,inode64,logbufs=8,logbsize=32k,noquota 0 0
```

Figure 2.7: /boot partition

Now, take a pendrive and insert it into the appropriate port. This media will be mounted automatically. A new entry related to this pendrive mount will be displayed when you view **/etc/mtab**. Try to find the new entry in **/etc/mtab**. At the bottom of the **/etc/mtab** file, a new entry will be added, which looks like *Figure 2.8*:

```
/dev/sdb1 /run/media/vkumar/RHEL-9-0-0-BaseOS-x86_64 iso9660 ro,nosuid,nodev,relatime,nojoliet,check=s,map=n,blocksize=2048,uid=1000,gid=1000,dmode=50
0,fmode=400 0 0
```

Figure 2.8: USB mount entry in /etc/mtab

The removable media is recognized as the **/dev/sdb1** device and is mounted on /**run/media/$USERNAME** using is the **9660** filesystem with listed attributes such as **ro** and **nosuid**.

Note: $USERNAME is the environment variable that stores username of the logged-in user.

/etc/fstab

/etc/fstab is a very important file and is used during system bootup. It stores mount information that is required to mount attached devices during boot. Take a look inside **/etc/fstab**. Type the following command and you will get the contents, as shown in *Figure 2.9*:

```
cat /etc/fstab
```

```
#
# /etc/fstab
# Created by anaconda on Tue Jul 26 18:49:38 2022
#
# Accessible filesystems, by reference, are maintained under '/dev/disk/'.
# See man pages fstab(5), findfs(8), mount(8) and/or blkid(8) for more info.
#
# After editing this file, run 'systemctl daemon-reload' to update systemd
# units generated from this file.
#
/dev/mapper/rhel-root   /                       xfs     defaults        0 0
UUID=257fd99f-6153-42c2-a330-37b953515646 /boot                   xfs     defaults        0 0
/dev/mapper/rhel-home   /home                   xfs     defaults        0 0
/dev/mapper/rhel-swap   none                    swap    defaults        0 0
[vkumar@192 ~]$
```

Figure 2.9: /etc/fstab file

The **/etc/fstab** file provides sufficient information to mount attached storage devices. This file describes the rules to mount and unmount various system devices. The file content shown in *Figure 2.9* clearly says that the **/dev/mapper/rhel-root** partition is mounted on **/** using the **xfs** filesystem. The **/dev/mapper/rhel-home** partition is mounted on /home directory using the **xfs** partition. As mentioned earlier, **/dev/mapper/rhel-root** and **/dev/mapper/rhel-home** are not traditional partitions but are LVM partitions. There is a line with UUID. It provides a label to a disk partition to identify it uniquely across reboots. This UUID is assigned to **/dev/sda1**, which is mounted on **/boot** using the **xfs** partition. The last line is related to swap partition that is used as swap area.

In *Figure 2.9*, you can also see the defaults option in each line. This says that the filesystem needs to be mounted using the default options. The default options that are used while mounting are **rw**, **suid**, **dev**, **exec**, **auto**, **nouser**, and **async**. There are many other options that can be used while mounting. They can be provided to **/etc/fstab** as a comma separated list. Some of them are as follows:

- **rw** means mount the device as read-write.
- **ro** means mount the filesystem read-only.
- **user** allows an ordinary user to mount the filesystem.
- **nouser** forbids an ordinary user from mounting the filesystem.

- **users** allows any user to mount and unmount the filesystems.
- **auto** means that partition can be mounted with the **-a** option when the mount command is used.
- **noauto** means that a filesystem can only be mounted explicitly (the **-a** option will not cause the filesystem to be mounted).
- **async**: All I/O to the filesystem should be done asynchronously.
- **sync**: All I/O to the filesystem should be done synchronously.
- **exec**: This permits execution of binaries.
- **noexec**: Do not permit direct execution of any binaries on the mounted filesystem.

Figure 2.9 also displays a number at the end of each line. These numbers have a special meaning. The first digit can be only 0 or 1 and is used to tell whether or not to dump the partition when the system goes down. Here, 0 means not to back up the filesystem. The last digit in each line of **/etc/fstab** determines the order in which the filesystem consistency check is performed during boot time. '**0**' means not to perform any file system integrity check for the related disk/volume during boot. 1 or 2 determines the order in which to perform filesystem consistency check. '**1**' means that the related device should be given priority over any other for filesystem integrity check.

Unmounting filesystem

Unmounting refers to removing mounted media from the main tree. All the filesystems are unmounted first during shutdown. This step is necessary before shutdown so that all filesystem data is written to disk beforehand to maintain the integrity of FS in clean shutdown. When you have performed your task in the mounted USB pendrive, you must unmount this drive from the system before detaching it, else you may lose your data. A familiar message that you receive is *Your device is now safe to remove*. This message makes everyone feel relaxed.

FileSystem space usage

When a new filesystem is created, it starts to consume disk space as and when new files are created. A filesystem can store as much data as it has free space. You can use the **df** command to view the disk space usage. We have already seen the output of the **df** command earlier in this chapter. Let's recall it again by typing **df -h** in the terminal window. Here, **h** stands for human readable format. The output contains 6 columns, as shown in *Figure 2.10*. The header of the column makes the functions of each of these columns clear. *Figure 2.10* shows that root partition is configured to use disk space up to 70G, of which 4.5G is used and the rest is free. Currently, only 7% of disk space is in use.

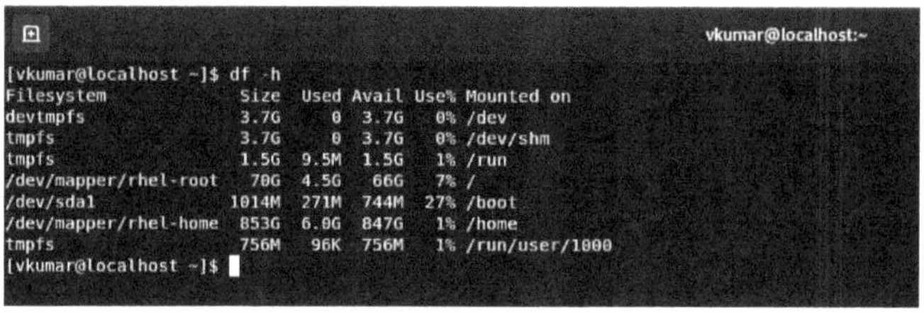

```
vkumar@localhost:~
[vkumar@localhost ~]$ df -h
Filesystem             Size  Used Avail Use% Mounted on
devtmpfs               3.7G     0  3.7G   0% /dev
tmpfs                  3.7G     0  3.7G   0% /dev/shm
tmpfs                  1.5G  9.5M  1.5G   1% /run
/dev/mapper/rhel-root   70G  4.5G   66G   7% /
/dev/sda1             1014M  271M  744M  27% /boot
/dev/mapper/rhel-home  853G  6.0G  847G   1% /home
tmpfs                  756M   96K  756M   1% /run/user/1000
[vkumar@localhost ~]$
```

***Figure 2.10:** df command displaying disk space usage*

Administering filesystem

So far, we have understood the Linux filesystem and its file structure. This section deals in creating and managing a filesystem. To understand this part, we will use USB pendrive. We will see how to create partition and filesystem on pendrive, and then mount and unmount this device. Since we have used all our disk space during installation and don't have any unused storage space on the hard disk, this section uses USB media. Only root can perform filesystem-related operations. So, you have to switch to root user by typing the following command:

```
su -
```

It will prompt you to enter root password. Enter the password that you provided while installing RHEL9.0.

Creating a partition

When a new storage device is added to the system, it must be partitioned and then formatted with a filesystem. Then, we can access it for read and write by mounting it to an appropriate directory in the main filesystem. We can use either **`fdisk`** or parted utility to create a new partition on a storage device. In this chapter, we will use the parted utility. Let's get started!

Attach your pendrive to the correct port. Be sure to back up all the necessary data because you will lose all the data in the pendrive with the activities that we are going to perform. Switch to root user and type the following command:

```
fdisk -l
```

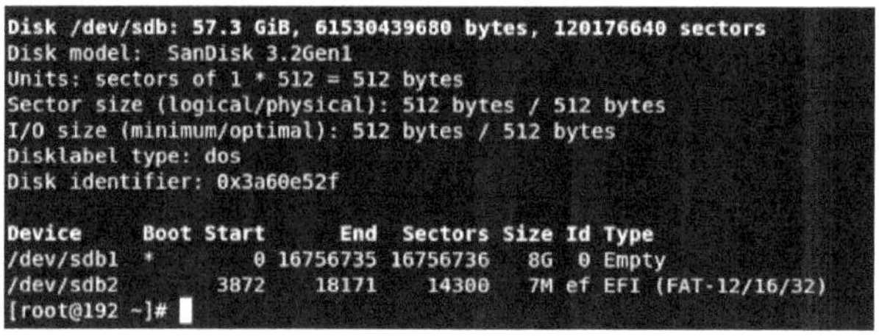

```
Disk /dev/sdb: 57.3 GiB, 61530439680 bytes, 120176640 sectors
Disk model:  SanDisk 3.2Gen1
Units: sectors of 1 * 512 = 512 bytes
Sector size (logical/physical): 512 bytes / 512 bytes
I/O size (minimum/optimal): 512 bytes / 512 bytes
Disklabel type: dos
Disk identifier: 0x3a60e52f

Device     Boot Start      End  Sectors Size Id Type
/dev/sdb1  *        0 16756735 16756736   8G  0 Empty
/dev/sdb2        3872    18171    14300   7M ef EFI (FAT-12/16/32)
[root@192 ~]#
```

***Figure 2.11:** fdisk describing the attached disk*

This command will give you the information of the attached hard disk and its partitions, regular as well as LVM, irrespective of whether or not it is mounted. Try to identify your attached USB media. In *Figure 2.11*, it is identified as **/dev/sdb**, highlighted in yellow.

Now, use parted to view and create the partition on **/dev/sdb**. Type this:

```
parted /dev/sdb
```

Where **/dev/sdb** is the name of the block device on which you are going to create a partition and create a filesystem.

```
[root@192 ~]# parted /dev/sdb
GNU Parted 3.4
Using /dev/sdb
Welcome to GNU Parted! Type 'help' to view a list of commands.
(parted)
(parted)
(parted)
```

***Figure 2.12:** Using parted*

The preceding command will give you an output similar to *Figure 2.12*. It displays a **(parted)** prompt. Type help to use the **help** command. You will find that the **print** command displays the partition table. So, type **print** in front of the **(parted)** prompt. You will get an output similar to *Figure 2.13*:

```
(parted) print
Model:  USB  SanDisk 3.2Gen1 (scsi)
Disk /dev/sdb: 61.5GB
Sector size (logical/physical): 512B/512B
Partition Table: msdos
Disk Flags:

Number  Start   End     Size    Type     File system  Flags
 2      1982kB  9304kB  7322kB  primary               esp
```

***Figure 2.13:** print to display partition table*

Figure 2.13 shows that it already contains a partition which is numbered as 2. If your drive also contains the partition already, delete it by typing the following command:

```
rm <partition number>
```

Reboot your machine if it says so. Type **quit** in the **(parted)** prompt, and reboot your machine. If you don't have any partition over there, you can skip the step of removing the partition and rebooting the machine.

If you have rebooted your machine, open **parted** again by typing the following command in the terminal:

```
parted /dev/sdb
```

Use **mkpart** to create the partition using **parted**. The following syntax is used:

```
(parted) mkpart partion-type name fs-type start end
```

Where:

- **partition-type** can be primary, logical and extended.
- **name** is the arbitrary partition name.
- **fs-type** is the filesystem type.
- **start** and **end** determines the starting and ending points of the partition; this ultimately determines the size of the partition.

This chapter only deals with the primary partition type. We will learn about the creation of logical and extended partitions in *Chapter 9, Partitioning in Linux*. On the **(parted)** prompt, type the following:

```
mkpart primary xfs 1MB 10000MB
```

The preceding command will create a primary partition of type **xfs** of size 10 GB. If you want to create the **ext4** filesystem, replace **xfs** with **ext4**. Let's verify partition by printing partition table using the **print** command in the **parted** prompt . It will show you the partition table as shown in *Figure 2.14*:

```
print
```

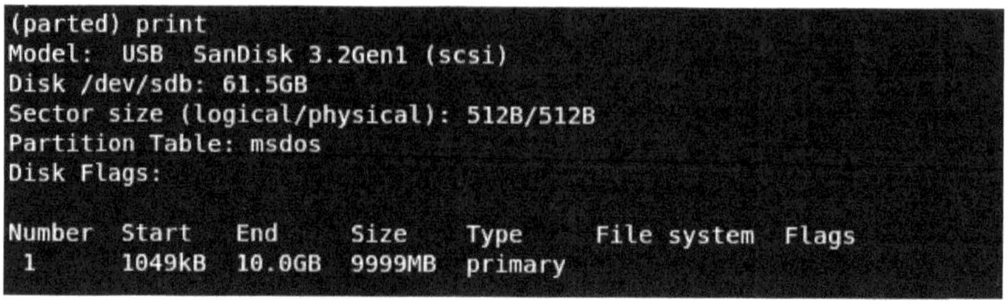

```
(parted) print
Model:  USB  SanDisk 3.2Gen1 (scsi)
Disk /dev/sdb: 61.5GB
Sector size (logical/physical): 512B/512B
Partition Table: msdos
Disk Flags:

Number  Start   End     Size    Type     File system  Flags
 1      1049kB  10.0GB  9999MB  primary
```

***Figure 2.14:** Partition table*

We have successfully created a 10 GB primary partition. Type **quit** to exit the parted prompt. Now, type the following command to register this change to the system:

```
#udevadm settle
```

Creating a filesystem

After we have created the partition, the next step is to create a filesystem on this partition. To create a filesystem, you can use the **mkfs.<fs type>** command. For each filesystem type, there is a respective **mkfs.<fs type>** command. For example, to create the **xfs** filesystem, you have to use the **mkfs.xfs** command. To create the **ext4** partition, you have to use the **mkfs.ext4** command. Now, let's create the **xfs** filesystem on the partition that we have just created using the following syntax:

```
mkfs.xfs <block device name >
mkfs.xfs </dev/sdb1>
```

It will create the **xfs** partition on **/dev/sdb1** with the default options. Type the following command to register this change to the system:

```
udevadm settle
```

You can verify the filesystem creation by printing the partition table again using the **parted print** command.

To create **ext4** filesystem, use the following:

```
mkfs.ext4 /dev/sdb1
```

Similarly, for the **ext2** and **ext3** filesystems, you can use the **mkfs.ext2** and **mkfs.ext3** commands, respectively.

Labelling filesystem

It is important to label all the storage devices because OS change device names across system reboots. When the system boots up, it identifies all the disks and assigns a name to each in the order that the disks are found. An OS may provide a different name to a disk after system reboot. This may cause problems in mounting the filesystem. So, it becomes very important for the system administrator to provide a unique name to all the devices so that all the devices are uniquely identified using the same identifier every time the system boots.

Each filesystem is provided with a unique name when an FS is created on a storage device. The unique name given to the device is written on the FS itself. It carries this identifier unless it is formatted again. Filesystem identifiers include the following:

- UUID
- Label

Again, we have different utilities or commands to administer different filesystem. To interact with the **xfs** filesystem, we have the **xfs_admin** command. To make changes to the **ext4** filesystem, we have tune2fs.

Let's verify UUID given to **/dev/sdb1** that we have just formatted. Type the following command:

```
xfs_admin -u /dev/sdb1
```

It will show output similar to *Figure 2.15*:

```
[root@192 ~]# xfs_admin -u /dev/sdb1
UUID = 61a2a2c9-c6fa-4852-8432-5a2cef828945
[root@192 ~]#
```

***Figure 2.15:** xfs_admin displaying UUID of xfs filesystem*

To view the label given, type the following command:

```
xfs_admin -l /dev/sdb1
```

UUID will be provided automatically when creating the **xfs** filesystem. No label will be assigned to the filesystem unless we provide it. Let's modify this filesystem to provide a new label and UUID. We have not mounted our device yet. To change the attribute of the filesystem, the device must not be mounted. If your device is mounted, you must unmount it. Mounting and unmounting commands are given in the next section. Type the following command to generate a new label or UUID:

```
xfs_admin -L xfsusb -U generate /dev/sdb1
```

```
[root@192 ~]# xfs_admin -L xfsusb -U generate /dev/sdb1
writing all SBs
new label = "xfsusb"
Clearing log and setting UUID
writing all SBs
new UUID = 78c2dfd5-dea7-4b92-8047-88e074ae5004
```

Figure 2.16: Modifying label and UUID of the xfs filesystem

Use the **-L** or **-U** options of the **xfs_admin** command to assign a new label or new UUID, respectively. In *Figure 2.16*, a new label named **xfsusb** is given to **/dev/sdb1**, and a new UUID is generated. You can see this new label in your desktop when you attach a USB device and mount it. After you have executed a command to change the FS attribute, remember to use the **udevadm** settle command to reflect your changes in the system.

To view and modify the label, UUID and other attributes given to the **ext4** filesystem, use the **tune2fs** utility. Use **man** to understand the options involved with this utility.

Mounting and unmounting filesystem

So far, we have successfully created an **xfs** filesystem on our USB media. Now it is time to access this media to perform read and write operations. To do so, it must be mounted. Let's mount it in **/media** using the **mount** command. The **mount** command uses the following syntax:

```
mount <disk name> <mount directory>
```

Where,

- **disk name** can be the absolute path of the disk partition / filesystem.
- **mount directory** is the directory where the filesystem is attached. This directory can be empty or non-empty. If you mount the filesystem in a non-empty directory, you cannot see the contents of that directory.

To mount **/dev/sdb1**, type the following:

```
mount /dev/sdb1 /media
```

Verify this mount using the **df -h** command. If the **mount** command fails saying that it does not recognize the filesystem of the device, you can use the **-t** option to specify the filesystem, as follows:

```
mount -t xfs /dev/sdb1 /media
```

You should also add the mount entry to **/etc/fstab** if you want the device to mount automatically. Open **/etc/fstab** as root and add the following line to it:

UUID=<UUID of the device> /media xfs defaults 0 0

Skip editing the **/etc/fstab** file for now if you don't know how to edit a file in Linux. We will learn editing in *Chapter 5, Handling and Managing Files*. If you have added an entry in the **/etc/fstab** file, you can mount the device by simply mentioning either the mount point or device name, as follows:

mount /dev/sdb1, or

mount /media

Now, you can move to **/media** and perform read and write operations on the filesystem on **/dev/sdb1**. Running **mount** without any option and arguments will give you list of all the mounted devices. This output is the same as the **/etc/mtab** file.

A filesystem can be mounted on multiple directories and can be accessed via any of these.

Do it yourself:

Attach storage media to your machine and verify automatic mount by using df -h. Note the mount directory, and again mount /dev/sdb1 on /media; verify this mount using the df -h command. Switch to /media and create a file abc on it by using the cat command. Create a new directory named /pendrive under '/'. Now, mount your /dev/sdb1 on the /pendrive directory. Have you successfully mounted your storage device from multiple mount points. Go to all the mount points one by one and verify whether the abc file exists there. What do you conclude?

After you have performed your task, you can detach the device from the tree by simply writing the following:

umount <device>, or

umount <mount directory>

Where **<device>** is the absolute path of the device and **<mount directory>** is the directory from which you want to detach the filesystem.

Simply put, you can unmount the device by either mentioning the device name or mount directory in the **umount** command. To unmount **/dev/sdb1**, simply write this:

```
umount /dev/sdb1
```

Or write this:

```
umount /media
```

Verify the unmounting of the filesystem using the **df -h** command.

Do it yourself

Mount your storage device from three different mount points. Verify using the mount command. Unmount it once, and print the contents of the abc file from another mount point. Are you successful? Detach the media only after unmounting it from all the mount points.

Checking filesystem

It is very important for a system administrator to ensure the consistency of the filesystem and repair it if it becomes damaged. RedHat provides a set of tools to check for FS consistency and repairing a filesystem. This tool is **fsck**. During system boot, **fsck** invokes and checks all the filesystems one by one for its inconsistency and repair if found. XFS and **ext4** both are journaling filesystems, which means they keep a record of filesystem operations in a journal before writing it into the super block. Journaling filesystems are crash safe. **fsck** takes a long time to repair a damaged filesystem, but sometimes, system admins have to use this utility for filesystem check. There can be many reasons to use **fsck** utilities manually. It can be due to the following:

- If system boot cannot solve filesystem inconsistencies
- When all the files or a single file on a specific disk is corrupted
- When there is a hardware error
- When the system does not boot

To check the health status of the external drives, **xfs_repair** utility is used**.** **xfs_repair** repairs the corrupted **xfs** filesystem. Extended filesystems such as **ext2**, **ext3** and **ext4** uses the **e2fsck** utility to perform filesystem checks and repair. You can also use **fsck.<fs-type>** utility to repair the filesystems, where **<fs-type>** is the name of a single filesystem. There are **fsck.ext2**, **fsck.ext3** and **fsck.ext4** utilities to repair the respective filesystems. Before using any of the filesystem consistency tools, the filesystem must be unmounted.

Conclusion

A Linux filesystem follows a hierarchical way of storing files and directories on storage devices. Each file path starts with / and descends toward other branches of the filesystem. To store data on storage devices, these devices must be partitioned first. Then, a filesystem is laid on them. Different filesystem types may reside on different partitions of a storage disk. Each filesystem type has different properties. You should use the appropriate filesystem for your need. To access a filesystem, they should be mounted on a mount directory. If you want to remove a filesystem from the main tree and attach it to some other tree or another Linux machine, you must unmount it first. Removing any attached device without unmounting it may cause corruption on the disk, or you may lose your data.

In the next chapter, we will learn about various basic and administrative commands that can be used by regular users and by the system administrator to perform their daily duties.

References

https://access.RedHat.com/documentation/en-us/red_hat_enterprise_linux/9/html/managing_file_systems

CHAPTER 3
Knowing Linux Commands

Introduction

Commands are a great way to perform everything from simple to complex tasks on a Linux machine. They are like the instructions given to the shell, which interact with the kernel on your behalf. The kernel then performs the instructions, and the shell displays the result on the screen. You can provide the instructions to the shell through built-in commands, user-created commands, or a shell script. This chapter focuses on several built-in commands. Commands are given to the shell in command line or graphical modes. In the command-line mode, commands are given in the command prompt when you open up a terminal. Graphical tools give you a feel of GUI like Windows OS, but all the graphical tools execute the respective commands internally. Most system administrators are fond of using command-line mode to perform admin-related activities. This book also focuses on various command-line utilities to demonstrate the concepts. A chapter on GUI is included in this book to let you understand how graphical mode works on RHEL9.

Linux supports multiple flavors of shell, like bash shell, Korn shell and C shell. By default, RHEL9.0 supports bash shell. All the commands discussed in this chapter work with bash shell. Their working with C and Korn shell is not guaranteed. You must read the respective shell's manual to know the correct Korn and C shell command.

Structure

In this chapter, we will cover the following topics:

- Understanding commands
- Standard input, standard output, and standard error
- Pattern matching and regular expression
- User commands
- Administrative commands
- Here document

Objectives

The objective of this chapter is to make the user aware of the essential commands in Linux. Give them a good understanding of the shell metacharacters and how they can match patterns in file names. Let them understand regular expressions and their usage in various commands for simple to complex pattern matching in strings and file names. Learn the usage of various user and admin commands.

Understanding commands

Several built-in commands allow a user to give instructions to the shell. Command is written at the command prompt. When you open a terminal after you log in to the Linux desktop, the following is how the command prompt looks:

```
[vishesh@192 ~]$
```

By default, command prompt contains the name of the logged in user, private IP of the machine, and the current working directory. Here, the current working directory is the home directory referenced by a tilde **(~)** sign. In *Chapter 7, Interacting With Bash Shell and Scripting*, we will see how users can change their command prompt. It can be set to the current date, the absolute path of the present working directory, or the way you like. Just change your directory and see how your command prompt changes.

Whatever is written at the command prompt is known as the command line. Each command in Linux is case-sensitive. Each command performs a specific operation. To operate, you must provide the existing command on the command line. You must know the name of the command for that specific purpose. If you type an invalid command on the command line, such as **DATE**, shell will throw you an error message saying the following:

```
bash: DATE: command not found...
Similar command is: 'date'
```

In the previous example, you may notice that shell would also guess the command name you might have wanted to execute instead. Each command is executed only after you press the **Enter key**. Shell interprets the command, simplifies the command line, and submits it to the kernel for its execution. Result is then displayed on the screen. Many commands do not give you any output; they work silently. The next command prompt on the screen signifies the completion of the last command, irrespective of whether or not it is successful.

Each command will have a return value. A return value of 0 means that the command is successfully executed, while a return value of 1 means that command exited with error. To know the return value of any command, you can just echo the value of **`$?`** environment variable, as follows:

```
echo $?
```

Commands may take several options and arguments. The options and arguments work as modifiers of the given command. They modify the default behavior of the command.

There is a fixed list of supported options with every command, and each option is used to generate specific behavior. The command options may start with a single or two dash. To modify the default behavior of a command, you must provide an option, followed by a space after the command name. When we write the **`ls -l`** command in the command prompt, **`ls`** is the command name, while **`-l`** is the command's option. Many options can be given together in a command line, as in the following command:

```
ls -la
```

The preceding command combines the **`-l`** and **`-a`** options of the **`ls`** command.

Each command option may be preceded either with a single dash **`(-)`** or two dashes **`(--)`**. The options that take single dash are generally one character long, while the options taking double dash are of one word. Two dashes are called as long format options. This book majorly demonstrates the command option using single dash. You can use manual pages to know about the long options a command supports. A command line may contain both the kinds of options (short format as well as long format).

Commands may support a varying list of arguments. They are generally many characters long or only one word. The words that are used as arguments are not fixed. One such argument can be filename. For example, the **`cat`** command displays the contents of the given filename. The supplied filename is an argument of the **`cat`** command.

Each command has an associated manual page, which gives detailed information about that command, the options it takes, and the number of arguments it may support. You can access these man pages whenever you stick around with a command. This acts as a support system for you. To read a manual related to a command, you have the **`man`** command.

Almost every command supports the **`--help`** option (preceded with double dash). This option provides quick help for the related command.

Each command in Linux also supports the **--version** option that prints the command's version information.

Some commands may take input, while some may run without any input. Input is usually given by typing from the keyboard. The input streams coming from the keyboard are called standard input. Here, we have visited a new term, *standard input*. What is it? We will discuss that later in this chapter.

Type of commands

We have two types of commands: internal and external commands. Internal commands are those that are built into the shell itself. External commands reside under one of the paths reserved for storing commands, such as **/usr/bin** and **/usr/sbin**. Internal commands are not stored in these locations. Whenever an external command is executed, the command is searched in the locations specified under the **PATH** environment variable. Following is the content of the **PATH** environment variable:

```
echo $PATH
```

```
/home/vishesh/.local/bin:/home/vishesh/bin:/usr/local/bin:/usr/local/sbin:/
usr/bin:/usr/sbin
```

When shell receives a command at the terminal prompt, it searches for it within its own list of commands, and if it finds one, search is not forwarded to search paths listed in the **PATH** variable. Suppose the command given does not match within its internal set. In that case, shell searches the directories specified in the **PATH** environment variable in sequence to search for the command. If the command is not found in any of the paths listed in this variable, shell throws the **command not found** error.

Using command terminal

For efficient working on the terminal, you must know different keystrokes to perform different operations on the terminal. The **stty** command will give you a list of your terminal settings and its characteristics. This command can also change terminal characteristics. If used with the **-a** option, it prints all the terminal settings and characteristics in human readable format. *Figure 3.1* lists several keystrokes that are important to remember for efficiently working on the terminal. While writing a command, you may end up with several mistakes. Now, you would like to erase all the line's content. Just do this by pressing *Ctrl* + *u*. This is a kill character.

```
[vishesh@192 ~]$ stty -a
speed 38400 baud; rows 53; columns 211; line = 0;
intr = ^C; quit = ^\; erase = ^?; kill = ^U; eof = ^D; eol = <undef>; eol2 = <undef>; swtch = <undef>; start = ^Q; stop = ^S; susp = ^Z; rprnt = ^R; werase = ^W; lnext = ^V; discard = ^O; min = 1; time = 0;
-parenb -parodd -cmspar cs8 -hupcl -cstopb cread -clocal -crtscts
-ignbrk -brkint -ignpar -parmrk -inpck -istrip -inlcr -igncr icrnl ixon -ixoff -iuclc -ixany -imaxbel iutf8
opost -olcuc -ocrnl onlcr -onocr -onlret -ofill -ofdel nl0 cr0 tab0 bs0 vt0 ff0
isig icanon iexten echo echoe echok -echonl -noflsh -xcase -tostop -echoprt echoctl echoke -flusho -extproc
```

Figure 3.1: *Usage of stty command showing terminal settings*

Many options are also listed in the output, as shown in *Figure 3.1*. Options that are prefixed with **-** are turned off and others are turned on. The **stty** command can also be used to change any of the terminal characteristics or settings, as follows:

```
stty intr ^I
```

The previous command would change the interrupt key from `^C` to `^I`. You can verify this change using the **`stty -a`** command.

When you start executing a command after pressing the enter key, you will get your next prompt only after its successful or unsuccessful completion. If a command is running for several minutes in your terminal, and you do not want to wait any more for its completion, you can terminate this by pressing *Ctrl + c*; your command prompt is back to accept the next command. This is interrupting character.

Many commands take input from the terminal, such as the **`cat`** command. If you want to stop giving input and execute command with this input, press *Ctrl + d*. This is **EOF** character. This will stop accepting more input from the keyboard and will execute the command.

Pressing the *Tab* key in the command line would serve as an assistant for you. It helps in completing the command line in fewer keystrokes. Typing *Tab* completes the incomplete command name or file name. It depends on what are you typing. Type **`ec`** in the command terminal and press *Tab* key; what happens then? **`ec`** will change into **`echo`**. It automatically finds all the command names that start with **`ec`** and complete the spelling of the command if it finds only one match. If it finds many commands starting with **`ec`**, the list of commands will be displayed for you to choose from. You can press *Tab* key again when typing further keys for the command name. Typing further letters and pressing the *Tab* key will restrict the list of matching commands. Repeating this key combination many times would complete the command name. The same applies to filenames. When we are about to write filenames in the command line, pressing the *Tab* key will complete the file name if only one match is found, or produce the list of filenames if more than one match found. Using the *Tab* key comes in handy if you do not remember the name of the command or the name of the file. Just type one or more characters; shell would give you a list of commands you would like to execute. You can choose your command from the list.

Do it yourself

Read the output of stty -a thoroughly; find the keystrokes to stop and suspend a command.

Type `ca` in the command prompt and press *Tab* twice; what happens?

Standard input, standard output, and standard error

In Linux system, a number known as file descriptor is assigned to each opened file, and the list of each opened file is kept inside the file descriptor table. This number starts from 0. Each command in Linux system opens three files, namely, standard input, standard output and standard error. These are known as standard files. Their file descriptors are 0, 1 and 2, respectively. Command sees these standard files as stream of characters. Each of these standard files has an associated default device file. When a command needs an input and is given from the keyboard, the device file associated with the keyboard is used to provide input to the command. Whatever is written on the standard input is displayed on your terminal. The input given from the keyboard is written as a stream known as standard input. When command produces an output, it is displayed on the terminal. Here, the device file associated with the terminal displays the command output. The command output is sent as a stream known as standard output, which, in turn, is displayed on the terminal. When the command throws an error, the message is also written as a stream in the third standard file known as standard error. Streams from standard error are also displayed on the terminal.

Thus, we can conclude that three standard files are always associated with the terminal. These files are standard input, output, and error. Each command completes its work using these three files only, and each of these standard files, in turn, are associated with a physical device. Standard input uses keyboard for input and is displayed on the terminal. Standard output and error use terminal to send output and error messages, respectively. We can redirect the standard input, output and error to the disk file instead of their default device file. Redirection operator **>** and **<** are used for this. The next section discusses how the redirection operator is used to disassociate the standard files from their default physical device and associate them to a disk file.

Redirection of standard I/O and error

cat command takes the standard input from the keyboard when we type the following:

```
cat file > file1
```

The **>** operator redirects the output to **file1** instead of being displayed on the terminal. Thus, standard output has been redirected from its default physical device to a disk file, but the file descriptor remains the same. We read that file descriptor (**fd**) for the standard output that is associated with the terminal is 1. The preceding command closes the terminal for standard output, and fd 1 is now assigned to **file1**.

```
echo > /dev/tty
```

The preceding command echoes a new line on the attached terminal. By default, standard output goes to the terminal. So, what is the implication here? **/dev/tty**[1] is a pseudo device that refers to the terminal to which the user is connected. All the commands that send their output to terminal can also be written by redirecting the standard output to **/dev/tty**. Check your terminal name by issuing the **tty** command, as we did in *Chapter 1, The First Step to Linux*. If you get **/dev/pts/0**, then the preceding command can be replaced with the following:

```
echo>/dev/pts/0
```

Real usage of redirecting to **/dev/tty** can be understood when we read shell scripting:

```
echo 1>file1
```

[1] *Any redirection to /dev/tty file does not increase its size. It always remains 0.*

1> and **>** are the same. There is no space between **1** and **>**. Here, 1 is the **fd** that refers to standard output.

When we type the following:

```
cat > file1
```

Or simply we type the following:

```
cat
```

The **cat** command takes its input from the standard input, that is, the keyboard:

```
cat < infile1
```

In the preceding command, the **<** operator is used to redirect standard input of cat command from the default keyboard device to a disk file, say, **infile1**. Here, the output is displayed on the terminal as standard output is not redirected. In the previous command, the **cat** command takes input from the file named **infile1** and **fd 0** is assigned to this file after disassociating standard input from the keyboard device file. The previous command can also be written as follows:

```
cat 0<infile1
```

Here, **0<** and **<** are the same. Both redirect the standard input from the default keyboard device to something else:

```
cat file1
```

The preceding command attempts to display the contents of **file1**. If the specified file does not exist, the command throws an error on the terminal. This is the default behavior. To redirect the standard error somewhere else, say to a disk file, the **2>** operator is used as follows:

```
cat file4 2> err
```

In the previous command, we attempted to view the content of **file4**. If **file4** does not exist, the associated error message is sent to the **err** file and not on the display because we have redirected the standard error to the file named, **err**, by using **2>** operator. There should be no space between **2** and **>**. Now, **fd 2** is assigned to a disk file, named **err**, and the original device file (terminal display) associated with **fd 2** is closed. All the error messages generated from the command will be written to the given file name, and only the output from the command will be written to the terminal.

We can also redirect the standard error and standard output to the same file, say **file.out.err**:

```
cat file1 >&file.out.err
```

In the previous command line, the output and error messages of the given command will be written to the file named **file.out.err** using the **>&** operator. This way, we have merged the standard output and standard input.

It is also possible to redirect the standard output wherever a standard error is going or vice-versa, as follows:

```
cat file1 > newfile1 2>&1
```

In the preceding command, the output is redirected to **newfile1**, and error messages are redirected to where the output is going using the **2>&1** operator:

```
cat file1 2> newfile >&2
```

The preceding command redirects the error message to **newfile** and standard output is redirected to where a standard error goes using the **>&2 or 1>&2** operator.

There may be times when you are not interested in knowing the errors or the output generated by the command; you may only be interested in its execution. If error messages or output printing on the screen are not of any interest for you, you can send them to a special device file **/dev/null** instead of redirecting them to a disk file. **/dev/null** nullifies any output written to it. Suppose you want to know whether a particular file exists; you can use the following sequence of commands:

```
cat f1 >& /dev/null
echo $?
```

The preceding command redirects the standard output and standard error to **/dev/null**, which stores nothing. The next command uses the last command's return value to verify whether the last command was successfully executed. Now, verify the contents of **/dev/null** by typing the following:

```
cat /dev/null
```

The file size of **/dev/null** always remains zero, even if you redirect very big output to **/dev/null**:

```
cat f1 f2 >merge1 2>/dev/null
```

Suppose you are assigned a task to concatenate the contents of two files on a regular basis. You need to execute the given task even if one of the files does not exist. Using the **cat** command on non-existent file always returns error. You can avoid this error by redirecting the standard error to **/dev/null** that does not show you any errors.

You have another requirement: creating a directory every few minutes while you are unaware of its existence at a particular time. In this case, you will not be interested in any error message, only in creating the directory. **/dev/null** will be very handy in this case:

```
mkdir dir1 2>/dev/null
```

The previous command will create a directory if it does not exist, else the error message will be redirected to **/dev/null**. In this case, you will need a shell script to automate this task every minute. We will see real usages of **/dev/null** when we will read shell script in *Chapter 7, Interacting With Bash Shell and Scripting*.

When we use the **1>** or **2>** operator to redirect the standard output and standard error to a file respectively, it overwrites the destination file, if it exists. Using **1>>** and **2>>** can prevent file overwriting. **>>** means append, which means the **>>** operator will append the disk file rather than overwriting it. Consider this example:

```
cat file1 >> newfile
```

In the preceding command, contents of **file1** are being redirected to **newfile**, however, **newfile** will not be overwritten but appended.

Do it yourself

1. What will the following command return if **file1** exists on the disk, while **file2** is non-existing?

   ```
   cat file1 file2>& file.out.err
   ```

   a. What is the output and error message of the preceding command. Name the standard output and standard error. Does the previous command require any standard input?

2. Store the current system date and time to file named **home.lst**. Next, list the contents of your home directory and store the output to **home.lst** using the **>** operator. View the contents of **home.lst**.

   a. Now, store the date and time again to **home.lst** while ensuring that the previous content on the file is not be overwritten.

3. Type the following command:

   ```
   cat home.lst f2 > filemerge 2>file.err
   ```

   here, **home.lst** is the existing file and **f2** is non-existing file. What content will **filemerge** contain, and what will be stored in **file.err**?

4. What is the difference between the following commands:

   a. **echo 1 > file1**

      and

   b. **echo 1> file1**

5. Write the command to pass the output of the **who** command to a file named **who.out**. Verify the contents of **who.out** by using the **cat** command.

Pattern matching and regular expression

Linux allows us to search the files on disk that match a pattern. This facility is not limited to files searching; strings matching a pattern can also be searched in a large file. Many operations can be performed after a successful file match or string match. But the question is how to define those patterns. The patterns are defined using the following:

- Various wild-card characters
- Meta characters
- Regular expressions

We will visit all these three concepts one by one and understand how they work in RHEL9.0.

Wild card characters

Wild card characters form simple to complex patterns to match one or multiple filenames in the command line. The wild card characters are not the same as regular characters; they are special characters that have some special meaning for shell. When a command is submitted to the shell, it interprets the command line to find wild card characters before the command is submitted to the kernel for execution. If the command line contains any wild-card character, shell translates and transforms it accordingly. Only after transformation of all wildcard characters is done, the command is executed.

There are three wildcard characters, *****, **?**, and **[]**, each having a special meaning or special interpretation by the shell. These characters are called wild-card characters because they are used to match many filenames at once. Any one or a combination of these wildcard characters can be used in a single command line to build generic patterns that can match many filenames.

* to match many files names

Let us talk about * first, which will give you a good idea of how wild card characters work. * is a wild card character that matches many filenames at once. Let us see what files reside in our working directory by issuing the **ls** command, as shown in *Figure 3.2*. Next, type the following command:

```
echo *
```

What will you get here? You will see all the filenames in the current working directory, as shown in *Figure 3.2*:

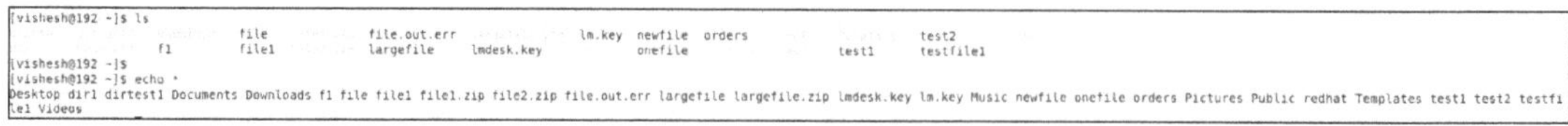
[vishesh@192 ~]$ ls
file file.out.err lm.key newfile orders test2
f1 file1 largefile lmdesk.key onefile test1 testfile1
[vishesh@192 ~]$
[vishesh@192 ~]$ echo *
Desktop dir1 dirtest1 Documents Downloads f1 file file1 file1.zip file2.zip file.out.err largefile largefile.zip lmdesk.key lm.key Music newfile onefile orders Pictures Public redhat Templates test1 test2 testfile1 Videos

***Figure 3.2:** Usage of * metacharacter*

The output will be same as that of the **ls** command. Here, * matches all the file names. That is why it is called a wild-card character. The **echo** command's behavior just echoes whatever string is passed to it. Here, shell sees *. Since * has a special meaning to the shell, it is in action now. It scans the command line to look for the wild card characters. It finds * and interprets it to match all the file names in the current working directory. So, * will be transformed to match all the filenames as follows:

```
echo Desktop dir1 dirtest1 Documents Downloads f1 file file1 file1.zip file2.
zip file.out.err largefile largefile.zip lmdesk.key lm.key Music newfile onefile
orders Pictures Public redhat Templates test1 test2 testfile1 Videos
```

Thus, shell expands the command line as if all the files from the current directory is listed. The command line is simplified now. This simplified line is submitted to the kernel for execution. Shell waits for the execution of the command to complete. After the command is executed completely, the user will receive the next prompt for their next command.

Exception to * wildcard character is that it does not match any hidden files or file starting with a dot **(.)**. Wild card character can match dot **(.)** anywhere in the filename but not at the beginning. Thus, if you want to view files that begin with **.file**, type the following:

```
ls .file*
```

The previous command will match all the hidden files whose name starts with **.file**. Type the following command:

```
ls file*
```

It would match filenames like **file1**, **file2** or filenames containing a dot, like **file.txt**. If you want to match all the files having an extension **.c**, type the following command:

```
ls *.c
```

Now, type the following command:

```
echo '*'
```

What will you get here? In the preceding command, an asterisk (*) character is echoed on the screen. Here, * is enclosed in single quotes. Single quotes are used to escape the meaning of the * symbol. When shell sees * enclosed in single quotes, it does not simplify it and * will match literally. Besides single quotes, double quotes and backslash character \ can also be used to escape its special meaning. The preceding command is same as:

```
echo \*
```

Or

```
echo "*"
```

Thus, if a string contains a special character that we want to print literally and do not want the shell to interpret it, you should hide its meaning for the shell by doing one of the following:

- Enclosing complete string character within a single or double quotes.
- Preceding each special character with a single backslash character or quote character.

  ```
  $echo '* is a wild-card character'
  * is a wild card character
  ```

  In the preceding command, the complete string is enclosed in single quotes, so * is matched literally. The previous command line is the same as follows:

```
echo \* is a wild card character
```

Or

```
echo '*' is a wild card character
```

Or

```
echo "*" is a wild card character
```

So, how would you decide whether to use quote character (' or ") or backslash character (****) to hide the meaning of wild-card character for shell. If a string contains more than one wild card character, enclosing the complete string in quotes would be the best option instead of escaping each character.

The next question is when to use single or double quotes. Singe quotes can escape all the special characters that shell supports. Double quotes cannot support some metacharacters. These are ` (backtick or backquote), **$** and ****. So, using these metacharacters, you must use a single quote to escape shell. We will study these metacharacters in the next section.

Now, we understood how does * work. Let us use it to create a generic pattern that matches one or more filenames. Using wild card characters to match many files simultaneously saves your typing efforts, and the command line also looks concise. Suppose we have many files whose names start with **sample**, and we want to concatenate these files; we would simply issue the following in that case:

```
cat sample1 sample2 sample3 sample4 sampletest sample
```

In the previous command, we must type all the required filenames as arguments to the **cat** command. No special characters have been used in this command line. No simplification by the shell will be done. To save yourself of the typing efforts, you can create a generic pattern that matches all these filenames, as follows:

```
cat sample*
```

In the preceding command, shell will attempt to match filenames starting with sample, which can end with any character and number of characters. Actually, * matches zero or more characters. The previous command could match file names like sample, **sample1**, **sample2**, **sample11**, **sample12**, **sample135**, **sampletest**, and so on. It will also match files named **sample***, if any exist. Thus, the search patten using * is not very restrictive and matches more than the required files. What if we want to match only **sample11** and **sample12**. We have to resort to another wild-card character **[]**, which we will see soon.

If no matching filenames are found with the preceding command executed, the word is left unchanged and the following error is thrown:

```
cat: 'sample'*: No such file or directory
```

? Matching a single character

Let us understand another wild card character **?**. **?** matches a single character. To match filenames like **sample1**, **sample2**, we can issue the following:

```
ls sample?
```

The previous command will list all the files whose names are 7-characters long and start with sample. **?** can match any character after **sample**. The preceding command will not match the **sample**. To match filenames like **sample11**, **sample12**, and so on, you must use the **?** wild card character twice, as follows:

```
ls sample??
```

Like *****, **?** do not match any files beginning with a dot **(.)** but can match dot **(.)** anywhere in the file name. To match filenames that are 5-characters long, type the following command:

```
ls ?????
```

This will match filenames like **file1**, **file2**, and the file names having period **(.)** as **f.txt**. Use the following to match file names that contain the **.txt** extension and have three characters before **.txt**:

```
ls ???.txt
```

When shell sees **?** in the command line, and if it is not quoted or escaped, shell transforms it to match a character. After all the **?** wild card characters are resolved to a matching character, the command line is submitted to kernel for execution. To match **?** literally and prevent shell from treating it in a special way, the same quoting method is used as described for the ***** wild card character:

```
echo '? is also a wild card character'
```

The previous command will print **?** literally, as follows:

```
? is a wild card character.
```

Can you guess what the preceding command does without quoting **?**. It will match all the filenames that are 1-character long. To match filenames whose extension is three characters long:

```
ls *.???
```

[] character class

We have seen that the ***** and **?** wild card characters create generalized patterns that match multiple filenames. When we use ***** and **?**, it is impossible to restrict our search to some matched files. When we use **sample***, it searches all the filenames starting with **sample** and ending with zero or more characters. What if we want to search only **sample12** and **sample21**. Similarly, **sample**? will search **sample1**, **sample2**, **sample3**, and so on. What if we want to match only **sample1** and **sample3** and not **sample2**. All these requirements can be satisfied using another wild card character called character class, a pair of square brackets **[ ]**. Character class matches only one character. The characters to match are listed under square brackets. Square brackets can contain a list of numbers, characters, special characters or combination of these three. Square brackets may also contain a range of alphabets or numbers. The contents of character class determine what to match. Let us understand character class by issuing the following command:

```
ls sample[13]
```

The preceding command will find only files named **sample1** or **sample3**. It matches file names that starts with **sample** and end in either 1 or 3. Thus, **character** class may contain many characters but will match any of them in file names.

If we want to match only **sample12** and **sample21** and **sample23**, the following solution will work:

```
ls sample[12][213]
```

The preceding command would match file names starting with **sample** followed by either 1 or 2 and ending in any of the given digits listed in the last character class. (2 or 1 or 3). You can also specify the range inside square brackets. The preceding command can also be written as follows:

```
sample[1-2][1-3]
```

Suppose we have the following files on disk:

```
samplea sampleb samplec sampled samplee samplef
```

To match only the files that start with **sample** and end with either **a**, **b**, or **c**, issue the following:

```
ls sample[a-c]
```

Thus, the preceding command matches the range **a-c** after **sample** in the file names. Thus, it searches **samplea**, **sampleb**, and **samplec**.

With character class, you have the option to negate the search criteria. **!** is used as the first character in the character class to negate the criteria as follows:

```
sample[!a-c]
```

The preceding command matches all the files that start with **sample** and do not end with alphabets that comes under range **a-c**. Let us match files using a numeric range. Suppose we have many files named **file1**, **file2**, **file3**, etc. To search for files whose names start with file and that have an ending range of 4-8, issue the following:

```
ls file[4-8]
```

To match the square brackets **[** or**]** literally and prevent shell from treating it as a special character, precede it with backslash, as **[#$\]]**, or specify it as the first character in the character class as follows:

```
[]$#]
```

The preceding pattern will match the **]** character literally under the character class. Suppose you have inadvertently created a file named **abc[123]**. To match this file, you will use the following:

```
'abc[123]'
```

If quoting is not provided, it can match **abc1**, **abc2**, or **abc3**. If neither of these files exist, the **abc[123]** is matched even without quoting. Quoting must match the file name only (**abc[123]**). The following are the few usages of these wild card characters:

- **ls *[!a-zA-Z]**: It will list all the files whose names do not end with any letter.
- **ls *.[!o][!t][!t]**: It lists all the files whose extension is of three letters long and the first, second and third letters of the extension are not **o, t, t** respectively. It can match **.pdf** files, **.zip** files, and so on if they exist on the current directory.
- **[$*?]**: It matches any special symbol like **$**, ***** and **?**. These special characters do not have any meaning when used inside character class.
- **[?*$\]]**: It matches special symbols like **?**, *****, **$** or **]**.

Metacharacters

Metacharacters are also special characters and have special meaning for shell. When shell sees any metacharacters, it translates them and transforms the command line accordingly. The following tables lists the metacharacters and their special meaning for shell:

Metacharacter	Meaning for shell
a.		A pipeline character
b. &	Used to run the command as a background job
c. ;	Used to separate two commands in a single command line
d. ()	Used to group two commands
e. <	Standard input operator
f. >	Standard output operator
g. {}	Used to enclose multiple arguments together in the command line
h. &&	To execute two commands in a command line; the command after && is executed only if the first command is executed successfully
i. $	Evaluates environment variable as used in echo
j. ``	Command substitution

Table 3.1: *List of metacharacters and their meaning for shell*

Executing commands together

We can use a single command line to execute two tasks together by using the **;** operator as follows:

```
cat > f3;cat f3
```

First, the preceding command creates a file named **f3**, and after the first command finishes, it also displays the contents of file **f3**. The second command is always executed irrespective of whether or not the first command executes successfully.

When two commands are combined using the **&&** operator, they work differently. The second command will be executed only if the first command finishes successfully and has an exit status of 0. If the first command exits with a non-zero status, the command next to the **&&** operator will not be executed. Refer to *Figure 3.3*, where we want to delete file **f3** if it exists. The first command line uses; where **rm** is executed even if the **cat** command fails. But in the second command line, where commands are separated by the **&&** operator, the **rm** command is executed only if the **cat** command is successfully exited.

```
[vishesh@192 ~]$ cat f3; rm f3
cat: f3: No such file or directory
rm: cannot remove 'f3': No such file or directory
[vishesh@192 ~]$
[vishesh@192 ~]$
[vishesh@192 ~]$ cat f3 && rm f3
cat: f3: No such file or directory
```

***Figure 3.3:** Usage of ; and && metacharacters*

Pipe (|) operator

This operator is used to pass the output of one command to another. There may be cases when we want to perform more tasks with the output of a command. The output of a command can be passed as the input of another command. The first command in *Figure 3.4* returns nothing on the screen. Can you guess why? Due to the pipe **(|)** operator, the output of the **date** command is not displayed to the standard output but is passed to the command next to the **|** operator. The output of the **date** command serves as the input for the next given command **cat**. Here, the **cat** command takes its input from the **date** command, not standard input, and writes it to file **f2**. Thus, **f2** will contain the output of the **date** command, that is, the system date and time. Pipeline worked with commands that give standard output and accept standard input. We can use pipe operator multiple times in a command line if we have complex tasks. We will use pipe operator to combine sequence of commands throughout the book.

```
[vishesh@192 ~]$ date|cat > f2
[vishesh@192 ~]$
[vishesh@192 ~]$ cat f2
Wednesday 14 December 2022 12:34:51 AM IST
```

***Figure 3.4:** Usage of pipe | operator*

Whitespaces (space, tabs, and new line)

Whitespace characters are those included in a file but not visible when the file's contents are printed. They consume space in the file but do not have any visible mark. Spaces, tabs, newline, form feed and carriage return character are called whitespaces:

Spaces and tabs

Shell performs its interpretive role when it finds multiple spaces or tabs between two words. It always replaces many consecutive space or tabs characters with one. If you want to preserve the multiple spaces, the same quoting method is used for shell wild cards discussed earlier. Consider this example:

```
$echo Hello, this is the world of Linux
```

It will echo the following on your terminal:

```
Hello, this is the world of Linux
```

All the extra spaces are truncated in the preceding output. If you want to preserve extra space, you can use the following command:

```
$echo 'this     is a world        of Linux'
this     is a world        of Linux
```

Here, shell did not interpret multiple spaces. Similarly, echoing a line with consecutive tabs will print single tabs. But the question that comes to mind is 'How will you print *Tab* character in your terminal?' *Tab* key will not do this as pressing *Tab* in the command line will help you complete the command line. You must press *Ctrl + v* and *Tab* key combination to print the *Tab* character.

Newline

The newline is generated by pressing the *Enter* key. When shell sees newline, it marks the command as complete and takes up the command line for its interpretation and execution. When we have some command that spans a line, you must type **** before pressing *Enter*, as follows:

```
\[Enter]
```

Pressing **** followed by the *Enter* key does not mark the end of the command, and the shell does not take over the command line. Instead, you will get a continuation prompt, **>**, where you can continue your command that spans a line. Take a look at this example:

```
echo "hello this is world of Linux\
> Read this book on Linux which is for beginners\
>you will get hand-on using Linux commands"
```

In the preceding example, pressing **** before the *Enter* key gives you a second prompt >, which is the beginning of the second line of the current command.

{} Giving multiple patterns in command line

Braces **{}** are used to provide more than one pattern in the command line, as follows:

```
cp {abc,xyz} redhat/
```

The preceding command copies files named **abc** and **xyz** to the **redhat** directory. Without this metacharacter, we must issue two commands to copy these two files.

Moreover, braces are also used to generate a series of strings based on the specified patterns. Consider this example:

```
touch file{1..5}
```

In the preceding command, braces are expanded to transform the given pattern and generate a set of filenames as **file1**, **file2**, **file3**, **file4** and **file5**. Then, the **touch** command is executed using expanded file names.

Command substitution

Back quote (`) is used in pairs and is called the command substitution character. It enables the execution of a command within a command. Suppose we want to print today's date; we would type the following command:

```
$ echo today's date is 'date'
today's date is Wednesday 14 December 2022 12:34:51 AM IST
```

The preceding command uses the command substitution character using the **date** command to display the current date and time. The **date** command is enclosed in backquote ('), which has been given special treatment by shell. Shell interprets it as a command substitution character. The value returned is printed in the message.

grouping commands

The parentheses **()** are used to group commands and apply some operation to all of them. See the following command line:

```
pwd;ls>listing
```

Here, two commands are executed in a single command line, and the output of the last command is passed to a disk file named **listing**, whereas the output of the first command will be displayed on the screen. What if we like to redirect the output of all the commands in the command line to the same disk file. We must group all these commands in parentheses as follows:

```
(pwd;ls)> listing
```

The preceding command would write the output of the **pwd** command and the output of the **ls** command to the same file.

Quoting the quote character

So far, we have seen that the escape character and the quote character are used to prevent the shell from interpreting the special symbols. But how can we print quote or **/** character literally? The answer is escaping them with a backslash \ character or quoting it with opposite quote, as follows:

```
$echo this is single quote \'
this is single quote '
```

In the preceding command, we have used the backslash character before ' to prevent the shell from interpreting this. You can also enclose complete string with double quotes, as follows:

```
$echo "this is single quote '"
```

What if your string includes double quotes and you want to print double quotes? This can be achieved by backspacing double quote character using either \ or by enclosing it in single quotes. Also, the complete `string` can be enclosed in single quotes to print double quotes on the screen. To print the \ character, an additional \ character has to be used, or \ character can be enclosed in single quotes to let the shell not to interpret it, as follows:

```
$echo this is backspace character //
this is backspace character /
```

Now, rewrite the preceding string in single quotes and see its output yourself. As we read earlier, double quotes does not escape the meaning of the / metacharacter.

Precautions when special characters are included in filenames

You should not create any file names that contain any of the characters that are special for shell. Suppose you have a file like **`sample?123`** or **`samplex123`**. Issue the following command:

```
cat sample?123
```

It will make shell interpret the **?** to match for filenames. It will show you the contents of both the mentioned files and not only **`sample?123`**. Thus, if you wanted to view the contents of only **`sample?123`**, you will inadvertently end up listing the contents of two files together, leaving you in a fix. This may also lead to losing important data if you want to delete only one file but inadvertently deleted two files without your knowledge. So, you must take precautions to deal with the files' names containing any special characters. If you want to access the file whose name includes any special characters, you must escape the special meaning of the special character by quoting or escaping technique that we read earlier.

Regular expression

We have seen that shell has some special meaning for some of its special characters. If used in the command line, the shell will always interpret these special characters, transforming or expanding the line accordingly. Some expressions are formed using these special characters consumed and understood by some commands. They are known as **Regular Expression** (**RE**). The shell has no role of interpreting them. These regular expressions match some patterns in filenames or file contents. Some useful commands that use REs are **`grep`**, **`sed`**, **`vi`**, **`awk`**, and **`tr`** .

Since patterns formed by RE use the same metacharacters as shell, you must always enclose them in quotes. These metacharacters have different meanings when used in RE. This chapter recommends always quoting RE using single quotes as we know that double quotes cannot escape some of the special characters for shell. To match any metacharacter literally inside RE, you can escape it by preceding it with a backslash.

In this section, we will see how REs are used by **`tr`** and **`grep`** commands. We will see the usage of REs throughout the book.

There are two types of regular expressions: **Basic Regular Expression** (**BRE**) and **Extended Regular Expression** (**ERE**). Some metacharacters form basic regular expressions, others form extended RE. Let us understand these regular expressions. After you understand these regular expressions, we will see their usages in various commands that will be discussed in the next section.

A period (.)

A period (`.`) is a part of BRE. It matches a single character. To match strings like **`ape`**, **`ate`**, **`axe`**, and so on, following regular expression can be used:

```
a.e
```

It will match strings that contain **`a`**, followed by any one character and then **`e`**. The match is performed anywhere in the string.

```
a....e
```

The preceding pattern will match strings that contains **`a`**, followed by any 4 letters and then a single **`e`**. To match it literally, precede with ****, as follows:

```
a\.txt
```

It will match the string that contains **`a.txt`**.

Character class

It is a regular expression where a list of characters is enclosed in `[` and `]`. It is a part of BRE. It matches any single character in the list. If the first character inside the brackets `[]` is `^`, it negates the list, meaning it matches the characters that are not in the list. For example, if we write `[`**`abcd`**`]`, it matches any one character in the list. If we write `[`**`^abcd`**`]`, it matches all those characters that are not inside `[` and `]` brackets.

We can also specify a range of characters or numbers inside **[]**, as follows:

```
[a-d]
```

It matches any characters from **a** to **d**. For numeric range, we may write this:

```
[1-6]
```

It matches any one digit from **1** to **6**. To match – in the string, write – as the first or the last character of the character class, as follows:

```
[TU-]
```

This will match either **T** or **U** the or – character. To include a **[** or **]** in the character class, you have to include it as the first or the last character. To match all the non-alphabetic characters, type the following command:

```
[^A-Za-z]
```

Named character classes

Named character classes are the name given to a character class that contains the list of all characters belonging to that class. We have certain named character classes that have predefined list of characters, as follows:

- **[:alnum:]**: This represents the characters containing letters and numbers.
- **[:alpha:]**: This represents the character class that contain only letters.
- **[:blank:]**: This represents the character class that contains spaces and tabs.
- **[:cntrl:]**: This represents the character class that contains control character.
- **[:digit:]**: This represents the class of characters that contains only digits.
- **[:graph:]**: This represents the character class that contains alphanumeric characters and punctuation.
- **[:lower:]**: This represents the class of characters that contains all the lowercase letters.
- **[:print:]**: This character class includes [:graph:] and space character.
- **[:punct:]**: This represents the character class that contains punctuation characters.
- **[:space:]**: This character class includes all white space characters.
- **[:upper:]**: This represents the class of characters that contains uppercase letters.
- **[:xdigit:]**: It represents digits in hexadecimal numbers.

Anchor characters

^ and **$** are anchor characters. **^** matches the string at beginning of the line and **$** matches the string at end of the line. It forms a part of BRE.

- **^h**: It matches the line that begins with letter **h**.
- **h$**: It matches the line that ends with **h**.
- **^hello$**: It matches **hello**; the only word in the line.
- **^$**: It matches empty lines.
- **^[^[:digit:]]**: It finds the lines that do not begin with digits.

To match any of the listed regular expression's metacharacters, you must escape them using the **** character. For example, to search for literal **(.)**, type the following:

```
\.
```

To search for ***** literally, type this:

```
\*
```

Special characters

The following are some of the special characters that you can use to form regular expressions.

- The symbols **\<** and **\>** match the strings at the start and end of the word, respectively.

  ```
  '\<apple\> '
  ```

  Preceding regular expression searches the whole word.

  ```
  \<az
  ```

  Preceding regular expression matches the word that starts with letter **a**.
- **\W** is a synonym for **[^_[:alnum:]]**. It searches for non-alphanumeric word character excluding _.
- **\w** is a synonym for **[_[:alnum:]]** . It matches alphanumeric word character including _.
- **\s** matches white space character. Whitespace character may be space, tab, form feed, new line and carriage return character.

Repetition

A regular expression may be followed by one of several repetition operators:

- **?**: The preceding item is optional and matched at most once.
- **.**: The preceding item will be matched zero or more times.
- **+**: The preceding item will be matched one or more times.

- **{n}**: The preceding item is matched exactly n times.
- **{n,}**: The preceding item is matched n or more times.
- **{,m}**: The preceding item is matched at most m times.
- **{n,m}**: The preceding item is matched at least n times, but not more than m times.

Among the preceding repetition operators, **+**, ?, and **{}** belong to ERE. The following are some common usages of these repetition operators:

- **a***: It matches zero or more occurrences of **a**. It can match no character or **a**, **aa**, **aaa**, **aaaa**, etc.
- **Book***: It matches the string that contains **Boo**, and **k** is optional. Thus, it can match **Book**, **Bookkkkk**, **Boo**, and so on.
- **b**?: It matches letter **b** zero or one time.
- **b+**: It matches letter **b** at least one time.

Matching the alternate expression

When two Res are joined using the **|** operator, they are matched. This belongs to extended sets of regular expression. Use this to find out lines that contain either apple or mango:

```
apple|mango
```

Grouping patterns

The parentheses **()** are used to group patterns that help you write simple to complex patterns. Grouping metacharacter is also the part of ERE:

```
(water|musk|star)melon
```

The preceding RE searches for either **watermelon**, **muskmelon** or **starmelon**.

Back-references and \(\)

\(and **\)** is used to identify multiple patterns by creating a grouped pattern that can later be reproduced using **\n**. The back-reference **\n**, where **n** is a single digit, matches the substring previously matched by the grouped expression. Each grouped patterns gets a numeric tag **n**. To print group **1**, **\1** is used; to print second created group, **\2** is used; and so on.

Now, we can end our discussion of regular expressions. In the next section, we will learn the usage of these regular expressions in commands. We have seen that some metacharacters form a set of basic regular expressions and some form a set of extended ones. As some of the metacharacters belonging to the extended family, such as **?**, **+**, **{**, **|**, **(**, and **)**, lose their special meaning in BRE, we can use the back slashed versions of these metacharacters as **\?**, **\+**, **\{**, **\|**, **\(**, and **\)**, when using BRE.

Do it yourself

1. **What is the difference between the following three commands?**
   a. echo '*'
   b. echo "*"
   c. echo *
2. **Explain what the following command will do, and explain the output.**
   a. echo all kids are stars *
   b. echo all kids are stars *
   c. echo 'all kids are stars *'
   d. echo all kids are stars*
3. **Suppose you have a file named stars1 in your current working directory; what does the following command do?**

   Echo all kids are stars*

   What will the preceding command print if:
   a. You do not have any files starting with stars.
   b. You have a file named stars*
4. **Create a file named my new project. To create this file, enclose the file name in quotes. How will you access this file using cat command and backslash character?**
5. **How will you find out the files whose names are three characters long?**
6. **Create two files named ??abc and xyabc. Add some contents in these files. How will you list these two files in one command line using wild card character. How will you list only the file named ??abc**
7. **Create a file named abc.txt. What does the following command do?**

   ls ???????

   Does the above command match abc.txt also?
8. **Create file named abc? and abc]. Now, write command to list the following:**
   a. Only abc] file,
   b. Only abc? file and
   c. Both the files
9. **What do the following commands do?**

   echo '$HOME'

   echo "$HOME"

User commands

This section discusses basic user commands and briefly discusses various useful commands that users can use in their daily activities. Each command is described with various useful options that go with it. Besides the command in this section, various other commands are covered throughout the book. Though most useful command options have been discussed in this book, you can always refer to man pages for other options and better understand commands.

date

We have already visited the **date** command in *Chapter 1, The First Step to Linux*. It prints the system date and time and displays the time zone. Type the **date** command on the command prompt, and you will get the following output:

```
Thursday 08 December 2022 11:42:46 AM IST
```

The **date** command displays the current date and time in the following format:

```
%A %d %B %Y %r
```

The interpretation of these options, along with other format modifiers, is listed as follows:

- **%A**: Full name of the weekday
- **%d**: Day of the month in two digits
- **%B**: Full name of the month
- **%Y**: Four digit of the year
- **%r**: Time in 12-hour format; also, timezone
- **%a**: Abbreviated weekday name
- **%b or %h**: Abbreviated month name
- **%B**: Full month name
- **%c**: Date and time, no timezone displayed
- **%C**: Two digits of century
- **%d**: Day of month in two digits
- **%H**: Hour (00..23)
- **%I**: Hour (01..12)
- **%j**: Day of year (001..366)
- **%m**: Month (01..12)

- **%M**: Minute (00..59)
- **%p**: AM or PM; blank if not known
- **%P**: Like %p, but lower case
- **%q**: Quarter of year (1..4)
- **%R**: 24-hour hour and minute; same as **%H**:**%M**
- **%S**: Second (00..60)
- **%T**: Time; same as **%H**:**%M**:**%S**
- **%u**: Day of week (1..7); 1 is Monday
- **%U**: Week number of year, with Sunday as first day of week (00..53)
- **%w**: Day of week (0..6); 0 is Sunday
- **%W**: Week number of year, with Monday as first day of week (00..53)
- **%y**: Last two digits of year (00..99)
- **%Y**: Four digits of year
- **%z**: +hhmm numeric time zone (for example, -0500)
- **%Z**: Alphabetic time zone abbreviation (for example, **EDT**)

The mentioned format modifiers can be used to control the output of the **date** command. The following command will print the name of the weekday, month in two digits and year in four digits:

```
date +'%A %m %Y'

Thursday 12 2022
```

To print the date and time in non-default format, mention the specifiers after the **+** symbol. If multiple specifiers have been used and are separated by space, they must be enclosed in single quotes. You can use many format modifier combinations to modify the **date** command output.

The **date** command may take the following options:

- **-d <string>**: Displays the date and time described by the given string; string can be like next Thursday, Tomorrow, Yesterday, and so on
- **-f <filename>**: Same as **-d**; the difference being that the list of string is given in a file; date displayed for each line in the file
- **-R**: Output date and time in RFC 5322 format
- **-r <filename>**: Display the last modification time of given filename

- **-s**: Used to set date and time
- **-u**: print UTC
- **--help and -version**: As mentioned earlier, all the commands support these two options

The following are some of the usages of the **date** command:

- Use the following to display the date and time that was on last Monday:

  ```
  [vishesh@192 ~]$ date -d 'Last Monday'
  Monday 05 December 2022 12:00:00 AM IST
  ```

- Use the following to display the date that belongs to next Thursday in non-default format:

  ```
  $ date -d 'Last Monday' '+%d %m'
  05 12
  ```

- Use the following to set the date to other than **now**:

  ```
  # date -s 'Friday 25 November'
  Friday 25 November 2022 12:00:00 AM IST
  ```

Verify the change in the date by typing the **date** command. Changing a date requires you to log in as root.

Pager

When commands produce big output that scrolls many screens upward, only the part of the result accommodated on the last screen is displayed. Pagers are useful and paginate the big output to many screens. It allows you to display the big output one screen at a time. Pagers not only work with commands but also with files. They allow you to view the contents of a large file one screenful at a time. Many built-in pagers are available in RHEL9.0, but we will discuss only two: **less** and **more**. Some of the commands, by default, use pager when presenting their output. One of them is the **man** command.

more

more can be used to view the large output of commands conveniently. Instead of sending large output to standard output, it can be sent to more pager using pipelining. By passing the large output of the command to **more**, the command's output will not scroll; the result will be displayed page-wise. Using the piping operator, the output of a command is sent to the `more` pager as follows:

```
env|more
```

In the preceding command line, the output of **env** is passed to the more pager, and you see the output one screenful at a time. One screenful of output will be in front of you unless you press the *Enter* key. Pressing the *Enter* key will show you the next screenful of output. You will automatically exit from pager after all the output is displayed on the screen. You have the option to exit at any screen by pressing *q*.

Let us view the contents of a large file by passing it in a pager, as follows:

```
cat /proc/cpuinfo |more
```

The preceding command can be written as follows:

```
more /proc/cpuinfo
```

This would also open a pager for you to view one screenful of file contents at a time. Pressing the *Enter* key will take you to the next page.

more pager offers many internal commands, allowing you to navigate the pages or search within pages. These internal commands are usually defined using one character. To move one screen forward, press *f*. Backward movement is not possible when **more** command is used in pipelines. That said, you can move backward by pressing *b* when more is used with files.

more pager also gives you the search capability. Pressing a forward slash **(/)**, followed by a keyword, will search the given keyword from the current cursor location. Pressing *n* will move the screen to the next match, if any. So, if you want to search the fourth occurrence of the search keyword, you must press *n* three times. more does not provide backward search capability:

```
/PASS
```

Typing the preceding keystrokes will search the supplied **PASS** pattern in the more pager. Pressing *n* will move to the next occurrence.

A number can precede many internal commands. This is known as a repeat factor. This will repeat the internal command with *n* number of times. To move four screens forward, type **4f**, instead of pressing *f* four times. Similarly, to find the fourth occurrence of the search keyword, you can simply type **4n**.

You can also execute a shell command within more pagers by using **!**, followed by the command name. Suppose you want to delete a file **f1**; just type the following:

```
!rm f1
```

Pressing **v** will open **vi** editor.

Pressing **(.)** repeats the previous command. For example, if you have typed **4f**, which moves four screens forward, pressing **(.)** will move another four screens forward.

To display a quick help on more internal commands, **press** *?* or **h**.

less

The **less** has more features than more. It includes almost all the facilities provided by more, plus some extra capabilities. By default, **man** command uses less pager. **less** command does not exit the pager even after scrolling all the pages. To quit the less pager, you must press **q**. You can move backward to screens even if less is used in pipelines. It also offers many commands not supported by more. The following is the list of **less** internal commands:

- **e or j or Down arrow key**: Forward one line or N lines when preceded by N
- **y or k or Up arrow key**: Backward one line or N lines when preceded by N
- **f or SPACE**: Forward one window
- **b**: Backward one window
- **d**: Forward one half-window
- **u**: Backward one half-window
- **Up arrow key**: One line upward
- **Down arrow key**: Scrolls one line downward

It also offers search capability like **more**, but **less** provides more than that. Unlike **more**, **less** can perform backward searching by pressing **?** followed by the search keyword. Pressing **n** will search in the current direction. Pressing **N** will search in the opposite direction. Unlike **more**, **less** highlights the search keyword found. When you type **&** followed by a search pattern, it will display only matching lines as used in following pattern:

```
&PASS
```

The preceding keystroke will display all the lines that contains **PASS**. You can also perform the search for non-matching lines by preceding the search pattern with !:

```
?!PASS
```

The preceding keystrokes will search all the lines that do not match **PASS** in backward direction. Unlike more, **less** cannot repeat the last command.

whereis

The **whereis** locates the binary, source, and manual files for the specified command name. Consider this example:

```
whereis date
date: /usr/bin/date /usr/share/man/man1/date.1.gz /usr/share/man/man1p/date.1p.gz
```

The preceding output lists the binary of the date command and two **man** pages. The following are the options that you can use with the **whereis** commands:

- **-b**: Search for binaries

- **-m**: Search for manuals
- **-s**: Search for sources

If you want to ask only for man pages of the specified commands, type the following:

```
whereis -m date
```

which

The **which** command shows the full path of the given executable, as follows:

```
[vishesh@192 ~]$ which date
/usr/bin/date
```

The output given with the **which** command specifies that when the command is executable at the shell prompt, it would be executed from the path that is listed in the output. In the preceding example, date binary will be executed from **/usr/bin/date**.

man

Linux contains manual documentation for each command line utility that is installed. It is like the system's reference manual. Any of the commands discussed throughout the book can be referred to **man**, which may give you a vast explanation of each option used with the commands. It dumps its output using the **less** pager. You can navigate to man pages in the same way you navigate when using the **less** pager with other commands. A utility or a program may contain many sections of man pages. Each section opens a different **man** page. For example, opening a man page on the **find** command by default displays section **1** of the available man pages. Section **1** includes the description of the command and options available. Use it as follows:

```
man find
```

Manual pages are divided into the following sections:

- Executable programs or shell commands
- System calls (functions provided by the kernel)
- Library calls (functions within program libraries)
- Special files (usually found in **/dev**)
- File formats and conventions, for example, **/etc/passwd**
- Games
- Miscellaneous (including macro packages and conventions), for example, **man(7)**, **groff(7)**
- System administration commands (usually only for root)
- Kernel routines [Nonstandard]

To view the explanation of the **/etc/passwd**[2] file and not the **passwd**[3] command, use section **5** as shown:

```
man 5 passwd
```

The preceding command opens section **5** of manual page related to the **passwd** utility.

A particular man page contains the following sections:

NAME, **SYNOPSIS**, **CONFIGURATION**, **DESCRIPTION**, **OPTIONS**, **EXIT STATUS**, **RETURN VALUE**, **ERRORS**, **ENVIRONMENT**, **FILES**, **VERSIONS**, **CONFORMING TO**, **NOTES**, **BUGS**, **EXAMPLE**, **AUTHORS**, and **SEE ALSO**.

The **-k** option with the **man** command searches for the man pages related to the given keyword and prints short descriptions of all the man pages it found. Type the following:

```
man -k find
```

It prints a short description of the manual page that is referenced by the word **find**. The **-f** option simulates the **whatis** command. To understand the man page, you can use the following:

```
man man
```

whatis

It displays a one-line definition of specified command from all the man pages found. Index databases are used during the search and are updated by the **mandb** program. If the database is not up to date, you would get the following message:

```
[root@192 ~]# whatis echo
echo: nothing appropriate.
[root@192 ~]# whatis date
date: nothing appropriate.
```

Now, update database using the **mandb** command, as shown:

```
[root@192 ~]# mandb
Processing manual pages under /usr/share/man/overrides...
Updating index cache for path '/usr/share/man/overrides/man3'. Wait...done.
Checking for stray cats under /usr/share/man/overrides...
Checking for stray cats under /var/cache/man/overrides...
Processing manual pages under /usr/share/man...
-----------------output truncated---------------------
Checking for stray cats under /usr/local/share/man...
```

---

2 */etc/passwd stores the name and details of all the existing users in Linux System. We will read about this file in Chapter6: Managing Users and File Permissions.*

3 *passwd* command is discussed in Chapter6: Managing Users and File Permissions

```
Checking for stray cats under /var/cache/man/local...
119 man subdirectories contained newer manual pages.
7805 manual pages were added.
0 stray cats were added.
0 old database entries were purged.
```

After updating the index database, execute the **whatis** command again on the **date** binary and **echo** binary, as follows:

```
[root@192 ~]# whatis date
date (1)       - print or set the system date and time
date (1p)       - write the date and time
[root@192 ~]#
[root@192 ~]# whatis echo
echo (1)       - display a line of text
echo (1p)       - write arguments to standard output
```

Both the commands display the definition from two man pages. The **whatis** command is equivalent to **man -f**.

apropos

It is same as follows:

```
man -k <keyword>
```

type

To know the type of the command, you can use the **type** command as follows:

```
type echo
echo is a shell builtin
```

The preceding output shows that **echo** command is an internal command. Use the **type** command with **date** as argument, as follows:

```
$ type date
date is /usr/bin/date
```

It shows that the **date** is an external command.

type command can also accept an alias name as follows:

```
type ll
ll is aliased to 'ls -l --color=auto'
```

It shows that **ll** is an alias.

history

The **history** command displays a list of the last 1000 commands executed in your terminal session. The default length of history cache is determined from the **HISTSIZE** environment variable. This list is stored in the **~/.bash_history** file. The size of this history file is determined on the basis of the **HISTFILESIZE** environment variable. When you execute the **history** command, each command displayed is preceded with the event number. You may repeat any command stored in history by pressing **!**, followed by command number, as follows:

```
$ !999
```

The preceding command will re-execute the command listed in line number 999 without typing it. To execute the last command in bash shell, use the following:

```
!!
```

If you want to execute the second last command, use the following:

```
!-2
```

To clear the history list from the cache, you can use the **-c** option. To display only the last **n** number of commands, type the following command:

```
history <n>
```

By default, command **history** is maintained in the history cache and is written to the **.bash_history** file only after the user exits the session. To immediately write all the commands executed since the beginning of the current shell session from the cache history to the history file, use the **-a** option.

Other useful options that can be used with the **history** command are as follows:

- **-r**: Read the contents of the history file and append them to the current history list
- **-w**: Write the current history list to the history file, overwriting the history file's contents

who

We already studied this command in *Chapter 1, The First Step to Linux*. This command shows who is logged in to the server. Simply type **who** on the terminal prompt, and you will get output as displayed in *Figure 3.5:*

```
[sam@192 ~]$ who
vishesh  tty2         2022-12-20 11:38 (tty2)
sam      tty3         2022-01-02 05:25 (tty3)
```

***Figure 3.5:** Who command*

The output displayed in *Figure 3.5* has four columns. The The first column shows the logged in username, the second column shows the terminal from which the user is logged in, third column shows the date and time of the login, and the fourth column displays the remote hostname of the user. Here, the user is logged in locally. So, the fourth column just displays the terminal name.

The following options can be used with the **`who`** command:

- **`-b`**: Time of the last system boot.
- **`-H`**: It prints output with column name.
- **`-q`**: All login names and total number of users logged on.
- **`-r`**: It prints the current run level.

Figure 3.6 displays the list of all the logged in usernames as well as their total count.

```
[sam@192 ~]$ who -q
vishesh sam
# users=2
```

Figure 3.6: *Usage of who command*

write

`write` command sends a message to another user. This utility allows you to send a message to another user's terminal by allowing you to write the message to your terminal. For example, to send a message to user **`sam`**, you will type as follows:

```
# write sam
```

Pressing the Enter key will wait for you to enter the input. After you type your message, press *Ctrl + D* at the end; this will send the message to **`sam`**. If the user is logged in from multiple terminals, you can specify the name of the terminal to which to send the message, as follows:

```
# write sam tty3
```

The preceding command will send the message to the **`tty3`** terminal of **`sam`** user.

Note: By default, only root can send messages from terminal to other users. Write access to terminal is restricted for non-root users due to security risk. If you want write access to the terminal, then the `TTYPERM` setting in the `/etc/login.defs` file must be modified by root or system administrator. We will discuss this configuration file in *Chapter 6, Managing Users and File Permissions.*

mesg

The **`mesg`** utility allows or disallows the messages from another user's terminal. If **`mesg`** allows the write access, the messages may appear to the terminal from another user's terminal. The **mesg** command may take two arguments: **y** or **n**. If you want no messages to appear in your terminal, you can issue the following:

```
mesg n
```

Else, use the following:

```
mesg y
```

Passing **y** to **mesg** will work only if access is provided in the **/etc/login.defs** file.

wall

The **wall** command displays the message to the terminals of all the logged in users. Users will receive the messages only if the messages are allowed on their terminal. Superusers can write on the walls of all the users even if messages are not allowed on a user's terminal.

set

The **set** command displays the list of all the available shell variables and shell functions. Type the following command:

```
set
```

The long list of variables and functions scrolls up. To view all the variables and functions, you can use a pager as follows:

```
set|less
```

From the output of this preceding command, you will notice that variables are displayed in the form of **variable=value**. Any new setting of the environment variable will be valid only for the current terminal session. There are some read-only variables that cannot be reset. To reset the value of an environment variable, say **HISTSIZE**, type the following:

```
[vishesh@localhost ~]$ HISTSIZE=2000
[vishesh@localhost ~]$ echo $HISTSIZE
2000
```

Many environment variables store set of values such as in **$PATH**. To append a new path to **PATH**, type:

```
[vishesh@localhost ~]$ PATH=$PATH:/bin
```

Verify the change using echo **$PATH**. The **set -o** prints the values of the current options. The meaning of some of the useful options is given here:

- **history**: It enables command **history**.
- **nocobbler**: If turned on, no file overwriting will take place when using the **>** operator.

- **`pipefail`**: If set, the return value of a pipeline is the value of the last (rightmost) command to exit with a non-zero status, or zero if all commands in the pipeline exit successfully.
- **`onecmd`**: It exits after executing one command.
- **`noglob`**: It disables pathname expansion.
- **`histexpand`**: If set, enable the **`! style`** command substitution.
- **`ignoreeof`**: If set, you will not exit from the terminal session if *Ctrl* + *d* is pressed. You must type exit to exit the session. This setting ensures that accidently pressing *Ctrl* + *d* will not lead you to exit your session.
- **`notify`**: Report the status of terminated background jobs immediately rather than before the next primary prompt.

Many other options will be discussed in the subsequent chapters. **`set +o`** prints a series of set commands to recreate the current option settings, as shown in *Figure 3.7*:

```
[vishesh@localhost ~]$ set +o
set +o allexport
set -o braceexpand
set -o emacs
set +o errexit
set +o errtrace
set +o functrace
set -o hashall
set -o histexpand
set -o history
set +o ignoreeof
set -o interactive-comments
set +o keyword
set -o monitor
set +o noclobber
set +o noexec
set +o noglob
set +o nolog
set +o notify
set +o nounset
set +o onecmd
set +o physical
set +o pipefail
set +o posix
set +o privileged
set +o verbose
set +o vi
set +o xtrace
```

***Figure 3.7:** Usage of set command*

In *Figure 3.7*, **`+o`** means that options are turned off, and **`-o`** is used to turn them on. So, to turn on any option like **`nocobbler`**, type the following:

```
set -o nocobbler
```

After you execute the preceding command, file overwriting will not take place if you would use the **`>`** operator. To override this behavior, you can use special redirection operator, **`>|`**.

cat

We have already used the **cat** command to view the contents of one file. The **cat** command can also take multiple filename arguments. It then displays the contents of all the specified files, concatenating each one together, as shown in *Figure 3.8*:

```
[vishesh@192 ~]$ cat f1
hello
[vishesh@192 ~]$ cat f2
vishesh  tty2         2022-12-13 22:07 (tty2)
[vishesh@192 ~]$
[vishesh@192 ~]$ cat f3
hello world
[vishesh@192 ~]$
[vishesh@192 ~]$ cat f1 f2 f3
hello
vishesh  tty2         2022-12-13 22:07 (tty2)
hello world
```

Figure 3.8: *Usage of cat command*

In *Figure 3.8*, the three files are concatenated together, and the contents of the concatenated files are printed. Typing the **cat** command without any argument means it will wait for the standard input, and whatever is given to the standard input will be displayed in the standard output.

When **-** is provided instead of the filename, **cat** reads the data from standard input:

```
cat -
```

The preceding command is the same as the **cat** command when runs without any arguments. The following options can be used with the **cat** command:

- **-n**: Print line numbers before each output lines.
- **-s**: Suppress repeated empty output lines.
- **-T**: Display *Tab* characters as **^I**.

```
cat > file1
```

No space is required before and after the **>** operator, as shell always truncates any extra spaces around when it sees metacharacter. So the preceding command can also be written as follows:

```
cat>file1
```

The **>** operator always overwrites the existing file or creates the specified file if it does not exist. We have the **>>** operator, which can be called as an append operator that appends into the output file rather than truncating it.

```
cat >> file1
```

The preceding command will append the data read from the standard input to **file1**, if it exists.

```
cat <file2 > file3
```

The **<** and **>** operators can also be used together, as shown in the preceding command line. Standard input and output have been redirected to the disk file. In the preceding command, **<file2** instructs the shell to read the content of the file named **file2** and use it as the standard input for the **cat** command, while **>file3** instructs the shell to write the standard output of the **cat** command to the file named **file3**. If **file3** exists, it will be overwritten using the contents of **file2**, else a new file named **file3** will be created.

The **>** operator is also used drastically by system admin to truncate a large file. Just type this:

```
>file1
```

The preceding command makes **file1** empty.

wc

The **wc** command reads the given file contents and print the number of lines, number of words and total characters that the specified file contains. The following is the basic usage of the **wc** command. It is used as follows:

```
[vishesh@192 ~]$ wc file1
11 9 53 file1
```

The preceding output shows that **file1** has 11 new line characters, 9 words and 53 characters. When **wc** is used without any argument or – is used instead of a filename, it reads the data from the standard input.

The following are the options that can be used with the **wc** command:

- **-c**: Prints the byte counts
- **-m**: Prints the character counts
- **-l**: Prints the newline counts
- **-w**: Prints the word counts
- **-L**: Prints the maximum line length

The following command can also take its input via pipeline operator. For example, to count the number of users that are currently logged in to the system, you can use the following:

```
who|wc -l
```

When the **wc** command runs with many file arguments, it also displays a sum total of each field for all the files in the last.

cut

The **cut** command removes the specified section from each line of specified file and prints it on the screen. That is, the **cut** command can be used to print only the selected part of the file on the screen. It can work on multiple file arguments. Suppose we have a file named **file1** that contains the following line of text:

```
Hello, this is the world of Linux
We will be using RHEL9.0 in this book
Many enhancemnets have been done on this version
```

```
[vishesh@192 ~]$ cut -c 5 file1
o
i

[vishesh@192 ~]$ cut -c 1-5 file1
Hello
We wi
Many
[vishesh@192 ~]$ cut -c 1,5 file1
Ho
Wi
M
```

Figure 3.9: *Usage of cut command*

Now, suppose we want to print only the first 5 characters of a file, say **file1**. In *Figure 3.9*, the first command prints the 5th character of each line of **file1**. We can also specify the comma-separated list of characters or a range of characters to print. In the second command of *Figure 3.9*, a range of characters are specified to be printed. The second command prints the characters from 1 to 5 from each line of the file. The third and the last command provides the comma-separated list of character positions to be printed.

Besides the number of characters, the **cut** command can make its selection based on byte position and field position in the file. So, we can say that the command works based on one of the three selection criteria:

- **-c <list of character position>:** We have seen that the **-c** option takes a comma-separated list of characters or range of characters to cut from the file.
- **-b <list of bytes positions>**: The **-b** option takes a comma-separated list of byte positions or range of byte positions to cut from the file.
- **-f < list of fields >**: This option cuts a part of the file on the basis of the specified field list or range of fields.

Take the following file:

```
cat emp
101,umesh,hr
102,nikki,fin
```

```
103,vishesh,ops
104,geeta,dev
```

The **emp** is a small datafile that contains the records of employees working in an organization. The preceding file stores the data in three fields, separated by comma **(,)**. The first field is employee id, the second one is employee name, and the third field stores the employee's department. We will use this file in the rest of our discussion of the **cut** command. Now, we will use the **cut** command to print only the selected fields from the **emp** file using the **-f** option. The default delimiter that is used by the **-f** option is the *Tab* character. In the real world, fields can be separated by **a** *Tab*, **a** comma, **a** semicolon, and so on. So, there must a way to inform the correct fields delimiter to the **cut** command, else the **cut** command may give you erroneous results. The **-d** is option is used with the **cut** command to specify the field delimiter. Our sample file contains **(,)** as the field delimiter. Now, print the 1st and 3rd fields from the emp file:

```
cut -d, -f 1,3 emp
101,hr
102,fin
103,ops
104,dev
```

The preceding command uses the **-d** option to specify the field delimiter. Here, the field delimiter used is '**,**'. The **-f** option is used to print only two fields 1 and 3 from the file **emp**. To print a range of fields, that is, from field number 1 to 2 from file **emp**, we will use the following:

```
cut -d, -f 1-2 emp
```

Range can also be specified in the form of **N-** or **-N**, where N is the byte or character, or field position.

- Use this to print all the fields starting from fields 2:

  ```
  cut -d, -f 2- emp
  ```

- Use the following to print all the fields from 1 up to the specified N:

  ```
  cut -d, -f -2 emp
  ```

When the **cut** command is executed without any filename or **-** is given as argument, it will read the data from the standard input.

paste

The **paste** command merges two or more files vertically. Using the **-s** option with the **paste** command will merge the file horizontally as merged in the **cat** command. We have the following two files:

```
[vishesh@192 ~]$ cat f1
hello world
[vishesh@192 ~]$ cat f2
vishesh tty2    2022-12-13 22:07 (tty2)
```

To merge the preceding two files, type the following:

```
[vishesh@192 ~]$ paste f1 f2
hello world  vishesh tty2    2022-12-13 22:07 (tty2)
```

In the preceding output, contents of the **f2** file are pasted along the side of contents from **f1**. Now, we will join two small datafiles together. The following is the content from the **dept** file:

```
$ cat dept
1,fin
2,hr
3,ops
4,dev
```

The **dept** file stores the department id and department name. Now, let us create a report that prints employees' information along with their department name, as shown in *Figure 3.10*:

```
[vishesh@192 ~]$ paste emp dept
101,umesh,hr     1,fin
102,nikki,fin    2,hr
103,vishesh,ops  3,ops
104,geeta,dev    4,dev
```

Figure 3.10: *Usage of paste command*

In the preceding output, the lines from the second file are merged with the respective lines from the first file. The **paste** command always merges all the characters from the second file to the first file.

sort

sort command sorts lines of text present in file. When multiple filenames are given with the **sort** command, it sorts the concatenation output of all the files. When no filename is given or **-** is given, instead of the filename, it reads the text from the standard input. Refer to *Figure 3.11*, which lists the contents of two files and then these two files are sorted together:

```
[vishesh@192 ~]$ cat f1
mango
orange
apple
[vishesh@192 ~]$ cat f2
watermelon
blueberry
berry
[vishesh@192 ~]$ sort f1 f2
apple
berry
blueberry
mango
orange
watermelon
```

***Figure 3.11**: Usage of sort command*

In *Figure 3.11*, **`f1`** and **`f2`** contain the name of fruits, and the **`sort`** command presents the name of fruits from both the files in sorted order.

The following options can be used with the **`sort`** command:

- `-f`: Ignore case
- `-i`: Ignore non-printing characters
- `-n`: For numeric sort
- `-r`: Sort in reverse order
- `-m`: Merge already sorted files; do not sort
- `-c`: Checks whether the file is sorted; reports if file is unsorted; when the file is sorted, no output is printed
- `-u`: Prints sorted unique records only and hides duplicate entries in the file

The following are some of the usages of the **`sort`** command:

- To sort the files numerically:

  ```
  sort -n smaple1
  1 february
  4 april
  26 october
  28 january
  ```

- If files are not sorted numerically, it would yield the following output:

  ```
  sort smaple1
  1 february
  26 october
  ```

```
28 january
4 april
```

- To sort the files in descending order:

```
sort -r f1
orange
mango
apple
```

- To perform numeric sort in reverse order:

```
sort -nr smaple1
28 january
26 october
4 april
1 february
```

time

The **time** command gives the resource usages information of the executed command when that command is preceded by the **time** command utility. To view the resource consumption by a command, you must begin the command line with **time**, as follows:

```
$ time ls *
```

Resource usage information is displayed at the end, after the output of timed command is displayed. That means, first, the output of the **ls** command is displayed, and then the resource usage information is printed on the screen, as follows:

```
//ls output truncated//
real   0m0.001s
user   0m0.000s
sys 0m0.001s
```

The preceding output displays three kinds of statistics. These statistics consist of the following:

- The elapsed real time between invocation and termination
- The user CPU time
- The system CPU time

xargs

The **xargs** builds and executes the command line dynamically. When **xargs** is executed without any command, it reads the arguments from the standard input and applies the text from the standard input as an argument to the **echo** command and executes it. Press *Ctrl + D* after you have finished giving standard input to the **xargs** command.

```
[vishesh@192 ~]$ xargs ls -l
dir1 emp dept f1 f2 f3
file
-rw-rw-r--. 1 vishesh vishesh 23 Dec 15 10:33 dept
-rw-rw-r--. 1 vishesh vishesh 57 Dec 14 23:44 emp
-rw-rw-r--. 1 vishesh vishesh  6 Nov 30 23:10 f1
-rw-rw-r--. 1 vishesh vishesh 46 Dec 14 00:45 f2
-rw-rw-r--. 1 vishesh vishesh 12 Dec 14 01:07 f3
-rw-rw-r--. 1 vishesh vishesh 38 Nov 29 23:53 file

dir1:
total 0
```

***Figure 3.12:** Usage of xargs command*

In *Figure 3.12,* the **xargs** command is executed with the **ls** command and its arguments. Arguments are supplied in the standard input. In the preceding figure, the **xargs** command line takes only the **ls** command and one of its options. Pressing the enter key will wait for the user to provide standard input. If you do not need to provide any further arguments to the **ls -l** command, you can immediately press *Ctrl + D*. But if you want to view the long listing of some of the specified files, provide the space separated or new line separated arguments of file names. After you have finished entering the text, press *Ctrl + D*, which then builds the command line using the text given in the standard input and then executes it.

The following options can be used with **xargs**.

-a <filename> reads the input from the specified file instead of using standard input. The **xargs** is mostly used with the **find** command.

```
find . -name 'apl*' -print|xargs rm
```

The preceding command searches for all files whose names start with **apl** and all the matched file names are passed to the **xargs** command as arguments to the **rm** command. The **xargs** deletes all the matched files by only a single invocation of the **rm** command.

-0 correctly processes filenames that contain new line or other white-space characters.

echo

Besides the known usages of the **echo** command, it can be used to print the strings containing many special key sequences. These key sequences are known as **escape sequences,** and they begin with ****. Each escape sequence has some special meaning. The name and meaning of supported escape sequences are listed as follows:

- **\a**: alert (BEL)
- **\b**: backspace
- **\c**: suppresses the trailing newline
- **\e**: escape

- `\f`: form feed
- `\n`: new line
- `\r`: carriage return
- `\t`: horizontal tab
- `\v`: vertical tab

To use the preceding escape sequences in bash shell, the **-e** option must be given in the command line. The string containing escape sequences must be quoted to not let shell interpret them. Refer to *Figure 3.13*, which shows usages of the **echo** command using escape sequences:

```
[vishesh@192 ~]$ echo -e "enter file name:\c"
enter file name:[vishesh@192 ~]$
[vishesh@192 ~]$ echo -e "hello\nthis is chapter3"
hello
this is chapter3
[vishesh@192 ~]$ echo -e "hello\rthis is chapter3"
this is chapter3
[vishesh@192 ~]$ echo -e "hello\tthis is chapter3"
hello   this is chapter3
[vishesh@192 ~]$ echo -e "hello\vthis is chapter3"
hello
     this is chapter3
[vishesh@192 ~]$ echo -e "hello\bthis is chapter3"
hellthis is chapter3
```

Figure 3.13: *echo command usage using various escape sequence*

In *Figure 3.13*, the first command uses **\c** which suppresses the new line character. The cursor blinks at this point. **\c** escape sequence can be used in shell scripts that ask for your input. The second command uses **\n**, which prints the new line. The third command uses **\r** (carriage return), which moves the cursor at the beginning of the current line. Similarly, **\t** and **\v** are used for horizontal and vertical tabs, respectively. The last command uses **\b**, which erases a single character *o*, here.

alias

You can create an alias of some commands that overrides their default behavior. Type **alias** simply in the command prompt; you will get output as shown in *Figure 3.14*:

```
[vishesh@192 ~]$ alias
alias egrep='egrep --color=auto'
alias fgrep='fgrep --color=auto'
alias grep='grep --color=auto'
alias l.='ls -d .* --color=auto'
alias ll='ls -l --color=auto'
alias ls='ls --color=auto'
alias xzegrep='xzegrep --color=auto'
alias xzfgrep='xzfgrep --color=auto'
alias xzgrep='xzgrep --color=auto'
alias zegrep='zegrep --color=auto'
alias zfgrep='zfgrep --color=auto'
alias zgrep='zgrep --color=auto'
```

Figure 3.14: *List of default aliases*

In *Figure 3.14*, we can see that many commands have been aliased. For example, the **ls** command is aliased such that it always gets executed by setting the **-color** option to **auto**. This is due to this alias that different colors are seen for different kinds of files in **ls** command output. In this example, alias is given the same name as the command. **ls** is one of the frequently used commands by system administrator for their day-to-day activities. So, it is very convenient to use this alias instead of typing the **ls** command along with the --**color** option again and again. To use **ls -l**, you can simply type **ll**, which is more convenient to type and eases typing effort. These aliases are easy-to-remember names and are created to make commands accessible using simple keystrokes.

You can create aliases for the command-option combinations that are used frequently in your daily activities. To create an alias that executes the **wc** command using the **-l** option, type the following:

```
alias wcl='wc -l'
```

Verify the creation of **wcl** alias by using the **alias** command. Now, if you want to view the number of lines in file **f1**, you can simply type the following command:

```
wcl file1
```

This will work as if the **wc -l file1** command has been executed. You can remove any alias anytime by using the **unalias** command. Say, you want to remove the **wcl** alias, type the following command:

```
unalias wcl
```

info

It presents the documentation in **info** format. It works as **man** pages. It also provides the feature of page linking. Pressing the *Enter* key will take you to the page that follows the hyperlink text *UNDER THE CURSOR*. To know more about info documentation, type **info**. To view information about find command in the **info** format, type the following command:

```
info find
```

bc

The **bc** is used as powerful command-line calculator. When you simply invoke the **bc** command, it waits for the user's input. Enter your mathematical expressions that you want to calculate, as follows:

```
bc

2+2

4

4*6

24
```

The **bc** is a calculation language that includes the **math** library, using which you can do any simple to complex mathematical calculations.

clear

It clears the terminal.

script

script command records all the commands run in the terminal session to the default file named **typescript**. It stores commands along with their output. To start the recording, simply type the following command:

```
script
Script started, output log file is 'typescript'.
```

You will get the preceding output. From then, any activity done on the terminal will be recorded in the given log file. To stop recording the session, type **exit** at the command prompt. Every time you run the script command, it overwrites the previous contents. So, you can use the **-a** option to append contents into the logfile.

To do the session recording to non-default file, specify the name of file as an argument to *script* as follows:

```
script sessinfo
```

The preceding command will record the terminal session into the **sessinfo** file. When you type **clear** on clear the terminal screen, all the info collected so far in the output logfile also gets cleared.

printf

It formats the supplied argument and prints it. It is basically used in shell scripts where we would like to print formatted messages in the standard output. The following formats can be used with the **printf** command:

- \": double quote
- \\: backslash
- **\a**: alert (BEL)
- **\b**: backspace
- **\c**: produce no further output
- **\e**: escape
- **\f**: form feed

- **\n**: new line
- **\r**: carriage return
- **\t**: horizontal tab
- **\v**: vertical tab

The meaning of the listed format specifiers is the same as that of the **echo** command. Use the following to print the value of environment variable **$USER**:

```
printf "Current user name is : %s\n" $USER
Current user name is : vishesh
```

In the preceding command, the following syntax is used:

```
printf format argument
```

$USER is given as an argument to the **printf** command and string format is specified in double quotes. **%s** is used to print a string. Let us use **%d** to print numbers:

```
[vishesh@localhost ~]$ printf "number of logged users is %d\n" 'who|wc -l'
number of logged users is 1
```

uname

uname prints system information. Typing **uname** without any argument displays the name of the operating system. Using **-a** option prints many system related information in the following order :

- kernel-name
- network node hostname
- kernel release
- kernel version
- machine hardware name
- processor type (non-portable) (this information is omitted if unknown)
- the hardware platform (non-portable) (this information is omitted if unknown)
- operating system

The following are other options that can be used with the **uname** command:

- **-s**: Prints the kernel-name
- **-n**: Prints the network node hostname
- **-r**: Prints the kernel release

- `-v`: Prints the kernel version
- `-m`: Prints the machine hardware name
- `-p`: Prints the processor type (non-portable)
- `-i`: Prints the hardware platform (non-portable)
- `-o`: Prints the operating system

To print the kernel version, you can type the following:

```
uname -v
#1 SMP PREEMPT Thu Apr 14 12:42:38 EDT 2022
```

To print the processor, type the following:

```
uname -p
```

To print the kernel release, type the following command:

```
[vishesh@192 ~]$ uname -r
5.14.0-70.13.1.el9_0.x86_64
```

tty

The **`tty`** command prints the file name of the terminal connected to standard input. Open three terminals by clicking on **+** symbol in the top-left corner of your GNU terminal. Check the filename of each of these terminals by typing the **`tty`** command on each of the open terminals.

sleep

It is used to wait for the specified number of seconds.

```
sleep 60
```

The preceding command would wait for 60 seconds. We will use this command many times throughout the book.

uniq

The **`uniq`** command prints only unique lines from the input filename. The **`uniq`** command requires sorted lines of text, so if your input file is unsorted, you must sort it first using the **`sort`** command for **`uniq`** commands to work properly. The following are the options that can be used with **`uniq`**:

- `-c`: Prints number of occurrences of each repeated line
- `-d`: Prints only duplicate lines

- **-i**: Ignore case
- **-u**: Prints unique lines only

```
[vishesh@192 ~]$ cat fruits
apple
mango
watermelon
berry
grapes
orange
apple
mango
```

Since the preceding file has unsorted text, we will sort it first, as follows:

```
sort fruits>fruitsort
```

Now, **fruitsort** has the sorted contents. Now, see *Figure 3.15*, which uses the said sorted file for the usages of options of **uniq**:

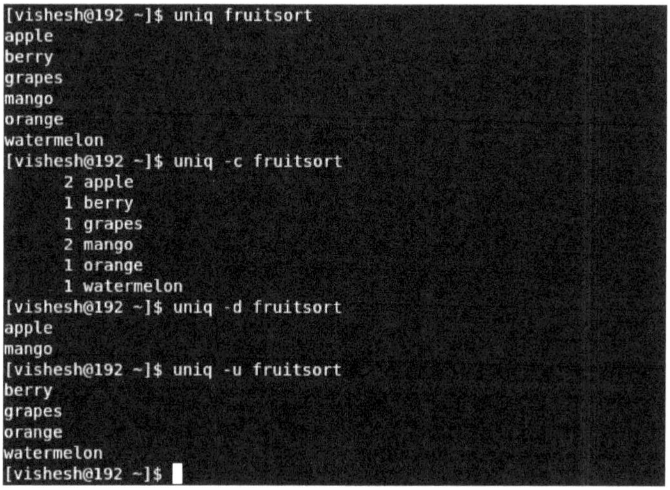

```
[vishesh@192 ~]$ uniq fruitsort
apple
berry
grapes
mango
orange
watermelon
[vishesh@192 ~]$ uniq -c fruitsort
      2 apple
      1 berry
      1 grapes
      2 mango
      1 orange
      1 watermelon
[vishesh@192 ~]$ uniq -d fruitsort
apple
mango
[vishesh@192 ~]$ uniq -u fruitsort
berry
grapes
orange
watermelon
[vishesh@192 ~]$
```

***Figure 3.15**: Usage of uniq command*

In *Figure 3.15,* the first command line shows the unique text from the **fruitsort** file, with duplicates removed. The next command line used the **-c** option, which displays the number of occurrences of each line. Here, each line appears only once along with the count of their occurrences. The third command line uses the **-d** option, which prints only the lines that are repeated. The repeated lines are printed only once. The last command line uses the **-u** option, which shows only the available unique lines. Duplicate lines are not printed even once.

at

It reads form standard input or a specified file, which are to be executed later. For example, to execute the command today at 11:00am, type the following command:

```
$ at 11:00am
```

The preceding command line will give you a secondary prompt:

```
at>
```

You will enter the command to be scheduled at the specified time.

```
[vishesh@192 ~]$ at 1:00 pm
warning: commands will be executed using /bin/sh
at> echo current time is $USER > daten
at> <EOT>
job 5 at Sat Dec 17 13:00:00 2022
```

Figure 3.16: *Usage of at command*

In *Figure 3.16*, the **echo** command is entered at the given **at>** prompt. After you have finished giving your standard input, press *Ctrl + D* to execute the **at** command. At the end, the command displays that job 5 has been created that will create a file **daten** at 1:00 pm on the same day. It can use keywords like **now**, **tomorrow**, **midnight**, **noon**, and so on.

To execute a command next day at the current time, type the following command:

```
$ at tomorrow
```

The preceding command will schedule the job tomorrow at the current time. You can also specify the date as follows:

```
at July 01
```

The preceding **date** command will execute the command specified in the standard input on 1 July at the same time. To execute the job at specific date at specific time:

```
$ at 10:00am July 01
```

Use the following to execute the job after 3 minutes from now:

```
$ at now+3 minutes
```

You can substitute minutes in the preceding command with hours, days, or weeks. To view the user's pending job, the **atq** command is used. To delete a job, **atrm** is used as follows:

```
atrm 5
```

You can also put the commands to be scheduled in a file and supply the name of that file with the **at** command using the **-f** option, as follows:

```
[vishesh@192 ~]$ at -f cmdsample 2:00 pm
```

```
warning: commands will be executed using /bin/sh
job 10 at Sat Dec 17 14:00:00 2022
```

The following are the options that go with the **at** command:

- **-l**: It is an alias for **atq**.
- **-d**: It is an alias for **atrm**.
- **-b**: It is an alias for **batch**.
- **-v**: It shows the time the job will be executed before reading the job.

batch

It executes commands when system load levels permit. This command does not require any time specification as the job scheduled is run when system load permits.

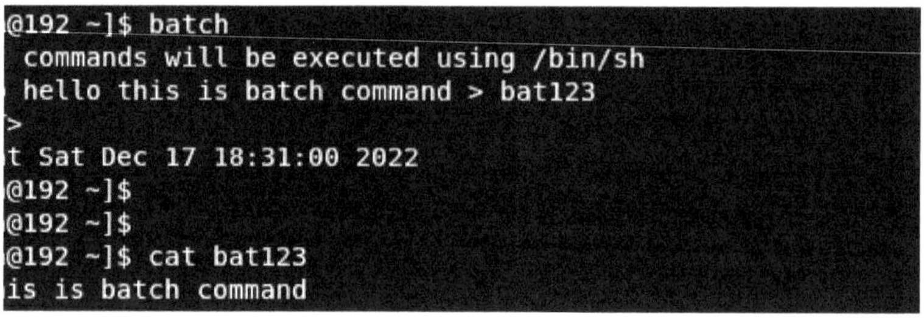

```
@192 ~]$ batch
 commands will be executed using /bin/sh
 hello this is batch command > bat123
>
t Sat Dec 17 18:31:00 2022
@192 ~]$
@192 ~]$
@192 ~]$ cat bat123
is is batch command
```

***Figure 3.17:** Usage of batch command*

In *Figure 3.17*, the **batch** command is executed without specifying a time. The command in *Figure 3.17*, would execute the **echo** command and then create a file **bat123**. Since the system had no load, the given job executed immediately.

grep

The **grep** command is used to find a word or a pattern within one or more files. It is frequently used by Linux users in their day-to-day activities. It will simply display the lines that matches the pattern. Patterns can be given as BRE, ERE or fixed strings. Let us create a file to quickly get hands-on to the **grep** command:

```
cat fruitsdesc
Apple is a good fruit. It is superfood. Eating an apple daily makes a doctor away.
Other fruits to add in daily habits are oranges, guava, kiwis, etc.
Pineapple is also liked by many. Pineapple flavor is also used in cakes which named as pineapple cakes.
Orange is good in vitamin c
```

Let us find the lines containing the word apple.

```
grep apple fruitsdesc
```

The **grep** command searches for apple in the given file **fruitsdesc** and prints the lines where the match is found. It matches the given pattern anywhere in the text. No regular expression is used in this example. Let us take an example where basic regular expression is used:

```
[vishesh@192 ~]$ ls|grep '^s'
s21
s2xyz
sam
sample
sample1
sample11
```

The preceding command searches for the lines in **ls** output that begin with **s**. Here are the options to use with **grep**:

- **-E**: To treat specified patterns as Extended REs
- **-F**: Interpret PATTERNS as fixed strings, not regular expressions
- **-G**: To treat specified patterns as basic REs; this is the default
- **-e**: Used to specify multiple patterns
- **-f <filename>**: Patterns are given in filename instead on the command line
- **-i**: Ignore case in pattern search
- **-v**: Inverse effect; shows non-matching lines
- **-w**: Searches the patterns that matches the whole word only
- **-x**: Select only those matches that exactly match the whole line
- **-c**: Only print the count of all the matching lines for each input files
- **-l**: Print the file names where match is found
- **-L**: Print the file names where match is not found
- **-m <NUM>**: Matches only specified NUMBER of matched lines in each file
- **-q**: Quiet; do not write anything to standard output; exit immediately with zero status if any match is found, even if an error was detected
- **-s**: Suppress error messages about non-existent or unreadable files

If **-** is given instead of the file name, it searches the pattern from the text read from standard input:

```
[vishesh@192 ~]$ grep '\(apple\).*\1' fruitsdesc
Pineapple is also liked by many. Pineapple flavour is alos used in cakes
which named as pineapple cakes.
```

The preceding example creates a grouped pattern using the **\(...\)** operator, and **\1** repeats the grouped pattern 1. The first pattern searches for *apple* anywhere in the text. It creates group 1. Dot (.) matches any one character, but **.*** matches any number of characters, and then it again searches for the grouped pattern 1 (that is **apple** here). In other words, the preceding command searches for lines having **apple**, then any number of characters, then again **apple**.

The following command echoes two lines matching the pattern(**apple**). **-i** makes the search case-insensitive, so it also matches lines having **Apple**:

```
[vishesh@192 ~]$ grep -i '\(apple\).*\1' fruitsdesc
Apple is a good fruit. It is superfood. Eating an apple daily makes a
doctor away.
Pineapple is also liked by many. Pineapple flavour is alos used in cakes
which named as pineapple cakes.
```

The following command searches the lines that do not contain **pineapple** in the specified file:

```
grep -v pineapple fruitsdesc
```

The following command will print the line number, along with the matched lines that contain some white-space character in the beginning, followed by **orange**. **\s*** is used to match zero or more white-space characters. The line performs case-insensitive search:

```
grep -ni '^\s*orange' fruitsdesc
4:     Orange is good in vtamin c
```

The following command searches for the lines that contain the word **apple**:

```
grep '\<apple\>' fruitsdesc
```

The following command matches the lines matching either **apple** or **mango**:

```
grep -E 'apple|mango' fruitsdesc
```

-F does not recognize the given metacharacters in the pattern as forming a regular expression but a fixed string. It finds the given pattern as string. So, ***** and **.** are not interpreted as a part of regular expression but a character to match literally:

```
echo '* and . is part of metacharacetr' |grep -F '* and .'
* and . is part of metacharacetr
grep -v '^$' file1
```

The preceding command does not show empty lines:

```
grep -l mail /var/log/* 2>err.our
```

The preceding command lists out all the filenames in the **/var/log** directory where **mail** is found. Become root if you do not have permission to access **/var/log**.

basename

The **basename** command is used to extract the actual file name from the specified relative or absolute path:

```
basename /home/vishesh/redhat
redhat
```

The preceding command extracts the actual filename **redhat** from the given argument. To remove trailing file extension, say **.key**, provide the second argument:

```
basename /home/vishesh/redhat.key .key
redhat
```

The basename command comes in handy when you want to perform some operations with many filenames in the same directory, such as renaming the extension of file name. Using shell scripting makes the task easier.

nl

It prefixes each line of the input file with the line number. Refer to *Figure 3.18*:

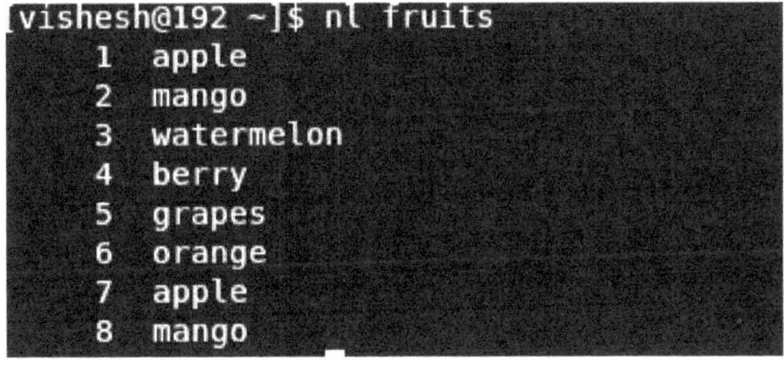

Figure 3.18: *Usage of nl command*

In *Figure 3.18*, line numbers are added starting from 1 to the contents of the file given. To add a string, say **$** after the line number, use the **-s** option as follows:

```
[vishesh@localhost ~]$ nl -s $ fruits
  1$apple
  2$mango
  3$watermelon
  4$berry
```

```
5$grapes
6$orange
7$apple
8$mango
```

eval

The **eval** command is used to execute the command passed to it as the argument. The command name and its arguments become the arguments of **eval**. Consider this example:

```
[vishesh@localhost ~]$ eval sort -r fruits
watermelon
orange
mango
mango
grapes
berry
apple
apple
```

This command comes in handy when the command name is passed dynamically in shell scripts.

expr

It evaluates the given expression. The expression may be arithmetic expression, integer and string comparison, or regular expression to match patterns. Let us use arithmetic operations in **expr** as shown in *Figure 3.19*. There should be spaces around all the operators used in the command line. Some of the operators are preceded with backslash character \ which escapes their meaning to prevent their interpretation by shell. The usage of many arithmetic expressions in **expr** is shown. After showing arithmetic expressions, it demonstrates some comparisons of strings as well as integers. **length** calculates the length of the given string and prints it. **substr** extracts the substring of length 10 starting from position 4.

```
[vishesh@localhost ~]$ expr 3 + 2
5
[vishesh@localhost ~]$ expr 3 \* 2
6
[vishesh@localhost ~]$ expr 3 % 2
1
[vishesh@localhost ~]$ expr 3 \| 2
3
[vishesh@localhost ~]$ expr 3 \& 0
0
[vishesh@localhost ~]$ expr 10 \> 9
1
[vishesh@localhost ~]$ expr 11 \< 9
0
[vishesh@localhost ~]$ expr length expression
10
[vishesh@localhost ~]$ expr substr expression 4 10
ression
[vishesh@localhost ~]$ expr expression : '\(....\)'
expr
```

Figure 3.19: Usage of expr command

The last command line uses regular expression for pattern match in given string. The string after **:** is the regular expression to match. Here, the **expr** command returns the string matching the pattern enclosed in **\(** and **\)**. Since (**.**) matches any characters, it returns the first four characters. If given regular expressions, do not use **\(** and **\)**; they return the number of characters matched or 0.

head

The **head** command prints the top 10 lines from the specified file/files. If **-** is specified, it reads from standard input.

Figure 3.20, displays the top 10 lines from the **/etc/passwd** file:

```
[vishesh@192 ~]$ head /etc/passwd
root:x:0:0:root:/root:/bin/bash
bin:x:1:1:bin:/bin:/sbin/nologin
daemon:x:2:2:daemon:/sbin:/sbin/nologin
adm:x:3:4:adm:/var/adm:/sbin/nologin
lp:x:4:7:lp:/var/spool/lpd:/sbin/nologin
sync:x:5:0:sync:/sbin:/bin/sync
shutdown:x:6:0:shutdown:/sbin:/sbin/shutdown
halt:x:7:0:halt:/sbin:/sbin/halt
mail:x:8:12:mail:/var/spool/mail:/sbin/nologin
operator:x:11:0:operator:/root:/sbin/nologin
```

Figure 3.20: Usage of head command

If you want to view a higher or lower number of lines, say 20 lines, specify that value with the **head** command, as follows:

```
head 20 /etc/passwd
```

The **head** can also take its input from the standard output of another command, so it can be used with pipe as follows:

```
mount|head
```

tail

The **tail** command prints the last 10 lines from the specified list of files or from standard input:

```
tail /etc/passwd
```

The preceding command displays the last 10 lines from the **/etc/passwd** file on standard output, as shown in *Figure 3.21*:

```
[vishesh@192 ~]$ tail /etc/passwd
manager1:x:1008:1010::/opt/home/manager1:/bin/bash
newmanager:x:1009:1011::/opt/home/newmanager:/bin/bash
redhat:x:1010:1012::/home/redhat:/bin/bash
ss:x:1011:1015::/opt/home/ss:/bin/bash
dd:x:1012:1016::/opt/home/dd:/bin/bash
ff:x:1013:1013::/opt/home/ff:/bin/bash
sam:x:1014:1017::/opt/home/sam:/bin/bash
hat:x:1015:1018::/opt/home/hat:/bin/bash
ma6:x:1016:1019::/opt/home/ma6:/bin/bash
redhatlinux:x:1017:1020::/opt/home/redhatlinux:/bin/bash
```

***Figure 3.21** : Usage of tail command*

If you want to view the specified number of last few lines, say 20 lines, use the following:

```
tail -20 /etc/passwd
```

The **tail** command is frequently used with the **-f** option by system administrators to view the growth of log file, as follows:

```
tail -f /var/log/maillog
```

Using the **-f** option with **tail** command opens the specified logfile at its tail, and the output is appended while it is growing. We can use the preceding command to view the progress of files and for troubleshooting or debugging.

id

Print user and group information of the user. When the **id** command is executed without any options and arguments, it displays the effective user ids and group ids of the current user. The following options can be used with the **id** command:

- **-g** : Prints only the effective group ID
- **-G**: Prints all group IDs
- **-n**: Print a name instead of a number, can only be used with **-u**, **-g** and **-G**

- `-r`: Print the real ID instead of the effective ID, with **`-ugG`**
- `-u`: Print only the effective user ID

Real uid is the **uid**, which initiated the command. All the commands run with a **real uid** and an **effective uid**. Most user commands have the same real and effective **user `id`**. But sometimes, some commands require a privileged user's permission to execute. At that time, the effective userid will not be same as the real user id. Effective user **`id`** will become equal to the id of root user.

od

The **`od`** command dumps the data in octal format. The **`od`** command takes one or more files as input and returns the file's contents in octal format. This command is used to display non-printing characters contained in a file. Let us create the following file that contains some non-printing characters:

```
This is tab [Ctrl-i] character

This is new line character [Enter]

This is formfeed character[Ctrl-l]
```

To insert the *Tab* character, you can press the *Ctrl* + *i* key combination. For the formfeed character, press *Ctrl* + *j*. For linefeed character, insert *Ctrl* + *L* key combination. *Enter* key always inserts a new line character. To print all these characters, we will pass the **`abc`** file to od, as shown in *Figure 3.22*:

```
[vishesh@192 ~]$ od -bc abc
0000000 124 150 151 163 040 151 163 040 164 141 142 011 040 143 150 141
          T   h   i   s       i   s       t   a   b  \t       c   h   a
0000020 162 141 164 145 162 012 124 150 151 163 040 151 163 040 156 145
          r   a   t   e   r  \n   T   h   i   s       i   s       n   e
0000040 167 040 154 151 156 145 040 143 150 141 162 143 141 164 145 162
          w       l   i   n   e       c   h   a   r   c   a   t   e   r
0000060 012 124 110 163 151 040 151 163 040 146 157 162 155 146 145 145
         \n   T   H   s   i       i   s       f   o   r   m   f   e   e
0000100 144 040 143 150 141 162 141 143 164 145 162 014 012
          d       c   h   a   r   a   c   t   e   r  \f  \n
0000115
```

Figure 3.22: od command showing non-printing characters

The command in *Figure 3.22* displays the octal value for each character in the file. The first value of each line is the offset in the file, which specifies the position of the current line . Thus, the *Tab* character is displayed as octal value 011 and the **`\t`** character. Form feed is displayed as 014 octal value and **`\f`** character. New line is displayed as the **`\n`** character using octal value of 012.

split

The **`split`** command splits a file into multiple files, with each file containing 1000 lines and named **`xaa`**, **`xab`**, and so on. Let us create a large file containing thousands of lines, as shown in *Figure 3.23*:

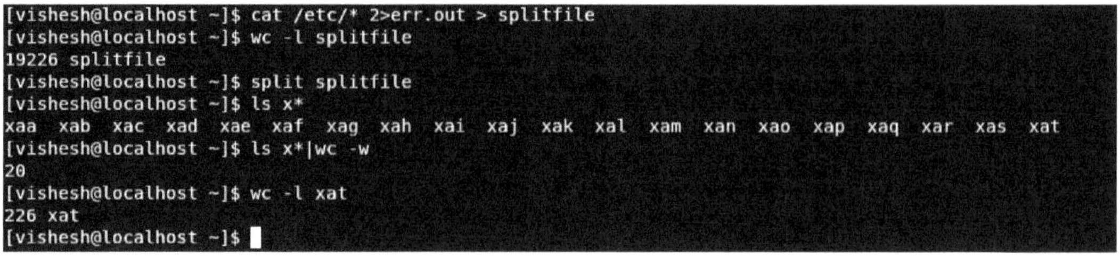

```
[vishesh@localhost ~]$ cat /etc/* 2>err.out > splitfile
[vishesh@localhost ~]$ wc -l splitfile
19226 splitfile
[vishesh@localhost ~]$ split splitfile
[vishesh@localhost ~]$ ls x*
xaa  xab  xac  xad  xae  xaf  xag  xah  xai  xaj  xak  xal  xam  xan  xao  xap  xaq  xar  xas  xat
[vishesh@localhost ~]$ ls x*|wc -w
20
[vishesh@localhost ~]$ wc -l xat
226 xat
[vishesh@localhost ~]$ 
```

***Figure 3.23:** Usage of split command*

In *Figure 3.23*, we have created a file named **splitfile** that contains the concatenated output of all the files under **/etc/**. Guess yourself why we used the **2>** operator in the first command line. The next command shows the total number of lines in **splitfile**. You can easily count the number of files that will be created with the split command. Since each file, by default, takes 1000 lines, the **split** command would yield 20 files. Next, we will use the **split** command to split the specified file. 20 files are created with the default prefix of **x** letter. The **ls x*** command verifies this. Files are created in the order of **xaa**, **xab**, **xac** and so on. The last file **xat** in this sequence would receive only the last 226 lines.

To create files using non-default prefix, specify the prefix at the end of the **split** command, as follows:

```
split splitfile spl
```

The preceding command creates files in the pattern of **splaa**, **splab**, **splac**, and so on. The default length of suffix of the created files is 2. If you want to create files having suffixes of length 3, use the **-a** option as follows:

```
split -a 3 splitfile spl
```

The preceding command will create the file sequence as **splaaa**, **splaab**, **splaac**, and so on. Thus, the specified prefix is suffixed with three letters. Other options to use with the **split** command is as follows:

- **-C**: Put at most C bytes of records in each newly created file
- **-d**: Use numeric suffixes starting at 0, not alphabetical
- **-x**: Use hex suffixes starting at 0, not alphabetic
- **-l**: Put specified number of lines/records per output file

strings

The **strings** are mainly useful for determining the contents of binary files and print the printable characters contained in the files.

sum

It prints the checksum and number of blocks in a file. Block count is given in terms of 1024 bytes block. Using the **-s** option will give you the number of blocks in 512 bytes block size. Let us count the blocks and checksum of the file, **splitfile**:

```
[vishesh@localhost ~]$ sum splitfile
44291 968
```

tee

It writes the standard input to standard output as well as to specified files:

```
tee message
```

When you write the preceding command line, **tee** will wait for the standard input. After you have entered the text as standard input, the entered text will be written to the file named **message** as well as to the standard output. You can verify the creation of the **message** file by the **cat** command. In the following command line, the list of files in the current directory is being saved to a disk file, and the output is also written on the standard output:

```
ls |tee listfile
```

More real usage of this command will be shown in *Chapter 7, Interacting With Bash Shell and Scripting.*

tr

The **tr** command is used to translate individual characters from one form to another. It takes input from standard input only. **tr** may use same escape sequences as used by the **echo** command.

Let us use the **emp** file that we created earlier to change **(,)** to the *Tab* character:

```
$ tr "," "\t"< emp
101	umesh	hr
102	nikki	fin
103	vishesh	ops
104	geeta	dev
```

The preceding command takes the **emp** file as standard input and converts field separator to the *Tab* character. **\t** must be quoted to prevent shell from treating it as special character. As a precautionary measure, you should always quote or escape the source and destination characters to save it from shell. **tr** can also take character classes as its argument.

```
$ tr [a-z] [A-Z] < dept
1,FIN
```

```
2,HR
3,OPS
4,DEV
```

This will convert small letters to big letters. The preceding command can also be written as follows:

```
tr [:lower:] [:upper:] < dept
```

You can also specify many sets of source or destination characters, as follows:

```
[vishesh@192 ~]$ tr '\n[a-z]' '-[A-Z]' <fruits
APPLE-MANGO-WATERMELON-BERRY-GRAPES-ORANGE-APPLE-MANGO-[vishesh@192 ~]$
```

The preceding command converts each new line character to – (dash) and also converts all the lower case letters to upper case. **tr** can also delete certain characters. The **-d** option is used for this. Let us delete all the digits from **emp**:

```
tr -d [:digit:]< emp
,umesh,hr
,nikki,fin
,vishesh,ops
,geeta,dev
```

The **-c** option can negate the specified pattern, as follows:

```
 [vishesh@192 ~]$ tr -cd [:alpha:] < emp
umeshhrnikkifinvisheshopsgeetadev[vishesh@192 ~]$
```

The preceding command deletes all the characters, including white-space characters (such as new line **\n**) from **emp**, except the alphabets. Use the following to retain only alphabets and new line characters:

```
tr -cd [:alpha:]'\n' < emp
umeshhr
nikkifin
visheshops
geetadev
```

The **-s** option can be used to squeeze the repetitive occurrence of given characters to single occurrence, as follows:

```
echo "This  is book on LInux " |tr -s " "
```

Do it yourself

1. Write the command to count the number of files in a directory.
2. What do the following commands do?
   a. **cat file1 - file3**
   b. **cat <file1 > file2**
   c. **cat < file1 >> file2**
3. Create a hidden file named **.abc**. Verify the same using **ls -a**.
4. Type **echo -e '\a'**. Do you hear a beep?
5. Split **splitfile** created in *Figure 3.22* into multiple files, each file taking at most 100K. Before running the **split** command, guess the number of files that would be created here. Now, execute your command. Calculate the total size of newly created files and compare it with the size of **splitfile**. Does the total size of tiny files equal the original file, **splitfile**.
6. Reset the environment variable **HISTSIZE** to 250. Also reset the number of lines in the **.bash_history** file to 500.
7. Set the **ignoreeof** option to on. Now, press *Ctrl* + *d* to exit the session. Does it work? Now, press *Ctrl* + *d* 10 times. What happens? What do you conclude?
8. Set the **noglob** option to on. What will happen when you execute **ls ***?
9. Modify the **dept** file such that the field separator '**,**' is converted to the TAB character, and save it to another file, say **dept_modi**.

Admin commands

So far, we have read about many useful commands that come in very handy for Linux users for file manipulation or for performing any simple to complex task. Throughout the chapter, you will be introduced to many admin commands that are useful for system administration tasks. This section will briefly discuss only a few of them. Admin command requires root privileges to be executed. Many admin commands can also be run by regular users but with restricted privileges.

su

This command literally means switch user. If you want to execute the command as another user, you can use the **su** command. You must know the password of the user you want to switch to. In *Chapter 2, Linux FileSystem and Administration,* we used the **su** command to switch to root user and saw that it asks for the root password. Similarly, it is always possible to switch to another user if you know their password to access files that they are allowed to access. Use the following to access the files that only user **sam** has access to:

```
su sam
```

The preceding command will ask you for **sam**'s password. After you have successfully entered the password, you will be logged in as **sam**, but **sam**'s login shell will not be executed. That means you will receive a mix environment where only some of the environment variables are reset. So, the correct way to use the **su** command is as follows:

```
su - sam
```

You will be logged in as **sam**, as if **sam** is logged in. You will get all the environment variables that **sam** receives when they log in. When you don't specify any username after **su -**, you will be attempting to log in as root and will be asked for the root password. A root user can use the **su** command to switch to another user without prompting for password. A root user uses the **su** command to get the user's environment for troubleshooting.

mkfifo

We have used pipes that connect a command's output to another command's standard input. **mkfifo** allows us to create named pipes:

```
mkfifo mypipe
```

The preceding command creates a special file named **mypipe**, which is a named pipe used for the communication between two processes. One process sends a message in the pipeline while another consumes it. To understand this, we will send the message in one terminal and see how another process launched in the second terminal consumes it. Type the following in the first terminal:

```
ls |wc -l >mypipe
```

The preceding command sends the command's output as a message to a named pipe, **mypipe**. Now, type the following command in another terminal:

```
cat <mypipe
```

Here, the process launched by the **cat** command consumes the message from **mypipe**, which displays the total number of files in the current directory. Now verify the pipe that you opened in the first terminal; it closes automatically since all the messages have been consumed. You can reuse this named pipe for communication between any two processes.

dd

Though the **dd** command can be used by non-root users, it is mainly used by the system administrator to copy a file from one place to another or an entire hard disk to another hard disk. Let us understand the usage of the **dd** command using the following example:

```
dd if=/home/vishesh/project.zip of=/tmp/prvishesh.zip
```

```
2048000+0 records in
2048000+0 records out
1048576000 bytes (1.0 GB, 1000 MiB) copied, 1.55972 s, 672 MB/s
```

From the preceding command line, it is clear that the **dd** command takes input value in the form of **option=value**. The **if** option is used to specify the source file, and the **of** option is used to specify the destination. Thus, the preceding command copies the **/home/vishesh/project.zip** file to **prvishesh.zip** under the **/tmp/** directory. At the end, the output shows the total number of bytes copied, the time taken to complete the copy operation and the transfer speed. It copies the file in 512- bytes blocks by default. 512 bytes is the default read and write block size that the **dd** command uses at a time. So, it has to read and write **2048000** records calculated as **1048576000/512**. You have to be careful when you specify your destination, as **dd** will overwrite the output file. Take the following example, where the entire disk is copied to another disk in non-default block size.

```
dd if=/dev/sda of=/dev/sdb bs=500M
```

The preceding command line performs the copy operation in 500M block and copies **/dev/sda** to another disk. The **bs** option is used to specify the block size to read and write at a time.

```
dd if=/dev/zero of=largefile bs=500M count=2
2+0 records in
2+0 records out
1048576000 bytes (1.0 GB, 1000 MiB) copied, 0.755281 s, 1.4 GB/s
```

The preceding command creates a file named **largefile** of size 1G in the current directory. Input source is **/dev/zero**, a pseudo-device, reading from which always yields zeros in the output file. The **count** option specifies the number of blocks to be copied. The preceding command will copy two 500M sized blocks. If we want to copy fewer blocks from the input file, the count option is useful.

The **dd** command can also be used to convert a file from one form to another. For example, use the following to convert all the text in a file to uppercase:

```
dd if=fruits of=fruitslc conv=ucase
```

The preceding command line use the **conv** option for conversion. **conv** is set to **lcase** here. **conv** can take the following comma-separated values:

- **noatime**: Do not update access time
- **ascii**: From EBCDIC to ASCII
- **ebcdic**: From ASCII to EBCDIC
- **ibm**: From ASCII to alternate EBCDIC
- **ucase**: Change lower case to upper case

- **excl**: Fail if the output file already exists
- **nocreat:** Do not create the output file
- **notrunc:** Do not truncate the output file
- **noerror:** Continue after read errors
- **fdatasync:** Physically write output file data before finishing
- **fsync**: same as **fdatasync** but also write metadata

By default, the **dd** command overwrites the existing file. If we do not want to truncate the existing file but append it, we can use the following command:

```
dd if=fruits of=fruitslc1 conv=lcase,notrunc oflag=append
```

The preceding command line uses **oflag** where it is set to **append**. So, write is performed in the **append** mode. **conv** must take **notrunc** for this option to work. The **iflag** and **oflag** options read and write, respectively, according to the given FLAG. Other values that are supported in FLAGS are as follows:

- **append**: Append mode
- **direct:** Use direct I/O for data
- **dsync**: Use synchronized I/O for data
- **sync:** Use synchronized I/O for data as well as for metadata
- **noatime:** Do not update access time

To view the progress of the copy operation, **status=progress** can be used, as follows:

```
dd if=largefile of=/tmp/largefile status=progress
```

The preceding command shows the running progress of the copy operation. Status option may also take the following values:

- **none** suppresses everything but error messages.
- **noxfer** suppresses the final transfer statistics.

Here are the other options that the **dd** command supports:

- **obs**: Write specified bytes at a time(default:512)
- **ibs:** Read up to specified bytes at a time (default:512); *bs* overrides **ibs** and **obs**
- **seek:** Skip specified **obs** sized blocks at the start of output; handy to skip some of the starting blocks while writing
- **skip**: Skip specified **ibs** sized blocks at start of input; handy to skip the read of some of the starting blocks

du

This command can be used to view the disk space consumption by a particular directory. It shows the disk usages of all the subdirectories recursively. At the end, it also displays the total disk space consumption of the directory itself. For example, if you want to view the current consumption of **/var/log**, type the following:

```
du /var/log
```

You will get the output shown in *Figure 3.24*. By default, the **du** command will not show the disk usages of any of the files residing under the subdirectories or the directory itself:

```
[root@192 ~]# du /var/log
0       /var/log/private
0       /var/log/samba/old
0       /var/log/samba
7748    /var/log/audit
20      /var/log/sssd
0       /var/log/speech-dispatcher
72      /var/log/rhsm
0       /var/log/insights-client
12      /var/log/cups
0       /var/log/gdm
0       /var/log/chrony
0       /var/log/qemu-ga
7612    /var/log/anaconda
23140   /var/log
```

Figure 3.24: *Usage of du command*

To also view the disk consumption by all the files, use the **-a** option as follows:

```
du -a /var/log
/var/log/README
/var/log/tallylog
/var/log/private
36 /var/log/lastlog
/var/log/samba/old
/var/log/samba
7748   /var/log/audit/audit.log
.....output truncated.....
```

The other options that can be used with the **du** command are as follows:

- **-h**: Prints size in human-readable format as **K,M** or **G**
- **-s**: Displays only the disk space usage of directory itself

The following command displays only the total space consumed by the specified directory itself:

```
[root@192 ~]# du -s /var/log
23152  /var/log
```

lastlog

It prints the last login of all the users. It gives information for all the users listed in the **/etc/passwd** file. See *Figure 3.25*, where the last login details of all the users are printed in four fields: **Username** displays the login name of the user, **Port** displays the port to which they log in. Since the users are logged in locally, terminal file is displayed. The **From** field is empty as the user logs in locally. The **Latest** field shows the last date and time when the user logged in.

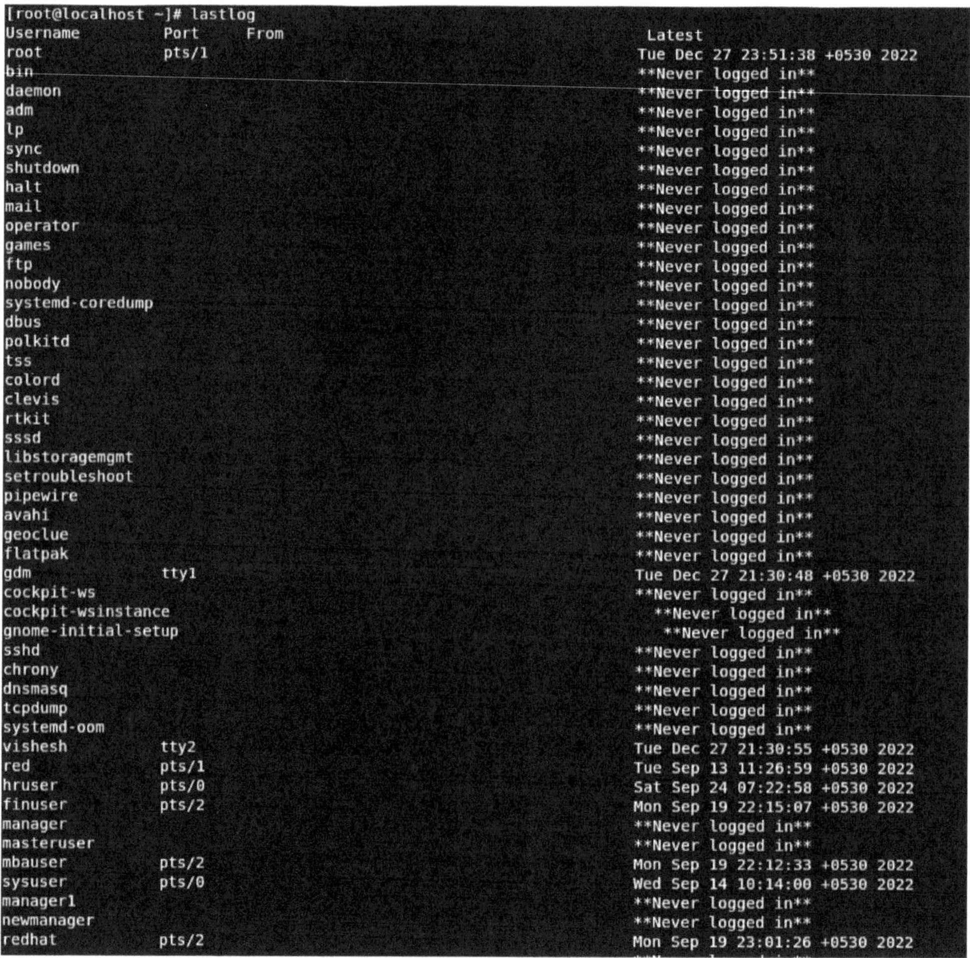

***Figure 3.25**: lastlog command displaying the last login of all the users locally*

Do it yourself

Type the following in the terminal:

```
tail -f <mypipe
```

Open another terminal and type the following:

```
echo "hello this is first message" > mypipe
```

Verify the message consumption by the `tail - f` command.

Again, pass an input message from the second terminal using `echo`. Verify the message read by the process running in the first terminal. Why is the `tail -f` process still open? What does this command do?

Here document (another way to read standard input)

So far, we have learnt many ways to give standard input to the command that requires it; these are keyboard, redirect symbol '**<**', and pipe. Besides these ways of standard input, we have the **here document**. The **here document** does not refer to any document but to the standard input that is given immediately along with the command.

```
cat < file
hello this is a book on Linux
CTRL+D
```

In the preceding command line, shell will wait for the user input. When we use the **here document**, no waiting will be there as input is given even before the shell comes into action:

```
[vishesh@192 ~]$ cat << EOI
hello this is a book on linux
written on 'date'
EOI
hello this is a book on linux
written on Saturday 31 December 2022 12:02:57 AM IST
```

In the preceding command, instead of the **<** operator, **<<** is used. This is **here document**. It means 'do not look anywhere for standard input; standard input is here only.' You have to specify the terminator for your standard input; we use **EOI**, but it can be of any name. When shell sees **<<**, it takes each line as input until it finds the limiting character **EOI.** On finding the limiting character **EOI**, it translates the input line, resolves any metacharacters and wild card characters that it finds. In the preceding command, it finds command substitution character, so it executes the command enclosed in `` and returns the output.

Real usages of the **here document** are in shell script, which we will see in *Chapter 7, Interacting With Bash Shell and Scripting*.

Conclusion

Learning Linux commands makes you efficient in performing simple to complex task on a Linux machine. All commands may use three stream files. They are standard input, standard output and standard error. Some commands use only standard input, some use only standard output and standard error, while some others use all the three streams. By default, standard input is accepted from the keyboard. Standard output and standard error are displayed on the terminal. Commands may also accept standard input from disk file (using **<** operator), pipe (using **|** operator) and the **here document** (using **<<** operator). The default destination for standard output can be changed using redirection operator (**>** and **>>**), which saves standard output to disk file. Another destination for standard output could be the input of another command (using pipe). When a command is submitted on the command prompt, shell comes into action and acts as a command interpreter that takes and executes the instructions when you type a command on the terminal prompt, followed by the *Enter* key. These instructions can be in the form of built-in commands, or user-created commands or a **`shell script`**. The command line may contain several special characters or symbols known as metacharacters or wild-card character that has special meaning for shell. To escape their special meaning, quoting or escaping is used on the command line. Some characters, like **`$`**, `'`, and **`\`** cannot escape their special meanings for shell when quoted using double quotes. So, they must be enclosed in single quotes. Single quote can escape the meaning of all the special symbols. Some commands use a regular expression, which is a pattern that describes one or many strings.

In the next chapter, we will read about system and user processes in RHEL9.0 and understand how they are managed.

Join our book's Discord space

Join the book's Discord Workspace for Latest updates, Offers, Tech happenings around the world, New Release and Sessions with the Authors:

https://discord.bpbonline.com

CHAPTER 4
Managing Processes and Services in RedHat Linux

Introduction

When a user runs a program, the operating system allocates this in memory, and the running program in memory is known as process. OS performs the role of process scheduling, keeps track of all running processes and allocates the required system resources to it, thus managing processes until it finished its execution. After the process is finished, it deallocates the resources assigned to it. When an OS boots, its target is to take the machine to the login prompt. During boot, multiple processes are launched to make the system ready for use. To manage the system initialization process, Linux OS uses system and service manager, also known as init system of Linux. Init system is responsible to manage all the processes running. SysV init daemon had been the main init system for Linux OS since many years. Now, most of the Linux distribution has replaced SysV init system with systemd for the system initialization. systemd provides many other features than its legacy SysV init system. In the earlier distribution of RHEL, system initialization process was managed by Sysv daemon. But since RHEL7, systemd replaced sysV init to manage services and processes running in system. In this chapter, you will see what are processes and services in RHEL9, how OS manages these processes and services using systemd, and what role a system administrator plays in managing the complete system.

Structure

This chapter has the following structure:

- Understanding process
- Viewing running process
- Searching process using pgrep
- Managing processes
- Running process in the background
- Setting priority of the process
- System and service manager
- Managing services by systemd

Objectives

Upon finishing this chapter, you will gain the ability to elucidate the process within RHEL9, understand the methods for observing and overseeing active processes, and proficiently comprehend systemd while effectively administrating Linux systems employing systemd as their init system.

Understanding process

Linux is a multi-user operating system where several users can run different programs simultaneously. Each program runs in memory as a process. A program is a passive entity as it is stored in a file on the storage disk. When a user starts a program to execute it, it copies the program in memory to create a process. Simply, a program in execution is a process. Each process is maintained by a unique identifier known as process ID. A process can give rise to many other processes. The Linux OS is responsible for managing of all these processes. But process is not just a copy of a file program; it is more than that. Everything that runs on Linux machine is a process. When you start a terminal in Linux system, you actually start a shell process, which waits for the user's input to serve it as a request. When you boot your machine, several processes start from the very beginning. Several processes are not needed after machine is started, so they die.

Process has a life. It moves to multiple stages since its birth. It is forked, then executed; it can become an orphan or a zombie or can die. There follows a parent-child relationship among running processes. A process can be either a child or a mother of a process. Each process is identified by its parent process ID (PPID) and its process ID (PID). The **pstree** command is used to view the parent-child relationship between the processes in hierarchical order. Execute the **pstree** to view who is the child of whom. Your output may scroll the screen. So, use pager, as follows:

```
$ pstree|more
```

The default output of **pstree** will not display the process ID of the processes. To print more information on the screen, execute the following command:

```
$ pstree -p|more
```

From the output, you can see that the process having pid 1 is **systemd**. And this is the mother/grandmother of all the running processes.

Creation of processes

A new process is created using fork system call. **fork()** creates a copy of the calling process, and what is created is known as the child process. The process that requests the kernel to create a new process is the parent process. A child process inherits the environment of its calling parent process. The child process copies the parent program into itself. But they still differ in the following sense:

- Child process and parent process runs in separate memory spaces.
- No pending signals and resource locks are inherited.
- Child process receives a new pid.
- Both child and parent processes are executed parallelly.

When the child process is successfully created, pid of the child is returned to the parent, else -1 is returned to the parent.

Zombie and orphan process

A child process in a user session can become orphan if its parent process is killed somehow. When a process running in your session becomes orphan, it is adopted by the **systemd** process. This is unlike a SysV init-based system, where an orphan process is adopted by the process, named as **init**, whose **pid** is 1. In SysVinit-based systems, init process is said to be the mother of all the orphan processes. In fact, it is the mother/grandparent of all other processes. In systemd-based systems, the **pid** of the **systemd** process that adopts the orphan process is not 1. So, you should not say that the next parent pid of the orphan user process is 1. To know the process ID of life saver mother in systemd-based systems, continue going through this chapter.

A process that is killed but has not been yet destroyed properly by its parent is called zombie or defunct process. The entry of this process can still be seen in the process table.

Viewing running process

After you open a terminal, just type the **ps** command to view your running processes. What do you see? Let us delve into this output.

```
[visheshkumar@192 ~]$ ps
  PID TTY          TIME CMD
   2704 pts/0    00:00:01 bash
   5004 pts/0    00:00:00 ps
```

Here, the output contains only two lines, and each line describes a process. The first line refers to the bash process that is started to serve your request when you open your terminal. This is clear from the last column of the output above. The second line refers to the command itself that you have just executed. You see four columnar outputs here. The details of each of these columns are as follows:

- **PID**: PID is the process ID of the executed program. In the first line, 2704 is the pid of the bash process. Command executed is bash. You will say that you have not run bash program. So, where does it come from? When you start a terminal, a bash program is executed. Second line is **ps** command, which you have just executed. This program is executed with the pid of **5004** and after execution, the process finishes.
- **TTY**: TTY is the name of the terminal from which you are logged in and to execute the program. In the preceding output, your terminal identifier is **pts/0**. **?** in the TTY column, which means the process is running without any terminal.
- **TIME**: This is the cumulative CPU time since the process has started.
- **CMD**: This is the actual program that is executed.

Process categories

Process can be broadly classified into two categories:

- **Foreground process**: Whatever command or program you are running while connected to the system, it creates a foreground process. You can run this program via terminal or using Desktop GUI. When you type the **ps** command, you actually start a foreground process that executes the **ps** command, returns the output in your terminal and then goes away. Foreground process may require user intervention.
- **Background process**: Background processes are the processes that run in the background. The idea behind this is that such a process doesn't require any user intervention. While it is being executed in the background, a user can run another task in the foreground. The process that takes time to execute and doesn't require user intervention can run as a background process. Further discussion on running background jobs is given later in this chapter.

Daemons

Daemons are a special type of background processes that start automatically and keep running forever. One important daemon in the rhel9 is systemd, which is always running. This is the system and service manager in RHEL9. Its pid is 1, and it is the parent/grand parent of all other processes. These daemon processes actually have **d** in the last character of their name. They are not associated with any terminal. You will notice a **?** in terminal column of **ps** output. We will deal with various daemons throughout this book.

Fetching process information

When **ps** is used without any option, it will display the processes associated with the same user and same terminal. You have seen that it outputs only a few columns. To output more columns that can give you additional process information, you can use the **-f** option with **ps**.

```
ps -f
[visheshkumar@192 ~]$ ps -f
UID          PID    PPID  C STIME TTY          TIME CMD
vishesh+    2704    2678  0 03:12 pts/0    00:00:01 bash
vishesh+    6158    2704  0 23:12 pts/0    00:00:00 ps -f
```

Now, let us see what all these columns mean:

- **UID**: It displays the uid of the user who owns the process. **+** in front of the username in UID column means that UID is truncated as it contains more than 7 characters. This is the limit of the **ps** command output. In the further reading, we will see how this limit can be overridden by using other options with the **ps** command.
- **PPID**: PPID is the parent process id. In the preceding output, you can see that the PPID of the **ps -f** command that you have just executed is 2704, which is the **pid** of bash process itself.
- **STIME**: This is the starting time of the process.
- **CMD**: This is the command that initiated this process. In the preceding output, pid 2704 is the session leader. Session leader means the first member pid of this session. Here, 2704 will be the session id of the user.

More options with ps command

There are many other options that you can use with the **ps** command to fetch extra information about each process; some are listed as follows. You can read man pages to know more options. Refer to the following list:

- `-e` or `-A`: Returns all the processes running for all the users; to view additional information of all the processes of all the users, you can use **`ps -ef`**
- `-a`: All user's processes with tty, except session leaders
- `a`: All processes with tty, including other users
- `-d`: All processes of all users except session leaders
- `r`: Only running processes
- `T`: All processes on this terminal
- `x`: List of all the processes owned by the current user; you will get a big list of the processes running
- `-p` or `p` **`<comma separated list of pid>`**: View the details of given comma-separated list of processes
- `-t` or `t` : It displays all the processes running on this terminal when only `-t` or `t` is used. You can also provide comma-separated list of terminals if you want to see processes running on a specific terminal
- `-u` or `U` : It displays all the processes run by the current user by default. You can also provide a comma-separated list of effective user ids or names if you want to see the processes running by specific users.
- `u` : It displays processes of the invoking user in user format.
- `-C` **`<cmdlist>`**: It displays the processes whose executable name is given in cmdlist.
- `--ppid`**`<comma separated list of ppids>`**: It selects processes by ppid.
- `-j`: It will show you the output in jobs format.
- `-F`: It will give you more information in extra full format.

Note: In all the options of ps, some require '-', while some options don't require any dash (-). They are the standard syntax and BSD syntax, respectively. a and -a will show you different results. BSD style options can be combined with standard style options. You have some long options also that start with --- (double dash). Use man pages to know them.

Output columns in ps

With the use of the appropriate option in the **`ps`** command, you will be able to fetch all the necessary information related to processes. Apart from the columns that we have understood earlier, there are many other columns that can be displayed with the usage of other options. Following are some of the output column's lists and the meaning of each column:

- **C**: CPU utilization
- **RSS**: Resident Set Size is non-swapped physical memory that process has used
- **PSR**: Processor that the process is currently assigned to
- **SZ**: Size in physical pages of the core image of the process, including text, data, and stack space
- **SIZE**: Virtual size of the process (code+data+stack); approximate amount of swap space that would be required if the process were to dirty all writable pages and then be swapped out
- **Vsz:** Virtual memory size of the process in kb
- %**CPU**: `cpu` utilization of the process
- %**MEM**: Ratio of the process's resident set size to the physical memory on the machine
- **STAT or S:** Display the status of the process; more on these status codes in the next section
- **PGID: Display the process group ID to which the process belongs. A process group is used to manage the group of processes together.**

Usages of ps options

One option can be combined with others to view the output according to your requirement. The following are some frequently used useful usages of these options:

- `ps -ef` or `ps ax`: This command can be used to list every process on the system. `ps -ef` is standard syntax, while the latter (`ps ax`) uses BSD syntax. If you want to view extra columns with `ps ax`, you can add the `-f` option, as follows:

  ```
  ps ax  -f
  ```

- `ps -f x`: This lists the process owned by you. The `-f` option can be combined here to display additional information.
- `ps -uvisheshkumar`: You will see a list of all the processes run by the named user.
- -o <format>: You can customize the output of `ps` the command using the `-o` option. This option allows you to specify a comma-separated list of `ps` output columns. The following are a few example usages.

If you want to view only the pid, ttys, and respective username of all the processes, use the following command:

```
ps -eo pid,tty,user
```

To view the resource usage information, you can use the following command:

```
ps -eo pid,user,rss,vsz,
```

To view pid of the specified process, use the following command:

```
 ps -C systemd -o pid
```

You will get the following output:

```
    PID
      1
   1881
```

You can also execute the preceding command by suffixing the "=" sign as below:

```
ps -C systemd -o pid=
```

You will get the following output:

```
      1
   1881
```

Header is not printed in the preceding output. You can also view the pid of a particular process by using the **pidof** command. For example, to find the **pid** of a process whose name is **systemd**, you can use the following command:

```
$ pidof systemd
1881 1
```

To find the pid of a process whose name is **gnome-terminal-server**, you can use the following command:

```
$ pidof gnome-terminal-server
2678
```

To view the details of a single process, type the following command:

```
$ ps 1881
    PID TTY      STAT   TIME COMMAND
   1881 ?        Ss     0:02 /usr/lib/systemd/systemd –user
```

or

```
$ ps -p 1881
    PID TTY          TIME CMD
   1881 ?        00:00:02 systemd
```

Besides the **ps** command, you can echo environment variables **$$** and **$PPID** to view the **PID** and **PPID**, respectively, for your session.

Searching processes using pgrep

To search a particular process, system administrator frequently uses the **ps -ef|grep <pattern>** command. Let us try to get information about a particular process whose name matches **bluetooth**.

```
[visheshkumar@192 ~]$ ps -ef|grep bluetooth
root        14946       1  0 Sep01 ?        00:00:00 /usr/libexec/          /         d
vishesh+    17651   15227  0 09:38 pts/1    00:00:00 grep --color=auto
```

Figure 4. 1: *ps with grep to search a process using a pattern*

In *Figure 4.1,* you can see the information related to **bluetoothd** daemon. An alternative way to search for a process is using **pgrep**. Type the following command:

```
$ pgrep system
```

```
[vishesh@192 ~]$ pgrep systemd
1
677
690
904
2102
```

Figure 4.2*: Usages of pgrep to search for a pattern*

Figure 4.2 will display all the **process id** having matching name **systemd**. Nothing is clear about the returned process ID in the preceding command's output. We have multiple options that can give you a clearer output. Use the **-a** option as follows:

```
 $ pgrep -a systemd
1 /usr/lib/systemd/systemd rhgb --switched-root --system --deserialize 31
677 /usr/lib/systemd/systemd-journald
690 /usr/lib/systemd/systemd-udevd
904 /usr/lib/systemd/systemd-logind
2102 /usr/lib/systemd/systemd -user
```

To view all the processes belonging to a single user, you can use the following command:

```
$ pgrep -uroot
```

To view the processes matching a pattern but belonging to a single user, type the following command:

```
$ pgrep -uroot systemd
```

There are many options that you can use with **pgrep** for advanced searching. To know more options, explore man pages.

Do it yourself

1. **Count the total number of all the processes running by all the users.**
2. **Sort the list of all the users' processes by pid**
3. **What is you session ID or session leader pid?**
4. **Open another terminal. What is your session leader pid here. Type ps a and find out all the session leaders here.**
5. **How will you view only the session leaders of all the sessions?**
6. **How will you format the ps output so that it displays username in full format? Hint: Use the `-o` option along with all those columns that you would like to display in ps output.**

Process state

The following is from the man page (empty lines truncated and output re-formatted).

```
PROCESS STATE CODES

       Here are the different values that the s, stat and state output
specifiers (header "STAT" or "S") will display to describe the state of a
process:

         D    uninterruptible sleep (usually IO)
         I    Idle kernel thread
         R    running or runnable (on run queue)
         S    interruptible sleep (waiting for an event to complete)
         T    stopped by job control signal
         t    stopped by debugger during the tracing
         W    paging (not valid since the 2.6.xx kernel)
         X    dead (should never be seen)
         Z    defunct ("zombie") process, terminated but not reaped by its
parent.

For BSD formats and when the stat keyword is used, additional characters
may be displayed:

              <    high-priority (not nice to other users)
              N    low-priority (nice to other users)
              L    has pages locked into memory (for real-time and custom IO)
              s    is a session leader
             l   is multi-threaded (using CLONE_THREAD, like NPTL pthreads do)
              +    is in the foreground process group
```

Managing process

A regular user can control the processes that are owned by him. They can stop or suspend or even terminate their processes anytime. A root user or administrator can control all the processes owned by any user. In this section, we will see how processes are managed.

Stopping a running process

To stop a foreground process, use the *Ctrl* + *C* key combination.

Suspending a process

To suspend a process for some time, use the *Ctrl* + *Z* key combination. After pressing these keys, you will get a prompt for your next task. Whenever you want to resume the suspended task, you can use the **fg** command as in *Figure 4.3:*

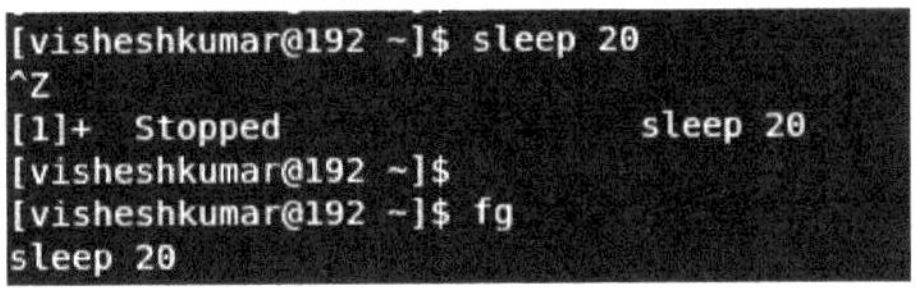

```
[visheshkumar@192 ~]$ sleep 20
^Z
[1]+  Stopped                 sleep 20
[visheshkumar@192 ~]$
[visheshkumar@192 ~]$ fg
sleep 20
```

Figure 4.3: *Suspending and resuming a foreground process*

Do it yourself

Create a new long running process in your terminal session using sleep 60. Suspend it. Create another long running process in the prompt that you get after suspending the first job. Use sleep 40 for the second job. Also, suspend the second long running job. Now, use the fg command to bring a job in the background. Which job resumes its operation? After the resume job finishes its operation, use the fg command again to resume the remaining job.

Terminating a process

Many times, a user needs to terminate its process if it is taking a long time. A normal user can terminate only processes that they own. In the case of system slowdown, a system administrator may also terminate a process if they find that a process is consuming all the system resources and is the main culprit for the system hanging.

To terminate or kill a running process, use the **kill** command. You will need the process ID of the job that you want to **kill**. Simply use the following command:

```
kill <pid>
```

This will send the **TERM** signal to the specified process by default. **TERM** would mean terminate. If a process is not terminated by using the **kill <pid>** command, you can also forcedly kill the process using the following:

```
kill -9 <pid>
```

Here, 9 refers to the **SIGKILL** signal. Type **kill -l** to view the list of available signals that can be sent. *Figure 4.4* shows you a total of 64 signals that can be sent to the processes. A normal user cannot use all these signals to terminate a process.

```
[visheshkumar@192 ~]$ kill -l
 1) SIGHUP       2) SIGINT       3) SIGQUIT      4) SIGILL       5) SIGTRAP
 6) SIGABRT      7) SIGBUS       8) SIGFPE       9) SIGKILL     10) SIGUSR1
11) SIGSEGV     12) SIGUSR2     13) SIGPIPE     14) SIGALRM     15) SIGTERM
16) SIGSTKFLT   17) SIGCHLD     18) SIGCONT     19) SIGSTOP     20) SIGTSTP
21) SIGTTIN     22) SIGTTOU     23) SIGURG      24) SIGXCPU     25) SIGXFSZ
26) SIGVTALRM   27) SIGPROF     28) SIGWINCH    29) SIGIO       30) SIGPWR
31) SIGSYS      34) SIGRTMIN    35) SIGRTMIN+1  36) SIGRTMIN+2  37) SIGRTMIN+3
38) SIGRTMIN+4  39) SIGRTMIN+5  40) SIGRTMIN+6  41) SIGRTMIN+7  42) SIGRTMIN+8
43) SIGRTMIN+9  44) SIGRTMIN+10 45) SIGRTMIN+11 46) SIGRTMIN+12 47) SIGRTMIN+13
48) SIGRTMIN+14 49) SIGRTMIN+15 50) SIGRTMAX-14 51) SIGRTMAX-13 52) SIGRTMAX-12
53) SIGRTMAX-11 54) SIGRTMAX-10 55) SIGRTMAX-9  56) SIGRTMAX-8  57) SIGRTMAX-7
58) SIGRTMAX-6  59) SIGRTMAX-5  60) SIGRTMAX-4  61) SIGRTMAX-3  62) SIGRTMAX-2
63) SIGRTMAX-1  64) SIGRTMAX
```

Figure 4.4: *List of signals that can be sent to the process to kill them*

An alternate way to kill the process is by using the **pkill** command. **pkill** would kill the processes matching the pattern by sending the **SIGTERM** signal by default. You can also specify the signal used to kill using the following syntax:

```
pkill <signal> pattern
```

For example, to terminate gnome-calculator, use the following command:

```
pkill -9 gnome-calculator
```

killall kills the process by name. For example, to kill all the bash processes, use the following command:

```
# killall bash
```

If you are not the root user, you cannot kill all the bash processes kept running by other users. So, this command will fail. To kill all the bash processes owned by you, use the following command:

```
killall -user <username> bash
```

You can use the **-9** option if the preceding command fails to kill the named process:

```
$ killall -9 -user visheshkumar bash
```

Do it yourself

- **Open gnome-calculator application in your terminal by typing gnome-calculator. Open another terminal and try to kill gnome-calculator that you ran in the first terminal. Use the killall command to do this.**

- **Use the ps -f command to note the pid of bash process that runs in your terminal. Use the killall command to kill bash process. Now, type the ps -f command again to verify whether the bash process is terminated. If it is still there, use killall with the -9 option to forcibly kill it. What do you see?**

Running process in background

If you have a long-running job to do, you can execute it in the background so that you can continue other operations on the same terminal. Let us use the **sleep** command to sleep the session for 500 seconds and switch it in the background using the **&** operand:

```
[visheshkumar@192 ~]$ sleep 500 &
[1] 11952
[visheshkumar@192 ~]$ sleep 600&
[2] 11961
```

You will get a number when you switch a process in the background. What to do with it? Here, the number in the square bracket '**[]**' is the number of background job. **[2]** means this is your second background job. And its **pid** is 11961; you have to use this **pid** to manage or kill this background job.

To switch job 2 back to foreground, use the following command:

```
$ fg 2
sleep 600
```

To switch this job in the background again, you must suspend it first. Press *Ctrl + z* to suspend it:

```
Ctrl+z
^Z
[2]+  Stopped                 sleep 600
[visheshkumar@192 ~]$
```

To resume it back in the background, use the **bg** command along with the job number that you want to switch.

```
bg 2
[2]+ sleep 600 &
```

After a background process is finished, it sends the following output while you are working in your terminal:

```
[1]-  Done                    sleep 500
```

This output will display the job number and process ID of the finished job.

Setting priority of a process: Nice and renice

The **nice** command is used to execute a process with the specified CPU priority. It is used to provide a process with more or less CPU time than any other process. Many times, you need to execute a program with higher priority as you may need to finish it earlier than any other program. You must execute this program using the **nice** command. If you want to finish a long-running program earlier, you can also modify the priority of a running program by using the **renice** command. Let us view what is default in the system.

```
# ps -o priority
PRI
 20
 20
# ps -o nice
 NI
  0
  0
```

By default, the priority of all the user processes is 20 and nice value is 0.

Niceness values range from -20 to 19. The processes with the lowest nice value would be prioritized by the CPU and would finish earlier than any other process. The process having a higher nice value will be given less priority by the CPU and would finish later. The con is that a lower nice value stresses on the CPU as the CPU would compete for the completion of the process sooner.

Start the **gnome-calculator** application by using the **nice** command, as follows:

```
nice -10 gnome-calculator
```

This will start the calculator application with a **nice** value of 10. To verify, execute the following:

```
$ ps -f -o user,pid,ppid,cmd,priority,ni
USER          PID    PPID CMD                         PRI  NI
vishesh+    12417   12254 bash                         20   0
vishesh+    12280   12254 bash                         20   0
vishesh+    12736   12280  \_ gnome-calculator         30  10
vishesh+    12822   12280  \_ ps -f -o user,pid,ppid,  20   0
vishesh+     1912    1860 /usr/libexec/gdm-wayland-se  20   0
vishesh+     1922    1912  \_ /usr/libexec/gnome-sess  20   0
```

See the line with gnome-calculator. This program has been started with CPU priority with 30 and nice value 10. This process would be given comparatively lower priority by the CPU.

A regular user is not allowed to start a process with negative nice value. Try starting gnome-calculator application using the following command as a regular user:

```
nice --1 gnome-calculator
nice: cannot set niceness: Permission denied
```

You receive a permission denied error. A root user can start a process with a lower nice value. Log in as root user and execute the following command:

```
nice --1 gnome-calculator
```

Verify the process creation by using the mentioned **ps** command as root. You will find that the calculator application is running with **-1** nice value and priority set to 19.

Now, let us renice the nice value of a running process to -19.

```
#  renice -n -19 -p 12736
12736 (process ID) old priority 10, new priority -19
```

A normal user cannot decrease the nice value of a process. So, you have to be root or use **sudo** to do the same. To verify the change in nice value, execute the following:

```
$ ps -f -o user,pid,ppid,cmd,priority,ni
USER          PID    PPID CMD                           PRI  NI
visheshm+   12417   12254 bash                           20   0
visheshm+   12280   12254 bash                           20   0
visheshm+   12736   12280  \_ gnome-calculator            1 -19
visheshm+   12934   12280  \_ ps -f -o user,pid,ppid,   20   0
visheshm+    1912    1860 /usr/libexec/gdm-wayland-se  20   0
visheshm+    1922    1912  \_ /usr/libexec/gnome-sess  20   0
```

See the output. It receives priority 1 by CPU, which is the top priority. This process will execute at the first priority. You should not leave this process priority to 1. Else, all other important processes may not be attended by CPU, leaving the system unusable. So let us immediately increase the nice value.

```
$ renice -n 1 -p 12736
12736 (process ID) old priority -19, new priority 1
```

System and service manager

Earlier versions of RHEL and other Linux distros used SysVinit as an init system, which is used for system initialization. Since RHEL7, Red Hat had moved to incorporating systemd in its Linux distributions. Systemd binaries are written in C, unlike SysVinit. SysVinit is used to handle startup process through various shell scripts in **/etc/rc.d/init.d**, but they are gone now. You can read the **/etc/rc.d/init.d/README** file. Systemd handles startup and system processes using service files that are smaller in size as compared to traditional SysV init script files. Look at **/sbin/init** that was used to manage the system in earlier SysVinit-based systems. Type the following command:

```
ls -l /sbin/init
lrwxrwxrwx. 1 root root 22 Apr  7 19:31 /sbin/init -> ../lib/systemd/system
```

In the preceding output, you see that init program points to **/lib/systemd**. Symbolic link is created here just to retain backward compatibility. Other binaries, such as **/usr/sbin**, that were used earlier to manage the system have been removed, and symbolic links pointing to systemd related binaries have been placed at their residing location to maintain backward compatibility. In *Chapter 1, The First Step to Linux*, we learnt to shut down the machine using **shutdown** command. Use **ls -l** to view the details of this binary.

```
ls -l /usr/sbin/shutdown

lrwxrwxrwx. 1 root root 16 Apr  7 19:31 /usr/sbin/shutdown -> ../bin/
systemctl
```

Systemd features

Systemd does not only initialize the system on boot but also provides several services after the system is ready. Major features of systemd are listed here:

- **Systemd daemon**: Systemd is a system and service manager for RHEL9 operating system.
- **systemctl:** It is a utility to gather information about many services and other entities (known as units) controlled by **systemd**.
- **systemd-analyze**: This utility is used to analyze a system's booting performance, the correctness of unit files, and the like.
- **Logging:** In a traditional **init** system, there was no way to store initial boot messages, and they were lost. Systemd provides its own logging mechanism, and all the logs, including boot time logs, are stored in its own journal. Log message stored on the systemd journal can be read by using a utility provided by **systemd** itself, that is, **journalctl**. Daemon name is **systemd-journald**. Run **ps -ef** and verify whether it is running. We will understand how to use logging in systemd in *Chapter 15, Performance Monitoring and Tuning*.
- **Socket-based activation**: At boot time, **systemd** creates listening sockets for all system services that support this type of activation and passes the sockets to these services as soon as they are started. These sockets remain accessible even if corresponding services are unavailable. This not only allows **systemd** to start services in parallel but also makes it possible to restart a service without losing any message sent to it while it is unavailable as the corresponding socket remains accessible, and all messages are queued.
- **udevd**: It listens to kernel uevents and manages devices via **systemd**.
- **loggingd**: It provides a logging daemon that is used to manage user logins.
- **Dependencies**: In legacy system, there was a fixed boot order for starting services. One service used to start at a time. Under the systemd system, no fixed order

of starting of services during booting is maintained. Rather, an explicit set of dependencies among the services is defined in systemd-related files. This fixed set of dependencies among the services is responsible to start these services whenever their dependencies are met. This way, many services can be started at the same time, making the boot process faster. Thus, it replaces legacy system's non-parallel approach of starting services during boot.

- **Activating services**: Services can be activated anytime, irrespective of whether or not they have been enabled on boot.
- **Resource management**: Systemd tracks processes and services using Cgroups instead of PIDs. Each process is placed in individual control groups named after the unit to which they belong. Cgroups use the concept of slices to divide the system resources among the services. Units that manage processes may be assigned to a specific slice. Certain resource limits are imposed to each slice, and these limits apply to all processes of all units contained in that slice.
- **Parallelism**: Since it uses socket-based activation, it provides parallel starting of services as soon as all the listening sockets have been activated during boot. It also provides on-demand service activation, providing faster boot than its legacy version.
- **Centralized management**: It provides centralized management of multiple system objects/entities such as devices, mounts, processes, services, and swap space. These entities that **systemd** manages are known as units.

Systemd units

The entities and resources that are handled by systemd are categorized into several unit types. Systemd provides a system that offers dependency between various entities or units. Each unit performs certain roles. Each unit encapsulates various objects that are relevant for its role. Each of these unit types is configured in a configuration file. The systemd unit types are listed as follows:

- **Device unit**: Devices that have been made visible to **udev** are exposed to **systemd** by device unit. The configuration filename ends in .device. This is used to define dependencies between devices and other units. Systemd will dynamically create device units for all kernel devices that are marked with the **systemd** udev tag.
- **Mounts units**: It dynamically mounts and unmounts filesystem.
- **Automount unit**: Automount units provide automount capabilities for on-demand mounting of file systems as well as parallelized boot-up.
- **Paths**: It checks the existence of **systemd** monitored files and directories, can create them as needed, and describes which unit to activate when the path is modified.

- **Services**: It starts a service by launching a service daemon and its related components and controls it.
- **Slices**: It is used in conjunction with cgroups to group related processes into one hierarchical tree for the management of resources such as CPU and memory.
- **Snapshot**: This unit is used to take the snapshot of the current state of the system.
- **Socket**: Socket unit encapsulates local IPC or network sockets in the system. It is used for socket-based activation.
- **Swaps**: Swap unit is used to manage swap partition.
- **Scope**: It is an externally created processes.
- **Target**: Target units are useful to group other units and determine the dependencies among them. You will learn more about targets in this chapter.
- **Timers:** It is a systemd timer and is used like **`crond`**. It triggers actions based on a timer.

Systemd Daemon

Systemd systems use systemd daemon as its **`init`** process whose **`pid`** is 1. Before proceeding further, verify whether systemd daemon is running on the system. Type the following:

```
$ ps -fp 1
UID          PID    PPID  C STIME TTY          TIME CMD
root           1       0  0 Aug24 ?        00:00:14 /usr/lib/systemd/
systemd rhgb --switched-root --system --deserialize 31
```

The preceding output shows that systemd daemon is the first process of the system whose **`pid`** is 1.

Whenever you fetch the list of all the running processes on the system, you may have noticed that there are multiple instances of systemd running. You can use following command to see multiple instances:

```
ps -F -C systemd
UID          PID    PPID  C    SZ   RSS PSR STIME TTY          TIME CMD
root           1       0  0 42962 15940   5 15:34 ?        00:00:08 /usr/
lib/systemd/systemd rhgb --switched-root --system --deserialize 31
vishesh+    2013       1  0  5621 14268   1 15:39 ?        00:00:00 /usr/
lib/systemd/systemd –user
```

Here, you will see more than one instance of systemd. Why is that? The **`systemd`** instance that has **`pid 1`** is the **`init`** system for your RHEL9 system; it serves as the system manager. We can say that this instance runs as **`system-mode systemd`**. For each user's login, a separate instance of systemd is created to manage user-related services. The **systemd --user** instance serves as user service manager. Only one user instance of systemd is displayed here because only one user logged in to this machine. This user instance is the child of systemd instance, which has **pid** 1. If a user process becomes orphan, it will not be adopted by **systemd** whose **pid** is 1 but will be adopted by the systemd that runs in user mode. Thus, **user-mode systemd** will be the next mother if any user process becomes orphan.

There are many other daemons running around systemd. Now, it is time to determine all the daemons that have **systemd** in their name:

```
ps -ef|grep systemd
```

Figure 4.5 shows you all the systemd-related processes as well as systemd itself. The **ppid** of all these systemd-related daemons is the main systemd instance itself. This is very clear in *Figure 4.5*, where the **ppid** of these daemons is 1. It lists out daemons like **journald**, **udevd**, **logind** and **systemd -user** (which is the user mode **systemd** used to manage user-related processes).

```
[visheshkumar@192 ~]$ ps -ef|grep systemd
root         1        0  0 Aug30 ?        00:00:44 /usr/lib/        /         rhgb --switched-root --system --deserialize 31
root       720        1  0 Aug30 ?        00:00:13 /usr/lib/        /         -journald
root       738        1  0 Aug30 ?        00:00:01 /usr/lib/        /         -udevd
root     10659        1  0 Sep01 ?        00:00:01 /usr/lib/        /         -logind
vishesh+ 11270        1  0 Sep01 ?        00:00:01 /usr/lib/        /         --user
vishesh+ 11345    11270  0 Sep01 ?        00:00:02 /usr/libexec/gnome-session-binary --       -service --session=gnome
vishesh+ 19788    18696  0 00:18 pts/0    00:00:00 grep --color=auto
```

Figure 4.5: *ps command showing systemd-related process running on the system*

Earlier in this chapter, we used the**pstree** command to view the processes in hierarchical order. The default output of the **pstree** command will give you process hierarchy of all the running processes on the system. To trace the path of a particular process from its root parent up to its last child in the hierarchy, you can use the following command:

```
pstree -sp <process id>
```

Now, we will try to trace the path of our bash process up to pid1. Get the id of your bash by running the **ps** command:

```
$ ps
    PID TTY          TIME CMD
   2870 pts/0    00:00:00 bash
   3251 pts/0    00:00:00 ps
```

It is 2870. Now pass this process ID in the **pstree** command as follows:

```
$ pstree -sp 2870
systemd(1)───systemd(2013)───gnome-terminal-(2844)───bash(2870)───pstr
ee(3264)
```

What do we see here? Bash process is the child process of gnome-terminal-server, which, in turn, is the child of `systemd` daemon. In the preceding output, 2013 is the `pid` of `systemd` daemon, which runs in user mode. User instance of `systemd` daemon is the child of main `systemd` instance having `pid` 1.

Do it yourself

- **Try to create another user, sam, using root login. Start a new session of user sam graphically by using the Switch User... option under the menu that pops up when you click the power button in the top-right corner of the screen. Don't log off with your current session. After you log in as sam graphically, open terminal and find out how many systemd instances are running here. Type this:**

  ```
  ps -F -C systemd
  ```

  What do you see now?

- **Create a background process by running**

  sleep 500 &

  in the terminal. Notice the pid and ppid of your bash shell and this background process. Note who is the parent of the sleep process. Now, from another terminal, kill bash that started sleep process in the background. Observe the ppid of sleep process again. Who is the parent now?

Configuration of systemd

Systemd stores the initialization configuration for each daemon in a configuration file (known as unit files). When run as a system instance, systemd interprets the configuration file `system.conf` and the files in `system.conf.d` under the `/etc/systemd` directories; when run as a user instance, systemd interprets the configuration file `user.conf` and the files in the `user.conf.d` directories under the `/etc/systemd` directory.

Systemd Unit Files

Systemd manages the units with several units files. A unit is defined in unit configuration file, which includes information about itself and about its role. Unit configuration file also describes how a unit is dependent on other units. These unit files are located in the following directories:

- `/usr/lib/systemd/system`: This directory contains all the installed unit files. You should leave it as default.
- `/run/systemd/system` : These unit files are created at runtime. This takes precedence over the preceding directory.

- **/etc/systemd/system**: The unit files in this directory are created by systemd enable as well as unit files added to extend a service. This directory takes precedence over the directory with runtime unit files. If you want to customize any of the unit files, modify this file and not the unit files that reside under **/usr/lib/systemd/system** as the files in the **/usr/lib/systemd/system** directory are installed by the distribution package manager.

The system administrator can also install the units locally under other directories. The details are as follows:

- **/usr/local/lib/systemd/system**: This contains system units installed by the administrator.
- **/usr/local/lib/systemd/user:** It contains user units installed by the administrator.
- **/etc/systemd/user:** It contains customization of user units that are installed by the administrator.

A unit file typically consists of three sections:

- **[Unit] section**: This section contains unit name, its type, behavior and set dependencies. Every unit field has a minimum of this section.
- **[<Unit Type>] Section**: This section is unit-type specific. If it is a service unit file, then this section would be named as **[Service]**. In this book, we will learn about the settings used in this section only for service unit type. Unit specific type section for other units is outside the scope of this book.
- **[Install] Section**: This contains information that is used by systemctl enable or disable commands.

The detailed description of all the directives contained in each of the sections are out of the scope of this book. In this chapter, we will discuss only a few of them for your understanding.

Systemd target

The set of services managed under a single unit are represented by a target name. Earlier, init system used runlevels, which determined what services to start to take the system to that runlevel on boot. Instead of runlevels, RHEL9 uses systemd targets to determine the desired state of the system after boot. Target unit's main purpose is to determine the dependencies among various systemd units. It sets these dependencies among the units via its unit file. A target can also be a part of another target. Thus, a target can be dependent on other targets.

Each target unit has a name and configures using its configuration unit file. Target unit file is stored in the **/usr/lib/systemd/system/** directory. Each target file name contains the **.target** extension at the end. If the target name is **graphical** target, then the related unit file name would be **graphical.target**. Explore this directory to see what target unit files you have. A target unit can have a corresponding directory **<target name>.target.wants** under the **/etc/systemd/**system. For **graphical.target**, you can find corresponding .wants directory **graphical.target.wants** under the **/etc/systemd/**system. Similarly, there can also be corresponding **.requires** directory under the **/etc/systemd/**system. The **.wants** and **.requires** directories set the requirement dependency for that target unit. When a service is enabled, a symbolic link to a service file is added to the corresponding target's **.wants** directory. Then, that service becomes a dependency of that target.

There are many target units available, but the system target can only be either multi-user target or graphical target. System target is determined by the **default.target** unit file, where a symbolic link is created to set the default target. So, if you want to change the default target, you can just edit symbolic link manually. Besides, you can also use the following set of commands to change that. Run the following command:

```
systemctl get-default
```

This command will show you the name of the default target. If you want to change the default target, you can use **systemctl set-default** command along with the name of the target. If you run **systemctl set-default** command as a non-root user, it will ask you for the password of a privileged user. Now, run the following command:

```
systemctl set-default graphical.target
```

The preceding command will set the default target to graphical target. To set the default target to multi-user target, use the following command:

```
systemctl set-default multi-user.target
Removed /etc/systemd/system/default.target.
Created symlink /etc/systemd/system/default.target → /usr/lib/systemd/system/multi-user.target.
```

The preceding output shows that it recreates the symbolic link of **default.target** to point to the specified target. Changes will be applied on the next boot.

What if you want to change the target of the running system immediately? Use the **systemctl isolate** command. It will stop all the unnecessary services and start all the services that are required to reach the new target. To modify the default target to **multi-user.target**, execute the following:

```
systemctl isolate multi-user.target
```

You will reach the text console screen in a short time. To change yourself back to **graphical.target**, use the following command:

```
systemctl isolate graphical.target
```

Now let us see what is inside the **graphical.target** file. *Figure 4.6* shows you the contents of **graphical.target** unit configuration file. You can see that this file only contains **the [Unit]** section.

```
[vishesh@192 ~]$ cat /usr/lib/systemd/system/graphical.target
#  SPDX-License-Identifier: LGPL-2.1-or-later
#
#  This file is part of systemd.
#
#  systemd is free software; you can redistribute it and/or modify it
#  under the terms of the GNU Lesser General Public License as published by
#  the Free Software Foundation; either version 2.1 of the License, or
#  (at your option) any later version.

[Unit]
Description=Graphical Interface
Documentation=man:systemd.special(7)
Requires=multi-user.target
Wants=display-manager.service
Conflicts=rescue.service rescue.target
After=multi-user.target rescue.service rescue.target display-manager.service
AllowIsolate=yes
```

Figure 4.6: *Contents of a unit configuration file*

Following is the description of the options contained in the `[UNIT]` section of this file:

- **Description**: This is a label that describes the unit.
- **Documentation**: This is the list of man pages and/or other documentation of the unit.
- **After**: The listed unit is fully started up before the configured unit is started.
- **Before**: Before is the opposite of after; it ensures that the configured unit is started before the listed unit begins starting up.

  After and before settings configure ordering dependencies between units. When two units with an ordering dependency between them are shut down, the inverse of the start-up order is applied. If two units have no ordering dependencies between them, they are shut down or started simultaneously, and no ordering takes place. Given two units with any ordering dependency between them, if one unit is shut down and the other is started up, the shutdown is ordered before the start-up.
- **Requires**: It implements stronger requirement dependency. Listed units must be activated first to activate this unit. Dependency of this type may also be configured by creating symbolic links to the corresponding **`.requires`** directory under the **`/etc/systemd/`**system.
- **Wants**: It sets weaker dependency than required. Units listed in this option will be started if the configuring unit is. If any of the listed units do not start, it does not have any impact on the unit activation. Units of weaker dependency can also be configured as a symbolic link under corresponding **`.wants`** directory under the **`/etc/systemd/`**system. Requirement dependencies are determined by **`Requires`** and **`Wants`**.
- **Conflicts**: It configures negative dependencies and is the opposite of requires. Conflict dependency means that when one unit needs startup, conflicting units have to be stopped.
- **AllowIsolate**: It takes 'Yes' or 'No'. If set to *Yes*, this unit may be used with the **`systemctl isolate`** command.

Thus, to achieve graphical target on boot, units listed in **multi-user.target** should have been started prior to it. The **multi-user.target** file shows that it requires **basic.target** to start successfully. To start **basic.target**, **sysinit.target** must have been started prior to it, and so on. You can open and read these unit files residing under the **/usr/lib/systemd/system** and understand the dependencies. After all the dependencies listed in unit files are met, the system is successfully boot in the desired state.

Using systemctl

Systemd-based init system provides the **systemctl** utility to manage the system and all the services running on the system. **systemctl** can be used to perform several admin-related tasks on the system. From starting the machine to managing the services, all the tasks can be performed by the **systemctl** utility. Now, it will be good to recap stopping of machine using **systemctl**.

systemctl poweroff: Poweroff performs a clean shutdown and powers off the machine.

systemctl halt: Halt performs a clean shutdown and halts the system but does not power off the machine.

systemctl reboot: It reboots the system.

The various usages of **systemctl** have been provided under a cheat sheet by RedHat itself. This cheat sheet is given at the end of the chapter. The following section describes the usages of **systemctl** utility, which you can use to perform your admin-related activity.

Listing Unit dependencies

To view the dependency of a particular unit, say **graphical.target**, use the following command:

```
systemctl list-dependencies graphical.target
```

In *Figure 4.7*, you can clearly see that **graphical.target** depends on many other targets. You will get a big output. Just scroll it and see what targets and services are dependent on each other.

```
graphical.target
● ├─accounts-daemon.service
● ├─gdm.service
○ ├─nvmefc-boot-connections.service
● ├─power-profiles-daemon.service
● ├─rtkit-daemon.service
● ├─switcheroo-control.service
○ ├─systemd-update-utmp-runlevel.service
● ├─udisks2.service
● ├─upower.service
● └─multi-user.target
●   ├─atd.service
●   ├─auditd.service
●   ├─avahi-daemon.service
●   ├─chronyd.service
●   ├─crond.service
●   ├─cups.path
```

Figure 4.7: *Target dependency*

Do it yourself

View the default target via command. What is it? Change that to the alternate target. View the symbolic link of the default.target file. It should point to the new target. Reboot the machine to verify the change. What do you see? If you have changed your default target to graphical target, you will see a graphical screen, else you will see a non-graphical console. Change default target back to the original mode and reboot the machine.

Listing before and after dependency

To view what units are ordered to start before a particular unit, use **`sshd.service`**:

```
systemctl list-dependencies --before sshd.service
```

To view what units are ordered to start after a particular unit, use **`sshd.service`**:

```
systemctl list-dependencies --after sshd.service
```

Listing all the active units

To list all the active units, use the following command:

```
systemctl list-units
```

It gives the same output when we run **`systemctl`** without any options.

Listing all the available units

The previous command only displays active units. To also see inactive units, use the following command:

```
systemctl list-units --all
```

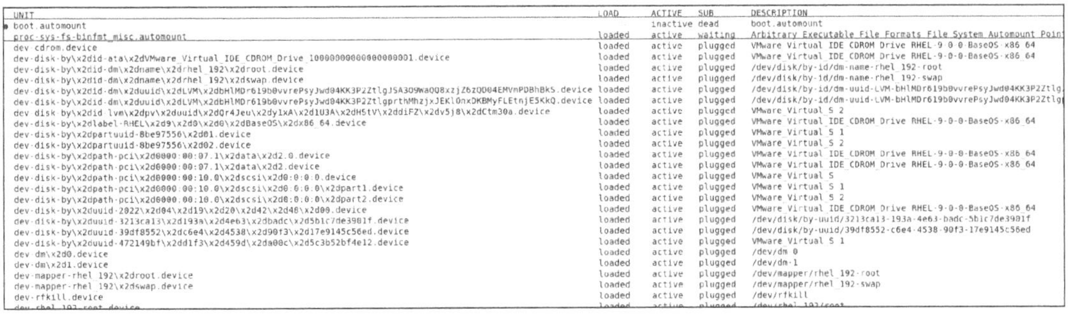

```
UNIT                                                                                          LOAD     ACTIVE   SUB      DESCRIPTION
● boot.automount                                                                                       inactive dead     boot.automount
  proc-sys-fs-binfmt_misc.automount                                                           loaded   active   waiting  Arbitrary Executable File Formats File System Automount Poin
  dev-cdrom.device                                                                            loaded   active   plugged  VMware Virtual IDE CDROM Drive RHEL-9-0-0-BaseOS-x86_64
  dev-disk-by\x2did-ata\x2dVMware_Virtual_IDE_CDROM_Drive_10000000000000000001.device         loaded   active   plugged  VMware_Virtual_IDE_CDROM_Drive RHEL-9-0-0-BaseOS-x86_64
  dev-disk-by\x2did-dm\x2dname\x2drhel_192\x2droot.device                                     loaded   active   plugged  /dev/disk/by-id/dm-name-rhel_192-root
  dev-disk-by\x2did-dm\x2dname\x2drhel_192\x2dswap.device                                     loaded   active   plugged  /dev/disk/by-id/dm-name-rhel_192-swap
  dev-disk-by\x2did-dm\x2duuid\x2dLVM\x2dbHlMDr619b0vvrePsyJwd04KK3P2ZtlgJSA3O9WaQQ8xzjZ6zQD04EMVmPDBhBkS.device loaded active plugged /dev/disk/by-id/dm-uuid-LVM-bHlMDr619b0vvrePsyJwd04KK3P2Ztlg
  dev-disk-by\x2did-dm\x2duuid\x2dLVM\x2dbHlMDr619b0vvrePsyJwd04KK3P2ZtlgprthMhzjxJEKl0nxDKBMyFLEtnjE5KkQ.device loaded active plugged /dev/disk/by-id/dm-uuid-LVM-bHlMDr619b0vvrePsyJwd04KK3P2Ztlg
  dev-disk-by\x2did-lvm\x2dpv\x2duuid\x2dQr4Jeu\x2dy1xA\x2d1U3A\x2dHStV\x2ddiFZ\x2dv5j8\x2dCtm30a.device loaded active plugged VMware_Virtual_S_2
  dev-disk-by\x2dlabel-RHEL\x2d9\x2d0\x2d0\x2dBaseOS\x2dx86_64.device                         loaded   active   plugged  VMware_Virtual_IDE_CDROM_Drive RHEL-9-0-0-BaseOS-x86_64
  dev-disk-by\x2dpartuuid-8be97556\x2d01.device                                               loaded   active   plugged  VMware_Virtual_S 1
  dev-disk-by\x2dpartuuid-8be97556\x2d02.device                                               loaded   active   plugged  VMware_Virtual_S 2
  dev-disk-by\x2dpath-pci\x2d0000:00:07.1\x2data\x2d2.0.device                                loaded   active   plugged  VMware Virtual IDE CDROM Drive RHEL-9-0-0-BaseOS-x86_64
  dev-disk-by\x2dpath-pci\x2d0000:00:07.1\x2data\x2d2.device                                  loaded   active   plugged  VMware Virtual IDE_CDROM_Drive RHEL-9-0-0-BaseOS-x86_64
  dev-disk-by\x2dpath-pci\x2d0000:00:10.0\x2dscsi\x2d0:0:0:0.device                           loaded   active   plugged  VMware_Virtual_S
  dev-disk-by\x2dpath-pci\x2d0000:00:10.0\x2dscsi\x2d0:0:0:0\x2dpart1.device                  loaded   active   plugged  VMware Virtual S 1
  dev-disk-by\x2dpath-pci\x2d0000:00:10.0\x2dscsi\x2d0:0:0:0\x2dpart2.device                  loaded   active   plugged  VMware Virtual S 2
  dev-disk-by\x2duuid-2022\x2d04\x2d19\x2d20\x2d42\x2d48\x2d00.device                         loaded   active   plugged  VMware_Virtual IDE CDROM Drive RHEL-9-0-0-BaseOS-x86_64
  dev-disk-by\x2duuid-3213ca13\x2d193a\x2d4e63\x2dbadc\x2d5b1c7de3981f.device                 loaded   active   plugged  /dev/disk/by-uuid/3213ca13-193a-4e63-badc-5b1c7de3981f
  dev-disk-by\x2duuid-39df8552\x2dc6e4\x2d4538\x2d90f3\x2d17e9145c56ed.device                 loaded   active   plugged  /dev/disk/by-uuid/39df8552-c6e4-4538-90f3-17e9145c56ed
  dev-disk-by\x2duuid-472149bf\x2dd1f3\x2d459d\x2da00c\x2d5c3b52bf4e12.device                 loaded   active   plugged  VMware_Virtual_S 1
  dev-dm\x2d0.device                                                                          loaded   active   plugged  /dev/dm-0
  dev-dm\x2d1.device                                                                          loaded   active   plugged  /dev/dm-1
  dev-mapper-rhel_192\x2droot.device                                                          loaded   active   plugged  /dev/mapper/rhel_192-root
  dev-mapper-rhel_192\x2dswap.device                                                          loaded   active   plugged  /dev/mapper/rhel_192-swap
  dev-rfkill.device                                                                           loaded   active   plugged  /dev/rfkill
  dev-rhel_192-root.device                                                                    loaded   active   plugged  /dev/rhel_192/root
```

Figure 4.8: List of available units

Figure 4.8 is the snap of first screen that you will receive when you execute the command to list all the available units. The first column is the unit name, the second column will show you whether it is loaded in the system, the third column will display whether it is currently active or inactive, and the next column will show you the current unit state and provide a short description about the unit in the last column.

List all the active units of a specific unit type

To view all the active units of a specific unit, say mount unit, type the following command:

```
systemctl list-units --type mount
```

Fetching information of a particular unit

To get information about a particular unit, say, **`run-user-1000.mount`**, use the **`systemctl status`** command as shown in *Figure 4.9*:

```
[root@192 ~]# systemctl status run-user-1000.mount
● run-user-1000.mount - /run/user/1000
     Loaded: loaded (/proc/self/mountinfo)
     Active: active (mounted) since Sun 2022-08-28 23:03:28 IST; 24h ago
      Until: Sun 2022-08-28 23:03:28 IST; 24h ago
      Where: /run/user/1000
       What: tmpfs
```

Figure 4.9: Systemctl status command to view the status of a mount unit

Output will be unit-type specific. *Figure 4.9* displays the information about a particular unit of mount type. It shows that unit name is **`run-user-1000.mount`** and related path is **`/run/user/1000`**. It also fetches unit information under the following headings:

- **Where**: The mount point
- **Loaded**: Shows whether unit is loaded and its config file, which is **`/proc/self/mountinfo`**
- **Active**: Shows whether the unit is currently active
- **Until**: Displays the time when it is mounted
- **What**: Displays the filesystem type of the mount

Listing installed unit files

To view all the installed unit files, use the following command:

```
sytemctl list-unit-files
```

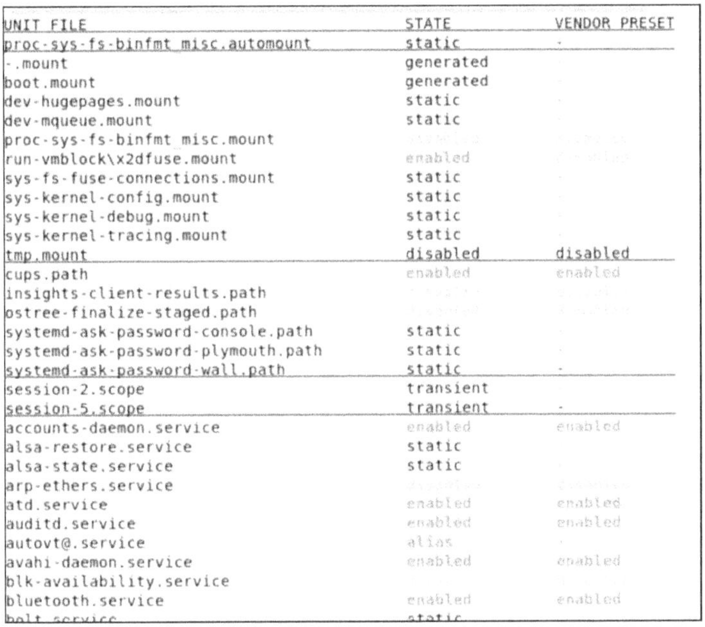

```
UNIT FILE                                 STATE        VENDOR PRESET
proc-sys-fs-binfmt_misc.automount         static       -
-.mount                                   generated
boot.mount                                generated
dev-hugepages.mount                       static
dev-mqueue.mount                          static
proc-sys-fs-binfmt_misc.mount
run-vmblock\x2dfuse.mount                 enabled
sys-fs-fuse-connections.mount             static
sys-kernel-config.mount                   static
sys-kernel-debug.mount                    static
sys-kernel-tracing.mount                  static
tmp.mount                                 disabled     disabled
cups.path                                 enabled      enabled
insights-client-results.path
ostree-finalize-staged.path
systemd-ask-password-console.path         static
systemd-ask-password-plymouth.path        static
systemd-ask-password-wall.path            static       -
session-2.scope                           transient
session-5.scope                           transient    -
accounts-daemon.service                   enabled      enabled
alsa-restore.service                      static
alsa-state.service                        static
arp-ethers.service
atd.service                               enabled      enabled
auditd.service                            enabled      enabled
autovt@.service                           alias        -
avahi-daemon.service                      enabled      enabled
blk-availability.service
bluetooth.service                         enabled      enabled
bolt.service                              static
```

***Figure 4.10**: List of installed unit files*

This command displays the output shown in *Figure 4.10*. It displays the name of the unit files and its state that will be displayed according to the unit type. For example, for service unit, it will show whether this is enabled or disabled. Other states are as follows:

- **Masked**: When the state is masked, it means that service is linked to **`/dev/null`**, and it is completely disabled and cannot be started by any means.
- **Static**: Static means that this unit file is dependent on other unit files and cannot be started or stopped by the user. They are controlled automatically. For static service, the **`[Install]`** section is missing in the service file, so you cannot enable or disable it.
- **Failed**: If unit is in failed state, **`systemd`** will try to start it again.

Viewing the contents of a unit file

The `systemctl` command can also be used to view the contents of a unit file, say **`auditd.service`**, using the following command:

```
systemctl cat auditd
```

Listing inactive units

To view only inactive units, type the following command:

```
systemctl list-units  --all --state=inactive
```

Use the **`--type`** option to view inactive units of a particular unit type.

Managing services by systemd

We have used the term service many times. But what is service in Linux OS? A service is a set of processes, service configuration file and other components that together perform one or many systems-related or user-related tasks . To make you work in the system, many services are already running in the background. You can also start many services later to perform your operations. Systemd provides the **systemctl** utility to manage services running on the system. **Systemctl** can only manage the services that have been started by **systemd**. If a system admin starts a particular service or daemon via the other way, **systemctl** is unable to manage this as it does not know the **pid** of its main process. When a service is started by **systemd**, **systemd** stores the PID of its main process to manage this service. And then it keeps track of these processes until the service is stopped.

Traditionally, services are stored in the **/etc/init.d** directory and then linked to different **runlevel** directories. Services with **systemd** are named **<servicename>.service** and are stored in the **/usr/lib/systemd/system** directory. When we enable the service to run in boot time, a symbolic link under the **/etc/systemd/system/multi-user.target.wants** directory is created for this service, which points to the service file under **/usr/lib/systemd/system**. Explore the **/etc/systemd/system/multi-user.target.wants** directory using **ls -l**; you will notice that whatever services and other units reside here are the symbolic links to those services and units under **/usr/lib/systemd/system**.

To check the status of a service and fetch other information about a service, say **sshd.service**, use the following command:

```
systemctl  status sshd.service
```

Or simply use this:

```
systemctl  status sshd
```

No.service extension is required for the unit of service type. To view the status of any other unit type, you have to use unit type extension:

```
[root@192 ~]# systemctl status sshd.service
● sshd.service - OpenSSH server daemon
     Loaded: loaded (/usr/lib/systemd/system/sshd.service; enabled; vendor preset: enabled)
     Active: active (running) since Mon 2022-08-29 11:43:37 IST; 1min 49s ago
       Docs: man:sshd(8)
             man:sshd_config(5)
   Main PID: 7107 (sshd)
      Tasks: 1 (limit: 48628)
     Memory: 1.7M
        CPU: 16ms
     CGroup: /system.slice/sshd.service
             └─7107 "sshd: /usr/sbin/sshd -D [listener] 0 of 10-100 startups"

Aug 29 11:43:37 192.168.88.128 systemd[1]: Starting OpenSSH server daemon...
Aug 29 11:43:37 192.168.88.128 sshd[7107]: Server listening on 0.0.0.0 port 22.
Aug 29 11:43:37 192.168.88.128 sshd[7107]: Server listening on :: port 22.
Aug 29 11:43:37 192.168.88.128 systemd[1]: Started OpenSSH server daemon.
```

***Figure 4.11**: systemctl status command displaying status of sshd service*

Figure 4.11 shows you the location of the unit configuration file. So, we can say that **/usr/lib/systemd/system/sshd.service** is the service config file. It also displays whether service is active and running, its man page, pid, and resources it is consuming. It is also displaying **Cgroup** fields, which shows the slice unit the service belongs to. It belongs to **system.slice**. By default, **systemd** creates a new cgroup under the **system.slice** for each service it monitors. Remaining lines are the recent lines fetched from the **systemd** journal.

To view whether the service is running, you can also use the following command, besides using the **systemctl status** command:

```
systemctl is-active sshd.service
```

To stop /start a service

Systemd only stops running services, whereas the earlier version stops all the available system services, irrespective of their current state. To stop a running service, say **sshd.service**, type the following command:

```
systemctl stop sshd.service
```

```
[root@192 ~]# systemctl stop sshd.service
[root@192 ~]#
[root@192 ~]#
[root@192 ~]# systemctl status sshd.service
○ sshd.service - OpenSSH server daemon
     Loaded: loaded (/usr/lib/systemd/system/sshd.service; enabled; vendor preset: enabled)
     Active: inactive (dead) since Mon 2022-08-29 11:43:27 IST; 4s ago
       Docs: man:sshd(8)
             man:sshd_config(5)
    Process: 7085 ExecStart=/usr/sbin/sshd -D $OPTIONS (code=exited, status=0/SUCCESS)
   Main PID: 7085 (code=exited, status=0/SUCCESS)
        CPU: 20ms

Aug 29 11:42:04 192.168.88.128 systemd[1]: Starting OpenSSH server daemon...
Aug 29 11:42:04 192.168.88.128 sshd[7085]: Server listening on 0.0.0.0 port 22.
Aug 29 11:42:04 192.168.88.128 sshd[7085]: Server listening on :: port 22.
Aug 29 11:42:04 192.168.88.128 systemd[1]: Started OpenSSH server daemon.
Aug 29 11:43:27 192.168.88.128 sshd[7085]: Received signal 15; terminating.
Aug 29 11:43:27 192.168.88.128 systemd[1]: Stopping OpenSSH server daemon...
Aug 29 11:43:27 192.168.88.128 systemd[1]: sshd.service: Deactivated successfully.
Aug 29 11:43:27 192.168.88.128 systemd[1]: Stopped OpenSSH server daemon.
```

Figure 4.12: *systemctl stop command stopping sshd service*

Figure 4.12 shows the **systemctl stop** command. To verify whether the service is stopped, you can use the **systemctl status** command.

To start a service, say *sshd*, you can use the following command:

```
systemctl start sshd.service
```

No output is displayed for the preceding command. The starting of the service is verified again using the **systemctl status** command.

Restarting a particular service

To restart a service, say, *sshd* service, use the following command:

```
systemctl restart sshd.service
```

Reloading the service

If you have made any changes to the config file, you can reload the configuration without any service disruption by using the **systemctl reload** command.

```
systemctl reload sshd
```

Disabling or enabling a service

Similarly, you can enable or disable a service that determines whether to start the service during boot time. Disable means service will not start during boot time. Enable means service will start during boot time. To disable a sshd service, use the following command:

```
systemctl disable sshd.service
```

```
[root@192 ~]# systemctl disable sshd
Removed /etc/systemd/system/multi-user.target.wants/sshd.service.
[root@192 ~]#
[root@192 ~]#
[root@192 ~]#
[root@192 ~]# systemctl status sshd.service
● sshd.service - OpenSSH server daemon
     Loaded: loaded (/usr/lib/systemd/system/sshd.service; disabled; vendor preset: enabled)
     Active: active (running) since Mon 2022-08-29 11:43:37 IST; 7min ago
       Docs: man:sshd(8)
             man:sshd_config(5)
   Main PID: 7107 (sshd)
      Tasks: 1 (limit: 48628)
     Memory: 1.7M
        CPU: 16ms
     CGroup: /system.slice/sshd.service
             └─7107 "sshd: /usr/sbin/sshd -D [listener] 0 of 10-100 startups"
```

Figure 4.13: systemctl status showing service is disabled to start on boot

Note the Loaded column in *Figure 4.13*; service is disabled now.

To enable a service, use the **systemctl enable** command. For example, to enable **sshd** service, type the following command:

```
systemctl enable sshd.service
```

```
Created symlink /etc/systemd/system/multi-user.target.wants/sshd.service →
/usr/lib/systemd/system/sshd.service.
```

The output displayed shows that a symbolic link pointing to service unit file is placed under the **/etc/systemd/system/multi-user.target.wants/** directory.

You can also view whether a service unit is enabled using the following command:

```
systemctl is-enabled <name>.service
```

We will learn to create a new service via service unit file in *Chapter 17, Web Server and Database Server Setup in Linux*. We will also learn to use timer unit and many other units in *Chapter 18, Miscellaneous*.

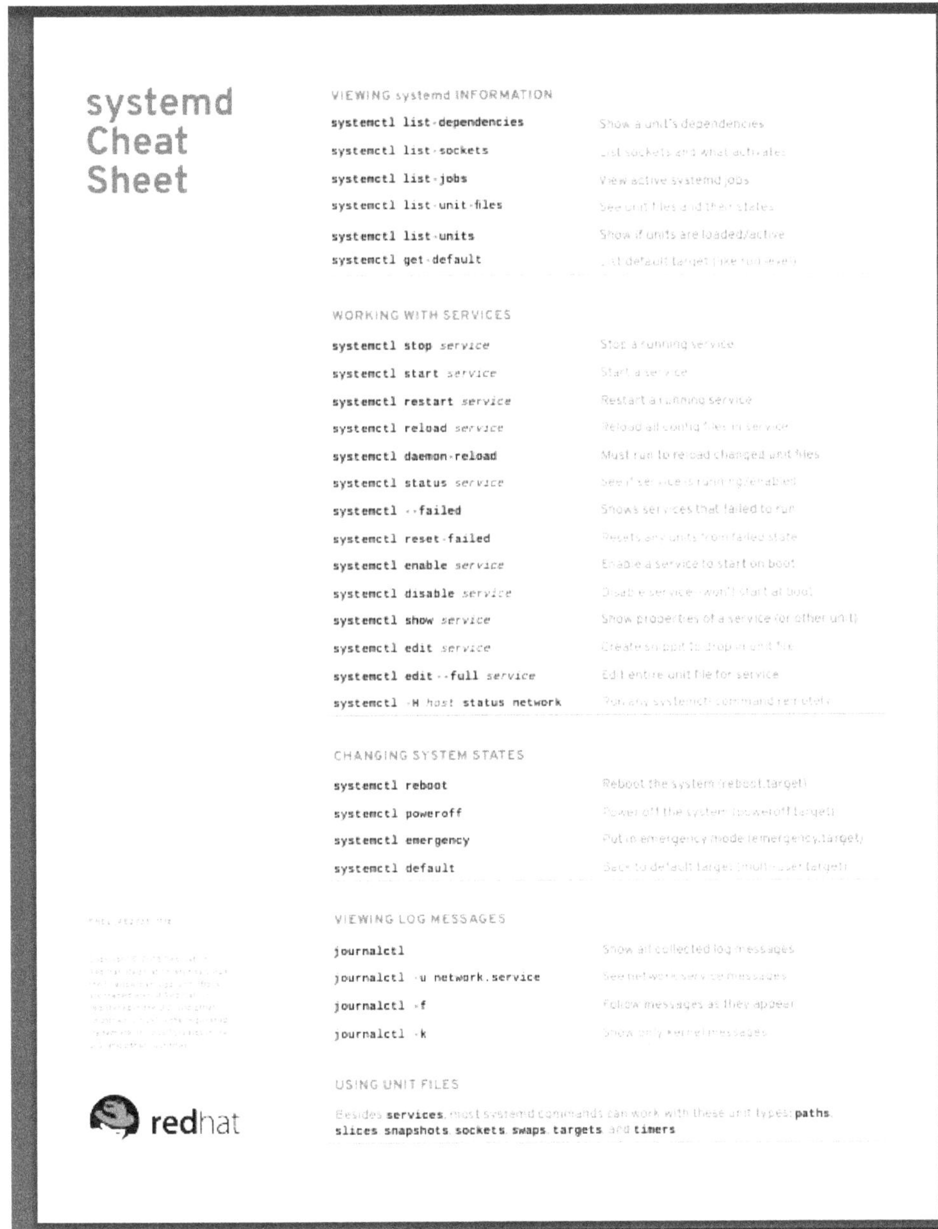

Figure 4.14: systemd cheat sheet as provided by Red Hat itself

Conclusion

When you execute a program, a running image of that program starts in memory; this is a process. Thus, process is an active execution of a program. It is an active entity, while a disk file or a program file on the disk is an inactive entity. Systemd, a service and system manager, is adopted by many Linux distros. Now it is also adopted in newer versions of RHEL. In earlier distros, SysVinit was used as an init system. Since RHEL7, RedHat replaces legacy init systems with systemd. It also replaces runlevels of the traditional init system. Systemd provides vast functionalities than provided by traditional init system. Systemd provides its own logging mechanism by journald daemon. All the logs, including boot time logs, are stored in its own journal. Systemd manages system components by using the concept of units. Each unit has a specific type, and each type performs its unit-specific role by using unit configuration file. Unit configuration files reside under the **`/usr/lib/systemd/system`** directory. This directory contains the units installed by the distribution package manager. Unit configuration files are also used to set dependency among several units. Units are configured in unit files by the use of several directives. A unit file has at least a **`[UNIT]`** section that describes the role and behavior of that unit. **`Before=`** and **`After=`** setting defines the order in which the units are started. **`Requires=`** and **`Wants=`** setting defines the requirement dependency. **`WantedBy=`** and **`RequiredBy=`** are used in the **`[Install]`** section to create **`symlinks`** in correspondinge **`.wants/`** and **`.requires/`** directories under the **`/etc/systemd/system`** directory. A **systemd target** is a set of systemd units to be managed as a single unit. Target unit is used to group other units so that they can be managed as a single unit. Systemd systems use **`systemd`** daemon as init daemon and provide **`systemctl`** utility to manage the services on system.

In the next chapter, we will learn about handling files and directories.

References

https://access.redhat.com/articles/754933

Join our book's Discord space

CHAPTER 5
Handling and Managing Files

Introduction

All the users in a Linux system generate data of some kind. It can be text-based data, binary data, images, audio and video files, and so on. All the data in the filesystem are stored into one hierarchical tree like structure that starts from `/`. Users access the data in the filesystem in the form of files. Everything in Linux is treated as a file. All the attached peripherals, storage devices, processors, memory and other objects related to Linux system interact with the Linux kernel in the form files. The files related to these objects are also stored in the same hierarchical tree as data and their access path starts with `/` (**`root`**). Every file is handled in the same way. Each file has some associated attributes that perform an important role in the overall functioning of the Linux filesystem. In this chapter, you will learn how the files are stored and accessed in the file system. You will understand various file attributes, their importance in storing and locating files, and how the creation and manipulation of file is done.

Structure

This chapter has the following structure:

- Object identity in Linux
- File-related attributes and inodes

- Working with regular files
- Navigating around the filesystems
- Operations related to files
- Text processing utilities
- Searching files

Objectives

The chapter aims to achieve several objectives, including gaining an understanding of file-related attributes, comprehending the structure of files and directories and their storage in the filesystem, acquiring knowledge on file access in Linux systems, mastering the manipulation of various file types and performing operations on them, enhancing proficiency in using the vim editor, and introducing users to file processing tools like sed and awk for executing simple to complex operations on text data stored in files.

Object identity in Linux

Each object in a Linux system is treated as a file. This object can be related to your regular data, directory or devices. This leads to the existence of four different types of files in Linux systems:

- Regular file
- Directory
- Device file
- Special files

Regular file

Any ordinary file that is created on the system is classified as a regular file. Any data that a user stores as plain text, all the compiled forms of any program, binary file, system configuration files, compressed or archive file, the actual program file, the audio files, image file, shell script file, and so on are categorized into regular files. It can be executable or non-executable. Regular file is identified by - in the first character in the first field of the **ls -l** output. Consider the following:

```
$ls -l abc
-rw-rw-r--+ 1 vishesh vishesh 0 Sep 27 11:03 abc
```

In the previous output, the first dash **(-)** signifies that **abc** file is a regular file.

We can also use the **stat** command to identify the file type. The third way to identify the file type is using the **file** command.

The regular file can or cannot contain an extension in their file name. Extension in the file name usually signifies the file type that starts with a period **(.)** after the file name, as **.txt** and so on. But in a Linux system, suffixing the file name with the extension is not required in every case. It may be required just for the system to know which application is suitable to open the file.

Directory

A set of related files, when grouped together in a folder, is called a directory in Linux system. This file type is identified in the **ls -l** output when the first character contains a **d**. A directory may contain one or more subdirectories.

Device files

Device files provide an interface to interact with the attached devices and device drivers through the kernel. Each attached device will have an entry inside the **/dev** directory. In *Chapter 2, Linux Filesystem and Administration,* we learnt that devices can be broadly categorized into two categories: block devices and character devices. Block devices such as hard disks read and write the data in terms of blocks with random access. Character devices such as terminal and keyboard perform input and output sequentially in terms of bytes. You can easily identify them by the first **b** or **c** character, respectively, in the **ls -l** output. Go to the **/dev** directory and type **ls -l**; you will get a screenful of output. Let's find out all the device files related to character devices. Type the following command:

```
ls -l |grep ^c|more
```

This is to view the character devices only. Following are a few lines from the output provided:

```
crw-rw-rw-. 1 root  tty    5,    0 Apr 7 2022 tty
crw--w----. 1 root  tty    4,    0 Apr 7 2022 tty0
crw--w----. 1 root  tty    4,    1 Oct 11 07:14 tty1
```

Notice the first character in the output. It's **'c'**, which denotes the file as character device file. In this case, the size column of **ls -l** output provides a comma-separated list of two numbers. This is the major and minor number of the device, respectively. Major number identifies a particular driver associated with the device, while the minor number refers to a particular device handled by that driver. The same device driver may be assigned to multiple devices. So, there must be some way to distinguish each device, and the minor number is used to uniquely identify a particular device.

To list out the block devices, type the following command:

```
ls -l |grep ^b
```

Your output may look like this:

```
brw-rw----. 1 root  disk  253,   0 Apr 7 2022 dm-0
brw-rw----. 1 root  disk  253,   1 Apr 7 2022 dm-1
```

```
brw-rw----. 1 root  disk  253,   2 Apr 7 2022 dm-2
brw-rw----. 1 root  disk  259,   0 Apr 7 2022 nvme0n1
brw-rw----. 1 root  disk  259,   1 Apr 7 2022 nvme0n1p1
```

In the preceding output, the first character is **b**, which denotes the block devices. Size column here refers to major and minor number, as we saw earlier.

There are a few pseudo-device files that exist under **/dev**, which are not the actual devices. Two of them are **/dev/null** and **/dev/zero**. Any write to **/dev/null** will be ignored. Any read from **/dev/zero** to write into the file will erase the file's data. We have already used these pseudo-devices in *Chapter 3, Knowing Linux Commands*.

Special files

- **Linked file**: Linked files are identified with a small **l** character in the leftmost side in the first field of the **ls -l** output. These are soft linked files.
- **named pipe**: We have read about named pipes in *Chapter 3, Knowing Linux Commands*. Named pipes are identified with the **p** character as the first character in the first field of the **ls -l** output.
- **socket file**: Sockets are used for inter-process communication. Small **s** in the first field of the **ls -l** command signifies a socket file.

Throughout the book, when we refer to the term **file**, it would mean that the context is referring to all types of files and not only the regular file unless specified.

File-related attributes and inode

Each file in Linux has an associated metadata stored on the disk. This metadata plays an important role in maintaining the files in the filesystem. The file's metadata specifies how the files are accessed. It stores the important information about the file and includes many file-related attributes but neither its actual data nor its name. Metadata is stored in a file data structure known as **inode**. The **inode** can be understood as the block that contains the file-related metadata. The metadata that it contains is listed here:

- **inode number**: **inode** number of the file
- **permission sets**: The permission that the file has
- **file size:** Determines the file size in bytes
- **timestamps**: Each file has associated timestamp fields such as last access time, last modification file and last change time of the **inode**
- **file type**: Stores the file type
- **user owner and group owner:** Stores the user and group owners of the file

- **count of link to the file:** Contains the number of hard links to the file
- **device id**: Device ID of the device in which the file resides
- **I/O block size**: The input and output block size for the filesystem
- **number of blocks allocated**: Number of allocated blocks in terms of 512-byte units

Inode

Inode refers to a file data structure where file-related attributes are stored, which, in turn, are used to access the file's contents. **Inode** is a unique number that is assigned to each file on creation. This number is used to identify the block that contains the **inode** where the file-related information is stored.

The functioning of Linux filesystem depends on the file and directory structure and not its name. So, it is important for us to understand file and directory structure in Linux filesystem. The directory to which a file belongs does not contain any file's data. Directory structure contains only the file's name and associated **inode** number. **Inode** contains the file-related metadata as well as the address of the disk blocks where the actual file's data is stored. The system never accesses the file by its name but by its **inode** number. By simple arithmetic, kernel can locate the block where the related **inode** is located. After reaching the **inode** block, kernel fetches all the associated data block where the actual file's data is stored. Humans can't remember the **inode** number of the file. So, they always access the file using its name and not by the **inode** number. When the user looks up a file by its name, directory entry is searched to map the file name to its **inode** number. This number is then used to fetch the **inode** where all the file's information and list of data blocks is stored. This is true for the directory itself and for any type of files and subdirectories residing in the directory.

Needless to say, the **inode** structure for the directory also stores the same information, that is, its attributes as well as the blocks where directory structure is stored.

For a clearer picture, refer to *Figure 5.1*.

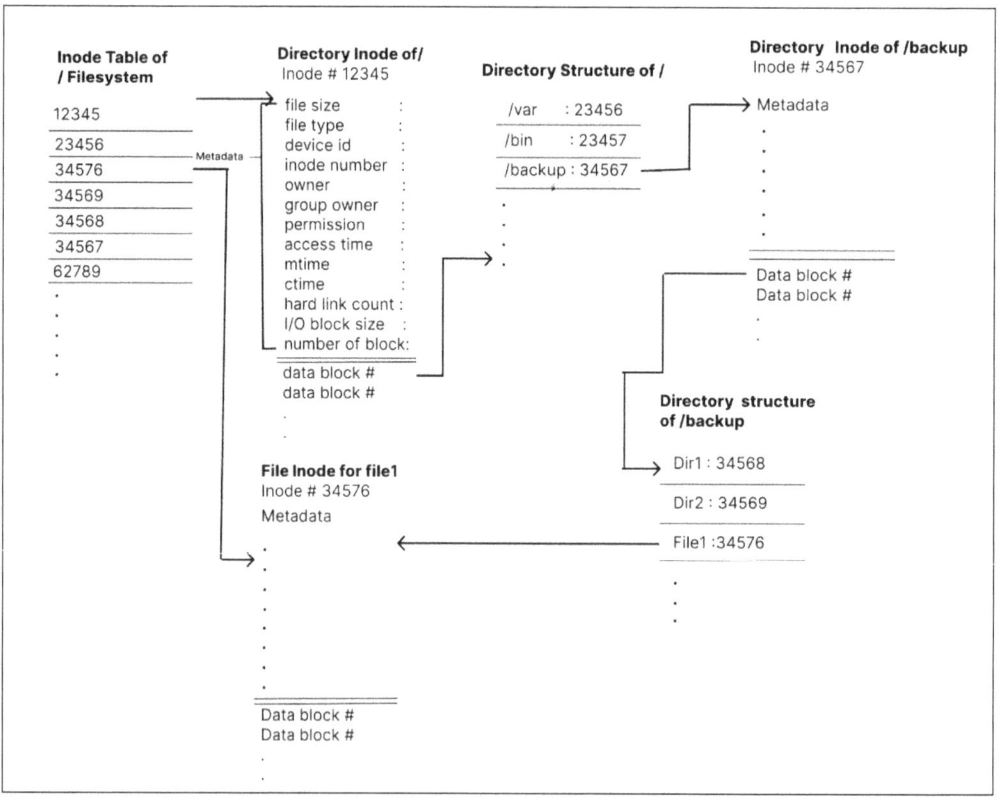

Figure 5.1: Relation between inode table, inode block and directory structure

It displays file **inode**, directory structure, and **inode** table. When a file system is created, a small portion in the beginning of the filesystem is reserved for **inode** table, which stores all the available **inodes**. **Inode** table may look as shown in *Figure 5.1*. When a file is created, an unused **inode** number is assigned to it. This **inode** number serves as the identification of the block where the related file's **inode** is stored. File data is stored in the data blocks and not in the **inode** blocks. Thus, any **inode** block contains two kinds of information: file attributes and the list of blocks where data is stored. In *Figure 5.1*, **inode** of the **/** directory is shown. This **inode** contains many attributes about the directory itself. The data block of that directory **inode** contains pointers to the block where the directory structure is stored. The directory structure of **/** contains all the top-level directories of **/**. This directory entry contains the names of all directories and files that it houses and their **inode** numbers. Look at the **/backup** entry and its associated number. This number points to the directory inode of the **/backup** directory. The directory **inode** of **/backup** also stores the metadata related to **/backup** and the address of data block that contains the directory structure of **/backup**. Similarly, the directory structure of **/backup** will also contain the name of its resident files along with their **inode** numbers. **Inode** of **/backup/file1** contains the attributes related to **/backup/file1** and a list of all the data blocks where the file's data is stored. So, it is clear from *Figure 5.1* that each directory entry stores the filename and an associated number.

Each number points to the **inode** where the file's attributes are stored. This **inode** is used to fetch the data blocks where either the file data or the directory structure is stored.

Since the number of inodes is determined at the filesystem creation time, the number of available inode is static. Consequently, the number of files that can be created in a single filesystem is also static. Though the range of inodes is very large, there is a cause for worry if you have created several smaller files on disk. Then, you may end up with all the available inodes in a short span of time. But this occurs rarely because of the larger range of inodes available.

You can use the **df** command, as in *Figure 5.2,* to view the **inode** usage on the various filesystems. It displays the **inode** usage for every mounted filesystem. It shows the total number of **inodes**, how many **inodes** are used and how many of them are free currently.

```
[vishesh@192 ~]$ df -ih
Filesystem               Inodes IUsed IFree IUse% Mounted on
devtmpfs                   1.9M   557  1.9M    1% /dev
tmpfs                      1.9M     1  1.9M    1% /dev/shm
tmpfs                      800K  1.2K  799K    1% /run
/dev/mapper/rhel-root       35M  138K   35M    1% /
/dev/mapper/rhel-home       42M   48K   42M    1% /home
/dev/nvme0n1p6             512K    22  512K    1% /boot
/dev/nvme0n1p1                0     0     0     - /boot/efi
tmpfs                      386K   156  386K    1% /run/user/1000
```

Figure 5.2: *df command showing inode usages on all the mounted filesystem*

Each filesystem has its own list of **inodes** created when the filesystem is built. Two filesystems may carry the same **inode** number, but within a filesystem, each **inode** number is unique. An **inode** number cannot be allocated twice within a filesystem. To provide unique identification to all the files of all the mounted filesystem, file system id is combined with the **inode** number.

Fetching file attributes

So far, we have used the **ls** command to fetch detailed information about any file in Linux. Since everything in Linux is treated as a file, the **ls** command comes in very handy to view the information of everything in Linux and is popular among Linux users. We have already fetched many of the listed attributes using the **ls -l** command. Besides, there are many other ways to view file-related information. One way is to use the `stat` command. This command will show you file-related metadata in greater detail, as shown in *Figure 5.3*. In *Figure 5.3*, metadata information related to the **abc** file is displayed. Output shows that **abc** is a regular file, is owned by user **vishesh**, and has 664 permissions set. The fields displayed are self-explanatory. Internally, the **stat** command returns the output from file's **inode**.

The next command that we can use to identify the file type is the `file` command.

```
$ file redhat
redhat: directory
```

To view the associated **inode** number for a file, you can use the **-i** option of the **ls** command where the first number of each listed file is the related **inode** number.

```
[vishesh@192 ~]$ stat abc
  File: abc
  Size: 0               Blocks: 0          IO Block: 4096   regular empty file
Device: fd02h/64770d    Inode: 387691      Links: 1
Access: (0664/-rw-rw-r--)  Uid: ( 1000/ vishesh)   Gid: ( 1000/ vishesh)
Context: unconfined_u:object_r:mozilla_home_t:s0
Access: 2022-11-18 06:41:43.130221917 +0530
Modify: 2022-11-18 06:41:43.130221917 +0530
Change: 2022-11-18 06:41:43.130221917 +0530
 Birth: 2022-11-18 06:41:43.130221917 +0530
```

***Figure 5.3:** stat command displaying file-related attributes*

Understanding timestamps in file

There are four timestamp fields related to the file that is stored in the file's **inode** block:

- **Access time**: Access time denotes the time when the file was last accessed or read.
- **Modification time**: Modification time denotes the time when the file was last modified. It is related to the file's contents. The modification time of file is updated whenever new data is added or replaced, or when older data is deleted. The modification time of directory is also changed whenever a file is added to or deleted from a directory.
- **Change time**: Change time denotes the time when the file's attributes were last changed. Modify time is related to modification in file's contents, while change time has no relation with changes in the file's contents or data. Change time or time is updated whenever any file-related attribute, such as user owner, group owner, and permission sets, are changed. Thus, change time is related to change in the **inode** information, such as, **owner, group,** and link count.
- **Birth time**: Birth time denotes the time when the file was created in the filesystem.

Working with hard links

In the previous section, we saw many file attributes stored in the **inode**. One of the attributes is the link count. This link count is the hard link count. Number of hard links specified in the **inode** block lets the system know the number of aliases or hard links the file has.

To create a hard link for a file or directory, the `ln` command is used as follows:

```
ln <name of the source file> <new link of the source file>
```

Let's create a hard link of the **abc** file, as shown in *Figure 5.4*. In *Figure 5.4*, an attempt to create a hard link of **abc** under **/tmp/** is made, but it fails as hard links are not allowed to span multiple filesystems. The next successful attempt is made to create a hard link under the **redhat** subdirectory. Then, on issuing **ls -li** in the **redhat** directory, we find that the hard link count of the **abc** file is increased to 2. Now, check the inodes of two hard linked files. You will find that both receive the same **inode**.

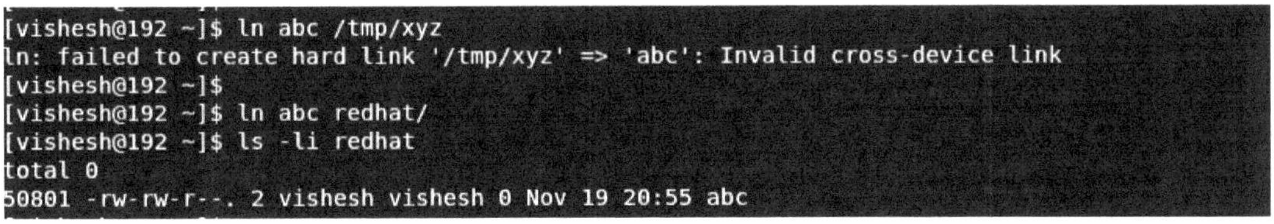

```
[vishesh@192 ~]$ ln abc /tmp/xyz
ln: failed to create hard link '/tmp/xyz' => 'abc': Invalid cross-device link
[vishesh@192 ~]$
[vishesh@192 ~]$ ln abc redhat/
[vishesh@192 ~]$ ls -li redhat
total 0
50801 -rw-rw-r--. 2 vishesh vishesh 0 Nov 19 20:55 abc
```

Figure 5.4: *ln command creating hard links within a filesystem*

When a directory is created, the directory is empty at the first sight. But actually it is not. An empty directory contains two special pointers or directories that point to itself and its parent directory. These pointers are **. (single dot)** and **.. (double dot)**. The first one refers to the current working directory, while the other refers to its parent directory. The **single dot (.)** is the reference to directory itself. Thus, the current directory is referred twice. One reference to the current directory is available inside the directory entry itself via a **single dot (.)**. Another reference to the current directory is located inside its parent directory. This is true for every new directory that is created. For a regular file, we have only one hard link by default. Type the following command:

```
$ls -l abc
```

And you will find the following:

```
-rw-rw-r--. 1 vishesh vishesh  0 Sep 27 11:03 abc
```

Notice 1 in the third field, which shows the number of hard links of the file.

You may have created several hard links for the file, but there will be only one **inode** block for that file. The file's data will be stored only once, and all the hard links will point to this data only. **Inode** block is independent of the file name, as a file may have multiple names in the same filesystem. Multiple names to a file can be given using hard links. It means that hard links are just the different names or aliases given to the same file. All these aliases point to the same **inode** block as they are just the same file. Hard links or aliases cannot span multiple filesystems or devices.

Hard links are opposed to symbolic linked files that we have already studied in *Chapter 2, Linux FileSystem and Administration*. Symbolic linked files do not receive the same **inode** as both are different files. So, they point to different **inodes**. The symbolic link file's **inode** block points to the **inode** block of the source file. Thus, data is stored only once. Moreover, symbolic link creation can span multiple filesystems. If we delete the source file of symbolic linked file, we will get a broken link. Any access to that symbolic linked file will fail in that case.

Do it yourself

1. **Create a file test1 in your home directory. Create a symbolic link file `/tmp/` sltest1 that points to the test1 file in the user's home directory. Does this command successfully execute? If yes, delete the original file `test1`. Issue `ls -l` on `/tmp/sltest1`. What do you see? Try to access `/tmp/sltest1` file.**
2. **Create a new directory `dirtest1` in your home directory. Issue `ls -lia` on this directory. How many file entries do you find here? What are they? Note the inode of the . (single dot) directory. Issue the `ls -lid` command on `dirtest1`. What does this command do? Note the inode number that is displayed by this command. Also note the hard link count that is displayed. Match both the noted inode numbers. What do you conclude? How many hard links count of the dirtest1 directory exist, and why?**
3. **What is the difference between these two commands:**
   (i) ln abc redhat, and
   (ii) ln abc redhat/

Working with regular files

In this section, we will look at the creation and handling of regular files.

Creation of regular files

So far, we looked at the creation of files using the **cat** command. To create a new file, the **cat** command requires a standard input. If you want to create an empty file, you have to use multiple keystrokes with the **cat** command. But there other ways to create an empty file with fewer keystrokes. We have the **touch** command to create an empty file. To create a file, this command does not require any standard input. Simply type the following command:

```
touch <filename>
```

Replace **<filename>** with the actual filename that you want to create. This is a very handy tool if you want to create a file faster. Let's create a new file named **test1** using the following:

```
$touch test1
```

Preceding command creates an empty file You can verify the creation of the **test1** file using the **ls** command.

There are other uses of the **touch** command. When the **touch** command is used on an existing file, it updates the access and modification time of the specified file. Now, issue the **stat** command to note down the access and modification time of the **test1** file that you have just created. Now, use the **touch** command on the **test1** file in the same way:

```
$touch test1
```

Again, use the **stat** command to verify the change in timestamps. The timestamp that is displayed in **ls -l** output is the modification time. You can use **ls -lu** to view the file access time, as follows:

```
$ls -lu test1
```

The **touch** command can also be used with the following options:

- **-a**: Change only the access time
- **-m**: Change only the modification timestamp
- **-d <date string>**: Use date string instead of the current timestamp. Date string can be in any human-readable format. It can take string like *yesterday, tomorrow, next Thursday* or *Sat, 15 Oct 2022 16:21:42 +0530*. It can also contain a string like day of the week, time of the day, relative time, and relative date.
- **-t <timestamp in number format>**: It changes the timestamp for the specified file to the specified time. It takes the following format:

  `[[CC]YY]MMDDhhmm[.ss]`

  Where,

  CC: The first two digits of the year

  YY: The last two digits of the year

  MM: Month of the year

  DD: day

  hh: hour

  mm: minutes

  ss: seconds
- **-c**: Do not create any files. By default, the **touch** command creates a file if it does not exist. Using the **-c** option disables this functionality, and no file is created.

The following are some of the usages of the **touch** command:

To change only the access time:

```
touch -a file1
```

To change only the modification time:

```
touch -m file1
```

To change the access time to the specified time and not to the current time, use **-d** along with the **-a** option.

```
touch -ad "yesterday" test
```

You can verify the change using either the **stat** command or the **ls -lu** command. To change the modification time to the specified time and not to the current time:

```
touch -md "tomorrow" test
```

To change both the timestamps to the specified time:

```
touch -d "October 10 7:00am" test
```

Access time and modification time will be updated to 10 Oct 7:00am. To change the timestamp using the timestamp format, use the **-t** option. The following command changes the timestamp of test file to 10 Oct, 1:00pm:

```
[vishesh@192 ~]$ touch -t 202010200100 test
[vishesh@192 ~]$
[vishesh@192 ~]$ stat test
 File: test
 Size: 7       Blocks: 8      IO Block: 4096   regular file
Device: fd02h/64770d    Inode: 2846158    Links: 2
Access: (0664/-rw-rw-r--) Uid: ( 1000/ vishesh)  Gid: ( 1000/ vishesh)
Context: unconfined_u:object_r:mozilla_home_t:s0
Access: 2020-10-20 01:00:00.000000000 +0530
Modify: 2020-10-20 01:00:00.000000000 +0530
Change: 2022-10-16 08:53:06.546632206 +0530
 Birth: 2022-10-13 21:48:23.252220492 +0530
```

The question that comes in mind is, 'Why do you ever require to update file's timestamp?' One reason could be to keep this file out of the rule of scheduled deletion policy of unused files from the **/tmp** directory. Consider a scenario where **/tmp** is low in space as it is cluttered with many unused files of many users, and these files have not been used for a while. If these unused files are not deleted, **/tmp** may become full, thus stalling the system. Before the system deletes them automatically, it is important for the administrator to schedule their deletion. The file deletion can be scheduled on the basis of the number of days for which the file has not been accessed. If some of the files lying in **/tmp** are important for the user and you want to keep it out of deletion rule, then the **touch** command can come in handy to change its access time to the current time.

We discussed the **touch** command enough. Now, the next thing is to write data to the file. We are already aware of two of the ways to do this: **cat** command and **echo** command that we learnt about in *Chapter 3, Knowing Linux Commands*. But they have the limitations. They do not provide any functionality to make an efficient edition to the file. The next section discusses these limitations and points out various editing tools.

Modifying file contents

We have looked at commands such as **cat** and **echo** that take inputs from the standard input and a file is created or appended. We have also seen how the output of some commands can be redirected or appended to a file. The major limitation of these methods is that contents can only be inserted or appended. File contents cannot be replaced or deleted from the middle of the file. So, the question is, 'How can we modify the contents, or delete some words, phrases or complete lines from the file?' The answer is that we will require an efficient file editing tool that allows us to handle file contents more easily. Editing tools are always appreciated for their efficient editing capabilities. The following are a few editing tools that regular users or system administrators can use for their daily file editing activities:

- **vi**: An older command-line tool to manipulate file contents
- **nano**: Another command-line tool to manipulate file contents
- **vim**: An improved version of **vi**; nowadays, **vim** is used as an alias of **vi**
- **gedit**: A graphical tool, as implied by the **g** in the beginning; opens a text editor just like the text editor opens in Windows OS
- **sed**: A Stream editor
- **Emacs**: Older command-line tool for file editing; can be used to perform complex operations on file

Among these, **vim** is popular among system administrators to edit the system files. We will learn to use this editor later in this chapter.

Viewing the contents of a file

To view the contents of a file, we have many commands; we have studied some of them earlier. If the file is small and the file contents can be accommodated into one screen, we can use the **cat** command. If file contents cannot be accommodated onto a screen, the **cat** command on that file will scroll the output. You have pagers to view the file contents that do not fit on one screen. *Chapter 3, Knowing Linux Commands,* discussed less and more pagers. We used them to view large command output page by page. Same pagers can also be used to view large files one screen at a time. These pagers can be used as follows:

```
more <filename>
```

```
less <filename>
```

When we pass a file name to a pager, one screenful of file content is visible at first. You have to press *Enter* for the next screenful of output.

These pagers also offer capabilities to search for some phrases on the file. Let us understand the use of both the pagers on a regular file.

less file1

Providing the `less` command to a filename will open a page that shows one screenful of the file's contents. On pressing Enter, the next screenful of file content is visible. This way, `less` allows you to read the contents page by page. The `less` pager does not exit after all the file's contents are scrolled. It will remain on screen unless you press `q` on the keyboard.

Pressing `/` will take you to search mode. It will do the search in forward direction. Type your phrase and press the Enter key; the first search keyword will be highlighted on the screen. Typing `n` will show you the next match on the screen in forward direction. Typing `N` will allow you to move backward to the search term.

To search a phrase in the backward direction, use `?` and not `/` before the search term. Press `n` to find the next search in the current direction. Pressing `N` will show the previous search but in the opposite direction.

Pressing `vi` will open the text editor, where you can make editions to the file.

more file1

Like the `less` pager, `more` can also be used to view a file page by page. Forward search can be performed in the same way as is performed using `less`. Unlike `less`, it does not highlight the search keyword when found. Unlike `less`, it will exit the pager automatically after all the file's contents have been scrolled. It provides limited backward search capability. Like `less`, pressing `vi` will open the text editor.

Navigating around the filesystem

For any logged in user, the home directory becomes the first working directory where they can perform any operation on the files and directories. They can create any number of directories in their home directory, and many levels of subdirectories can be created beneath these directories. They can create files or directories in other locations as well if they have the permission to do so. To access the files and directories residing in any location, you should have access path to that location, which will allow you to move into that location. You will use the `cd` command to reach your desired location. To access a particular file or subdirectory, you must specify either their absolute path and/or relative path with the `cd` command.

The absolute path is the complete access path starting from `/` down toward the tree up to the desired file location. Suppose the user wants to access the file residing in the `redhat` directory which, in turn, is located in their home directory; they can use the `cd` command as follows:

```
#cd /home/vishesh/redhat/
```

This way, your current working directory is changed to **/home/vishesh/redhat**. Now, you can access the files and any subdirectories residing beneath the **redhat** directory. It is not necessary to move to that location to access the files residing there. You can access the file in any location and perform any operation on the file without switching your current location, as follows:

```
$touch /home/vishesh/redhat/chapter1
```

In the preceding example, we have successfully created a file named **chapter1** without changing our current working directory. What we have specified is the absolute path of the directory where the file is to be created. So far in this book, we have used absolute path to access our files and directories.

Relative path does not start from root **(/)** but from the location relative to the current one. Let us say you are in your home directory currently and want to access the **chapter1** file, which resides under the **redhat** subdirectory. Just type the following command:

```
cat redhat/chapter1
```

In the preceding example, the path starts from the location relative to the location where you are; no `'/'` in the beginning of the path. Now, create a subdirectory **Book** inside the **redhat** directory:

```
cd redhat
mkdir Book
cd Book
```

You are inside the **book** subdirectory under the **redhat** directory of your home directory. To switch back to your parent directory, you can use **..** (double dot) with the **cd** command that we looked at earlier:

```
cd..
```

The preceding command says 'move me one level up to the parent directory'. To move two levels up, use the following:

```
cd../..
```

Now, you will be moved to **/home /vishesh**, the parent directory of **Book**.

You can move many levels down using the **cd** command and then use multiple double dot notations to move up in the hierarchy.

If you are inside **/tmp** and want to move back to your home directory, you can use the **~** symbol, which refers to the home directory, as follows:

```
cd ~
```

Here, '~' signifies the current user's home directory. Suppose you are root and want to move into the home directory of user **sam**; you could just type the following:

```
cd ~sam
```

You can use the tilde symbol to move inside any subdirectories under the home directory, as follows:

```
cd ~vishesh/redhat
```

You will be moved inside the **redhat** directory under **vishesh** user's home directory, irrespective of your current location.

Do it yourself

Go to your home directory. Create a directory dir1, if it does not already exist. Inside dir1, create two subdirectories: sub1 and sub2. Now, change your working directory to dir1/sub1 using relative location starting from your home directory. Now, change to dir1/sub2 from the current location. Hint: use the .. notation.

Working with directory

In this section, we will see how we can create and handle directories and subdirectories in Linux.

Creating a directory and a subdirectory

We know that an empty directory can be created by just issuing the following command:

```
mkdir <dir name>
```

An empty directory is created wherever you are in the filesystem. To create a directory in a location other than your current location, just provide the absolute or relative path with **<dir name>**:

```
mkdir /tmp/redhat
```

The preceding command creates the **redhat** directory under **/tmp** irrespective of the current working directory.

Suppose you are in your home location and want to create a subdirectory under **redhat/Book**; issue the following:

```
mkdir redhat/Book/Chapter1
```

Here, **Book** is the subdirectory under **redhat**, and **Chapter1** is, again, the subdirectory of **Book**. Thus, here, directories are nested at 3 levels inside the home directory of the user.

It is also possible to create many levels of parents concurrently when using **mkdir**. Suppose you want to create a directory named **/home/vishesh/Book/Chapter1/headings/heading1/heading2**, which is nested many levels down but sequence of its parents does not exist, then issue the following command:

```
mkdir -p /home/vishesh/Book/Chapter1/headings/heading1/heading2
```

The preceding command will create all the non-existent parents that come in the path of creating the **heading2** subdirectory. If all the parents already exist, the **-p** option has no effect, and the specified directory is created.

To delete an empty directory, you can use the **rmdir** command:

```
rmdir <dir path and name>
```

To delete a non-empty directory, you can use the **rm** command, which we will see later in this chapter.

Listing the contents of a directory

To view what files and subdirectories exist in a directory, the **ls** command is used. By default, directory contents are displayed in alphabetical order. To view file-related metadata, you have the following options to use with the **ls** command:

- **-a**: Lists hidden files, those starting with a period (or a dot)
- **-c**: Displays the directory contents sorted by **ctime** and not sorted alphabetically, which is the default display order
- **-d**: Lists directory itself and not its contents; you will see a single dot (**.**), which refers to the current directory itself
- **-i**: Displays the inode number of each listed file
- **-l**: Displays the directory contents along with many of the attributes of each file
- **-r**: Displays the directory contents in reverse order
- **-R**: Lists the directory contents recursively; it will list all the subdirectories and files that reside underneath each of the listed directories; the list will recursively move up to many levels downward the tree, unless all the files are listed
- **-s**: Displays the size of each file in blocks
- **-S**: Shows the directory contents sorted by file size
- **-h**: Displays the file size in user-readable format when used with other options
- **-t**: Displays output sorted by modification time; **-t** determines which timestamp field to use for sorting the listing; by default, it sorts the listing by **mtime**
- **-u**: Displays access time
- **-1**: Lists one file per line

The following is the most frequent usage of the **ls** command:

```
$ls -l
```

The preceding command displays file-related information in multiple fields, as shown in *Figure 5.5*.

```
[vishesh@192 ~]$ ls -l
total 3759644
-rw-rw-r--. 2 vishesh vishesh          6 Nov  8 13:19 abc
drwxr-xr-x. 4 vishesh vishesh         40 Sep  6 16:29
drwxr-xr-x. 2 vishesh vishesh          6 Sep  6 04:48
drwxr-xr-x. 6 vishesh vishesh       4096 Nov  7 21:09
-rw-rw-r--. 1 vishesh vishesh          5 Oct 17 11:15 file1
drwxrwxr-x. 2 vishesh vishesh          6 Sep 24 07:23
-rw-rw-r--. 1 vishesh vishesh       1697 Oct 17 23:00 lmdesk.key
-r--------. 1 vishesh vishesh       1675 Oct 17 23:00 lm.key
drwxr-xr-x. 2 vishesh vishesh          6 Sep  6 04:48
drwxr-xr-x. 2 vishesh vishesh       4096 Sep 25 15:36
drwxr-xr-x. 2 vishesh vishesh          6 Sep  6 04:48
drwxrwxrwx. 3 vishesh vishesh         40 Nov  8 13:14
drwxr-xr-x. 2 root    root             6 Nov  7 17:39
drwxr-xr-x. 2 vishesh vishesh         21 Sep  6 22:45
-rw-rw-r--. 2 vishesh vishesh          6 Nov  8 13:19 test
drwxr-xr-x. 2 vishesh vishesh          6 Sep  6 04:48
-rw-rw-r--. 1 vishesh vishesh 3849846784 Oct 13 12:20 zyx
```

***Figure 5.5**: ls command with the -l option listing some file attributes in seven fields*

Let's understand each field it displays. *Figure 5.5* shows the default output of the **`ls -l`** command, displaying a total of seven fields:

- **Permission sets**: The first field contains the permissions sets associated with the file. We will understand file permission in the next chapter. The first character of the first field refers to the file type, as we studied earlier. Here, **`abc`** is a regular file as it contains **a** '**-**'. Desktop is a directory as it contains **`d`** as the first character.
- **Hard link count**: The second field shows you the hard link count.
- **Owner name**: The third field displays the username.
- **Group owner**: The fourth field displays the **group owner** of the file.
- **File size**: The next field displays the file size in bytes.
- **timestamp**: It displays the date and time of file modification time in the **`mon dd hh:mm`** format, where **`mon`** is the three-letter abbreviation of month name, **`dd`** is the date in two digits, **`hh:mm`** is the hour and minute of the day separated by **`:`**.
- **filename**: The last field will show you the file name. This field may show you extended output if any of the files has any symbolic links.

To view the information of the current working directory , say **`redhat`**, use the **`-d`** option with **`ls -l`**:

```
[vishesh@192 redhat]$ cd redhat
[vishesh@192 redhat]$ ls -ld
drwxrwxrwx. 3 vishesh vishesh 40 Nov 8 13:14.
```

The preceding command displays the information of the current working directory. It shows you the permissions of the **`redhat`** directory in the first field. The first field contains a **d** in the first character, which clears that the output is that of a directory. And the directory name listed as a single dot (**.**). The next six fields can be interpreted in the same way as we have just discussed for the regular file. Starting from the second field, it displays the hard link count, owner and group owner of the directory, size of the directory, and modification time of the directory in sequence. The directory name is listed as single dot(**.**) in the last field.

```
ls -h
```

The **ls -h** will show you the size column suffixed with units such as K, M, and G . By looking at the output, you can easily determine the files taking gigabytes of disk space.

```
ls -li
```

Using the **-i** option along with the **-l** option of **ls** will give you an additional column, which displays the **inode** number of each listed file.

```
ls -lc
```

The preceding command lists the change timestamp or the **ctime** field instead of the default timestamp.

```
ls -lu
```

The preceding command displays the access timestamp instead of the default timestamp.

To list the contents ordered by the access time, use the following command:

```
ls -ltu
```

To view the directory contents ordered by change time, use the following command:

```
ls -ltc
```

Operations related to files

In this section, we will see how we can move, rename, copy, delete, and compress or decompress the files.

Renaming file and directory

The **mv** command can be used to rename or move a file to a different location. To rename or move a file, the following syntax is used:

```
mv <source> < destination>
```

Here, **source** and **destination** can be filenames or directory names, along with their access path. Path can be relative or absolute.

To rename a regular file named **abc**, simply use the following command:

```
mv abc xyz
```

The preceding command would just rename **abc** to **xyz**.

If **abc** is a directory, then that directory will be renamed as **xyz**, and all the contents of **abc** will be moved to **xyz**. If the **xyz** directory do exist, then **abc**, along with all its contents, will be moved under **xyz** with the same name. If **abc** is a file and **xyz** is an existing directory, then the **abc** file will move under it.

Now, to move **abc** to different location, say **/tmp/redhat/**, type the following command:

```
mv abc /tmp/redhat/
```

Here, **abc** will move under **/tmp/redhat**.

If you want to change the name of the **abc** file under the **redhat** directory, supply the new name of the **abc** file as follows:

```
mv abc /tmp/redhat/xyz
```

Caution: Note that mv would overwrite the destination file if it already exists, so be cautious while using the mv command.

To avoid overwriting destination file and directory silently, use the **-i** option of the **mv** command. It will ask you to confirm whether to overwrite the existing file. Press **y** or **n**.

Following are a few other options that can be used with the **mv** command:

- **-v**: Turns on verbose mode; use **-v** with the mv command to know what is going on behind the scene
- **-u**: Moves the files to destination only if source is newer or destination file does not exist

Do it yourself

What is the difference between these two commands: (i) mv abc dir and (ii) mv abc dir1/, if abc is a regular file and dir is an existing directory.

Copying files and directory

To copy files from one location to another, we have the **cp** command. It has the following syntax:

```
cp <source filename and path> <destination filename and path>
```

If **abc** is a regular file, to copy **abc** from the current location to another, say the **redhat** directory, simply type the following command:

```
cp abc redhat/
```

The preceding command will copy the **abc** file under the **redhat** directory. If the source file does not exist, it will throw an error saying the following:

```
"cp: cannot stat 'abc': No such file or directory"
```

If the destination directory does not exist, it will send the following error message:

```
cp: cannot create regular file 'redhat/': Not a directory
```

The **cp** command can also be used to rename the file while copying, as follows:

```
cp abc redhat/xyz
```

Here, the **abc** file will be copied under the **redhat** directory with a different name: **xyz**.

To copy the directory from one location to another, the same syntax is used, as is used to copy the regular file. Say you have a **test** directory in your home location and you want to copy it under the **redhat** directory that exists in the same location:

```
cp test redhat/
```

This command executes successfully only if the source directory is empty, else it throws the following error:

```
cp: -r not specified; omitting directory 'test'
```

The error message also specifies for you to use the **-r** option of the **cp** command if you want to copy a non-empty directory, as follows:

```
cp -r test redhat/
```

With the preceding command executed, the **test** directory will be copied to the **redhat** directory with all its contents recursively.

Caution: Like mv, the cp command also overwrites the destination file if it exists. So, use the cp command cautiously.

To avoid overwriting of destination files and directory silently, use the **-i** option of the **cp** command. It will ask you whether to overwrite the existing file; press **y** or **n**.

Following are a few other options that you can use with **cp**:

- **-v**: Turns on verbose mode; use **-v** with the **cp** command to know what is going on behind the scene
- **-u**: Copies the files to destination only if source is newer or destination file does not exist
- **-s**: Creates symbolic link instead of copying
- **-l** : Creates hard link instead of copying

For more options and usages of the **cp** command, explore man pages.

Deleting file and directory

The **rm** command is used to remove any file and directory from the system. To delete a regular file, say **abc**, simply type the following command:

```
rm abc
```

If **abc** is a non-empty directory, this command will fail, giving you the following error message:

```
rm: cannot remove 'abc': Is a directory
```

Use the **-r** option to remove a non-empty directory along with its contents. Type the following command:

```
rm -r abc
```

The **rm** command works silently; it will not confirm with you before deletion. To remove only files and subdirectories from a directory, say, **redhat**, and not the directory itself, use the following command:

```
rm -r redhat/*
```

It will remove all the files and directories recursively lying under the **redhat** directory.

Caution: Be cautious while using the rm -r * command, as it will delete whatever exists in the current location. The system may become unusable if you issue this command without thinking twice, as rm never confirms with you before deletion.

The following are a few other options that you can use with the **rm** command:

- **-i**: It will ask you before deleting each file and directory. This option can be used with recursive deletion (using **-r**) for safe removal of files and directories.
- **-v**: It deletes the file in verbose mode.
- **-f**: Never prompt for non-existent files or when the files are write-protected.

Comparing two files

This section discusses the following tools to let you understand comparing two files:

- **diff**
- **cmp**
- **comm**

cmp

The **cmp** command is used to compare two files byte-by-byte. It will return the first differing byte, as shown in *Figure 5.6*:

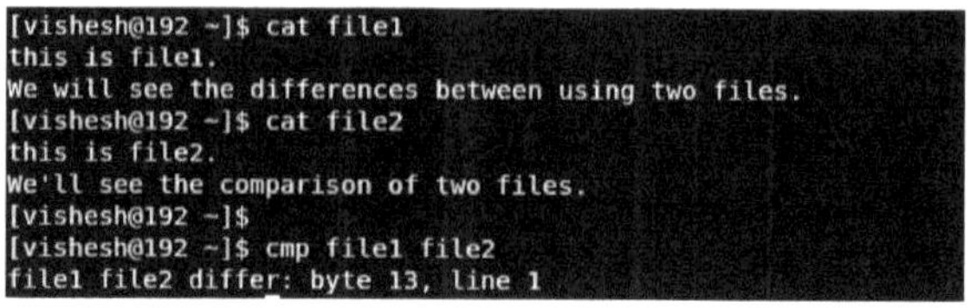

```
[vishesh@192 ~]$ cat file1
this is file1.
We will see the differences between using two files.
[vishesh@192 ~]$ cat file2
this is file2.
We'll see the comparison of two files.
[vishesh@192 ~]$
[vishesh@192 ~]$ cmp file1 file2
file1 file2 differ: byte 13, line 1
```

Figure 5.6 *usage of cmp command*

comm

It takes two sorted files and compares them line by line. It produces 3-columnar output. The first column contains lines unique to the first file, the second column contains lines unique to second file, and the third column contains lines common to both files. If the files are not sorted, it will not work as desired. It will throw the following message:

```
comm: file 1 is not in sorted order
```

You must sort the given files prior to passing it to **`comm`** utility, as shown in *Figure 5.7*.

```
[vishesh@192 ~]$ cat f1
redhat
enterprise
linux
9.0
[vishesh@192 ~]$ cat f2
Redhat
Enterprise
linuz
9.0
[vishesh@192 ~]$ sort f1>test1
[vishesh@192 ~]$ sort f2>test2
[vishesh@192 ~]$ comm test1 test2
                9.0
enterprise
        Enterprise
linux
        linuz
redhat
        Redhat
[vishesh@192 ~]$ 
```

***Figure 5.7**: comm utility comparing two sorted files*

Here, both the unsorted files are sorted first using the **`sort`** command-line utility. Then, the generated sorted files are passed to **`comm`** utility. The output generated does not seem to be aligned, so it could leave you perplexed. You have the following options for generating any one or two of the columns to understand your output in a better way:

- **`-1`**: Suppress column 1
- **`-2`**: Suppress column 2
- **`-3`**: Suppress column 3

It means that if you want to see only common lines between two files, you will issue the following:

```
comm -12 test1 test2
```

The preceding command will suppress columns 1 and 2, displaying only column 3. To view only lines unique to **file1**, you can issue the following:

```
comm -23 test1 test2
```

Similarly, you can combine these options in other ways according to your requirement.

diff

It compares two files line by line but does not require them to be sorted, unlike **comm**. It will show you the differences between the two files while instructing you on how can these files be made identical. It uses special symbols and characters to let you know how **file1** can be changed to make it identical to **file2**, as shown in *Figure 5.8*. Here, the **diff** command is used to find the differences between the two files **f1** and **f2**. The first line **1,2c1,3** means that line numbers 1 to 3 in **file1** have to be changed with line numbers 1 to 3 from **file2**. Here, **c** refers to **change**. The number given before character **c** points to the line numbers of **file1**, and the numbers given after the **c** character are the line numbers referring to **file2**. Other symbols that **diff** command may return are **a**, which refers to **append**, and **d**, which refers to **delete**. The **<** symbol signifies that the lines are from **file1**, and **>** signifies that the lines are from **file2**.

```
[vishesh@192 ~]$ diff f1 f2
1,3c1,3
< redhat
< enterprise
< linux
---
> Redhat
> Enterprise
> linuz
```

Figure 5.8*: diff command displaying the difference between two files and how two files can be made identical*

Compressing file

If your files are big and consuming too much of disk space, you would be worried about how to handle big files. You could not think of moving them from the system as they are important files for you. You can keep these files on the same system by compressing them; compression saves disk space. Compression utilities are also useful when you have large system backups and want to preserve them in case restoration is required. You can compress your large backups and keep these compressed files at a safer place for future use. You can uncompress them whenever required. There are many command-line utilities, such as **zip**, **gzip**, **bzip2**, and **xz**, that you can use to compress large files. This section discusses only the **zip** and **gzip** commands to compress files and folders. You can use **man** pages if you want to learn about the **bzip2**, **xz**, and so on built-in compression utilities.

zip

The **zip** command-line utility takes one or more filenames as arguments and compresses them in a single package file known as **archive**. Archive created with **zip** command contains a**.zip** extension. If you find any file having an extension**.zip**, you must use the **unzip** command-line utility to uncompress it before you can read and use this file. You can move or copy the **.zip** file in any safe location for storing. You can uncompress it back whenever and wherever required. It usually takes the following syntax:

```
zip <name of the destination file> <one or more source file name>
```

Let us quickly create a large file using the following command:

```
dd if=/dev/zero of=largefile bs=1M count=2
```

The previous command will create a file named **largefile** of size 2MB.

To compress this file, simply type the following:

```
zip largefile.zip largefile
```

It outputs the following:

```
 adding: largefile (deflated 100%)
```

The preceding command will compress the **largefile** file and create a compressed file named **largefile.zip**, leaving the original file intact. Suffixing the compressed file name with its extension is not necessary in the preceding command. The first filename argument provided is interpreted as a compressed filename by the **zip** utility. You can add more files to the same archive by supplying the name of the existing **.zip** file. Say, to compress a file named **onefile** and add it to the same archive, use the following command:

```
zip largefile onefile
```

It will give you the following output:

```
adding: onefile (deflated 100%)
```

The **onefile** will be added to an already existing archive **largefile.zip**.

Now, to compress two or more files together, type the following command:

```
zip a.zip onefile twofile
```

The preceding command will create **a.zip** file that compresses the two listed files, **onefile** and **twofile**, in a package. Now, to uncompress these two files from **a.zip**, use the **unzip** command as follows:

```
unzip a.zip
```

The **.zip** extension is not necessary here. The preceding command will give you the following output:

```
Archive: a.zip
 extracting: onefile
 extracting: twofile
```

It may prompt you to replace the extracted file if the same file or a file having the same name already exists in the extracted location.

```
Archive: a.zip
replace onefile? [y]es, [n]o, [A]ll, [N]one, [r]ename: A
```

Press **y** to replace, **n** to not replace, **A** to replace all the files, **N** to not to replace any of the files, and **r** to rename the file.

To extract only one file, say **onefile**, from a zipped archive, say **a.zip**, simply use the following command:

```
$unzip a.zip onefile
Archive: a.zip
 extracting: onefile
```

If you have modified a file that is already compressed, and you want to update the **.zip** file with the newer version of the uncompressed file, you have to use the same command that is issued to compress it for the first time. Say you have modified **onefile** and want to update the zipped version of this file; issue the following:

```
zip largefile onefile
```

It will give you the following output:

```
updating: onefile (deflated 100%)
```

Following are few other options that can go with the **zip** command:

- **-r**: Compresses directory structure along with its contents
- **-v**: Turns on verbose mode
- **-u**: Updates the compressed file only if uncompressed file is newer; without this option, zip always readds the uncompressed files in the zipped package
- **-m**: Deletes original uncompressed file when compressing them

For more options, you can explore man pages or use the **-help** option.

gzip

gzip is another compression utility used to compress one or more files together. Unlike zip, it replaces the original file with its compressed version and creates a file having extension **.gzip**. Unlike **zip**, it does not combine all the supplied input files into one package; instead, it creates a **gzip** file for each file. To **gzip** two files together, say **largefile** and **onefile**, simply use the following:

```
gzip largefile onefile
```

The **largefile.gz** and **onefile.gz** are created in the same location. To decompress them, use the **gunzip** command as follows:

```
gunzip largefile.gz onefile.gz
```

To decompress all the files ending with `.gz`, you can use gunzip `*.gz`.

Following are a few options that can be used with the **gzip** command:

- **-v**: Turns on verbose mode
- **-r**: Recursively compresses each file in a folder and replaces each file under the folder with its **gzip** version; unlike **zip**, it does not impact the folder name; it remains intact
- **-k**: Compresses the file leaving input files intact
- **-d**: Decompresses the file

Explore man pages for more options. You also have the **--help** option for quick assistance:

Text editor: vim

Vim is a text editor to edit all kinds of plain text files very efficiently. It provides you with the capability to perform many operations on the files. To open a file to edit, simply type the following command:

```
vim <filename>
```

It opens a buffer that displays the existing contents, if any, and places the cursor at the very first character of the buffer. The location where the cursor is placed is said to be the current location of the file where any action can take place. The name of the file is displayed at the bottom-left corner of the screen.

If you have not provided any filename, **vim** opens an empty buffer and places the cursor at the very first character of the buffer. **vim** works in many modes. Each mode has an associated keystroke, pressing which will switch you to that mode and let you perform operations specific to that mode. Some of the modes and their respective keystrokes, along with their brief descriptions, are given in *Table 5.9*:

Mode	Key combination	Explanation
Normal mode	*[ESC]* key	Simple navigation can be performed.
Insert mode	*I*	Pressing the small `i` character takes you to the insert mode, where you start typing characters from the current location.

Mode	Key combination	Explanation
Command-line mode	:	It is used to give various commands to the editor, such as save the file and quit the editor.

Table 5.1: vim modes with their associated keys

When a file is opened in **vim**, you are in normal mode, where you can perform simple navigation using the arrow keys and *Home* and *End* keys. Pressing the colon (`:`) in the normal mode takes you to the command-line mode, where you can issue commands such as save the file or exit the editor. Pressing the *ESC* key will take you back to the normal mode. Pressing `i` (small `i` character) takes you into the editing mode, where you can insert or delete the character. When you are in insert mode, you will see the following at the bottom-left corner of the screen:

```
--INSERT--
```

You can start typing now. You will see the typed characters on the screen.

To save the file, switch to command mode by pressing the **ESC** key and then the colon (`:`) character. You will see the following at the bottom-left corner of the screen.

```
:
```

Now press `x!` or `wq` to save the file and exit the editor. Once you type any command after colon (`:`) in the command mode, you must press the Enter key. Thus, following are the few keystrokes that you must remember to start working with `vim` editor.

After you open a vim editor, press *ESC* just to ensure that you are in normal mode. Press `i` once to switch to insert mode and start typing. Then, to save and exit, press *ESC* and then `:wq` or `:x!`.

Thus, to switch from one mode to another, you must press the [*ESC*] key. Then, you can execute any command related to the current mode.

Options in command mode

Some of the other keystrokes that you can use in the command mode are as follows:

- `<number>`: To go to a specific line number, say 10, type 10 after `:` character, as follows:

  ```
  :10
  ```

- `set <number>`: It displays line number at the start of each line.

- `w`: saves the file. If you want to save the file with another name, then supply the file name after `w`, as follows:

  ```
  :w abc
  ```

If **abc** already exists, it will throw you the following message:

```
E13: File exists (add ! to override)
```

If you want to forcefully write on the existing file, type the following:

```
:w! abc
```

To write only the range of lines as the line number from 2-5 to another file, say **abc**, use the following command:

```
:2,5w abc
```

To save a single line to another file, precede the **w** with the line number and press Enter. **q:** is used to quit the editor. It will not exit the editor if you have unsaved changes. To quit the editor while discarding the changes, use the **!** symbol after **q**, as follows:

```
:q!
```

This will forcefully exit the editor. This command is also very handy if you have done something messy in the file and want to restore the original file. It quits the editor without saving any modifications.

. and **$** are some special characters in command mode. Their description are as follows:

- **.** (dot): A single dot refers to the current line.
- $: This will take you to the last line. Type

  ```
  :$
  ```

Taking help

Typing **help** in the command mode opens the user manual for general help. If you want to look for a specific keyword or the context, provide that keyword after the **help** command, as follows:

```
:help w
```

This will show you manual for the **w** command.

To take help on searching within the file, type the following:

```
:help searching
```

While scrolling the help page, if you find any hyperlinked text, the press **Ctrl** + **]** to read the related contents.

Opening multiple files in vi window

You can open multiple files in the same **vim** window. Use the **split** command to open the specified file horizontally, as follows:

```
:split file1
```

This will open another file named **file1** horizontally.

The **vsplit** command opens the specified file vertically. To switch between files, press **Ctrl** + w + **`<direction keys>`** in normal mode. Direction keys are **`h, j, k, l`** and are used in the same way as used for navigating cursor.

Searching and replacing

To search and replace the word in the file, you can use the **`s`** command as follows:

```
:s/<word to replace>/<replacement word>
```

For example, to change the first matching **`book`** to **`books`**, type the following:

```
:s/book/books
```

The previous command will just replace the first matching keyword in the current line. To apply this operation to all the matching words in the current line, add **`/g`** next to the preceding command, as follows:

```
:s/book/books/g
```

Here, **`g`** refers to globally.

To apply the previous operation to the whole file, prefix the preceding command with **`%`**:

```
:%s/book/books/g
```

Options in Normal mode

Following are some of the other keystrokes that can be used in normal mode. Most of the following keys or key combinations can be preceded with a number. The interpretation of this number must be made according to its following key.

Besides using arrow keys for navigation, **`vim`** also provides some keys to be used specifically for navigation. Below are some of the keystrokes that can be used for navigation in normal mode :

`h`: left

`j`: down

`k`: up

`l`: right

We can precede these keys with a number, such as pressing **`5j`** will move the cursor 5 lines down.

Following are some other keystrokes that can be used in normal mode to perform some action:

- **`dd`**: Deletes the current line; can be preceded by a number to delete the specified number of lines
- **x:** Deletes the current character; can be preceded with a number to delete that number of characters

- **X**: Deletes character to the left of the cursor
- **y**: Copies the current line or the selected characters or words
- **p:** Pastes the data from the clipboard
- **o:** Inserts a new blank line following the current line; will also take you to the insert mode where you can do editions; can also be preceded by a number to insert that number of lines following the current line
- **O**: Inserts a new blank line above the current line; will also take you to the insert mode; can be preceded by a number to insert that number of lines following the current line
- **a:** Takes you to the insert mode. Text is actually appended after the current cursor location. When you press **i** to switch to insert mode, text is inserted before the current cursor location.
- **A:** Appends the character in the last character of the line; can be preceded a with number to repeat the inserted characters that number of times
- **I:** Inserts text before the first non-blank character of the line
- **w:** Moves the cursor to the start of the next word; can also use number key, like **2w**, which moves the cursor to two words ahead
- **b:** Moves the cursor to the beginning of the previous word; can precede **b** with **a** number also, as in the **w** command discussed earlier
- **e:** Moves the cursor to the end of the current word
- **ge:** Moves the cursor to the end of the previous word
- **dw**: Deletes the current word
- **G:** Moves to the end of the file; preceding G with a number will move you to the **n**th line; for example, **40G** will move you to the 40th line
- **$:** Moves to the end of the current line; preceding **$** with a number will move the cursor forward up to that number of lines, such as **4$**
- **^**: Jumps to the first non-blank character of the line
- **0**: Jumps to the start of the line
- **gg**: Moves to the start of the file; 1G will also jump to the first line
- **/**: Takes you to search mode
- **u**: Undo the last change; pressing **u** again will revert the second last modification made, and so on. If you want to revert the last 4 modifications made, press **u** four times

- **CTRL+R**: Used to redo; will revert the last undo
- **U:** Undo all the changes made to the last line that was edited
- **r**: Replaces the character under the cursor
- **s**: Replaces the character under the cursor with many characters
- **R**: Replaces all the characters from the current cursor position upto the position you want; pressing **R** will switch you to the **Replace mode**. You can enter and replace as many characters as you want; to switch to the normal mode, you have to press **[ESC]**
- **S**: Replaces the entire line
- **J:** Merges two lines; deletes line break from the current line
- **CTRL + f:** Scrolls a screen forward
- **CTRL + b**: Scrolls a screen backward
- **CTRL + U:** Scrolls half a screen upward
- **CTRL + D:** Scrolls half a screen downward

Searching a pattern within vi

To search for a particular word or phrases, switch to normal mode and then press **/**. The **/** character will be displayed at the bottom-left of the screen. Now, type your search keyword as follows:

```
/Redhat [ENTER]
```

The preceding entry will search for the **Redhat** keyword, and if found, all the matching phrases will be highlighted on the current screen. The cursor will move to the first match found. To move the cursor to the next match, press **n**. To find the third, and so on, press **n** that number of times. You can also precede **n** with a number. Say, you want to find the 3rd match, then press **3n**.

To search backward, press **?**, unlike **/**, which is used to search in the forward direction. Press **n** to perform the next search in the same direction. **N** performs the search in the opposite direction.

The following key sequence finds the words **Redhat**, **Redhat9** and **ELRedhat**.

```
/Redhat [ENTER]
```

To match only the whole word, use **\>**, as follows:

```
/\<Redhat\>
```

To search **Redhat** at the end of a word, type the following command:

```
/Redhat\>
```

It will match **Redhat** and **ELRedhat** but not **Redhat9**.

If search contains special characters that have special meaning in **vim**, precede that character with a **** (backslash). The characters with special meaning are as follows:

```
.*[]^%/\?~$
```

Suppose you want to search for a word **one$**; type the following in normal mode:

```
/one\$
```

You can also specify the search pattern using a regular expression. A few examples are as follows:

To search a specific word, such as **Linux** at the end of the line, type the following:

```
/Linux$
```

To search for a particular word, say **Linux**, when it is the only word in a line, type the following:

```
/^Linux$
```

To search the word **Linux**, where the first letter can be in lower or upper case, use the following command:

```
/[L|l]inux
```

Similarly, you can form simple to complex patterns here to perform your search.

Copying and pasting in vi editor

Pressing **y** in normal mode selects the current line. To copy more lines or a few characters in a line, you must select the range at first by pressing **v** and using the arrow keys to select the desired area to be copied. After you have done the selection, press **y**. Pressing **y** will copy the selection to the clipboard. Now to paste it, move to the desired area by using navigation keys, and press **p**.

Repeating the last command

To repeat the last command at the current cursor location, press a single dot (**.**). If you will press **4**. (a dot after 4), then the last command will be repeated 4 times. Pressing **.** (dot) again will repeat your last command, which is **4.** (a dot after 4).

Other important key combinations

- **d$**: Deletes the line from the current cursor location upto the end of the line
- **dw**: Deletes the current word starting from the current cursor location only; to delete a whole word, place the cursor at the beginning of the current word and then press **dw**
- **`**: Use backtick to jump back to your older position; very handy when you jump to the end of the file or any line number in the file using **G** keystrokes
- **''**: Moves among two positions

Do it yourself

- **Create two files using vim editor: file11 and file22. Save 6-8 lines of text in these files. Open file11 in vim editor. Save line number 2 to file22. Look at the contents of file22 to verify whether older contents are replaced. Is file11 still open? Next, move the cursor 3 lines forward. Write only the current line to file22. Verify the changes made in file22 again. Next, save only the last line from file11 to file22. Verify this change as well. You can open another terminal to verify the changes made in file22 each time.**

Text processing

In *Chapter 3, Knowing Linux Commands*, we read about the **grep** command, which can be used to search a patten within one or more files. Besides **grep**, we have the **awk** and **sed** utilities that also act as filters in Linux. The **sed** utility searches the pattern, process it and then transforms it in some form. The **awk** utility is not just a filter but also an input processing language. In this section, we will discuss **sed** and **awk** one by one.

gawk

The **gawk** command is an alias of awk in Linux. It is a very powerful utility to search for a given pattern within the file and take certain action on it. **awk** is more than this. It is said to be a programming language using which you can perform most of your data processing tasks. It provides several predefined variables and programming constructs. You can create several variables, apply programming logic to process the data and even create formatted reports on a small datafile. Let us take a simple example. The following command finds all the lines matching **Linux** in file **file1**:

```
[vishesh@192 ~]$ awk '/Linux/ {print}' file1
```

In the preceding command, whatever is provided inside single quotes can be termed as the instructions that are given to the **awk**. It operates on the instructions given. Instructions have two parts: search criteria and action. In the previous command, action statement is given inside curly braces, and search criteria or a pattern is provided between two forward slashes ('/'); both are enclosed in single quotes. The preceding command will print all the lines containing **Linux**. Clearly, **awk** follows the given syntax:

```
awk <options> 'search criteria {action}' <filename>
```

If no search criteria are specified, it prints all the lines of the file. If action is not given, it prints the lines matching the criteria. If the input file name is not given, it takes input from the command line. The following command will print all the lines from the given input file:

```
[vishesh@192 ~]$ awk '{print}' file1
Welcome to the world of Linux
```

```
RHEL9.0 is teh latest version
We are using RedHat Enterprise Linux9.0
RHEL is widely adopted among the Linux flavours by enterprises.
RedHat incorporates several benefits for its enterprise version of Linux.
```

awk is also capable of dividing each line of the file into multiple fields and can format each field to give you beautiful reports. Let's divide each line of the **file1** file into multiple fields:

```
[vishesh@192 ~]$ awk '{print $3}' file1
the
teh
using
widely
several
```

In the preceding command, **awk** divides each line into multiple fields and uses a single space as field separator. The default field separator that **awk** uses is single space. Any number preceded by a **$** symbol refers to a variable for that particular field number. Here, **$3** refers to field 3, and the output shows all the lines from field 3 only.

To understand the strength of **awk**, let us create a small datafile storing orders information, as follows:

```
[vishesh@192 ~]$ cat orders
101	Dining Chair	6	3000
102	3 seater sofa set	1	27000
103	table lamp	1	5000
106	Adhsive racks	2	600
105	shoe rack	1	5000
104	wooden almirah	1	45000
```

The first field is order ID, the second field belongs to product name, the third field is the quantity ordered, and the last field is the total cost of the order. In the preceding file, the field separator used is *Tab*. If your input has a non-default field separator, you must specify the same to **awk**. Use the **-F** option to specify the field separator. Let us print order id and product name for the records where product name contains **rack** in their name:

```
[vishesh@192 ~]$ awk -F '\t' '/rack/{print $1, $2}' orders

106 Adhsive racks

105 shoe rack
```

It prints all the lines that contains **rack**. If you want to match only the whole word **rack** and not **racks**, you can use the following command:

```
[vishesh@192 ~]$ awk -F '\t' '/\<rack\>/{print $1, $2}' orders
105 shoe rack
```

You can search for any pattern from the input file using the regular expressions that you have already studied. It supports both BRE and ERE.

To match the lines that contain either **sofa** or **lamp**, type the following:

```
$awk -F '\t' '/sofa|lamp/{print $1, $2}' orders
102 3 seater sofa set
103 table lamp
```

There is much more to learn in **awk**. We will revisit awk in *Chapter 7, Interacting With Bash Shell and Scripting*, where the programming features of this tool will be discussed.

Stream editor: sed

sed is a stream editor. It processes all the lines of the given file one by one, according to the given instructions. **sed** can be used to perform insertions, modifications, replacements or simply searches on the given input file. It means that all operations that can be performed in a **vi** editor can be performed with sed without opening the file. It does not save the result of the processed lines in the original input file; instead, the result of these modifications are displayed on the screen. **sed** is used to manipulate the file contents but does not overwrite the file unless you direct it to do so. When you are satisfied with the output, you can redirect the **sed** command to a file to save the processed lines. **sed** works at the supplied commands which it applied on the given input file line by line. These commands instruct **sed** to take that particular action line by line on the given input file. If no input file name is provided, then it applies the given command on the standard input. See the following file:

```
[vishesh@192 ~]$ cat file1
Welcome to the world of Linux
RHEL9.0 is teh latest version
We are using RedHat Enetrprise Linux9.0
RHEL is widely adopted among the Linux flavours by enterprises.
RedHat incorporates several benefits for its enterprise version of Linux.
```

We will look at a few examples of sed on the basis of this file. Let's print all the lines of the file on the screen. Use the following command:

```
sed p file1
```

See *Figure 5.9*, where **sed** is given the **p** command on the **file1** file.

```
[vishesh@192 ~]$ sed p file1
Welcome to the world of Linux
Welcome to the world of Linux
RHEL9.0 is teh latest version
RHEL9.0 is teh latest version
We are using RedHat Enetrprise Linux9.0
We are using RedHat Enetrprise Linux9.0
RHEL is widely adopted among the Linux flavours by enterprises.
RHEL is widely adopted among the Linux flavours by enterprises.
RedHat incorporates  several benefits for its enterprise version of Linux.
RedHat incorporates  several benefits for its enterprise version of Linux.
```

***Figure 5.9**: sed command printing all the lines from the file twice; to avoid the printing of all the lines, use the -n option*

The **p** command instructs **sed** to print all lines from the file, but it prints each line twice. This is because **p** always prints the given patten and all lines from the given input. Here, all the lines of the file belong to the patten space as we have not specified any line numbers or a matching criterion to take action on. To avoid printing of pattern space, use the **-n** option as follows:

```
sed -n p file1
```

The preceding command does not produce any line twice. This was a very simple example. Now, let us use **sed** to print the lines matching a criterion, say **RedHat**:

```
sed -n '/RedHat/p' file1
```

The previous line would only print the lines matching the specified criteria. Using the **-n** option suppresses the printing of all the lines from the file.

Here, **sed** follows this syntax:

```
sed options '/search pattern/command' file1
```

Thus, instructions are given to **sed** in search pattern and command combinations that are always enclosed in single quotes. There are many other commands that we can give to **sed** to manipulate text in the file. Following is the list of some of these commands:

- **d**: To delete the matching lines and print all other lines on the screen
- **i**: To insert a new line before the matched lines
- **c**: To change the complete line with the given text
- **r**: To read the contents of the specified file into the input after the current line
- **w <filename>**: To write the current pattern space to file name
- **W <filename>**: To write the first line of the current pattern space to filename
- **y/source/destination/**: To translate the matched criteria from source character to the destination character.
- **s/source/destination/**: To substitute or replace the search pattern from source to destination

- `n`: To apply the command to the line following the current line in the buffer
- `=`: To print the current line number

To negate the search criteria, you can use **!** just before the command, as follows:

```
sed -n '/RedHat/!p' file1
```

The preceding command prints the line that does not match **RedHat**. Let's delete all the lines matching the criteria, as follows:

```
sed  '/RedHat/d' file1
```

Let us insert a new line before the line that matches the search pattern, say **RedHat**, as follows:

```
sed  '/RedHat/i\hello' file1
```

See *Figure 5.10*, where the **i** command is used to insert a new line.

```
[vishesh@192 ~]$ sed   '/RedHat/i\hello world \
> lets explore unix' file1
Welcome to the world of Linux
RHEL9.0 is teh latest version
hello world
lets explore unix
We are using RedHat Enetrprise Linux9.0
RHEL is widely adopted among the Linux flavours by enterprises.
hello world
lets explore unix
RedHat incorporates  several benefits for its enterprise version of Linux.
```

***Figure 5.10:** Usage of sed command for inserting a new line before each selected line*

After the **i** command, you must provide a backslash ****, followed by your text.

To insert multi-line text, terminate each line with a ****, except the last one, as shown in *Figure 5.11*.

```
[vishesh@192 ~]$ sed   '/RedHat/i\hello' file1
Welcome to the world of Linux
RHEL9.0 is teh latest version
hello
We are using RedHat Enetrprise Linux9.0
RHEL is widely adopted among the Linux flavours by enterprises.
hello
RedHat incorporates  several benefits for its enterprise version of Linux.
```

***Figure 5.11**: sed command inserting multiple-line before each selected line*

In this figure, two lines are inserted using the **i** command. The **i** command is followed by a **/**, as used earlier. To provide multi-line text, separate the lines by a **** and press the Enter key. The last line to be inserted should not end with ****. The text should be inserted before each matched line.

Likewise, we can use the **a** and **c** commands to append the text after the current line and to change the current line with other text, respectively. The current line is the line that is currently being processed by **sed**.

Besides the search pattern, we can provide line addresses to **sed** to act upon. To delete line 2 from the **file1** file, use the following:

```
sed '2d' file1
```

To delete a range of lines, say 2-4, provide starting and ending range, separated by a comma as follows:

```
sed '2,4d' file1
```

To refer to the last line, you can use the **$** symbol if you don't know the total line numbers of the given input file. Besides line numbers, a range of lines to act upon can also be specified using a search pattern, as follows:

```
sed -n '/102/,/106/p' orders
```

The previous command will print all the lines lying between the lines that matches 102 and 106, as shown in *Figure 5.12*:

```
[vishesh@192 ~]$ sed -n '/102/,/106/p' orders
102     3 seater sofa set       1       27000
103     table lamp      1       5000
106     Adhsive racks   2       600
```

***Figure 5.12**: sed command displaying only the selected range of lines*

To translate a character to another, use the **y** command as follows:

```
sed '/Linux/y/L/l/' file1
```

The preceding command will replace **L** with a small **l** for all the lines that match the criteria. After the **y** command, press **/** to provide the source and destination character, separated by a **/**. Destination character must also end with a **/**.

Let us use the command that performs substitution of the text within the file. To substitute the word **Linux** with **linuz**, use the **s** command as follows:

```
sed '/Linux/s/Linux/linuz/' file1
```

The preceding command will substitute the **Linux** word in each matched line with **linuz**. Only the first occurrences of the word **Linux** on all the matched lines are replaced. To apply the substitution on all the occurrences of a line, suffix **g** at the end of the command, just before the closing single quote, as follows:

```
sed '/Linux/s/Linux/linuz/g' file1
```

The syntax of the **s** command is the same as that used in the **vi** editor.

Following are the options that can be used with the **sed** command:

- **-e**: To perform multiple edits with a single command
- **-E**: allows to use ERE.
- **-i**: To perform edits in the original file; the contents will not be printed on the screen
- **-f <file name>**: To read the instructions from the given file instead of the command line

Following are some of the useful usages of the mentioned options:

- **Giving two instructions at one go**

  ```
  sed -e '2d' -e 's/101/110/' orders
  ```

  The preceding command makes two manipulations on the data. Firstly, it deletes line number 2 and substitutes order ID 101 with 110.

- **Using file to give instructions**

  If we have many instructions to give to **sed** in a one command, we can save these instructions in a file and use this file in the **sed** command by using the **-f** option. Each instruction will be placed on a new line. You can also use **-e** to provide additional instructions on the command line, besides the instructions given with the **-f** option. See the following file:

  ```
  [vishesh@192 ~]$ cat prg1
  $d
  s/Adhsive/adhesive/
  [vishesh@192 ~]$sed -e 's/\<rack\>/racks/' -f prg1 orders
  ```

  The preceding command executes the instructions given from the **prg1** file and what is given in the command line.

  So far, we have seen that **sed** command made the changes on temporary buffer only. You can use the **-i** option if you want to make any manipulation in the input file itself. When you are satisfied with the output displayed on the screen, either use the **-i** option to do all the manipulation in the file itself or redirect the output to a file to save the transformation done.

  Suppose you want to delete lines 2-4 from the **file1** file; follow these steps:

  ```
  sed '2-4d' file1 > /tmp/file1.tmp
  mv /tmp/file1.tmp file1
  ```

Searching files: find

In *Chapter 2, Linux FileSystem and Administration*, we saw how a particular file is located in the Linux filesystem, given its name or a pattern. In this section, we will see how to find a file based on other file attributes. Files are searched according to some tests performed against the specified criteria. You can perform your search according to a particular file type, according to a specified timestamp, according to a specific file permission, and so on. The following expressions are useful to perform tests for file searching:

- **`-type`**: To search the files that belong to a specific file type; uses the following arguments:
  - o `b`: Block devices
  - o `c`: Character devices
  - o `d`: Search only the directories
  - o `p`: Named pipe
  - o `f`: Regular file
  - o `l`: Symbolic link
  - o `s`: Socket-based
- **`-atime <n>`**: Searches for the files that are **`n`** days ago; **`n`** can also be **`+`** or **`-`**; **`+n`** means greater than **`n`**, and **`-n`** means less than **`n`**
- **`-amin <n>`**: Searches for the files that are accessed in last **`n`** min
- **`-cmin <n>`**: Searches for the files that are changed in last **`n`** min
- **`-ctime <n>`**: Searches for the files whose statuses have been changed **`n`** days ago
- **`-mmin <n>`**: Searches for the files modified in the last **`n`** minutes
- **`-mtime <n>`**: Searches for the files that are modified **`n`** days ago

All the preceding options related to timestamp can take **`n`** as mentioned in **`-atime`**:

- **`-newer <filename>`**: Find the files whose modification time is newer than the given file
- **`-anewer <filename>`**: Find the files whose access time is newer than the given file
- **`-empty`**: Searches the empty file or directory
- **`-executable`**: Searches for the files and directory which are executable
- **`-gid <n>`**: Searches for the files having the given group id
- **`-group <name>`**: Searches for the files owned by the given group name
- **`inum`**: Searches the files having the given **inode** number
- **`-links <n>`**: Searches the files whose hard link count is same as the given number

- **-perm<octal notation>:** Searches for the files whose permission bytes match the given octal notation
- **-size <n>**: Searches for the files whose size is exactly **n** units

The **find** command may also take certain actions on the files found. These actions are specified using the following expressions:

- **-delete**: Deletes matched files; never provide this argument as the first expression after specifying the starting point, else it will delete everything following the starting point
- **-exec <command>**: Executes the specified command on the matched files; command is run once for each matched file; if the directory name is specified in the path, the specified command is executed in the starting directory only
- **-ls**: Lists matched file in **ls -dils** format on standard output
- **-ok <command>**: Works like **exec** but asks the user for confirmation before running the command
- **-execdir**: Is like **-exec**, but the specified command is run from the subdirectory containing the matched filename
- **-okdir**: Like **-execdir** but asks the user for confirmation before executing the command on each matched file
- **-print**: Prints the full file name on the standard output; is the default action that **find** command takes
- **-print0**: Interprets the file names that contain new lines or other white space characters

The following are the other options that you can use with the **find** command:

- **-depth**: Process each directory's contents before the directory itself; the **-delete** action also implies **-depth**
- **-maxdepth <levels>**: Descend at most specified levels of directories following the starting points; using **-maxdepth 0** means only applying the tests and actions to the starting points themselves
- **-mindepth <levels>**: Do not apply any tests or actions at levels less than the specified levels; using **-mindepth 1** means processing all files except the starting points

Many of the options that take **n** as their argument may also take **+n** or **-n**. **+n** would mean more than the specified **n**, and **-n** would mean less than the specified **n**.

When an option is preceded by **!**, it negates that condition. Multiple options can be used together while using the **find** command. When multiple options are combined, **AND** operator is assumed. To join the conditions using the **OR** operator, use the **-o** option between the two conditions.

Following are a few example usages of the **find** command:

- **Negating conditions in find**

  To negate the specified conditions in the **find** command, use the **!** operator before the given option. To view all the files except **zip** files, type the following:

  ```
  find / ! -name *.zip
  ```

- **Merging two conditions using OR**

  Say you want to list all the files starting from the **/opt** location which have not been accessed for the 7 days or the files that are larger than 50M.

  ```
  find /opt -size -atime +7 -o -size +50 -ls
  ```

- **Finding files satisfying the specified range**

  Use the following to view only the files whose size is between 50M and 100M:

  ```
  find / -size +50M -size -100M -exec ls -l {} \; 2>/dev/null
  ```

  Here, the **-exec** command is used to execute the **ls -l** command on each matched file. All the arguments after **-exec** until the **\;** symbol are treated as the command name, its options and arguments. **{}** is used as a placeholder for the current file name, which is being processed. Semicolon mark (**;**) is treated as the marker that represents the end of the command arguments. You must escape **;** with **** to protect semicolon **(;)** from shell's expansion. **2>/dev/null** at the end throws all the errors to **/dev/null**.

- **Finding files according to their timestamp**

  It is very easy to find the files that are accessed, modified, or changed at a particular time. To view files that have been modified 7 days ago and execute the **ls** command on them, use the following

  ```
  find /home -mtime 7 -ls
  ```

  Use the following to view the files that have been modifies less than 7 days ago:

  ```
  find /home -mtime -7
  ```

  Use the following to find the file that has been modified more than 7 days ago and back them up to the **/backup** directory:

  ```
  find $HOME -mtime +7 -exec cp {} /backup \;
  ```

  Use this to find all the files that have been accessed less than 24 hours ago:

  ```
  find /home -mtime 0 -ls
  ```

- **Finding files by inode number**

  Use the following to find the files that have **inode** 1234:

  ```
  find. -inum 1234
  ```

This is very handy if you want to look for all the files having the same **inode** number or that are hard links to each other.

- **Finding the file of a particular type**

  If you want to search for files that belong to a specific file type, use the **-type** option of the **find** command. For example, to find all the files of regular file type in your home directory, type the following:

  ```
  find /home -type f
  ```

  If you are the administrator and want to search for all files of the socket type, use the following command:

  ```
  #find / -type s
  ```

- **Finding the files according to permission type**

  Use the following to find all the files having permission **777** and restore their permission to 664:

  ```
  find / -perm 777 -ok chmod 664 {} \;
  ```

  It will ask for your confirmation for each listed file and will change the file mode to **664** when you press **'y'**. To find all the regular files having **777** permissions, use the **-type** option as well:

  ```
  find / -perm 777 -type f
  ```

- **Using xargs with find**

  The following command will find regular files named **sample** under **/tmp** and delete them:

  ```
  find /tmp -name sample -type f -print | xargs /bin/rm -f
  ```

- **Deleting matched files**

  ```
  find /tmp -name sample -type f -delete
  ```

  The previous command will find the files named **sample** under **/tmp** and delete them more efficiently and faster than in the previous example.

Do it yourself

1. **Go to /opt. As a regular user, use the find command to search for files that are of regular file type. Have you successfully accessed all the files in all the subdirectories of /opt. If not, why?**

Conclusion

Everything in a Linux system is identified as a file. The processor, RAM, peripheral devices like keyboard, mouse, printer, storage devices, and so on are identified as files, and they can be accessed in the same hierarchical tree as data. To access a file, a related **inode** block is fetched where all the attributes related to that file are stored. This **inode** block does not store the file's data. Instead, it contains the list of disk storage blocks where the file data is lying. For directory **inode**, **inode** contains the data block where the directory structure is stored. Directory structure contains the name of the file that resides under it and the **inode** number of each file. This number serves as the identification of the blocks where all the file-related information is stored. There are several ways to create a new file and insert data into it. An editing tool such as **vim** provides you with an efficient way to edit files. You can use **cp** to copy files from one location to another, **mv** to move files from source to destination, and the **rm** command to delete files. To save disk space, you can use one of the built-in compression utilities such as **zip**, **gzip**, and **bzip2** to compress very large files. **sed** is a powerful text processing tool that you can use to process text in a file in any way you like. **awk** is another powerful text processing tool that can process data and create beautiful reports for you.

In the next chapter, we will discuss how the concept of limited privileges is followed by restricting file access to users. The next chapter will also discuss user and password management.

CHAPTER 6
Managing Users and File Permissions

Introduction

One of the most important tasks of the Linux system administrator is to manage users and their access rights. Each user is provided with a limited set of privileges that are just enough to do their task. This is the principal of least privilege, which is followed on almost every kind of system. Sharing information is restricted to the users who need to know it to perform their duties according to their role. Public information is shared with everyone. To prevent unauthorized access to other users' privacy, a user is given only the required privileges and permissions. Only limited data is shared with them. Users can only access the files that they are allowed to access. They have all the rights on the files/directories that are owned by them. In Linux systems, root is the user who can read other users' files as well. Root user account comes with greater power and thus, greater responsibilities. Any access to root account is at high risk as the root account can do anything on the system either mistakenly or intentionally. So, use of root account by the system administrators to perform day-to-day operations is highly discouraged. Thus, as a precaution, root account should be temporary accessed when needed. So, a normal account should be created to perform daily admin activities, and the required administrative privileges should be given to these accounts.

Each file and directory on the Linux system is owned by a user and a group. Users performing similar roles are given similar kind of privileges and access rights on certain files and directories. These can be easily managed by the concept of groups. The set of users can be kept in the group and can enjoy all the access permissions and privileges assigned to the groups.

In this chapter, we will see how the new users are created, how they are managed and how they are assigned limited privileges. This chapter also lets you know how the file permissions are managed in Linux systems.

Structure

This chapter has the following structure:

- Your identity as a Linux user
- Creating new users
- User groups
- Modifying users and group attributes
- Deleting users and groups
- Privilege delegation
- Understanding permissions on files
- Modifying file permissions

Objectives

By the end of this chapter, you will grasp the following concepts: understanding users and groups, effectively managing them, adjusting attributes associated with users and groups, delegating privileges, ensuring secure root access, comprehending file permissions, and methods for modifying them.

Your identity as a Linux user

In a Linux operating system, a user is identified by a **user ID** (**UID**) and a **group ID** (**GID**). When a new user is created, they are assigned a new **UID** and a primary group by default. The number associated with **UID** and **GID** are generated on the basis of the last number that has been used up for **UID** and **GID**, respectively. It means that the new user will be assigned with a new **ID** and **GID**, which is one number higher than what has been used up. This is the default action when a new user is created without specifying any **user ID** and **group ID**.

Users in Linux OS can be divided into two categories: **normal/regular** users and system users. Regular users are ones whose **user ID** starts from 1000. The regular user's **UID** can be between the range of 1000 and 60000, which is set using the **`GID_MIN`** and **`GID_MAX`** variables, respectively, in the **/etc/login.defs** file. Look at the **user ID** of the first user that you had created during the installation. Log in from the first user and type the **id** command on the terminal.

```
[vishesh@192 ~]$ id
uid=1000(vishesh) gid=1000(vishesh) groups=1000(vishesh) context=unconfined_u:unconfined_r:unconfined_t:s0-s0:c0.c1023
[vishesh@192 ~]$ 
```

***Figure 6.1:** id command displaying user's information*

In *Figure 6.1*, the **id** command displays user-related information that identifies a user. It outputs information in various fields:

- **UID**: Displays **UID** of the logged in user. **UID** 1000 represents that **vishesh** is the first non-root user of the system.
- **GID**: Displays the **group ID** of the user. This field displays the **primary group** of the user to which the user belongs. *Figure 6.1* shows that the **primary group ID** of the user is 1000.
- **Groups**: A user may be a member of other groups. This is called the **secondary group**. In Figure 6.1, the current user named **vishesh** is only a member of one group which is itself his primary group.
- **Context**: This is the security context of the user. We will read about security context in *Chapter 8, Security and Networking in Linux*.

System users are the owners of the various system services running on the system. The **user ID** of owner of these services often follows 1000. Thus, we can say that standard **user ID** following 1000 are related to system users and any **user ID** equal to or above 1000 is related to a regular user. That said, the default range of system and regular **UID** can be changed.

Viewing users list

Users' information is stored in the **/etc/passwd** file. A normal user can read the contents of this file. This file has many fields. Let's view a few lines of this file; type the following:

```
$head /etc/passwd
```

```
[vishesh@192 ~]$ head /etc/passwd
root:x:0:0:root:/root:/bin/bash
bin:x:1:1:bin:/bin:/sbin/nologin
daemon:x:2:2:daemon:/sbin:/sbin/nologin
adm:x:3:4:adm:/var/adm:/sbin/nologin
lp:x:4:7:lp:/var/spool/lpd:/sbin/nologin
sync:x:5:0:sync:/sbin:/bin/sync
shutdown:x:6:0:shutdown:/sbin:/sbin/shutdown
halt:x:7:0:halt:/sbin:/sbin/halt
mail:x:8:12:mail:/var/spool/mail:/sbin/nologin
operator:x:11:0:operator:/root:/sbin/nologin
```

***Figure 6.2:** Contents of /etc/passwd file*

Figure 6.2 displays 10 lines from the **`/etc/passwd`** file. Each line in this file contains the information of a user. There are multiple fields in this file, separated by a semicolon (**`:`**) character. Following is the description of these fields:

- The first field is username.
- The second field displays just an **`x`** and is not used currently. In earlier Unix-like systems, encrypted passwords were stored in this field only. Now, passwords are stored under **`/etc/shadow`** in encrypted format. An **`x`** is retained in the **`/etc/passwd`** file just as an indication or a placeholder for passwords that stored in **`/etc/shadow`**.
- The third field is **user ID**.
- The fourth is primary **group ID**.
- The fifth fields contain user information in GECOS format. This may contain users' full name, phone number, and so on.
- The sixth field lists the absolute path of the home directory of the user.
- The seventh and last field is the absolute path of the login shell of the user.

The first line contains information about the root user whose **UID** is 0, belongs to primary group 0. Home directory of root is **`/root`** and not **`/`**. Other lines in these files are the system users. Notice their **user ID**. They use a shell named **`nologin`** shell. The **`/sbin/nologin`** shell is absolute path of the **`nologin`** shell, which is used to disallow any login to the user. These system users essentially do not need any logins, and any attempt to login by these users fails. The output in *Figure 6.2* does not list regular users. Regular users are listed after all the system users. New user entries are created at the end. Use the tail command on **`/etc/passwd`** to fetch the list of regular users.

Creating a new user

A system administrator is required to create users, giving them appropriate permissions, and then delete these users when they are no longer required or when they leave the organization. Root login is required to create a new user. We read earlier that when a new user is created, the corresponding user's home directory is also created, which is named after the user's name under the **`/home`** directory. **`/home`** is always used a base directory for the user's home when a new user is created. Home directory provides a place where the user can store their files. They can do anything with the files that are created by them in their home directory. On user creation, the home directory is populated with many default files or directories. The place from which these default files and directories are copied over to the user's home directory is called **skeleton directory**. Default skeleton directory is **`/etc/skel`**. In *Chapter 2, Linux FileSystem and Administration,* we have seen what file or directories are created under the user's home directory by default.

You have to be rooted to create a new user. Type the following:

```
$su -
```

It will ask you the password for the root user; enter the root password. The steps to create a user are two-fold:

- Adding the user in the system
- Setting the password

Adding the user in the system

To add a new user, the **useradd** command is used as follows:

```
useradd <new user name>
```

This command will create a new user, make its entry in **/etc/passwd**, create a home directory and place all the defaults files under it.

Default file and configuration

Default options to create users with the **useradd** command can be overridden when we use options in the command line. Without any option, the **useradd** command uses the default option set in the **/etc/default/useradd** and **/etc/login.defs** file.

Figure 6.3 displays the contents of the **/etc/default/useradd** file that will be used when the **useradd** command is used without any options. Following is the description of the contents of this file:

```
GROUP=100
```

If the user specifies the **-n** option with the **useradd** command to not create the same **group ID** as its **login ID**, then the user will be assigned to group 100.

```
[vishesh@192 ~]$ cat /etc/default/useradd
# useradd defaults file
GROUP=100
HOME=/home
INACTIVE=-1
EXPIRE=
SHELL=/bin/bash
SKEL=/etc/skel
CREATE_MAIL_SPOOL=yes
```

***Figure 6.3**: Default contents of /etc/default/useradd file*

```
HOME=/home
```

This line mentions the default base directory to create a user's home. By default, a new directory having the same name as the username is created under this base directory.

```
INACTIVE=-1
```

Above line specifies the number of days after a password has expired before the account will be disabled. -1 means that account will never be disabled.

```
EXPIRE=
```

This line specifies the date on which the user's password expires. Empty string means the password will never expire.

```
SHELL=/bin/bash
```

This line describes the default login shell:

```
SKEL=/etc/skel
```

This line describes the default **skeleton** directory to be used with the **useradd** command:

```
CREATE_MAIL_SPOOL=yes
```

This line describes whether to create the `mail spool` directory. *Figure 6.4* shows the contents of the **/etc/login.defs** file, which plays a major role in creating user account with **useradd**.

```
[vishesh@192 ~]$ cat /etc/login.defs |tr -s '\n'|grep -v '^#'
MAIL_DIR        /var/spool/mail
UMASK           022
HOME_MODE       0700
PASS_MAX_DAYS   99999
PASS_MIN_DAYS   0
PASS_WARN_AGE   7
UID_MIN                  1000
UID_MAX                 60000
SYS_UID_MIN               201
SYS_UID_MAX               999
SUB_UID_MIN            100000
SUB_UID_MAX         600100000
SUB_UID_COUNT           65536
GID_MIN                  1000
GID_MAX                 60000
SYS_GID_MIN               201
SYS_GID_MAX               999
SUB_GID_MIN            100000
SUB_GID_MAX         600100000
SUB_GID_COUNT           65536
ENCRYPT_METHOD SHA512
USERGROUPS_ENAB yes
CREATE_HOME     yes
HMAC_CRYPTO_ALGO SHA512
```

***Figure 6.4**: Default contents of /etc/login.defs file*

Table 6.1 provides the description of some of the options listed in this file, along with their default values:

Setting	Default value	Description
MAIL_DIR	**/var/spool/mail**	Determines the base mail spool directory
UMASK	**022**	The mode of the home directory if HOME_MODE is not set
HOME_MODE	**0700**	Permission for the home directory

Setting	Default value	Description
PASS_MAX_DAYS	99999	The maximum number of days a password may be used; if the password is older than this, a password change will be forced; - disables the restriction
PASS_MIN_DAYS	0	The minimum number of days allowed between password changes; any password changes attempted sooner than this will be rejected; 0 means user can change their password anytime
PASS_WARN_AGE	7	The number of days warning is given before a password expires; 0 means warning is given only upon the day of expiration, a negative value means no warning is given; if not specified, no warning will be provided
UID_MIN	1000	Minimum **UID** to use for the creation of regular user account
UID_MAX	60000	Maximum limit for **UID** of regular user account
SYS_UID_MIN	201	Minimum **UID** to use for system user
SYS_UID_MAX	999	Maximum **UID** to use for system user
GID_MIN	1000	Minimum **GID** to use to create first regular group
GID_MAX	60000	Maximum **GID** to use for the creation of regular group
SYS_GID_MIN	201	Minimum **GID** of system group
SYS_GID_MAX	999	Maximum **GID** for system group
ENCRYPT_METHOD	SHA512	The name of the algorithm to use to encrypt password
USERGROUPS_ENAB	Yes	If yes, a group will be created for the user, with the same name as their login name; if set to no, `useradd` will set the primary group of the new user to the value specified by the GROUP variable in `/etc/default/useradd`, or 100 by default
CREATE_HOME	Yes	Determines whether to create a user's home directory on account creation
HMAC_CRYPTO_ALGO	SHA512	Select the HMAC cryptography algorithm

Table 6.1: *Default options in /etc/login.defs file*

Options with useradd

You can provide non-default settings when creating a new user account. To create a user with non-default setting, use the following options along with the **useradd** command:

- **-D**: Prints or modifies the contents of the **/etc/default/useradd** file
- **-d <home directory>**: Creates the user account in a non-default home directory
- **-b**: Specifies new base directory to create home directory of the user; if this option is not used, **/home** is used as the base directory to create each user's home directory
- **-e <YYYY-MM-DD>**: Specifies the date on which the user account will be disabled; the date is specified in the **YYYY-MM-DD** format
- **-f <number of days>**: Specifies the number of days after a password has expired before the account will be disabled; a value of 0 disables the account as soon as the password has expired, and a value of **-1** disables the feature
- **-g <gid or group name>**: Name or ID of the primary group of the new account
- **-G <comma-separated list of supplementary groups>**: List of supplementary groups of the new account
- **-k <skeleton directory>**: Specifies the location of alternative <**skeleton directory**>
- **-m**: Creates the user's home directory
- **-M**: Does not create the user's home directory
- **-N**: Does not create a group with the same name as the user
- **-r**: Creates a system account; home directory will not be created for system account
- **-s<shell>**: Login shell of the new account; the default is **/bin/bash**
- **-u<uid>**: **User ID** of the new account
- **-U**: Creates a group with the same name as the user
- **-Z < seuser>**: The SELinux user for the user's login; the default is to leave this field blank, which causes the system to select the default SELinux user

Following are some of the usages of options with the **useradd** command:

- **To change default**

  To change the default values in the **/etc/default/useradd** file, use the **-D** option with **useradd**, as follows:

  ```
  useradd -D options
  ```

For example, to change the home directory to **/opt/home**, use the following command:

```
#useradd -D -b /opt/home
```

From then on, the **home** directory of newly created users will be created under the **/opt/home/** directory.

- **To create home directory in non-default location**

  To create a user account that uses a home directory in a non-default location say **/opt/home**, use the following command:

  ```
  useradd -d /opt/home/hruser hruser
  ```

  The preceding command will create a user named **hruser** whose home directory is **/opt/home/hruser**.

- **To change the base of home directory**

  To change the base directory of the user's directory location, use the following command:

  ```
  useradd -b /opt/home finuser
  ```

  The preceding command will create a user account named **finuser**, but home directory is created under **/opt/home**. Thus, the home directory of this user will be **/opt/home/finuser**.

- **To create a system user**

  To create a system user named **sysuser**, use the following command:

  ```
  #useradd -r sysuser
  ```

  The preceding command will create a system user, but no home directory will be created. And this user cannot log in to the system. **UID** following 1000 will be assigned to it. Type the following:

  ```
  #grep sysuser /etc/passwd
  ```

  To verify the system user creation, the following is what you will use:

  ```
  #sysuser:x:977:977::/opt/home/sysuser:/bin/bash
  ```

  The **/etc/passwd** file will display the home directory, but this directory does not actually exist. In this example, **sysuser**'s home directory is set under **/opt/home** as base of the **home** directory is modified in the **/etc/default/useradd** file in this machine.

Setting the password

So far, we have just created a user account. This user account is inactive unless a password is set. So, let us move to the second step. Root must set the password to make that user log in to the system. Use the **passwd** command as follows:

```
passwd <username>
```

The password will not be visible on the screen when you type, not even '*', as in older Unix systems. Thanks to this feature, no one can guess your password or its properties, such as its length. The system never stores the password in its original unencrypted format; it is encrypted and stored in the **/etc/shadow** file. The **/etc/shadow** file not only stores password information but also its aging information. A normal user cannot read the contents of the **/etc/shadow** file, so you have to become root to fetch its contents. Following are the top few lines of **/etc/shadow**:

```
[root@192 ~]#
[root@192 ~]# head /etc/shadow
root:$6$sfojbuGDtK9u3xXw$WX6mJgmWCl13.HX9/MuxmRJefwo5YkgAedL3XuRnhz6jpgIzH0FY83ieE418G9cwR2P1gDyibMEeuvhJKexeh.::0:99999:7:::
bin:*:18849:0:99999:7:::
daemon:*:18849:0:99999:7:::
adm:*:18849:0:99999:7:::
lp:*:18849:0:99999:7:::
sync:*:18849:0:99999:7:::
shutdown:*:18849:0:99999:7:::
halt:*:18849:0:99999:7:::
mail:*:18849:0:99999:7:::
operator:*:18849:0:99999:7:::
[root@192 ~]#
```

Figure 6.5: *Top few lines of /etc/shadow file*

Figure 6.5 shows some of the lines fetched from the **/etc/shadow** file. Each line refers to a user account. The first line clearly shows the password-related information for the root user. Rest of the lines are related to system users. After system users, normal users are listed (not displayed in *Figure 6.5*). This file stores password information in multiple fields, and each field is separated by a colon (**:**). The description of each field is given below:

- **name**: The first field is the name of the user account.
- **password**: The second field is the encrypted password. '*' or '**!**' in this field means that the user cannot log in via password. A password field that starts with '**!**' indicates that the password is locked, and the remaining characters display the password that existed just before the locking.
- **Date of last password change**: This is the date of the last password change, expressed as the number of days since Jan 1, 1970 00:00 UTC. The value 0 means that the user should change their password the next time they log in to the system. An empty field means that password ageing features are disabled.
- **Minimum password age**: This is the minimum number of days after which the password is allowed to change.
- **Maximum password age**: This is the maximum number of days after which the password has to change. An empty field means that there is no maximum password age. If the maximum password age is lower than the minimum password age, the user cannot change their password.
- **Password warning period**: This is the number of days a warning is given before a password expires. An empty field or 0 means there is no warning period.

- **Password inactivity period**: This is the number of days for which the password is accepted after it expires. Users should be asked to change their password on the next login.
- **Account expiration date**: This is the date on which the account expires. It is expressed as the number of days since Jan 1, 1970 00:00 UTC.
- **Reserved field**: This field is reserved for future use.

The **passwd** command can also be used by any regular user to change their password. A normal user cannot change any other user's password, but root can.

When a normal user tries to change their password, they will be asked for the current password and then a new password. The system won't allow you to enter very easy passwords. It is intelligent to analyze the password entered for its complexity. From the security perspective, the password should be strong enough so that it cannot be easily guessed. A strong password may be one with the following features:

- Not the same as the username
- Not the same as the name of any other person
- Not the dictionary-based word
- Not be a very simple pattern, such as **aaaa**, or **abcdefghi**
- Equal to or more than 8 characters
- Not contain previous password in any form
- A combination of alphabets, numbers and special symbols.

Create a new user **sam**, as shown in *Figure 6.6*:

```
[root@192 ~]# useradd sam
[root@192 ~]# passwd sam
Changing password for user sam.
New password:
BAD PASSWORD: The password is shorter than 8 characters
Retype new password:
passwd: all authentication tokens updated successfully.
[root@192 ~]#
```

Figure 6.6: *User creation steps*

Figure 6.6 demonstrates all the steps of user creation. The new user, **sam**, is created using the **useradd** command. Then, the **passwd** command is used to set the password. In *Figure 6.6*, the **passwd** command shows **BAD PASSWORD** message on the screen as the user enters a very weak password. Th output displays the following message at the end:

```
All authentication tokens updated successfully
```

This message means that the user password is successfully set. You can verify the creation of a new user entry by finding a new username inside the **/etc/passwd** file, as shown in *Figure 6.7*. The following figure confirms that you will be assigned to **/home/sam** as your home directory, you will be assigned to **/bin/bash** shell on your login, and your **user id** is 1001 and primary group is 1001:

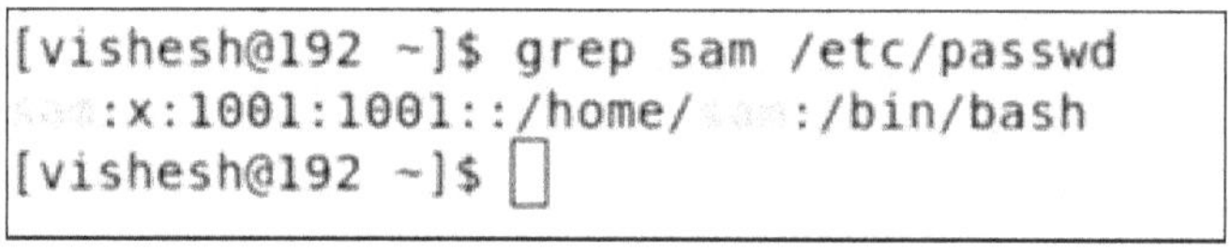

```
[vishesh@192 ~]$ grep sam /etc/passwd
:x:1001:1001::/home/ :/bin/bash
[vishesh@192 ~]$ 
```

Figure 6.7: /etc/passwd file displaying a new user entry

Options in passwd

The following options can be used with the **passwd** command. To use the following options with the **passwd** command, you have to be root:

- **-e**: It will expire the password immediately and force the user to change it on next login attempt.
- **-x <days>**: This is the maximum number of days a password may be used. If the password is older than this, a password change will be forced.
- **-n <days>**: This is the minimum number of days allowed between password changes.
- **-w <days>**: This is the number of days before password expiration that a warning is received.
- **-i <days>**: This is the number of days after password expiration when an account becomes disabled.

Do it yourself

1. **Create a user account named hruser with the non-default skeleton directory. This skeleton directory must exist. So, create a new directory named hrskel in /opt. Copy .bash_profile from /etc/skel to /opt/hrskel. Now, create a new user account using this skeleton directory. Go to the home directory of the new user and check what files are created there.**
2. **Change the SKEL variable to /opt/hrskel in the /etc/default/useradd file using the -D option of the useradd command. Now, create a new user. Don't provide any option in the command line. Verify what files are created under their home directory.**
3. **Become root. Note the entry related to hruser in /etc/shadow. Execute command to expire the password of hruser using the passwd command. Again, note the related entry in /etc/shadow. What change do you notice and in which field. Now, log in from hruser from another terminal. What do you see?**

4. **Become root. Create a new user manager1; don't set the password. Now look at the password entry under the /etc/shadow file for this user. What does the password field indicate? Now, set the password for this user. Again, verify the same inside /etc/shadow. Also notice other field values. One of the fields contains 7 as its value. What does 7 indicate in this field?**

User groups

We have seen that each new user is assigned a **user ID** and is added to a primary group. When a new user account is created in the system, a new group is with the same name as the username is also created. The user's primary group is also known as user private group. No other user is the member of the user's private group. Each group is identified by a **group id**. Like **user id**, **group id** is also generated according the next available id in the system. The regular user's **GID** can be between the range of 1000 and 60000, which are set using the **`GID_MIN`** and **`GID_MAX`** variables, respectively, in the **`/etc/login.defs`** file. That said, this range can be modified if required.

Some users need to share the same file because this file is part of the same project they belong to. Users who belong to the same project usually need the same set of privileges and access permissions on the project-related files. Instead of assigning a set of privileges and permissions to all these users one by one, they can be added to a common group, and the required permissions can be given to this group. This group will become the secondary group for its user members. All the user members of the group can enjoy all the privileges that are assigned to the group. To share the project files among the members of a group, the files have been assigned the same group. The members will have access rights to the files that belong to the same group to which they belong. We will learn to assign group ownership to files later in this chapter.

Any **group ID** following 1000 represents system groups, and other ones represent regular groups. System **group ID** ranges are determined by the **`SYS_GID_MIN`** and **`SYS_GID_MAX`** variables in the **`/etc/login.defs`** file, but they can be changed.

Creating a new group

Just like user creation, root login is required to create groups. Group information is stored in **`/etc/group`**. To create a new group, use the **`groupadd`** command as follows:

```
groupadd <group name>
```

For example, to create a group **`hr`**, use the following command:

```
#groupadd hr
```

This will create a new regular group and assign it a **group ID**, which is the next available number greater or equal to 1000. By default, no member will exist in the newly created group.

Viewing user groups

User group information is stored in **/etc/group**. Each line in the **/etc/group** file belongs to a particular group. Let's view a few lines of the **/etc/group** file. Refer to *Figure 6.8*:

```
[vishesh@192 ~]$ head /etc/group
root:x:0:
bin:x:1:
daemon:x:2:
sys:x:3:
adm:x:4:
tty:x:5:
disk:x:6:
lp:x:7:
mem:x:8:
kmem:x:9:
```

Figure 6.8: *Top few lines of /etc/group*

Figure 6.8 shows the top 10 lines of the **/etc/group** file. It contains four fields, the description of which are given here:

- The first field is the group name itself.
- The second field was used in the earlier days to store group password. Now, the password is stored in the **/etc/gshadow** file. **x** in the second field means that passwords are no longer stored here.
- The third field is the id of the group itself.
- The fourth field contains the list of members belonging to this group. In *Figure 6.8*, all of the groups displayed have no members. The first line refers to the group belonging to the root user. It is clear from the first line that no other users are members of the root group. Other lines are related to the default available system group.

Whenever you create a new user, we know that a new private group is created with the same name. The information of the newly created group is stored at the last line of the **/etc/group** file. Initially, the newly created group will not have any members.

Options in groupadd

- **-r**: Creates a system group
- **-g <gid>**: Uses this gid for the new group
- **-U <comma-separated list of user members>**: Specifies the list of members of this group

Following are some of the usages of options in **groupadd**:

- **To create a group adding few members**

  To create a group named **finance** and add two members inside the new group, use the following command:

  ```
  #groupadd -U sam,finuser finance
  ```

  Before executing the above command, **sam** and **finuser** usernames must exist. On viewing **/etc/group**, we will find the following:

  ```
  finance:x:1009:finuser,sam
  ```

  Contents of **/etc/group** specify that a group named **finance** is created with **group ID** 1009. **finuser** and **sam** are the members of this group. The **finance** is the supplementary group for these two users.

- **To create a system group**

  To create a system group, use the **-r** option as follows:

  ```
  #groupadd -r sysgrp
  ```

  The preceding command will create a system group named **sysgrp**. Verify the system group creation in the **/etc/group** file by typing the following:

  ```
  #grep sysgrp /etc/group
  ```

  The previous command will display the following output:

  ```
  sysgrp:x:977:
  ```

  It is clear from the output that **sysgrp** is a system group as it is assigned 977 as its GID.

Modifying users and group attributes

By default, the **useradd** command creates a home directory under **/home**, creates a **/bin/bash** shell for each user login, and creates a new **user id** and groups for them.

These default parameters/settings that apply to **useradd** or **groupadd** commands are stored in the **/etc/login.defs** file. The default setting of this file can be changed by the system administrator if they know the implications of doing that. This file would also allow you to change the starting range of the **UID** and **GID** that a new user is assigned to. It means that you can modify the settings such that the minimum **userid** and **gid** ranges start from 5000 instead of 1000.

usermod

Any of the attributes related to a user account can be modified using the **usermod** command:

- **-d <new home directory>**: New home directory for the user account
- **-e <expire date>**: Set account expiration date

- **-f < number of days>**: The number of days to disable the account after a password expires
- **-g <group name>**: Use specified group name as new primary group of the user
- **-G <comma-separated list of supplementary groups >**: New list of user's supplementary groups; list should contain user's older membership as well as new group information, else the membership from the older group is removed
- **-a**: Append the user to the supplemental groups mentioned by the -G option without removing the user from other groups
- **-l <new login name>**: New value of the login name
- **-L**: Lock the user account
- **-m**: Move contents of the home directory to the new location (use only with **-d**)
- **-s <shell>**: New login shell for the user account
- **-u <UID>**: New **UID** for the user account
- **-U**: Unlock the user account
- **-Z**: New SELinux user mapping for the user account

Following are some of the usages of the **usermod** command:

- **To add a user to new supplementary group**

  To add a user to new supplementary groups, use the **-G** option as follows:

  ```
  usermod -G <group name> <user account name>
  ```

  Here, **<group name>** must exist. For example, To add user **sam** to a new group named **hr**, use the following command:

  ```
  #usermod -G hr sam
  ```

  The previous command will add the user to the **hr** group, where the **hr** group must exist. This command will remove the user from any of the other supplementary groups they are a member of, and they would become the member of the new specified group. You can also specify a comma-separated list of supplementary groups after the **-G** option. If multiple group names are specified with the **-G** option, the user will become the member of all these groups, and the membership of older supplementary group will be removed. If you don't want to remove the user from the older groups, then you must specify the name of all the older supplementary groups along with the names of the new groups. Along with the **-G** option to add a user to additional groups, you can use the **-a** option, which will append the user membership to other groups.

  Figure 6.9 demonstrates an example. In *Figure 6.9*, user **sam** is modified so that he becomes a member of **hr** group. His earlier membership to other supplementary groups is removed. Next, the **sam** account is appended with a new **finance** group membership. You can use the ID command to verify the same:

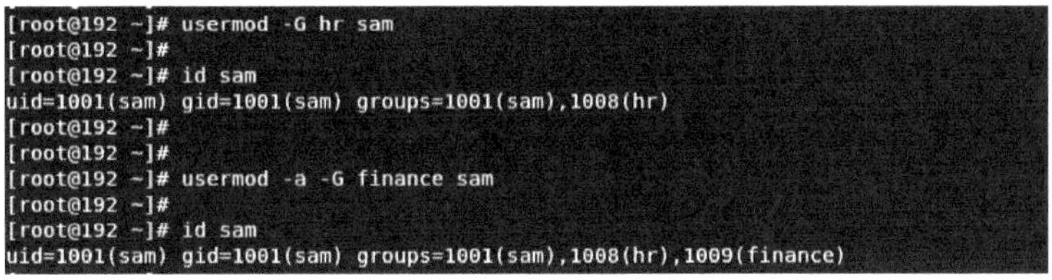

```
[root@192 ~]# usermod -G hr sam
[root@192 ~]#
[root@192 ~]# id sam
uid=1001(sam) gid=1001(sam) groups=1001(sam),1008(hr)
[root@192 ~]#
[root@192 ~]#
[root@192 ~]# usermod -a -G finance sam
[root@192 ~]#
[root@192 ~]# id sam
uid=1001(sam) gid=1001(sam) groups=1001(sam),1008(hr),1009(finance)
```

Figure 6.9: *usermod usage to add a user to a supplementary group*

- **To change the working or login directory of the user**

  To change the user to a new login directory, use the following command:

  ```
  usermod -d <new login directory of the user> <login name>
  ```

  Here, the <new login directory of the user> must exist. To change the login directory of the user **sam**, use the following:

  ```
  #usermod -d /opt/home/sam sam
  ```

  The previous command will change the login directory of the user **sam** to **/opt/home/sam**, but the home directory will not be changed. This means that the user will be logged in to the new login directory and not to their home directory. The files and directory that belong to that user under the home directory will not move here, but the user can still access them.

- **To change the home directory of the user**

  To change the home directory and not only the login directory, use the **-m** option along with **-d**, as follows:

  ```
  usermod -m -d <new home directory> < login name>
  ```

  In the preceding command syntax, **<new home directory>** will be created if it does not exist. Say we want to change the home directory of user **sam** from **/home/sam** to **/opt/home/sam**; use the following:

  ```
  #usermod -m -d /opt/home/sam sam
  ```

  The preceding command will create the user's home directory under **/opt/home** and move all the contents of the older home directory to the new home directory. Also, this command will remove the older home directory of the user.

groupmod

Similarly, group attributes can be modified using the **groupmod** command. The following options go with **groupmod**:

- **-a**: Append the users mentioned by the **-U** option to the group without removing the existing user members

- **-g <new gid>**: Change the **group ID** to **new gid**
- **-n <new group name>**: Change the name of the group to new group
- **-U<comma separated list of users>**: List the user members of this group

Do it yourself

- **Become root. Create a group named manager. Create a few user accounts, such as man1, man2, man3 without any non-default option. Verify the creation of a new group and all the three user accounts using their respective files. Modify user account man1 to become a member of manager group. Verify this change using the id command. Also, verify the group information again using the /etc/group file. What do you see? How many members are currently there in the manager group? Now, append the member user list of manager group such that all the three users, man1, man2 and man3, are the members of this group**

Deleting users and groups

If a user leaves an organization, the system administrator must remove that user's entry from the system to prevent any future login attempt. The same applies to groups. If a group is no longer required, it has to be removed. We have the **userdel** command to delete the user account and the **groupdel** command to delete the group. The **userdel** command will only delete the user if that user is not currently active.

To delete a user account, **userdel** is used as follows:

```
userdel <user account to delete>
```

When the **userdel** command is used without specifying any option, it will delete all the entries of the specified user from the system. But it neither deletes user-owned files from the home directory nor from any other place.

To delete a user account along with all the user-owned files inside their home directory, use the **-r** option as follows:

```
userdel -r <user account to delete>
```

To delete a user account **sam** from the system, along with all the user-owned files in their home directory and the home directory itself, use the following:

```
#userdel -r sam
```

The preeding command won't delete the user-owned files outside their home directory. Any files related to the deleted user outside of the home directory can only be accessed by root and have to be found manually to be deleted.

The **groupdel** command deletes the specified group from the system by removing all the entries that refer to that group. It can be used as follows:

```
groupdel <group to delete>
```

The specified group must not be the primary group of any user. To delete the group named **hr**, use the following:

```
#groupdel hr
```

You have to manually scan the entire system to verify that no files owned by the deleted group remain.

Privilege delegation

Each user in a system is provided with privileges that are just enough for them to perform their tasks. Root is a person of greater power; with great power comes greater responsibilities. So, every user cannot become root or be given system administration rights. Root account should be used only when necessary.

To perform day-to-day operations, the system administrator or root user can delegate some of the privileges to non-root user accounts. Then they can do their daily chores using these non-root accounts and log in to the root account only when necessary. These non-root user accounts or regular accounts can elevate their privileges temporarily by using the **sudo** command, which is the safest way to delegate responsibility. Every user is not allowed to use the **sudo** command. This cap on the **sudo** command is maintained by the **sudoers** file. The command can only be used by the user accounts whose entries are listed in the **sudoers** file. The **sudoers** file allows regular users to use the **sudo** command to execute some of the administrative-level commands.

A regular user can only execute admin commands that they are allowed to execute via the **sudoers** file. The **sudoers** file is located under **/etc**. As the name of the file suggests, this file describes who can run the **sudo** command. So, what is the **sudo** command really? Literally, **sudo** means **superuser**. This file describes which user can run which commands. Listed users can run specified admin commands as the root user without needing to enter the root password. When you type the **sudo** command, you will be asked to enter your password and not the root password. It is a great feature that secures root password. Everyone knowing the root password may intentionally or mistakenly harm the system. Any attempt to use the **sudo** command by users who are not allowed to do so will be recorded in the journal log, and the user executing the command will receive this information on the screen. This discussion may have helped you understand the difference between the **sudo** command and the **su** command to become root. So far, we have used the **su -** command to become root, which asks for the root password. So, the user executing the command should know the root password. On the other hand, when we use the **sudo** command to become root, it asks the password of the user executing the command and not the root command. Thus, it brings you the safest approach. **Sudo** is followed by the actual command that you want to execute with elevated privileges.

Now, it's time to look at the contents of the **/etc/sudoers** file. A normal user cannot view or open the **/etc/sudoers** file. One must become the root user to read and edit this file. This file has two types of contents: **Aliases** and command rules. It is the command rule that specifies who can run what. Command rules are listed after the **aliases**.

Some sample aliases given in the file are listed in *Figure 6.10*:

```
## Host Aliases
## Groups of machines. You may prefer to use hostnames (perhaps using
## wildcards for entire domains) or IP addresses instead.
# Host_Alias     FILESERVERS = fs1, fs2
# Host_Alias     MAILSERVERS = smtp, smtp2

## User Aliases
## These aren't often necessary, as you can use regular groups
## (ie, from files, LDAP, NIS, etc) in this file - just use %groupname
## rather than USERALIAS
# User_Alias ADMINS = jsmith, mikem


## Command Aliases
## These are groups of related commands...

## Networking
# Cmnd_Alias NETWORKING = /sbin/route, /sbin/ifconfig, /bin/ping, /sbin/dhclient, /usr/bin/net, /sbin/iptables, /usr/bin/rfcomm, /usr/bin/wvdial, /sbin/iwconfig, /sbin/mii-tool

## Installation and management of software
# Cmnd_Alias SOFTWARE = /bin/rpm, /usr/bin/up2date, /usr/bin/yum
```

Figure 6.10: *Sample aliases as given in the /etc/sudoers file*

Figure 6.10 lists three kinds of aliases:

- **Host aliases**: Aliases like **`FILESERVERS`** and **`MAILSERVERS`** are used to group two or more file servers together.
- **User aliases**: Aliases like **`ADMINS`** are used to group related users together.
- **Command aliases**: Aliases like **`NETWORKING`** and **`SOFTWARE`** are used to group sets of related commands together.

These **aliases** can be used in the later section of the file to apply command rules on them. Let's see the bottom section of the file, which lists the sample command rules as displayed in *Figure 6.11* :

```
[root@192 ~]# tail -25 /etc/sudoers
##
## The COMMANDS section may have other options added to it.
##
## Allow root to run any commands anywhere
root    ALL=(ALL)       ALL

## Allows members of the 'sys' group to run networking, software,
## service management apps and more.
# %sys ALL = NETWORKING, SOFTWARE, SERVICES, STORAGE, DELEGATING, PROCESSES, LOCATE, DRIVERS

## Allows people in group wheel to run all commands
%wheel  ALL=(ALL)       ALL

## Same thing without a password
# %wheel        ALL=(ALL)       NOPASSWD: ALL

## Allows members of the users group to mount and unmount the
## cdrom as root
# %users  ALL=/sbin/mount /mnt/cdrom, /sbin/umount /mnt/cdrom

## Allows members of the users group to shutdown this system
# %users  localhost=/sbin/shutdown -h now
# vishesh ALL=/usr/bin/umount
## Read drop-in files from /etc/sudoers.d (the # here does not mean a comment)
#includedir /etc/sudoers.d
```

Figure 6.11: *Lists of sample command rules from the /etc/sudoers file*

You can edit sample command rules to specify any rule for any users or groups. Each command rule follows the syntax given here:

```
user   MACHINE=COMMANDS
```

The first phrase refers to a user or a group. If it refers to a group, then the group name will be preceded by a **%** sign. The second phrase specifies the machine name, and the last one is a command or a list of commands on which the rule applies. This can also list the command-line arguments that are allowed to run with the named command by the specified user or group. Note that the specified command must be mentioned with its absolute path.

The syntax of the rule can be understood better by looking at the following entry from the **/etc/sudoers** file, which is uncommented by default:

```
root   ALL=(ALL)     ALL
```

This entry allows the root user to run all the commands on all the servers. Value **ALL** in parentheses refers to the **runas user**. **Runas user** specifies the user name using whom privileges the command run as. This allows a user to execute commands with the privileges of another user. If no value is specified in parentheses, then root is assumed. The following entry uses command aliases:

```
%sys ALL = NETWORKING, SOFTWARE, SERVICES, STORAGE, DELEGATING, PROCESSES,
LOCATE, DRIVERS
```

The previous line means that sys group is allowed to run listed command aliases on all the servers.

The following line allows all the users in the **wheel** group to run all the commands. If you want to assign a few users the admin role to perform admin tasks, you can uncomment the entry that contains wheel group. Then, all the users who are members of wheel group can use **sudo** to run any command.

```
%wheel ALL=(ALL) ALL
```

Trick: If the password of the root user is forgotten, then any user who is the member of wheel group can change the root password using sudo passwd root.

The following entry allows all the members of the users group to run listed commands in all the machines:

```
 %users ALL=/sbin/mount /mnt/cdrom, /sbin/umount /mnt/cdrom
```

Notice the absolute path of the command used. If the preceding line is uncommented, members of the users groups can **mount** and **unmount /mnt/cdrom**.

```
# %users localhost=/sbin/shutdown -h now
```

The previous line, if uncommented, allows members of the `users` group to immediately shut down the local machine. The following line, when uncommented, allows a normal user **vishesh** to perform unmount operations on all the machines.

```
#vishesh ALL=/usr/bin/umount
```

vishesh user will be allowed to elevate his privileges temporarily to run the **umount** command as the root user. When the **runas** username in parentheses is not specified, then each command runs as root user by default.

To edit this file, you can use the **visudo** command, which opens a **vi** like editor to edit the **sudoers** file. Let's edit the **sudoers** file to allow **sam** user to create a user account and then set the password. Add the following line:

```
sam ALL=/usr/sbin/useradd
```

After making successful entry to the **/etc/sudoers** file, log in to **sam** account and try to add a new user account, as shown in *Figure 6.12*:

```
[sam@192 ~]$
[sam@192 ~]$ sudo useradd ma6

We trust you have received the usual lecture from the local System
Administrator. It usually boils down to these three things:

    #1) Respect the privacy of others.
    #2) Think before you type.
    #3) With great power comes great responsibility.

[sudo] password for sam:
[sam@192 ~]$ sudo passwd ma6
Sorry, user sam is not allowed to execute '/bin/passwd ma6' as root on 192.168.1.9.
```

Figure 6.12: *A regular user is executing sudo command to add a new user*

In *Figure 6.12*, **sam** user tries to elevate his role to add a user account **ma6** using the following command:

```
$sudo useradd ma6
```

After giving you some speech, it will prompt you to authenticate yourself by entering your password instead of the root user's password.

When an attempt is made to set the password for **ma6** user, a warning message appears on the screen saying that **Sam** is not allowed to set the password of any user. To make this work, you must add a new rule in the **sudoers** file, which will allow him to execute the **passwd** command as well.

Do it yourself

1. **Add user sam to the wheel group. Uncomment the entry related to wheel group in the /etc/sudoers file. Now, log in via sam user and create a new user account using sudo. Have you successfully created a user account using sam user login?**
2. **Use sam account to reset the password of the root user.**

Understanding permissions on files

The users and the groups have access permissions on some set of files. By default, a regular user can only access the files that are created by them. A user has all the right to create and delete the files inside their home directory. They can also create files at other locations if appropriate permissions on the respective directory are set. By default, besides the home directory, all users are allowed to create files under the **/tmp** directory also. They can do anything with the file that they create either in his home directory or in any other location. They are called the owner of the file. To access other files that are not owned by them, appropriate permissions should be given to the file. Each file has an owner and group owner. It is possible for the user to access the file if they are the owner of that file or are the member of the same group to which the file belongs.

Access rights on a file or a directory are managed by three sets of permissions:

- **read**: Read permission on a file allows users to read the contents of a file or a directory. Read permission is represented by the `r` character.
- **write**: Write allows the users or groups to write to the file or directory. Write permission is represented by the `w` character. Write permission on directory means to add or remove files in the directory.
- **execute**: The meaning of **execute** differs for a file and a directory. In terms of a file, it allows the users to execute the contents, and in terms of a directory, it allows the users to access the contents. Any file can only be executed if it has **execute** permission. **Execute** permission is represented by the `x` character.

Each of these permissions can be given to a file either individually or in conjunction with each other. The file permissions to **read**, **write** and **execute** are given at three levels:

- **user**: User is a single user who is the owner of the file. User owner is represented by the `u` character.
- **group:** Group is the group owner of the file. Group owner is represented by the `g` character.
- **Others**: They are users that are not the owner of the file and do not belong to the group to which the file belongs. The access permissions of **other users** on the same file are determined at the third level. **Other users** are represented by the `o` character.

Thus, access rights of a user on a file are determined by two factors: the sets of permissions given to files, and the assigned user owner and group owner of the file. Users can perform actions on these files according to the set permissions.

Default permissions

Let's create a file in your home directory and verify what default permissions are given to this file. In *Figure 6.13*, the **`touch`** command is used to create a file named **`xyz`**. To check the file permission, the **`ls -l`** command is used. The first field in the output determines the permission bits set on the file. Let's extract the first field here:

```
-rw-rw-r–
```

```
[vishesh@192 ~]$ touch xyz
[vishesh@192 ~]$ ls -l xyz
-rw-rw-r--. 1 vishesh vishesh 0 Sep 25 03:55 xyz
[vishesh@192 ~]$
```

***Figure 6.13:** Permission bits of a regular file*

We know that first '-' specifies that the current listing is a regular file. For a directory, it contains a **d** character. Leaving the first bit, the rest of the bits in the first field specify the file permissions in multiple groups of three bits. In a group, the first bit always refers to **read permission**, the second bit always refers to **write permission**, and the third bit always refers to **execute permission**. A '-' in any of the bit's place means that the respective permission is not set. Leaving the first character, following are the three groups extracted from the first field that specifies permissions at three levels:

- **rw-**: The first group of three bits determines the permission at user owner level. The owner of the file can read and write on the file. The third bit contains a '-'. This bit is reserved for execute permission. A '-' in the place of **x** means that no permission is set at that place. The file cannot be executed because it doesn't have **x** bit set. The file owner can set the execute bit if required.
- **rw-**: The second group determines the permission at group owner level. The group owner of the file can read and write on the file.
- **r--**: The third group determines the permission for **other users**. **Other users** are those users who are neither the owner of the file nor members of the group which owned the file. **Other users** can only read the contents of the file.

Now, it's time to view the default permission of a directory on creation. So, create a directory in your home directory and look at its default sets of permissions:

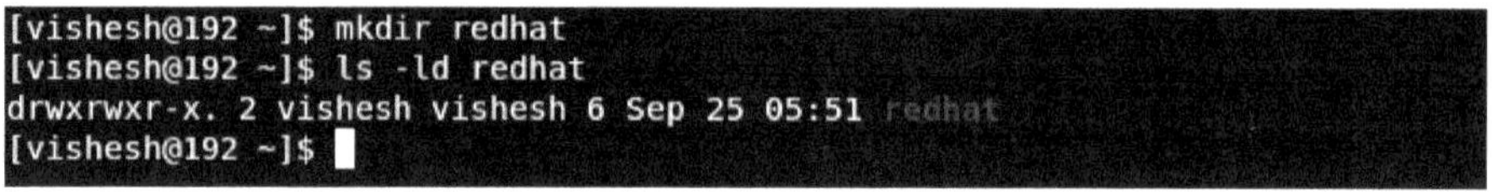

```
[vishesh@192 ~]$ mkdir redhat
[vishesh@192 ~]$ ls -ld redhat
drwxrwxr-x. 2 vishesh vishesh 6 Sep 25 05:51 redhat
[vishesh@192 ~]$
```

Figure 6.14: Default permission sets of the newly created directory

In *Figure 6.14*, a new directory is created and the **ls -ld** command is used to look at the directory information. Dividing the first field (leaving the first **d** character) in three groups, we get the following:

- **rwx**: The first group refers to the user owner. The user owner can **read** and **write** in a directory. They can also access the contents of a directory as they have **execute** permission on it.
- **rwx**: The second group refers to group owner. The group owner also has all sets of permissions on the directory.
- **r-x**: The third group refers to **other users**. Others have only **read** and **execute** permissions on the directory. This is not writable to others.

If you see a group of 3 dash '---', it means that no permission is set for that level.

A. (dot) in the last bit of the first field, as shown in *Figure 6.14*, means that SELinux security context is set for the file.

Octal representation of file permissions

We have seen the character or symbolic representation of the file permissions in the form of **rwx**. File permissions can also be represented by **octal notations**. The following octal values are used to represent file permissions:

- Execute refers to 1
- Write refers to 2
- Read refers to 4

These permission bits, when combined in a group, determine the permissions at all access levels. Use the **stat** command on the file that you just created in your home directory.

```
[vishesh@192 ~]$ stat xyz
  File: xyz
  Size: 0               Blocks: 0          IO Block: 4096   regular empty file
Device: fd02h/64770d    Inode: 662164      Links: 1
Access: (0664/-rw-rw-r--)  Uid: ( 1000/ vishesh)   Gid: ( 1000/ vishesh)
Context: unconfined_u:object_r:user_home_t:s0
Access: 2022-09-25 03:55:58.908915661 -0400
Modify: 2022-09-25 03:55:58.908915661 -0400
Change: 2022-09-25 03:55:58.908915661 -0400
 Birth: 2022-09-25 03:55:58.908915661 -0400
```

***Figure 6.15**: Output of stat command on a regular file*

In *Figure 6.15*, notice the access field. This field displays the access details of the file. Here, it is **0664/-rw-rw-r--**. Thus, the default **octal notation** for a regular file is 0664. Leaving the first digit 0, 664 is the file permission. The first digit, which is 0 here, refers to special permission bits that we will learn about in *Chapter 8, Security and Networking in Linux*. Among the remaining values, the first octal value 6 applies to user owner, the second octal value applies to group owner, and the third octal value applies to others.

To create the permission in **octal notation**, you have to perform some simple calculations, according to the following table:

Character representation	Octal Value	Explanation
rw-	4+2=6	
r-x	4+1=5	
rwx	4+2+1=7	All permissions
-wx	2+1=3	
---	0	No permission

***Table 6.2**: Octal notation of file permissions*

Table 6.2 displays the octal values for sets of permissions. **rw-** is represented by octal value 6 (4 for read + 2 for write), and **r-x** is represented by octal value 5(**4** for **r** + **1** for **x**). Similarly, **rwx** is represented as 7 in **octal notation**, and **-wx** is represented as 3.

Thus, if we break default permission 664 into three groups, it would be interpreted as follows:

- `6`: User owner has **read** and **write** permissions on the file.
- `6`: Group owner has **`read`** and **write** permissions on the file.
- `4`: **Other users** have only **read** permission on the file; they cannot write on and **execute** the file.

Default **Octal notation** for a directory is: 0775. Leaving 0, the **octal notation** for actual permission is 775. This octal value would be interpreted in the same way as the **octal notation** for the file. Its character representation thus becomes **`rwxrwxr-x`**. The character notation can be divided into three groups:

- `rwx`: It refers to all permissions for user owner. It is represented by octal value 7, the first number in the default **octal notation** (775) of a directory.
- `rwx`: It refers to all permissions for group owner. It is represented by octal value 7, the second number in the default **octal notation** (775) of a directory.
- `r-x`: It refers to read and execute. It is represented by octal value 5, the third number in the default **octal notation** (775) of a directory.

Base permissions and umask

Base permission is different from the default permissions that are assigned to newly created files and directories. The default permission of a file and a directory that we have read so far is based on base permission and **umask**.

Base permission of a directory is **`777 (drwxrwxrwx)`** and of a file is **`666 (-rw-rw-rw-)`**.

The user file-creation mode mask (**`umask`**) is a variable that controls how file permissions are set for newly created files and directories. The **`umask`** automatically removes permissions from the base permission value to increase the overall security of a Linux system.

Default **`umask`** for the standard user is **`0002`** and that for a **`root`** user is 0022.

The first bit of the **`umask`** is, again, the special permission bit that we will read about in *Chapter 8, Security and Networking in Linux*. Leaving the first bit of the **`umask`**, the next three bits represent the permission bits that are subtracted from the base permissions to assign the default permissions to the file and directory. Among the last three bits, the first bit represents the permission of user owner, the second bit represents the permission of group owner, and the last bit represents the permission for others.

As we have learnt that base permission of a file is 666 and **umask** for standard user is 002, the default permission of the file would yield 666-002=664. In symbolic notation, it is the same as **`-rw-rw-r--`**.

Similarly, base permission of a directory is 777 and **umask** for standard user is 002; the default permission of directory would yield as 777-002=775. In symbolic notation it is same as `-rw-rw-r-x`.

If **umask** is set to 000, then all permissions, 777, will be assigned to file. It means that no permission bits are subtracted from the base permission. Note that, by default, regular files are not given execute permission unless explicitly assigned.

Viewing and setting the umask

To view the **umask**, use the following command:

```
$umask -S
```

The preceding command displays the **umask** in symbolic notation. Type the following to display the **umask** in **octal notation**:

```
$umask
```

If you want to change the default permissions that are given to newly created files and directories, you must change **`umask`** in the **`/etc/login.defs`** file. The **`umask`** setting in **`/etc/bashrc`** is related to non-login shell. User-specific **`umask`** value is set in the **`.bashrc`** file that resides in each user's home directory. Add the following line in the **`.bashrc`** file if you want to set **`umask`** for a user:

```
umask <octal value>
```

Modifying file permissions

The default file permissions have to change according to one's requirement. To change file and directory permissions, the **`chmod`** command is used. This utility can change file permissions using **octal notation** or symbolic value notation. The **`chmod`** command can change the file permissions in three ways:

- **Adding new permission using the + operator**: To fill any empty permission bit, the **+** operator is used.
- **Removing an existing permission using the – operator** : To remove any set permission bit, the `'-'` operator is used. It will then replace the permission bit to a dash `(-)`, meaning empty permission bit.
- **Assigning new permissions using the = operator:** The `'='` operator is used to remove the older set of permission and assign new sets of permissions.

The previous operations can be performed at the following levels:

- **User owner** : The `u` character value is used when using symbolic notation. **u** is used to change the permission of user owner only.

- **Group owner**: The **g** character value is used when using symbolic notation. **g** is used to change the permission of group owner only.
- **Others:** The **o** character value is used when using symbolic notation. **o** is used when you want to change the permission of **other users** only.
- **All:** The **a** character value is used when using symbolic notation. **a** is used when you want to change the permission for all the mentioned levels together.

Using the chmod command

A user can **read**, **write**, **execute** the file and modify the permission of the files owned by them. They cannot change the permission of the file that are not owned by them. A root user can change any other user's file permissions. The **chmod** command can be used modify any permission bit for any level. This section will demonstrate some of the usages of the **chmod** command.

- **Removing a permission bit**

  If you want to remove a permission bit from a file, use the following syntax:

  ```
  chmod <level>-<permission bit to remove> <absolute path of the file>
  ```

  By default, **other users** have **read** permission on the file. Let's remove this permission by using the **chmod** as follows:

  ```
  $chmod o-r xyz
  ```

  The preceding command uses the **-** operator to remove read permission (**r**) from others (**o**) for the **xyz** file. You can verify the same using the **ls -l** or **stat** command.

  ```
  [vishesh@192 ~]$ ls -l xyz
  -rw-rw----. 1 vishesh vishesh 0 Sep 25 03:55 xyz
  ```

  One or more levels as well as one or more permission bits can be combined to change multiple permissions at multiple levels at one go. The following example provides read and write permissions to **other users** on the **xyz** file:

  ```
  $chmod o+rw xyz
  ```

  To remove all permissions from group and others, use the following:

  ```
  $chmod go-rwx xyz
  ```

  To remove **read** and **execute** from **other users** for the **redhat** directory that we created in the earlier section, use the following:

  ```
  $chmod o-rw redhat
  ```

  To verify the permission of the **redhat** directory, use the **ls -ld** command. To remove all the permissions from a file, use the following:

  ```
  $chmod a-rwx redhat
  ```

- **Adding a permission bit**

  To add execute permission to the **`xyz`** file for owner level, use the following:

  ```
  $chmod u+x xyz
  ```

  To provide all the permissions to a file, use the following:

  ```
  chmod ugo+rwx xyz
  ```

  The previous command will provide **read**, **write** and **execute** permissions to all the users on the **`xyz`** file. Thus, this file is world accessible now. Since this is not safe from the security perspective, immediately remove the extra permission.

  If a file or directory already has the specified permission bit set or is unset, the **`chmod`** command does not apply on those bits.

- **To set absolute permission**

  To provide **`rwx`** to all the users on the **`redhat`** directory, use the following:

  ```
  $chmod a=rwx redhat
  ```

  The preceding directory will give all the permissions to all the users. In **octal notation**, it will be 777.

  To provide **read** permission to **other users** on the **`xyz`** file, use the following:

  ```
  chmod o=r xyz
  ```

  All the other permissions to **other users** would automatically be removed.

  So far, we have learnt to modify the permissions using symbolic notation. You can also modify the permission using **octal notation**. The **+** or **-** operator cannot be used here. For example, use the following to provide only **read** and **write** permissions to the owner and remove all the values from group and **other users**:

  ```
  $chmod 600 xyz
  ```

  This is just like mentioning absolute permission for a file or a directory. To give all permission to the **`redhat`** directory, use the following:

  ```
  $chmod 777 redhat
  ```

Conclusion

Managing users and their access rights on file is one of the fundamental tasks of a Linux system administrator. Each file has a user owner and a group owner. The owner of a file can do anything with the file. Other users should not be allowed to see the files that do not belong to them. The root user can see any user's file and can do anything with their files. To implement file security, only a limited set of privileges are assigned to the file. If other users are not required to see the contents of files that are not owned by them, restrictions are placed at the file level by modifying the file permissions using the **`chmod`** command. Each user belongs to a private group. Besides this, users can be added to supplementary groups if required, so that they can enjoy all the privileges that are assigned to the group to which they belong. Root is the account of high privileges and carries high risk. This account should not be accessed by everyone. It should be protected and used only when necessary. Instead, the system administrator can create a regular user account and assign regular admin task-related privileges to this account; the use of this account can be made to perform system admin tasks. To summarize, the principle of least privilege should be followed to achieve the best security.

In the next chapter, we will learn how to interact with bash shell and how to write simple to complex scripts.

References

https://access.redhat.com/documentation/en-us/red_hat_enterprise_linux/9/html/configuring_basic_system_settings/assembly_managing-file-permissions_configuring-basic-system-settings#user-file-creation-mode-mask_assembly_managing-file-permissions

Join our book's Discord space

Join the book's Discord Workspace for Latest updates, Offers, Tech happenings around the world, New Release and Sessions with the Authors:

https://discord.bpbonline.com

CHAPTER 7

Interacting with Bash Shell and Scripting

Introduction

Shell is a beautiful piece of the Linux operating system that made Linux loved by all. It is an important pillar that keeps Linux/Unix the most preferable OS. It sits as an agent between you and the kernel and executes any task on the system. Shell allows you to do anything on a Linux system. When you open a terminal and type the **ps** command, you will find that the process named **bash** is always running, and that process is your shell. So, bash is just the name of your shell that is, by default, available in RHEL9.0. Your Linux system may support many shell flavors, such as **Korn**, **C**, and **Bourne shells**. This book focuses on bash shell only.

Bash acts as a command interpreter that accepts commands from you, interprets them, and then submits them to the kernel for execution. Bash shell also provides a default but flexible working environment for your task that you can customize according to your needs. Besides, bash provides essential programming features and various programming constructs. So, you can also use it as a programming language. To use bash to your benefit, you must understand its basic functionality and the various features that it provides. This chapter tells you about bash shell, its capabilities, and how to interact with it. It also demonstrates how you can use programming features in bash and write beautiful shell scripts to make your life easier.

Structure

In this chapter, we will cover the following topics:

- Introducing Bash
- Bash default environment
- Bash shell facilities
- Bash scripting
- Here document
- Debugging shell script
- Awk revisited

Objectives

By the end of this chapter, you should have a comprehensive understanding of the bash shell and various methods to interact with it. You should gain insights into the shell's default environment and learn how to modify it according to your requirements. Moreover, you should acquire the skills to perform a wide range of operations within your shell, from simple tasks to complex operations. Additionally, you should be able to write scripts efficiently, enabling you to automate various tasks on your Linux machine. Lastly, you should develop proficiency in writing awk programs, further expanding your capabilities to process and manipulate data effectively.

Introducing Bash

Bash shell is abbreviated as GNU bourne-again shell. It includes some useful features of other shells, such as Korn, C, and Bourne shells. The bash shell starts and runs in the background as soon as you log in. Any command you execute after that will give rise to a new shell called **child shell**, which will inherit its parent shell's environment. You can also spawn a new child shell by typing bash[1] in your terminal. Execute the bash command followed by the **ps** command, and you will see two bash processes running. This can be descended to further levels. Thus, many levels of parent-child relationship exist in a terminal session. Any new program that you type in the terminal will give further rise to a new shell process. Then, the image of the new shell process will be overwritten with the image of the new program[2]. Then the program is executed.

---

1 *Bash is name of your shell program which runs via /bin. It has a symbolic link named sh. So, instead of bash, you can also type sh command. Both will give rise to bash shell.*

2 *Here, exec system call is in action which is actually responsible to replace the current image of the shell process with the new program image.*

Bash shell is very user-friendly. You can easily modify your profile or working environment by editing text-based configuration files. When we type commands on the terminal, you give instructions to the bash shell. This is the interactive way of using the shell. We can also use the shell non-interactively by writing shell scripts. A shell script is a group of instructions written in a plain text file that can be executed like any built-in command. If you have some repetitive tasks to perform regularly, you can automate this via shell script. You can write any simple or complex shell script if you understand the shell's programming features. In the next section, we will first understand the bash shell's features and its default configuration settings and see how you can modify the bash's configuration. In the later section, we will view bash shells programmatically and learn to write shell scripts.

Bash default environment

Bash gives you a working environment where you execute your commands, though you can customize your environment according to your needs. The working environment includes your terminal settings, history settings, user profile, command aliases, built-in environment variables, and so on. You can also redefine how wild-card characters and redirection operators work. The pre-defined variables bash supports are called **environment variables,** as they define the behavior of the commands you execute. They are also called **global variables** as they are always made available to the child shell recursively at all levels. We have encountered many environment variables in the earlier chapters, such as home and path. And we also know that any variable in the bash shell can be accessed by prefixing the variable name with the **$** symbol. But you are not restricted to using global variables. You have all the freedom to create and use user-defined variables. User-defined variables are created using the following syntax:

```
<variable_name>=<value>
```

There should not be any spaces around the **=** sign. A variable created this way is called a **local variable,** as it is only available to the current shell. Any child shell created after that cannot access local variables defined in the parent shell. To make any user-defined variables available to the child shell, we must make it global. Any variable defined in the current shell can be made global using the **export** command. Exporting these user-defined variables using the **export** command in the current shell will make them available to the child shells at all the further levels.

Let us create a variable and make it global, as shown in *Figure 7.1*.

```
[vishesh@localhost ~]$ vara=10
[vishesh@localhost ~]$ varb=20
[vishesh@localhost ~]$ export vara
[vishesh@localhost ~]$ bash
[vishesh@localhost ~]$ echo $vara
10
[vishesh@localhost ~]$ echo $varb
```

***Figure 7.1:** Creating local and global variables*

In *Figure 7.1*, two variables, **vara** and **varb**, are created in the parent shell, and **vara** is exported only. Then, a new child shell is spawned using the **bash** command. In further commands, you can notice that the value of **vara** is echoed in the child shell, but the value of **varb** is not, as it is not exported. Exporting a variable makes it global and can be accessed like any environment variable. Vara is available globally up to all levels downward to child shells. A variable can also be exported during its creation, as follows:

```
export vara=10
```

The above-mentioned command creates a global variable named **vara**.

Any global or local variable can be reset by its creator shell only. The child shell can read global variables, but it cannot reset them. Resetting it in the child shell will create a new variable having the same name in the child shell and make it locally available. Its value is not visible to the parent. In *Figure 7.2*, a global variable **varc** is created and assigned a value of **10**. Then, a new child shell is created. The child shell can access the value of a global variable. It tries to reset the value of **varc** to **12**. Exiting the child shell does not make the new value of **varc** available to the parent, as the new value of **varc** is only locally available to the child shell. Refer to the following figure:

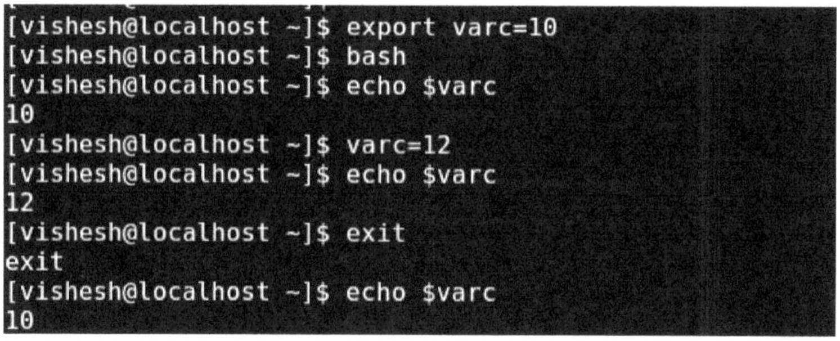

```
[vishesh@localhost ~]$ export varc=10
[vishesh@localhost ~]$ bash
[vishesh@localhost ~]$ echo $varc
10
[vishesh@localhost ~]$ varc=12
[vishesh@localhost ~]$ echo $varc
12
[vishesh@localhost ~]$ exit
exit
[vishesh@localhost ~]$ echo $varc
10
```

***Figure 7.2**: Demo showing restricted access of global variables to child shell:*

Child shell can only read into the value of the global variable; it cannot change it

Typing the **set** command on the terminal will show you the list of all the available variables, global and local. You also have the **env** and **printenv** commands that display only global variables, pre-defined and user defined.

Bash shell provides many pre-defined variables you can reset according to your needs. *Table 7.1* lists some useful pre-defined variables, along with their meaning:

Variable Name	Description
BASH	Current shell in use
BASHOPTS	The list of options that are turned on by built-in program named *shopt*[3]
BASH_VERSION	Current bash version in use

[3] *Shopt command is discussed later.*

Variable Name	Description
PPID	Parent pid of the current bash shell
PROMPT_ COMMAND	Stores command to be executed just before the shell displays the prompt
PATH	Stores the sequence of paths where the binary of the commands is to be searched
PWD	Stores the path of the current directory
OSTYPE	Stores the name of the operating system
PS1	Determines the primary prompt
PS2	Determines the secondary prompt, which is shown as the line continuation character when we press the Enter key without completing the command line
PS4	Used to echo the command line when shell debugging is used
PS0	Executed before the command displays its result
UID	Stores the UID of the user who is currently logged in to the terminal.
USERNAME	Stores the name of the user who is currently logged-in to the terminal.
USER	This also stores the name of the user who is currently logged-in to the terminal unless you have executed sudo command to elevate your privileges. Thus, the difference between $USER and $USERNAME environment variables is that $USER stores the effective user id while the latter stores the real user id. [4]
SHELL	Path of the shell in use
LOGNAME	Stores the name of the currently logged-in user in the terminal.
MAIL	Stores the path of the user's mailbox
MAILCHECK	Determines how often to check for the new mail in the $MAIL; default is 60 seconds
Lines	Determines the terminal width
LANG	Determines the system language
IFS	Determines the character to be used for word-separator in the command line as well as when taking input by bash
HOSTNAME	Stores the hostname of the system
HOSTTYPE	Determines the processor type
HOME	Stores the home directory of the user
HISTFILESIZE	Determines the size of bash history file

[4] *Effective user id changes if user executes sudo command to elevate his privileges or he execute any program that require privileged user's permissions.*

Variable Name	Description
`HISTFILE`	Stores the path of history file
`HISTCONTROL`	Stores the options related to history
`EUID`	Stores the effective user id
`DISPLAY`	Used for Xserver display; to be covered in *Chapter12, Graphical User Interface*
`COLUMNS`	Determines the number of columns in the terminal
`SHELLOPTS`	Contains a list of enabled shell options, as determined by the built-in program named *set*.

***Table 7.1:** List of a few environment variables*

You can reset all the environment variables using the **`variablename=value`** syntax. However, read-only variables cannot be reset. **`BASHOPTS`** and **`SHELLOPTS`** are among the few read-only variables among the pre-defined list of environment variables. Any variable can be removed by using the **`unset`** command:

```
unset vara
```

Bash configuration

To change the default environment variable, aliases, and default settings, you need to understand how bash is configured when it first starts. The bash process starts at user login. The first shell that starts on user login is known as **login-shell**. Any other shell that starts after it without any login is called a **non-login shell**. Non-login shell is started when you execute the **`bash`** command on the terminal, run a script, or create a new terminal session. That means the shell that starts without authenticating the user is called a non-login shell. If you are logged in to a Linux machine using the graphical mode, then opening your first terminal would start a non-login shell, as the login shell would already have started when your first GUI window appeared after you authenticated yourself. How will you determine whether your current shell is a login shell or a non-login shell? Use the **`$0`** variable at the terminal prompt; type the following:

```
echo $0
```

If the output renders **`bash`**, then it is a non-login shell. But if you find bash preceding with – as: **`-bash`**, then your shell is a login shell. You can easily find a login shell if you have remotely logged in to a Linux server or if you have you have authenticated to a Linux server using the non-graphical console. You can easily verify this. Just change the target of your box to a **`multi-user.target`**, as we studied in *Chapter 4, Managing Processes and Services in RedHat Linux*.

```
sytemctl isolate multi-user.target
```

And you will switch to text mode. Log in with your user. After you have successfully logged in, type the following:

```
echo $0
-bash
```

Here it is. You see **`-bash`**, as this is the login shell. Type the **`bash`** command again and verify the value of **`$0`**. What do you see? Now, you can switch yourself back to **`graphical.target`**.

Bash initialization files

When you first log in, various bash-related configuration files initialize your shell, thus determining your environment. There are two groups of initialization files: **profile files** and **rc files**. Each file has two levels of versions: system-wide file and user-specific file. System-wide profile and rc file reside in the **`/etc`** directory, while user-specific files reside under the user's home directory. Let us discuss the two groups of files.

/etc/profile : system-wide profile file

`/etc/profile` stores the system-wide environment settings. This file is read when the shell is identified as a login shell. It stores the environment settings that applies to all the users upon login. This file does not get executed when non-login shell starts. Thus, if you want to make changes in any environment variable and want to persist it so that the same can be applied to all the users upon login, you can put your changes in this file.

~/.bash_profile : user-specific profile file

This file corresponds to system-wide **`/etc/profile`** and stores user-specific environment settings. This is a hidden file stored under each user's home directory. After **`/etc/profile`** runs, the **`.bash_profile`** file is searched under the user's home directory and is executed if it exists. Thus, this file is also executed on each log in.

.bashrc : user-specific rc file

This is a hidden file stored under each user's home directory. This file stores user-specific functions and aliases. For each new non-login shell session, the user's home directory is searched for **`.bashrc`**, and it is executed once found.

/etc/bashrc : system-wide rc file

It stores system-wide functions and aliases that apply to all the users. **`.bashrc`** invokes **`/etc/bashrc`** for each new non-login shell session. Any aliases that you want to make available system-wide can be stored here. **`/etc/profile`** also executes the **`/etc/bashrc`** file at the end so that all the settings given here can be applied to login sessions as well.

.bash_logout : user-specific logout file

This file is searched for under each user's home directory when the user logs out. It stores commands to execute when the user logs out.

Changing configuration in bash

If you want to make changes in default environments that persist across logins and reboots, you can make changes to any of the bash initialization files discussed in the previous section. Let us change the **HISTSIZE** environment variable to **500** so that this change becomes available each time you log in.

Open **.bash_profile** under your home directory and add the following in the last line:

HISTSIZE=500

Your .bash_profile should look like:

```
# .bash_profile
# Get the aliases and functions
if [ -f ~/.bashrc ]; then
        . ~/.bashrc
fi
# User specific environment and startup programs
HISTSIZE=500
```

You do not need to export this environment variable as HISTSIZE environment variable among others, has already been exported by the shell before reaching this line. Do not bother about other contents available in this file as we will study shell scripting later in this chapter. The new value of **HISTSIZE** will be available only to new log-ins, and thereafter to all the child shells. To apply the changes made in **.bash_profile** in any of the running sessions, just execute the file in that session using the following command:

source .bash_profile

or

. .bash_profile

The **.** (dot) command or **source** command reads the given file and executes all the commands written inside it in the session where the above command is executed.

If you want to make any new setting available to all the users upon log in, make the entry in the **/etc/profile** file. Add the new setting of the **HISTFILE** environment variable that we used in the earlier example at the bottom of this file.

Let us change your primary prompt using the **PS1** environment variable in your current session. To make changes to your prompt, various escape sequences are used. The default primary prompt is as follows:

[\u@\h \w]\$

Where:

- **\u** refers to username.
- **\h** refers to the hostname up to the first dot(.).
- **\w** refers to the present working directory and is changed according to your change in the present working directory.
- **\$** represents the **$** symbol if effective user is non-root.

Let us change your primary prompt that displays the current date and time as well as the present working directory, as follows:

```
PS1='<\d \t \w>'
```

After you press the *Enter* key, the prompt would become the following:

```
<Tue Feb 07 11:25:18 ~>
```

This is clear that **\d** refers to the date, **\t** refers to the current time in 24-hour format, and **\w** refers to the present working directory. Thus, your prompt will change every second with the change in clock time, and you will also notice changes in the present working directory as you change into another directory.

This change is available only to the current bash process and not to any child shell that is created thereafter. You must export it with the **export** command to pass this variable to future child shells, as follows:

```
export PS1='<\d \t \W>'
```

To make this change persistent, you must add this line to one of the configuration files of bash. And PS1 will go to **~/.bashrc** and not to **~/.bash_profile**. Add the previously mentioned PS1 related line to **.bash_profile** and verify yourself. Your PS1-related setting will not apply if you add it on **.bash_profile** file[5]. So, add the line to **.bashrc**, and all the new sessions thereafter will take this change. Open a new terminal and verify your new prompt. To apply this setting for all the users, add this line to the **/etc/bashrc** file. System-wide **bashrc** and user's specific **.bashrc** file run for each new non-login session, while changes to the system-wide profile file and user's specific profile file apply only when the user logs in.

To apply any change made in **~/.bashrc** or **/etc/bashrc** immediately to your current bash process, type the following:

```
. .bashrc
```

Or

```
source bashrc
```

Let us use **.bashrc** file to store aliases. We will create the following alias in user-specific **.bashrc** that resides under a user's home directory:

```
alias wcl='wc -l'
```

[5] *But same does not apply to other environment variables as we have seen in our earlier example when we add HISTSIZE environment variable to profile file.*

Add the mentioned line at the bottom of the **.bashrc** file. Any change in **.bashrc** will immediately apply for each new session created thereafter.

If you want to bring a new global variable into the picture every time a user logs in. You have to put the variable setting in the **.bash_profile** file. Suppose you have added a new global variable MSG to the **.bash_profile** file by typing the following:

```
MSG="hello"
```

The mentioned command creates a user-defined variable named MSG. Variable names are case-insensitive but as a standard, they are generally created in all caps. We have not exported *MSG* variable in our **.bash_profile** yet, so change will be visible only to all the login bash shells and not to any child shell or non-login shells. To apply the same to child shells, you must export it in your **.bash_profile** file.

Bash shell facilities

After we have understood how bash is configured, we will see some of the facilities provided by bash except programming facility, which is the subject of our next section. Knowing these facilities will help you take the most out of your bash shell.

Redirection facility and various metacharacters

We have learnt about various wild cards and metacharacters that are available for bash shell. Bash also provides us with a redirection operator, which redirects standard input, standard output, and standard error from the default terminal to the specified disk file or to pipe operator.

Logical && and || operator to execute the commands

The logical **&&** and **||** operator can be used to execute two commands together. We saw the **&&** operator in action in *Chapter 3, Knowing Linux Commands*. The logical **&&** operator executes the second command only if the first command exits successfully and returns **0** status. The **||** operator works like the logical **OR** operator, which executes the second command only if the first command returns false. The latter operator means either execute command **A** or command **B**.

```
ls BOOK* || echo "error in finding file"
```

The given command will print the message **"error in finding file"** only if the **ls** command returns an error.

Exit status of each executed command

Each command returns an exit status that can range from 0 to 255. When a command executes successfully, its return status is always **0**. If any command fails, it may return a non-zero value depending on the error. If the command terminates with a fatal error, it returns the exit value of 128+<signal number>. Suppose you press *Ctrl+C* in the middle of the command's execution, the command receives signal number 2(**INTERRUPT** signal) and thus, returns **130** exit value. You can see the signals list by issuing the **kill -l** command. To check the exit value of the last command executed, issue the following:

```
echo $?
```

You can also pass exit value **n** to the **exit** command to return the specified **n**. We will the use **exit** command with **n** in our shell scripts.

Changing shell options using set and shopt

We have learnt about the **set** command, which is used to customize shell environment and enable and disable many settings. We also have looked at **shopt**, which is available in newer versions of bash and is also used to turn on and off many bash-related settings. Many settings that are manipulated by the **set** command are also available to be manipulated by **shopt**. The settings that are turned on by **shopt** are listed in the **BASHOPTS** environment variable. Typing **shopt** will show you all the options available and display whether they are on or off. Type this:

```
shopt -p
```

It will list the current bash settings, along with the **-u** or **-s** switch, as follows:

```
shopt -u autocd
shopt -u assoc_expand_once
shopt -u cdable_vars
shopt -u cdspell
shopt -u checkhash
shopt -u checkjobs
shopt -u compat44
shopt -s complete_fullquote
..........output truncated.......
```

The given output signifies the commands that can be executed to recreate the same setting. **-u** indicates that the option is unset, and **-s** indicates that the option is set. To reverse any of the option settings, just reverse the switch. For example, to turn **cdable_vars** to on, issue the following:

```
shopt -s cdable_vars
```

This will make the argument given to the **cd** command be treated as a variable name and will expand this variable if the specified directory in **cd** does not exist.

A few other options are listed here:

- **cdspell**: Minor errors in the spelling of the **cd** directory are ignored. For example, if you have missed a letter in the directory name, the **cd** command ignores that and switches to the directory that matches the most.
- **dotglob**: If enabled, it also matches the filenames that begin with a dot(.), when using globs. It does not include special filenames "**.**" and "**..**".
- **interactive_comments**: If set, comments starting with **#** are allowed in the command line.
- **nocaseglob**: If set, it matches filenames ignoring the casing.
- **xpg_echo**: If set, **echo** in bash does not require the **-e** option to expand backslash sequences.
- **autocd** : If this is set and a directory name is given as a command, it **cd** into that directory.

Special bash shell parameters

The Bash provides some special environment variables, as listed here:

- **$$**: Stores the current shell's pid
- **$!**: Stores the pid of the last background job
- **$?**: Stores the exit value of the last command
- **$0**: Stored value determines whether the shell is a login shell or non-login shell

Let us know the pid of your current shell. Use the **$$** built-in variable:

```
echo $$
3435
```

This is the same pid that you get after executing the **ps** command.

Read-only variables

Any variables that we have created so far can be reset or unset. We have the facility of creating read-only variables as well. You have the **readonly** command to accomplish that. Just precede your usual variable assignment statement with **readonly**, as follows:

```
readonly ABC=hh
```

And **ABC** is created as a local **readonly** variable.

```
unset ABC
-bash: unset: ABC: cannot unset: readonly variable
```

You cannot unset or reassign a read-only variable. The same read-only rule applies to global variables. We also have the **declare** command to work with variables. Simply typing declare in the command line provides the list of all the global and local variables. **declare** can also be used to create a new variable, as follows:

```
declare ans='y'
echo $ans
y
```

Here, **ans** is a local variable to the current shell and is also displayed in the **set** command output. To make it global or environment variable, use the **-x** option when creating variables, as follows:

```
declare -x ans
```

The mentioned command will change the attributes of the **ans** variable to global. The **declare** command also offers the **-r** option, which makes the variable read-only.

Do it yourself

1. Type the following:

   ```
   ls *.bash*.
   ```

   Does the mentioned command match any hidden files? Now, turn the **dotglob** option to on. Again, issue the mentioned **ls** command. What do you see?

2. Execute the following command:

   ```
   cd #this moves you to your home directory
   ```

   Does the mentioned command execute successfully? Check the current value of **interactive_comments** by issuing this:

   ```
   shopt -p interactive_comments
   ```

   Disable **interactive_comments** if it is enabled.

   Issue the mentioned **cd** command again. What do you get? Switch this setting to its original mode.

3. Execute a large command, say, the following:

   ```
   find / -name mo* 2>/dev/null
   ```

   And then immediately press *Ctrl+c* to interrupt it in the middle. Check the value of $.

   Note the value of the PS2 environment variable. Now, issue the following command as specified:

   ```
   echo "this is \[ENTER]
   world of Linux"
   ```

The first line is terminated by a backslash (\), followed by the *Enter* key. What continuation prompt string do you get when you type the command line? Now, change the PS2 environment variable to %%. Now, type the mentioned command again. What do you see in the secondary prompt?

Bash scripting

In this section, we will see shell as a programming language. Shell script helps system administrator to automate most of their regular tasks, helping them focus on other non-regular but important and critical tasks. Here, bash acts as a program interpreter, which reads the instructions from the program file one line at a time, interprets it and executes it. If a line contains an error, it displays the error on the standard output and then continues to the next line for its execution. Usually, a shell script filename ends in **.sh**, but this is not necessary.

Let us create a script file **demo.sh**, as shown in *Figure 7.3*:

```
#!/bin/bash

# this script will print values of selected environment variables.

date #this line prints current system data and time

#Below few lines echoed the values of some of the environment variables.

echo "HOME is set to $HOME"
echo "PATH is set to $PATH"
echo "USER is set to $USER"
echo "current shell is $SHELL"
```

Figure 7.3: *Simple bash script*

The first line of the shell script in *Figure 7.3* is called an **interpreter line**, which always starts with **#!**. It specifies the shell to use as interpreter for script execution. If you want to use a shell other than bash, then you can specify the full path of that shell here. The script executes using the specified shell. The second line that starts with **#** is the comment line. Any script or program in any language should be commented properly so that its usages and purpose are understood. There can be a comment for each line of the script file for better understanding. Comments can also be given in the same line, as in line 3 of the script. Line number 3, which contains the **date** command, provides the comment on the same line. Any character after **#** is treated as a comment of the current line. Rest of the lines are very clear. Many **echo** commands are used to print the values of some of the environment variable on the screen.

Now, let us execute our first demo script. You must make it executable before you can execute the **demo.sh** file. So, use the following command:

```
chmod u+x demo.sh
```

The mentioned command adds execute privilege on the **demo.sh** file. To run the script, provide the name of the script along with its location:

```
./demo.sh
```

The mentioned command executes **demo.sh** from the current directory. If your script is located in the current directory, and the directory path is not given in the **PATH** variable, then to execute the script, you must precede the script name with ./, which means *search the script name inside the current directory*. Our script is currently running from our home directory as it resides there. To run script from any location just by invoking it using its name, we have to add the location of the script to our **PATH** environment variable. Let us create a directory called **scripts** and move **demo.sh** to this location:

```
mkdir scripts
mv demo.sh scripts
```

Add the location of your script file in the **PATH** environment variable:

```
PATH=$PATH:/home/vishesh/scripts
```

Now, you can execute your script just like any command. Type the following:

```
demo.sh
```

The **demo.sh** file will be successfully executed. You can store the modified setting of $PATH in your **.bash_profile** file so that the new setting becomes available to all the new logins and across the reboots.

To run any script located inside the current directory without using **./**, you must add dot (.) in the **PATH** environment variable. We will store all the script created in this book to the *scripts* folder so that it will be executed like a command.

Like a command, a shell script also runs with a new child shell. When the script is executed till the end, the control returns to the parent shell. The preceding script can also be executed as follows:

```
bash  demo.sh
```

Using the preceding method, the script can be run in the shell of your choice. Here, we have used bash shell to invoke **demo.sh**. If the script is executed this way, the interpreter line given inside the file is ignored. The preceding command does not require execute permission to execute the script file.

Our **demo.sh** script is very simple, and it does not take any user input or perform any calculations or other operations. The next few sections will help you learn about more features of bash shell that will help you in writing an enhanced script that will perform some useful tasks for you.

Reading user input

If your script requires user input, you can use the **`read`** command, which accepts user input from the keyboard and stores it into a variable so that you can perform some operations on the input. See the script in *Figure 7.4*, which asks for the directory name and displays the number of files residing in the directory:

```
#!/bin/sh

#countfiles.sh display the numner of files residing in th current directory.

#Usage: countfiles.sh

echo -e  "Enter the full path of the directory to see the count of files residing there> \c"
read a                                          # accepts input from the user and store into variable named a.
cd $a                                           # move into the entered directory path
count=`ls|wc -l`
echo "the number of file residing in the selected path is $count"
```

Figure 7.4: Sample bash script showing usage of read command

Note how the script given in *Figure 7.4* is properly commented. The **`countfiles.sh`** script in *Figure 7.4* shows the usage of the **`read`** command, which waits for the user input and accepts it until user the presses *enter* key. Thus, it accepts a line and will split the line into multiple words, with each word separated by the delimiter specified in the IFS environment variable. By default, arguments that read from the keyboard are separated by space or tab character. If you specify multiple space-separated words as input, all the words will be assigned to the variable named **`a`**. The **`cd`** command in the preceding script will fail if you pass many words because the **`cd`** will see it as multiple arguments, but it accepts only one directory path as its argument. Just provide two directory paths as its input and see how this script results in the wrong file count. Error related to the **`cd`** command will be thrown on the standard output, and the further line will be executed. No checks have been given in this script to validate user input. We can enhance the functionality of this script by adding some checks for validating user input. The enhanced script should not print erroneous information count; instead, it should exit with non-zero status if a user does not provide valid input. In the next section, we will learn validation of input data in bash script.

Before proceeding further, let us learn more about the **`read`** command. The **`read`** command may accept multiple arguments, and each argument may be assigned to a separate variable at once. Take a look at this:

`read a b c`

Suppose the user types the following:

```
hello this is linux world
```

The given variables will receive the values as follows:

```
a = "hello",
b = "this"
c = "is linux world"
```

Each word will be assigned to a listed variable in sequence. If the number of words supplied exceeds the specified variable, the last variable will accept all the remaining words. The extra variables will take null data if the number of inputs given is less than the number of specified variables. You can also assign a multi-word argument to any variable by enclosing that in single quotes. The **`read`** command will treat the argument enclosed in single quotes as one argument. Let's see below usage:

```
read a b c
```

Suppose the user keyed in the following:

```
Hello "This is linux world"
```

And then they pressed the *enter* key. The variable **`a`** gets **`Hello`** and variable **`b`** gets **`"This is Linux world"`**, while variable **`c`** receives null.

Evaluating expressions in Bash

In this section, we will discuss how bash evaluates and compares various numerical or string expressions. The **`test`** command is used in shell scripting to evaluate one or more expressions. The following is the list of various comparison operators that are used with the **`test`** command to compare two operands; if there are two numerical variables, namely `a` and `b`, these tests can be performed:

- **$a -eq $b**: Tests whether **`$a`** equals **`$b`**
- **$a -ne $b**: Tests whether **`$a`** is not equal to **`$b`**
- **$a -ge $b**: Tests whether **`$a`** is greater than or equal to **`$b`**
- **$a -gt $b**: Tests whether **`$a`** is greater than **`$b`**
- **$a -le $b**: Tests whether **`$a`** is less than or equal to **`$b`**
- **$a -lt $b**: Tests whether **`$a`** is less than **`$b`**

In the preceding list, **`-eq`**, **`-ne`**, and so on are operators, while the numerical variables are the operand. The listed comparison operators compare two numeric values and return 1 if the comparison is true and 0 if it is false.

If **`str1`** and **`str2`** are two strings, then we can use the following operators to compare them:

- **str1 == str2**: Tests whether **`str1`** equals **`str2`**
- **str1 != str2**: Returns true if **`str1`** is not equal to **`str2`**
- **-n str**: Checks whether length of the string is non-zero
- -z: Returns true if length of string is zero

The listed comparison operators compare two strings and return 1 if the comparison is true and 0 if it is false.

The **test** also provides us with the operators that test the conditions on attributes of the given file. Here are the file test operators:

- **-d file**: Checks whether the file exists and is a directory
- **-e file**: Checks whether the file exists
- **-f file**: Checks whether the file exists and is a regular file
- **-g file**: Checks whether SGID bit is set
- **-r file**: Checks whether you have read permission on files
- **-s file**: Checks whether the file is non-empty
- **-u file**: Checks whether the file has suid bit set
- **-k FILE**: Checks whether the file exists and has sticky bit set
- **-L FILE**: Checks whether the file exists and is a symbolic link
- **-w file**: Checks whether the file is writeable by you
- **-x file**: Checks whether you have executed permission on files
- **-O file**: Checks whether you are the owner of the file
- **-G file**: Checks whether you belong to the same group as the file
- **file1 -nt file2**: Checks whether the file is newer than **file2**
- **file1 -ot file2**: Checks whether file1 is older than **file2**

After testing integer values, strings, or file attributes, we can simply use the value of **$?** to check the exit status of the **test** command. Using the **$?** variable, we determine whether the given condition is true or false, as follows:

```
[vishesh@localhost ~]$ a=10;b=10
[vishesh@localhost ~]$ test $a -eq $b
[vishesh@localhost ~]$ echo $?
0
```

In the preceding sequence of commands, since **a** equals **b**, the **echo** command returns **0** status.

The **test** command can be replaced with **[]** (a pair of square brackets), as follows:

```
[ $a -eq $b ]
```

There should be spaces around **[' and ']**. Let us take an example of string comparison:

```
[ 'hello' == 'hello' ]
```

The preceding command uses the equality operator for string comparison. For equality comparison of two integers, we have used the **-eq** operator.

While performing any operation on a file in your script, you should check for the existence of the file or other file-related attributes. This check is important if you do not want your script to throw file errors.

```
[ -f fruits ]
```

The preceding command checks whether the file named **fruits** is a regular file.

```
[-r fruits ]
```

The preceding command checks whether you have read permission on the given file.

The **test** command also provides you various compound operators to check two conditions, as follows:

```
expression1 -a expression2
```

Here, **-a** signifies the **AND** operator. The preceding expression returns true if both the expressions are true.

```
expression1 -o expression2
```

In the preceding expression , **-o** signifies the logical **OR** operator. It returns 1 if either **expression1** or **expressio2** is true. You can use the **!** operator that negates the given expression, as follows:

```
[ ! -f redhat ]
```

The preceding expression returns true if **redhat** is not a regular file. Similarly, you can negate numerical and string expressions as follows:

```
[ $a -gt 100 -a $a -le 200 ]
```

The preceding command shows how we can use a compound operator to join two conditional expressions.

Arithmetic operations in bash

In *Chapter 3, Knowing Linux Commands*, we looked at the **expr** command to perform athematic calculations. Bash also provides you with another way to perform arithmetic calculations, which is simpler than **expr**; no need for escaping special characters with backslash. The **let** command is easier to use than **expr**. You can provide any arithmetic expressions after the **let** command, as follows:

```
let var1++
let ++var1
let var1--
let --var
let var1+var2
```

```
let var1-var2
let var1*var2
let var1/var2
let var1%var2
```

No spaces are allowed around the operators. The variable name does not need to be preceded by the **$** symbol. Refer to the following command:

```
let i = i + 2
```

It will return the following:

```
bash: let: =: syntax error: operand expected (error token is "=")
```

To avoid the preceding error, you can put the expression in double quotes, as follows:

```
let "i = i + 2"
```

Alternatively, you can avoid any space in the **let** expression, as shown here:

```
let i=i+2
```

Like the **test** command, the **let** command can be written in a simpler way using parentheses, as follows:

```
((expression))
```

Where expression is any arithmetic expression, as follows:

```
((i=i+2))
```

Spaces are allowed anywhere within the parenthesis:

```
(( i = i + 2 ))
```

The preceding command will not return any error and will work as expected.

Do it yourself

1. **Let us write a script that accepts two numbers and calculate their product. Use expr.**
2. **Write another version of the preceding script without using expr.**

Flow control

Usually, a program file is executed from top to bottom in order. You can change the flow of this order if required. Bash provides us with many constructs that control the order of execution of the lines written in the script. If our script is involved in decision-making or uses looping, flow control of the script will change accordingly. In this section, we will study the *if*, *for*, *while*, and *case* constructs.

Validating conditions using if

If your script uses the **if** construct, it will validate certain conditions, and if the conditions evaluate to true, the list of commands is executed. After executing the given list of commands, control comes to the lines written after the **fi** keyword. An **if** block always ends with the **fi** keyword; **if** helps us to use a decision-making approach. We have seen how to test commands to evaluate numerical and string expressions. It results in only true or false status. If we want to take certain actions based on the exit status of the **test** command, we must use the **if** operator. It takes the form given in *Figure 7.5*. The **if** construct may also contain many optional **elif** blocks and an optional **else** block. The main **if** block and each **elif** block contains the **then** keyword, followed by a set of commands. **if** takes an expression, which, if evaluates to true, executes the command set given after the **then** keyword. Refer to *Figure 7.5*, where all the commands after the **then** keyword until the first **elif** keyword are executed if **condition1** given in the **if** line evaluates to true. **Elif** means **else if**, which may be used to provide us with a way for multi-way decision-making. If **condition1** evaluates to false, control comes to the **elif** block, if it exists, and the condition next to the **elif** keyword is evaluated. In *Figure 7.5*, **if condition2** evaluates to true, all the commands from **command1** up to command n are executed until the second **elif** block is reached. The second **elif** block also works the same way. Control comes to this **elif** block if the earlier two conditions are evaluated to be false. If **condition3** evaluates to true, all the commands given after the **then** keyword are executed until the **else** block is reached. Control comes to the **else** block if neither of the earlier conditions is evaluated to be true. All the commands given after the **else** keyword up to the **fi** keyword are executed if control comes to the **else** block. If there is no **elif**, and the **else** blocks and **condition1** evaluates to false, control immediately goes to the line given after the **fi** keyword. Refer to the following figure:

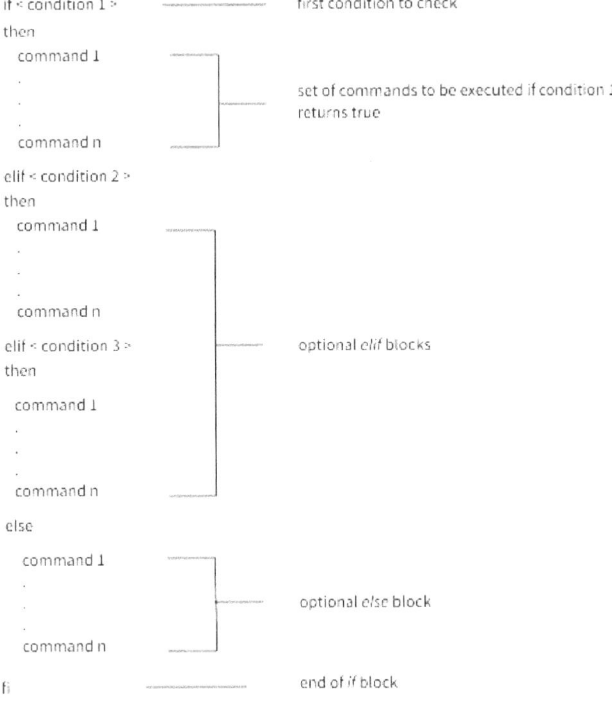
if < condition 1 >
first condition to check
then
command 1
command n
set of commands to be executed if condition 1 returns true
elif < condition 2 >
then
command 1
command n
elif < condition 3 >
then
command 1
command n
optional *elif* blocks
else
command 1
command n
optional *else* block
fi
end of *if* block

***Figure 7.5**: if construct*

Thus, **if** construct may take four forms:

- if-fi
- if-elif-fi
- if-else-fi
- if-elif-else-fi

Figure 7.6 extends our script given in *Figure 7.4* to add input validation. In *Figure 7.6*, after the user supplies their input, it is validated for the number of input words given. The following line counts the number of words in input variable **a**:

```
input=`echo $a|wc -w`
```

```
#!/bin/sh

#countfiles.sh display the numner of files residing in th current directory.

#Usage: countfiles.sh

echo -e  "Enter the full path of the directory to see the count of files residing there> \c"
read a                                            # accepts input from the user and store into variable named a.
input=`echo $a|wc -w`                             # checks the number of words in user's input. If it is more than one word, script will exit.
if [ $input -gt 1 ]
then
echo "you have entered more number of arguments, but cd taked only one"
exit 1                                            # script exists with exit status 1 to the parent
else

# move into the entered directory path
cd $a
count=`ls|wc -l`
echo "the number of file residing in the selected path is $count"
fi
```

Figure 7.6: Script showing usage of the if construct

The *if* construct is used to trigger an action based on the value of the input variable. The **if** command uses the **[** command to test for the given condition. If the given expression evaluates to true, the statements under the **then** block are executed. If the user enters more than one input argument, control enters the **if** block and the **echo** command after the **then** keyword is executed. The next command is **exit**, as follows:

```
exit 1
```

The preceding command returns the **exit** status of **1** to the parent. Thus, the script terminates with the exit status of **1** if a user gives invalid input. If the expression given in the **if** statement evaluates to false, then control comes to the **else** block. The working directory is changed to the path given in the input, and then the count of files is performed and is displayed to the user.

Out script is not up to the mark yet. It may throw an error if the user provides a non-existing directory path or directory name. So, we must perform some more validation on our input data. Let us extend the **if** condition as shown in *Figure 7.7*.

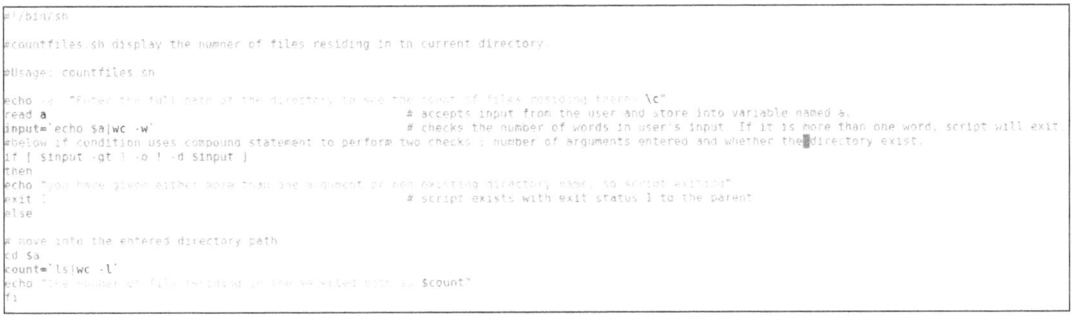

```
#!/bin/sh

#countfiles.sh display the numner of files residing in th current directory.

#Usage: countfiles.sh

echo -e "Enter the full path of the directory to see the count of files residing there: \c"
read a                                      # accepts input from the user and store into variable named a.
input=`echo $a|wc -w`                       # checks the number of words in user's input. If it is more than one word, script will exit.
#below if condition uses compound statement to perform two checks : number of arguments entered and whether the directory exist.
if [ $input -gt 1 -o ! -d $input ]
then
echo "you have given either more than one argument or non existing directory name, so script exiting"
exit 1                                      # script exists with exit status 1 to the parent
else

# move into the entered directory path
cd $a
count=`ls|wc -l`
echo "the number of file residing in the selected path is: $count"
fi
```

Figure 7.7: Script showing input validation using the if construct

The **`if`** condition uses a compound statement that combines two expressions using the **`-o`** option. If either **`expression1`** or **`expression2`** is true, the commands given under the **`then`** block will be executed. If the expression given in the **`if`** line evaluates to false, then the commands under the **`else`** block are executed.

Let us take an example where **`if`** uses optional **`elif`** also. **`elif`** is used when you must take different actions based on different criteria. In *Figure 7.8*, multiple **`elif`** blocks have been added. At first, the **`if`** condition validates our input. If it evaluates to false, then control is passed to the first **`elif`** block. It checks the given condition, and if it is true, then all the commands next to the `then` keyword are executed. Otherwise, control goes to the second **`elif`** block, and the same flow control rule applies here. Similarly, further **`elif`** blocks are checked using the same logic. If the condition of any of the **`elif`** block does not return true, then the commands given in the **`else`** block are executed. Execute this script using some valid and invalid inputs, and then you can conclude that this script is behaving correctly with valid and invalid inputs. This script should also handle incorrect number of arguments and exit itself if the user enters wrong number of arguments. Refer to the following figure:

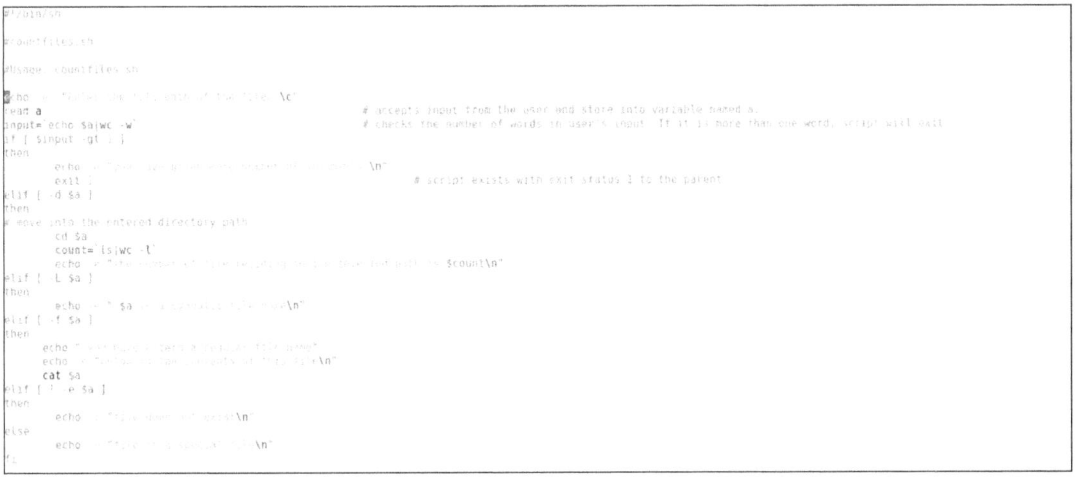

```
#!/bin/sh

#countfiles.sh

#Usage: countfiles.sh

echo -e "Enter the full path of the file: \c"
read a                                  # accepts input from the user and store into variable named a.
input=`echo $a|wc -w`                   # checks the number of words in user's input. If it is more than one word, script will exit
if [ $input -gt 1 ]
then
        echo -e "you have given more number of arguments \n"
        exit 1                                      # script exists with exit status 1 to the parent
elif [ -d $a ]
then
# move into the entered directory path
        cd $a
        count=`ls|wc -l`
        echo -e "the number of files residing in the above entered path is: $count\n"
elif [ -L $a ]
then
        echo -e " $a is a [illegible]\n"
elif [ -f $a ]
then
      echo " you have entered a regular file name"
      echo -e "below are the contents of this file\n"
      cat $a
elif [ ! -e $a ]
then
        echo -e "file does not exist\n"
else
        echo -e "file is a [illegible]\n"
fi
```

Figure 7.8: Script showing the if-elif-else-fi form of the if construct

You may also nest one **if** construct inside another for added programming logic. Nesting can be done up to multiple levels.

Looping in Bash

Looping is used in programming languages to keep executing a set of commands until a certain condition is met. In this section, we will understand looping using two commands: **while** and **for**.

Looping using *for*

for takes a list of elements and performs set of instructions on the items in the list one by one. *Figure 7.9* shows a simple **for** construct:

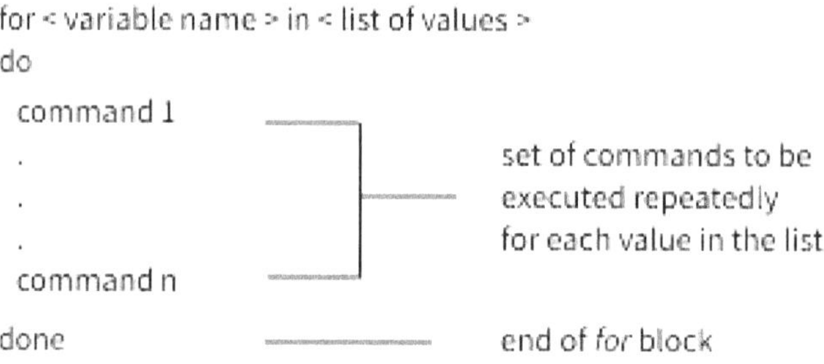
for < variable name > in < list of values >
do
command 1
.
.
.
command n
done
set of commands to be executed repeatedly for each value in the list
end of for block

Figure 7.9: for construct

The foremost line of the **for** construct contains the **variable name** and a space-separated list of values that is assigned to the given **variable name** one by one. List of values and **variable name** is separated by the **in** keyword. For each value assigned to variable, all the commands listed after the **do** keyword up to the **done** keyword are executed. Each **for** construct ends with the **done** keyword. All the commands between the **do** and **done** keywords are called the **loop body,** which executes repeatedly until all the items in the list have been processed. Here, **command 1** up to **command n** are executed for each element of the list. Thus, the given commands are executed as many times as the number of elements in the list. If the given list provides five values, then the listed commands are executed five times for each value. The list can be formed by simply listing many word values separated by a delimiter specified under the IFS environment variable. It can also be formed by using any patterns that shell understands. It can be a list of filenames, strings, numeric values, variables, and so on. A list can also be generated by using the command substitution feature of bash shell. The following example generates the square of the specified numbers:

```
for i in 1 2 3 4 5
do
b='expr $i \* $i'
echo $b
done
```

The preceding shell script will print the square of numbers from 1 to 5. The numbers from 1 to 5 are assigned to the **i** variable one by one. Loop body first calculates the square of the first number and stores it in variable **b**, and then the result is echoed on the screen. The same execution will proceed with the second number and so on. Square will be calculated for all the numbers specified in the sequence. After all the numbers have been used up in the **for** loop, the loop will exit.

In the preceding script, we had to specify each number specifically. If our list of numbers is long, then the task of providing numbers in the **for** list becomes tedious. We have a special expression to specify the range where numbers between the specified ranges are auto-generated . Refer to the following shell script, which is just a modification of the earlier script:

```
for i in {1..10}
do
      b='expr $i \* $i'
      echo $b
done
```

In the preceding script, curly braces are used to enclose the start and end range to produce a list of numbers automatically. The start range and end range are separated by two dots(**..**). The square will be calculated for numbers between the given range, including the range itself.

Take a look at the following example:

```
#! /bin/bash
# filecopy.sh: This script will copy the files matching 'sample' to /backup
#usage : filecopy.sh
for file in sample*
do
   cp $file /backup/ 2>/dev/null
   status=$?
   if [ $status -eq 0 ]
   then
      echo  "$file copied successfully"
   else
      echo  "$file:copy operation failed"
   fi
done
```

The preceding script copies the selected files to **/backup** and determines whether file copy operation is successful. **for-list** is produced using shell's wild-card characters, which are expanded to matching files. Each file name is assigned to the **file** variable in sequence. Each file is then copied to the **/backup** variable. Status of the copy operation is checked using the **if** command and is displayed on the screen. Many features have been accommodated in this script. Error messages of the **cp** command have been redirected to **/dev/null** so that the **cp** command does not throw error messages on the screen on failure. Next, we saw that the **if** construct has been nested under the **for** construct for added programming logic. Likewise, any programming construct can be nested in another construct.

The preceding shell script can copy only files whose name start with sample. We can enhance this shell script by allowing users to input source and destination files dynamically, as shown in the following script:

```
#! /bin/bash
# filecopy.sh: This script will copy the files to /backup
#usage : filecopy.sh
echo -e "enter source file to copy\c"
read orig
echo -e "enter destination directory\c"
read dest
        if [ -d $dest ]
        then
                for file in $orig
                do
                        cp $file $dest 2>/dev/null
                        status=$?
                        if [ $status -eq 0 ]
                        then
                                echo  "$file copied successfully"
                        else
                                echo  "$file:copy operation failed"
                        fi
                done
   else
                echo "you have not entered an existing directory name"
                exit 1
        fi
```

In the preceding modified version of our **filecopy.sh** script, the user is asked for the source and destination files, and their input is stored in the **orig** and **dest** variables, respectively. Our script then checks whether our destination is an existing directory using the **if** construct. If the **if** condition returns true, control enters the **for** loop, else script exits with exit status of 1.

Next, we will look at an example where the list of elements is generated and supplied to **for** by using a command, as follows:

```
for i in 'cat /etc/passwd|tr -d ' ''
do
username='echo "$i"|cut -f1 -d:'
echo $username
done
```

The preceding example uses command substitution to generate the **for** list. The command given under backquote (**'**) is executed, and the output is given to the **for** list. The preceding script **echoes** all the usernames available in the **/etc/passwd** file. You should now be able to interpret all the given lines yourself.

While loop

While loop is used to execute a set of commands repeatedly till some conditions are true. The **while** command accepts a condition and evaluates it. If the given condition evaluates to true, it enters the loop and executes all the commands given after the **do** keyword until the **done** keyword is reached. Commands given between the **do** and **done** keywords are called the **loop body**. After the **done** keyword is reached, control again goes to the **while** condition and checks whether the condition is still true. If the condition evaluates to true, it enters the loop again. The process continues unless the given **while** condition evaluates to false. It has the following structure:

```
while condition
do
command 1
.
.
command n
done
See below example:
#! /bin/sh
# while loop example : the script will print the square.
Num=1
while [ $num -le 5 ]
do
(( b=num*num ))
```

```
echo "square of $num is $b"
(( num ++ ))    #increments num by 1
done
```

In this script, the **[** command is used as a conditional expression for **while**. The given condition checks whether **$num** is less than **5**. Since this evaluates to true, control enters the **while** loop and all the commands between **do** and **done** are executed. The **num** variable is incremented in each iteration after calculating the square of its value, and the condition is checked for incremented **num** every time. The loop exits when the given condition evaluates to false.

It is a good time to enhance the functionality of our script named **filecopy.sh** that we have used in the looping using the **for** section. This script previously copied files only once. Now, the script in *Figure 7.10* can perform multiple copy operations. In the given script, when the loop starts the first time, it receives a predefined user input via the **ans** variable. So, the condition will be true on first entering the loop. Here, it takes compound conditional expression to test multiple forms of user input. It then asks for the source and destination files to perform the copy operation. After successful or unsuccessful copy operation, our script would not exit. It would continue to prompt the user for more copy operation. User input is read again by the **read** command. Our script can accept many forms of user input. Refer to the following figure:

```
#! /bin/bash
# filecopy.sh: This script will ask you for the source and destination to perform  one or multiple copy operation
#usage : filecopy.sh
ans='y'
while [ $ans == 'y' -o $ans == 'yes' ]
do

echo -e "enter source file to copy \c"
read orig                                # You can also input patterns to match many filenames
echo -e "enter destination directory \c"
read dest
        if [ -d $dest ]                  # checks whether destination directory exist
        then
                for file in $orig
                do
                        cp $file $dest 2>/dev/null
                        status=$?
                        if [ $status -eq 0 ]
                        then
                                echo  "$file copied successfully"
                        else
                                echo  "$file:copy operation failed"
                        fi
                done
        else
                echo "you have not entered an existing directory name"

        fi
        echo -e "do you want to do more copy operation?(Y/N)\c"
read input
ans=`echo $input |tr [A-Z] [a-z]`
echo "you input $ans"
done
```

***Figure 7.10**: Script showing usage of while loop*

Our script ensures that user input be modified such that all the uppercase letters are converted into lowercase. This is an important consideration to make as a user may give their answer in uppercase or lowercase or in abbreviated form. If a user enters *YES* or simply *Y*, then our script can convert it to *yes* or y, respectively, without the user knowing this change. The following line in the script ensures this:

```
ans=`echo $input |tr [A-Z] [a-z]`
```

Running infinite loop

So far, we have used **while** and **for** to run only finite number of times. Suppose we are in a situation where we want to establish a process that constantly looks for a particular directory's existence and move it on the **/backup** directory when it arrives. Alternatively, we may have a situation where we want to put an eye on our disk space consumption and compress large files if disk space reaches a threshold. All these requirements need an infinite loop that constantly looks for a particular directory's existence and disk space usage, respectively. The **while** loop can be used easily and efficiently to establish an infinite loop, as in the following script:

```
#! /bin/sh
#infinite.sh
while true
do
        if [ -d ~/redhat/mydir ]
        then
                d='date +'%Y%m%d%H%M%s''
                mkdir /backup/$d
                mv ~/redhat/mydir /backup/$d/ 2>/dev/null
        fi
   sleep 300
done
```

To make an infinite loop, we can use the **true** command of Linux, which always **exit** with status **0**. Thus, the **while** condition always remains true, and the script never exits and runs infinitely. The user can initiate termination of the script by pressing *Ctrl+C* or by adding some conditions within the infinite loop that exit the loop. We will see a mechanism that we can use to break the infinite loop in the next section.

It is good practice to run an infinite loop in the background by adding **&** after the **done** keyword as `done` **&**; this will make our infinite loop run as a background task.

Break and continue in loop

The **break** keyword is used in looping to break the execution of the loop in the middle. When **break** is used, the control exits from the loop and is passed to the commands listed after the **done** keyword. The **continue** keyword is used to pass the control back to the start of the loop, leaving all the commands after the **continue** keyword unattended. Let's see the following script:

```
#! /bin/bash
#square.sh:finds the square of numbers from 2 to 10
```

```
n=2
while [ 1 ]
do
   (( a = n * n ))
   echo "square of $n is $a"
   (( n++ ))
   if [ $n -eq 11 ]
   then
      break
   else
      continue
   fi
done
```

As is clear from the comment line, this script will calculate the square of numbers ranging between 2 to 10. Here, **`while [1]`** is equivalent to saying **`while true`**. It calculates the square using the value of **`$n`**. The preceding script will exit the loop when **`$n`** becomes **`11`**, else it will continue the loop and go to the beginning of the loop again and calculate the square.

Case in bash

Case is an easier alternative for the **`if-elif-else`** construct. Like **`if-elif-else`**, it also provides us with the way to make a decision when we have multiple conditions to choose from. It follows the form as given in *Figure 7.11*.

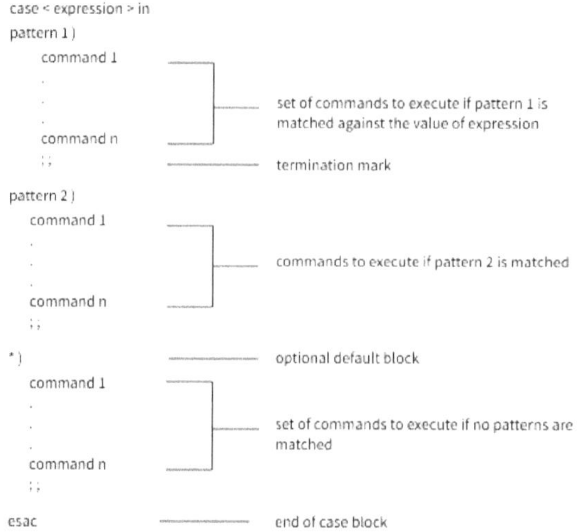
case < expression > in
pattern 1)
command 1
.
.
.
command n
;;
set of commands to execute if pattern 1 is matched against the value of expression
termination mark
pattern 2)
command 1
.
.
.
command n
;;
commands to execute if pattern 2 is matched
*)
optional default block
command 1
.
.
.
command n
;;
set of commands to execute if no patterns are matched
esac
end of case block

***Figure 7.11:** case construct*

case accepts an expression that, when evaluated, can match a pattern. Each **case** has an ending **esac** keyword that signifies the end of **case** construct. When the **case** expression matches a pattern, the related list of commands that ends with a pair of semicolons is executed. Patterns are delimited by a closing parenthesis. The expression given in **case** can be a variable name, a command substitution or arithmetic expression, and so on. After evaluating the given expression, the resulting value is matched against each pattern given. If the resulting value of the expression matches **pattern 1**, the sequence of commands specified after **pattern 1)** upto termination character **;;** are executed. In the given figure, you can see that each pattern is delimited by **')'**, and a pattern block is terminated by **;;** (double semicolons). Each pattern block includes a list of commands (**command 1** to **command n** in *Figure 7.11*) to execute when the pattern matches the expression given in **case**. If **pattern 1** is not matched, then **pattern 2** is checked against the expression in **case**. If **pattern 2** is matched, then all the commands listed after **pattern 2)** upto **;;** are executed. If no patterns are matched, then all the commands listed after ***)** are executed until **;;** is found. The expression ***)** can be referred to as the default pattern block.

Refer to the following figure:

```
#! /bin/bash
echo -e "What do you want to do?"
echo -e "1. addition of two numbers"
echo -e "2. multiplication of two numbers"
echo -e "3. division of two numbers"
echo -e "Enter 1 or 2 or 3"
read ans
case $ans in

        1)
                echo "enter your numbers separated by space\c"
                read a b
                (( i = a+b ))
                ;;
        2)      echo "enter your numbers separated by space\c"
                read a b
                (( i = a*b ))
                ;;
        3)      echo "enter dividend \c"
                read div
                echo "enter divisor \c"
                read dis
                (( i = div/dis ))
                ;;

        *)      echo "you have entered a wrong choice, so exiting"
                exit 1
esac

echo "Result is $i"
```

Figure 7.12: case usage in generating menus

Figure 7.12 shows a sample example of the **case** construct. This script is used to generate menus to the user. A user must choose one option from the displayed menu. After displaying the menu, the script prompts the user to press either **1** or **2** or **3**. The user's response is read into the **ans** variable. If the user supplied **1** in their response, then commands under **1)** block are executed. If the user supplied 2 in their response, then commands under **2)** block are executed, and so on. If the user's response does not match any of the given patterns, the default pattern block is executed. The default pattern block is the block that has ***)** as a pattern. If the user enters wrong choice, the default block exits the script after printing the related message on the screen. The remaining lines in the script should be self-explanatory to you.

We can also use **case** construct to verify user input, as shown in *Figure 7.13*. The script shown in this figure is just the modification of the script given in *Figure 7.10*. Refer to the following figure:

```
#! /bin/bash
# filecopy.sh
#usage : filecopy.sh

ans='y'
while [ $ans == 'y' ]
do

        echo -e "enter source file to copy \c"
        read orig
        echo -e "enter destination directory \c"
        read dest
        if [ -d $dest ]
        then
                for file in $orig
                do
                        cp $file $dest 2>/dev/null
                        status=$?
                        if [ $status -eq 0 ]
                        then
                                echo  "$file copied successfully"
                        else
                                echo  "$file : copy operation failed"
                        fi
                done
        else
                echo "you have not entered an existing directory name"

        fi
        while true
        do

                echo -e "do you want to do more copy operation?(Y/N) \c"
                read input
                case $input in
                        y|Y|[yY][Ee][Ss]) ans='y'
                                break;;
                        n|N|[Nn][Oo]) ans='n' exit 0;;
                        *) echo "you entered wrong choice, enter your choice again"
                esac

        done
done
```

Figure 7.13: *Script showing usage of case in verifying a user's response*

You can easily note the modification that we have made in the main while loop condition. The next modification you will notice is at the place where the user is asked whether they want to continue. We have used the case command here to check for the user's answer.

See how the user input is being verified by using | to check all forms of *yes*. | is used to separate multiple patterns in the **case** pattern list. Our script is also capable of checking all forms of *no*. A user can say *yes* when they type y or *Y* or *YEs*, and so on. Our script is well crafted to match users' responses properly. The **break** command is required here to break the inner **while** loop when user says *yes*, and control goes to statements listed after the end of the current **while** loop. In our case, there is no command after the **done** keyword, so control goes back to our main **while** loop. Our script exit if a user responds negatively.

Redirection in script

So far, all the output and error messages of the script are either going to the terminal or are being redirected to **/dev/null**. This mechanism always loses information regarding the last run of the script. What if we want to view the messages printed by the previous run of a script. We have to devise a way to store all the error messages and output messages of each run of our script to a disk file. You can call the script as follows:

```
script1 > scriptlog
```

The preceding command will redirect all the output generated while running the script to a file named **scriptlog**.

Similarly, we can rewrite the preceding command to also redirect all the errors to another file named **script1.err** as follows:

```
script1 >scriptlog 2> script1.err
```

Now, what can we do if we want to display some of the messages printed through the script on the screen also? The solution is to redirect those messages to a special file called **/dev/tty**. **/dev/tty** is pseudo file that represents a user's terminal. Each user has access to different terminal files; user A may be writing to **/dev/pts/0**, while user B may be attached to **/dev/pts/1**. But both the users can access their terminal using **/dev/tty**. Writing to **/dev/tty** will send the data to the terminal to which the user issuing the command is associated.

You can rewrite commands printing messages on the script, as follows:

```
echo "print this message on screen " > /dev/tty
```

If *script1* contains the preceding line, the **echo** command will send the message to our screen; the remaining commands will send their output to the **scriptlog** file.

Redirection of standard output to a file can also be achieved by adding the redirection operator to **while** loop, **if** or **case** construct, as shown here:

```
done > logfile
```

Adding the redirection operator to the **done** keyword redirects all the output messages printed within the loop to **logfile**. Only the messages that have been explicitly redirected to **/dev/tty** will be printed on the terminal.

Similarly, take a look at the following:

fi >logfile

This will send all the messages printed within the **if** construct to logfile. Now, refer to the following:

esac > logfile

It will redirect all the messages printed within the **case** construct to logfile.

All these ways to redirect the messages to a log file allow you to explicitly send any message to the terminal by redirecting it to **/dev/tty**.

Using the preceding mechanism will redirect the messages from the script either to the terminal or to the file. What if we want to send a message in our file as well as in our terminal. In *Chapter 3, Knowing Linux Commands,* we have learnt about the **tee** command that is specifically used to send the output to a file as well as to the terminal. See the following script:

```
while true
do
    if [ -d ~/redhat/mydir ]
    then
        d='date +'%Y%m%d%H%M%s''
        mkdir /backup/$d
        if [ $? -eq 0 ]
        then
            echo "directory named $d created successfully"|tee /dev/tty
            mv ~/redhat/mydir /backup/$d/ 2>/dev/null
            echo "directory is copied to /backup as $d"|tee /dev/tty
        fi
    fi
done
```

Consider calling the script as follows:

scrip1>logfile

It will send the commands output to **logfile**, and the messages with the **tee** command included will also be written to the terminal.

Running shell script with arguments

While running the script in the command line, we can pass some arguments to it, known as **command line arguments** or **positional parameters**. These arguments are then accessed inside the script to do your task. Each argument given in the command line is assigned a number starting with 1. The first nine arguments can be simply accessed by preceding each number with the **$** symbol, as follows:

$1 , $2 , $3 …. $9

If you have provided a greater number of arguments, they can be accessed as follows:

${10}, ${11} .... and so on.

Bash also provides us some special parameters like **#,@** and *****:

- $#: It stores the number of arguments supplied.
- $*: It stores the complete list of supplied arguments as a string.
- $@: It also stores the complete list of supplied arguments as a string, but it treats multi-word argument as a single argument. **$*** splits multi-word arguments into separate arguments. So, **$@** is preferred over **$***.
- **$0**: It stores the name of the script itself.

Each argument specified in the command line is separated from others by a separator specified under the IFS environment variable. Let us create a script that uses these parameters effectively:

```
cat pos1.sh
#!/bin/bash
# usage: $0 arg1 arg2 ..... argn
if [ $# -eq 0 ]
then
   echo "you have not entered any arguments"
   echo "usage : $0 arg1 arg2 ... argn"
   exit 1
else
   echo " you have entered $# arguments"
fi

for val in $*
do
echo '======= $* ======='
echo $val
done
for val in $@
```

```
do
echo '======== $@ ========'
echo $val
done
for val in "$*"
do
echo '======= "$*" =========='
echo $val
done
for val in "$@"
do
echo '========== "$@" ==========='
echo $val
done
```

The preceding script starts by checking the number of arguments the user entered using the `if` construct. The **`$#`** environment variable is used to verify the same. If the user entered no arguments, then our script prints the usage message to the user. The **`$0`** environment variable is used to show the usage of the script. Before discussing remaining lines of script, let us run the script with no arguments and see how our **`$#`** and **`$0`** environment variables are working:

```
[vishesh@localhost scripts]$ ./pos1.sh
you have not entered any arguments
usage : ./pos1.sh arg1 arg2 ... argn
```

Now, execute the script in many runs and see how it behaves with different inputs:

- **First run**

  `./pos1.sh hello`

  In this run, only a single one word argument is passed to the script. Then, **`$#`** is used to print the number of arguments. Next, our script uses quoted and unquoted versions of the **`$*`** and **`$@`** environment variables to pass all the command-line arguments to the **`for`** loop. The output makes it clear that **`$*`**, **`$@`** and their quoted version handle one argument correctly.

- **Second run**

  `./pos1.sh hello there`

  In the second run, two arguments are passed in the command line. From the execution, you will find that **`$*`**, **`$@`** and **`$@`** handle this correctly. **`$*`** treats the whole text entered in the command line as a single string, so it is not displaying us the correct result. So, what is purpose of **$***? You can use this parameter if you want to act upon all the arguments as a string.

- Third run

  `./pos1.sh "hello there"`

  In the third run, only one argument is passed but is multi-word. From the execution, we can see that only $* and $@ are able to handle this correctly. But for the reason mentioned above, $* is not reliable. The unquoted versions $* and $@ do not work here as expected, as they split each argument into several space-separated words and treat each word as a single argument.

- Fourth run

  `./pos1.sh "hello there" this`

  The output of this run shows that only one form $@ succeeded, in this case, in displaying the correct result. So, we can conclude that among all the four runs of the script, $@ always works correctly. So, you should always use $@ and not $* or "$*" or $@.

Setting positional parameters automatically

We have used the **set** command to display default environment variables. In this section, we will see another strength of the **set** command, which will make your life easier. The **set** command can be used to easily separate fields from the output of a command into special variables. Say, you want to work with some or all the fields of the **/etc/passwd** file. To accomplish your task, you can use the following:

```
set `head -1 /etc/passwd|tr ':' ' '`
```

The **/etc/passwd** file contains colon (**:**)as the delimiting character to separate fields. When you execute the preceding command, all the colon characters will be changed into single space characters and will be passed to the **set** command. Now, when set sees words separated by IFS, it treats each word as an argument and assigns them to positional parameters. After issuing the preceding command, just use **echo** to view the value of positional parameters, as follows:

```
echo $1
echo $2
echo $3
```

Here document

We know that we can provide standard input to the command by either using keyboard or the redirect symbol **<** or pipe. Apart from these ways of standard input, we have here document. **Here document** does not refer to any document; it refers to the standard input that is given immediately along with the command. Suppose we use the following:

```
cat < file1
```

In this case, shell will wait for user's input. When we use here document, no waiting will be there as input is given even before the shell comes into action:

```
[vishesh@192 ~]$ cat << EOI
hello this is a book on linux
wriiten on 'date'
EOI
hello this is a book on linux
wriiten on Saturday 31 December 2022 12:02:57 AM IST
```

In the preceding command, instead of the **<** operator, **<<** is used. This is **Here document**. It means 'do not look anywhere for standard input; standard input is here only'. You have to specify the terminator for your standard input. We use EOI, but it can be of any name. When shell sees **<<**, it takes each line as input until it finds the delimiting character EOI. On finding the limiting character EOI, it translates the input line by resolving any metacharacters or wild card characters that it finds. The preceding command line uses command substitution, which is interpreted by shell even before execution of the script.

Real usages of **here document** are in shell script. Many times, the inputs that user may give to the script are predefined and limited. In this case, you can instruct the shell to accept the input from here document rather than waiting for the input from the keyboard. You can use **here document** when executing a script, as follows:

```
./filecopy.sh << END
> square
> /tmp
> y
> file1
> /tmp
> n
> END
enter source file to copy enter destination directory square copied successfully
do you want to do more copy operation?(Y/N) you input y
enter source file to copy enter destination directory file1:copy operation failed
do you want to do more copy operation?(Y/N) you input n
```

Earlier, we used the **`filecopy.sh`** script such that it will not wait for the user's input and all the inputs will be accepted from the command line itself. Our script asks input from the user in multiple places, and you must provide all the inputs in sequence to here document, else our script will fail. From the preceding output, it is clear that all the input was provided beforehand, and the script ran successfully. If you want to replace only a few input variables with here document, you can use here document inside the script to read the data directly from the script itself. For example, assume that our destination directory is always the same: **/tmp**. So, we can modify the line in the script that asks for the user input as follows:

```
echo -e "enter destination directory \c"
read dest << INPUT
/tmp
INPUT
```

Now, your script will prompt the user for all the inputs except the destination directory. Run your script after making the preceding modification and see the result yourself.

Debugging shell script

Bash also provides you with a debugging feature that helps you troubleshoot the script. When your script is not working as expected and you are unable to find the problem in the script, turn on debugging mode in bash before running the script, as shown here:

```
bash -x script
```

The preceding command will turn debugging mode on, and any script that you run afterward will print each command before it is actually executed. Each line from the script, when printed, is preceded by the prompt character specified in the PS4 environment variable. Each line is then followed by the output of the command, if any.

This is especially useful in debugging the script line by line. This helps you in identifying the line in your script that is the problem.

Error handling in Bash

We have seen that the shell script does not terminate in between when it receives an error by executing any line. If any line throws an error, the script continues its execution until the last line. It returns 0 exit status if the last line of the script executes successfully. This approach of bash shell may give you erroneous results that are intolerable most of the time. So, you must develop a mechanism to handle errors in the script.

Bash shell itself provides you with the option of error handling in the script. Adding the following line inside the script would halt the execution of the script if it finds any error, without continuing to the next line:

```
set -e
```

Another way to handle errors in bash is using the **trap** command. The **trap** command can be used to catch any signals that the shell receives and take appropriate action. It has the following syntax:

trap command signal

Here, signal is the signal that you want to catch.

Command is any command that you want to execute when bash receives the specified signal. For example, refer to the following script:

```
#! /bin/bash
trap "echo \"signal received; but can't quit\"" SIGINT
i=5
while [ $i -gt 0 ] ; do
    sleep 10
    (( i-- ))
Done
```

This script catches an interrupt signal (**SIGINT**) using the **trap** command. When you press **Ctrl+C** (keystroke for interrupt signal) on your keyboard, script will not terminate; rather, the message given under the **trap** command would just be echoed.

Awk revisited

By now, you should be able to write shell scripting to automate many routine tasks. There can be some complex requirement, which makes writing shell scripting a very difficult and tedious task. Your shell script might contain many lines of code to solve this problem. You can use awk if you have a complex requirement that cannot be easily coded into shell scripts. You can make your task simpler by using awk, which provides all the features of a programming language. Mastery to awk can be achieved with practice. As the scope of this book is limited, advanced programming using awk is not covered.

In *Chapter 5, Handling and Managing Files*, we learnt the basic usage of awk. In this section, we will explore more facilities provided by awk. Awk works on the given pattern, which is searched for in the input file, and then it takes specified actions on the lines matched. In awk parlance, each line of the input is known as a **record**. The records are separated by new line characters. Each record may have one or more fields, and space character is used as the default field separator. Like any other programming language, awk also supports variables and other programming constructs. Awk also provides you with a set of built-in variables. Here are a few of them:

- **NR**: Stores the line number that the awk is currently processing
- **FS**: The input field separator
- **NF**: The number of fields in the current input record
- **OFS**: The output field separator
- **ORS**: The output record separator

- **FNR**: The input record number
- **RS**: The input record separator
- **$0**: Stores the whole record; the action statement **{print}** is equivalent to **{print $0}**

Awk can be given one or more instructions to work on at a single command, as follows:

```
awk -F ',' '/fin/{print $1}/hr/{print $2}' dept
```

In the preceding command, two instructions have been provided enclosed in single quotes. Each instruction follows a pattern-action set. The first instruction prints field 1 from lines matching **fin**, and the next instruction prints field 2 from lines matching **hr**.

Sometimes, we have many instructions to give to awk, and specifying those in the command line becomes very clumsy and makes the code unreadable. So, you can use the **-f** option to let the awk read instructions from the file instead of the command line, as follows:

```
awk -f prgfile orders
```

Where **prgfile** contains the following:

```
cat prgfile
/sofa|lamp/{print $1, $2}
/racks/
```

Here, two instructions are provided to awk via a separate program file named **prgfile**. Awk will print field 1 and field 2 from the record that matches either **sofa** or **lamp** or both. The second line of **prgfile** indicates that it will print all fields of the records where it contains **racks**.

Besides regular expression, we can specify ranges of patterns to search from the given input source, as follows:

```
awk -F '\t'  '/Dining Chair/,/table lamp/{print}'  orders
```

The **orders** file that had been created earlier, is used in the preceding command. The preceding command will print all the records that fall between the lines containing **'Dining Chair'** and **'table lamp'**.

You can also specify the line numbers to print, as follows:

```
awk -F '\t' 'NR==3{print}' orders
```

The preceding command uses the **NR** variable to print only the record number **3**. Note the '==' operator. Here, our search criteria should not be enclosed in \ forward slashes. We can also provide the line number range as in following example:

```
awk -F '\t' 'NR==3,NR==5{print}' orders
```

The preceding command prints line numbers from **3** to **5**.

Patterns in **awk** may also contain any expression, as shown here:

```
awk -F '\t' '$3>5{print $0}' orders
```

The preceding command will print those records from the **orders** datafile where quantity ordered is greater than **5**. Here, the quantity ordered is field3. Let us use string in an expression:

```
awk -F '\t' '$2=="table lamp"' orders
```

As you just saw, string must be enclosed in double quotes. The **==** operator matches the **table lamp** as a whole string that contains a field. It will not match the **table lamp** embedded in a field, but the entire field must contain the given string only.

If you want to match a string embedded in the field, you must match it as a regular expression pattern using the **~** operator. **~** is used to match regular expression in a specific field. We also have the **!~** operator, which prints those lines that are not matched:

```
awk -F '\t' '$2~/lamp/' orders
awk -F '\t' '$2!~/lamp/' orders
```

Patterns can be combined using the logical **AND** or **OR** operator, as follows:

```
awk -F '\t' '$3>=1 && $3<=2' orders
```

The preceding command prints those records where field3 is between the range 1 and 2, inclusive. Similarly, you can use the **||** logical operator signifying the **OR** operator, as follows:

```
awk -F '\t' '$3>5 || $4>25000{print}' orders
```

You can also use the logical **NOT** (**!** operator) to negate any expression, as shown here:

```
awk -F '\t' '!($3>5)' orders
```

It matches the records where the **$3 > 5** condition returns false.

Let us print all the records from **orders** file, with each record preceded by its record number:

```
awk -F '\t' '{print NR , $0}' orders
```

In the preceding command, we used **NR** to print the line number and then the record. **$0** is a special variable in **awk** that holds the current record. In the output, record number and the whole record are separated by a space as OFS is set to a space by default. Let us change OFS such that the line number and the whole record ae separated by ' **:** ', as follows:

```
awk -F '\t' -v OFS=' : ' '{print NR,$0}' orders
```

The preceding command uses the **-v** option to give new assignment to a variable.

Print action not only prints the value of a specific variable or field but can also print formatted strings, as follows:

```
awk -F '\t' '{print "record number" NR ": " $0}' orders
```

The preceding command combines given string and numeric variable named **NR** and prints formatted string on the screen very easily. But a string needs to be enclosed in double quotes, while the same does not apply to variables.

The **awk** command applies the given action to all the matching lines. What if we want to give a heading to our report. The printing of heading does not require any extra processing of lines. It should have been printed even before **awk** starts processing each line. Similarly, we may have a need to print the sum of a numeric field at the end. This sum must be printed after all the records have been processed. To accomplish this task, we have the **BEGIN** and **END** keywords that we can specify at the beginning and end of our **awk** program, respectively as follows:

```
awk -F '\t' 'BEGIN{print "\n*******Order information*********\n"}
{print $0} END {print "\nTotal number of records are " NR"\n"}' orders
```

You can note that actions that need to take place in the **BEGIN** and **END** sections must be enclosed in their respective **{}**. The complete awk program must be enclosed in single quotes. See how the beautiful report is generated in *Figure 7.14*. **BEGIN** and **END** are case-sensitive. **BEGIN** can also be used to create a new variable and assign or reassign values to variables. The middle **{}** is the main program body, where you can write any statements, not only print. Refer to the following figure:

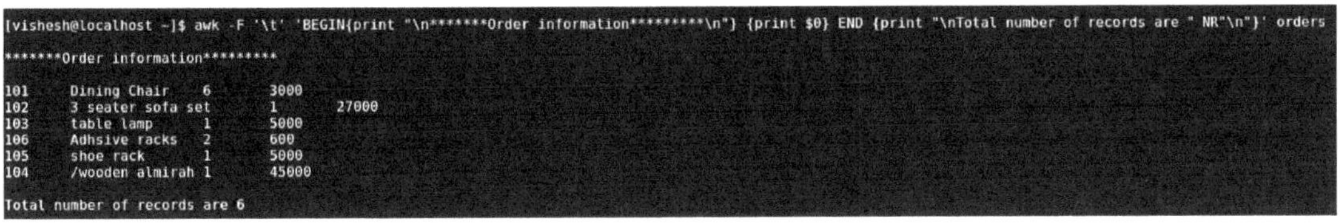

```
[vishesh@localhost ~]$ awk -F '\t' 'BEGIN{print "\n*******Order information*********\n"} {print $0} END {print "\nTotal number of records are " NR"\n"}' orders

*******Order information*********

101     Dining Chair    6       3000
102     3 seater sofa set       1       27000
103     table lamp      1       5000
106     Adhsive racks   2       600
105     shoe rack       1       5000
104     /wooden almirah 1       45000

Total number of records are 6
```

Figure 7.14: awk program showing the usage of the BEGIN and END keywords

Suppose you want to print the total of all the ordered quantity and the grand total of all orders:

```
awk -F '\t' 'BEGIN {sum=0;total=0} { sum=sum+$3;total=total+$4 }END {print
"total quantity ordered is " sum; print "total cost of all the orders is "
total}' orders
```

```
total quantity ordered is 12
total cost of all the orders is 85600
```

All the blocks in the preceding **awk** program take multiple statements, and each statement is terminated with a semicolon (**;**). For each record, **$3** is added to the **sum** variable and **$4** is added to **total** variable, and no other action is taken. The middle **{}** is doing the processing of all the lines, as no pattern or conditional expression is specified. Let us rewrite the preceding **awk** program that prints the aggregations for only those orders where quantity ordered is more than 1:

```
awk -F '\t' 'BEGIN {sum=0;total=0}$3>1{ sum=sum+$3;total=total+$4}END
```

```
{print "total quantity ordered is " sum; print "total cost of all the
orders is " total}' orders
```

In the preceding command, a criterion is added just before the middle **{}** section so that **sum** will be calculated only for matching lines.

awk also supports several built-in functions; a few of them are described here:

- **int(expr)**: Truncates to integer
- **rand()**: Returns a random number N, between zero and one
- **sqrt(expr)**: Returns the square root of **expr**
- **length([s])**: Returns the length of the string **s**; if **s** is not supplied, it returns the length of **$0**
- **substr(s, I [, n])**: A substring of length **n** is extracted from string **s** starting from position **I**; if **n** is not supplied, it extracts all the characters of the string starting from position **i**
- **index(s,t)**): Extracts the position of the substring **t** from string **s**
- **tolower(str)**: Converts the string to lowercase
- **toupper(str)**: Converts the string to uppercase

Let us use few functions in the **awk** program:

```
awk -F '\t' '{print "The length of line no " NR " is : "length}' orders
awk -F '\t' 'length($2)>10 {print substr($2,11,3)}' orders
```

If you want to be an advanced programmer, you can learn advanced shell and **awk** programming using books that focus on this.

Conclusion

There are many built-in shells around a Linux machine, such as C shell, Korn shell, bourne shell, and bash shell. RHEL9.0 uses bash shell by default. This is the bash shell that is running on the terminal when we first open it. It provides a default environment for your task that you can easily customize according to your requirements. Bash is a scripting language and a command interpreter that takes a script file and reads, interprets, and executes each line one by one. Performing repetitive tasks is a good candidate for shell scripting. Bash shell supports many built-in variables and several programming constructs, with which you can write efficient shell programs. Many of the complex tasks can be easily performed using awk programming.

In the next chapter, we will discuss the concepts of networking and how networking is implemented in Linux. We will also learn how Linux servers and networks can be made more secure to protect the organization from many kinds of internal and external threats.

CHAPTER 8
Security and Networking in Linux

Introduction

Securing any system is the need of the hour. Information management is an integral part of all organizations, whether large or small. Information is a critical part of any organization that must be protected from losses. An enterprise must protect itself from the theft of information, disruption of services, or complete damage of the system. Multi-level security is needed to protect a system entirely. You must implement security at the hardware level, OS level, application level, file level as well as user level. Security managers must ensure that the system should be running all the time and providing continuous services. In *Chapter 6, Managing Users and File Permissions,* we have seen file-level and user-level security. User-level security is implemented by authenticating any user logged in. File-level security is implemented by protecting the file's permission bits. In this chapter, we will see how we can implement extra layers of security. This will provide limited access to data stored on the system when the host is accessed locally or remotely. Securing your system only at the OS level or securing only the application is not enough. Today, each machine is on the network, so network security is of utmost importance. In this chapter, we will see how security is implemented in Linux systems at all levels. This chapter will also help you understand networking concepts and how they are implemented and secured in Linux systems.

Structure

This chapter has the following structure:

- Securing Linux
    - o DAC vs MAC
    - o SELinux as MAC
- Networking concepts
- Configuring network
- Viewing network connectivity information
- Securing network
- Wireless network and profiles
- Monitoring logs
- Global security benchmarks for Linux

Objectives

By the end of this chapter, you should have acquired the skills to implement diverse security measures on a Linux box. You should also be proficient in setting up networking on a Linux host using network manager utilities. Additionally, you should know to utilize secure services like SSH, SCP, and SFTP for secure data transfer. Furthermore, you should be able to effectively monitor your network and its traffic to identify and counter external threats. With the knowledge gained, you can safeguard your organization's network by implementing firewalls. Moreover, you should develop the ability to comprehend and analyze networking logs for efficient troubleshooting. This comprehensive understanding of network security and management should empower you to handle various challenges in the Linux environment confidently.

Securing Linux

Linux has inherent security features; still, each host in your organization must have proper access control methods implemented so that sensitive information is accessible only by the user who is authorized to access it. An organization must protect each Linux system from malware, viruses, and internal and external threats. Disallowing root login locally or remotely, complex password policy, password aging policy, securing files, and restricting user permissions are some ways to implement basic Linux security that must be known to each system administrator. In the previous chapters, we learnt that the admin should not use a root account to perform their administrative task. Instead, they should use regular users' accounts and can raise their privileges only for highly privileged tasks by using **sudo**. A complex password policy must be established so that users' passwords cannot be guessed easily. Password aging policy forces the user to change their password regularly so that unauthorized access to the system can be prevented. Besides, proper access control must be in place to protect the files. And users must be properly authenticated. We have already learnt this basic security mechanism. In this section, we will learn other available mechanisms for securing our system.

Access control list

Each file has a user owner and a group owner, and they access the files and perform operations on them according to the set file permission bits. Besides the owner and group owner of the file, each file may also have a set of permissions for all other users. The permissions to other users are specified using file permission bits set for the "other" category. File permission bits set at the "other" level are generic, that is, they apply to all other users on the system who are neither the owner of the file nor the group owner. This generic feature gives us no option to apply the file access permissions to only select users. This is where **Access Control List** (**ACL**) comes into the picture. By using ACL, a file can even be made accessible to individual users who are neither the file owner nor the member of the group owner of the file.

To view the current ACL of the **xyz** file, use the **getfacl** command as follows:

```
$getfacl xyz
```

It will give the following output:

```
[vishesh@192 ~]$ getfacl xyz
# file: xyz
# owner: vishesh
# group: vishesh
user::rw-
group::rw-
other::r--
```

Currently, there is no ACL set in this file as the output only displays permissions of user, group and other. This is the same output as is displayed with the **ls -l** output. Let us assign some ACL to this file. To do this, the **setfacl** command is used in the following way:

```
$setfacl -m u:<username>:<permission> <filename>
```

To assign the user **sam** write permission on the **xyz** file, use **setfacl** as shown here:

```
$setfacl -m u:sam:rw- xyz
```

To verify the ACL, use **getfacl** command as shown here:

```
getfacl xyz
# file: xyz
# owner: vishesh
# group: vishesh
user::rw-
user:sam:rw-
group::rw-
mask::rw-
other::r--
```

A new entry can be seen in the preceding output, which allows **sam** to read and write on the file. Besides **sam**, only the owner and member group of the file have read and write access to the file. But to access the specified file, you should ensure that **sam** has appropriate permission in the related directory. Let us view the output of **ls -l** again once.

```
-rw-rw-r--+ 1 vishesh vishesh 0 Sep 27 11:03 abc
```

Now, you will see that a **+** symbol is added to the last bit of the first field. The **+** symbol indicates that there is some ACL property attached to this file.

To remove ACL entry for the user **sam**, use the **-x** option with the **setfacl** command, as follows:

```
$setfacl -x u:sam xyz
```

Do it yourself

Create a file under /tmp. This is a directory accessible to all users. Now, notice the default permission of the file using ls -l. Remove any permission from the other level. After you have set empty permission bits for others, grant an extra layer of permission using ACL such that sam can read and write on this file. Verify that sam can write on the file. Also, verify the ACL using the getfacl command.

Special permission bits

In this section, we will discuss other important permission bits. Following are the three special bits that are used to enhance the file system's security:

- **suid**
- **sgid**
- **sticky bit**

Let us understand each of them one by one.

suid

This bit is set at user access level. When a command or script having **suid** bit set is run, that command runs as the owner of the file rather than as the user who invokes the command. Thus, the effective user ID becomes the **uid** of the owner of the file. To understand **suid**, let us see how **passwd** command works. The **passwd** command can be used by every user in the system to set their password. The **passwd** command writes into the **/etc/shadow** file. Let us check the permission bits of the **/etc/shadow** file:

```
$ls -l /etc/shadow
----------. 1 root root 2618 Sep 24 15:12 /etc/shadow
```

This file does not have any permission bit set, and user and group owner are root. So, how is it possible for the **passwd** command to write to the **/etc/shadow** file whenever any regular user invokes this command. It is due to the fact that the **passwd** binary has **suid** bit set at user access level. Let us use **ls -l** to verify the permission bits of **/usr/bin/passwd**.

```
ls -l /usr/bin/passwd
-rwsr-xr-x. 1 root root 32648 Aug 10  2021 /usr/bin/passwd
```

See the **s** character at the user owner level. Instead of execute (**x**) bit, it displays a **s**. This small **s** indicates that **suid** bit is set along with the execute bit. Anyone can run the **passwd** command with effective user ID set as the owner of the command file and not as the invoking users. Thus, **Effective User ID (EUID)** becomes root when the **passwd** command is executed by a regular user.

If the user does not have permission to execute the file, then big **S** is displayed.

sgid

The **sgid** bit works at group level. When a file having sgid bit set is executed, then it runs as the file group owner and not as the user who initiated the command. A small **s** is displayed at group level if the file has **sgid** bit set.

When a **sgid** bit is set on a directory, any file created on that directory will have the same group ownership as that of the directory. Its purpose is to make project files shareable among the users.

If a group does not have execute permission, then big **S** *is* displayed to represent **sgid** bit.

Sticky bit

Any user can store their files in **/tmp**, but the files created can only be accessed by the owner of the file, who can perform any operation on them. Other users are not allowed to delete the files under **/tmp**, but the root user can delete any file lying on **/tmp**.

/tmp is a world-writable directory. This directory has all the permission bits set at all the levels. All the users have read, write and execute permission on this directory. If a directory has read, write and execute permission set for all the users, then any user can read and modify the contents of the directory. They can create new files on the directory and delete any files. All these operations can be performed by a user even if the files residing in the directory do not belong to them. This is where sticky bit comes into picture. The /tmp directory has sticky bit set, which prevents any other user from deleting the files that are not owned by them.

Verify the permission sets of the /tmp directory by using the following:

```
ls -ld /tmp
drwxrwxrwt. 24 root root 4096 Sep 27 14:14 /tmp
```

Notice t in the place of x at the other access level. This t indicates that /tmp has a sticky bit set, which means that no one but the owner and root can delete the files inside /tmp.

If you notice big T instead of small t at other access level, then it would mean that the sticky bit is set without execute privilege for others.

Setting the special permission bit

We know that the preceding bit in octal notation is used to set special permission bits. The following digits are assigned to these special permission bits:

```
SUID= 4
SGID= 2
Sticky Bit= 1
```

The **chmod** command is used in the same way to set special permission bits as it is used to set regular permission bits. Thus, to set suid on a regular file, you will use the following:

```
chmod 4xxx <filename>
```

Where xxx is the permission bits for user, group and other. The first digit, 4, is used to set suid.

To set sgid on a file, you can write this:

```
chmod 2xxx <filename>
```

To set sticky bit on a file, you can use the following syntax:

```
chmod 1xxx <filename>
```

See the permission of the **passwd** command file in octal format; you will get the following:

```
4755
```

Where 4 is the indicator of **suid** bit.

The following is the permission **of /tmp** in octal format:

```
1777
```

Here, the first digit in octal notation contains 1, which is the indicator of sticky bit set.

Do it yourself

Become root. Create a new directory `/temp`. Assign all permissions at all levels to this directory. Verify the value in octal. Do you see 777? Now, log in to your regular user account. Create a file named test under `/temp`. Log in as sam now. Try to access the file inside `/temp` as sam. Did you succeed in accessing the file? Write to the file as sam. Were you successful in writing? Now, try to delete the file as sam. Are you able to delete the file?

Now, set the sticky bit on the `/temp` directory. Verify the sticky bit creation. Again, create a new file named `test2` in this directory using your regular user account. Now, log in as sam. Try to read and write on the test2 file as sam. Are you successful? Now, delete the `test2` file as sam.

What do you conclude?

DAC vs MAC

The access control system that we have seen so far is **Discretionary Access Control** (**DAC**), as access to the files is granted at user discretion. User owner can control what access should be allowed to other users for the files that are owned by them. **Mandatory Access Control** (**MAC**) is an access control system where the operating system enforces access to various resources of the system. It provides strict access control with a high level of security. With DAC, users can grant any permission to any user over any file at their will. With MAC, the user cannot alter any access to the resources by themselves. Only the administrator can alter and enforce the access to resources. The resources or the files in the system are assigned a security label and categorized into hierarchy levels according to their confidentiality. Each user is also assigned a security label and a hierarchy level. When access is requested, the user level and security label is checked against the file's security label and confidentiality levels, and access is granted only when the user belongs to the same or higher level. Access is denied if the requesting user's security level is lower than that of the file's. Users with higher level in the hierarchy can access the resources at the same level or any of the lower levels.

In the next section, we will look at the mandatory access control-based model, **SELinux**, which is compiled into the Linux kernel itself. The problem with MAC is that it is complex to set up and does not scale easily when a new user is added to the system because configuration needs to change with each new user. So, many organizations use DAC and MAC together. You can protect highly sensitive data with MAC, while a regular user's file can be protected by DAC.

Security context

SELinux is a security mechanism built into the Linux kernel that provides MAC. By default, SELinux comes with few predefined access policies that provide restricted access to certain system resources. These policies have certain rules specified, and if a rule is violated, access is denied. If no written rule is available for a specified action, access is denied. By default, SELinux is enabled with these predefined policies. Any access to any file is allowed by a particular process or user only if it is specifically allowed by the written rules. If both DAC and MAC are in place, DAC rules are checked first, and then SELinux rules are checked. If DAC allows the access but the SELinux policy denies it, then access is not provided. If DAC rules deny the access, then SELinux rules are not checked.

Configuration of SELinux

The main configuration file for SELinux is **`/etc/selinux/config`**. This file contains several directives to control the status of SELinux. Two important directives are SELINUX and **SELINUXTYPE**.

The **SELINUX** directive specifies whether SELinux is enabled or disabled. SELinux is said to be enabled if this directive contains one of the two values: permissive or enforcing. The **`Permissive mode`** does not enforce any security policy but raises a warning in log file that a security policy rule is violated. The log file used is **`/var/log/messages`**. The **`Enforcing mode`** enforces the defined security rules and allows access to system resources according to these rules. Enforcing mode is the default setting.

The **SELINUXTYPE** directive can take one of the three values that are discussed below:

- `targeted`: With targeted, only the specific processes and services are confined to the SELinux policy. These services and processes run in restricted mode. All other processes can access system resources according to DAC. This is the default policy.
- `minimum`: This is a modification of the targeted policy. Only the selected processes are protected.
- `mls`: It implements multi-level security. All the processes, resources and users are assigned a category and a security level.

We will not discuss minimum or mls policy in this book; we will learn the default **`targeted`** policy in brief.

To check the current status of SELinux on your system, just type the following:

```
sestatus
SELinux status:            enabled
SELinuxfs mount:           /sys/fs/selinux
SELinux root directory:        /etc/selinux
Loaded policy name:          targeted
Current mode:              enforcing
Mode from config file:       enforcing
Policy MLS status:           enabled
```

```
Policy deny_unknown status:   allowed
Memory protection checking:   actual (secure)
Max kernel policy version:   33
```

It shows the output in multiple fields. Note that in the first field, **SELinux** is enabled. Refer to the **Current mode** and **Mode from config file** fields in the preceding output that shows that **SELinux** is enabled in the **enforcing** mode. Another important field in the preceding output is **Loaded Policy Name**, which is set to **targeted**. This field is controlled by the **SELINUXTYPE** directive in the configuration file.

You can use the **setenforce** utility to switch between the **permissive** and **enforcing** modes. The **getenforce** utility can be used to view the current mode. Any change made with **setenforce** does not persist across reboots. Passing **0** to **setenforce** will set the **SELinux** policy to **enforcing**, and passing **1** will change it to **permissive**. You should run these utilities as the root user, as shown here:

```
[root@localhost ~]# setenforce 0
[root@localhost ~]# getenforce
Permissive
[root@localhost ~]#
[root@localhost ~]# setenforce 1
[root@localhost ~]# getenforce
Enforcing
```

User and file context

Files created in a user's home directory are labelled with the **user_home_t** type. Any new file created will take the labelling rule according to its parent directory.

In Red Hat Enterprise Linux, users are mapped to the **SELinux unconfined_u** user by default. All processes run by **unconfined_u** run in the **unconfined_t** domain. This means that these processes and users are not confined by any **SELinux** policy and can access files across the system according to the DAC policy.

Since **SELinux** is enabled by default, any new user created will be mapped to a predefined security context: **unconfined_u**.

To view the mapping of SELinux user to the existing users, run the following command as root:

```
semanage login -l
Login Name      SELinux User     MLS/MCS Range     Service
__default__     unconfined_u     s0-s0:c0.c1023     *
root         unconfined_u     s0-s0:c0.c1023     *
```

Figure 8.1 displays all the available SELinux user list using the following command:

`semanage user -l`

```
[root@localhost ~]# semanage user -l

                Labeling   MLS/       MLS/
SELinux User    Prefix     MCS Level  MCS Range                      SELinux Roles

guest_u         user       s0         s0                             guest_r
root            user       s0         s0-s0:c0.c1023                 staff_r sysadm_r system_r unconfined_r
staff_u         user       s0         s0-s0:c0.c1023                 staff_r sysadm_r system_r unconfined_r
sysadm_u        user       s0         s0-s0:c0.c1023                 sysadm_r
system_u        user       s0         s0-s0:c0.c1023                 system_r unconfined_r
unconfined_u    user       s0         s0-s0:c0.c1023                 system_r unconfined_r
user_u          user       s0         s0                             user_r
xguest_u        user       s0         s0                             xguest_r
```

***Figure 8.1**: SELinux default users list*

Under SELinux, all the users, files, processes and devices are assigned specific labels known as security contexts. These contexts are stored in the extended attributes of the file system.

Check the security context of your ID by passing **`-Z`** to the **`id`** command, as follows:

`id -Z`

`unconfined_u:unconfined_r:unconfined_t:s0-s0:c0.c1023`

Security context contains four fields in the following format:

`user:role:type:security level`

The fields are described as follows:

- **`user`**: It defines the **`SELinux`** user to which the Linux user is mapped. In the preceding example, the current user is mapped to the **`unconfined_u`** user.
- **`role`**: It describes the role for which the mapped **`SELinux`** user is authorized.
- **`type`**: The **`type`** defines a domain for processes and logged in users and a type for files. By default, each process runs in its own domain. By default, all the **`SELinux`** users run in the **`unconfined_t`** domain.
- **`security level`**: **`s0`** is the default security level existing, and all users are labelled with **`s0`**. **`c0-c1023`** is the access category type. This is MLS range and is used when the **`SELinux`** security policy is set to MLS and is not targeted.

To view the security context for each file in the current directory, use the **`-Z`** option of the **`ls`** command as shown here:

`ls -Z`

```
[sam@vmachine ~]$ ls -Z
 unconfined_u:object_r:user_home_t:s0    unconfined_u:object_r:user_home_t:s0     unconfined_u:object_r:user_home_t:s0
 unconfined_u:object_r:user_home_t:s0   unconfined_u:object_r:audio_home_t:s0     unconfined_u:object_r:user_home_t:s0
 unconfined_u:object_r:user_home_t:s0    unconfined_u:object_r:user_home_t:s0
 unconfined_u:object_r:user_home_t:s0    unconfined_u:object_r:user_home_t:s0
```

***Figure 8.2:** Security context of files*

Figure 8.2 shows the output of the preceding command, which lists each file in the current directory along with its security context. The output shows that all the files residing in your home directory fall under the **user_home_t SELinux** type.

```
ls -Z /bin/passwd
system_u:object_r:passwd_exec_t:s0 /bin/passwd
```

The preceding command displays the security context for a system file. It is clear from the output that the **object_r** role is assigned to this file, but this role does not apply to the file. In the preceding output, **system_u** is the special **SELinux** user identity that is used for system processes and services. The file type is **passwd_exec_t**.

Now, start a **passwd** process by typing the **passwd** command in another terminal. Do not finish the process. Now, enter the following in the previous terminal:

```
ps -eZ|grep passwd
unconfined_u:unconfined_r:passwd_t:s0-s0:c0.c1023 16229 pts/2 00:00:00
passwd
```

In the preceding scenario, when a **passwd** utility labelled with the **passwd_exec_t** type is executed, it starts a **passwd** process in the **passwd_t** domain.

Let us check the security context for one of the system processes, say **atd**:

```
ps -eZ|grep atd
system_u:system_r:crond_t:s0-s0:c0.c1023 1212 ? 00:00:00 atd
```

For system processes, the **system_r** role type is used, and the domain differs for each process. **atd** runs in the **crond_t** domain. Similarly, other system services, such as web servers, are confined by the **SELinux** policy and run in their own domain. When the processes run in their own domain, they can only access the files that are allowed for them to access. They cannot access the files used by other processes. The advantages of using SELinux are that if the web server is compromised, then the files used by the web server are damaged. The attacker cannot use web server processes to access the other resources or files available in the system.

Chroot jail

Chroot jail restricts the process and ensures that it runs in a restricted directory tree only. This directory tree will be viewed as a root directory for that process. The mechanism of assigning a new root to a process is called **chroot jail**, as this process is restricted to run in a jail of a particular directory tree. The new root directory will be used for pathnames beginning with **/**. It cannot access any resources outside the directory tree where it has chrooted. This also applies to all child processes spawned by the process running under chroot jail.

Networking concepts

When computers talk to each other, we say that they are on a network. A network can be made up of only two computers or may contain thousands or millions of computers. Computers in a network may be located close to each other, within a house, on separate stories within a building, or at distant locations across the city, country or anywhere in the world. A network does not include only computers; it may also contain printer, drives, and other computing resources. Each of the computing resources, when connected to each other via any means, forms a network. The connection medium may be ethernet cable, fiber optic cables, telephone lines, or wireless. The network requirement is so diverse today that you cannot think of running a computer without a network. It is used as a communication medium nowadays. Due to the existence of networks, you do not have to buy a powerful mini or mainframe computer. You can efficiently achieve their benefits by just connecting to a network using cheaper desktop computers. You may need to connect to a network if you want to access and download the files that are stored in another system. If you want to use the printer service provided by a printer on the network, if you want to send an email to someone with another machine, or if you want to use any service that is not available on your stand-alone machine, you can do so. To accomplish all these tasks from your single machine, you must connect all those resources together in a network.

Today, we are all connected to the internet, which is the network of networks. Using the internet, we can talk to a person sitting anywhere in the world. You can also connect to the internet for web browsing, FTP services, interactive chatting, sending e-mails, tweeting, connecting with your friends via social networking sites and much more. This section provides you with a brief overview of networking concepts, and the next section will demonstrate how the network is configured.

Client/server model

A network can be formed in such a way that your machine, called **local machine**, is able to talk to a far-away computer, called **remote machine**, in such a way that the local machine can use the services of the remote machine. The machine that provides you with a service is called the **server**, and the machine that uses these services is called the **client**. This is known as the **client/server model**. A single computer may provide you with many services, where each service is configured to run on different ports. Services usually run as a daemon. Each daemon listens on a specific port number for the client's request. The client can use any port number to send any request to the server. For example, FTP service has two components: FTP client and FTP server. FTP server is the server that stores many public files to be downloaded by other computers, called FTP clients. FTP daemon runs on port 21. Any communication between client and server occurs via this port. When a connection is made to FTP server, it is established at port 21 on the server end, and the client may use any port number to connect to the server.

TCP/IP

For two or more machines to talk to each other, they must understand each other's language. So, they must follow the same set of rules for communication. The set of rules or the standard that computers use to communicate with each other is called **protocol**. Linux uses the TCP/IP protocol. TCP/IP is not a protocol but a protocol suite that bundles many protocols. It consists of two main protocols: the **Transmission Control Protocol (TCP)** and the **Internet Protocol (IP)**.

TCP is responsible for establishing a reliable, connection-oriented data transfer between two devices. It ensures that the data is transmitted in a correct order, with no loss or duplication of packets. TCP also includes flow control, congestion control, error detection, and correction mechanisms to ensure that data is transmitted efficiently and accurately.

IP is responsible for addressing and routing packets of data between devices on a network. Other protocols in the TCP/IP suite include **User Datagram Protocol (UDP), Internet Control Message Protocol (ICMP)** and **Address Resolution Protocol (ARP),** which we will discuss now:

- **UDP** is a connectionless, unreliable protocol that is used for transmitting data and does not provide guaranteed delivery.
- **ICMP** is used for sending error messages and operational information about network conditions.
- **ARP** is used to translate between IP addresses and physical addresses on a local network.

IP addresses

Each computer on the network carries a unique 32-bit address, which is known as its **IP address**. An IP address is assigned to the network interfaces available with the machine. A computer may have several interfaces, to which a unique IP address can be assigned. An IP address has two parts: network address and host address. If you connect two machines via a LAN cable and do some network configuration (which we will be talked about later), then they will be on the same network. The network part of the IP address will be the same for both the computers, but their host part will differ. An IP address can be given in decimal dotted notation, where every eight bytes are separated by a dot(`.`), as follows:

```
192.168.2.1
```

Each eight byte is converted into decimal form and is represented here. Each decimal number can have a range between 0-255.

All the valid IP addresses are divided into five classes: A, B, C, D, and E. Among the five classes, only class A, B and C are used for TCP/IP networks. Class D is used for multicasting, while class E is reserved for future use. Their ranges are specified in *Table 8.1*:

Class	Range	Number of bits for network address	Number of bits for host address
A	0.0.0.0-127.255.255.255	8 bits	24 bits
B	128.0.0.0-191-255.255.255	16 bits	16 bits
C	192.0.0.0-223.255.255.255	24 bits	8 bits

Table 8.1: *IP Address classes*

The classification of IP addresses into classes is based on the number of bits used for network address and host address. Among this range, some addresses are always reserved for the following:

- **Loopback address**: 127.0.0.1
- **Network address**: 192.168.88.0
- **Broadcast address**: Broadcast address is always assigned to the last IP address in the range; for example, 192.168.88.255 can be used as broadcast address for the network address 192.168.88.0. Broadcast address is used to send broadcast messages to all the machines on local network.

When multiple devices at home or at office are connected, a private network is formed. Computers in the private network can communicate with each other and can share data. But they are not connected to the outside world. No one outside the private network can access the data transmitted on the internal network. If the office or home network needs to connect to another network, a special device called **router** is required. Each computer in the internal network will get a private IP address to communicate with computers in the same network. For the network that never communicates with the outside world, any IP address range can be used. However, there are reserved sets of IP addresses that can be used for these kinds of private networks:

- 10.0.0.0 – 10.255.255.255
- 172.16.0.0 – 172.31.255.255
- 192.168.0.0 – 192.168.255.255

To communicate with the host outside the network, private IP addresses will not work. Any communication with other networks can be made using only the public IP address. So, a host can be assigned two IP addresses: public and private.s

Packets

Any information sent over the network is not transmitted as a whole stream; it is conveyed by breaking into several discrete pieces. Each piece is then added with some overhead, like source and destination address, error correction bits, and more. These pieces, with added overhead, form a packet. Each packet is then sent to the network, but they may arrive at the destination out of order. There may be huge traffic in the network while sending some of the packets, so each packet can follow a different route and may reach the destination out of order. Each packet, when it arrives at the destination, is checked for error correction. If any packets are corrupted while travelling, then the sender is requested to resend them. After all the packets arrive without any errors, they are assembled in the original order at the destination, and are then received by the host as the entire information.

Besides IP address, each machine has its **MAC** address, which is the address assigned by the manufacturer. TCP/IP protocol works in many layers. The IP address is used at the network layer of the TCP/IP protocol. At the lowest level, data transmission takes place by MAC address. Each machine on a network is also uniquely identified by its MAC address. An IP address can be assigned to any machine or host, but MAC address is machine-specific and is fixed for a machine. Before a destination receives a packet, the IP address is mapped to the MAC address, and then data is transferred to the receiving host.

Communication across the network

To make communication between two networks possible, a special device called router is required; it connects one network to another either directly or indirectly. A router must be used at the exit point of the network. The machine on the network should know about the router present at its gateway to the network so that the packet can be sent to another machine available outside the network. The router is assigned with a public IP address so that it can send the packets to another network. If two networks are connected directly using the same router, the router sends the packet directly to the destination network. When the two networks are not connected directly, a packet may reach the destination using many routers in between. Multiple paths may exist for a packet to reach the destination. The router, on receiving the packet, must decide on the best available path using various criteria, such as the shortest distance, network traffic and more, and send the packet accordingly.

A router can connect two networks together using two of its ports. Each port is assigned a unique IP address. Refer to Figure 8.3, where two networks NetA and NetB are connected directly via router R1. One port of R1 is connected to NetA, and another port of R1 is connected to NetB. If any machine on NetA wants to communicate with another machine on NetB, all the traffic will be sent via R1.

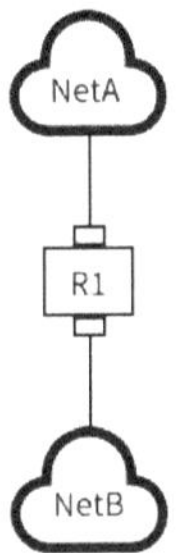

Figure 8.3: *Sample Network configuration*

Look at another network configuration given in *Figure 8.4*, where router R1 connects three networks via three ports. All the three ports are configured with three public IP addresses. Using R1, NetA, NetB, and NetC can communicate with each other directly. NetD and NetB are directly connected using router R2. NetD and NetA are also directly connected using router R3. There is no direct connection between NetC and NetD in the same figure. There are multiple paths available between these two networks. Traffic between NetD and NetC can be routed either via R2 and R1 or via R3 and R1. If a machine on NetD sends a packet to a machine on NetC, router R2 finds that it is not directly connected to the destination network, so it will determine the best available path to send the packet to NetC. Each packet can be delivered to NetC using different routes.

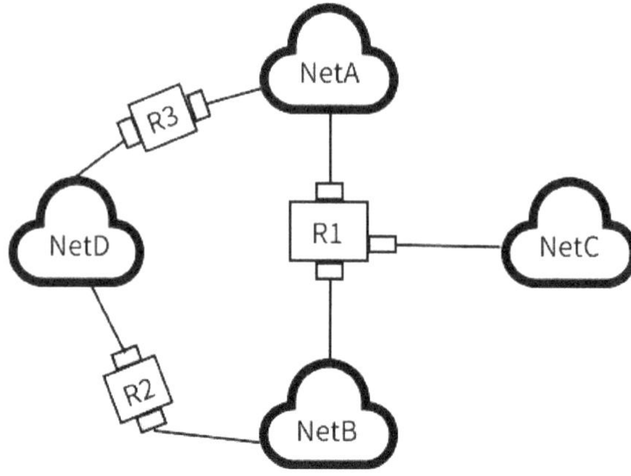

***Figure 8.4**: Sample network configuration connecting many networks*

Intranet

If an office has several branches at different locations of the city, the local network for all the branches needs to connect all of them for their daily tasks. This forms an intranet, and it represents an organization's internal network.

Loop back address

Each computer has a special address that points to itself. This is known as the loop back address. You can use this loop back address to test whether some networking services work properly on your machine.

Internet

The internet is the network of networks that spreads throughout the world. It connects billions to trillions of computers together using TCP/IP. In today's world, constant connectivity to the internet is a given, thanks to our mobile phones and portable devices.

Even at home, we can enjoy live streams of shows on our televisions, all made possible through the internet. The vast resources available online are easily accessible from the comfort of our homes using a web browser. Sending emails to people far away becomes effortless through the internet. Additionally, downloading public files hosted on servers is a breeze. To access these valuable resources, we simply reach out to our **Internet Service Provider (ISP)** for an internet connection. The internet has truly transformed the way we interact with information and stay connected in our daily lives.

A router is placed inside your home or office, and a public IP address is assigned to this router by the ISP that you choose. When any packet is destined for the internet, it is transmitted to this router, which, in turn, sends the packet to your ISP network. Thus, any traffic to the internet will travel via your ISP network. Therefore, any packet that is sent to the internet will reach your destination via your ISP network. All the IP addresses are being taken care of by an authority: **Internet Assigned Numbers Authority (IANA)**. They assign blocks of IP addresses to **Regional Internet Registries (RIRs)**, which, in turn, assign them to ISPs when they request.

IPv4 vs IPv6

The addressing scheme that we studied earlier is related to IPv4, where IP addresses are categorized into many classes, and each class has specific ranges and a fixed number of IP addresses that it supports. It provides a total of 2^{32} (which is approximately 4.3 billion) unique IP addresses. This range will not be able to fulfil the demand for IP addresses with growing internet connectivity. So, a new addressing scheme with **Internet Protocol V6 (IPv6)** is implemented. IPv6 provides a much larger address space than IPv4. IPv6 addresses are 128-bits long, which provides a total of 2^{128} (approximately 3.4×10^{38}) unique addresses. This allows for a virtually unlimited number of devices to be connected to the internet.

Host naming

If you have many machines on your local network, you cannot access a machine's resource by its IP address since it is difficult to remember the IP address of each machine. An easy-to-remember name is assigned to each host on the network. To communicate with another machines, you can use its name instead of IP. These names must be mapped into an IP address because each machine is uniquely identified by its IP address. The sender must have some name resolution mechanism in place that resolves the given hostname to a valid IP address. Here, the **/etc/hosts** file comes into the picture. The **/etc/hosts** file resides on every computer, which is used for name resolution. You can place the hostname and IP address combination in this file. Open this file and see what it contains:

```
cat /etc/hosts
127.0.0.1  localhost localhost.localdomain localhost4 localhost4.
localdomain4
::1      localhost localhost.localdomain localhost6 localhost6.
localdomain6
```

This file contains the default entries. The first line is the loopback address that the machine is using. This loopback address is mapped to a default host name, that is, **`localhost`**. **`localhost.localdomain`** is the full name of this machine. This full name is termed as FQDN, which we will talk about later. Thus, **`localhost`** is just the alias. **`localhost4`** is another alias, and **`localhost4.localdomain4`** is yet another alias. The entries in this file contain the IP address, followed by space- or tab-separated host names and aliases. The other line is related to **IPv6 addressing scheme**.

Suppose you want to communicate with a machine whose hostname is **`rmachine`** and IP address is 192.168.88.54. Add the following line at the bottom of your **`/etc/hosts`** file:

```
192.168.88.54       rmachine
```

After adding this line, you will be able to send a message using host's name instead of its IP address. Similarly, if you have many computers on the network, you can specify each computers's host name and IP address mapping to this file. The same can be done on other machines of the network so that they can also access any machine via its name.

When a new machine is added to the network, the **`/etc/hosts`** file on all the machines must be updated to reflect the new host entry.

We will learn how the host name is assigned in the upcoming sections.

WWW

You use the web browsers to access the vast resources available on the internet. The **World Wide Web** service is used to access web pages or other resources available on the internet. This service is based on the simple client server model, where web clients such as your browser request for a specific web page using a URL, and the web server listens on port 80 for web page requests. A **Uniform Resource Locator (URL)** is the fully qualified address of a web page. A URL specifies the website address as well as the path of the resource that you want to access. A URL may be of the following form:

```
Protocol://fqdn of host/full path of the page
```

For example, look at the following web address:

https://www.redhat.com

This is the fully qualified name of the web host. This address uses the HTTPS protocol that is used to fetch a web page from the web server. Now, if you want to access the contact page from this web page, the URL will be converted to the following:

https://www.redhat.com/en/contact

The protocol used in URL can either be http or https. It could also be FTP if you want to access files residing on the host.

HTTP/HTTPS

HyperText Transfer Protocol (HTTP) is used for communication between web clients and the web server. The web server listens on port 80 to for clients' web page requests and responds to the requests by sending the web page. HTTP is not a secure protocol, so any data sent over HTTP is vulnerable to interception and manipulation by third parties. This can increase your risk if you are transmitting sensitive information, such as passwords or credit card details over the internet.

HTTPS (HTTP Secure) is the secured version of the HTTP protocol that does not transmit data in plain text. It uses encryption to transmit the data securely between the two parties. With HTTPS, a secure connection is established to the web server and all the data transfer takes place over an encrypted session.

HTTP uses port 80, while HTTPS uses port 443.

FTP

File Transfer Protocol (FTP) is a protocol used for transferring files between computers on a network. It is based on client/server architecture. An FTP server hosts many files and is used for uploading and downloading files to and from the FTP server. FTP servers listen on port 21 for an FTP request, and an FTP client sends requests for files uploading or downloading to the FTP server. FTP transmits the login credentials in plain text, which can be intercepted during transmission, so it is an insecure protocol. As a result, a secure alternative, SFTP is now used for file transfers between two computers.

CIDR

In earlier days, classes schemes were used for IP addresses. Large organizations were assigned class A blocks, mid-sized organizations were assigned class B blocks, and smaller organizations are assigned class C blocks of addresses. As a result, numerous addresses within the assigned range remained unusable. Class C supports 2^8, that is, (256) hosts minus the two reserved addresses (network address and broadcast address), which makes the total to 254 hosts. If you have been assigned with a class C network, and you have only 100 hosts that need IP addresses, 154 IP addresses would be wasted. This inefficient use of IP addresses cannot accommodate the increasing number of computers on the internet. So, a new scheme of IP addressing, called **Classless Inter-Domain Routing (CIDR)** was invented. CIDR includes 32 bits address with dot notation, followed by a forward slash (/) and a number that specifies the number of bits reserved for network prefix.

For example, IP address **`192.168.88.128/24`** represents an IP address where 24 bits are reserved for network addresses. Here, the network prefix 24 is the netmask. **Netmask** determines the number of hosts available in the network. So, the number of hosts that can be accommodated is 2^8. Among this range, two IP addresses are always reserved:

192.168.88.0 and **192.168.88.255**. The first is the network address, and the second is the broadcast address.

Thus, CIDR provides more efficient use of IP addresses that allows organizations to request the number of addresses needed instead of looking for an IP address range based on classful addressing scheme.

Configuring network

In order to connect a machine to a network, the network administrator must configure the machine's networking settings to enable it to communicate with other machines on the network. A machine has several network interfaces, using which it talks to another machine. An IP address is assigned to these network interfaces and not to the host. A network administrator has to configure these interfaces properly to enable networking on the machine. RHEL9, by default, uses the **NetworkManager** utility that makes the work of the network administrator easier. In this section, we will learn how networking is configured in RHEL9 using the **NetworkManager** tool.

Networking configuration tools

NetworkManager (NM) is the default tool in RHEL that simplifies the configuration and management of network connections and devices. NM provides the following tools:

- **nmcli**: A command-line interface to configure network interfaces and network devices
- **nmtui**: A text-based user interface where navigation is done using cursor keys
- **nm-connection-editor**: A graphical user interface to use NM utility

You can use any of the listed tools at your end. In this chapter, we will use **nmcli** to configure networking.

NM stores configuration information in the **keyfile** format. These keyfiles are created in **/etc/NetworkManager/system-connections**.

We also have **IP** utilities where we can use the **ip addr** command to view connection profiles, **ip add** to add a connection, and more.

Besides these, we will see many other tools throughout the chapter to configure and monitor our network.

Assigning host name

Each machine is identified on the network by its IP address. It is difficult for us to access every machine on the network using its IP address, so each host on the network can be assigned an easy-to-remember name, called **hostname**. Let us find the hostname assigned to your machine using the following command:

```
nmcli general hostname
```

If you see a blank line, it means no hostname is set currently. To set a hostname, issue the following command:

```
nmcli general hostname vmachine.example.com
```

Let us now verify the hostname of your machine by issuing the following command:

```
nmcli general hostname
vmachine.example.com
```

Hostname is also visible via the `hostname` command and is permanently set in the `/etc/hostname` file.

```
ip route show
```

The preceding command displays the default router that will be used to access other networks, as shown in *Figure 8.5*. Here, the default gateway is **192.168.88.2**.

```
[visheshkumar@localhost ~]$ ip route show
default via 192.168.88.2 dev ens33 proto dhcp metric 100
192.168.88.0/24 dev ens33 proto kernel scope link src 192.168.88.128 metric 100
```

Figure 8.5: *IP command showing default route*

Configuring network interfaces

Before configuring network interfaces, let us identify the network interfaces that are available in your machine using the **ip** utility, as follows:

```
ip addr
```

```
[visheshkumar@localhost ~]$ ip addr
1: lo: <LOOPBACK,UP,LOWER_UP> mtu 65536 qdisc noqueue state UNKNOWN group default qlen 1000
    link/loopback 00:00:00:00:00:00 brd 00:00:00:00:00:00
    inet 127.0.0.1/8 scope host lo
       valid_lft forever preferred_lft forever
    inet6 ::1/128 scope host
       valid_lft forever preferred_lft forever
2: ens33: <BROADCAST,MULTICAST,UP,LOWER_UP> mtu 1500 qdisc fq_codel state UP group default qlen 1000
    link/ether 00:0c:29:e2:07:37 brd ff:ff:ff:ff:ff:ff
    altname enp2s1
    inet 192.168.88.128/24 brd 192.168.88.255 scope global dynamic noprefixroute ens33
       valid_lft 1579sec preferred_lft 1579sec
    inet6 fe80::20c:29ff:fee2:737/64 scope link noprefixroute
       valid_lft forever preferred_lft forever
```

Figure 8.6: *IP command showing available network interfaces on a Linux host*

The output in *Figure 8.6* gives us the details of two types of interfaces. The first interface is loopback type whose device name is **lo**. The second interface name is **ens33**, which is your ethernet card.

The output shows that the ethernet card is already configured. The **link/ether** field displays the MAC address. The IP address of **ens33** is 192.168.88.128/24, as displayed by the **inet** field. 192.168.88.128/24 is the CIDR notation of IP addressing scheme. This IP address is suffixed by a forward slash (/) and a number 24. 24 is the netmask that signifies the number of bits reserved for the network address. /24 means that the first 24 bits from the IP address is your network address. **/24** is the abbr of netmask 255.255.255.0. In binary format, subnet mask would have all 1s in the network part. Thus, you are part of the network whose address would be 192.168.88.0.

In the same figure, **brd** signifies broadcast address, which is 192.168.88.255 for ethernet card. For each network, the last address in the IP address range is reserved for broadcast address. In binary format, the host part field is all 1s in case of the **brd** address. Broadcast address is used to broadcast on a local network. The **inet6** field displays the IPv6 address.

You can also view the **nm** utility to view available network interfaces:

```
[visheshkumar@localhost ~]$ nmcli device
DEVICE TYPE   STATE   CONNECTION
ens33  ethernet connected ens33
lo    loopback unmanaged --
```

NetworkManager manages all the identified network-related devices except the loopback address. In the preceding output, **lo** is set to unmanaged, meaning it is not managed by NM. To set any other device to unmanaged, you can switch its state to **unmananged**, then that device will not be managed by NM but manually.

You can also use the **ip link** command to identify your ethernet card device name.

For the demonstration of configuring a network interface, we will add a network adaptor to our virtual machine. Go to **Virtual Machine Settings** and click the **Add** button that is displayed on the left panel. **Add Hardware Wizard** will open; select **Network Adaptor** from the **Hardware Types.** Click on the **Finish** button. Now, click on **ok** to close this window and apply the new settings to your virtual machine. Issue the **nmcli device** command again. This is what you will find:

```
nmcli device
DEVICE TYPE   STATE     CONNECTION
ens33  ethernet connected   ens33
ens36  ethernet disconnected --
lo    loopback unmanaged   --
```

A new ethernet card named **ens36** is added. This card is disconnected from the network. Let us configure it and bring it into the network. Issue the following set of commands:

```
nmcli connection add con-name ens36 ifname ens36 type ethernet
Connection 'ens36' (d983c299-7ec0-4bfd-8629-cbe9ac8c6924) successfully
added.
```

The preceding command creates a connection named **ens36** using **ens36** network interface. The related files are also automatically updated by the network manager with the preceding command. Any changes that are made to this network interface will be made using its connection name, which is just an arbitrary name.

Now, provide the **ipv4** address:

```
nmcli connection modify ens36 ipv4.addresses 192.168.200.46/24
```

The preceding command configures the **ens36** connection with CIDR IP address 192.168.200.46/24.

Set connection method to manual:

```
nmcli connection modify ens36 ipv4.method manual
```

Set the default gateway as follows:

```
nmcli connection modify ens36 ipv4.gateway 192.168.200.254
```

Activate the connection profile as follows:

```
nmcli connection up ens36
```

To display the details of a specific network connection, execute **nmcli connection show** command as follows:

```
nmcli connection show ens36
```

The preceding command will give you all the details of the specified network connection.

This way, we have configured networking on one computer. If you have other computers to configure, follow the same sequence of commands on all the computers but with different IP addresses.

To bring down any network connection, use the following:

```
nmcli connection down ens36
```

The files that are affected by these commands are listed here:

```
/etc/resolv.comf
/etc/NetworkManager/system-connections/ *.nmconnection
```

DHCP

Dynamic Host Configuration Protocol (DHCP) is a network protocol that is used to automatically assign IP addresses and other network configuration information to all the hosts on a network. This information is automatically made available to all the hosts. It puts little overhead on the network manager to allocate different network information to hosts. Any human error may cause the same IP addresses to be provided to two machines if it is configured manually, but DHCP server prevents any human error.

If you want to assign addresses dynamically using the **dhcp** server, execute the following command:

```
nmcli connection modify ens36 ipv4.dhcp-hostname dhcp-server
```

Replace **dhcp-server** with the address of the DHCP server. IP address and other details will be assigned dynamically. No manual configuration is required by network administrators.

Domain Name System

Domain Name System (DNS) is a method to map the IP address to hostnames. For a smaller network, you can add a name to address the mapping for all the hosts in the **/etc/hosts** file. You can place the same **/etc/hosts** entry in all the hosts. As the number of hosts increase on the network, it becomes a tedious task to manage the changes in the **/etc/hosts** file of all the existing hosts. If you connect to the internet, it is impossible to put entries of unlimited hosts on a local file. So, you have to switch to DNS. DNS manages this mapping through a distributed database. A set of servers, called **name servers**, accept requests for name resolution and work in collaboration for resolving host names to the correct IP addresses.

Your machine must be aware of the nameserver that will resolve your request of mapping hostname to IP address.

By default, the network manager automatically manages settings for DNS server by using activated connection profiles. Whenever network request is made using hostname, resolver comes into picture. It will either use **/etc/hosts** or DNS for name resolution. It first looks in **/etc/hosts** for name resolution. If name is not found in **/etc/hosts**, it sends resolution request to one of the nameservers it knows. The **/etc/resolv.conf** file contains the list of IP addresses of name servers to use for host name resolution. You can list up to three name servers. In case one is down, another in the list is searched for name resolution. It may contain the entries like this:

```
nameserver 192.168.88.127
nameserver 192.168.88.126
```

It first sends the request to the first nameserver listed; if it cannot be contacted or is down, then another server is contacted for the purpose. If one nameserver does not have the answer to this query, then it forwards the request to another. Thus, with the cooperation of many name servers, host name is resolved to a valid IP address.

You can access your machine by either using its host name as **server1** or its **Fully Qualified Domain Name** (**FQDN**) as **server1.example.com**. The part after the first dot is called the domain name. **Domain name** is assigned to an organization by the assigning authority, called **Internet Corporation for Assigned Names and Numbers (ICANN)**. This authority will give you the domain name, and you will be responsible for your host part. The rightmost string after the last period(.) is the **Top-Level Domain** (**TLD**). The remaining part in the domain name identifies the organization that is an unused name chosen by the organization and assigned to it by ICANN accredited registrar. The domain name may contain more than two strings also.

The host name, that is, **`server1.example.com`**, is a FQDN. Here, **`com`** is a top-level domain, **`example`** is a subdomain and **`server1`** is the host name.

Domains and subdomains form as hierarchy in a DNS system, starting with the root domain, which is represented by a dot (.). There are several top-level domains, such as **gov, com, in, edu,** and **org** available under root domain. In this example, **`com`** acts as a top-level domain that resides under the root domain. Within each TLDs, we may have several sub-domains. Here, **`example`** is subdomain residing under the **`com`** domain. In **`amazon.com`**, **`amazon`** is a subdomain residing under the **`com`** domain. This hierarchy can be descended to further levels.

TLDs represents the type of organization. For example, **`edu`** represents a educational organization, **`gov`** represents a government organization. Some two-letter TLDs refer to the country; for example, **`in`** refers to India.

FQDN can be quite long as it may contain more than two dots containing many levels of subdomains. It might be tedious to type long FQDNs. So, you can choose an alias for the FQDN and write it in your **`/etc/hosts`** file. Add the following line at the bottom of the / **etc/hosts** file:

```
192.168.88.50 vmachine vmachine.example.com
```

The preceding entry will give an alias **`vmachine`** to **`vmachine.example.com`**.

Type the **`dnsdomainname`** command on your terminal; it will return **`example.com`**.

Use the following to set the DNS for your network connection:

```
# nmcli connection modify ens36 ipv4.dns dns-server-ip-address
```

In the preceding command, replace **`dns-server-ip-address`** with the IP address of your DNS server. If you have multiple DNS servers, then specify the comma-separated IP addresses enclosed in double quotes.

You can perform DNS lookup for the given name by using **`host`**, **`nslookup`** or the **`dig`** command. Here, we will use **`dig`**, which is mostly used by Linux administrators to understand DNS lookup.

```
dig google.com
```

The preceding command contacts one of the name servers listed in **`/etc/resolv.conf`**, which coordinates the other name server and fetches the IP addresses that corresponds to the preceding domain. The **`host`** command can also do **reverse lookup** when you provide IP address as its argument.

Viewing network connectivity information

In this section, we shall discuss the utilities that can be used to verify whether the network is properly configured and is available.

Ping

After you have configured network interfaces successfully, it is time to check whether your machine can send any packets to another machine; use the following command:

```
ping <your hostname>
```

You can also use **ping** to check whether a particular host is running. Use the **ping** command, as follows:

```
ping vmachine
PING vmachine (192.168.88.50) 56(84) bytes of data.
64 bytes from vmachine (192.168.88.50): icmp_seq=1 ttl=64 time=0.322 ms
64 bytes from vmachine (192.168.88.50): icmp_seq=2 ttl=64 time=0.197 ms
2 packets transmitted, 2 received, 0% packet loss, time 1002ms
```

Using *Ctrl+C*, you will get statistics at the end. 0% packet loss means everything is configured properly at your end. You can also use this command to check network connectivity form the localhost to remote host. Also, notice how the name **vmachine** is resolved to IPaddress 192.168.88.50. Resolver reads the **/etc/hosts** file first to resolve names. If it is not available here, then it fetches the information from name servers from **/etc/resolv.conf**.

Finding port

Finding the port number on which a particular service is running on the host is one of the regular tasks of a network administrator. Use the **ss** utility to display detailed information about network sockets and connections. Use the following command to display all the sockets that listen over TCP:

```
ss -tl
```

It will give you the output shown in *Figure 8.7*:

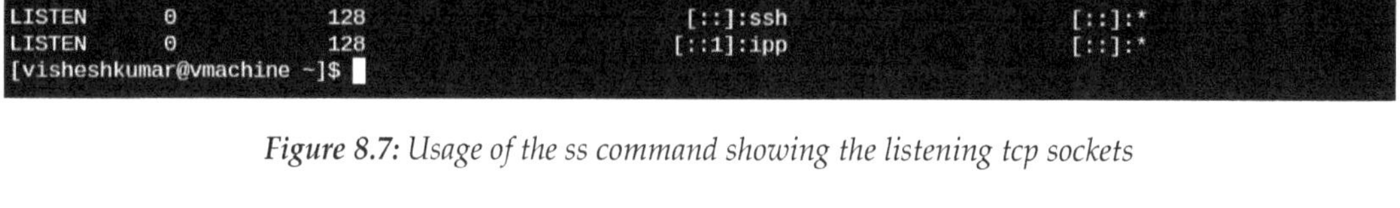

```
[visheshkumar@vmachine ~]$ ss -tl
State      Recv-Q      Send-Q          Local Address:Port          Peer Address:Port      Process
LISTEN     0           128                   0.0.0.0:ssh                0.0.0.0:*
LISTEN     0           128                 127.0.0.1:ipp                0.0.0.0:*
LISTEN     0           10                          *:rfb                      *:*
LISTEN     0           128                    [::]:ssh                     [::]:*
LISTEN     0           128                   [::1]:ipp                     [::]:*
[visheshkumar@vmachine ~]$
```

Figure 8.7: Usage of the ss command showing the listening tcp sockets

Here, all the sockets that listen over TCP are listed. The **-t** option lists TCP sockets, and the **-l** option lists only listening sockets. The preceding output is not displaying the port number on which the service is running. To display the port number, execute the following command:

```
ss -tnl
```

It will give you the output shown in *Figure 8.8*:

```
[visheshkumar@vmachine ~]$ ss -tnl
State      Recv-Q      Send-Q          Local Address:Port           Peer Address:Port      Process
LISTEN     0           128                   0.0.0.0:22                  0.0.0.0:*
LISTEN     0           128                 127.0.0.1:631                 0.0.0.0:*
LISTEN     0           10                          *:5900                      *:*
LISTEN     0           128                      [::]:22                     [::]:*
LISTEN     0           128                     [::1]:631                    [::]:*
[visheshkumar@vmachine ~]$
```

Figure 8.8: *Usage of the ss command showing service to port mapping*

Other useful options that you can use with **ss** utility are listed here:

- **-a**: Display both listening and non-listening sockets
- **-u**: Display UDP sockets
- **-p**: Display processes information using sockets

Tracing the path

The **tracepath** command-line utility can be used to test network connectivity problems. **tracepath** replaces the earlier traceroute utility. The **tracepath** utility traces the path that will be followed to reach a packet to the destination. Let us use **tracepath** to trace the route from your localhost to **google.com**, as follows:

```
tracepath google.com
```

After you press *Enter*, it will begin tracing the route and listing out IP addresses of all the routers through which the packet passes on its way to the remote host. Along with the IP address of each router, it prints the time taken by the packet to reach that router.

Securing network

After you have configured the networking on your host, you cannot sit back to relax, as you are now more prone to external threats by hackers. Your data, including information and passwords, if traveling in plain text, can be seen and altered by any intruder on the network. So, network security is of utmost importance to you. When you connect yourself to the network or internet, you must think of securing your network at the most prioritized job. In recent versions of RHEL, all the utilities that transmit the data in plain text have been disabled. In the earlier version of RHEL, we had the **telnet** utility to remotely log in on another host and run commands on a remote server. We had the **ftp** utility to copy the files from and to the FTP server. The problem with these utilities was that all the information from source to destination was transferred in plain text. Anyone with access to network traffic can easily intercept and read the data, including login credentials and other sensitive information. So, **telnet** and **ftp** are not recommended for use over the internet or any other untrusted network. Instead, you can use their secure alternative: the **Secure Shell (ssh)** protocol. This protocol ensures that information is never transferred in plain text. All the data transfer takes place between client and server in an encrypted session. It also ensures that if any packet is intercepted by an intruder in transit, message contents cannot be altered. Thus, information will reach the destination in its original form. To understand how this protocol works, we must first understand cryptography, which is the basis of any secure protocol. In this section, we will first understand what cryptography is and how it protects your information, and then we will discuss various secure services that you can use to access the resources safely over the internet.

Cryptography

Cryptography is a method used to hide the original data in transit so that if the packet is intercepted, the hacker cannot restore the actual information and thus, cannot modify its contents. Thus, it ensures that the information is sent to the destination in its original form. It is used to protect information in transit as well as in rest. The data in storage media can also be hidden so that if the storage device is stolen, the data on it cannot be read by any unauthorized person. Cryptography methods convert the plain text into an unintelligible form that cannot be easily decoded by the thief; only the intended recipient can restore it back to the original plain text and read it. When any message or information is converted into an unintelligible form that is hard to decode by an unauthorized person, it is called **ciphertext**. The process of generating ciphertext from plain text is called **encryption**. Thus, ciphertext means **encrypted text**. The process that converts the encrypted text back to its original intelligible form is called **decryption**. Cryptography uses various algorithms to hide sensitive information. Cryptography algorithms use various mathematical operations and a set of rule-based calculations to encrypt information. The source and destination parties must agree on the algorithm used. The information encrypted with one algorithm can only be decrypted with the same algorithm. Each cryptography algorithm requires a **key,** which is used to encrypt the data. The same key is also used to decrypt the data, so the intended receiver must also know the key to decrypt the encrypted text. The key must be large enough so that the encrypted message is almost impossible to decode in timely manner. Brute-force attacks is the most common technique to guess the key. Timely correct guesses of the key will make all the information readable and create a nuisance for an organization. The longer the key, the stronger is the ciphertext. If it takes a long time to decrypt the data, the information might become void in the long run and not lead to any business loss. If our key is 128-bit long, then the attacker will try 2^{128} combinations to guess the correct key. It takes many days to try all the combinations and create intelligible text from the ciphertext. Today, algorithms are strong enough to ensure that by looking at the ciphertext, an attacker will not be able to guess the property of the ciphertext or the actual key itself. Cryptography techniques become more important when performing banking transactions on the internet.

Objectives of cryptography

It has the following objectives:

- **Confidentiality**: It means that the message can only be read and understood by the intended recipient.
- **Integrity**: It means that the information in transit is not altered. Thus, it ensures that the receiver receives the original message sent by the source party.
- **Non-repudiation**: The sender cannot deny that they sent the message.
- **Authentication**: It always authenticates the sender and thus, the recipient is assured that the message is indeed from the sender.

Type of cryptography

Cryptography is the technique of secure communication between the two parties over untrusted networks. There are three types of cryptography; let us look at each one.

Symmetric key cryptography

This ensures that a single key will be used to encrypt the message in transit or at rest. The receiver and sender must agree on the secure key, which must be transferred via a secure means over the untrusted network. If not transferred securely, it could be intercepted and accessed by someone else in the network, compromising the transmission. Some of the algorithms of symmetric key are **Advanced Encryption Standard (AES)** and **Data Encryption Standard (DES)**. It can be used in encrypting large disk to protect the data in rest. When you protect the data in rest with a symmetric key, that key has to be placed in a safe location and should not be lying along with the actual ciphertext. If you store the key and ciphertext together, anyone who has unauthorized access to your storage media can view the key, decrypt all your data, and read the sensitive information, which may lead to business loss. As an added security, you should never store your encryption key in plaintext format. .

Asymmetric key cryptography

Asymmetric key cryptography is also called **public key cryptography**, and it uses a pair of two keys: **private key** and **public key**. The public key is known to all, even to an intruder. The private key, on the other hand, is never transferred to anyone. In this technique, the public key of the receiver is used to encrypt the data, which can only be decrypted by the private key of the recipient. Thus, anyone who intercepts the data in transit cannot decrypt this as they do not have the private key. Private key is known to its owner only, so only they can decrypt the data. This mechanism is used to encrypt the key for symmetric encryption. One of the communicating clients generates the session key and encrypts it with the public key of another client. The encrypted key is sent over the unencrypted network, which can only be decrypted by the private key of the intended recipient. After the session key is shared securely between the two parties, all the communications can be made between two parties via the symmetric algorithm using this key. A widely used algorithm for asymmetric key cryptography is **Rivest, Shamir, Adleman (RSA)**. The name RSA comes from the names of the inventors of this algorithm.

Another usage of public key cryptography is in authentication. User A signs their message with their private key, and anyone with User A's public key can decrypt the signed message. Successful decryption of the message gives assurance that message is indeed sent from user A only.

Hash functions

It ensures data integrity. A hash function is a mathematical function that takes a message of arbitrary size as its input and produces a fixed-size output called a **hash**, **hash value**, or **message digest**. Hash function is one-way function, meaning the hash generated cannot be retrieved to its original form by any means. Hash functions are used to verify the integrity of data to the recipient. The hash value of the message is sent along with the message by the sender party. At the receiving end, the hash value is calculated from the received message and compared with the original hash value. If the hash value of the information is the same as the received hash, it indicates that the data has not been tampered with in transit. Hash function is also used to store passwords on computers in hashed form. If password is stored in plain text, it can be seen by anyone else who gets unauthorized access to the system. When a user is logging in, the entered password is hashed and then verified against the stored hash. If it is the same, login is allowed. Common examples of hash functions are SHA-1, SHA-256, MD5, and HMAC.

Secure services

RHEL provides a **OpenSSH** tool for secure communication and data transmission over unsecured networks. OpenSSH implements the SSH protocol. OpenSSH suite includes secure services like **`ssh`**, **`sftp`**, **`scp`**, and more that enable secure remote login, secure file transfer and more on encrypted connection. It implements cryptography principles to provide all the secure facilities. Let us discuss some of the useful utilities provided by OpenSSH.

Secure shell

SSH is used for secure remote login. It provides a secure tunnel for transmission of data between the sender and receiver. It replaces the older unsecured application, telnet, which sends password in plain text. It is used to log in on the remote machine and execute commands over there.

When the user wants to log in to the remote machine, they must prove their identity to the remote machine. You can connect to a remote machine using the password or the key. Use of keys is much safer than the use of password because the latter can be guessed more easily. You need the IP address or host name of the remote machine and a user name to log in with.

To connect to the remote server, **OpenSSH Daemon (sshd)** must be running on it. SSH daemon listens for client requests on port 22.

It uses cryptography for transmitting data and asymmetric encryption for key distribution. To authenticate host, it uses asymmetric encryption, while to transfer bulk data, it uses symmetric encryption.

To access a machine named `machine1.example.com`, you will type the following:

```
ssh vmachine.example.com
The authenticity of host 'vmachine.example.com
(fe80::20c:29ff:fee2:737%ens33)' can't be established.
ED25519 key fingerprint is
SHA256:Isk0s3326GHLdfB8TsYCgho9DwN56R297E0KtfuKX+o.
This key is not known by any other names
Are you sure you want to continue connecting (yes/no/[fingerprint])? Yes
Warning: Permanently added 'vmachine.example.com' (ED25519) to the list
of known hosts.
visheshkumar@vmachine.example.com's password:
Activate the web console with: systemctl enable -now cockpit.socket
Register this system with Red Hat Insights: insights-client -register
Create an account or view all your systems at https://red.ht/insights-
dashboard
Last login: Tue Mar 28 11:17:06 2023
```

The preceding command will log you to the remote server using the same user to which you are currently logged-in. If the user with the same name also exists on the remote server, login is allowed. To specify a different user, type this:

```
ssh user@machinename
```

During the connection, the server transfers its host key to the client to identify itself. If the client is communicating with the server for the first time, the host key is unknown to it. So, you will be asked whether you trust the host, and if you type `yes`, the key is added to the `~/.ssh/known_hosts` file. It will then prompt you for the password of the remote user. From then on, connection to the same server will check the host key against the saved host key. If the host key matches, it assures that you are indeed communicating to the same host. Next time, when you try to logging in to the same host using the `ssh` command, it would prompt you to enter only the password, and the server will automatically be trusted.

By default, your connection request will try to connect to a remote server on port 22. If the remote server is using a different port, say 27, to run ssh daemon, specify the port number using the **-p** option in your connection request, as follows:

```
ssh -p 27 user@machinename
```

The preceding connection request is using password-based-authentication. The problem with password-based authentication is that the password can be seen by the intruder in transit. To alleviate this limitation, you can use key-based authentication where you provide key to authenticate yourself to the server. Key-based authentication also eliminates the need for you to retype the password again and again. To use key-based authentication, SSH key pairs must be generated for each user.

Figure 8.9 displays the process of public-private key pair generation:

```
[visheshkumar@vmachine ~]$ ssh-keygen
Generating public/private rsa key pair.
Enter file in which to save the key (/home/visheshkumar/.ssh/id_rsa):
Enter passphrase (empty for no passphrase):
Enter same passphrase again:
Your identification has been saved in /home/visheshkumar/.ssh/id_rsa
Your public key has been saved in /home/visheshkumar/.ssh/id_rsa.pub
The key fingerprint is:
SHA256:TdgPpXjhUbCgdZAZq8Aqac3s1kWRUp+GDheZqxKJHHQ visheshkumar@vmachine.example.com
The key's randomart image is:
+---[RSA 3072]----+
|.. E  .+O==oo    |
| ... . *BO.*     |
|. o +.o+=+O      |
| +++ .=o.+ o     |
|o..+. ooS . .    |
|.......          |
|   o..           |
|  .              |
|                 |
+----[SHA256]-----+
```

Figure 8.9: *ssh-keygen command generating key pairs for asymmetric cryptography*

For generating public and private key pair, we have used **ssh-keygen** utility as in figure 8.9. By default, RSA key-pair is generated. Your private key is saved as **id_rsa** and public key is saved as **id_rsa.pub** under **~/.ssh/**. It asks you for the pass phrase that will encrypt your private key and keep it safe if your storage media is accessed by an unauthorized party. Your keys must have restricted permission of octal value 600 so that no one else can access and read the keys except the owner.

After you have generated ssh key pairs, the next task is to transfer public key to the remote server. There are many ways to do this. One of the widely used methods is to send the public key to server admin via email. Another way could be using **scp**, which we will look at later. Your public key contents will look as shown in *Figure 8.10*:

```
[visheshkumar@vmachine ~]$ cat .ssh/id_rsa.pub
ssh-rsa AAAAB3NzaC1yc2EAAAADAQABAAABgQCG7ZusRo6QeuDRLOQ2paBRdcFrTKutaQj8kOak6XKlJ8BzMGxT79FjVIAvga/88SfxeE6WY3C
q5zuVRls5/pwBVYyOlfKa8bLm5yrt+0FA409mc6UJnP49EzU0X1k8efsGyVHBwcx7o1hJuFJ5YaY6f2RNrPhEluSVdT02hcyZB5nCAO/InJvThs
TmvvkBkQLBPfY5col/RwPY3aTrRbVwF6gL//HwFSvty1HXJU8btLaN557MtsLzXw+qdwCdWqsvLCe8HH7n2ffWPAkP/SePByXUvxsVCwXEkDx1c
9Vq9iH2tcaYrN1WGJ3eHyfMQVG9Io/2dku5mBc3v2osGZqfsYnEhL7cCjScZ0+FxyQYyzQ88/StPQygSDPYx45gxszocJSc7ba4qWgxp4KGEhjS
87wa05oY9KxdRFFTZKNnAktplKlPI44km+SqNxzwjQbxBDNdiyXTl5Z046a40gaRM4WqAjpPsKtHwQfaWwbCKcs7BWj6dpmhZk5h7swQD+8= vi
sheshkumar@vmachine.example.com
[visheshkumar@vmachine ~]$
```

Figure 8.10: *Public key format*

Public key must be copied to the remote server's user account **~/.ssh/authorized keys** file. Your key must be copied at the end of this file on the server. The permission of this file must be 600. If file permission is not restricted, then **ssh** access is not allowed.

Now, for key-based login to remote server, just type this:

ssh user@machinename

You will get the output shown in *Figure 8.11*:

```
[visheshkumar@vmachine ~]$ ssh  vmachine.example.com
Activate the web console with: systemctl enable --now cockpit.socket

Register this system with Red Hat Insights: insights-client --register
Create an account or view all your systems at https://red.ht/insights-dashboard
Last login: Wed Apr  5 10:53:35 2023 from fe80::20c:29ff:fee2:737%ens33
```

Figure 8.11: *ssh command to remote login*

The preceding command will use your private key to authenticate you. By default, it will search for the **.ssh/id_rsa** file under the user's home directory. After you are successfully authenticated, you will be logged in to the remote machine. You will then be on the remote machine and can type **exit** anytime to exit it.

If your key is located in a non-default location or uses a different name in the default location, then specify the **-I** option to specify the key-pair path and file name.

If the server does not find any key file, it will ask you for the password. To completely disable password-based authentication so that the password never travels over the network in plain text, open the **/etc/ssh/sshd_config** file on the server and change the following line:

#PasswordAuthentication yes

to

PasswordAuthentication no

View the default permission of the **~/.ssh** directory. This is 700 just to ensure the safety of this file.

You can also use **ssh** to execute a command without getting a terminal shell prompt into the remote server. Suppose you want to delete a file name **file1** from remote machine; type this:

ssh vamchine.example.com rm file1

The preceding command will delete the file named **file1** after authenticating the user while the user is still on their local shell session.

The destination of the remote host can also be specified as follows:

URI of the form ssh://[user@]hostname[:port]

Configuration of ssh

System-wide configuration is stored under the **/etc/ssh** directory, while the user's specific configuration is stored in **~/.ssh**. **/etc/ssh/ssh_config** is the client-side configuration file, while **/etc/ssh/sshd_config** is the server-side config file.

Scp

Ssh also provides **scp** utility used to copy files from remote machine to local machine and vice-versa. Since **scp** is part of **ssh** package, the **ssh** daemon should be running on the remote machine. Any configuration of **ssh** also applies here. With **scp**, the same keys pairs you generated earlier are used. The way of authenticating the user is same as **ssh**.

The following command will copy **/tmp/file1** from the remote host to **/tmp** on the local computer:

```
scp user@host:/tmp/file1 /tmp/
```

The following command copies the **/tmp/1.sh** file from local host to the remote host under the **/tmp** directory:

```
scp /tmp/1.sh user@host:/tmp/
```

Here are the options that you can further use with **ssh**:

- **-P**: To use non-default port
- **-r**: To copy the entire directory recursively
- **-i**: For key-based authentication if the key file resides in a non-default location

SFTP

This is OpenSSh secure file transfer. It is a secure alternative to FTP. It performs all the file transfer operations over an encrypted **ssh** transport. The destination may be specified either as **[user@]host[:path]** or as a URI in the **sftp://[user@]host[:port][/path]** form.

Since **sftp** runs as a part of the **ssh** utility, any configuration for **ssh** also applies here.

sftp uses the FTP protocol to transfer a file from remote to local on the same or another network and vice versa. But this file transfer takes place in an encrypted session. The difference between **scp** and **sftp** is that **sftp** requires you to log in to the remote machine to transfer the files, but **scp** allows you to transfer the files without logging in to the remote machine.

Other options include the following:

- **-P**: Port number using which to connect to the FTP server
- **-p**: Preserves modification times, access times, and modes from the original files transferred
- **-r** : Recursively copies entire directories when uploading and downloading

We can use sftp in interactive and non-interactive mode. In the interactive mode, commands are case-insensitive. To learn commands that are used in an interactive FTP session, see man pages.

To connect to SFTP server, say **vmachine** execute following command:

```
sftp vmachine
Connected to vmachine.
sftp>
```

The preceding command will simply log you in using the same authentication method as used for **ssh** and start a secure interactive session between you and the remote server. The **sftp>** prompt will be displayed to you, to enter set of commands. Your working directory will be set to the remote user's home directory.

```
sftp vmachine:/tmp
```

The preceding command will open an FTP session between you and remote host **vmachine**, and you will change into the **/tmp** directory. From then on, you can interact with the server using various commands. To get a list of commands, type **?** at the **ftp** prompt. The file transfer will take place in encrypted mode. Type **quit** or **exit** to close the interactive session.

```
sftp vmachine:/tmp/no_see_lead
```

The preceding command will automatically fetch the **/tmp/no_see_lead** file from the remote server and copy it to your local server under the current directory. An interactive session will not be started in this case.

For non-default port, use the **-P** option. The **-i** option is used to specify key file.

Firewall

Firewall provides a mechanism where the internal network of company is protected from any outside intrusion. It is rule-based. Firewall monitors any incoming traffic and allows the traffic to enter the company's network only if is it allowed by the specified rules.

RHEL9.0 uses **firewalld** daemon to support firewall. It is enabled by default. Issue this:

```
systemctl status firewalld
```

You will get the output shown in *Figure 8.12*. The output shows that the **firewalld** daemon is active and running with default rules. Earlier versions of RHEL used **iptables**, which are less flexible and less user-friendly than the **firewalld**.

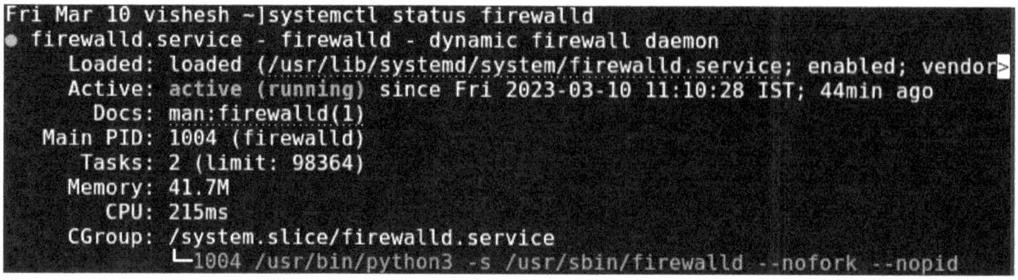

```
Fri Mar 10 vishesh ~]systemctl status firewalld
● firewalld.service - firewalld - dynamic firewall daemon
     Loaded: loaded (/usr/lib/systemd/system/firewalld.service; enabled; vendor>
     Active: active (running) since Fri 2023-03-10 11:10:28 IST; 44min ago
       Docs: man:firewalld(1)
   Main PID: 1004 (firewalld)
      Tasks: 2 (limit: 98364)
     Memory: 41.7M
        CPU: 215ms
     CGroup: /system.slice/firewalld.service
             └─1004 /usr/bin/python3 -s /usr/sbin/firewalld --nofork --nopid
```

***Figure 8.12**: Systemctl utility showing firewalld status*

firewalld uses a set of rules to determine what traffic is allowed to enter the network and what traffic is disallowed. Discussion of firewall configuration and related tools is beyond the scope of this book.

Wireless network and profiles

Today, most modern hardware include Wi-Fi devices. This modern hardware may or may not have any Ethernet card. If they do not have any Ethernet card, you can configure Wi-Fi devices for networking. We will use the same utility tool **nmcli** to configure a Wi-Fi device.

Finding out Wi-Fi device

Type the following:

```
nmcli device
DEVICE    TYPE   STATE     CONNECTION
wlo1     wifi   connected   TuxAcademy_5G
p2p-dev-wlo1 wifi-p2p disconnected --
lo       loopback unmanaged   --
```

You will get a list of all the available Wi-Fi devices with your hardware. Output shows that **wlo1** is available and **NetworkManager** has already configured it when we attempted to connect to the network the first time. You can view network connections file under **/etc/NetworkManager/system-connections/**.

Configuring Wi-Fi device

If you want to configure your Wi-Fi device assuming that your Wi-Fi device is not already configured, it is a prerequisite that you have Wi-Fi network. Another requirement is that your Wi-Fi device must be enabled in **NetworkManager**. To check whether your Wi-Fi device is enabled, type this:

```
nmcli radio
WIFI-HW WIFI   WWAN-HW WWAN
```

```
enabled enabled enabled enabled
```

If the output shows that the Wi-Fi device is disabled, then you can turn it on by typing the following:

```
nmcli radio wifi on
```

Now, to view available Wi-Fi networks, type this:

```
nmcli device wifi list
```

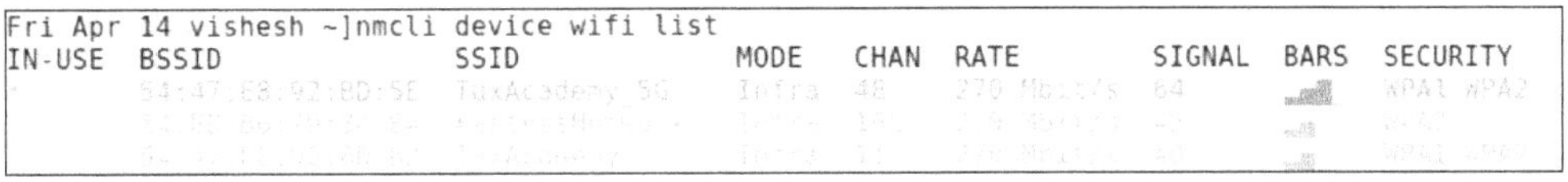

```
Fri Apr 14 vishesh ~]nmcli device wifi list
IN-USE  BSSID              SSID            MODE   CHAN  RATE        SIGNAL  BARS  SECURITY
*       54:47:E8:92:BD:5E  TuxAcademy_5G   Infra  48    270 Mbit/s  64            WPA1 WPA2
```

Figure 8.13: nmcli utility usage - showing available Wi-Fi devices on the host

The output in *Figure 8.13* shows the available Wi-Fi networks in SSID column.

Let us try to connect to a Wi-Fi network if you are not already connected. Type the following:

```
nmcli device wifi connect wifi-network-name --ask
```

Replace wifi-network-name with the Wi-Fi network name to which you want to connect. Here, the ask option will prompt you for the Wi-Fi password. Type the password and press the *Enter* key. If the preceding command does not work, you have to do manual configuration, as follows:

```
nmcli connection modify TuxAcademy ipv4.method manual ipv4.addresses
192.168.1.60/24 ipv4.gateway 192.168.1.1 ipv4.dns "103.62.236.85
103.62.236.84"
```

Now, activate your connection using the preceding profile, as shown here:

```
nmcli connection up TuxAcademy
```

View the connection settings using the following:

```
nmcli connection show TuxAcademy
```

Monitoring logs

For monitoring the system for some events, logging is important. Security hardening is not enough; you must have ways to find unauthorized access attempts made on the system, packets that arrived on your network, events occurred on the system, and suspicious user activities so that any security breaches can be prevented. System logs are a great place to look for various authorized and unauthorized events that occur on your server. To protect yourself from network breaches, faults, non-availability of services and future panics, network monitoring is important.

Each network device sends some logging information that can be stored and analyzed later by the system admin. Any logging system stores messages based on the timestamps of events. Logging makes it possible to view events that occurred on specific dates. It discloses various kinds of system information to system admin. They use it for troubleshooting. Two of the logging systems that we will discuss here are **Rsyslog** and **systemd** journal.

Rsyslog

Syslog can be said to be a protocol or a standard used to store various messages and diagnostic information generated from various applications/daemons or network devices running on the system. Syslog defines a format and semantics by which messages are formatted. **rsyslog** is an improvement or extension of syslog. Both have been used for log management in Linux for ages.

Applications should be aware of the syslog server if they need to send diagnostic messages to it. Syslog logs the messages according to specified rules. Some default rules are already written in its config file. Rules specify what facility will write what level of logs. Facility is the subsystem or the program that generates the logs. Each line of log written in the log file has some severity level. Log levels can be any of the following:

- **Emerg**: The log contains emergency messages, which signifies that the system is in emergency mode and is not usable.
- **Alert**: An alert condition needs to be acted on immediately.
- **Crit**: System is in critical state.
- **Err**: Critical errors are stored.
- **Warn**: Warnings are logged.
- **Notice**: It generates notice that are important for the user to know.
- **Info**: Informational messages are stored.
- **Debug**: It stores more drastic information which is used for system or application troubleshooting purpose.

These levels have corresponding integer values in the range of 0–7. 0 has the highest severity. Increasing levels of log information means more information for administrator to diagnose the problems. More information in the log files means more disk space consumption, so you should consider your needs. If you really want to debug some problems in the application, then you can turn on debug log level. After you have resolved your problems, you can turn it off. Some applications are configured to send only **emerg** messages. Emergency messages are written to the log file only when certain emergencies occur. Some applications are configured to send only **info** level.

The available facilities are as follows:

- **kern**: Kernel messages
- **user**: User process related messages

- **mail**: All the messages related to mail subsystem
- **daemon**: All the messages send by daemons
- **auth**: Security / authorization messages
- **syslog**: Messages generated by syslogd itself
- **lpr**: Line printer subsystem
- **news**: Usenet news subsystem
- **uucp**: UUCP subsystem
- **cron**: Clock daemon: **crond** and **atd**
- **authpriv**: Private authorization messages
- **ftp**: FTP daemon
- **local0 to local7**: Reserved for local use

```
#### RULES ####

# Log all kernel messages to the console.
# Logging much else clutters up the screen.
#kern.*                                                 /dev/console

# Log anything (except mail) of level info or higher.
# Don't log private authentication messages!
*.info;mail.none;authpriv.none;cron.none                /var/log/messages

# The authpriv file has restricted access.
authpriv.*                                              /var/log/secure

# Log all the mail messages in one place.
mail.*                                                  -/var/log/maillog


# Log cron stuff
cron.*                                                  /var/log/cron

# Everybody gets emergency messages
*.emerg                                                 :omusrmsg:*

# Save news errors of level crit and higher in a special file.
uucp,news.crit                                          /var/log/spooler

# Save boot messages also to boot.log
local7.*                                                /var/log/boot.log
```

Figure 8.14: Contents of /etc/rsyslog.conf file showing default rules

The main configuration file is **/etc/rsyslog.conf**. Syslog works on set of rules. It clearly defines what services or facilities will be logged into which files and what level of logging info will be logged. Let us view the default rules written inside the configuration files, as shown in *Figure 8.14*. In *Figure 8.14*, * refers to either all log levels or all facilities. **cron.***

refers to all of **cron** subsystem's logs. ***.emerg** refers to emergency messages generated from any of the facilities. The **none** keyword means do not log any level of log. **/var/log/messages** consist of generic messages. **/var/log/secure** contains authentication messages. Thus, the rules have the following form:

```
Selector action
```

Selector contains facilities and priority, both separated by a period(.). The **action** field specifies what to do with the message. For example, in *Figure 8.14*, all the logs generated from the **cron** subsystem will be written to the **/var/log/cron** file.

```
kern.*                                    /dev/console
```

The preceding line sends all the levels of messages to the user's console while they are working so that any kernel-related info will be received by them immediately.

```
*.info;mail.none;authpriv.none;cron.none         /var/log/messages
```

The preceding line stores logs of severity **info** or higher level (notice, warning, error, critical, alert, emergency) to **/var/log/messages**, but logs from mail **authpriv** and **cron** subsystem will not be logged into **/var/log/messages**. **/var/log/messages** will also receive logs from kernel. If they want to view kernel info sometimes later, such as during downtime, it can be found in this file.

```
*.emerg                                    :omusrmsg:*
```

The preceding line sends any emergency-level messages to all users. **: omusrmsg:*** refers to the wall of all the logged in users.

```
mail,cron.info /var/log/otherlog
```

The preceding command will log the logs of severity **info** or higher to **/var/log/otherlog**.

Using **rsyslog**, remote logging is possible. It can send messages generated at a local machine to a centralized syslog server. All the logs from all the machines can be collected at one place and seen and analyzed from one place by the admin without logging in to other machines on the network. It listens for incoming syslog traffic at UDP port 514 or TCP 1468.

To send log messages to a remote host, provide the name of the remote host prepended by the @ symbol in the **action** field. For example, to send kernel logs to other hosts, add the following to the configuration of file:

```
kern.crit @server1.example.com
```

It uses UDP to transfer messages to another host, though it is less reliable; it is simple. To forward it via TCP, use @@, as follows:

```
kern.crit @@server1.example.com
```

Structure of log

rsyslog writes logging info in text form, which can be easily viewed using any of the file viewing utilities, such as **less** and **cat**. You can also filter the required events from these files using **grep** and more.

Any logged message contains at least a timestamp, a hostname field and the program name that logs that particular information. To understand the logging information, let us view a few lines of **/var/log/messages**:

```
Apr 2 07:36:14 vmachine systemd[1]: Started SSSD Kerberos Cache Manager.
Apr 2 07:36:14 vmachine sssd_kcm[8565]: Starting up
Apr 2 07:40:44 vmachine chronyd[902]: Forward time jump detected!
Apr 2 07:42:27 vmachine systemd[1]: Starting dnf makecache...
Apr 2 07:42:28 vmachine dnf[8574]: Updating Subscription Management repositories.
Apr 2 07:42:28 vmachine dnf[8574]: Unable to read consumer identity
Apr 2 07:42:28 vmachine dnf[8574]: This system is not registered with an entitlement server. You can use subscription-manager to register.
```

Here, the first line is written by **systemd** on Apr 2 at 07:36:14 by the host named **vmachine**. The number in square brackets [] is the pid. Similarly, you can translate other lines of logs.

Journal log

Systemd, the default service manager in RHEL9, includes the **systemd-journald** daemon for log management. **Systemd-journald** stores the log messages generated by different programs in a collective log known as **journal log**. It stores the messages from different sources, such as kernel logs, boot messages or applications and other service-related logs. It also collects logging messages from standard output and standard error of service units.

The default configuration of **systemd-journald** is set during compile time. **/etc/systemd/journald.conf** contains default configuration entries but commented out. By default, the log stored in systemd journal does not persist to disk; rather, it is stored in memory. You can find temporary journal file under **/run/log/journal**. **Storage** configuration option determines where to store journal log. The default value of **storage** option is **auto**, which means that journal log is stored on persistent location at **/var/log/journal**, if it exists, else it is stored in a volatile location. Since default installation does not create the mentioned persistent location, journal logs are stored in volatile location. Other values that the **storage** directive may take are **volatile, persistent**, and **none**. **none** will not drop all the logs. **volatile** will write logs to volatile location, which is created if required. **persistent** will record logs under persistent storage, which is created if needed. If the location is not writable, then it switches to volatile location. After you make any changes to default configuration in the main configuration file, restart the **journald** service using the following:

```
systemctl restart systemd-journald
```

Journald stores the messages in binary format, which can only be viewed by special utility known as **journalctl**. Just type **journalctl** in the command prompt and see how the logs labelled with timestamp are being displayed. It uses the log levels of standard syslog daemon. Default log level that is written to journal log file is debug. The maximum log level is determined by the **MaxLevelStore** directive, which is set to debug by default. All the logs of severity level emergency also go to the wall of all the logged in users.

To view only the massages generated by a specific program, say **sshd**, use **grep** as follows:

```
journalctl |grep shh
journalctl -f
```

opens the log at its tail, and new messages are displayed on the screen as it is being written into.

```
journalctl -n
```

displays last 10 events logged.

To view the last 20 events, issue the following:

```
journalctl -n 20
Journalctl -r
```

The preceding command reverses the output such that the newest entries are displayed first.

```
journalctl -b
```

shows the journal messages from the current boot.

```
journal -u <systemd unit or pattern>
```

The preceding command displays the messages gathered from the specified **systemd** unit.

Using the **-k** option retrieves only kernel messages.

Using the **-p** option shows you only the logs of the log level equal to the specified severity level or higher.

Consider this example:

```
journalctl -p 4
```

It displays the log messages of severity log level 0 to 4, which include **emerg**, **alert**, **crit**, **err**, and **warning**.

```
--since=
```

The preceding option shows entries starting from the specified date or newer.

`--until=`

The preceding option shows entries until the specified date. Date specifications should in of the format "2012-10-30 18:17:16". It may also accept strings like "today", "tomorrow", "yesterday" and "now".

Forwarding of journal log to syslog

Journal log entries can be sent to syslog by using **`ForwardToSyslog=`**. When this is set to '**`yes`**', messages are automatically forwarded to syslog. The **`MaxLevelSyslog`** directive determines the maximum log level forwarded to syslog. By default, it is set to debug.

You can also use the rsyslog and systemd journals together. While, rsyslog provides a centralized system to view the logs from multiple servers, rhe systemd journal compiles the logs from multiple services into one place.

Viewing NetworkManager Logs

Debug logging is helpful for network administrators to troubleshoot network problems. Use the following to view the logs related to network manager:

```
journalctl -u NetworkManager
```

You can also change the log-level at runtime via the following:

```
nmcli general logging level TRACE domains ALL
```

The logging level of **`NetworkManager`** is controlled by two options in the **`NetworkManager`** configuration file **`/etc/NetworkManager/NetworkManager.conf`**. These options are level and debug.

Domain means message category to record. Logs are recorded for many domains, such as WIFI, DHCP4, DHCP6, DNS, SYSTEMD, and more.

Level determines which log level to use to record the messages generated from different domains. Level may contain one of the following: OFF, ERR, WARN, INFO, DEBUG, TRACE.

Figure 8.15 displays the current status of logging information generated by **`NetworkManager`**. It shows that all the domains will generate log messages equal to INFO level or higher level. This means it will also record messages of ERR level as well as WARN level.

```
[visheshkumar@vmachine ~]$ nmcli general logging
LEVEL  DOMAINS

INFO   PLATFORM,RFKILL,ETHER,WIFI,BT,MB,DHCP4,DHCP6,PPP,IP4,IP6,AUTOIP4,DNS,VPN,SHARING,SUPPLICANT,AGENTS,SETTINGS,SUSPEND,CORE,DEVICE,OLPC,INFINIBAND,FIREWAL
L,ADSL,BOND,VLAN,BRIDGE,TEAM,CONCHECK,DCB,DISPATCH,AUDIT,SYSTEMD,PROXY
[visheshkumar@vmachine ~]$
```

***Figure 8.15**: nmcli usage to view logging status of NetworkManager*

The following command will change all the domains to log messages of severity level INFO or higher:

```
nmcli general logging level info domains ALL
```

To change the log level of specific domains, say DNS, use this:

```
nmcli general logging level info domains DNS
```

The preceding command will disable the logging of all the other domains. Use the following to preserve the settings of other domains and change the logging level of only the specified domain:

```
nmcli general logging level keep domains
DEVICE:info,SYSTEMD:err,CORE:debug
```

Security Information and Event Management

Syslog server collects the data from different clients, with each client providing logging information from many services or facilities. This way, vast amounts of log data is collected at the rsyslog server end. They are of no importance if this is not analyzed. **Security Information and Event Management (SIEM)** is a great tool to track and analyze the logs received from different sources and not only syslog. It can be used to identify potential security threats so that corrective actions can be taken. It collects the log, processes them, and creates an alarm based on the rules defined by security admin. SIEM is a software solution category that can perform centralized management of security events and raise security alarms based on defined rules.

Global security benchmarks for Linux

Benchmarking means evaluating a system against some established standard and best practices. There are several global security benchmarks for Linux that are widely recognized and used in the industry. **Center for Internet Security (CIS)** benchmarks are comprehensive, consensus-based security configurations developed by cybersecurity experts around the world. They provide detailed instructions for securing various Linux distributions, including Red Hat Enterprise Linux, Ubuntu, and others. You can use CIS standards to maintain the security of your system. Other security standards that are used industry-wide are NIST, ISO/IEC 27001 and PCI-DSS.

Conclusion

Information security is the foremost requirement of any enterprise. Local security is implemented by establishing proper access control system. You can choose between DAC and MAC. Restricting file permissions and user permissions falls under DAC. RHEL9 provides SELinux to implement MAC. Today, each computer is on the network, and networking makes computers talk to each other so that various resources such as printers, scanners, software and files can be shared. Moreover, an application can be shared and distributed among multiple hosts to ensure reliability and high performance. Networking ensures that if one of the computers goes down, another computer in the network is still up and running and continues the work without any disruption of services. When the load on one computer increases, it can be shared with other hosts, providing high performance. Network requirement is vast, but it is not secure. Anyone can attack your data when it travels on the unsecured network, so you must use secure services on the network. To maintain the network and its security log, monitoring is important.

In the next chapter, we will discuss how a disk can be partitioned and formatted in Linux.

CHAPTER 9

Partitioning in Linux

Introduction

Data on Linux systems lies on various formatted storage devices. Linux provides you with many options for storing data; there can be local storage, remote storage, or cluster-based storage. Local storage is directly attached to or installed on the host. Local storage can support filesystems like **`xfs`**, **`ext4`**, and more. To store any filesystem on a storage disk, it must be partitioned first. As a storage administrator, you need to create a storage pool, create partitions, format them, mount the disk, and resize it on demand. Partitioning is a good idea for the following reasons:

- Partitioning divides a storage disk into many logical sections, each dedicated to different types or formats of data. You can format each section/partition with a different filesystem. If the whole disk is treated as one partition, space would be wasted if the data is not large. In this case, the remaining space cannot be used for another type of filesystem. Thus, Linux partitions provide efficient storage space usage by dividing the disk into many logical sections of varying sizes. One partition can be used to store user-related data; the second partition can be used to store logs; the third partition can be used to store operating systems; the fourth partition can be used to store backups.
- Since partitioning divides the disk into two or more logical areas/disks, you can manage separate, smaller size logical disks more easily than the larger single disk. Thus, it makes the management of storage disks easier.
- Using partitioning, different filesystems can be kept in one storage disk.

In this chapter, we will learn how to use different tools to create different partitions on block storage devices and look at how to manage storage space.

Structure

This chapter has the following structure:

- Partitioning in RHEL9
- Partition types
- Logical Volume Management
- Managing LVM
- Storing data in partitions

Objectives

By the end of this chapter, you should be able to create and manage regular partitions. You should know how to use LVM to manage storage space more efficiently. This chapter will equip you to become a proficient storage administrator who can manage storage devices, create a storage pool, and make provisioning of space on demand.

Partitioning in RHEL9

RHEL default installation begins with the partition of the storage device into three parts: **/(root filesystem)**, **Swap** and **/boot**. Type **fdisk -l** to view the partitioning default layout. Given here are the starting few lines from the output:

```
Disk /dev/sda: 20 GiB, 21474836480 bytes, 41943040 sectors
Disk model: VMware Virtual S
Units: sectors of 1 * 512 = 512 bytes
Sector size (logical/physical): 512 bytes / 512 bytes
I/O size (minimum/optimal): 512 bytes / 512 bytes
Disklabel type: dos
Disk identifier: 0x8be97556
Device     Boot   Start      End  Sectors Size Id Type
/dev/sda1  *       2048  2099199  2097152   1G 83 Linux
/dev/sda2       2099200 41943039 39843840  19G 8e Linux LVM
```

Here, the disk is identified as **/dev/sda**, which has a size of 20 GiB and is divided into two partitions: **/dev/sda1** and **/dev/sda2**. Both partitions are of different types. **/dev/sda1** is labelled as Linux type, meaning it is a regular Linux partition. This is a boot partition and is mounted on **/boot**. Type **df -h**, and you can verify the same. **/dev/sda2** is the Linux **Logical Volume Management (LVM)** type. LVM provides you with an alternate way to manage storage space. It is a more efficient method than the regular partitioning tools, such as **fdisk** and **parted**. LVM divides the partition into further logical partitions. The following are the next set of lines in the output of the **fdisk -l** command:

```
Disk /dev/mapper/rhel_192-root: 17 GiB, 18249416704 bytes, 35643392
sectors
Units: sectors of 1 * 512 = 512 bytes
Sector size (logical/physical): 512 bytes / 512 bytes
I/O size (minimum/optimal): 512 bytes / 512 bytes
Disk /dev/mapper/rhel_192-swap: 2 GiB, 2147483648 bytes, 4194304
sectors
Units: sectors of 1 * 512 = 512 bytes
Sector size (logical/physical): 512 bytes / 512 bytes
I/O size (minimum/optimal): 512 bytes / 512 bytes
```

The above subset of output displays the two logical partitions that are part of LVM. It shows that **/dev/sda2** is further divided into two logical partitions: the first is identified as **/dev/mapper/rhel_192-root**, and the second is identified as **/dev/mapper/rhel_192-swap**. The identifier is the absolute path of the related device file. The first logical partition is mounted as **/** (root partition), while the latter is mounted as **swap** area.

Among the three partitions created during the default installation, **/boot** is created as a regular partition, while **/** and **swap** are created as a part of LVM. In this chapter, we will first discuss regular partition and then learn the usage of LVM.

The location and size of each disk partition are stored in the **partition table,** which is stored in the starting sector of the hard disk. You can choose between two partition table types: **GPT** and **Master Boot Record (MBR)**.

On a device formatted with the MBR partition table, you can have the following combination of partitions:

- Up to four primary partitions
- Up to three primary partitions, one extended partition
- Many logical partitions within the extended partition

GUID Partition Table (GPT Partition Table) table type will give you up to 128 partitions.

In this book, we will learn to create an MBR partition table type. It is labeled as **msdos** when you print the partition table. **Msdos** is used for generic Linux. Refer to the output of the **fdisk -l** command that was printed earlier. The **Disklabel type** field is **dos**. This field shows the partition table type that this disk is labeled with.

Partition types

We can have one of the following three partition types that may exist on a single partition:

- **Primary**: Each primary partition is managed as a single entity. Only four primary partitions can be created on a single drive.
- **Extended**: Extended partition divides a partition into one or more logical partitions. It has its own partition table, which stores the location and size of all the logical partitions created under this. If you have already created four primary partitions, you cannot create an extended partition. With a maximum of three primary partitions, one extended partition can be created.
- **Logical**: An extended partition consists of one or more logical partitions.

Creating a regular partition

You can use either the **fdisk** or the **parted** utility to create and manage partitions. In this book, we will use **parted** utility to create and manage partitions.

In *Chapter 2, Linux Filesystem and Administration*, we learnt how to create a primary partition using our portable USB drive. In this section, we will, again, use the same portable device to create additional partitions. You must log in as the root user to create and manage partitions.

Now, attach your pen drive and identify the device name by typing either:

```
parted -l
```

or

```
fdisk -l
```

After identifying your portable device, you can invoke the **parted** command as in *Figure 9.1* using the device name you identified in the previous step:

```
[root@vmachine ~]# parted /dev/sdb
GNU Parted 3.4
Using /dev/sdb
Welcome to GNU Parted! Type 'help' to view a list of commands.
(parted)
(parted)
(parted)
(parted) p
Model:  USB  SanDisk 3.2Gen1 (scsi)
Disk /dev/sdb: 61.5GB
Sector size (logical/physical): 512B/512B
Partition Table: msdos
Disk Flags:

Number  Start  End  Size  Type  File system  Flags

(parted)
```

Figure 9.1: Parted utility showing an empty partition table and its type

In *Figure 9.1*, the **`parted`** command is executed on **`/dev/sdb`**. This opens the **`parted`** utility in interactive mode. You receive the **`(parted)`** prompt. Type **`h`** to view commands that can be used in the **`(parted)`** prompt. Type **`p`** to print the partition table. The **`Partition Table`** field is marked as **`msdos`**. This label is used for MBR. To change the partition table type to **`gpt`**, use the following command:

```
mklabel gpt
```

Replace **`gpt`** with **`msdos`** for vice versa.

After this, a warning will be generated for you, saying all the disk data will be lost and your confirmation will be needed if you want to continue. Press **yes** to format the disk with the new partition table type.

The output in *Figure 9.1* shows that you do not have any existing partition yet. Let us create your first primary partition quickly using the **`mkpart`** command:

```
(parted) mkpart primary xfs 1MB 10000MB
```

The preceding command will create a primary partition of size 10G. The starting location of this partition is specified at 1M, and the ending location is specified at 10000MB. The filesystem given is **`xfs`**.

Type the **`p`** command on parted prompt to view the new partition created. It shows the data in several fields:

- **Number**: This is the partition number; it will be displayed as **`1`** as it is the first partition for the **`/dev/sbd`** device.
- **Start**: Partition starts at the specified position of disk.
- **End**: Partition ends at the specified position.
- **Size**: This is the size of the partition created.
- **Type**: Partition type is primary.
- **File system**: Filesystem is recognized as **`xfs`**.
- **Flags**: This displays the flags set.

Let us create one extended and two logical partitions in this exercise.

To create an extended partition type, use the **`extended`** keyword with the **`mkpart`** command, as shown in *Figure 9.2*:

```
(parted) mkpart extended
Start? 10G
End? 20G
(parted) p
Model:  USB  SanDisk 3.2Gen1 (scsi)
Disk /dev/sdb: 61.5GB
Sector size (logical/physical): 512B/512B
Partition Table: msdos
Disk Flags:

Number  Start   End     Size    Type      File system  Flags
 1      1049kB  10.0GB  9999MB  primary
 2      10.0GB  20.0GB  9999MB  extended               lba
```

Figure 9.2: *mkpart utility creating an extended partition*

Once you type **mkpart extended**, it will prompt you for further details that are required to create a partition. Input the start and end points for the new partition when prompted, as shown in *Figure 9.2*, and your partition will be created. Type **p** to view the partition table with a new partition entry. The output shows that the partition, numbered as **2**, is created with type set to **extended**.

Now, let us create a logical partition within this extended partition. Use the following command in the **(parted)** prompt to create a logical partition:

```
mkpart logical
```

Note that the keyword that will be used to create a logical partition is **logical.** When you execute the preceding command to create a logical partition, you will be prompted for the start and end locations of the new partition, as shown in *Figure 9.3*. It will also prompt you for the filesystem type; enter **xfs** when prompted.

```
(parted) mkpart logical
File system type?  [ext2]? xfs
Start? 10G
End? 15G
(parted) p
Model:  USB  SanDisk 3.2Gen1 (scsi)
Disk /dev/sdb: 61.5GB
Sector size (logical/physical): 512B/512B
Partition Table: msdos
Disk Flags:

Number  Start   End     Size    Type      File system  Flags
 1      1049kB  10.0GB  9999MB  primary
 2      10.0GB  30.0GB  20.0GB  extended               lba
 5      10.0GB  15.0GB  4999MB  logical   xfs          lba
```

Figure 9.3: *The mkapart command creates a logical partition*

Similarly, you can create as many logical partitions as you want. *Figure 9.4* shows the creation of an additional logical partition and then prints the partition table. We now have one primary, one extended and two logical partitions on **/dev/sdb**.

```
(parted) mkpart logical xfs
Start? 15G
End? 20G
(parted) p
Model:  USB  SanDisk 3.2Gen1 (scsi)
Disk /dev/sdb: 61.5GB
Sector size (logical/physical): 512B/512B
Partition Table: msdos
Disk Flags:

Number  Start   End     Size    Type      File system  Flags
 1      1049kB  10.0GB  9999MB  primary
 2      10.0GB  30.0GB  20.0GB  extended               lba
 5      10.0GB  15.0GB  4999MB  logical   xfs          lba
 6      15.0GB  20.0GB  4999MB  logical   xfs          lba

(parted) q
Information: You may need to update /etc/fstab.
```

***Figure 9.4:** mkpart creating a logical partition and viewing partition table*

Logical volume management

It provides you with another way of achieving storage management. LVM creates logical devices from physical devices. It provides elasticity in storage, which means we can easily increase the storage size in LVM even without unmounting the file system. This is not easily possible with regular partitions.

Follow these steps to create logical storage volumes:

1. Create one or more **Physical Volumes (PV)** out of the available storage space. One PV cannot span more than one hard disk partition or a hard disk.
2. A **Volume Group** (**VG**) is created using one or more PVs. A VG can create a storage pool out of one or more PV. If a VG consists of PVs from different hard disks, that VG can span more than one hard disk.
3. Then we create **Logical Volumes** (**LV**) out of VGs. An LV is where the filesystems are designed and mounted. The space of LVs can be increased by allocating unused extents[1] from VGs. If there is no space available in a VG, we can improve its size by adding more PVs.

The advantages of LVM are as follows:

- LVM aggregates many individual storage disks or partitions into one storage volume. Thus, a filesystem can have many devices. A logical volume can be larger than the available physical space. Thus, it supports filesystems of bigger capacity by efficiently utilizing storage space.
- Additional storage space can be made available dynamically.

[1] *An extent is the fixed unit of storage space that is assigned to logical volume from VG.*

- It provides user-friendly device naming. Users can provide easy-to-remember names to LV.

Creating a physical volume

As a first step, you must initialize a device as a PV. A PV can be created on the whole hard disk without partition. But this is not an ideal approach. You should create partitions on physical media, and then you can initialize chosen partitions as PVs.

Let us use the regular partition number 5 that we created earlier. We will use the **pvcreate** command to initialize partition **5** (designated as **/dev/sdb5**) as PV. LVM will use all the available space to create PV.

```
[root@vmachine ~]# pvcreate /dev/sdb5
  Physical volume "/dev/sdb5" successfully created.
```

The preceding command initializes **/dev/sdb5** as PV.

Let us create one more PV using **/dev/sda6**, as follows:

```
[root@vmachine ~]# pvcreate /dev/sdb6
  Physical volume "/dev/sdb6" successfully created.
```

To view PV, we have the **pvs**, **pvdisplay**, and **pvscan** commands. Just type the name of any of these utilities, and you will have the list of all the existing PVs, default and non-default. The following is the output from **pvscan**:

```
[root@vmachine ~]# pvscan
  PV /dev/sdb5                      lvm2 [4.65 GiB / 4.65 GiB free]
  PV /dev/sdb6                      lvm2 [4.65 GiB / 4.65 GiB free]
  PV /dev/sda2    VG rhel_192             lvm2 [<19.00 GiB / 0    free]
  Total: 3 [28.30 GiB] / in use: 1 [<19.00 GiB] / in no VG: 2 [<8.00
GiB ]
```

The preceding output displays two newly created physical volumes: **/dev/sdb5** and **/dev/sdb6**. **/dev/sda2** is the default physical volume created during installation, while **/dev/sda2** falls under **rhel_192** VG. The other two PVs do not fall under any VG as they have not yet been added to any.

Creating a volume group

A volume group creates a storage pool from which space for logical volumes is allocated, on which a filesystem is created. It is created using one or more PVs. Let us create a VG, named **STORAGEBANK**, using **/dev/sdb5** and **/dev/sdb6** PVs, as follows:

```
[root@vmachine ~]# vgcreate STORAGEBANK /dev/sdb5 /dev/sdb6
  Volume group "STORAGEBANK" successfully created
```

To view all the available volume groups, we have the **vgscan**, **vgdisplay**, and **vgs** utilities. You can use any of them to view the volume groups available. Here is the output from the **vgscan** command:

```
[ root@vmachine ~]# vgscan
  Found volume group "STORAGEBANK" using metadata type lvm2
  Found volume group "rhel_192" using metadata type lvm2
```

You can use the **pvscan** command to view the PVs involved under VG **STORAGEBANK**, as follows:

```
root@vmachine ~]# pvscan
  PV /dev/sdb5   VG STORAGEBANK      lvm2 [4.65 GiB / 4.65 GiB free]
  PV /dev/sdb6   VG STORAGEBANK      lvm2 [4.65 GiB / 4.65 GiB free]
  PV /dev/sda2   VG rhel_192           lvm2 [<19.00 GiB / 0    free]
  Total: 3 [28.30 GiB] / in use: 3 [28.30 GiB] / in no VG: 0 [0   ]
```

Creating logical volume

The last step is to create a logical volume out of the storage pool that we created earlier. We have created a storage pool in the form of VG: **STORAGEBANK**. This is the LV on which the filesystem is created. You can easily extend LV on demand from the storage space in VG. If VG is created using PVs from different drives, then an LV can be spread across other storage devices. Let us use the **lvcreate** command to create logical volume, as follows:

```
[root@vmachine ~]# lvcreate -L 3G STORAGEBANK -n DATAVOLUME1
  Logical volume "DATAVOLUME1" was created.
```

In the preceding command, the **-L** option is used to specify the size of the logical volume. The **-n** option is used to specify the name of LV. Here, LV named **DATAVOLUME1** is created by allocating 3G from our VG **STORAGEBANK**.

To view LV, use the **lvscan**, **lvs**, or **lvdisplay** command as follows:

```
[root@vmachine ~]# lvscan
  ACTIVE            '/dev/STORAGEBANK/DATAVOLUME1' [3.00 GiB] inherit
  ACTIVE            '/dev/rhel_192/swap' [2.00 GiB] inherit
  ACTIVE            '/dev/rhel_192/root' [<17.00 GiB] inherit
```

The output of the preceding command shows the logical volume we just created. It also shows the device's file path. Default logical volumes for **/root** and swap areas are also displayed. All the device files reside under path starting from **/dev**.

Managing LVM

In this section, we will discuss how the various components of LVM are managed. We will see how the dynamic storage space allocation is done in LVM.

To increase the size of LV, use the **lvextend** command:

```
[root@vmachine ~]# lvextend -L +1G /dev/STORAGEBANK/DATAVOLUME1
  Size of logical volume STORAGEBANK/DATAVOLUME1 changed from 3.00 GiB
(768 extents) to 4.00 GiB (1024 extents).
  Logical volume STORAGEBANK/DATAVOLUME1 successfully resized.
```

The preceding command allocates an additional 1G to our LV **DATAVOLUME1** using unallocated extents from VG **STORAGEBANK**.

If you do not have sufficient space in VG, then increase the size of VG by adding a PV. **To resize VG,** add a PV using the **vgextend** utility, as follows:

```
[root@vmachine ~]# vgextend STORAGEANK /dev/sdb7
  Volume group "STORAGEANK" successfully extended
```

To reduce the size of the Volume Group, remove an unused physical volume from VG by using the **vgreduce** utility as follows:

```
vgreduce STORAGEBANK /deb/sdb7
```

The preceding command will remove PV **/dev/sdb7** from **VG STORAGEBANK**. Precaution is required while removing a physical volume. No data should reside in the PV.

To remove a VG, use the **vgremove** command as follows:

```
vgremove STORAGEBANK
```

To remove LV

You can remove any unused LV using the **lvremove** command. Take precautions while removing so that it does not contain any critical data. Unmount it before executing the **lvremove** command.

Removing LVM label

If you want to remove a device from the LVM category, use the **pvremove** command to remove any metadata regarding PV on it. To remove **/dev/sdb6** from LVM, type the following:

```
pvremove /dev/sdb6
```

Storing data in partitions

Each regular or LVM partition is formatted to store any data in it. Formatting was discussed in *Chapter 2, Linux File System and Administration*. After formatting a partition with specific filesystem, they need to be mounted on a specific mount point so that the filesystem can be accessed from one hierarchical tree. If **/dev/sda5** is mounted on **/home**, then all the files under **/home** will physically reside on **/dev/sda5**. There can be more than one partition lying under a particular directory, say **/var.** **/dev/sda2** might be mounted on **/var**, while **/dev/sda3** may be mounted on **/var/log**.

To mount logical volume, say **DATAVOLUME1**, to **/mnt** mount point, type the following:

```
mount  /dev/STORAGEBANK/DATAVOLUME1  /mnt
```

After mounting any filesystem, identify that it is mounted correctly using the **df** command.

Conclusion

Partitioning allows you to create different logical sections on a storage device, each of which can be formatted with a specific filesystem. Each partition appears as a logical disk to the OS and can be managed as an entity. You can delete one partition without affecting the other. We have regular partitions created by **fdisk** or **parted**. We also have logical partitions, called logical volumes, created under LVM. By default, the installation process creates a boot partition as a regular partition and / and swap partitions within LVM volumes. LVM provides a flexible way to manage disk storage in Linux. With LVM, you can easily resize logical volumes, add or remove physical volumes, and increase the size of volume groups.

In the next chapter, we will learn what is a container in Linux and how you can use it.

Join our book's Discord space

Join the book's Discord Workspace for Latest updates, Offers, Tech happenings around the world, New Release and Sessions with the Authors:

https://discord.bpbonline.com

Chapter 10
Containers

Introduction

Suppose you are developing an application on a laptop. Developing an application requires specific environment settings, libraries, dependencies, and the application itself. If you want to shift your application to a testing host or production host, you need to set up that host to satisfy all the requirements to run the new application. This requires many man-hours on your part. You will try to match the system environment, libraries, and settings according to those running on your laptop. Any mismatch may result in the application misbehaving when it runs.

Let us consider one more scenario. The production environment has some standard set of files, environments, and settings. All the applications need to run in the same set of standard environments. You must simulate the same environment in your development task. This will, again, take a huge effort on your part.

Another problem that an organization may face is that the resources required to run your newly-built application are limited, and more investments cannot be made to buy them.

The solution is to bundle all application requirements in a collection, and what is formed is known as a **container**. Containers represent a process that is created from the image stored locally or remotely. A **container image** holds application-related files, required libraries, and all of its dependencies together in a very small-sized package. This image can then be ported very easily to another machine, such as a production machine. When this image is run, the running process is known as a container. The application runs inside the container by isolating itself from the rest of the process running on the system.

In this chapter, we will learn to work with containers and see how the container solves many real problems that an organization faces.

Structure

The chapter covers the following topics:

- Understanding containers and container image
- Container orchestration

Objectives

By the end of this chapter, you should be able to understand and use containers, and you should know various container tools, such as **podman**, **buildah**, **skopeo** and build containers, images and manage them.

Understanding containers and container image

Containers run like a regular Linux process but are isolated from the rest of the process running on the system. A container holds the required libraries, their dependencies, and the necessary files to run an application in itself. They provide you with a form of virtualization. Virtual machines also provide you with complete isolation from the host. Unlike virtual machines, containers do not require a copy of the OS. With virtualization, you run an OS on top of the main OS. These virtual machines do not disturb other virtual machines' processes and the process running on the main OS.

Containers do not hold OSes. Many containers can be made available on a single host. Each container interacts with the main OS's kernel, still isolating itself from the rest of the system.

Containers run like a process that is created from files located in the container image. All the files necessary to run the container, such as libraries, dependencies and required files, are bundled in the form of a package, known as an **image**. Container images are of small size. Thus, Linux containers are portable. You can simply move images from development to testing and testing to production and run the container.

Since this does not contain a full OS and is created from very small-sized images, containers are very lightweight and are of a small size measuring only a few megabytes and thus, less resource-intensive. The only restriction to move containers to different machines is that they should have the same OS.

Tools for containers

Many community projects, organizations and individual contributors have created several container tools and technologies to be interoperable. They follow the standards defined by **Open Container Initiative (OCI)** so that containers created by one tool can also be managed using another.

OCI defines the set of standards to build, run and manage containers. It defines the format of container image files, their meta data and the standard process to create containers. OCI-compatible container tools run and manage containers successfully across the platform.

Earlier versions of RHEL use **Docker** to build and manage containers. Since RHEL8, it has been removed and replaced with another set of command-line tools such as the following:

- `Podman`
- `Buildah`
- `Skopeo`
- `Runc`
- `Crun`

All the mentioned tools are OCI-compatible. So, they can also be used to manage containers that are created by Docker or other OCI-compatible tools. All the mentioned tools, together, will help you work with containers more easily.

`Podman` is a tool that provides a way to run, manage, and deploy containers. It is designed to replace **Docker**, with a similar command-line interface as used by **Docker**.

`Buildah`, on the other hand, is a tool for building and managing container images. It provides a way to create container images from scratch, and modify and inspect existing container images. `Buildah` can be used to build images using Dockerfile-like scripts or by directly manipulating the contents of a container image. `Podman` can also be used to build an image, but `Buildah` provides more functionality than Podman. Podman uses Buildah internally to create container images. Both tools share image storage, so each can use or manipulate images created by the other.

Together, `Podman` and `Buildah` provide a complete container management solution that can be used to create, run, and deploy containerized applications. They are both designed to be lightweight and secure, focusing on running containers without needing a separate container daemon or root privileges. Though they are designed to replace Docker, they are compatible with Docker.

`Skopeo` can be used to transfer container images from one registry to another.

`Crun` and `runc` are the container runtimes used to start and run containers. They also conform to OCI specifications. `runc` is a lightweight and portable runtime that provides basic features for creating and managing containers, such as process isolation, resource limits, and networking. **crun**, on the other hand, is a newer and more modern container runtime developed as an alternative to **runc**. It was designed to be faster and more lightweight than **runc**, with a smaller codebase and lower memory footprint.

These tools run without any root user privilege. Thus, they provide the feature of **rootless** container and are secure. These tools are **daemon less** tools. While Docker requires a daemon to run always, the Podman only runs when the container process is started. It runs integrated with systemd. It also uses cgroups to provide isolation.

Configuration files

The default configuration that is used by **Podman** and **Buildah** is defined in **containers.conf**, which is read from the mentioned locations in the following order:

- **/usr/share/containers**
- **/etc/containers**
- **$HOME/.config/containers (Rootless containers only)**

Setting specified in **containers.conf** file that is read later will override the previous **containers.conf** settings. By default, you will have the **/usr/share/containers/containers.conf** file in your Linux box.

Storage directory for data, including images, can be stored under **/var/lib/containers/storage** for UID 0 or **$HOME/.local/share/containers/storage** for non-root users. Storage-related settings are configured in **/etc/containers/storage.conf**.

Setting up containers

To set a container, you need to start with the container image. Container images can either be made from scratch or pulled from the registry server. The registry server holds the repository for many container images.

As a newcomer, you can begin by fetching a container image from a registry server. Afterward, you can use that image to create your container, run it, and then make any necessary modifications. Once you are satisfied with the changes, you can save them by committing them to a new image. Finally, you can share the new image by pushing it to the same or a different registry server, making it available for other users to access and utilize. Container images are cached on your host when downloaded. This local cached container image can be used to build any new containers. It helps you to build containerized applications.

Many vendors maintain registry servers to provide you with the images. There are two types of container images available on the registry server that is maintained by RedHat, which are as follows:

- RedHat Enterprise Linux base images (RHEL base images)
- RedHat Universal Base images (UBI images)

An advantage of using RHEL provided container image is that it is supported by RedHat itself. RedHat provides timely updates to container image and is properly catalogued.

In this book, we will use the **Podman** tool to work with images and containers. We will use various **Podman** commands to use its features and functionalities. To create a rootless container, we will set up containers using a regular account. Follow these steps to create your first container:

1. Become root and add a user:

   ```
   useradd poduser
   passwd poduser
   ```

2. Log in to new user as follows:

   ```
   ssh poduser@vmachine.example.com
   ```

   Avoid logging in using the `su -` command as it does not set environment variables properly.

3. Now, we will pull the container image using `podman pull` to pull image from the registry server.

   We will use the `registry.access.redhat.com` registry server to pull the base image. `registry.access.redhat.com` is the FQDN of the registry server.

   ```
   [poduser@localhost ~]$ podman pull registry.access.redhat.com/
   ubi9/ubi
   Trying to pull registry.access.redhat.com/ubi9/ubi:latest...
   Getting image source signatures
   Checking if image destination supports signatures
   Copying blob 72d37ae8760a done
   Copying config 8e9c11168e done
   Writing manifest to image destination
   Storing signatures
   8e9c11168e6d9de29f6bbd7e59eca89f868cab89028f266dae17c684046b1479
   ```

   The preceding command requires you to have internet running on your machine. It fetches the base image named **ubi** from the specified registry server. **Ubi9** is the namespace under which image named **ubi** exists. Namespace is used to distinguish the images uploaded by the different vendors or individuals. When the two images carry the same name, namespace distinguishes them.

There can be multiple images existing with the same name, even in one namespace. In these cases, you can specify the tag. By default, the **podman pull** command pulls the image with the **latest** tag. Notice **registry.access.redhat.com/ubi9/ubi:latest** in the output. There could be different versions residing for the same image name. So, the **latest** tag would refer to the latest version. This image will be cached locally.

4. As the next step, we will use the **podman run** command to run the container using the given image that is cached locally. If the image is not loaded, it will pull the image in the same way as **podman pull** and run the container using this image.

```
podman run --name=cont1 registry.access.redhat.com/ubi9/ubi cat /
etc/os-release
```

The preceding command runs the container named **cont1** and also executes the **cat** command with the given argument . It will display the OS version. The **Podman run** command runs the process in the new container. After running the command, the container stops running. If you do not specify the container name using the **--name** option, **Podman** will automatically provide a fancy container name.

Using podman

Podman commands are simple and easy to learn. To learn how to use **Podman** commands, just use the **--help** option, as follows:

```
podman --help
```

It will show you the list of commands and options to use with **Podman**. Proper description for each command is also given in this menu. Choose a command that you want to use; suppose you choose **container**. If you require any further help on the **podman container** command, type this:

```
podman container --help
```

It will show you another set of commands that can be used with **podman container**. Let us say you choose the **start** command. Now, you can again use the **--help** option to take further help on the **start** command, as follows:

```
podman container start --help
```

It will show you the proper usage of the **start** command and the options available.

Working with containers

Podman has a rich set of commands that can be used while working with containers.

To view the list of loaded containers, use the **podman container** command:

```
podman container list
```

This command will list all the running containers. The preceding command is the same as the **podman ps** command.

To view all the loaded containers, whether running or not, use the **-a** option at the end, as shown in *Figure 10.1*. It shows that the container named **cont1** was created **5 minutes ago**. Status field contains **Exited**, meaning that container has been stopped and is not running right now. You will also receive a container ID, with which you can manage the container.

```
[poduser@localhost ~]$ podman container list -a
CONTAINER ID  IMAGE                                   COMMAND     CREATED        STATUS                    PORTS       NAMES
b73fc151b7a5  registry.access.redhat.com/ubi9/ubi:latest  /bin/bash   5 minutes ago  Exited (0) 5 minutes ago              cont1
```

Figure 10.1: *podman command usage: displaying all the containers*

We can **start an existing container,** say **cont1**, using Podman in either of the following ways:

- **podman container start** command
- **podman start** command

You can use any one of the previously mentioned ways to start one or more containers.

podman container start cont1

podman start cont1

Both the preceding commands work the same way to start the specified container. You can verify the start of container, **cont1** by using **podman container list** command. It will show the output as in *Figure 10.2*:

```
[poduser@localhost ~]$ podman container start cont1
cont1
[poduser@localhost ~]$ podman container list
CONTAINER ID  IMAGE                                   COMMAND     CREATED         STATUS             PORTS       NAMES
b73fc151b7a5  registry.access.redhat.com/ubi9/ubi:latest  /bin/bash   23 minutes ago  Up 4 seconds ago               cont1
```

Figure 10. 2: *podman usage: starting a container*

Now, container **cont1** is up and running. Let us use it interactively by passing the **-i** and **-t** options. The **-i** option is used to run the container in interactive mode. The **-a** option is used to attach the pseudo-terminal to the standard input and standard output of the container.

[poduser@localhost ~]$ podman container start -ai cont1

[root@b73fc151b7a5 /]#

You will get a prompt as you just saw. Now, you are placed inside the root directory of the container. You can run any Linux commands here. Type **ls** to find the default files lying in the container's filesystem. You can also use the **-ai** option with the **podman start** command.

Type **exit** to exit out of the container.

To stop a running container, say **cont1**, you have two options: the **podman container stop** command and the **podman stop** command.

```
podman container stop cont1
```

or

```
podman stop cont1
```

To stop the running container, you can run the preceding commands using the **-a** option, as follows:

```
podman container stop -a
```

To inspect a container, say **cont1**, use this:

```
podman inspect cont1
```

The preceding command will show you all the details regarding the **cont1** container.

To remove a container, say **cont1**, you can use the **podman rm** command or the **podman container rm** command, as follows:

```
podman rm cont1
```

or

```
podman container rm cont1
```

To remove a container, it must not be running. Verify the status of the container using the **podman container list** command. If the **status** column displays **Exited**, then the container can be removed.

To remove all the stopped containers, use the **-a** option with the preceding command, as follows:

```
podman rm -a cont1
```

or

```
podman container rm -a cont1
```

To create a container using the specified image, type this:

```
[poduser@localhost ~]$ podman create --name cont2 registry.access.
redhat.com/ubi9/ubi:latest
dcb2eba2764d3d3f3aa0772b4e2ce64e32f7276177227ae39e5a81aa6ad53aa9
```

The preceding command uses the same image that was fetched earlier. You can verify the creation of container named **cont2** using the **podman container list** command. If you do not provide a container name, **podman** will automatically assign a name to container.

You can learn to use more **podman** commands using the **help** option as described earlier.

Working with images

So far, we have pulled **ubi** images. You can also pull the non-ubi images provided by vendors other than RedHat. You can specify just the image name or image **fqdn**. If just the name of the image is provided, then it is searched in the list of registry servers given in the **/etc/containers/registries.conf** file.

To view all the images pulled at your local system, use the **podman image** command as shown here:

```
[poduser@localhost ~]$ podman images
REPOSITORY                    TAG      IMAGE ID    CREATED    SIZE
registry.access.redhat.com/ubi9/ubi latest   8e9c11168e6d 2 weeks ago
219 MB
```

To pull non-ubi images, use this:

```
podman pull centos
Resolved "centos" as an alias (/etc/containers/registries.conf.d/000-
shortnames.conf)
Trying to pull quay.io/centos/centos:latest...
Getting image source signatures
Copying blob 7a0437f04f83 done
Copying config 300e315adb done
Writing manifest to image destination
Storing signatures
300e315adb2f96afe5f0b2780b87f28ae95231fe3bdd1e16b9ba606307728f55
```

To fetch the **centos** image, alias file **/etc/containers/registries.conf.d/000-shortnames.conf** is consulted to resolve **centos**. After the image name is resolved, it is fetched from one of the registry servers, that is **quay.io**, listed under **/etc/containers/registries.conf** file.

Verify your image using the following:

```
podman images
REPOSITORY          TAG      IMAGE ID    CREATED    SIZE
quay.io/centos/centos   latest   300e315adb2f 2 years ago 217 MB
```

To inspect pulled images, use this:

```
podman inspect quay.io/centos/centos
```

You can also specify the image ID instead of the image name.

Use the following to tag your locally-stored images:

```
podman tag 300e315adb2f centos
```

Here, the **podman tag** command is used to provide tag **centos** to the specified image ID. Let us verify the same, as follows:

```
podman images
REPOSITORY          TAG      IMAGE ID   CREATED   SIZE
quay.io/centos/centos latest   300e315adb2f 2 years ago 217 MB
localhost/centos    latest   300e315adb2f 2 years ago 217 MB
```

You can again provide another tag as shown here:

```
podman tag 300e315adb2f centos:9
```

Again, verify the new tag as follows:

```
podman images
REPOSITORY          TAG      IMAGE ID   CREATED   SIZE
quay.io/centos/centos latest   300e315adb2f 2 years ago 217 MB
localhost/centos    latest   300e315adb2f 2 years ago 217 MB
localhost/centos    9      300e315adb2f 2 years ago 217 MB
```

All the three tags refer to the same image as they carry the same image ID.

To remove the local image, use the **podman rmi** command, as follows:

```
[poduser@localhost ~]$ podman rmi quay.io/centos/centos
Untagged: quay.io/centos/centos:latest
```

The preceding command deletes the specified image. Verify that the image is deleted by issuing the **podman images** command.

To remove images that have multiple tags associated, use this:

```
[poduser@localhost ~]$ podman rmi -f 300e315adb2f
```

The preceding command deletes all the images that have the specified tag. Again, verify the result by issuing the **podman images** command:

```
[poduser@localhost ~]$ podman images
REPOSITORY TAG     IMAGE ID  CREATED   SIZE
```

Saving a container as image

Container is a runtime process that holds all your data in memory. When the container is stopped, all the changes are lost. Suppose you have executed many commands that made changes in the container. If you want to save your changes on the disk, you must save the container as an image. Later, you must start the container using the image that has the saved changes so that the changes are visible in the new container. To commit the changes on the new image, use the **podman commit** command as follows:

```
podman commit <containerid>
```

The **podman commit** command creates a new image using the modified container. Replace **<containerid>** with the actual container ID or name in the preceding command.

Managing a container network

To establish communication between containers, networking needs to be configured among them. Use the following to list all the networks available:

```
podman network ls
NETWORK ID   NAME     DRIVER
2f259bab93aa podman   bridge
```

Here, the network name is **podman**, as in **NAME** field. To view the network settings for the podman network, use this:

```
podman network inspect podman
```

To create a new network, use **the podman network create command:**

```
podman network create mynet
```

The preceding command will create a network named **mynet**.

To remove a network, use the following command:

```
podman network rm <network name>
```

To remove all unused networks, use the **podman network prune** command. The following command will remove networks that have no containers connected to it, but it does not remove the default podman network.

```
podman network prune
```

To inspect network information, use the **podman inspect** command as follows:

```
podman inspect podman
```

To view an individual item from the above command, use the **--format** option:

```
podman inspect --format='{{.NetworkSettings.IPAddress}}' containerName
```

The preceding command displays the IP address for the specified container.

Attaching disk in container

By default, container writes all the data into a volatile location. To save the changes to the disk, you must commit it as an image. Later, this image can be used to create the container using the saved image. This is a two-step process. Instead, you can attach a disk to the container and write all the data to the attached disk. No more data loss will take place. As a first step, you have to create a volume that later acts as a mount point.

Create a volume using the following command:

```
podman volume create
```

This will give you a name for the new volume. You can assign an easy-to-remember name to the volume while creating it, as shown here:

```
podman volume create tempdata
```

Here, the volume named **tempdata** is created.

To verify the volume created, use the following command:

```
podman volume list
DRIVER   VOLUME NAME
local
3dcf225f84a437159c0aeba6cdab10f16054e463b02e117259ce53ab4770ef93
local    tempdata
```

To get detailed information about a volume, use the **podman volume inspect** command as follows:

```
[poduser@localhost ~]$ podman volume inspect tempdata
[
   {
     "Name": "tempdata",
     "Driver": "local",
     "Mountpoint": "/opt/home/poduser/.local/share/containers/storage/
volumes/tempdata/_data",
     "CreatedAt": "2023-04-25T01:22:48.688607716+05:30",
     "Labels": {},
     "Scope": "local",
     "Options": {},
     "MountCount": 0,
     "NeedsCopyUp": true,
     "NeedsChown": true
   }
]
```

In the preceding output, notice the mountpoint located under the **/opt/home/poduser/.local/share/containers/storage** directory.(**/opt/home/** is the home directory set for the new user in the demo machine).

The next task is to assign a disk to this data volume. You can do this while running the container as follows:

```
podman run -it --name=perm1 --mount type=volume,src=tempdata,dst=/
backup ubuntu
```

The preceding command uses **/backup** to mount the volume. Now, you are inside the root directory of the container. Type **ls** to verify the volume creation. You will find the **backup** directory here. Let us create a file here:

```
cd backup
touch abc
```

Type **ls** and verify the file creation. Everything stored within the **backup** directory inside the container can also be found in the directory that belongs to the **tempdata** volume (**/opt/home/poduser/.local/share/containers/storage/volumes/tempdata/_data**). You can find the volume path using the **podman volume inspect** command. This data will be shared between other containers if they start with the same volume. The data will also persist when a container is restarted. Storing data in any other directory will also persist.

To delete a volume, use the **podman volume rm** command as follows:

```
podman volume rm <volume name>
```

Use the **-a** option to delete all the unused volumes:

```
[poduser@localhost ~]$ podman volume rm -a
```

The preceding command will delete only unused volumes, any volume being used by even a single container will not be removed.

The scope of this book is limited, so all the aspects of the container cannot be covered in this book. You can explore more about containers using the official documentation.

Do it yourself

Start the perm1 container that was created earlier in this section interactively. View the directories inside the root directory of container. Create a file named file1 inside the home directory. Stop the container and start it again interactively. Then, view the files under the home directory. Did you still find file1 there?

Now, use the same container to create a file xyz under its backup directory. Open another terminal to log in as poduser. Type ls to view the files inside /opt/home/poduser/.local/share/containers/storage/volumes/tempdata/_data. What files do you find here?

Next, start a new container, perm2, interactively using the same volume. Look into its backup directory. What files are there? Do you find xyz here? What do you conclude?

Container orchestration

Since containers are of small sizes, there can be many containers running on a host; you must manage all. If their number is in hundreds, the manual way to manage all the containers is clumsy. You can use **container orchestration**. Container orchestration refers to automation of deployment, management, and networking of containers on one or many hosts. It provides maintenance of containers across several hosts. It treats each container as an entity and starts, stops or manages them. One of the popular container orchestration tools is **Kubernetes**. It helps in building and managing containers and containerized applications. It also helps in managing containerized storage and networking, ensuring that containers have access to the necessary resources and can communicate with each other. Pod, a group of Podman containers, is the smallest compute unit that you can create, deploy, and manage in Kubernetes environments.

Conclusion

Containers provide a lightweight and isolated environment that allow applications to run on the same operating system kernel as the host, having their own virtualized environment. Containers are a popular technology for deploying and managing applications, as they provide a standardized and portable way of packaging and running software across different environments. Some of the popular containerization technologies are Docker, Kubernetes, LXC/LXD, Podman, and Buildah. These technologies allow you to build and manage containers across different host environment. All these tools are OCI-compatible, which makes them interoperable. The containers built by one tool can be run and managed by another tool. In earlier versions of RHEL, Redhat supported Docker to build and manage containers. Since RHEL8, Podman and Buildah have replaced Docker. While Docker requires a domain, Podman is daemon less, and its rootless feature makes it more secure. Creating a container requires you to pull the image from the registry server and start the container using that image. By default, Podman pulls the image with the latest version and by default, provides the latest tag to the pulled container image. This image is then cached on the host. The data created by one container can be shared with other containers.

In the next chapter, we will learn the concept of cloud computing.

Join our book's Discord space

Join the book's Discord Workspace for Latest updates, Offers, Tech happenings around the world, New Release and Sessions with the Authors:

https://discord.bpbonline.com

Chapter 11
Cloud Computing

Introduction

In the previous chapter, we discussed containers that provide virtualization to deploy and run your application. Suppose you want to run an application without modifying the current libraries and environment settings of the host. In that case, you need containers that run your application without interfering with the host environment. If you have a huge workload that your local computer cannot handle, you can transfer that to a robust remote server that can handle the increasing workload. When the workload increases, you can connect several remote computers to distribute the workload among them, delivering high performance; this is known as **cloud computing**. These remote servers may or may not run the application using containers. Cloud computing is different from containers. It is known as cloud computing when you store and process data on several remotely connected computers and access them via the internet. Today, cloud computing is the need of the hour. Organizations use it to distribute the workload to meet the increasing demand. Widespread use of the internet gave a boost to cloud computing. Since the internet is available to all, users can easily access any services provided over the internet. An increasing number of users on the internet leads to increasing demand for investment in infrastructure by organizations, rendering them higher costs to run their services. Organizations may take the support of various cloud providers instead of investing in local infrastructure. Switching to cloud computing automatically reduces their operational and maintenance costs.

In this chapter, you will understand cloud computing, its advantages, and its features provided in Linux, specifically in RHEL9.

Structure

This chapter covers the following topics:

- Understanding the terminology
- Advantages of cloud computing
- Types of cloud computing services
- Models of cloud computing
- Images and instances
- Networking in cloud
- Cloud features provided in RHEL9

Objectives

After completing this chapter, you should have acquired the knowledge and understanding necessary to delve into cloud computing. The core concepts of cloud computing should be well within your grasp, enabling you to comprehend the fundamental principles that underpin this innovative technology. Moreover, you should have gained insights into the main components of cloud computing and should develop a clear understanding of how the cloud operates. With this newfound knowledge, you should be ready to explore the vast possibilities and potential cloud computing applications.

Understanding the terminology

The term **cloud** in cloud computing refers to using a network of remote servers to store, manage, and process data. These servers are accessed over the internet, allowing users to access their data and applications from anywhere with an internet connection. The cloud is a virtual space that provides access to computing resources, such as servers, storage, and applications, over the internet. Thus, **cloud computing** is a model for delivering services using a network of remote servers rather than local servers or personal devices. With cloud computing, organizations and individuals do not need to rely on their infrastructure. The remote servers are maintained by third-party providers, called **cloud providers,** responsible for managing and securing them while organizations can focus on their core tasks.

Many cloud providers offer cloud computing services to organizations and individuals. The most popular cloud providers are **AWS**, **Microsoft Azure**, **IBM Cloud**, **Google Cloud**

Platform, and **Oracle Cloud**. You can choose a cloud provider according to your needs, workload, and cost.

These cloud providers provide you with many forms of computing services that you can choose from. You do not need any investment in setting up infrastructure and maintaining it. You only need a little to keep the uptime of the system and availability of the services all the time, as your cloud provider incurs the overhead of these complexities and offers you reliable and efficient computing services at a significantly lower cost. You have to pay only for the resources that you use.

Suppose you buy a mini or a mainframe computer to run your application and later realize that the server's capacity is not being fully utilized as the actual workload you are getting is not very high. You must wait to scale it down as you have already invested a large amount of money. Now, you are in a dilemma. Cloud relieves you of this dilemma, as any resources you have allocated can be deallocated if unused.

Advantages of cloud computing

Cloud computing benefits organizations of all sizes, enabling them to become more efficient, flexible, and responsive to changing needs. It offers a cost-saving advantage to small organizations that cannot invest in IT infrastructure. They also provide benefits to mid-size organizations that cannot afford more investments when scalability is required in case workload increases. Moreover, cloud computing delivers the following benefits to all organizations:

- **Reduced cost**: Individuals and organizations have to pay only for the resources they use; they do not need to invest their capital in buying local servers. It also reduces their maintenance cost, which is incurred by the cloud providers. Thus, it reduces their overall cost.
- **Scalability**: Increasing demand can be accommodated at a lower cost by allocating more resources from the cloud provider. Organizations do not need to buy more resources locally, which may lead them to incur higher charges.
- **Flexibility**: With cloud computing, you can increase or reduce computing resources on demand. Any computing resources, if unused, can be deallocated at any time. Cloud providers allow customers to choose resources and specific services according to their requirements.
- **Easier resource management**: Organizations can focus on their core operations rather than focusing on maintaining their IT infrastructure. Customers need to choose the required resources only, and they can use them without worrying about their maintenance. Cloud providers offer them a more accessible interface where they can allocate or deallocate any computing resources as required.

- **Easier accessibility of the services**: Cloud computing allows users to access their data and applications from anywhere with an internet connection.
- **Reliability**: Organizations spend a lot to maintain the uptime and reliability of their local servers. With local infrastructure, you need to storm your head to keep the uptime of the system, and a proper backup recovery plan should be in place all the time to reduce the **mean time to recovery** (**MTTR**) on failure. Cloud computing relieves you by providing high levels of reliability and uptime, with redundant backup systems and disaster recovery plans to ensure that data is not lost in case of an outage or system failure.
- **Performance**: Without downtime of infrastructure, the cloud provides an option to increase the capacity of CPU, disk, and memory. The CPU count of any machine can be increased if the system faces any performance issues due to computing constraints. If you have a machine performing complex mathematical calculations during the daytime but a lesser amount of processing during the night, you can make provisions in the cloud such that the CPU count of the machine increases in the daytime and reduces in the nighttime. Performance issues could also be related to network and disk I/O. For high network performance, cloud providers provide you with the option to select a machine with a network interface supporting network offloading. Network offloading reduces CPU overhead for TCP/IP-related network operations. The network controller itself performs all the processing of the TCP/IP stack. Cloud also provides an option to select **Input Output Operations Per Second** (in short , **IOPS**) for disks. High IOPS disks are required where a high volume of read/write operations are required. You can use the facility of higher IOPS at a higher price.
- **Security**: Cloud computing providers invest heavily in security measures to protect user data, including encryption, firewalls, and intrusion detection systems. They also comply with industry standards and regulations to protect data. Thus, little overhead to implement security is incurred on the part of customers.

Types of cloud computing services

Cloud computing provides you with a virtualized environment, but it appears to the user as if it is a local environment. Cloud computing offers different kinds of services, each with different levels of control over your resources. You can choose any of the following types of cloud computing services as per your business needs.

Infrastructure as a Service

Infrastructure as a Service (**IaaS**) provides access to virtualized computing resources like servers, storage, and networking on demand. Customers can configure and manage these resources themselves, providing the greatest level of flexibility and control over their computing environment. IaaS allows them to configure and manage these resources as their own infrastructure by paying a small amount. Popular IaaS providers include **Amazon Web Services (AWS)**, **Microsoft Azure**, and **Google Cloud Platform**. AWS's EC2 is an example of IaaS.

IaaS can be a cost-effective way for businesses to access computing resources without having to invest in and maintain their own infrastructure. IaaS providers offer a range of services that allow customers to configure and manage their own infrastructure, including the following:

- **Virtual machines**: IaaS providers offer virtual machines that customers can use to run their own operating systems and applications. Customers have a variety of options to choose from: configuration of the machine, processor type, memory size, storage type and size, OS, and more. After they choose the configuration, they can start and run their virtual machine instances and deploy their applications on them. They can provide a public IP address to this machine and perform networking-related chores. Then, they can migrate your workload to this machine. They can create as many virtual machines as the workload demands. The cloud provider offers an easy-to-use interface where customers can scale up and down the number of VMs very easily.

- **Storage**: IaaS providers offer different types of storage, including block storage for data that requires high performance, object storage for unstructured data, and file storage for organizing data in the hierarchical format of files and folders. Choose the one when you create a virtual machine instance according to your needs.

- **Networking**: IaaS providers offer virtual networks that customers can use to connect their virtual machines and other cloud resources.

- **Security**: IaaS providers typically offer security features such as firewalls, encryption, and identity and access management to help customers secure their infrastructure, data, and applications.

- **Load balancing**: IaaS providers offer load balancing services to help customers distribute traffic across their virtual machines and ensure high availability, performance, and scalability.

IAAS is a popular choice for businesses that need to quickly scale up or down their infrastructure to meet changing demands or those that want more control over their computing environment.

Platform as a Service

Platform as a Service (PaaS) provides a platform for developers to build, deploy and manage their applications using the infrastructure provided by the cloud service provider. Users do not need to worry about the setting up of infrastructure and the required libraries to run the application. They can focus on the development task of their application, while cloud providers handle the infrastructure, operating system, and middleware. They have little control over their computing environment and the infrastructure. Popular PaaS providers include **Heroku**, **Microsoft Azure**, and **Google App Engine**.

PaaS providers provide a range of services, including the ones listed here:

- **Development tools and frameworks**: PaaS providers offer preconfigured development environments, application frameworks, and other tools to simplify the application development process. This can include programming languages like Java, Python, and Node.js, and tools for testing, debugging, and deployment. Customers can use these tools to write and test their applications and can deploy them to the cloud provider's infrastructure with just a few clicks.

- **Scalability and availability**: PaaS providers typically offer automatic scaling and load balancing, ensuring that applications can handle increasing traffic and demand. PaaS providers also offer high availability and disaster recovery capabilities to ensure that applications are always available.

- **Database management**: PaaS providers offer database management services that allow customers to store and manage data for their applications. It allows customers to create, manage, and scale their databases without having to manage the underlying infrastructure. This includes tools for database backup, recovery, and replication. This can include databases, data analytics tools, and other data management services. **Relational Database Service** (**RDS**) provided by AWS comes under PaaS.

- **Web hosting**: PaaS providers offer web hosting services, allowing customers to host their applications and websites on the cloud provider's infrastructure. This includes tools for load balancing, autoscaling, and traffic management.

- **Integration**: PaaS providers offer integration services, allowing customers to connect their applications to other cloud services, on-premises applications, and external data sources.

- **Security**: PaaS providers offer security services such as firewalls, encryption, and access controls to protect customers' applications and data.

PaaS can be a cost-effective way for businesses to develop and deploy applications without having to manage the underlying infrastructure.

Software as a Service

Software as a Service (**SaaS**) provides access to ready-to-use software applications that are hosted on the cloud provider's infrastructure, such as email or project management tools. With SaaS, customers do not need to install and manage the software themselves. Examples of SaaS applications include **Gmail** and **Microsoft Office 365**. Popular SaaS providers include **Microsoft Office 365**, **Google Workspace**, and **Adobe Creative Cloud**. Customers can use the software services provided under SaaS irrespective of the language used in the software.

SaaS providers typically offer a range of software applications, including the following:

- **Productivity software**: SaaS providers offer productivity software such as email, word processing, spreadsheets, and presentation tools. Examples of popular productivity software are Microsoft Office 365, Google Workspace, and Zoho Workplace.
- **Collaboration software**: SaaS providers offer collaboration software such as team messaging, video conferencing, and project management tools. Examples of popular collaboration software are Slack, Zoom, and Trello.
- **Customer relationship management (CRM) software**: SaaS providers offer CRM software that allows businesses to manage their interactions with customers and prospects. It also allows businesses to manage customer data, track sales, and automate marketing campaigns. Examples of popular CRM software are Salesforce, HubSpot, and Zoho CRM.
- **Enterprise resource planning (ERP) software**: SaaS providers offer ERP software that helps businesses manage their core business processes, such as accounting, inventory, and order management. Examples of popular ERP software are Oracle NetSuite, SAP Business ByDesign, and Microsoft Dynamics 365.
- **Human resources (HR) software**: SaaS providers offer HR software, allowing businesses to manage employee data, payroll, and benefits. Popular examples are Zenefits and Workday.

SaaS applications are typically licensed on a subscription basis, with customers paying monthly or annual fees for access to the software.

Models of cloud computing

There are three primary types of cloud computing deployment models: public, private, and hybrid cloud. Choosing the right cloud deployment model depends on the specific needs and requirements of the organization.

Public cloud

In a public cloud model, computing resources are owned and operated by a cloud service provider and made available to customers over the internet. These resources are typically shared by multiple customers, and customers pay for the resources they use on a subscription or pay-per-use basis. Examples of public cloud providers include **Amazon Web Services** (**AWS**), Microsoft Azure, and Google Cloud Platform.

The benefits of the public cloud include the following:

- **Scalability**: Public cloud providers offer virtually unlimited computing resources that can be quickly and easily scaled up or down based on customer needs. This makes it easy for businesses to handle sudden spikes in demand without having to invest in additional hardware or infrastructure.
- **Cost-effectiveness**: Public cloud providers typically offer pricing models that allow customers to pay only for the resources they use, which can be more cost-effective than investing in and maintaining their own hardware and infrastructure.
- **Flexibility**: Public cloud providers offer a wide range of services and applications that can be easily accessed and used by customers anywhere in the world with an internet connection.
- **Geographical reach**: Public clouds have a global network of data centers, making it easy for customers to deploy services and applications in multiple regions worldwide.
- **Maintenance**: Public cloud providers are responsible for maintaining and updating the infrastructure and software, which frees up time and resources for businesses to focus on their core operations.
- **Security and compliance**: Public cloud providers typically have robust security and compliance measures to ensure customer data security and privacy. This feature puts little overhead on customers in maintaining the security of the resources.

Private cloud

Private clouds, on the other hand, are owned and operated by a single organization for their use. They are typically hosted on-premises or in a third-party data center. Private clouds provide more control over security, compliance, and performance than public clouds but require more management and maintenance. Organizations with strict data security or regulatory requirements often use private clouds. They offer several benefits:

- **Security and control**: Private clouds offer greater control and security than public clouds, as organizations have complete control over their computing environment and can customize security policies and protocols to meet their specific needs.
- **Customization**: Private clouds allow organizations to customize their computing environment, including hardware, software, and networking infrastructure, to meet their specific requirements.
- **Compliance**: Private clouds are well suited for organizations with strict regulatory or compliance requirements, as they provide greater control over data privacy and security.

- **Performance**: Private clouds can provide better performance and reliability than public clouds, as resources are dedicated to a single organization rather than being shared by multiple customers.
- **Cost**: While private clouds require more management and maintenance than public clouds, they can be more cost-effective for organizations with steady, predictable workloads over time.

Popular private cloud software include OpenStack and VMware vSphere. Private clouds are well suited for organizations with strict security or compliance requirements and those with steady, predictable workloads over time.

Hybrid cloud

Hybrid clouds combine elements of both public and private clouds. In a hybrid cloud model, computing resources are spread across both public and private clouds, allowing organizations to make the most of both. For example, an organization might use a public cloud for scalable computing resources and a private cloud for sensitive data storage. Hybrid clouds allow organizations to maintain control over sensitive data while taking the flexibility and cost-saving advantages of public clouds.

Hybrid clouds offer several benefits, including the following:

- **Flexibility**: Hybrid clouds offer a high degree of flexibility, allowing organizations to choose the best deployment model for their specific needs and workloads.
- **Scalability**: Public clouds offer unlimited scalability, while private clouds provide greater control over data privacy and security. Hybrid clouds allow organizations to take advantage of both, scaling up or down as needed while maintaining control over sensitive data.
- **Cost-effectiveness**: Hybrid clouds can be more cost-effective than private clouds, as organizations can use public clouds for scalable workloads and only pay for the resources they use.
- **Security**: Hybrid clouds provide higher security than public clouds alone, as sensitive data can be stored in a private cloud and accessed only through a secure, encrypted connection.
- **Compliance**: Hybrid clouds are well suited for organizations with strict regulatory or compliance requirements, as they provide greater control over data privacy and security.

Popular hybrid cloud providers include **Amazon Web Services** (**AWS**), Microsoft Azure, and Google Cloud Platform. Hybrid clouds are well suited for organizations with a mix of workloads.

Images and instances

Images and instances are fundamental components of cloud computing, and they are used to create and manage virtual infrastructure in the cloud. In cloud computing, an image can be thought of as a pre-configured template of a **virtual machine** (**VM**) that contains an OS, all the necessary settings, and software applications to run a specific workload or application. This image can be used to create a virtual machine instance that is the running copy of the image.

When creating an instance, users select an image and then determine the instance type, network settings, and storage options. Cloud service providers offer several choices for instance types. The VM instance is assigned computing resources such as CPU, RAM, and storage based on the selected instance type.

When a user requests an instance of a particular instance type, the cloud provider provisions a virtual machine with computing resources, including CPU, memory, and storage, based on the image type selected by the user. The user can then configure the machine to bring it into the network and access the instance through a remote connection using SSH through a local computer and then use this instance to run applications or workloads.

Images are typically created and maintained by cloud service providers and can be customized by users to include specific software or configurations and the required security settings. Each instance runs independently and can be started, stopped, resized, and terminated as needed.

Multiple instances can be created from the same image, allowing for easy scaling of applications and services. They offer several benefits, including the ability to quickly and easily create and deploy virtual machines with pre-configured settings and software applications. This can help reduce deployment time and complexity and enable more efficient use of computing resources.

Networking in cloud

Networking is another essential component of cloud computing, as it enables communication and data transfer between different components of cloud infrastructure, including instances, storage, and databases.

In a cloud environment, networking is typically managed through a virtual network that is abstracted from the underlying physical infrastructure. This virtual network is designed to provide flexible and scalable connectivity between different computing resources, regardless of their physical location.

There are several networking components and services in a cloud environment, including the following:

- **Virtual Private Cloud** (**VPC**): A VPC is a private network that is logically isolated from the public internet and other customers' networks. It provides a secure and isolated environment for instances and services to communicate with each other. It allows organizations to create their own network topology, define subnets, and configure security groups. We will see a brief overview of many concepts related to VPC, such as security groups and route tables, in this section.
- **Firewall**: A firewall is a hardware- or software-based device that monitors and controls traffic at the network level. They are used to secure a cloud environment by controlling inbound and outbound network traffic based on predefined security policies. They can be used to block traffic from specific IP addresses or ranges, restrict traffic to specific protocols or ports, and prevent unauthorized access to the network.
- **Security groups**: Security groups is yet another way to control access to instances and other resources in the cloud. A security group is a virtual firewall that controls inbound and outbound traffic to instances in a specific VPC. It operates at the instance level and allows administrators to specify which protocols, ports, and IP addresses are allowed to communicate with the instance. Security groups can be configured to allow traffic from specific IP addresses or ranges or from other security groups within the same VPC. They can also be used to block traffic from known malicious IP addresses or to restrict traffic to specific protocols or ports. The main difference between security groups and firewalls is that security groups operate at the instance level, while firewalls operate at the network level. Security groups are specific to a single VPC and are used to control traffic to instances within that VPC, while firewalls can be used to control traffic between different VPCs or between a VPC and an on-premise network.
- **Route table**: A route table determines the routing path, which will be followed by all the network traffic originating from your subnet. The main route table automatically comes with your VPC. A custom route table can be created according to your needs.
- **Load balancers**: Load balancers distribute incoming network traffic across multiple instances to optimize resource utilization and ensure high availability and reliability.
- **VPN**: **Virtual private network** (**VPN**) allows organizations to securely connect their on-premises infrastructure to their cloud environment over the public internet.
- **Direct connect**: Direct connect enables organizations to establish a dedicated, private connection between their on-premises infrastructure and their cloud environment.
- **Network interface**: Each VM instance is assigned one or more network interfaces that you can configure to bring the machine into the interface.

Cloud providers such as AWS, Microsoft Azure, and Google Cloud Platform offer a range of networking services and tools that enable organizations to manage their cloud network infrastructure efficiently and securely.

Cloud features provided in RHEL9

RHEL 9 provides an image builder service. Using this service, we can create images that can run in major cloud provider environments, including Amazon Web Services, Google Cloud Platform, Microsoft Azure, and VMware. RHEL 9 is distributed with the Windows Azure Linux Agent, which involves monitoring the health of RHEL instances running on the Azure cloud.

Conclusion

Cloud computing is the need of the hour. It provides on-demand computing resources like storage, CPU, OS, and more without the need for users to manage these resources themselves. Cloud computing is beneficial for small to large organizations. When the computing resources from your end are not enough to handle the workload and more investment in computing resources is not affordable, you can switch your workload to use the infrastructure provided in the cloud. It will incur little cost as you need to pay only for what you use. There are many organizations that provide cloud services. AWS and Microsoft Azure are among the popular ones. The cloud provider offers many kinds of cloud computing services, such as IaaS, PaaS, and SaaS. The main components of any cloud service are instances and images. Instances are running virtual machines created from images in a cloud computing environment. The cloud provider offers their customers many images to choose from. Each image is a bundle of a specific OS, libraries, and packages installed into it. Networking is another essential component of cloud computing. It enables communication and data transfer between different components of the cloud infrastructure. Overall, cloud providers help organizations optimize their performance and bring reliability and availability to their infrastructure all the time.

In the next chapter, we will learn to use and configure graphical user interface on a Linux host.

Join our book's Discord space

Join the book's Discord Workspace for Latest updates, Offers, Tech happenings around the world, New Release and Sessions with the Authors:

https://discord.bpbonline.com

CHAPTER 12
Graphical User Interface

Introduction

So far, we have used command-line interface to complete our task on the Linux system. We have visited many commands to perform different kinds of activities. Suppose you are fond of using graphical user interface or love the desktop nature of the Windows operating system. In that case, you can learn to use the desktop environment provided with some Linux distributions. You can execute almost any task using various menu options with just a mouse click, as you performed in Windows. Different Linux distributions provide different GUI features by supporting different kinds of desktop environments, like GNOME, KDE, and more. Each desktop environment has its own set of features and capabilities. In this chapter, we will learn to use the GNOME desktop environment, the only desktop environment supported in RHEL9.

Structure

This chapter covers the following topics:

- GNOME: The desktop environment
- Knowing your desktop
- Opening applications in GNOME

- Facilities in GNOME
- More in GNOME
- Accessing remote desktop
- File-related operations
- Adding applications in favorites
- Setting up networking and Bluetooth
- Desktop background and general settings
- Application-related settings
- Privacy
- Screenlock
- Managing users using GNOME GUI
- Changing date and time in GNOME
- Browsing remote files
- Customising the locals
- Keyboard and mouse
- Default applications
- Managing software in GNOME
- Log viewer
- Managing disk in GNOME
- System monitor
- GNOME Virtual File System

Objectives

By the end of this chapter, you should understand the GNOME desktop environment. You should be able to configure various system settings graphically. You can install, uninstall, and update various software graphically. Needless to say, by reading this chapter, you can perform almost any administration-related task on the Linux system using graphical user interface.

GNOME: The desktop environment

To perform all your tasks and run your applications in a graphical interface, you can use the desktop environment that is shipped with your Linux distribution. The only desktop environment available in RHEL9 is **GNOME**. The desktop environment determines how the various graphical elements, such as menus, icons, mouse pointer, and user interface, are rendered on the screen. Each desktop environment has its own **display server** responsible for managing the graphical display and input devices, such as the monitor, keyboard, and mouse. By default, Red Hat uses **GNOME shell** as its display server. Any display server follows a protocol that provides a framework for rendering graphical elements, managing windows, and handling input. By default, RHEL9 provides a standard GNOME environment using **GNOME shell on Wayland protocol**. Since RHEL7, **X11 protocol** was in place; it uses **XOrg** as the display server. The graphic is displayed according to the protocol used. You can switch to XOrg at any time. After you log yourself out, the screen will show you the list of users to select. Select the user from which you want to log in. Next screen will prompt you for the password. At the bottom right, there is a **gear** button. Pointing this button will open the list of menu options to choose from, as follows:

- Standard (Wayland display server)
- GNOME Classic
- GNOME Classic on Xorg
- Custom
- Standard (X11 display server)
- User script

By default, **Standard (Wayland display server)** is selected. This option provides GNOME Shell that uses Wayland protocol and creates a GNOME standard environment. You can choose Standard (X11 display server) if you want to use X11 as your display protocol. Any selection that you will make here will persist across all your logins as well as reboots. Besides GNOME standards, Red Hat allows you to choose a **GNOME Classic** environment that will give you a traditional look and feel. GNOME Classic can also work with both the protocols: Wayland and X11.

To disable Wayland for all the users of the system, edit the **`/etc/gdm/custom.conf`** file; change the following line:

```
#WaylandEnable=false
```

to

```
WaylandEnable=false
```

by uncommenting this line and rebooting the system.

However, legacy X11 application may behave differently if run using the Wayland protocol. RHEL9 is already shipped with XWayland. The main purpose of XWayland is to translate the **X11** protocol into the **Wayland** protocol and vice-versa. XWayland helps X11 legacy applications to work properly even with display server based on the **Wayland** protocol.

Knowing your desktop

The default installation of RHEL9 gives you standard environment. Let us understand how this environment looks when you first log in. Upon logging in, you find a blank screen and a top bar. The top bar contains the following:

- The **Activities** button at the extreme left side, clicking on which will lead to the following:
    - o A display of the preview of all the open applications windows; this is called the **Activities Overview** feature.
    - o A display of a panel at the bottom. This panel contains **Favorites** tools, icons of the applications running and the **Show Applications** button. The **Show Applications** button will give access to all the installed applications.
    - o A display of a search bar at the top, which can be used to search for any application or file. Just type something, and the search bar gets activated.
- **The Date and Time** panel in the middle, clicking on which allows access to scheduled events and important system notifications.
- **System Menu** at the extreme right, which gives you options to manage network connections, Bluetooth, user logouts, system shutdown, and other system settings.

Opening applications in GNOME

When you use the **GNOME Classic** mode, you will find two menu options in the top panel; **Applications** and **Places**. Click on **Application** and a sub-menu pops up that shows the list of categories from where you can choose your application and launch it. While in the **Standard** mode, you can open any application in one of the following ways:

- Click on **Activities** in the top menu: It shows a set of menus to choose from in the bottom bar. Click on **Show Applications** to select and run the software applications of your choice.
- By using the search bar displayed under **Activities Overview Window**: For example, to open the calculator application, type `calculator` in the search bar under the **Activities Overview** window and click on the appropriate search result. It opens up a calculator window.

- By using terminal commands: Many of the utilities that we run in GNOME have their corresponding commands that can be typed in the terminal. For example, to open the calculator via command line, type **`gnome-calculator`** in the terminal and the calculator utility will open up.

Table 12.1 shows the list of commands using which a few GNOME utilities can be accessed:

GNOME-related commands	GNOME utilities/application
`gnome-calculator`	Opens GNOME calculator
`gnome-characters`	Opens characters application that is GNOME's character map and is used to display characters that are not available via your keyboard
`gnome-control-center`	Opens GNOME's control center
`gnome-disks`	Opens the **`Disks`** application that is used to view, modify and configure disks
`gnome-extensions`	Is a command line tool for managing GNOME extensions
`gnome-help`	Opens the **`Help`** window, which acts as a hands-on guide to understand GNOME features and utilities
`gnome-logs`	Opens the **`Log`** utility, which acts as a log reader.
`gnome-session`	Starts a GNOME-session
`gnome-terminal`	Starts the GNOME terminal, which is the same terminal on which we have worked so far
`gnome-system-monitor`	Opens up the **`System Monitor`** utility, which is used to monitor the utilization of various resources on the system
`gnome-software`	Opens **`Software`** application, which is used to install, remove, and manage software on the system
`gnome-shell`	Starts GNOME shell, which is an essential component of the GNOME desktop environment

Table 12.1: *Various terminal gnome commands*

We will the talk about the usage of a few of the mentioned applications in this chapter.

Facilities in GNOME

This section discusses the facilities and features provided by GNOME version 40 used in RHEL9. Further discussion is related to the standard GNOME environment that is available by default in RHEL9.

Activities overview

Clicking on the **Activities** button displays the overview of your current activities. All the running applications and windows are displayed here. This is called the **Activities Overview** feature. Using this feature, you can switch between the running windows. **Activities Overview** also shows you the search bar at the top, which you can use to find any files or applications in the system. You can use **Activities Overview** many times throughout your work to switch between applications, search for files, open applications, and modify settings.

Virtual workspace

One important feature of the GNOME desktop environment is that it provides you with many **virtual workspaces**, where each workspace can be used to launch one application. You do not need to open many applications on a single desktop. Instead, you can segregate your work into multiple virtual workspaces. This approach does not clutter up your desktop with many open application windows. You can use one workspace to launch all the applications related to one project, while the second workspace can be used to work with another project. This way, you can work with two projects simultaneously by switching from one workspace to another.

Initially, you have two workspaces. To switch between workspaces, click on the **Activities** button. You will get an overview of your current activities in your current workspace, and another empty workspace will also be visible in the right corner. Hover your mouse on the second workspace to view the overview of open windows, and click on that workspace to activate it. Whenever one workspace is used, it automatically starts another empty workspace for you. When you utilize all the open workspaces, it starts yet another empty workspace for you. It automatically closes a workspace if no application is running on that. Since workspaces are automatically added and removed, they are called **dynamic workspaces.**

To switch between multiple workspaces, you can click on the workspace previews in the **Activities Overview** or use keyboard shortcuts *Ctrl+Alt+Left/Right arrow.*

Users can also move the running application's windows between workspaces by dragging and dropping them between the workspace previews available under **Activities Overview**.

Uncluttered desktop

No icons are placed in the GNOME desktop. In fact, it does not support any folder/file icons nor application shortcuts to be placed on the desktop. Thus, it never clutters your desktop. Rather, you use your desktop to view the running application windows and switch between them. You always get a clean desktop.

GNOME Extensions

You can increase the functionality of your GNOME Shell by installing **GNOME Extensions**, which add more features to your desktop. **GNOME Extensions** are add-ons or plugins that extend the functionality and customize the GNOME desktop environment. They allow users to modify the default behavior, appearance and functionality of GNOME Shell, enhancing the overall user experience.

GNOME Extensions are typically developed by the GNOME community and third-party developers. The GNOME community maintains a website: **https://extensions.gnome.org/**. It serves as a centralized platform where users can discover, install, and manage GNOME Extensions.

There are various popular **GNOME Extensions** that are widely used by the GNOME community; examples include **Dash to Dock** (which adds a dock for launching and switching between applications) and **User Themes** (allows custom themes).

GNOME Extensions are specific to the GNOME desktop environment and work with GNOME Shell. Users are required to update the extensions when they are available so that the GNOME desktop environment works properly.

Installing and managing **GNOME Extensions** can affect system stability and performance, so you should carefully review extension descriptions to ensure that the selected **Extensions** are well maintained and are delivered from trusted sources.

User productivity

Overall, GNOME facilities make users more productive. On login, you will see the **Activities Overview** page, which will give quick access to your favorites app that you may want to open. You can also select an application to open using the search bar or the **Show Applications** button that is displayed on the **Activities Overview** page. To open another app, you will again access the **Activities Overview** page, where you can choose your next app in the same way and also decide the workspace on which you want to open it. The search bar in **Activities Overview** allows you to search for an app or file quickly. Thus, everything is very easily accessible in GNOME, and you do not need to look around to search for an app or file, which savesw your time and effort and hence, increases your productivity.

In the upcoming sections, we will learn to use GNOME features, get hands-on with various GNOME utilities, and modify some of the system settings graphically.

More in GNOME

There is a lot in GNOME to understand and explore. This section covers some more handy features included in GNOME.

System menu in GNOME

To modify system and user settings, modify desktop appearance and behavior, manage applications and notifications, and more, you can access **System Menu** any time; it is visible in the top-right corner. This is the button containing the **Volume** icon, **Power** button icon, and more. Clicking on **System Menu** shows current system and network state at first. *Figure 12.1* shows the sub-menus generated on clicking **System Menu**. It shows your wired or wireless network settings, Bluetooth state as well as power settings. The next section of this sub-menu contains the **Settings** menu, which gives you access to various user- and system-related settings that could be customized as needed. We will use the **Settings** menu in various places in this chapter to customize our GNOME environment and to modify various system settings.

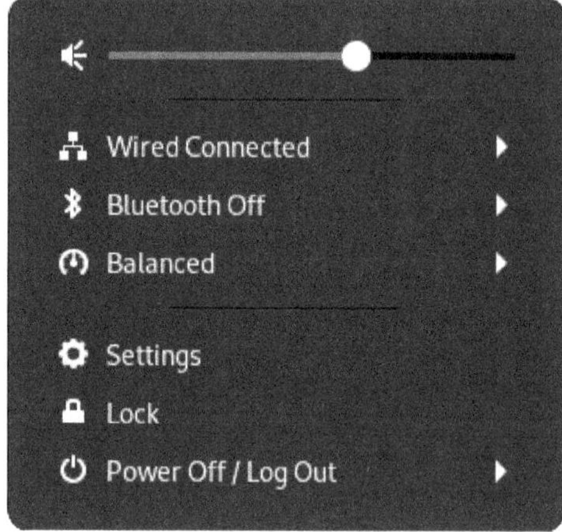

Figure 12.1*: System Menu*

Clicking on **Lock** will lock your screen. From a security perspective, if you are leaving your machine unattended, you must lock it.

Finally, we have sub-menu option related to system shutdown and reboots as well as user logouts. Clicking on **Log Out** closes all your running applications and logs you out safely. You can click on the **Switch User** option if you want to switch to another user without logging yourself out.

Searching in GNOME

GNOME provides a handy search feature for its users. You can search for anything using the search bar shown in the **Activities Overview** page. You do not need to look around anywhere else to search for anything. You can search for any type of file or application. Just start typing the search term on the **Activities Overview** page and search bar becomes activated. GNOME search can also provide the matching search result, even from within the application.

Result of the search term is shown in the following order:

- **Settings**: The result from the GNOME control-center is displayed. It displays any matching setting options from the control-center.
- **Files**: Matching results from **Files** application are displayed. It display file names that includes matching characters
- **Calculator**: Result from the **Calculator** application is displayed.
- **Character**: Matching characters from **Character** application are displayed.
- **Software**: Name of the installed software that matches the search term is displayed.
- **Terminal**: The matching terminal name is displayed, if found.

You can control the order of the displayed search result by going to **Settings** | **Search**. It will open the window as in *Figure 12.2*:

***Figure 12.2**: Search settings page*

The order given in *Figure 12.2* determines the order of search result displayed under the **Activities Overview** 's search bar. You can change the order of results by moving appropriate application names up or down. You can also choose to disable any application by clicking on the **disable** toggle button if you want the result from that application to not be displayed under the search result. The **Search Locations** button at the top bar of the **Search** window is discussed later in this chapter.

The search feature of GNOME is so powerful that you can also open the window in *Figure 12.2* by typing `search` in the search bar. In fact, any setting listed under **Settings** can be searched for and opened via the search bar of **Activities Overview**.

Modifying user/system settings

To access the **Settings**, click on the **System Menu** icon on the right of the top panel. In the menu that pops up, click **Settings**. This will open the **Settings** window, showing you the various system and user settings on the left side that you can modify. Clicking on each of the items on the left side of the **Settings** window opens the corresponding window on the right side. This window is the **GNOME's control center** where most aspects of GNOME are managed. You can also open **Settings** by typing **`settings`** or **`control center`** in the search bar of the **Activities Overview** page.

Any setting can also be opened by simply typing the name of that setting in the search bar of the **Activities Overview** page. For example, to open network-related settings, it is not necessary to go to **Settings | Network**. Rather, just type **`network`** in the search bar and choose **Network** from the search result to open the **Network** settings page.

In the upcoming sections, we will learn to view and modify various system-, user- and gnome-related settings. We will also discuss how the various system- and user-related operations can be performed in GNOME.

Accessing remote desktop

To get terminal access of the remote server and run commands over there, we have learnt to use SSH. SSH will not let you access the remote server graphically. You must use a different tool that allows you to access the desktop of the remote server. **Virtual Network Computing** (**VNC**) server allows you to access remote desktop by using the URI of the following form:

```
vnc://<computer name>
```

The following procedure needs to be performed on remote desktop to give remote desktop access to the other users:

1. To access remote desktop, sharing must be enabled on the remote desktop. Go to **Settings** and click on **Sharing** from the left panel. **Sharing** window pops-up on the right panel. You will notice that **Screen Sharing** is set to off. Click on **Screen Sharing** to open the **Screen Sharing** window, as shown in *Figure 12.3*:

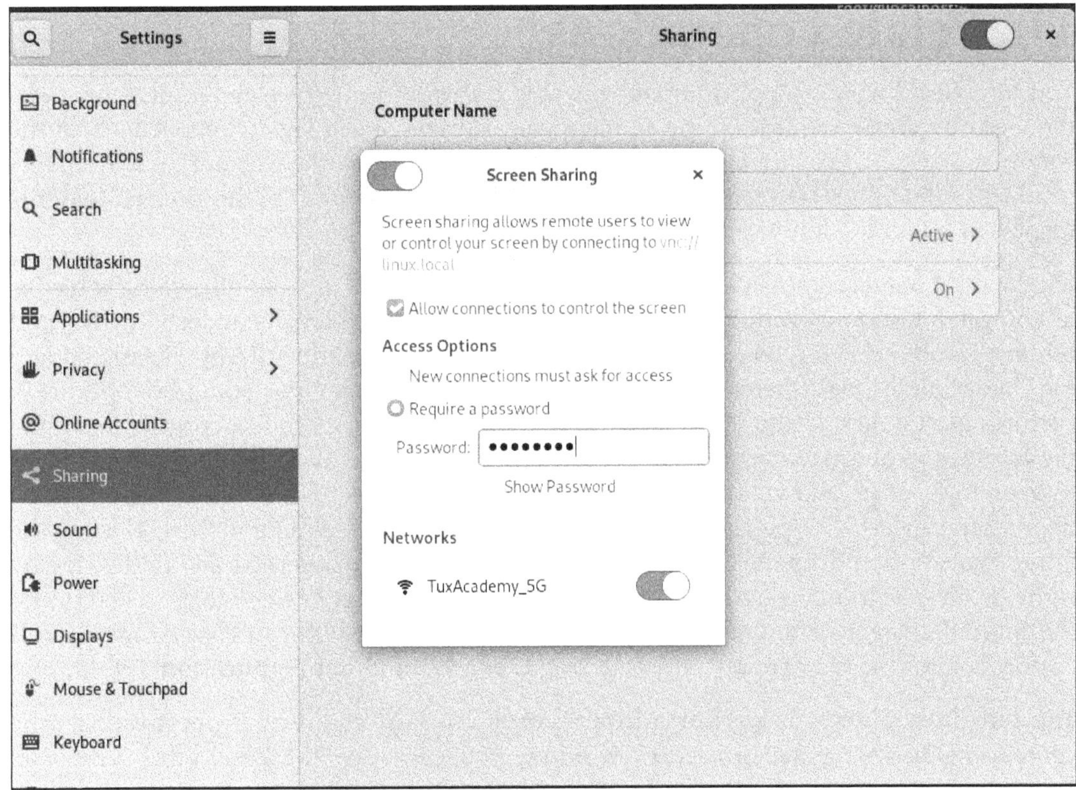

Figure 12.3: Sharing setting page from GNOME control-center

2. Click on the **Screen Sharing** switch button given in the top panel of this window to enable it.
3. Select **Allow connections to control the screen**. This option allows other people to move the mouse cursor, run applications and browse and view files on this computer. This window gives you two access options:
   - **New connections must ask for access**: If you enable this option, you will be asked permission to allow someone to access your desktop.
   - **Requires a password**: Enter the password. If you do not set the password, anyone can attempt to view your screen without entering the password.

Note that to connect to a remote desktop using VNC, you require the **Connections** software installed on your machine. **Connections** is a remote desktop client for the GNOME desktop environment. Installing the software will be discussed later in this chapter.

File-related operations

You can select the **Files** application to view and browse for any files and folders. To make the file searching easier, the application appears in two panels. The left panel lists out the common places where files can reside. The right panel display the lists of files and folders residing in the folder selected in the left panel. The directory path of the selected folder is displayed under the folder path bar.

On the right panel, right-clicking or left-clicking on a file will give you the same behavior as you get in Windows. A double-click will open the folder to view its underlying files and folders. Double-clicking on a file opens it in its default application. Right-clicking on any file/folder on the right panel opens the context menu, which gives you more options to perform on the files. Using the context menu, you can rename the file, copy or move the file to other locations, compress the files, and more. You can also choose the application to open the files in, and you can cut, copy and paste the files to other locations. All these operations can easily be performed by right-clicking on a file/folder and then selecting the appropriate option from the context menu generated. You can also star any folder/file by right-clicking on its name and selecting **Star**. The starred folder or files will be listed under the **Starred** category shown in the left panel. Additionally, you can change the default application for the file to open in by selecting **Open With Other Application**.

You can also view the properties/attributes of the files by choosing **Properties** from the context menu. Using the **Properties** window, you can view the basic attributes, such as file type, file size, and timestamp. This window also allows you to view or change the permission of the file/folders. It lists the owner of the file, the group owner and the permission to all the access level category.

Moreover, you can choose the default application to open the file using the **Properties** window.

You can add any folder that you frequently access in the bookmark for easier accessibility. Go to the folder; the selected folder should be displayed in the folder path bar. Click on the dropdown given next to the folder name in the folder path bar and select **Add to Bookmarks**, and that folder name will be visible in the left panel. You can click on that folder name to open it in one go.

Folder views

There are two views on which folder contents are displayed in the **Files** application window: list view and grid view. You can switch to one view from another by clicking on the **Show list/Show grid** button from the top-right panel.

Grid view or icon view is the default display. It allows you to sort the folder contents using various criteria, including alphabetically, by selected timestamps, size or type.

Under the list view, only the file name, file size and modification time are displayed. You can choose what columns/file attributes to display in the list view by selecting column names from the **Visible Columns** menu option listed under the drop-down button next to the **Show list/Show grid** button.

The search bar given in the **Files** application window comes in very handy if you want to search for any file: Start typing its name and the search bar is activated.

Right-click in the empty area inside the **Files** application, and you will get the **Open in Terminal** menu option in the generated context menu. This option allows you to open the terminal with the current working directory set to the selected folder.

Setting preferences

Click on the **Menu** button at the top-right corner right before the **Close** button. In the first row, you will have a few useful icons, such as the **New Window** icon that will open the file browser application in a new window, a **New Tab** button that will open the same application in a new tab in the same window. The last icon is used to create a new folder in the current folder.

The next row contains the **Edit** menu option, which gives you the options to cut, copy and paste the selected files or folders.

If you enable **Show Hidden Files**, then all the hidden files will also be listed. By default, this is set to off. **Show Sidebar** displays the side panel.

Preferences allows you to set file and folder preferences. Clicking on the **Preferences** menu option opens the **Preferences** window, as shown in *Figure 12.4*.

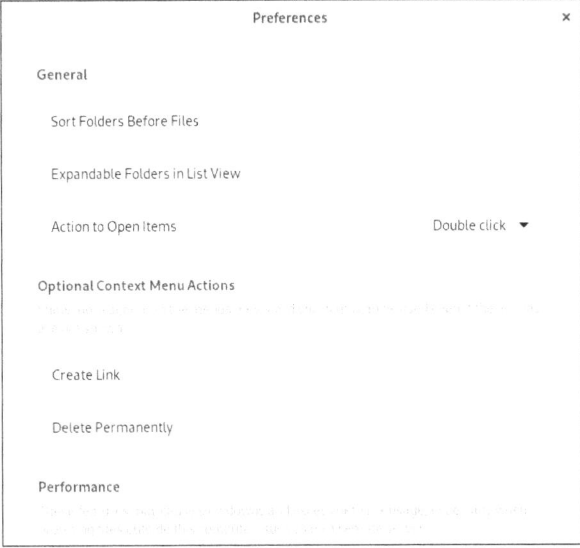

Figure 12.4: *Files Preferences Window setting preferences for File application*

This window is divided into several categories. The general panel allows you to set your view preferences, where you can determine your sort order. Enable **Sort Folders before Files** if you want to list folders before files under the **Files** application browser window. Enabling **Expandable folders in List View** will display the folders in a list view, preceded by the expand symbol. This is called the **expandable view**. In the last row, you can choose whether to open files with a double-click or single click.

The next set of rows allow you to add more options in context menus generated when a folder/file is right-clicked on. You have two buttons:

- **Create Link**: This will be displayed whenever a folder or file is right-clicked. This is used to create a link of the same folder. This link will be a hard link.
- **Delete Permanently**: This option is used to delete the files permanently. By default, when you delete a file/folder, it will move to trash.

You can enable these buttons if you want to display related options under the context menus.

The next set of options determines how the search is performed. Refer to *Figure 12.5* where **Search in Subfolders** determines where to search for file names. By default, the search displays only the files belonging to the local computer. If you want to list the files belonging to all the locations, choose **All locations** from the dropdown given in **Search in Subfolders**. If you want to limit your search to the current folder, choose **Never**. The same applies to **Show Thumbnails** and **Count Number of Files in Folders**. The selection in this section impacts the performance of browsing. The next section is related to icon view. By default, only the folder names are displayed beneath the **folder** icon. This section allows you to choose what other information can be displayed beneath the folder name in sequence. You can specify a maximum of three attributes to be listed below the folder icon under icon view. Choose the desired attributes using the dropdown, in **First**, **Second** and **Third**.

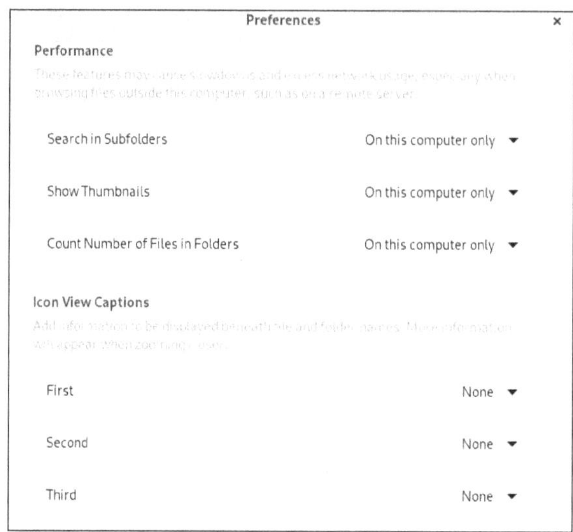

***Figure 12.5**: Files Preferences page (in continuation of Figure 12.4)*

Searching for files

You have the **Magnifier** button in the **folder view**. Click this button to search for any folder or file. You can also apply certain criteria using the dropdown given next to the search bar. You can specify the date range for file search under the **When** list button. You can also specify the type of file that you want to include in the search result by using the **What** dropdown button.

Customizing search results

You can customize the search result by determining what directories are to be included or excluded from searches. Go to **Settings | Search**. This will open **Search** window panel in the right pane. In the header bar, you have the **Search Locations** button. Clicking on it opens the **Search Locations** window, as shown in *Figure 12.6*:

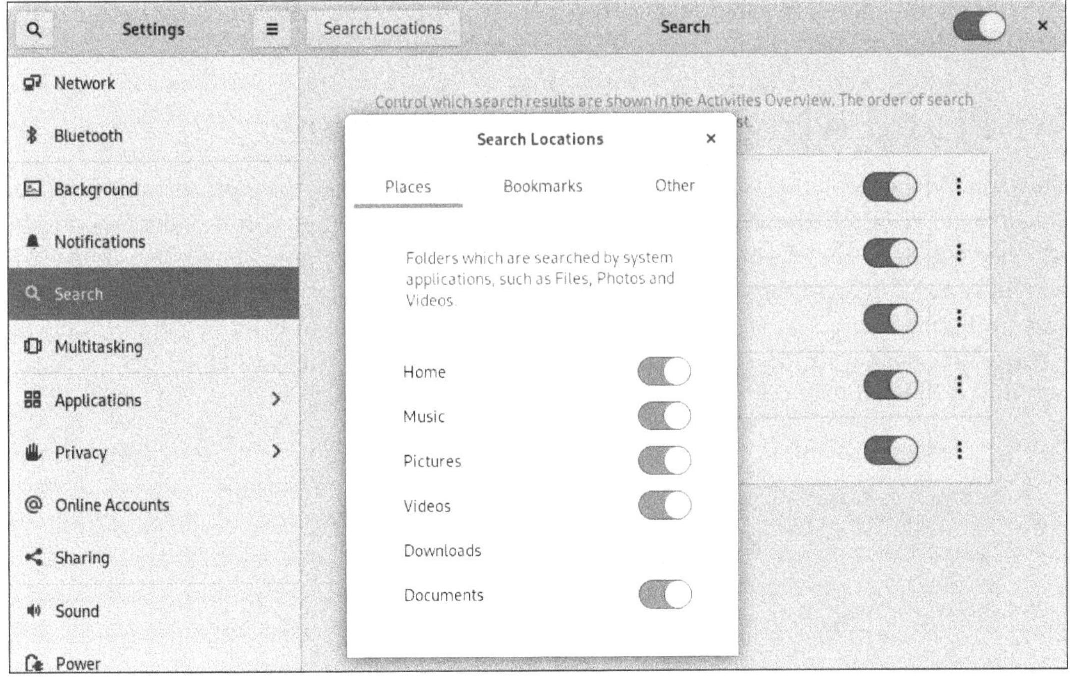

***Figure 12.6**: Search setting page: Determining Search Locations*

It opens with three tabs: **Places**, **Bookmarks**, and **Other**. The search will be performed in the folders that have the **Enable** button enabled. *Figure 12.6* shows that **Downloads** is not enabled. This means that search will not be performed on the **Downloads** folder. Under the **Bookmarks** tab, you can select which bookmarks should be searched for the files/ folders. Using the **Other** tab, you can include other folders or areas where the folder/file search can be performed.

Adding applications in Favorites

Open **Activities Overview** and type the name of the application that you want to add in favorites. Whatever you type in **Activities Overview** will automatically be typed under the search box. Right-click on the application icon in the search result. Select **Add to Favorites**. Your application will now be visible under the **Favorites** panel under **Activities Overview**.

Setting up networking and Bluetooth

We have seen that NetworkManager is used in RHEL9 to configure and manage network connectivity of a machine. It provides command-line utility, **`nmcli`** and text-based interface, and **`nmtui`** to interact with NetworkManager daemon. To configure and manage networking using GUI, use networking tools provided by gnome. Under **Settings**, the top three options in the left panel give you access to Wi-Fi, network- and Bluetooth-related settings.

Wi-Fi and wired network connections

Click on **Wi-Fi** from the left panel. The right pane gives you the option to connect or disconnect Wi-Fi, Bluetooth and mobile broadband by turning on/off the airplane mode. All the visible Wi-Fi networks will also be listed on the right pane. It will also detect the networks to which you are currently connected. Choose one of the listed WiFi networks and configure settings by clicking on the **Settings** button given in front of the Wi-Fi name. Choose **Network** from the left panel of **Settings** option, which allows to set up the wired network, VPN and network proxy. The **Network** window will look as shown in *Figure 12.7*:

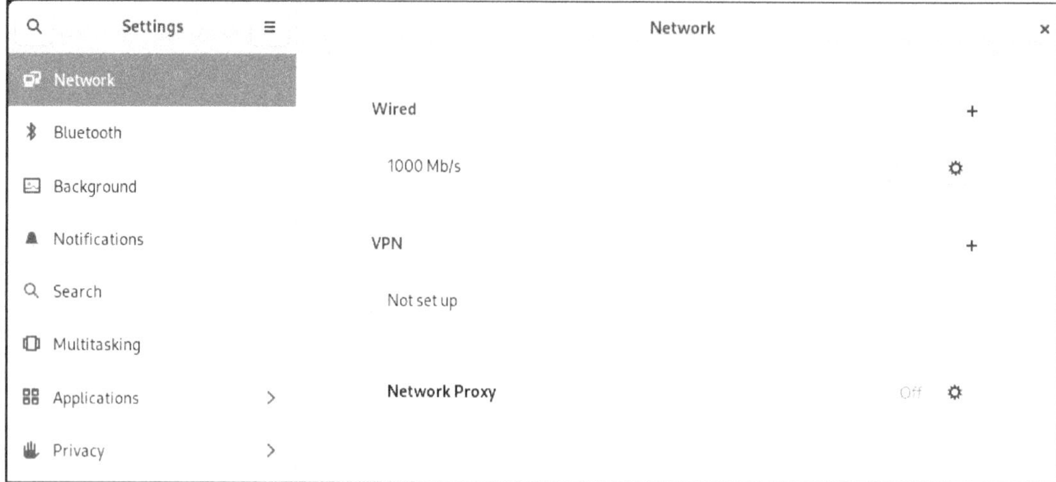

***Figure 12.7**: Network setting page showing network-related settings*

To add a new connection, click the + button given in the **Wired** panel. Similarly, to add a VPN connection, click the + button given in the **VPN** panel. To edit the properties of an existing connection, click the **gear wheel** icon given for the existing connection name. Whatever we have done in the earlier chapters using **`nmcli`** can be done via this window. Any setting that we configured here is visible to the **NetworkManager**.

Using nm-connection-editor

This can be used to configure any existing connections with additional features that are not provided by the control center. Just type **`nm-connection-editor`** in the terminal, and the **Network Connections** window will open. This will give you the option to add a new connection, or edit or delete an existing connection. At the bottom panel of this window, clicking on + will add, **-** will remove and the **gear wheel** button will change the settings.

Changing the hostname

To change the hostname using GNOME GUI, you can use one of the following ways:

- Open **Settings**, click on **Sharing** and type the computer name in the given text box in the right panel.
- Choose **About** from the left panel of the **Settings** menu, and enter the hostname in the **Device Name** text box given at the right panel.

Bluetooth

To turn on Bluetooth, click on the **Bluetooth** option in the left panel, and on the right, you will find the **Bluetooth enable** button at the top bar. Just click on the button to enable Bluetooth and search for nearby devices to share files across the Bluetooth enabled devices.

Desktop background and general settings

The next set of options under **Settings** allows to change the desktop background and themes, notification, and various other settings. The **Background** setting gives you the various desktop backgrounds to choose from. The **Notifications** settings enables you to choose the applications that can display send notifications on the lock screen. Use the **Enable toggle** button to enable **Lock Screen Notifications**. The next setting is related to **Search**, which we have already used. The **Multitasking** button gives you control over various other settings. You can choose to configure a number of workspaces here. By default, **Dynamic workspaces** is enabled.

Application-related settings

Settings | Application allows you to view and modify the settings related to each of the available applications. Choosing **Applications** in the left pane opens a list of all the installed applications in the same pane. Select one of the applications from the left pane to view the related settings in the right pane. From the right pane, you can control whether to display the notification from the application. From here, you can also control whether the **Search** feature will list out the matches from this application. Click the **Enable toggle** button if you want this application to be included in the search result, else do vice-versa. At the top of the right pane, there is a button named **Open in Software**, clicking on which opens the **Software** application with the overview window of the selected application in front.

Privacy

The next option gives you access to privacy-related features. Clicking on **Settings | Privacy** opens a set of other related settings in the left pane.

Application permissions

You can determine which applications are allowed to access location services, microphone, camera, and more by choosing **Location Services**, **Microphone** and **Camera** from the left pane of the **Privacy** window. By default, no application is given access to these system resources until asked for. The applications that have been allowed to access these resources will be listed here.

File history and trash

Under the privacy settings itself, you can manage the history of the files that you have used. Maintaining file history makes it easier for you to search for the files that you might want to use. You can modify file history duration from here. By default, file history duration is set to **Forever**. You can modify it by selecting another value from the corresponding drop-down list. You can also clear the history by clicking on the **Clear History** button.

Another important setting in this window is **Deleting of** trash and temporary files. By default, temporary files created under `/tmp` are never deleted unless the system is rebooted. It will delete only the system's temporary files. If your system is up since many days, these temporary files may be consuming too much of space, causing disk space usage problem. Trash may also be consuming too much of disk space. You can set to automatically delete temporary files and trash contents at a specified period. Click on the **Empty Trash** button to empty the trash. Clicking the **Delete Temporary Files** button purges the temporary files.

Screen lock

Another important setting under **Privacy** is related to **Screen Lock**. From a security perspective, you should not leave your laptop/computer unattended. If you are leaving it for a while, then your screen must be turned off. To lock your screen, click on **System Menu** from the top-right panel on your GNOME desktop and then select **Lock**. You can also arrange to automatically lock your screen if it remains idle for a specified period of time, say 1 minute. To specify the idle time after which your screen should lock, choose **Screen Lock** under **Privacy**, enable **Automatic Screen Lock** if it is not enabled, and choose the period for **Automatic Screen Lock Delay** from the drop-down list, as shown in *Figure 12.8*:

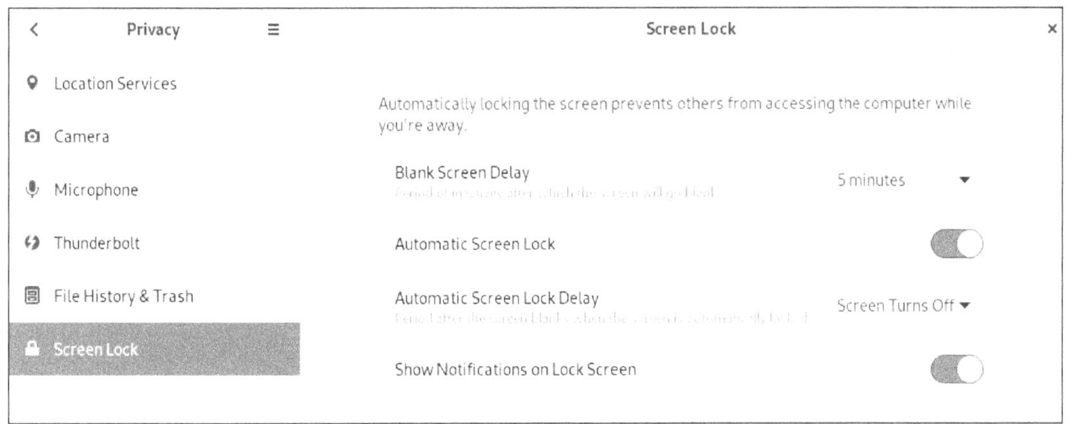

***Figure 12.8**: Privacy setting: displaying setting related to Screen Lock*

Managing users using GNOME GUI

You can create, manage, and delete user accounts using GNOME GUI. We have already visited related commands in the earlier chapters. To manage user accounts using GUI, open **Settings** and choose **Users** from the left panel. On the right panel, **Users** window will pop up. It displays the list all the available user accounts. It will ask you for the password if any setting requires administrator-level privilege. For example, if you want to add a new user, you have to click the **Unlock** button displayed at the top. You can change the username by clicking on the **pen** icon given after the current username. You can change the profile photo by clicking on the **picture** icon and browsing the image file. This screen also allows you to change your password. To add a new user, click on **Add User** at the top panel of the **Users** window. This button will only be visible if you have unlocked this option by entering the administrator's password. This window will also let you provide administrative privilege to a standard user. You can do this by enabling the **Administrator** button under the **Account Settings** section on the **Users** panel. You can also remove a user by clicking on the **Remove User** button. On enabling the **Automatic Login** button, the selected user account will be logged in automatically when the computer is started.

Changing date and time in GNOME

To change date and time, go to **Settings** | **Date & Time**, and the **Date & Time** setting window will be in front of you. You must unlock this setting to modify the date and time. Press **Unlock** and type super user password. Date and time will be updated automatically with an internet connection if you have the **Automatic Date & Time** option enabled. Alternatively, you can set date and time manually. You can also select **Time Zone** to be updated automatically using the internet connection or set it manually. Additionally, you have the option to select whether the time is displayed in the 24-hour format.

Browsing remote files

We have used the **Files** application in earlier sections to browse files and directories stored in your local computer. In the same application, look at the bottom of the left panel. You will find an entry named **+Other Locations**, which is used to browse files over the network.

At the bottom of this window, you will see a text box, **Connect to Server**, where you can provide the address of the server that you want to access. Click on the **?** icon given next to the text box. It will show you the format of the URL and the available protocols, using which you can establish a connection to the server. For example, to do `ssh` or `sftp` on remote server, say **vmachine.example.com** for file transfer, use the following URL:

```
ssh://vmachine.example.com/home/vishehskumar
```

Click on the **Connect** button. The preceding command will establish the connection to the given server and file browser path set to `/home/visheshkumar`, and all the folders and files under this directory will be visible under browser window of **Files** application.

An icon related to the connected server is visible in the left panel. There, you will notice a **Mount/Unmount** button in front of the server connection name. You can easily disconnect from the server by pressing the **Unmount** button. Your connection will be listed under the **Networks** section under **+Other Locations** option of **Files** application.

Customizing the locals

You can determine how date and time format, currency and languages are displayed. You can customize their display according to your locale or other region. Go to **Settings** | **Region** and the **Language and Settings** page will open with the **Region and Language** panel in the right. Using the **Language and Formats** section, you can customize the locals.

Keyboard and mouse

You can change your keyboard layout and the behavior of your mouse using **Keyboard and Mouse** and **Touchpad** settings, respectively, under the **Settings** window.

Default applications

Default Applications on the **Settings** page will show you the default application that will be used to open some file types. Default applications of the following file types are listed:

- **Web**: Default application to open the web page is Firefox.
- **Mail**: No application is set here to view mails, as no mail client is installed yet on this machine.
- **Calendar**: Text editor can be used to view Calender.
- **Music and Videos**: **Videos** application can be used to play audio and video files.
- **Photos**: To view photos, **Image Viewer** can be used.

You can change the default applications to view these file types by clicking on the related drop down button, as shown in *Figure 12.9*, and choosing your favorite application.

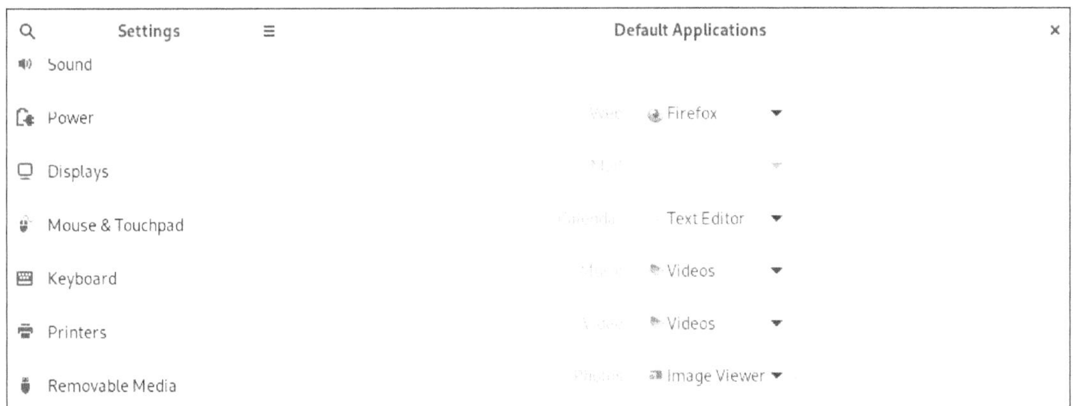

***Figure 12.9**: Default Applications settings page*

You can also change the default application of any file type from the **File** application. Right-click on any file for which you want to modify the default application. From the context menu that pops up, click on **Properties**. Go to **Open With** tab and choose the desired application name from the **Other applications** section. Click on the **Set as default** button. From then on, your file will run using that application.

Managing software in GNOME

We will learn about installing and managing software via commands in *Chapter 14, Package Installation*. In this section, we will learn to view the list of installed software and add or remove the software using GNOME.

Listing installed software

Open the **Software** application by typing `Software` in the **Activities Overview** page. Choose **Software** from the search result and the **Software** application will pop up. After the **GNOME Software** application opens up, you will see three tabs: **Explore**, **Installed**, **Updates**. Under the **Explore** tab, you will find application divided into various categories. To find an application, you must either choose the category or use search button given in top-left corner and type the name of the application. Suppose you choose **Create**; then, all the installed as well as uninstalled applications under this category are listed.

Adding or removing software

If you have not registered your system to Red Hat subscription service during installation, you will be prompted to register the system every time you log in. Click on **Register System** in the prompt window. You can also subscribe by going to **Settings** | **About** | **Subscription**. **Subscription** allows you to install additional software or update the exiting software.

To install an application, choose the category and find the desired application. If your application is listed, click on it to open the **Overview** page of the selected application. Then, click on the **Install** button.

To uninstall any application, go to the desired application, and the overview window of the selected application will opens up. Click on the **Trash** icon given in this window. It will confirm whether you want to uninstall the application. Click on the **Uninstall** button if you want to do that. If an application is not installed, then it will show you the **Install** button that you need to click to install it.

If any software that you want to install is not listed here, it can be downloaded from the concerned repository and can then be installed. Any software for RHEL is distributed in the form of packages, known as **rpm packages**. Package installation via commands is the subject of *Chapter 14, Package Installation*. If you have any downloaded rpm package, open the folder that contains the rpm file in **Files** application, and you can install it by simply double-clicking on it.

You can also install any rpm package by typing its name in **Activities Overview**. Click on the desired result and the software will open in the **Software** application. Click on the **Install** button to install it.

Log viewer

To view the system logs, RHEL9 provides a built-in graphical tool, **Logs**, which is used to view and monitor system log files. It provides a user-friendly display of the system logs. This log viewer shows events from the systemd journal and divides the events into categories such as hardware and applications. You can view detailed information about each event by clicking on it. *Figure 12.10* shows you a sample of system logs with **Important** logs in display. From

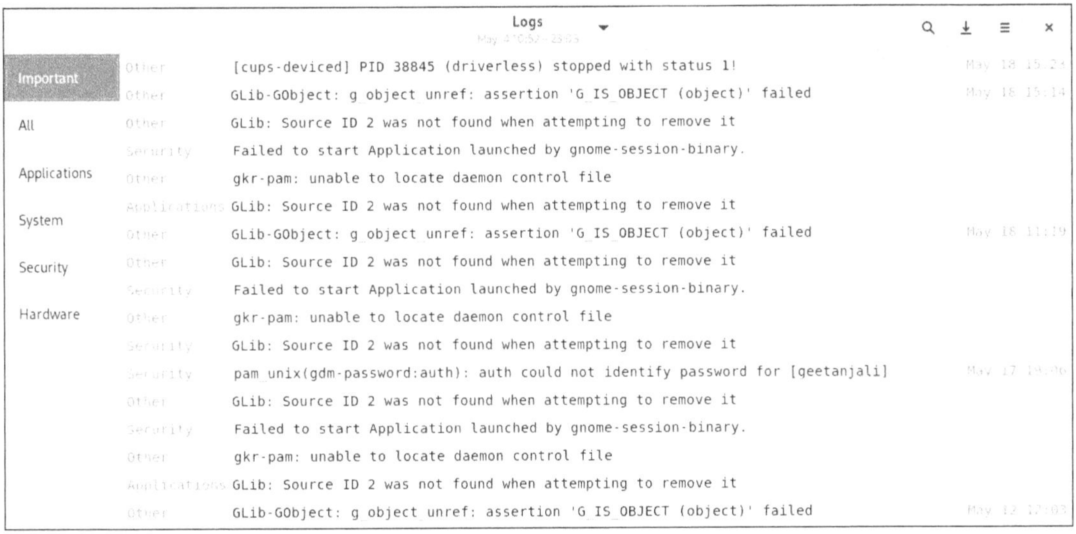

***Figure 12.10**: GNOME Log viewer displaying system logs from systemd journal*

the left panel, you can also choose to view either **All** the logs or only the logs related to **Applications** or **System** level logs or security-related logs or hardware-related logs. You can click the **search** button given on the title panel to search for logs matching the search term. You can type your search term in the search box. The dropdown given next to the search bar can be used to filter the specific journal filed and select the timestamp range for which to view logs. You can also save displayed logs to a file on disk by clicking the **Download** button next to **Search** button.

You can also open logs application by typing **`gnome-logs`** in the command terminal.

Managing disk in GNOME

The **Disks** application is used to manage and configure various disk and media graphically. It can be used to format a disk; create, delete and manage partitions; and even to create filesystems on them. GNOME also provides you with the **Disk Usage Analyzer** tool to analyze disk usage.

System monitor

System monitor application is used to view current processes and monitor system state. Gnome-system-monitor is the terminal command to start the **System Monitor** application. We will learn to use this tool in *Chapter 15, Performance Monitoring and Tuning*.

GNOME Virtual File System

GNOME Virtual File System (**GVFS**) is a technology used in the GNOME desktop environment for providing a virtual file system layer that allows access to various remote file systems and resources in a consistent and uniform manner. By using GVFS, applications can access files and directories from different locations without needing to be aware of the specific file system or protocol being used. It allows users to access files and directories seamlessly, regardless of their actual location, regardless of whether they are stored locally or on remote servers. GVFS allows users to mount remote file systems, such as FTP, SFTP, WebDAV, and SMB, so that they can be accessed and manipulated as if they were local file systems. This enables users to browse, open, save, and manage files on remote servers using their favorite GNOME applications. GVFS integrates tightly with the GNOME desktop environment and its applications. It integrates with other GNOME components and applications, such as the Nautilus file manager, to provide a consistent and user-friendly file browsing experience. You can mount a particular resource in virtual file system by using **Files** | **Other Locations** | **Connect to server**. In the earlier section, we have seen how a resource using the SFTP protocol is mounted. GVFS was in action here.

Conclusion

GNOME is a popular desktop environment that is used in many Linux distributions, including RHEL. It provides a modern and user-friendly interface that is designed to be easy to use and highly customizable. GNOME desktop environment includes GNOME Shell using the Wayland protocol. Using the GNOME control-center, we can modify various GNOME settings. GNOME Extensions allow users to modify various aspects of the GNOME Shell and add new features to it. Using GNOME Extensions' official website, users can search for extensions, read their descriptions, and install them with a single click. Most clickable feature of GNOME desktop environment is virtual workspaces. You can open and work with many workspaces at a time. Clicking on the **Activities** button display the overview of your current activities. **Activities Overview** also includes a robust search bar that is capable of finding almost anything from the system. Any GNOME application can be opened by clicking on the **Show Applications** button under **Activities Overview** or directly by typing the application's name in the search bar. The search bar is all-rounder as it can be used to find and open any file, setting, or application. To install a software and manage it graphically, choose to open the **Software** application. It lists out software divided into multiple categories. Clicking on each category will show you the list of the available software under that category. System log viewer is a graphical user interface to monitor system logs. If you want to share your desktop with another person sitting on another computer, you must enable screen sharing on your desktop. Screen sharing will allow other users to view and control your desktop.

In the next chapter, we will learn to manage the RHEL Network and discuss the system patching process.

Chapter 13
Software Updates and Patch Management

Introduction

An important task of the IT team is to keep all the machines updated. Updating the system ensures the security of the system. Today, with the increasing use of internet, the threat of viruses and cyberattacks has also increased. This may lead to vulnerabilities on some machines of the organizations. Vendors provide patches as regular support to their customers. Updating your system using these patches is important to keep it safe against any potential security-related attacks. If regular updates are not in place, entire organizations' infrastructure is at risk. If you are managing several machines, updating all these machines regularly is a cumbersome task without proper patch management in place. In this regard, you can opt for RedHat's subscription management service if you want to have planned software updates and patch management for your organization. You must take subscription for the products that you are using to download and apply the related patches on your machines. Subscription also provides technical support from your vendor that can be helpful if you want to patch your machine without unexpected errors or downtimes.

In this chapter, we will see how the software on RHEL systems are updated with the latest patches using RedHat Subscription Management Service.

Structure

- Understand patching
  - Patching process in RHEL9
  - Patch management in RHEL9
- Tools for subscription management
  - Managing subscription in RHEL9
  - Adding system to RHSM

Objectives

By the end of this chapter, you should understand the need for patching. You should also be able to manage subscriptions using RHSM. Additionally, you should know how to register RHEL machines to RHSM and apply for a subscription. This will assist you in searching for the latest available patches to be applied to registered machines.

Understanding patching

Patch is a small software code that is written to override an identified bug or security flaw in the software. A bug can be minor or major. Patches may be of several types: There are patches that fix a bug found in the software or patches that add a new feature in the software that can enhance its functionality or improve its performance. There are security patches that are used to fix security-related vulnerabilities/bugs found. **Patching** means updating the system with the latest security patches and software updates.

New software are never perfect. It has bugs and vulnerabilities that come into the picture during its course of usage with changing industry standards and requirements. A patch provides fixes to remove these vulnerabilities from the software. These vulnerabilities/bugs may hamper the proper functioning of the software, and the software may not deliver its functionality if bugs are not handled on time. If the vulnerability is security-related and if a software is not patched in a timely manner, its known vulnerabilities may be exploited by intruders to gain unauthorized access to the system. Thus, patching is one of the prioritized tasks for the IT department.

Patching is required due to the following reasons:

- Patches are required to keep the system protected against the detected viruses. Viruses, once attached to a machine inside an organization, may affect all the machines of the organization. They can create some vulnerabilities on the machines, making the whole system unusable. Other types of cyberattacks, such as **Denial of Service (DOS)** attacks, phishing attacks, and social engineering attacks, might also impact the organization if security-related measures are not implemented properly on all the machines. To prevent viruses or other cyberattacks from damaging the complete system, all the machines of the organizations must be updated regularly with the latest security-related software updates.

- Bugs are inherent in software. Loopholes can be found while using a software, due to which it may not deliver its functionalities, which can lead to disinterest in software among its users. So, the fixes are developed to rectify any bugs.
- Updating the software with the latest patches is also important for software compliance, which are the standard benchmarks that must be met by organizations.
- Patching is also required to update the software with new features that enhance its functionality.

To keep your system up to date with the latest bug releases, you must take vendor subscription for the product that you are using. Subscription allows you to download the latest patches from the vendor's site so that they can be applied to your machine. Usually, patching involves the following steps:

1. Identifying the non-compliant, non-patched, and out-of-date systems is the first step. You must scan your systems daily for the identification of all the machines that need patching. Scanning on a daily basis is important because if any machine is left unidentified, it may become vulnerable to inside or outside threats.
2. Downloading patches from vendor sites is the next step. Vendors publish bug fixes, patches, or security updates regularly. Some vendors release patches at regular intervals, while some have no timeline. Check for the latest updates from the vendor's site and download the patches matching your machine's architecture and platform.
3. Applying patches to all the machines that are identified in Step 1 is the final step.

Performing all of the mentioned phases may be messy for the IT team if they work with many servers, and they must ensure that all the servers get patched with the latest updates. Besides, they have many security patches and bug fixes to apply to those many servers. To ensure proper patching without any faults, they must keep track of all the inventory that they have, including which systems have already been patched and which ones need patching. Any system, if left unpatched, can create compliance issues and security vulnerabilities. Thus, there arises a need for a properly defined **patch management system** that keeps track of the following:

- The inventory that the organization has
- Which systems have applied patches
- Where the patches have failed, and thus, the machines are non-compliant
- Ongoing patching process

Maintaining a record of all the inventory and patching is also important for auditing and compliance purposes. IT administrator is responsible for providing accurate inventory information to the patch management system so that patches be applied to all the machines properly. To avoid any faults, the following things should be considered before applying patches:

- The entire **organization's assets must be scanned** on a daily basis to identify the potential machines requiring patching.
- **There are many patches available at a time. You must prioritize them according to their** significance, the risk involved, and time.
- You must test the patches in the test environment that matches the production environment. Any configuration mismatch in test environment in terms of hardware, software, library versions or workloads may result in strange behavior after patches are applied in production. So, test environment should be designed properly.
- **You must have a proper patch rollback plan in place before applying patches in production. Patching in a test machine may succeed, but it may fail when deployed in a production environment.** It may fail due to a resource constraint such as lower disk space, less memory, and more production machines. You might have bad user permissions. Sometimes, applying patches may cause issues that can have cascading effects on other running applications, and due to business reasons, you may have to roll back applied patches.
- **Logs** are an important place to look at if patching fails in the first place. So, logging should be turned on before starting the patching process. Logging may help you find out the differences between the test and production environments, and verify the list of packages installed on both the machines and the version of the packages installed. Any mismatch in the libraries installed and their versions may be the culprit for the failure of the patching process.
- One of the classifications of patches is **security patches**. Deployment of security patches sometimes comes with high priority and needs to be installed on machines on an urgent basis. Security patches' urgency is determined by the vulnerabilities addressed by that patch. If vulnerability is high in nature, then security patches need to be applied without much delay.

On RHEL9, patches are done using **`dnf`** or **`yum`**. **`dnf`** is the default package manager in RHEL9, while **`yum`** is the traditional utility supported on earlier RHEL versions. **`yum`** is still there as a symbolic link to the newer *dnf* utility. We will discuss the usages of the **`dnf`** utility in greater detail in the next chapter. In the upcoming section, we will discuss how patch management is performed using RedHat Support.

Patching process in RHEL9

In **Red Hat Enterprise Linux 9 (RHEL 9)**, patching is performed using the `dnf` package manager and the **Red Hat Subscription Manager**. Become a root user and perform the following steps for patching your system:

1. **Register the system**: Earlier, we mentioned that patches are downloaded from the vendor's site. Before downloading patches for your RedHat machine, you must have a valid account on the RedHat Customer Portal, and your machine must be registered to it. You must also purchase a subscription for the products installed on your machine so that you can get access to related patches and bug fixes. RedHat customer portal, along with RedHat Subscription Manager, assists you in the patching process. In the next section, we will see how registration and subscription management is performed using RedHat Subscription Manager.
2. **Enable repositories**: Use the `dnf config-manager` command to enable the necessary repositories for software updates and security patches. Consider this example:

   ```
   # dnf config-manager --enable rhel-9-server-rpms
   ```
3. **Scan your network:** Identify computers that have the missing patches and test the patches in a group of test computers.
4. **Update the system**: After you have identified your machines, you can update the system using the `dnf update` command:

   ```
   # dnf update
   ```
5. **Reboot**: After the updates are installed, it is recommended to reboot the system to ensure that all the changes take effect:

   ```
   # reboot
   ```

Always consult the official documentation or contact Red Hat support for the most accurate and up-to-date information on patching and updating RHEL 9 machines.

Re-mentioning that applying patches and updates should be done with caution, and it's advisable to have backups and a testing environment in place before applying updates to production systems. You must also make sure that you have the necessary permissions and administrative access to perform these actions.

Patch management in RHEL9

Red Hat does not have a fixed timeline for releasing patches as many other vendors have. Patches are released whenever they become available. **RedHat Subscription Management (RHSM)** notifies you when any updates are released.

RedHat uses RHSM to maintain network repository, which allows licensed RHEL 9 machines to download software and security patches. If you have taken a license/subscription for a RedHat product, then you will receive downloadable content and updates, access to the vast knowledge base, technical support for your product, and notifications for the latest bug fixes. To achieve all this for your installed product, you must register your machines to the Redhat Subscription Management service so that RHSM knows about your machine. Registering the machine also lets RHSM know about the software/products installed on it as well as knowledge of the machine's architecture. This information is important for RHSM to suggest available bug fixes related to that product.

Red Hat Subscription Management also keeps track of the following things:

- All the hardware that the organization has
- The software that is installed
- The Red Hat product that your organization has purchased or subscribed to
- The systems on which subscribed products are installed
- What subscriptions are available to your organization
- The status of your subscription
- How many copies are active
- When do the subscriptions expire

RHSM also helps in tracking updates and new releases of software. Whenever an update or bug fix is available, a notification email is sent to you if you have subscription for the associated product. The whole process of subscription management is as follows:

- A valid user account on Customer Portal buys a subscription to a product, which gives them access to the patches, upgrades, and support.
- A subscription is valid only for some amount of time and can be applied for a fixed number of times.
- A server is registered to the inventory of the subscription management. Once the system is added, the subscription management service receives all the necessary information about the machine, such as the OS installed, the machine's architecture, and the installed products and their versions.
- A matching subscription is then attached to the registered system so that the system becomes eligible to receive the vendor's support services and download the bug fixes and patches for the products installed. An available subscription is attached to the machine that matches the system's installed products and architecture.

- The subscription is renewed after the said validity period. Then, renewed subscriptions must be attached again to the system. If the new products are installed on a machine, and a subscription for that product is purchased, then that subscription is also attached to the system.

Thus, RedHat provides support to its customers by issuing subscriptions for its products. After a customer purchases a subscription for a product, two important steps are followed to use the RedHat Subscription Management service and receive support and updates for bug fixes of the subscribed product:

1. Registering the machine to RHSM
2. Attaching subscription to registered machine

After the machine is registered and a related subscription is attached to the machine, your organization is ready to use the services provided by RHSM. Different tools can be used to register the machine and attach the subscription to it. The next section discusses the tools to use for viewing and managing subscriptions.

Tools for subscription management

Red Hat Subscription Management provides the following tools for subscription management:

- **Red Hat Subscription Manager** client tool that runs locally to display system and subscription information
- **Red Hat Subscription Management integrated with the Customer Portal** that provides a web-based interface for viewing and managing available subscriptions
- **Red Hat Satellite** as an on-premise solution for systems that may not regularly check in

All the mentioned tools always run as root.

Managing subscription using portal

IT administrators need to track what subscriptions are available, how they are attached to systems, how many quantities of subscriptions are left, and how many of them are consumed. All this information can easily be tracked by using the Customer Portal. To view and manage subscriptions, log in to the **Red Hat Customer Portal** and navigate to the **My Subscriptions** link. Opening the **My Subscriptions** link will open the **Red Hat Subscription Management** page. The **Overview** tab gives you a high-level summary of your subscriptions, as shown in *Figure 13.1*. Currently, there are no **Active Subscriptions** and 0 machines registered.

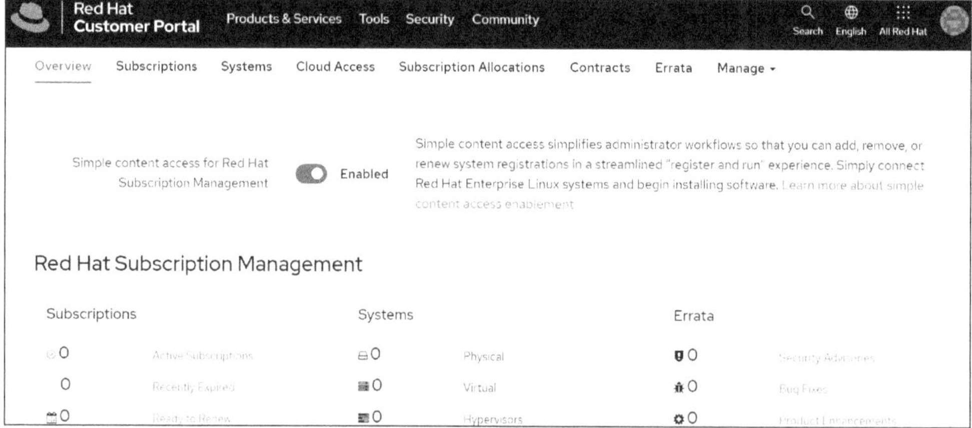

Figure 13.1: Overview of subscription for logged in user account

with the logged in account. You have access to other tabs such as **Subscriptions** to view and manage your subscriptions, **Systems** to view registered machines, and attaching and detaching subscription to them, and more. Other tabs may give you information about your subscriptions, their statuses, and so on.

You can opt to receive email notifications of security updates, bug fixes, and enhancements. This is known as **Errata**. To turn on **Errata** notifications, click on the *profile* icon given in the top-left corner of the **Customer portal** page. Click on **Account Details**. This will open a page showing account information. This page is divided into two panes. Select **Errata notifications** from the left pane. Select **Enable notifications** for the selected errata types radio button listed under the **Notification control** section, as shown in *Figure 13.2*. Choose what notifications you want to receive. You have the option to be notified of security updates, bug fixes, and enhancements. You can also select the event that triggers notifications under **Notify me when** section. You can also choose to set N**otification frequency** either to **Immediate**, **Daily Summary** or **Weekly Summary**. Click on **Save** to save your changes.

Figure 13.2: Turning on Errata using RedHat Customer Portal

Adding system to RHSM

Once you buy a subscription for a product that you are using, the system is registered to subscription management system. Then subscription is attached to the registered system. Once a subscription is attached to a system, that system is allowed to download and install updates, and receive support for that software product. By default, registration and attaching subscription to the machine are performed at the same time when using subscription management. When you register your machine to the RHSM, the subscription that matches the best with the system's architecture and currently installed products is applied to it automatically. **RedHat Subscription Manager** client tools perform both task registration as well as subscription management. This tool is available in both GUI as well as CLI. This is a local subscription manager client that connects the system to the RHSM service. **Subscription Manager** performs the following:

- It registers your systems to the **Red Hat Subscription Management** service and adds the system to its inventory.
- It applies the best-matched available subscription to the registered machine. Once a system is registered and subscribed, it can receive updates based on its subscriptions.
- It lists all the available subscriptions.
- It lists subscriptions that are consumed.
- It allows administrators to attach or detach specific subscriptions to a system.

Subscription to RHSM using GUI

Here, we will use GNOME to register our machine to the vendor's portal. Follow these steps for the registration and subscription of a machine:

1. Open **Activities Overview** and type `register`. The search result lists **About** option of **Settings.** Select it, and the **About** window from **Settings** pops up on your screen.
2. Click on **Subscription** and **Register System** dialog box opens up. Choose **Red Hat** as your **Registration Server**. You can also choose to enter a custom address if you are not using Red Hat Server.
3. Next, you need to choose **Registration Type**. You can choose to register either by using **Activation Keys** or **Red Hat Account**.
4. Choose **Red Hat** account and enter information asked under the **Registration Details** section.
5. Activation keys allow you to register your machine without specifying your RHSM **Login** and **Password**. If you have an activation key and want to register

using **Activation Keys**, then choose Activation Keys in step 3 and enter your activation keys under the **Registration Details** section.

6. Click on the **Register** button.
7. If everything works fine, your machine will be registered to RHSM and all the matched subscriptions will automatically be attached to your machine depending on the OS and products installed.

Subscription to RHSM using CLI

`subscription-manager` is a command-line utility used to register the system to subscription management service and then attach and manage subscriptions for software products.

It supports several commands and a set of options to interact with RHSM.

The **`subscription-manager register`** command registers a new system to the subscription management service as follows:

```
subscription-manager register --username=admin --password=secret
```

The preceding command registers the machine to RHSM and applies the matched subscription, if available, automatically. When the **`--activationkey`** option is used, it is not necessary to use the **`--username`** and **`--password`** options.

The **`subscription-manager remove`** command removes specified subscriptions from the system.

The **`subscription-manager list`** command lists all the subscriptions for the system. Options to use with **`list`** are as follows:

- **`--installed`**: Shows current subscriptions and products installed on the system. By default, the **`list`** command is the same as using the **`--installed`** option.
- **`--available`**: Lists available subscriptions that are not yet attached to the system.
- **`--all`**: Lists all possible subscriptions that have been purchased, even if they do not match the architecture of the system. This is used with the **`--available`** option.

Subscription using the RHSM client tool

On **Activities Overview**, type **`subscription`**, and you will get icon for the client tool. Click on it to open. On the **Subscriptions** window that opens, click on the **Register** button, and the **Register System** dialog box will open up. Select the registration method to **Account** under the **Method** section. Give your user name and password that exists on RedHat Customer Portal. Leaving other settings to default, click on the **Register** button.

Your machine will now be registered to RHSM service, and an available subscription will be automatically applied to your machine. After you have successfully registered, you will get the window shown in *Figure 13.3*. The figure shows the disabled subscription status on this machine, as no subscription is available yet.

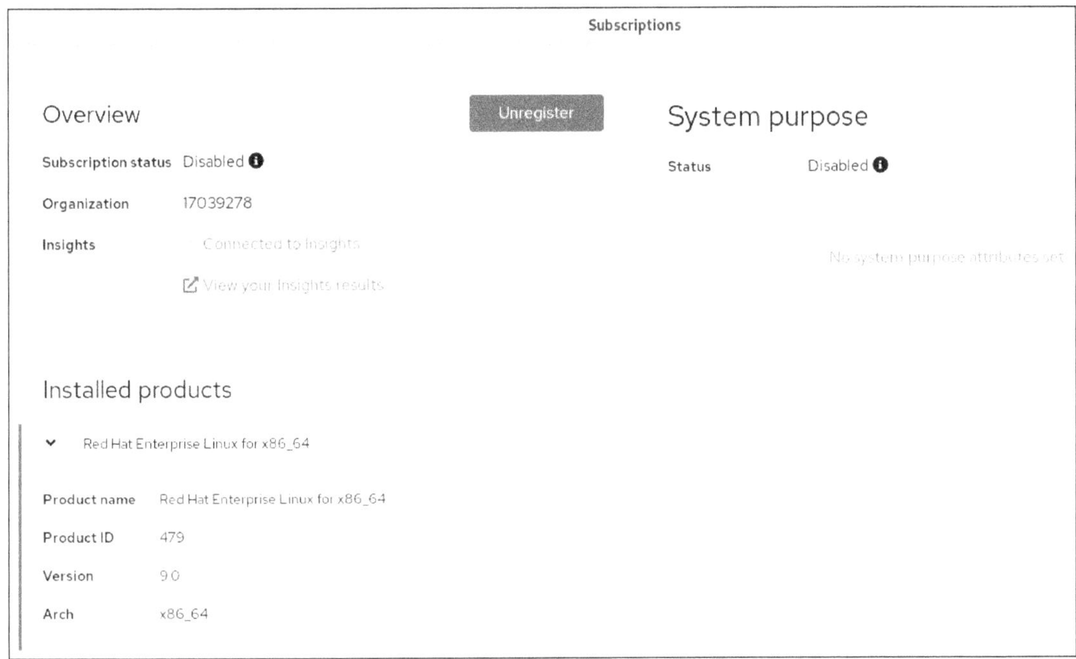

***Figure 13.3**: RHSM client tool showing that machine is registered and no subscription is yet applied to it*

After you have successfully registered and subscribed to your machine, you can receive notification for the latest patch releases for related products on this machine.

The **Subscription Manager** client tools use the **`/etc/rhsm/rhsm.conf`** file for configuration.

You can unregister your system by choosing **Settings | About | Subscription**. On the **Registration Details** screen, the **Unregister** button will be shown if the system is registered. Click the **Unregister** button.

Conclusion

Patching is a process of applying a short code, called a patch, to the software so that it either fixes it or adds a new feature to it. No software is perfectly developed. After software is released, many bugs are identified, which may create disinterest in the software among people if not fixed. They may resist using the software. So, the timely application of patches is important. Patching must be replicated on all the machines of the organization. Many security flaws can be identified while using the software. If these security flaws are not acted upon, attackers can exploit the software vulnerability to gain unauthorized access to the system. So, security patches are also developed, which fix the identified security-related vulnerabilities in the software. Thus, patch management is one of the important tasks of an IT Administrator. Red Hat provides support to its products via a subscription-based license. You must buy a subscription for the installed product to receive updates for the product and download the latest patches from the vendor's site. RedHat product subscription provides you with all the kind of support required to run your RHEL server perfectly all the time. It provides you with technical support and guidance, bug fixes and patches, software updates, etc. To get updates and notifications about new patches for the related product, you must register your RHEL machine to the RedHat Customer Portal using the RedHat Subscription Manager client tools. After your system is registered, you must attach a valid subscription to your machine. The subscription manager handles the registration of a system to the RedHat Subscription Management service and applies the subscription to the machine for the installed products. It is the responsibility of the organization to maintain and provide accurate information about their software assets to the RHSM to ensure that all the systems up to date. This will also make systems comply with regulatory standards such as PCI-DSS.

In the next chapter, we will see how the packages are installed and updated using the **`dnf`** utility, the default package manager in RHEL9.

Join our book's Discord space

Join the book's Discord Workspace for Latest updates, Offers, Tech happenings around the world, New Release and Sessions with the Authors:

https://discord.bpbonline.com

CHAPTER 14
Package Installation

Introduction

Installing a software update when required is another important task for a system administrator. The administrator must be aware of the package management tools that can find and install dependencies for the package before installing them to save time. Earlier, we talked about Gnome's software application that can be used to install and manage software easily. This chapter discusses the command-line package management utility, known as **`dnf`**, which is the default package manager in RHEL9. The earlier versions of RHEL used yum to manage packages. Since RHEL8, **`dnf`** has replaced yum as the default package management tool. In Linux, software is installed using RPM packages. An RPM package is a collection of many related files and associated metadata. A RPM package has a **`.rpm`** extension. In this chapter, we will learn to install RPM packages using the **`dnf`** utility on the RHEL machine.

Structure

This chapter has the following structure:

- Package management in RHEL9
  - DNF configuration
  - Viewing configuration

  - Adding a new repository
  - Creating a repository
  - Handling repository
  - Getting information about repository and packages
  - Installing software
  - Updating software
  - Listing packages
  - Removing a package
- Package groups
- Using transaction history

Objectives

By the end of this chapter, you should be able to explain RPM packages. You will learn to use the subscription manager to install, update, or remove packages. This chapter will also equip you with the knowledge of how to use the `dnf` command-line utility for package management. You should also understand how to work with package repositories, create new repositories, enable or disable repositories as well as handle package groups.

Package management in RHEL9

All software or applications on a RHEL system are made available via RPM packages. The **RPM Package Manager (RPM)** is a package management system that runs on RHEL, CentOS, and Fedora. When software is developed for RHEL-based systems, all its libraries, dependencies, and other necessary files are bundled together in what is known as RPM. RPM provides a standardized format for packaging software, including executable files, libraries, documentation, and other related files. Each software package is represented by an RPM file with a `.rpm` extension. Thus, an RPM file includes all the necessary information about the package, such as its name, version, dependent packages, libraries, and installation instructions. RPM is used to distribute the software that you have created for CentOS, RHEL, or Fedora. An **RPM package** can be easily installed, upgraded, or removed. For other OSs, different format of software packaging is used. For example, Ubuntu uses Debian packages.

Many packages are installed during RHEL installation. We have done basic installation in the first chapter of the book. Besides, your Linux distributor provides many other built-in packages via its **Red Hat Subscription Manager** (**RHSM**), which we have already learned in the previous chapter. Packages are delivered to you in repositories. A **repository** is a collection of packages and refers to a centralized location from where users can download the packages and install it. Each of the Linux distributors may provide you with official repositories. RHEL9 software / contents are made available using two main repositories:

- **BaseOS**
- **AppStream**

Some of the RHEL9 content is also shipped via another repository: **CodeReady Linux Builder**. There are also third-party repositories from where you can download and install packages that are not available with official repositories.

Using RPM gives you the following advantages:

- You can easily install, reinstall, remove, upgrade and verify packages with standard package management tools, such as yum or **`dnf`**.
- It stores information about installed packages in a database that can be queried anytime to get any kind of information about them.
- It allows the use of metadata that describes packages, installation instructions, and more.
- It allows you to package software source code, related files, and all the dependencies into source and binary packages. In this chapter, we will focus on binary packaging, known as RPM.
- You can easily add packages to **`dnf`**/ yum repositories.
- Package can be digitally signed using **GNU Privacy Guard (GPG)** signing keys.

RHEL provides two ways to manage software/packages: the **`dnf`** command utility and the **GNOME Software** application. We have learnt to use package installation and management using **GNOME Software** in earlier chapters. In this chapter, we will learn to manage packages using the **`dnf`** command-line utility.

Using dnf: the default package manager

`dnf` is the default package management tool in RHEL9. **`dnf`** can query package information from the database, fetch packages from repositories, install and uninstall them, and update a specific package or upgrade the complete system to the latest available version. It automatically performs dependency resolution when updating, installing, or removing packages and thus, never leaves the system in an unstable state.

If you have a subscription for the installed product, you can easily download, install, and update packages to their latest version using the **`dnf`** utility. If you have not subscribed to any product installed on your machine, you will not be able to access any of the official repositories maintained by your Linux distributor. In that case, you can build your local repository and install packages on your machine using that repository. In this section, we will learn how to handle repositories, and install and manage packages using **dnf**.

dnf supports many commands that perform package management tasks. You must be root to perform package management tasks. Important files that are used by package management tools in RHEL9.0 are listed in *Table 14.1*:

File purpose	File name	Description
Cache file	/var/cache/dnf	
Main configuration file	/etc/dnf/dnf.conf	Main configuration file to be used by dnf utility; all the global directives are specified in this file and apply to all the repositories.
Repository	/etc/yum.repos.d/	Repository-specific files having the .repo extension reside in this directory. Each repo file is applicable only to the repositories listed in this file. Any directives used in this file override the directives used in the main configuration file.

Table 14.1: *Files used by package management tools in RHEL9*

To troubleshoot any problems or errors related to the **dnf** utility, log files are a good place to see. The default log file that **dnf** writes on is **/var/log/dnf.log**.

To view the list of commands available with **dnf**, type the following:

```
dnf --help
```

To take the help of one of the **dnf** commands, type the following:

```
dnf <command name> --help
```

In the upcoming section, we will see many commands supported by **dnf** and learn their usage.

DNF configuration

The configuration information for the **dnf** utility is located at **/etc/dnf/dnf.conf**. This file contains a **[main]** section, which enables you to set directives that have a global effect. The **[main]** section is mandatory section, and there can be only one **[main]** section in this configuration file. This configuration file may also include one or more **[repository]** sections, which are used to set repository-specific options. **[repository]** signifies the repository ID, which must be unique across all available repositories.

But it is recommended that you set repository-specific options in separate files that have the **.repo** extension under the **/etc/yum.repos.d** directory. All the files under this directory are read by **dnf**. **/etc/yum.repos.d** contains many **.repo** files. Each **.repo** file may contain many **[repository]** sections.

You have a default **.repo** file named **redhat.repo** existing under the **/etc/yum.repos.d/** directory. This file is used by the RHSM to manage repositories in this file. This file is used if your system is registered and subscribed.

Before we begin with **dnf** utility usages, let us see the default configuration of **dnf** by issuing the following command:

```
dnf config-manager --dump
```

The preceding command displays the current global settings of **dnf**. Global settings are placed in the **/etc/dnf/dnf.conf** file under the **[main]** section. If you want to change any of the global settings of **dnf**, add the settings in this file. *Figure 14.1* displays some of the settings of **dnf** available globally:

```
Updating Subscription Management repositories.
===================================== main =====================================
[main]
allow_vendor_change = 1
assumeno = 0
assumeyes = 0
autocheck_running_kernel = 1
bandwidth = 0
best = 1
bugtracker_url = https://bugzilla.redhat.com/enter_bug.cgi?product=Fedora&component=dnf
cachedir = /var/cache/dnf
cacheonly = 0
check_config_file_age = 1
clean_requirements_on_remove = 1
color = auto
color_list_available_downgrade = magenta
color_list_available_install = bold,cyan
color_list_available_reinstall = bold,underline,green
color_list_available_upgrade = bold,blue
color_list_installed_extra = bold,red
color_list_installed_newer = bold,yellow
color_list_installed_older = yellow
color_list_installed_reinstall = cyan
color_search_match = bold,magenta
color_update_installed = red
color_update_local = green
color_update_remote = bold,green
config_file_path = /etc/dnf/dnf.conf
countme = 0
debug_solver = 0
debuglevel = 2
defaultyes = 0
```

***Figure 14.1:** Default configuration of dnf*

Listed here are the semantics of some of the **dnf**-related settings:

- **gpgcheck**: This option is used to specify whether **dnf** should perform a GPG signature check on packages. 1 will enable checking of the GPG signature on all packages in all repositories, while the value of 0 disables this checking. The default is 1.
- **installonlypkgs**: It lists install-only packages separated by a comma. Install-only packages are the packages that can only be installed but never updated.
- **installonly_limit**: It determines the number of install-only that can be installed at the same time. If you want to have different versions of the same package available on your machine at the same time, this option is useful. The default value is set to 3.
- **clean_requirements_on_remove**: The default is true. It removes dependencies that are no longer used when removing packages.
- **best**: The default is **True**. If set to **True**, **dnf** either uses a package with the highest available version or fails. On **False**, it will not fail if the latest version cannot be installed, but it continues with the lower version.
- **skip_if_unavailable**: The default is set to **False**. If set to **False**, **dnf** will stop running if one of the repositories becomes unavailable.
- **assumeno**: If enabled, **dnf** assumes "No" for user responses and will not prompt for user confirmation. The default is **False**.
- **assumeyes**: If enabled, **dnf** will assume "Yes" for user responses and won't prompt for user confirmation. The default is False.
- **config_file_path**: It specifies the path of main configuration file. The default is **/etc/dnf/dnf.conf**.
- **defaultyes**: If enabled, the default answer to user confirmation prompts will be "yes". The default is False.
- **logdir**: It specifies the directory where the log files will be stored. The default is **/var/log**.

Viewing repository

Repositories can be online/remote or local/offline. Online repositories are those that are made available to you by your vendor if you are subscribed. Though there are also third-party providers that provide freely available online repositories, local/offline repositories can be created on your local machine.

To see the repositories enabled on your system, use the **dnf repolist** command using a root user account.

```
[root@vmachine ~]# dnf repolist
Updating Subscription Management repositories.
No repositories available
```

If you do not have any subscription to your product, no repos will be made available for you, and you will get output similar to the preceding output.

If you are not connected to RHSM, you can use a third-party repository to install packages to your machine, but for learning purposes only. This book does not recommend using any third-party repository to manage RHEL contents in a production environment.

By default, the **dnf repolist** command displays only the enabled repository. To view only disabled repositories, use the following:

```
#dnf repolist --disabled
```

Other options that can be used with this command are as follows:

- **--all**: Show all repos (enabled as well as disabled)
- **--enabled**: Show enabled repos (default)
- **--disabled**: Show disabled repos

Adding a new repository

To install new packages or update older packages, you need to access a repository; local or remote. We will see the creation of local repositories in this section. Later, we will use these repositories to install packages.

By default, all the packages are not installed. In the first chapter, we did only the basic installation. You can use RHEL9 installation media or image file any time after the installation to install additional packages that are available with it. So, the installer file has to be configured to be used as our local repository. In this chapter, we will use the same RHEL9 image file to add the repository that we have downloaded to install RHEL9. There are two ways to add a repository:

- Manual method of configuring repository
- By using the **dnf config-manager** command, which is an automatic method

Manual method of adding repository

In the manual method, the user has to do all the chores of configuring repositories. The user must be aware of configuration parameters to use in a **.repo** file. You can follow these steps:

1. Mount installation **DVD/iso** file.
2. Identify mount point of your installation media. If you are using a virtual machine and iso image file is available on the host machine, iso image will usually be mounted on **/run/media/$USER/**. You can use mount command to find out the mount of your installation iso file, as follows:

   ```
   mount
   ```

   The following line displays the mount point of iso file:

   ```
   /dev/sr0 on /run/media/visheshkumar/RHEL-9-0-0-BaseOS-x86_64 type iso9660 (ro,nosuid,nodev,relatime,nojoliet,check=s,map=n,block-size=2048,uid=1000,gid=1000,dmode=500,fmode=400,uhelper=udisks2)
   ```

3. Explore the contents of the **/run/media/visheshkumar/RHEL-9-0-0-BaseOS-x86_64** directory. This mount contains two repositories: **BaseOS** and **AppStream.**
4. Let us configure **BaseOS** as our local repository. Create a file **rhel9.repo** in the **/etc/yum.repos.d** directory. Add the following contents to this file:

   ```
   [rhel9iso]

   name=RHEL_9_iso

   baseurl="file:///run/media/visheshkumar/RHEL-9-0-0-BaseOS-x86_64/BaseOS"

   gpgcheck=0

   enabled=1
   ```

   Let us understand the directive used in the **.repo** file.

   [rhel9iso] is the unique repository ID. Under this section, many repository-specific directives can be used.

   name=: This specifies the name of the repository.

   baseurl=: This specifies the URL of the repository, local or remote.

   gpgcheck=: It determines whether a GPG signature check should be performed on packages found in this repository. 0 disables GPG verification.

   enabled=: Enables this repository so that it can be used during the installation of packages.

5. Verify the repository creation by issuing the **dnf repolist** command as follows:

   ```
   dnf repolist
   ```

This should show the newly created repository.

A **.repo** file under **/etc/yum.repos.d/** may contain more than one **[repository]** sections. Let us add the **AppStream** repository found in our dvd iso in **rhel9.repo** file that we have just created. Obviously, the same can be added to a new **.repo** file. Let us add the following line in **rhel9.repo** file:

```
[appstreamiso]
name=appstreamiso
baseurl=file:///run/media/visheshkumar/RHEL-9-0-0-BaseOS-x86_64/AppStream/
gpgcheck=0
enabled=1
```

Again, verify the repository addition by issuing the **dnf repolist** command, and you will get the following output:

```
[root@vmachine ~]# dnf repolist
Updating Subscription Management repositories.
repo id                     repo name
appstreamiso                  appstreamiso
rhel9iso                    RHEL_9_iso
```

It displays two-columnar output: the **repo id** column displays the repository ID, which is taken from the text mentioned under []; and the **repo name** column shows the name of the repository and is taken from the **name=** directive mentioned in the **.repo** file. The output lists two repositories.

Let us use a newly added repository to install packages. Here, we will install the **createrepo** package. This will give you the **createrepo** binary/command that we will use to create a repository from a set of packages. Use the **dnf install** command to install the **createrepo** package, as shown in *Figure 14.2*. The following command is used to install the **createrepo** package:

```
dnf install createrepo
```

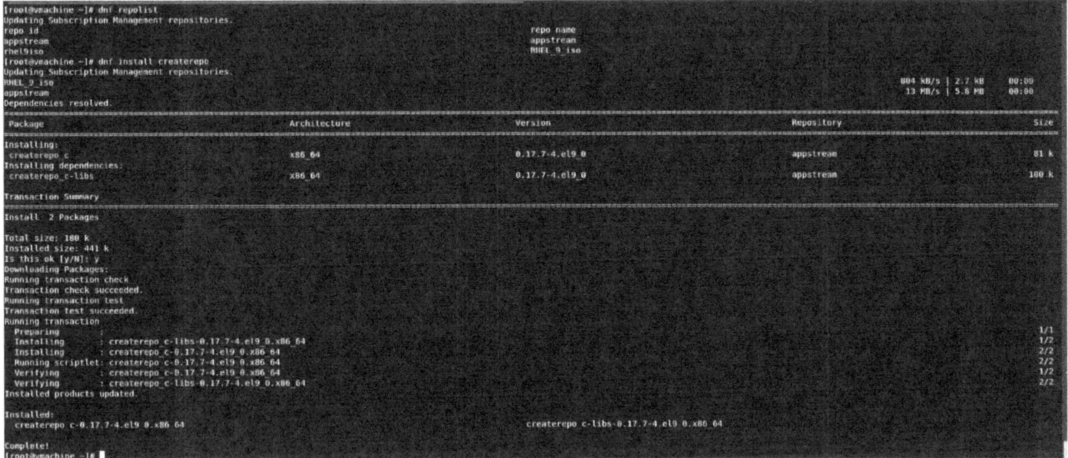

*Figure 14.2: **dnf** command usage: installing a package named createrepo*

dnf searches for the specified package in all the repositories available and installs it from the repository where the package is found.

Automatic method of creating a repository

Another way to add a repository is to use the **dnf config-manager** command. Here, the configuration file is created automatically with all the required parameters, and the repo is enabled. Provide the location in URI format as an argument with this command, as follows:

```
dnf config-manager --add-repo file:///run/media/visheshkumar/RHEL-9-0-0-BaseOS-x86_64/AppStream/
```

The preceding command adds the *AppStream* repository from the installation media without the need to make any configuration. The preceding command also creates the corresponding **.repo** file, as shown here:

```
cat /etc/yum.repos.d/run_media_visheshkumar_RHEL-9-0-0-BaseOS-x86_64_AppStream_.repo
[run_media_visheshkumar_RHEL-9-0-0-BaseOS-x86_64_AppStream_]
name=created by dnf config-manager from file:///run/media/visheshkumar/RHEL-9-0-0-BaseOS-x86_64/AppStream/
baseurl=file:///run/media/visheshkumar/RHEL-9-0-0-BaseOS-x86_64/AppStream/
enabled=1
```

Use the **dnf repolist** command to verify the addition of repository:

```
dnf repolist
```

Figure 14.3 shows the output after you added **BaseOS** and **Appstream** repositories both by manual and automatic methods.

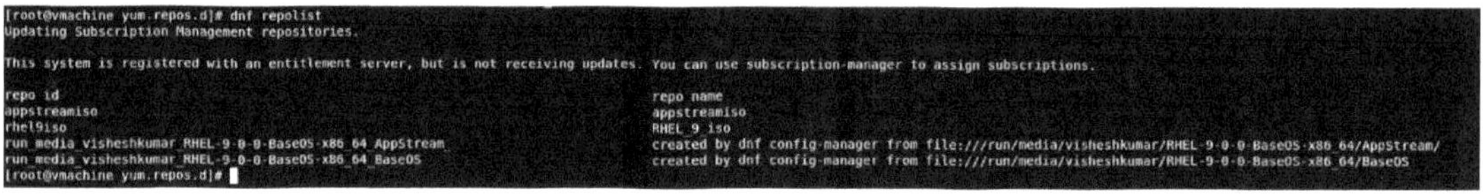

```
[root@vmachine yum.repos.d]# dnf repolist
Updating Subscription Management repositories.

This system is registered with an entitlement server, but is not receiving updates. You can use subscription-manager to assign subscriptions.

repo id                                                   repo name
appstreamiso                                              appstreamiso
rhel9iso                                                  RHEL_9_iso
run_media_visheshkumar_RHEL-9-0-0-BaseOS-x86_64_AppStream created by dnf config-manager from file:///run/media/visheshkumar/RHEL-9-0-0-BaseOS-x86_64/AppStream/
run_media_visheshkumar_RHEL-9-0-0-BaseOS-x86_64_BaseOS    created by dnf config-manager from file:///run/media/visheshkumar/RHEL-9-0-0-BaseOS-x86_64/BaseOS
[root@vmachine yum.repos.d]#
```

Figure 14.3: *dnf repolist command displaying enabled repositories on the system*

Creating a repository

In the preceding section, we added some repositories from the RHEL9 installation dvd to the configuration file. After it is configured in the configuration file, the repository can be used for package installations that have not been installed during the installation of RHEL9. Not only installation iso, you can add any existing repository, local or remote, to the configuration file provided that the base must be correct and exist.

Besides, **dnf** allows you to create your own repositories containing RPM packages for download and installation. In this section, we will create a new repository and add packages to it.

Here, we will use our installation media to copy all the provided packages to create a repository. Follow these steps as the root user to create a new repository and add it to the system:

1. Create a directory where our repository will lie:

   ```
   #mkdir -p rhel9_repo/BaseOS/
   ```

   The preceding command creates a directory at **/root**. You can choose another location.

2. Now, copy all the packages from the installation media to the newly created directory. Later these packages will be used to build a new repository at this location. We will use packages from the **BaseOS** repository as our package source. Under the **BaseOS** subdirectory, copy the contents of the **Packages** sub-directory to a new directory location, as follows:

   ```
   #cp /run/media/visheshkumar/RHEL-9-0-0-BaseOS-x86_64/BaseOS/
   Packages/* \ rhel9_repo/BaseOS/
   ```

3. You can also create a repository using packages from the **AppStream** repository available in the installation media. Let us create a directory to store **Appstream** packages, as follows:

   ```
   #mkdir rhel9_repo/AppStream/
   ```

   Then, copy all the packages from **AppStream/Packages** subdirectory to the new sub-directory location as:

   ```
   #cp \
   /run/media/visheshkumar/RHEL-9-0-0-BaseOS-x86_64/AppStream/
   Packages/* \ rhel9_repo/AppStream/
   ```

   You can skip this step if you do not want packages provided by this repository.

4. Now, use the **createrepo** command to create a repository using the preceding directories:

   ```
   createrepo rhel9_repo AppStream
   createrepo rhel9_repo BaseOS
   ```

5. Now, add a new entry at the bottom of the **/etc/yum.repos.d/rhel9.repo** file, as follows:

   ```
   [base]
   name=base_local
   baseurl=file:///root/rhel9_repo/BaseOS/
   ```

```
gpgcheck=0
enabled=1
[appstream]
name=appstream_local
baseurl=file:///root/rhel9_repo/AppStream/
gpgcheck=0
enabled=1
```

After adding the preceding contents, your **/etc/yum.repos.d/rhel9.repo** file looks like *Figure 14.4*:

```
[root@vmachine ~]# cat /etc/yum.repos.d/rhel9.repo
[rhel9iso]
name=RHEL_9_iso
baseurl="file:///run/media/visheshkumar/RHEL-9-0-0-BaseOS-x86_64/BaseOS"
gpgcheck=0
enabled=1

[appstreamiso]
name=appstreamiso
baseurl=file:///run/media/visheshkumar/RHEL-9-0-0-BaseOS-x86_64/AppStream/
gpgcheck=0
enabled=1

[base]
name=base_local
baseurl=file:///root/rhel9_repo/BaseOS/
gpgcheck=0
enabled=1

[appstream]
name=appstream_local
baseurl=file:///root/rhel9_repo/AppStream/
gpgcheck=0
enabled=1
```

Figure 14.4: Contents of **.repo** *file*

6. Now, list your repository:

```
$ dnf repolist
Updating Subscription Management repositories.

repo                  repo name
appstream    appstream_local
appstreamiso       appstreamiso
base         base_local
rhel9iso     RHEL_9_iso
```

Getting EPEL repository

You can install extra packages for RHEL using the **Extra Packages for Enterprise Linux** (**EPEL**) repository. EPEL repository provides packages that are not available with default installation media and are made available via the EPEL repository. The EPEL repository is provided by the Fedora community. You can fetch EPEL repositories using the following URL:

https://dl.fedoraproject.org/pub/epel/epel-release-latest-9.noarch.RPM

You can install the EPEL repository directly via the given URL using the **`dnf install`** command, as follows:

```
dnf install https://dl.fedoraproject.org/pub/epel/epel-release-
latest-9.noarch.RPM
```

Press '*y*' when it prompts, as shown in *Figure 14.5:*

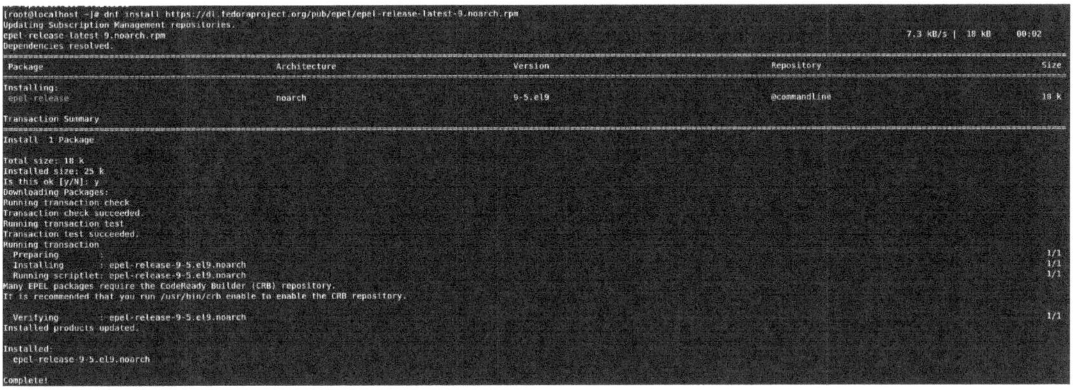

Figure 14.5: *dnf install command installing package using remote location*

Then, typing the following command must list the **`epel`** repository, and you will have the **`epel.repo`** file created automatically under **`/etc/yum.repos.d/`**.

```
dnf repolist
```

Handling repository

In this section, we will learn about enabling and disabling repository. To disable a **`dnf`** repository added to your system, use **`dnf config-manager`** with the **`--disable`** option:

```
dnf config-manager –disable <repository id>
```

To enable a **`dnf`** repository that is added to your system, use the **`dnf config-manager`** subcommand with the **`--enable`** option and the name or ID of the repository as follows:

```
dnf config-manager --enable <repository_id>
```

Do it yourself

Use the /etc/yum.repos.d/rhel9.repo file to disable appstreamiso and rhel9iso repositories. Type the dnf repolist command. Do you find the preceding two repositories in the list? If not, why? Use the dnf repolist command again to view disabled repositories only. Enable them again and verify them using the dnf repolist command.

Hint: Set enabled=0 in a .repo file to disable the said repositories.

Getting information about repository and packages

In this section, we will learn ways to query repositories and metadata for additional information.

To get detailed information about the repository, use the following:

```
$ dnf repoinfo
```

The output of the preceding command would look as follows:

```
Repo-id      : base
Repo-name     : base_local
Repo-revision   : 1686821137
Repo-updated    : Thu 15 Jun 2023 14:55:37 IST
Repo-pkgs     : 1,131
Repo-available-pkgs: 1,131
Repo-size     : 929 M
Repo-baseurl    : file:///root/rhel9_repo/BaseOS/
Repo-expire    : 172,800 second(s) (last: Thu 15 Jun 2023 15:40:33 IST)
Repo-filename   : /etc/yum.repos.d/rhel9.repo

Repo-id      : epel
Repo-name     : Extra Packages for Enterprise Linux 9 - x86_64
Repo-revision   : 1686793888
Repo-updated    : Thu 15 Jun 2023 07:24:21 IST
Repo-pkgs     : 16,101
Repo-available-pkgs: 16,101
Repo-size     : 14 G
Repo-metalink   : https://mirrors.fedoraproject.org/metalink?repo=epel-9&arch=x86_64&infra=$infra&content=$contentdir
```

```
Updated      : Thu 15 Jun 2023 15:49:27 IST
Repo-baseurl    : https://epel.excellmedia.net/9/Everything/x86_64/ (36
more)
Repo-expire    : 172,800 second(s) (last: Thu 15 Jun 2023 15:49:27 IST)
Repo-filename   : /etc/yum.repos.d/epel.repo
```

All the available repositories are listed with the preceding command.

You can also use the following command to get the detailed information about the repositories:

```
dnf repolist -v
```

If you want to find which repo provides a particular package or which package provides a particular value, say **thunderbird**, use the **`dnf provides`** command as follows:

```
dnf provides thunderbird
```

Output in *Figure 14.6* shows that the **thunderbird** package is available from the **Appstream** repository that we added from the installation media in the earlier section. The output also displays the package name that provides the given value. Actually, **dnf provides** lists all the repositories that provide the given package.

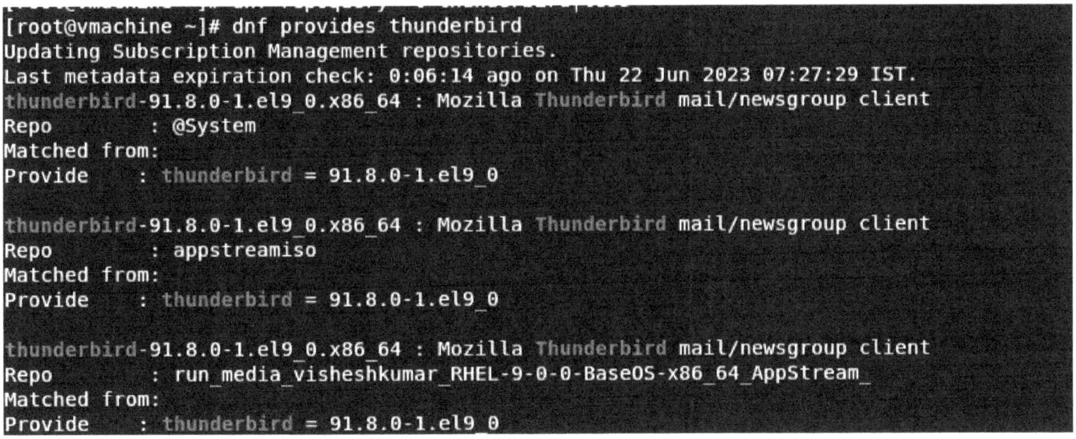

```
[root@vmachine ~]# dnf provides thunderbird
Updating Subscription Management repositories.
Last metadata expiration check: 0:06:14 ago on Thu 22 Jun 2023 07:27:29 IST.
thunderbird-91.8.0-1.el9_0.x86_64 : Mozilla Thunderbird mail/newsgroup client
Repo        : @System
Matched from:
Provide    : thunderbird = 91.8.0-1.el9_0

thunderbird-91.8.0-1.el9_0.x86_64 : Mozilla Thunderbird mail/newsgroup client
Repo        : appstreamiso
Matched from:
Provide    : thunderbird = 91.8.0-1.el9_0

thunderbird-91.8.0-1.el9_0.x86_64 : Mozilla Thunderbird mail/newsgroup client
Repo        : run_media_visheshkumar_RHEL-9-0-0-BaseOS-x86_64_AppStream_
Matched from:
Provide    : thunderbird = 91.8.0-1.el9_0
```

***Figure 14.6:** dnf provides command searching for repositories against a package name*

`dnf provides` can also be used to search the package name against the given binary file name, as shown in *Figure 14.7*. In the figure, the **`dnf provides`** command searches for the package that provides the specified file, here, **`/usr/bin/gzip`**. If multiple repositories provide that package, it lists them all.

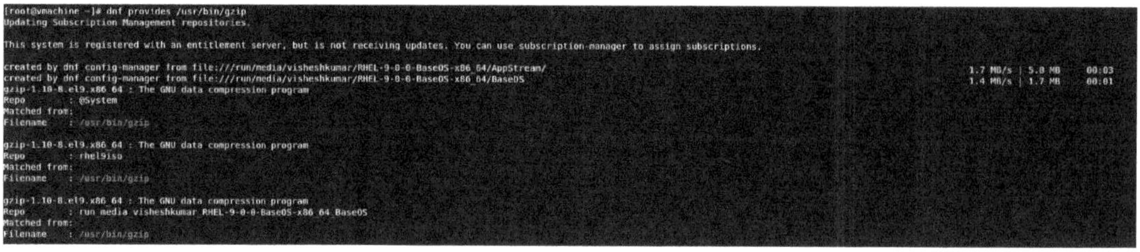

```
[root@vmachine ~]# dnf provides /usr/bin/gzip
Updating Subscription Management repositories.

This system is registered with an entitlement server, but is not receiving updates. You can use subscription-manager to assign subscriptions.

created by dnf config-manager from file:///run/media/visheshkumar/RHEL-9-0-0-BaseOS-x86_64/AppStream/    1.7 MB/s | 5.8 MB     00:03
created by dnf config-manager from file:///run/media/visheshkumar/RHEL-9-0-0-BaseOS-x86_64/BaseOS       1.4 MB/s | 1.7 MB     00:01
gzip-1.10-8.el9.x86_64 : The GNU data compression program
Repo        : @System
Matched from:
Filename    : /usr/bin/gzip

gzip-1.10-8.el9.x86_64 : The GNU data compression program
Repo        : rhel9iso
Matched from:
Filename    : /usr/bin/gzip

gzip-1.10-8.el9.x86_64 : The GNU data compression program
Repo        : run_media_visheshkumar_RHEL-9-0-0-BaseOS-x86_64_BaseOS
Matched from:
Filename    : /usr/bin/gzip
```

Figure 14.7: dnf provides command searching for a package that provides given filename

To list the files provided by a package, use the **dnf repoquery** command as follows:

```
dnf repoquery -l thunderbird|less
```

The preceding command uses the **-l** option with the **dnf repoquery** command, which lists out all the files provided by the specified package.

The **dnf repoquery** command comes in very handy for querying packages or repositories for any information. Using the **-i** option with **dnf repoquery** provides detailed information about the specified package. Type the following:

```
dnf repoquery -i thunderbird
Updating Subscription Management repositories.
Last metadata expiration check: 0:15:41 ago on Thu 22 Jun 2023 07:27:29 IST.
Name      : thunderbird
Version    : 91.8.0
Release    : 1.el9_0
Architecture : x86_64
Size      : 98 M
Source     : thunderbird-91.8.0-1.el9_0.src.RPM
Repository  : appstreamiso
Summary    : Mozilla Thunderbird mail/newsgroup client
URL      : http://www.mozilla.org/projects/thunderbird/
License    : MPLv1.1 or GPLv2+ or LGPLv2+
Description : Mozilla Thunderbird is a standalone mail and newsgroup client.
```

It provides detailed information about the **thunderbird** package. If many repos provide the package, then it lists information using all repos.

We can also use the following command to view the detailed information of a specified package:

```
dnf info thunderbird
```

Use the **-s** option to view the source RPM that provides the package as follows:

```
dnf repoquery -s dnf
Updating Subscription Management repositories.
Last metadata expiration check: 0:29:50 ago on Thu 22 Jun 2023 07:27:29 IST.
dnf-4.10.0-5.el9_0.src.RPM
```

Other options that you can use with the **dnf repoquery** command are listed here:

- **--conflicts:** Display capabilities that the package conflicts with
- **--depends:** Display capabilities that the package depends on
- **--provides:** Display capabilities provided by the package
- **--location:** Shows a location where the package could be downloaded from
- **--requires**: Display capabilities that the package depends on
- **--file <filename>**: Display the package that owns the specified file
- **--whatprovides:** List the packages that provide the specified capabilities
- **--provides:** Display capabilities provided by the package

Suppose you want to know what capabilities are provided by the **dnf** package itself; you can type the following command:

```
dnf repoquery --provides dnf
Updating Subscription Management repositories.
Last metadata expiration check: 0:14:58 ago on Friday 23 June 2023 01:12:01 PM.
dnf = 4.10.0-5.el9_0
dnf-command(alias)
dnf-command(autoremove)
dnf-command(check-update)
dnf-command(clean)
dnf-command(distro-sync)
dnf-command(downgrade)
dnf-command(group)
dnf-command(history)
dnf-command(info)
dnf-command(install)
dnf-command(list)
```

```
dnf-command(makecache)
dnf-command(mark)
dnf-command(provides)
dnf-command(reinstall)
dnf-command(remove)
dnf-command(repolist)
dnf-command(repoquery)
dnf-command(repository-packages)
dnf-command(search)
dnf-command(updateinfo)
dnf-command(upgrade)
dnf-command(upgrade-to)
```

Use the following command to check which package provides the listed specification/capability:

```
dnf repoquery --whatprovides vim
Updating Subscription Management repositories.
Last metadata expiration check: 0:17:57 ago on Friday 23 June 2023
01:12:01 PM.
vim-enhanced-2:8.2.2637-15.el9.x86_64
```

The preceding command lists the package name that provides the *vim* capability.

Suppose you want to know which package owns the given file; use the **--file** option with the **dnf repoquery** command, as follows:

```
dnf repoquery --file /var/log
Updating Subscription Management repositories.
Last metadata expiration check: 0:20:01 ago on Friday 23 June 2023
01:12:01 PM.
filesystem-0:3.16-2.el9.x86_64
```

The preceding output shows that **/var/log** is owned by the **filesystem-0:3.16-2.el9.x86_64** package.

Do it yourself

You want to run the iostat command. You typed the iostat command in the terminal. But you noticed that this is not available. What will you do? Try to install it using dnf install command, as follows:

```
dnf install iostat
```

What did you find? Is dnf able to find a match for iostat? If no, you need to identify the package that provides iostat binary? How will you identify the same? Write the command that will show you the package name that provides iostat binary. Now, install the listed package. Note the dependent packages that will be installed along with it. If installation is successful, execute the iostat command on the terminal. Does the command execute successfully this time? Ignore the output and other details of this command as we will be learning about this command in the later chapters.

Hint: Use the dnf provides command.

Installing software

To install a software or a package, use the **`dnf install`** command. The **`dnf install`** command takes many forms of argument: name of the package, file path, or the URL from where to install package. Earlier, we talked about installing the package specifying its name and URL. In this section, we will see the software installation in further detail.

Software is always installed using a repository that makes it available. You can verify whether available repositories contain the specified package. Use the **`dnf search`** command to confirm whether the package is in the available repository. If you know the name of the package to install, provide its name or just part of its name as an argument to the **`dnf search`** command. Let us search whether any repository provides packages whose names start with **`thunder`** software:

```
$ sudo dnf search thunder
Updating Subscription Management repositories.
Last metadata expiration check: 0:07:29 ago on Thursday 22 June 2023
06:34:55 AM.
=========================================================================
============== Name & Summary Matched: thunder ========================
plasma-thunderbolt.x86_64 : Plasma integration for controlling
Thunderbolt devices
thunderbird.x86_64 : Mozilla Thunderbird mail/newsgroup client
=========================================================================
===================== Summary Matched: thunder ========================
bolt.x86_64 : Thunderbolt device manager
```

In the preceding command's output, the given expression matches with two packages: **`plasma-thunderbolt`** and **`thunderbird`**.

Suppose you type the following:

```
dnf install <package name>
```

It automatically resolves all the dependencies that are required to install the specified package. Then, it displays the list of all the uninstalled dependencies. It also calculates and displays the total disk space required to install dependencies along with the actual package. It prompts you for the confirmation. If you have the required disk space available and want to proceed with all the listed packages and libraries, press '*y*'. After your response, DNF will proceed with the installation and display a 'complete' message if the transaction succeeds. Refer *to Figure 14.2, where the createrepo* package is installed with all its dependencies. It displays a table providing information about the given package as well as the dependent packages that it is going to install.

The table given in *Figure 14.8* is the snippet from *Figure 14.2*.

Package	Architecture	Version	Repository	Size
Installing:				
createrepo_c	x86_64	0.17.7-4.el9_0	appstream	81 k
Installing dependencies:				
createrepo_c-libs	x86_64	0.17.7-4.el9_0	appstream	100 k
Transaction Summary				
Install 2 Packages				

***Figure 14.8**: dnf install command providing detailed information about each package to be installed in tabular format*

The table as given in *Figure 14.8* is very handy for you to review the packages that **`dnf`** will install. The first section in the table displays the information about the package that will be installed. The second section lists all the dependent packages that will be installed. The table displays the architecture and version of each package that will be installed. It also displays the repository that will be used to install the listed package. The last column displays the size of the package. Then, it will ask you for confirmation on whether the information given is okay to you. After your response, it downloads the package, performs some checks, and installs the package.

You can install one or more packages by specifying their names as follows:

```
dnf install <package1 packgae3 …>
```

This will lead to the installation of the package along with all their dependencies.

You can also use glob expressions to install packages with matching patterns.

You can also provide file names to **`dnf install`**. If you know the name and location of the binary you want to install but not its package name, you can use the **`dnf install`** command providing path name as its argument. Type the following:

```
dnf install /usr/sbin/named
```

`dnf` searches through its database to find the package that provides the specified file. If it finds any package, it will ask you whether you want to install it.

```
dnf -y install thunderbird
```

The preceding command uses the **`-y`** option to install package. **`-y`** is used to presume user responses to **`'y'`** and does not prompt the user for any confirmation.

Other options that you can use with the **dnf install** command are listed here:

- **--nogpgcheck:** Skip checking GPG signatures on packages.
- **--noautoremove:** Disable removal of dependencies that are no longer used. It sets the **clean_requirements_on_remove** configuration option to **False**.
- **--assumeno:** Automatically answer 'no' for all prompts.
- **--downloadonly**: Only download packages.

dnf also allows the installation of a package from the specified location. Suppose you have already downloaded the RPM package from remote repository and you want to install the package using the downloaded RPM. To do this, you must specify path to the RPM file as follows:

```
dnf install ~/Downloads/samplepackage-0.RPM
```

It automatically resolves all the required dependencies and installs them from the available repositories before installing the package.

If you do not provide the correct package name to **dnf**, it automatically finds all the matching package names. For example, when you type the **dnf install createrepo** command, **dnf** automatically recognizes that the actual package name is **createrepo_c** and installs this.

To get more information on the **dnf install** command, use the **--help** option as follows:

```
dnf install --help
```

Updating software

dnf allows you to check for any pending updates. Using **dnf**, you can update all packages at once. You can also choose to update a single package or multiple packages together. Along with the specified packages, **dnf** updates all its dependencies.

The following command updates all installed applications along with their dependencies:

```
$ dnf upgrade
```

To update just a single package, say cheese:

```
$ dnf upgrade cheese
```

To see which installed packages on your system have updates available, use the following command:

```
dnf check-update
```

To update security-related packages, type the following:

```
dnf upgrade --security
```

To get more information on the dnf upgrade command, use the following:

```
dnf upgrade --help
```

Listing packages

You can use the **dnf list** command to list out all the packages, available or installed. A package is said to be installed if it is installed on the system. A package is said to be available if it not installed but is available to install in the repositories that **dnf** knows about.

To list packages, the **dnf list** command is used as shown here:

```
dnf list|less
```

you will get a very long list in the result, so you have to to use **less** to view the output. The preceding command shows the installed as well as available packages, as shown in *Figure 14.9*:

```
Updating Subscription Management repositories.
Last metadata expiration check: 8:18:13 ago on Thursday 22 June 2023 06:55:35 AM.
Installed Packages
ModemManager.x86_64                              1.18.2-3.el9             @anaconda
ModemManager-glib.x86_64                         1.18.2-3.el9             @anaconda
NetworkManager.x86_64                            1:1.36.0-4.el9_0         @anaconda
NetworkManager-adsl.x86_64                       1:1.36.0-4.el9_0         @anaconda
NetworkManager-bluetooth.x86_64                  1:1.36.0-4.el9_0         @anaconda
NetworkManager-config-server.noarch              1:1.36.0-4.el9_0         @anaconda
NetworkManager-libnm.x86_64                      1:1.36.0-4.el9_0         @anaconda
NetworkManager-team.x86_64                       1:1.36.0-4.el9_0         @anaconda
NetworkManager-tui.x86_64                        1:1.36.0-4.el9_0         @anaconda
NetworkManager-wifi.x86_64                       1:1.36.0-4.el9_0         @anaconda
NetworkManager-wwan.x86_64                       1:1.36.0-4.el9_0         @anaconda
PackageKit.x86_64                                1.2.4-2.el9              @AppStream
PackageKit-command-not-found.x86_64              1.2.4-2.el9              @AppStream
PackageKit-glib.x86_64                           1.2.4-2.el9              @AppStream
PackageKit-gstreamer-plugin.x86_64               1.2.4-2.el9              @AppStream
PackageKit-gtk3-module.x86_64                    1.2.4-2.el9              @AppStream
abattis-cantarell-fonts.noarch                   0.301-4.el9              @AppStream
accountsservice.x86_64                           0.6.55-10.el9            @AppStream
accountsservice-libs.x86_64                      0.6.55-10.el9            @AppStream
acl.x86_64                                       2.3.1-3.el9              @anaconda
adcli.x86_64                                     0.9.1-7.el9              @anaconda
adobe-mappings-cmap.noarch                       20171205-12.el9          @AppStream
adobe-mappings-cmap-deprecated.noarch            20171205-12.el9          @AppStream
adobe-mappings-pdf.noarch                        20180407-10.el9          @AppStream
```

Figure 14.9: *dnf list command displaying list of all the installed packages, followed by the available packages*

The output in *Figure 14.9* lists all the installed packages, followed by a list of the available packages. (The available packages are not displayed in the given figure). The rightmost column in the output lists the repository from which the package was retrieved.

The following are the options available with the **dnf list** command:

- **--all** : This is default and shows all packages (installed as well as available).
- **--installed**: The shows only installed packages.
- **--available** : This shows only the available packages in all the enabled repositories.
- **--extras**: This shows only extras packages.

- **--updates** or **--upgrades**: This shows only the upgrades packages.
- **--autoremove**: This shows only autoremove packages.
- **--recent**: This shows only recently changed packages.

To list packages matching glob expression, type the following:

```
dnf list <glob>
```

To find all the packages whose name starts with **Network**, you can type the following:

```
dnf list Network*
```

Removing a package

To uninstall a particular package, use the **dnf remove** command. This command also removes any packages that depend on it. Use **dnf** remove as follows:

```
dnf remove <package_name>
```

The **dnf remove** command allows you to remove several packages at once by adding more package names to the command.

You can use the following options with the **dnf remove** command:

- **-y** or **--assumeyes:** Automatically answer yes for all questions
- **--assumeno**: Automatically answer no for all questions

When you are removing a package, say **thunderbird**, **dnf** automatically removes packages that depend on it. *Figure 14.10* demonstrates the package removal process. It resolves the dependency and lists all the packages that will be removed.

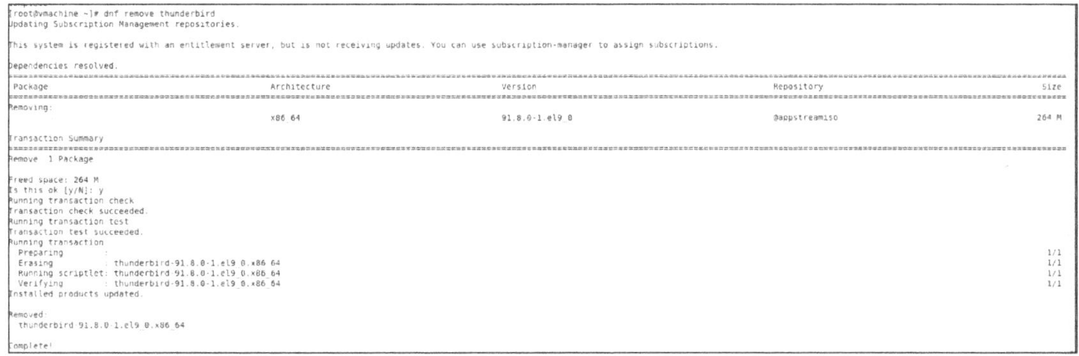

[root@vmachine ~]# dnf remove thunderbird
Updating Subscription Management repositories.
This system is registered with an entitlement server, but is not receiving updates. You can use subscription-manager to assign subscriptions.
Dependencies resolved.
Package Architecture Version Repository Size
Removing:
x86_64 91.8.0-1.el9_0 @appstreamiso 264 M
Transaction Summary
Remove 1 Package
Freed space: 264 M
Is this ok [y/N]: y
Running transaction check
Transaction check succeeded.
Running transaction test
Transaction test succeeded.
Running transaction
Preparing : 1/1
Erasing : thunderbird-91.8.0-1.el9_0.x86_64 1/1
Running scriptlet: thunderbird-91.8.0-1.el9_0.x86_64 1/1
Verifying : thunderbird-91.8.0-1.el9_0.x86_64 1/1
Installed products updated.
Removed:
thunderbird-91.8.0-1.el9_0.x86_64
Complete!

***Figure 14.10**: dnf remove command usage*

In *Figure 14.10*, no dependent packages are listed, as **dnf** did not find any dependent packages. It calculates and displays the disk space that will be freed after the removal of the listed packages. It then prompts your confirmation before uninstalling the said packages.

If you are sure to delete all the listed packages, type 'y' to proceed with the uninstallation. After the installation completes, it displays the 'Complete!' message.

Do it yourself

In the previous DO IT YOURSELF exercise, you installed the sysstat package. Now, uninstall it and note what packages will be uninstalled. Compare it with the packages that you noted during its installation.

Package groups

A package group is a collection of related packages. *System Tools* or *Sound and Video* are examples of package groups. When packages are grouped together based on their functionality and purpose, they form a package group. Package groups provide an efficient way to manage software on the system. Installing a package group automatically pulls a set of related packages as well as all the dependent packages in a single operation. Thus, it saves a considerable amount of time and effort.

The `dnf groups` command is used to work with package groups:

```
[root@vmachine yum.repos.d]# dnf group
Updating Subscription Management repositories.
Last metadata expiration check: 0:45:12 ago on Thu 15 Jun 2023 15:49:27 IST.
Installed Groups: 2
Available Groups: 13
```

The preceding command displays the number of installed and available groups.

To list all installed and available groups, use the following:

```
dnf group list
```

It will display the output shown in *Figure 14.11*:

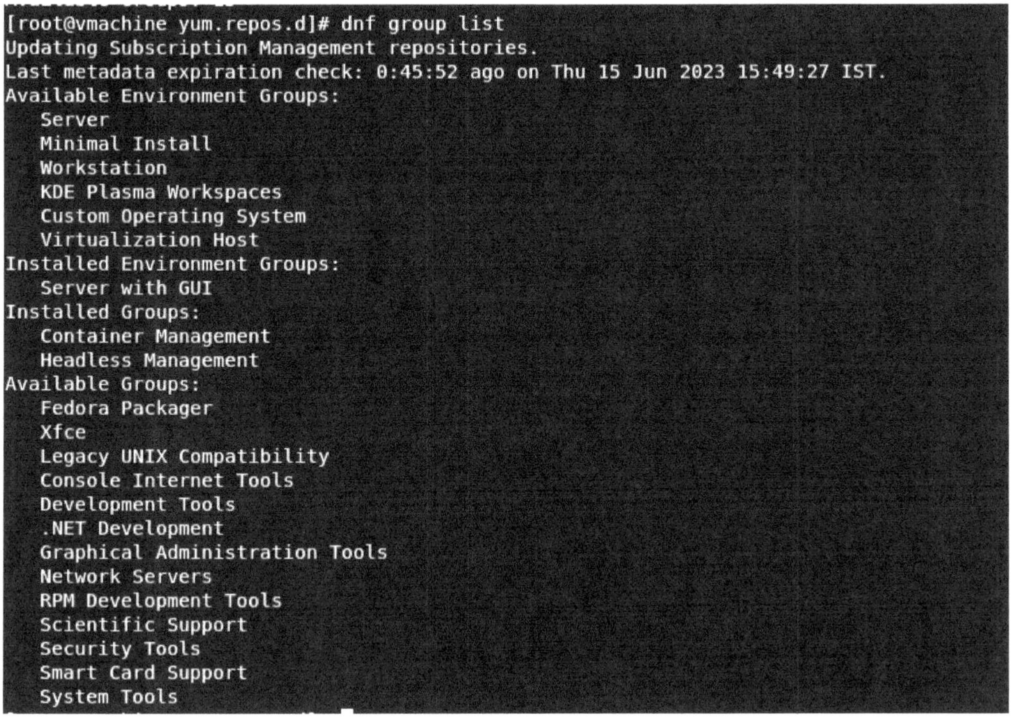

```
[root@vmachine yum.repos.d]# dnf group list
Updating Subscription Management repositories.
Last metadata expiration check: 0:45:52 ago on Thu 15 Jun 2023 15:49:27 IST.
Available Environment Groups:
   Server
   Minimal Install
   Workstation
   KDE Plasma Workspaces
   Custom Operating System
   Virtualization Host
Installed Environment Groups:
   Server with GUI
Installed Groups:
   Container Management
   Headless Management
Available Groups:
   Fedora Packager
   Xfce
   Legacy UNIX Compatibility
   Console Internet Tools
   Development Tools
   .NET Development
   Graphical Administration Tools
   Network Servers
   RPM Development Tools
   Scientific Support
   Security Tools
   Smart Card Support
   System Tools
```

Figure 14.11: *dnf group list command showing the list of available and installed package groups*

Use the following to install a package group:

```
dnf group install <group name or group id>
```

Use the following command to update a package group:

```
dnf group upgrade <group-name>
```

Type the following to remove a package group:

```
dnf group remove <package name or package id>
```

Use the following to view the detailed information about a particular group:

```
dnf group info <group name>
```

For instance, to view the detailed information about the **System Tools** group and the packages contained in it, use the following:

```
dnf group info "System Tools"
```

You will get output similar to *Figure 14.12*.

```
Updating Subscription Management repositories.
Last metadata expiration check: 10:13:06 ago on Thursday 22 June 2023 06:55:35 AM.
Group: System Tools
 Description: This group is a collection of various tools for the system, such as the client for connecting to SMB shares and tools to monitor network traffic.
 Default Packages:
   NetworkManager-libreswan
   chrony
   cifs-utils
   libreswan
   nmap
   openldap-clients
   samba-client
   setserial
   tigervnc
   tmux
   zsh
 Optional Packages:
   PackageKit-command-not-found
   aide
   autofs
   bacula-client
   chrpath
   convmv
   createrepo_c
```

Figure 14.12: Output of dnf group info command showing the details of the System Tools package group

Using transaction history

DNF keeps track of the operations that you perform. By maintaining the list of older transactions, **dnf** allows you to review past transactions, undo changes, or restore the system to a previous state if needed. You can also use the **dnf history** command to undo or redo the transactions.

To view the list of recent transactions, type the following:

```
dnf history
```

Transactions are shown sorted by the latest to oldest, with the oldest transaction being numbered as 1.

The preceding command is the same as issuing the following:

```
dnf history list
```

See *Figure 14.13* for a sample transactions list. It lists transactions that occurred in the past.

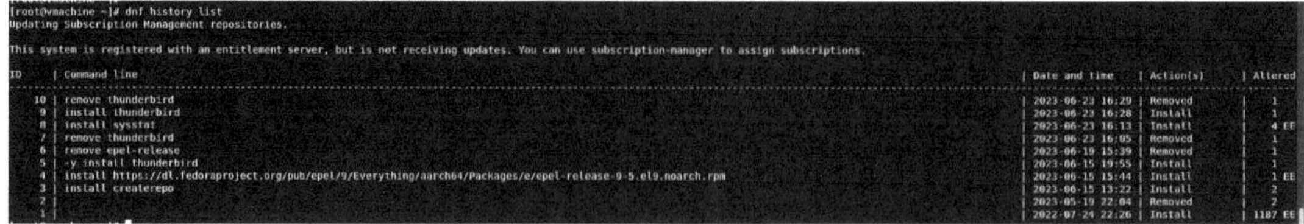

Figure 14.13: Usage of the dnf history command

Figure 14.13 gives the following information about the older transactions:

- **ID**: It represents the ID of the transaction. Each transaction is identified by a unique identifier in the transaction history. The recent transactions will receive larger values.
- **Command line**: This displays the command that made the transaction.

- **Date and time**: It displays the date and time when the trsaction occurred.
- **Action(s):** This displays the action that the transaction took.
- **Altered**: It displays the number of packages that are altered due to the transaction.

You can also list only the transactions related to a particular package as follows:

```
dnf history list <package name>
```

You can also provide the glob expression in the preceding command line.

Use the following to display the details of a particular transaction:

```
dnf history info <transactionID>
```

Type this to display information about the five oldest transactions stored in the history database:

```
dnf history list 1..5
```

Use this to view the first transaction:

```
dnf history list 1
```

Issue the following to view the second oldest transaction:

```
dnf history list 2
```

The **`--reverse`** option is used to display the history list in reverse order, as follows:

```
dnf history list --reverse
```

The **`dnf history info`** command provides detailed information about the last transaction:

```
dnf history info 8
```

The preceding command provides detailed information for the transaction whose ID is 8, as shown in *Figure 14.14*:

```
[root@vmachine ~]# dnf history info 8
Updating Subscription Management repositories.

This system is registered with an entitlement server, but is not receiving updates. You can use subscription-manager to assign subscriptions.

Transaction ID : 8
Begin time     : Fri 23 Jun 2023 16:13:11 IST
Begin rpmdb    : d6bb8a3c00f910a761e2cc44a5a81d7d930b3c9461337657737f964fb79d7932
End time       : Fri 23 Jun 2023 16:13:17 IST (6 seconds)
End rpmdb      : c6491691bbda07bcd3719ffc9b27a050f23e3f83024e4d44da904c412bd91b9b
User           : vishesh kumar <visheshkumar>
Return-Code    : Success
Releasever     : 9
Command Line   : install sysstat
Comment        :
Packages Altered:
    Install lm_sensors-libs-3.6.0-10.el9.x86_64 @appstreamiso
    Install pcp-conf-5.3.5-8.el9.x86_64         @appstreamiso
    Install pcp-libs-5.3.5-8.el9.x86_64         @appstreamiso
    Install sysstat-12.5.4-3.el9.x86_64         @appstreamiso
Scriptlet output:
   1 Created symlink /etc/systemd/system/multi-user.target.wants/sysstat.service → /usr/lib/systemd/system/sysstat.service.
   2 Created symlink /etc/systemd/system/sysstat.service.wants/sysstat-collect.timer → /usr/lib/systemd/system/sysstat-collect.timer.
   3 Created symlink /etc/systemd/system/sysstat.service.wants/sysstat-summary.timer → /usr/lib/systemd/system/sysstat-summary.timer.
```

Figure 14.14: *dnf history showing detailed information of a specified transaction*

```
dnf history redo <transactionID>
```

Using the preceding command repeats the specified transaction.

```
dnf history undo <transactionID>
```

The preceding command rolls back all the operations performed under the specified transaction. If the specified transaction installed a new package, the preceding command uninstalls it. If this transaction uninstalled a package, **dnf history undo** installs it again.

The **dnf history rollback** command reverts all the **dnf** transactions performed between the specified transaction and the last transaction.

```
dnf history rollback <transactionID>
```

The preceding command rolls back all the transactions performed after the specified transaction.

Conclusion

RHEL uses RPM-based packages and employs the **yum** and **dnf** utilities for package management. DNF is the enhanced version of yum and is now the default package management tool.

DNF uses easy-to-remember commands like **dnf install** and **dnf remove** to install and remove packages, respectively. **install** and **remove** are the subcommands of **dnf**. It provides its functionality by using many subcommands. Each subcommand can be learned using **dnf <subcommand> --help**. RHEL9 provides RPM-based packages using repositories like BaseOS and Appstream. The installed packages need to be updated from time to time. If you have subscribed to RHSM, you can receive updates for the packages installed. DNF allows you to check for pending updates and apply the updates if available. If your machine is subscribed, **dnf** also lets you install packages from repositories maintained by the vendor. DNF allows you to roll back or replay older transactions from the transaction history. It also provides you with a command to search for packages that provide a specified binary or text file, to search for repositories that provide a particular package, to view complete information for all the installed and available packages, and more.

In the next chapter, we will learn about the tools to monitor system health and performance, and ways to improve the system's overall health.

CHAPTER 15
Performance Monitoring and Tuning

Introduction

A system administrator spends most of their time monitoring the system's performance and tuning it. A proper performance monitoring system must be in place to ensure that the system is always performing properly. If the system is running slow, monitoring tools help identify the areas that can be bottlenecks. After a bottleneck point is identified, tuning actions are taken. The areas that could create performance problems can be related to CPU, memory, and IO. RHEL9 provides several useful tools for monitoring system performance and identifying potential performance problems before they create a nuisance and halt the system. This chapter gives an overview of various system monitoring tools and discusses how you can use them to diagnose performance problems so that tuning areas can be found.

Structure

The chapter discusses the following topics:

- Identifying performance problems
- System monitoring tools
    - o **`/proc`** filesystem
    - o Command-line tools like **`sar`**, **`top`**, **`free`**, **`vmstat`**, **`iostat`**

- Gnome's system monitor
- Performance logs

- Perform root cause analysis of slow response
- Setting alerts using **cron**

Objectives

By the end of this chapter, you will be able to monitor system performance, and identify potential problems and tune them. After learning various ways to monitor the system and its components, you will be able to automate the monitoring task using scripting and set alerts in **cron** to receive notifications when the performance goes below the specified threshold.

Identifying performance problems

A system administrator ensures that the system is performing well all the time. The administrator cannot sit back and relax after the system has become stable. Continuous monitoring of the system is important to identify any potential performance problems. If a problem is not identified in time, everything could be halted, which is never acceptable. Therefore, constant monitoring is required so that any performance-related problems can be identified before they start to slow down the application and create any disinterest in users about the applications they are using. You must identify the bottleneck points whenever this situation arises. Proper system analysis is required to know the area that causes performance issues. The system may be performing poorly due to problems in one or more of the following areas:

- CPU
- Memory
- Disk I/O

After identifying the problematic domain, you must drill down your analysis to the subdomains to identify the root cause. Identifying the root cause of a problem is the only way that can lead to the correct solution. This also ensures that you tune in the right direction. Proper tuning requires a good knowledge of the system. Modifying any system setting or making changes in hardware without proper knowledge may further degrade the problem.

Various monitoring tools assist you in monitoring and analyzing the system's performance. Before we delve into these tools, let us determine the overall system health by issuing the **uptime** command, as follows:

```
$uptime
13:22:46 up 2 days, 12:07, 1 user, load average: 0.11, 0.04, 0.01
```

The preceding command displays various system-related information, as follows:

- **Current time**: The first field displays the system's current time.
- **How long the system has been running**: The output shows that this system is up and running for 2 days, 12 hours, and 7 minutes.
- **Number of logged in users**: The third field displays the number of currently logged in users.
- **Load average**: The last field shows the load average on the system during the past 1, 5, and 10 minutes. The output shows that load averages for the past 1, 5, and 10 minutes are 0.11, 0.04, and 0.01, respectively.

What do we conclude with the given values of load average? They signify the ratio of the system capacity and the tasks assigned. They indicate which of the following categories the work assigned to the system falls in:

- Higher than the capacity of the system
- Lower than the capacity of the system
- Aligned with the capacity of the system

We can correlate the capacity of the system with the number of CPUs. If the system has two CPUs and the load average at a particular time is less than two, then it is considered that the system is fairly used. Suppose the load average is consistently more than 2 for a specific period. In that case, there is an immediate need to make a proper analysis of the system to identify the root cause of the high load and the area where the problem arises. Sometimes, no tuning actions are required, and the load becomes normal automatically. Always rely on multiple executions of the **`uptime`** command. The output of the first execution may vanish until the second execution. No need to storm your head if this is a transient situation, but proper diagnosis is required if it is recurring and users are complaining about slowness.

The **`w`** command gives you the same information as the uptime command. Additionally, it provides information about the users logged in currently and their running processes. See *Figure 15.1* for a sample output of the **`w`** command:

```
[visheshkumar@vmachine ~]$ w
 11:01:35 up 5 days,  3:52,  1 user,  load average: 0.34, 0.35, 0.21
USER     TTY        LOGIN@   IDLE   JCPU   PCPU WHAT
visheshk tty2      13Jun23 24days  0.11s  0.11s /usr/libexec/gnome-session-binary
```

***Figure 15.1**: w command usage*

In *Figure 15.1*, the first line displays the same information as the **`uptime`** command. Next, it shows the list of logged in users and the processes they are running.

The output of the **`uptime`** and **`w`** commands can give you some hints to determine whether any performance problem exists currently. In the next section, we will look at various tools that help us identify problematic domains so that appropriate actions are taken in the right place to tune the system.

System monitoring tools

RHEL provides many system monitoring tools, using which you can identify performance problems, if any. In this section, you will learn the usage of various command line as well as Gnome tools that can be used to diagnose system problems. You can then move to optimizing the throughput and latency of the RHEL system.

/proc filesystem

/proc is a virtual filesystem that holds the current state of the kernel. We discussed it in *Chapter 2, Linux Filesystem and Administration*. It stores the current status of system components such as CPU, memory, and disk. It is important to revisit this directory here, as all the monitoring tools that we will discuss produce their beautiful reports by analyzing data gathered under various files available under the **/proc** directory. It contains more than 300 files, each storing some kind of system information. Following are a few files residing under the **/proc** filesystem:

- **/proc/stat:** Contains system statistics
- **/proc/uptime:** Contains system uptime
- **/proc/diskstats:** Contains disk statistics
- **/proc/self/mountstats:** Contains statistics for network filesystems
- **/proc/meminfo**: Stores current memory usage
- **/proc/partitions**: Contains information about block allocation of all the partitions
- **/proc/interrupts**: Stores CPU interrupts
- **/proc/<pid>**: Contains a directory related to each running process, which further stores the statistics related to each process in multiple files; this is what is beautifully represented with the **ps** command

An interrupt is an event that gets immediate CPU attention by blocking all the running processes. In legacy systems, network events such as packets in/out require immediate CPU allocation and generate interruptions to the CPU. But in modern systems, **Network Interface Card** (**NIC**) has a built-in packet processor, which reduces interruptions to the system CPU.

sar

This utility is provided by the **systat** package. To use the **sar** command, the **sysstat** package must be on the system. We already installed this package in *Chapter 14, Package Installation*. The **sar** command stands for **System Activity Reporter** and is a powerful tool for system administrators to monitor and analyze system activity. It collects system performance data, resource utilization and other metrics over a period of time and reports them in a user-readable format. It helps in identifying bottlenecks, troubleshooting performance issues, and optimizing resource utilization on Linux systems.

It runs as a daemon and collects data every 10 minutes from various sources, including the kernel and system monitoring tools like the **System Activity Data Collector** (SADC). These sources provide information such as CPU usage, memory usage, disk activity, and network activity. It collects the data in binary format and saves it in various files under the **/var/log/sa/** directory. By default, data is stored in files named **sa##**, where **##** represents the day of the month. When we issue the **sar** command, it reads from the current day's data file (**sa##**) by default. Upon issuing the **sar** command, you will see the output shown in *Figure 15.2*:

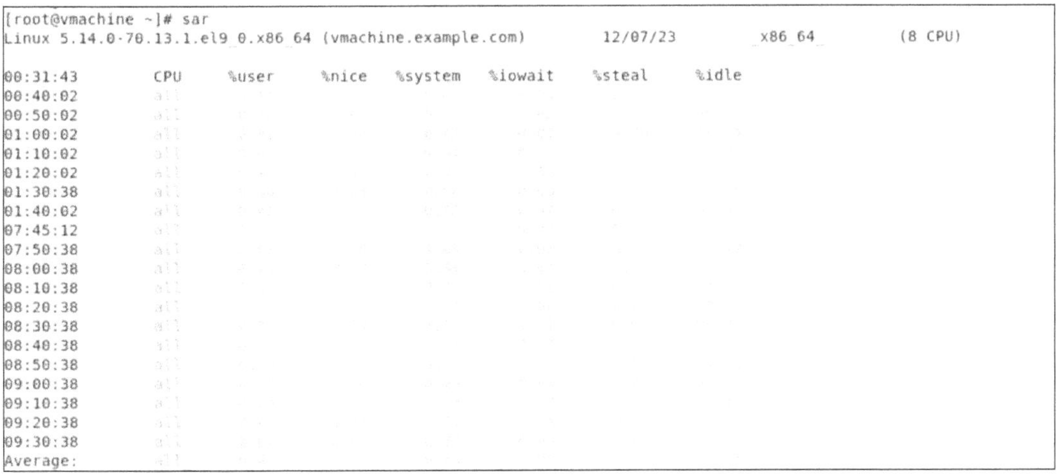

```
[root@vmachine ~]# sar
Linux 5.14.0-70.13.1.el9_0.x86_64 (vmachine.example.com)      12/07/23      _x86_64_      (8 CPU)

00:31:43        CPU     %user     %nice   %system   %iowait    %steal     %idle
00:40:02        all
00:50:02        all
01:00:02        all
01:10:02        all
01:20:02        all
01:30:38        all
01:40:02        all
07:45:12        all
07:50:38        all
08:00:38        all
08:10:38        all
08:20:38        all
08:30:38        all
08:40:38        all
08:50:38        all
09:00:38        all
09:10:38        all
09:20:38        all
09:30:38        all
Average:        all
```

Figure 15.2: *sar command shoring system-wide CPU usages for the current day*

The first line displays the system information like kernel name, kernel release, kernel version, hostname, current date, processor type, and number of CPUs on the system. It then displays the CPU statistics. By default, the **sar** command displays all the gathered data related to CPU statistics for the current day. It uses the current day's **sa** file to process its data and display it on the terminal. *Figure 15.2* displays the processed data in the following fields:

- **Timestamp:** The first field shows the time when the data is collected.
- **CPU:** This field mentions the specific CPU for which the statistics are shown. Here, **all** means the average of all CPUs is displayed.

- **%user**: This shows the percentage of CPU utilization that occurred while executing user processes.
- **%nice:** This shows the percentage of CPU utilization that occurred while executing user processes with nice priority.
- **%system:** It shows the percentage of CPU utilized at the system level.
- **%iowait:** This shows the percentage of time for which the CPUs were idle, during which the system had an outstanding disk I/O request.
- **%steal:** It shows the percentage of time the virtual CPU is waiting for hypervisor attention.
- **%idle:** This shows the percentage of time that the CPUs were idle for, and the system did not have an outstanding disk I/O request.

At last, it also displays the average of all the values displayed so far. Additionally, you can choose the time range for which statistics to display using the **-s** and **-e** options of the **sar** command. The **-s** option specifies the starting range, while **-e** specifies the ending range.

To view the current day's data starting from 13:00 to 14:00, use the following command:

```
# sar -s 13:00 -e 14:00
```

The preceding command displays the CPU statistics stored in the current day's file between the specified time.

You can also specify the data file from which you want to retrieve information. It processes the data captured in the specified files and presents it in a tabular format. To view the CPU utilization for the past day, provide the name of the last day's file using the **-f** option, as follows:

```
#sar -f /var/log/sa/sa12
```

Just suffix the last day's two-digit date after **/var/log/sa/sa**, and you will be able to retrieve the data for the desired date. You can also get the data for any day by providing numeric days, such as -1, -2, and -3. To view the last day's data, you can use the following:

```
#sar -1
```

The preceding command reads and processes the data saved in yesterday's system activity file. To view the data from 5 days ago, type the following:

```
#sar -5
```

The **sar** command also supports the **interval** and **count** parameters, where interval gathers CPU statistics at each specified interval, and count is the number of times the statistics are gathered:

```
sar <interval> <count>
```

To view the current CPU usage with the interval of 2 seconds, type the following:

```
#sar 5
```

The preceding command gathers CPU-related stats every 2 seconds, but it keeps gathering statistics for an infinite number of times. You must press the *Terminate* key to terminate the execution.

```
# sar 2 5
```

The preceding command starts collecting the data and displays it on the terminal every 2 seconds for 5 times. Data gathered this way is not saved in any file. To save the collected data on disk, specify the filename using the **-o** option, as follows:

```
# sar -o CPU_sar_2sec -u 2 5
```

Now, the data collected with the preceding command is saved in the **CPU_sar_2sec** file. To view the data collected in the non-default file, use the **-f** option of the **sar** command. The **sar** command does not only collect CPU statistics but also data related to other system activity. To report on memory utilization, you can use the **-r** option, as follows:

```
# sar -r
```

For the meaning of the fields, read man pages. To view statistics of all the system activity, use the **-A** option, as follows:

```
# sar -A|less
```

By default, the **sar** command displays the system statistics by averaging all the CPUs. To view the system statistics for the specified CPU, use the **-P** option as shown:

```
# sar -P 1
```

The preceding command displays the statistics only for processor 1 (CPUs are numbered from 0). To view the statistics details of all the CPUs individually, specify **ALL** with the **-P** option, as follows:

```
# sar -P ALL
```

Following are the other options that can be used with the **sar** command to view the specific metrics:

- **-B**: Reports paging statistics
- **-b**: Reports I/O statistics
- **-d**: Reports activity for each block device
- **--dev=<dev_list>**: Specifies the comma-separated block devices for which statistics are to be displayed
- **--fs=<fs_list>**: Specifies the comma-separated filesystems for which statistics are to be displayed

- **--iface=<iface_list>**: Specifies the comma-separated list of network interfaces for which statistics are to be displayed.
- **-S**: Reports swap space utilization statistics
- **-u**: Reports CPU utilization

You can learn more about the **sar** command using man pages.

Note: Suppose you see the following error when running the sar command: **Cannot open /var/log/sa/sa07: No such file or directory**

Please check if data collecting is enabled

Restart systat service as follows:

```
# systemctl restart systat
```

Do it yourself

- **Write the command to report the memory utilization between 13:00 to 14:00.**
- **Write the command that shows the memory utilization statistics collected 2 days ago between 8:30 am and 11:00 am.**

top

The **top** command displays a dynamic view of the running processes. By default, the processes are sorted according to the percentage of CPU usage. So, you can easily know the most CPU-intensive processes. Earlier, we used the **ps** command to view running processes and their details. The **ps** command provides a single snapshot of data, while the **top** command presents a real-time view of all the running processes and their additional information. It also displays the resource utilization by the process. It keeps refreshing itself and shows real-time data until you press the **q** key.

You can use the **top** command interactively or use command-line options. Interactive use of the **top** command is mostly liked by system administrators. So, we will discuss the interactive mode only. Typing **top** in the terminal opens the real-time view of the processes in interactive mode.

Pressing **h** in the interactive mode will take you to the help window that displays the help of interactive commands. Using interactive commands, you can sort the list or **kill** a process.

To run the **top** command, type the following at a shell prompt:

```
# top
```

It will display the real-time view, as shown in *Figure 15.3*. The first line of the **top** command provides output similar to that provided by the **uptime** command.

The second line displays the number of tasks started on the system, the number of running tasks, the number of sleeping tasks, and the number of stopped and zombie tasks.

The third line displays the overall utilization of CPU in percentage. It displays the following statistics:

- **us**: Percentage of CPU utilization that occurred while executing user processes
- **sy**: Percentage of CPU utilized at the system level
- **ni**: Percentage of CPU utilization that occurred while executing user processes with nice priority
- **id**: Percentage of time that the CPUs were idle and the system did not have an outstanding disk I/O request
- **wa**: Percentage of time CPU had waited for I/O completion
- **hi**: The time spent servicing hardware interrupts
- **si**: The time spent servicing software interrupts
- **st**: Percentage of time virtual CPU was waiting for hypervisor attention

The fourth and fifth lines are related to RAM and **swap** space utilization. Next, the **top** command displays the list of processes and information related to each listed process presented in the following fields:

- **PID**: Process ID
- **USER**: The effective username of the process owner
- **PR**: The priority
- **NI**: The nice value
- **VIRT**: The amount of virtual memory the process uses
- **RES**: The amount of non-swapped physical memory the process uses
- **SHR**: The amount of shared memory the process uses
- **S:** The process status field
- **%CPU**: The percentage of the CPU
- **%MEM**: Memory usage
- **TIME+**: The cumulated CPU time
- **COMMAND:** The name of the executable file that initiates the process

In *Figure 15.3*, note that the top CPU-consuming running process is **gnome-shell**. If you want to view the processes consuming the highest amount of memory, press **M**. To sort it

CPU-wise, press **P**. Pressing **T** will sort the list by the **TIME+** field. Pressing **P** will sort the display by PID.

```
top - 14:36:20 up 2 days, 12:45,  1 user,  load average: 0.17, 0.18, 0.10
Tasks: 288 total,   1 running, 287 sleeping,   0 stopped,   0 zombie
%Cpu(s):  1.2 us,  0.6 sy,  0.0 ni, 96.4 id,  0.0 wa,  1.4 hi,  0.5 si,  0.0 st
MiB Mem :   9512.9 total,    325.0 free,   1420.0 used,   7767.8 buff/cache
MiB Swap:   2048.0 total,   2045.0 free,      3.0 used.   7767.2 avail Mem

    PID USER      PR  NI    VIRT    RES    SHR S  %CPU  %MEM     TIME+ COMMAND
   1539 vishesh+  20   0 6178232 374084 133208 S   6.6   3.8  53:34.70 gnome-shell
   1929 vishesh+  20   0  546032  49440  34168 S   2.3   0.5  66:14.06 vmtoolsd
  22757 vishesh+  20   0  778064  61672  44540 S   2.3   0.6   0:13.00 gnome-system-mo
    915 root      20   0  530268  11376   7572 S   2.0   0.1  54:36.75 vmtoolsd
  22809 root      20   0  226032   4312   3464 R   1.0   0.0   0:00.18 top
     14 root      20   0       0      0      0 I   0.7   0.0   0:56.00 rcu_preempt
   2304 vishesh+  20   0  782076  62872  45716 S   0.7   0.6   7:03.29 gnome-terminal-
  22510 root      20   0  270860  40248   8376 S   0.3   0.4   0:00.67 sssd_kcm
      1 root      20   0  173352  17848  10556 S   0.0   0.2   0:16.66 systemd
      2 root      20   0       0      0      0 S   0.0   0.0   0:00.64 kthreadd
      3 root       0 -20       0      0      0 I   0.0   0.0   0:00.00 rcu_gp
      4 root       0 -20       0      0      0 I   0.0   0.0   0:00.01 rcu_par_gp
      6 root       0 -20       0      0      0 I   0.0   0.0   0:00.00 kworker/0:0H-kblockd
      9 root       0 -20       0      0      0 I   0.0   0.0   0:00.00 mm_percpu_wq
     10 root      20   0       0      0      0 S   0.0   0.0   0:00.00 rcu_tasks_kthre
     11 root      20   0       0      0      0 S   0.0   0.0   0:00.00 rcu_tasks_rude_
     12 root      20   0       0      0      0 S   0.0   0.0   0:00.00 rcu_tasks_trace
     13 root      20   0       0      0      0 S   0.0   0.0   0:00.73 ksoftirqd/0
     15 root      rt   0       0      0      0 S   0.0   0.0   0:05.17 migration/0
     16 root      20   0       0      0      0 S   0.0   0.0   0:00.00 cpuhp/0
     17 root      20   0       0      0      0 S   0.0   0.0   0:00.00 cpuhp/1
     18 root      rt   0       0      0      0 S   0.0   0.0   0:06.01 migration/1
     19 root      20   0       0      0      0 S   0.0   0.0   0:00.39 ksoftirqd/1
     21 root       0 -20       0      0      0 I   0.0   0.0   0:00.00 kworker/1:0H-events_highpri
     22 root      20   0       0      0      0 S   0.0   0.0   0:00.00 cpuhp/2
     23 root      rt   0       0      0      0 S   0.0   0.0   0:05.40 migration/2
     24 root      20   0       0      0      0 S   0.0   0.0   0:00.15 ksoftirqd/2
```

Figure 15.3: top command in interactive mode displaying various system statistics and running processes

free

The **free** command displays the memory utilization of the system. Type **free**, and you will get the output shown in *Figure 15.4*:

```
root-~ 23:38:44] free
               total        used        free      shared  buff/cache   available
Mem:         9741164     1321716     3225372       59092     5194076     8053372
Swap:        2097148        4180     2092968
```

Figure 15.4: free command showing memory utilization

The **free** command displays various statistics for memory utilization, physical as well as swap, in the following fields:

- **total**: The total amount of physical **memory** and **swap** in the system
- **used**: The amount of used physical **memory** and **swap** space

- `free`: The amount of **memory** and **swap** space that is free and idle
- `shared`: The amount of physical **memory** that is used by shared **cache**
- `buff/cache`: The amount of physical **memory** that is used by **buffer cache**
- `available`: The amount of available physical **memory**

The mentioned information is gathered by parsing `/proc/meminfo`.

One should not be afraid if the value given in the `free` column is close to zero. A low value in the `free` field does not indicate that the system does not have enough memory when needed.

Notice the `available` field. If it gives a high value, it means that the system has sufficient memory, which can be allocated when required. This is the part of the memory allocated to the shared cache and buffer cache, which can be immediately reclaimed on demand.

Some useful options that can be used with the `free` command are as follows:

- `-b`: Displays the information in bytes
- `-k`: Displays the amount of memory in kb; this is the default
- `-m`: Displays the amount of memory in MB
- `-g`: Displays the amount of memory in GB
- `-h`: Displays the output in human-readable format
- `-t`: Displays total at the last
- `-s`: Specifies the time interval in seconds
- `-c`: Specifies the number of times the report is printed

To print the **memory** and **swap** utilization report 5 times every 2 seconds, type the following:

```
# free -s 2 -c 5
```

vmstat

The `vmstat` tool reports the processes, virtual memory statistics, block I/O, interrupts, and CPU activity across the system. Type the `vmstat` command, and you will get output similar to *Figure 15.5*:

```
[visheshkumar@vmachine ~]$ vmstat
procs -----------memory---------- ---swap-- -----io---- -system-- ------cpu-----
 r  b   swpd   free   buff  cache   si   so    bi    bo   in   cs us sy id wa st
 1  0   4180 3218264   3824 5190592    0    0     3     3    9    1  1  1 98  0  0
```

Figure 15.5: *vmstat command showing wide range of system statistics*

The output in *Figure 15.5* displays the average statistics since system reboot. If you specify the interval in seconds, it will gather the statistics after every specified interval of seconds, as follows:

```
# vmstat 2
```

The preceding command gathers the statistics after every 2 seconds and displays the output to the terminal until it receives the interrupt signal. You can also specify the number of times the statistics are to be gathered, as follows:

```
vmstat 2 5
```

The preceding command gathers the statistics every 2 seconds, 5 times. By default, the **vmstat** command displays information in the following fields:

- `procs`
    - `r`: The number of processes ready to run (they are in run queue)
    - `b`: The number of processes blocked waiting for I/O to complete
- `memory`
    - `swpd`: Amount of swap memory used
    - `free`: Amount of unused memory
    - `buff`: Amount of memory used as buffer
    - `cache`: Amount of memory used as cache
- `swap`
    - `si`: Amount of memory swapped in from disk per second
    - `so`: Amount of memory swapped to disk per second
- `io`
    - `bi`: Amount of blocks read from a block device per second
    - `bo`: Amount of blocks written to a block device per second
- `system`
    - `in`: The number of interruptions per second, including the clock
    - `cs`: The number of context switches per second
- `CPU`
    - `us`: Percentage of total CPU time spent running user code
    - `sy`: Percentage of total CPU time spent on running system code

- o **id**: Percentage of total CPU time spent idle
- o **wa**: Percentage of total CPU time spent waiting for IO to complete
- o **st**: Percentage of total CPU time stolen from a VM

Some of the options to use with **vmstat** are listed as follows:

- **-d:** Report disk statistics
- **-D:** Report some summary statistics about disk activity
- **-p <device>**: Partition-specific statistics

The **vmstat** command can help administrators determine whether the I/O subsystem is responsible for any performance issues. If the **b** field in the **vmstat** command's output is higher than the **r** field, it is concluded that I/O subsystem is responsible for reduced performance. In this case, administrators can use the **iostat** tool to determine the I/O device creating the bottleneck.

iostat

The **iostat** command displays the I/O statistics for all devices attached to the system. The **sysstat** package provides the **iostat** utility.

Typing **iostat** in the terminal gives you the output shown in *Figure 15.6*:

```
root-~ 07:07:45] iostat
Linux 5.14.0-70.13.1.el9_0.x86_64 (vmachine.example.com)        16/07/23        _x86_64_        (8 CPU)

avg-cpu:  %user   %nice %system %iowait  %steal   %idle

Device             tps    kB_read/s    kB_wrtn/s    kB_dscd/s    kB_read    kB_wrtn    kB_dscd
dm-0
dm-1
sda
sr0
```

Figure 15.6: iostat command displaying the I/O statistics of devices

The first line of output depicts the average CPU statistics of all the CPUs since the system reboot. We have already noted the meaning of the given fields in the earlier sections. The next set of lines shows the I/O statistics of all the devices and partitions. The meaning of the I/O statistics-related fields that are displayed are as follows:

- **Device**: Lists the device (or partition) name as listed in the **/dev** directory
- **tps**: Indicates the number of transfers per second
- **kB_read/s**: Indicates the amount of data read from the device expressed in kb per second

- **kB_wrtn/s**: Indicates the amount of data written to the device expressed in kb per second
- **kB_dscd/s**: Indicates the amount of data discarded for the device expressed in kb per second
- **kB_read**: The total amount of data read, in kilobytes
- **kB_wrtn**: The total amount of data written, in kilobytes
- **kB_dscd**: The total amount of data discarded, in kilobytes

The first execution of the **iostat** command generates the I/O statistics report since the system reboot. So, one should ignore the first report when diagnosing I/O-related problems. Subsequent execution provides the statistics since the last execution.

To view the I/O statistics over a period of time, specify interval and count parameter in the command line to generate the statistics at the specified time interval and gather the statistics To view the report at the specified interval of seconds for the specified number of times, type the following:

```
# iostat 2 5
```

The preceding command line gathers I/O statistics every 2 seconds, 5 times. If no count parameter is specified, the report is generated an infinite number of times. The frequently used option by the system administrator is **-x**; it displays extended statistics. After the system administrator identifies the bottleneck in the I/O subsystem, they usually issue **iostat** using the **-x** option, as follows:

```
#iostat -x
```

The previous command shows additional columns from each displayed device/partition, as shown in *Figure 15.7*.

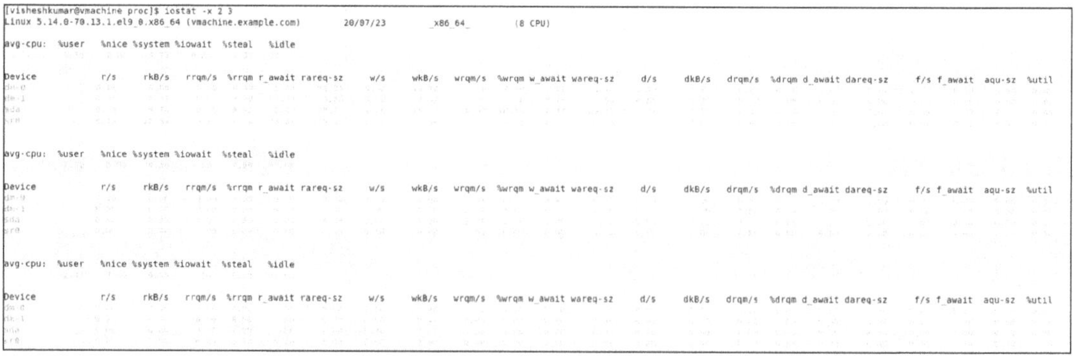

```
[visheshkumar@vmachine proc]$ iostat -x 2 3
Linux 5.14.0-70.13.1.el9_0.x86_64 (vmachine.example.com)     20/07/23     _x86_64_     (8 CPU)

avg-cpu:  %user   %nice %system %iowait  %steal   %idle

Device            r/s     rkB/s   rrqm/s  %rrqm r_await rareq-sz     w/s     wkB/s   wrqm/s  %wrqm w_await wareq-sz     d/s     dkB/s   drqm/s  %drqm d_await dareq-sz     f/s f_await  aqu-sz  %util

avg-cpu:  %user   %nice %system %iowait  %steal   %idle

Device            r/s     rkB/s   rrqm/s  %rrqm r_await rareq-sz     w/s     wkB/s   wrqm/s  %wrqm w_await wareq-sz     d/s     dkB/s   drqm/s  %drqm d_await dareq-sz     f/s f_await  aqu-sz  %util

avg-cpu:  %user   %nice %system %iowait  %steal   %idle

Device            r/s     rkB/s   rrqm/s  %rrqm r_await rareq-sz     w/s     wkB/s   wrqm/s  %wrqm w_await wareq-sz     d/s     dkB/s   drqm/s  %drqm d_await dareq-sz     f/s f_await  aqu-sz  %util
```

Figure 15.7: iostat in extended mode

You should ignore the first report given in the figure. The important field to monitor is **%util**, which reports the utilization of all the listed devices. A high value (say 96 to 100) in **%util** indicates the need for further diagnosis of that particular device.

Following are some of the other options supported by the **`iostat`** command:

- **`-d`**: Display only the device utilization report
- **`-c`**: Display only the CPU utilization report

You can focus on viewing the I/O utilization report of a particular device by providing the name of the device in the command line, as follows:

```
iostat -x sda
```

Gnome's system monitor

Gnome provides a GUI tool to monitor system resources and their utilization in a graphical representation. It displays real-time data of resource utilization like the **`top`** command. To start the system monitor tool, do either of the following:

- Type **`gnome-system-monitor`** at the terminal
- In **Activities Overview**, type **`system monitor`** and press *Enter*.

The **System Monitor** tool appears as shown in *Figure 15.8*:

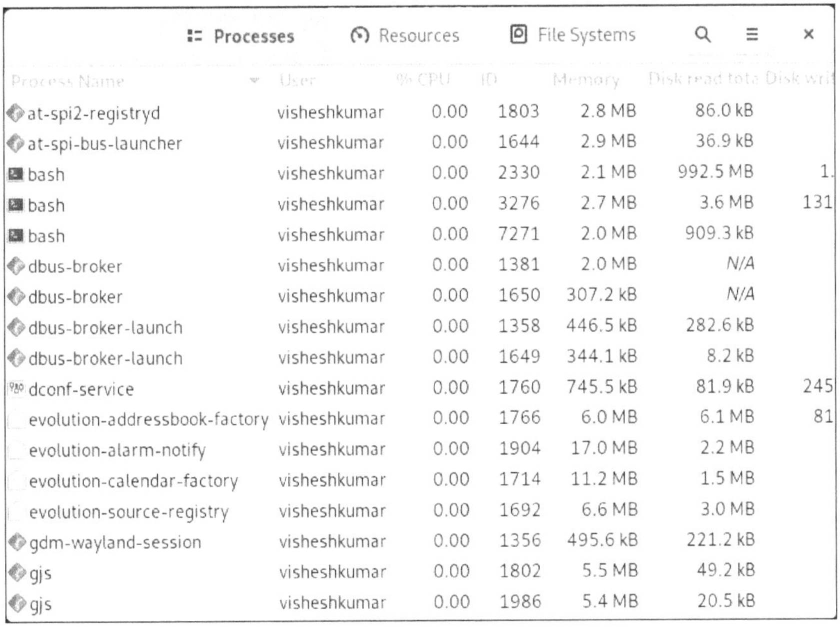

Processes | Resources | File Systems

Process Name	User	% CPU	ID	Memory	Disk read tota	Disk wri
at-spi2-registryd	visheshkumar	0.00	1803	2.8 MB	86.0 kB	
at-spi-bus-launcher	visheshkumar	0.00	1644	2.9 MB	36.9 kB	
bash	visheshkumar	0.00	2330	2.1 MB	992.5 MB	1
bash	visheshkumar	0.00	3276	2.7 MB	3.6 MB	131
bash	visheshkumar	0.00	7271	2.0 MB	909.3 kB	
dbus-broker	visheshkumar	0.00	1381	2.0 MB	N/A	
dbus-broker	visheshkumar	0.00	1650	307.2 kB	N/A	
dbus-broker-launch	visheshkumar	0.00	1358	446.5 kB	282.6 kB	
dbus-broker-launch	visheshkumar	0.00	1649	344.1 kB	8.2 kB	
dconf-service	visheshkumar	0.00	1760	745.5 kB	81.9 kB	245
evolution-addressbook-factory	visheshkumar	0.00	1766	6.0 MB	6.1 MB	81
evolution-alarm-notify	visheshkumar	0.00	1904	17.0 MB	2.2 MB	
evolution-calendar-factory	visheshkumar	0.00	1714	11.2 MB	1.5 MB	
evolution-source-registry	visheshkumar	0.00	1692	6.6 MB	3.0 MB	
gdm-wayland-session	visheshkumar	0.00	1356	495.6 kB	221.2 kB	
gjs	visheshkumar	0.00	1802	5.5 MB	49.2 kB	
gjs	visheshkumar	0.00	1986	5.4 MB	20.5 kB	

Figure 15.8: *Gnome's system monitor displaying processes' list and related information*

The **Processes** tab is displayed by default. It allows you to view the running process and additional information related to them. Right-clicking on the process name allows you to take many actions, such as changing the priority of a process, stopping, and continuing or killing the processes. By default, the **System Monitor** tool displays a list of processes that are owned by the current user. You have a view menu given at the right corner of the top bar. This menu gives you a set of options, such as the following:

- **Active Processes**: To view only active processes
- **All Processes**: To view all processes
- **My Processes**: To view only the processes belonging to the current user
- **Show Dependencies**: To also view process dependencies

The **Resources** tab shows resource utilization, as shown in *Figure 15.9*:

Figure 15.9: *Gnome's system monitor displaying CPU and memory utilization graphically*

Under the **Resources** tab, the **Memory** and **Swap History** section displays a graphical representation of the **memory** and **swap** usage history. It also shows the total amount of physical **memory** and **swap memory** on the system, and the amount of **free** and used **memory**. The **CPU History** section, under the **Resources** tab, displays a graphical representation of the CPU usage history and the current CPU utilization for all the CPUs.

The last section of the **Resources** tab contains the **Network** section, displaying network performance. The **File Systems** tab of the system monitor displays the usage of all the available devices. The **Preferences** option under the view menu is available for each tab of the **System Monitor**. It allows you to set refresh intervals for all the windows.

Using performance logs

Performance logs are a good source for performance monitoring. Many performance-related logs are stored under **`/var/log`**. Some of the important logs that may be of great help with regard to performance analysis are listed here:

```
/var/log/messages
/var/log/sa/*
/var/log/maillog
/va/log/cron
```

We read that **journald** is the default log manager in RHEL9. To view the logging information related to any **systemd** unit, just specify the name of the unit with the **journalctl -u** command. You can also use Gnome's Logs to view all the logs gathered by the **journald** at one place.

Performing root cause analysis of slow response

This section describes ways to troubleshoot a given performance problem. But there is no one-stop solution for a problem; each problem is specific and requires proper diagnosis on your part.

You are sipping coffee when you find that everything is running fine. Suddenly, the user complains about the system being slow. You start exploring the system to identify the actual problem. First of all, you may choose to check the overall system health just by issuing an **uptime** command. You find that the CPU is highly utilized. Then, you start to drill-down on this. You choose to run the **top** command to identify which processes are consuming high CPU power. If a system process consuming high CPU power is identified, you can debug it by looking at all the aspects of that process. Suppose you find that a backup job running in the background is the main culprit of the high CPU consumption. You should tackle this. As a solution, you can schedule the backup job to run at a time when there is less or no activity on the system. You can choose to run a backup job after midnight. You can also choose to increase the nicer value of this process so that it runs with less priority. If you find that all the running processes are working properly but the system is overloaded, then you can consider increasing the CPU power.

If system analysis shows high memory usage, then find the top memory consumers. If it is a user process, then you can ask the user to tune the related application. If the application does not require any tuning and everything else is running fine, then consider increasing system memory.

If the **vmstat** command shows a high value in the b field, it means that processes are blocked for disk r/w operations. A high value in the b field specifies that they are waiting for some I/O operations to be completed. Disk can be a bottleneck here. So, your next step will be to issue an **iostat** command. Run the **iostat** command in extended mode, as follows:

```
iostat -x
```

Consider running the preceding command multiple times. If **util%** is high all the time, identify which processes are responsible for high disk utilization. Try to tune or remove the identified responsible process or consider increasing disk IOPS.

If the **vmstat** command shows a high **swap in** and **swap out** (the **si** and **so** fields, respectively), then consider increasing the RAM.

Setting alerts using cron

We have seen many monitoring tools for resource consumption. Practically, it is not possible to keep executing monitoring commands all the time to get hints of the performance problem. Instead, you can place a mechanism on the system that monitors the resource utilization in the background and automatically alerts you about the resource utilization if it reaches a set threshold. We can use a system scheduler for this task. **cron** is a Linux system scheduler that allows you to run a task at regular intervals. Tasks scheduled under **cron** are known as **jobs**. A daemon named **crond** is responsible for running a scheduled job. This daemon should be running to use the **cron** service. To check the current status of this daemon, type the following:

```
# systemctl status crond.service
```

If it is not running, then start it as follows:

```
# systemctl start crond.service
```

You can provide the jobs to **crond** via commands or scripts and schedule to run each command or script at specific intervals. The file where the **cron** jobs and their schedules are specified is called **crontab**. **cron** searches for **crontab** files under the **/var/spool/cron** directory, where files named after user accounts are stored. If you have created a job using a login account named **Bob**, then the job will be entered in a file named **/var/spool/cron/bob** and owned by user **Bob**.

You can create a **cron** job to run every minute, hourly, every day, weekly, or monthly. **crond** checks **cron** entries every minute. If it finds any job scheduled for that minute and executes it. You can create monitoring and alerting scripts for your purpose and schedule them via **cron**. To create a new **cron** entry, you must use the **crontab** command as follows:

```
$ crontab -e.
```

The **crontab** command provides an interface to make **cron** job entries to the crontab file. You cannot directly write onto crontab files under the **/var/spool/cron** directory if you are not the root user.

The preceding command will open a temp file in the *vi* editor to create a new **cron** job entry. A user can specify many **cron** jobs. Each **cron** entry must start in a new line. When you save your entry using **:w** as in the **vi** editor, the **cron** job will be created and saved to the user account who initiated the **crontab**. If **Bob** starts the previous command, the file will be saved with his account name under the **/var/spool/cron** directory.

A **cron** entry has the following format:

```
* * * * * <command or script to execute>
```

It shows six fields. The first five fields having `*` determine the date and time the given command must be executed. This asterisk represents the minute, hour, day of the month, month, and day of the week, respectively. The last field accepts the command or the script to execute. To ensure that your scheduled task runs successfully, you should provide the full path of the command or script.

The first five fields must take valid integer values; allowed values are listed in *Table 15.1*:

Field name	Valid values
Minute	0-59
Hour	0-23
Day of the month	1-31
Month	1-12
Day of week	0-7 where 0 and 7 is Sunday

***Table 15.1**: cron job fields related to date and time*

An asterisk in any of the fields given in *Table 15.10* matches all the respective valid values. Each of these fields may also accept the following:

- `','`: Many integers can be provided to a single field separated by a comma. For example, 2, 4, 6 in the hour field means that the command will be executed at 2, 4, and 6 hours only.
- `'-'`: You can also specify the range. If 12-15 is mentioned in the day of the month, it means that the task will be executed on the 12th, 13th, 14th, and 15th day of the month.
- **`*/<number>`**: This is used to specify the step values. If you want to run a job every two hours, you can write **`*/2`** in the hour field.

Let us schedule a job in the **`cron`** as follows:

```
*/2 * * * * echo "hello"
```

The preceding **`cron`** job is scheduled to run every 2 minutes. This job's purpose is to print **`hello`**. This **`cron`** job does not specify where the job's output must go. The **`cron`** will not disturb the user by sending its output to the user's console every time it executes the scheduled job; the output is sent to the user's mailbox, and the user is alerted of the new mail with the following message displaying on the screen:

```
You have mail in /var/spool/mail/visheshkumar
```

Whenever a new mail arrives, you will get the preceding message on the console while you are working. Here, **`cron`** sends you a mail after it executes the scheduled job. You can use a configured email client to check your mail[1].

[1] If no email client is yet configured on your machine, follow the steps given on Chapter 18: Miscellaneous, where mutt email client is configured. Here, you will also learn to how to read and send a mail using email-client, *mutt*.

You can also send the output, if any, to a disk file, as the following **cron** job does:

```
*/5 * * * * uptime >> /tmp/uptime.out
```

The preceding **cron** job runs the **uptime** command every 5 minutes and redirects the output to the specified file. You can later review this file for performance monitoring purposes.

Suppose you have a script that is performing some cleaning task, and you want to schedule it at 2 am only on Saturday and Sunday; this is how your **cron** job will look:

```
0 2 * * 6,7 clean.sh
```

Script named **clean.sh** is scheduled to run at 2 am every Saturday and Sunday. To execute the job on 10, 15, and 30 minutes of every hour, provide a comma-separated list of minutes, as follows:

10,15,30 * * * * sar

You cannot create a **cron** job from another user. Only the root user is allowed to create a job for another user, by using the **-u** option as follows:

```
# crontab -u bob -e
```

The preceding command creates **crontab** entries under the user account **bob**.

To delete all the **cron** jobs owned by you, type the following:

```
$ crontab -r
```

To display all the **cron** jobs owned by you, type the following:

```
$ crontab -l
```

The script given in *Figure 15.10* has been created for you to understand the automation of the monitoring process. This is a very simple script capturing I/O statistics every 2 seconds. It captures the io stats five times, verifies the **util%** field, and sends a mail to the user if **util%** crosses 95 for any of the devices listed. You can now place this script and schedule to run it at specific intervals. You can modify this script to increase its functionality.

```
[visheshkumar@vmachine ~]$ cat perfio.sh
#! /bin/sh

d=`date +%d-%m-%y-%T`
filename=$d"_io.sar"

iostat -dxy 2 5|tr -s ' ' |awk -F ' ' '$23>95{print }' > `echo $filename`
if [ -s $filename ]
then
        cat $filename|mutt -s "io critical" visheshkumar@vmachine.example.com
fi
```

Figure 15.10: *Sample script to automate process monitoring*

Conclusion

Identifying bottlenecks when the system is running slow is important. Various monitoring tools are helpful in this regard. The **`uptime`** command is often used to check the system's uptime and get a quick overview of the system's load. The **`sar`** command in Linux is used to collect, report, and analyze system activity data. The **`sar`** command collects a wide range of information on system resources and presents it in user-readable format. The **`sar`** command is mostly used to view CPU usage. To view the system memory utilization, you have the **`free`** command. The **`vmstat`** command is another useful monitoring tool that details resource consumption. **`iostat`** is mainly used to view I/O statistics. Constant monitoring of the system and its performance is required so that you can perform troubleshooting proactively and preventing them from causing panic among end users.

In the next chapter, we will read about procedures to take backup on Linux filesystem and ways to troubleshoot when system failure occurs.

Join our book's Discord space

Join the book's Discord Workspace for Latest updates, Offers, Tech happenings around the world, New Release and Sessions with the Authors:

https://discord.bpbonline.com

CHAPTER 16
Backup and Troubleshooting in Linux

Introduction

Taking a backup of the system is an essential task for Linux system administrators. In case of hardware or system failure, backups are used to restore the system to recover any data loss. So, the organization must have an efficient backup plan in place so that restoration can be done with minimum downtime. A proper backup plan ensures that you always have a good backup when a failure occurs. During failure, recovery can be made up to the last good backup available. So, backup must be taken at regular intervals. Several older backups can be maintained in the system to keep historical data and ensure version control. Older backups are useful if historical data is required at any point.

In this chapter, you will learn ways to take backups in a Linux system and how to restore damaged files.

Structure

This chapter has the following structure:

- Backup needs
- Backup tools
    - `rsync`
    - `tar`

- Restoring lost files
- Troubleshooting using LogFiles
- Recovering system

Objectives

By the end of this chapter, you will be able to use various backup tools efficiently, schedule frequent backups, and restore the lost files. Logs are important for monitoring and troubleshooting purposes, so it is important to retain them as well. By going through this chapter, you will also learn about logs archival and retention. You will learn about the **`logrotate`** system service, which is responsible for rotating logs at predefined intervals. You will also learn system troubleshooting in rescue mode.

Backup needs

Regular backups of the user and system data are important for a reliable system. They are important to avoid any loss of important data from the system if any hardware or system failure occurs. System failure may occur due to corruption of data, mistaken deletion of data, hardware failure, network-related exploits, and more.

You aim to keep downtime as minimal as possible, so you must have an efficient backup and restoration process in place. You are hired to keep all the data and information of the system protected, not only from network-related exploits but from any system failures. If you cannot recover your system from any failure while keeping the mean time to recover as low as possible, then you could lose your job. The system must be configured to have a backup schedule. The system can be recovered only if you have a valid backup available so that it can be recovered up to the last backup available.

What to back up

Usually, taking backups is a time-consuming and CPU-intensive process. If the system has a large amount of data, backups will also consume a lot of space. You can create your backups in less time and make it space-saving by choosing what files to back up. You can ignore the non-important files and also avoid creating backups of the files that can be easily recreated. Here are the suggested areas of the filesystem that can be avoided in your backup plan:

- **`/tmp`**: The files under this directory are deleted during boot, so they are short-lived and do not need to be backed up.
- **`cache`**: The contents of the **`/var/cache`** or **`~/.cache`** directories can be excluded, as their content can be regenerated by applications.

- **Swap area:** Avoid backing up of swap partition, as this is used for swapping purposes only.
- **Runtime data**: Avoid backing up the `/run` or `/var/run` directories, as they are used to store runtime data.
- **System files**: Avoid backing up system files that are created during installation, as they can be recreated using installation media. This is true if no customizations have been made in system files.
- You can identify other large files that the system generated, but it is not important to back them up.

You should back up user and application data, system configuration files, web content, and other important data and related settings of the system to ensure that you can successfully make the system usable after a system crash or any data loss.

Considerations when taking backups

Keeping backups is a lifesaver, and you should consider the following points for efficiency when planning a schedule for backup:

- Regularly schedule backups to ensure that up-to-date copies of data are always available.
- You can maintain older copies of data to maintain historical data or version history.
- You must keep your backup in multiple backup locations to safeguard against hardware failures in one location.
- If the backup contains sensitive data, consider encrypting it to maintain privacy and security.
- Test your backups periodically by restoring some files and verifying that the restoration process successfully finishes restoring the data.
- Automate backup processes via script in cron.
- Backups can be scheduled daily, weekly, or twice a day or twice a week, or as per requirement. It depends on how critical the data is, how much disk space you have, the size of your data set, and more.
- You can compress the backup to save disk space. Restoration would require decompressing backup files first.

Backup types

A Linux system provides you with two types of backups to choose from:

- **Full back up**: It is the backup of the entire system. The time for completion varies according to the size of the data set. For a large data set, it consumes large disk space. You can compress your backup files after the backup is completed to conserve disk space. If we want to restore only one file, the entire backup needs to be searched for, thereby taking more time for restoration, and thus, high downtime. It will take even more space if the backup policy is to keep more than one backup.
- **Incremental backup**: It is not a complete backup. It refers to the backup of any modifications made or the files added since the last backup. Since it backs up only the modifications since the last backup, it starts with taking a full backup at first. Next, it continues with making incremental backups, that is, backing up only the changes made since the last full or incremental backup. It is faster and consume less disk space. If you have lost the entire filesystem, then restoration will first require restoring the last full backup, followed by all the incremental backups taken since then to recover as much data as possible. Thus, the process of restoring the whole filesystem is longer.

Backup tools

Linux provides a variety of options to take full or incremental backups. Earlier, we used `dd` and `scp` commands to copy data from one location to another. We have seen how `dd` command can be used to copy all the data from a disk to another location or backup disk. But the process is slow and cannot be used for large-scale backups. The `scp` can be used to transfer files from a local to a remote location or from a remote to another remote location. It can be used only for simple backups and cannot be used as a full-fledged backup tool. There are many efficient tools provided by RHEL 9.0. This book discusses the widely used tools `tar` and `rsync`.

rsync

`rsync` is used to back up data locally or remotely. It is an incremental backup tool that backs up only the changes made since the last incremental or full backup. It can copy files from:

- Local server to remote
- Remote to local server
- One place to another on a local machine

It cannot copy the files from one remote server to another.

Simply type the following for local file transfer:

```
$ rsync book/* /tmp/
```

The preceding command will transfer all files from the book folder to the **/tmp/** directory on the local machine. If any of the files already exist on the remote system, then **rsync** will update the file by sending only the differences in the data.

To copy data to a remote machine named **vmachine1**, use the following command:

```
$ rsync book/* vmachine1:/tmp/
```

This will transfer all the files from the **book** folder to the **/tmp/** directory on the remote machine named **vmachine1**. By default, **rsync** uses **ssh** for network communication.

Delta-transfer algorithm works behind the scenes and copies only the differences between the source files and existing files in the destination. Thus, **rsync** sends reduced data over the network.

If only the source is specified, files are listed in the **ls -l** format, and no file copying operation occurs. To copy all the files from the directory as well as the directory itself, use the **-r** option as follows:

```
$ rsync -r book /tmp/
```

The preceding command will copy the **book** directory recursively to **/tmp/**. To transfer multiple files from the source, specify the list of required files on the source, as follows:

```
$ rsync iostat.out io.out vmachine1:/tmp/
```

The preceding command copies files named **iostat.out** and **io.out** from the current directory to **/tmp** on the remote machine.

To transfer multiple files from the remote host to the local machine, specify the list of files as given in the following command:

```
$ rsync vmachine1:iostat.out vmachine1:io.out /tmp/
```

The preceding command will copy the **iostat.out** and **io.out** files from the current user's **home** directory on remote machine **vmachine1** to the **/tmp/** directory on the local machine. In the preceding command, the repeated hostname can be omitted to shorten the command line, as follows:

```
$ rsync vmachine1:iostat.out :io.out /tmp/
```

Besides, you can use the following options with **rsync**:

- **-a**: Archive mode; preserves file ownership, timestamp, and file attributes
- **-l**: Copies symlinks as symlinks
- **-p**: Preserves permissions
- **-t**: Preserves modification times

- **-o**: Preserves owner
- **-g**: Preserves group
- **-U:** Preserves access (use) times
- **-z:** Compresses file data during the transfer
- **--progress:** Shows progress during transfer
- **--list-only**: Lists the files instead of copying them
- **--delete:** Deletes extraneous files from the backup location
- **--exclude:** Excludes some of the specific files or folders during backup

Let us view a few more usages of the **rsync** command. Use **-v** to view verbose output as in *Figure 16.1*. If a file named **cpustat** is not available in the destination, **rsync** assumes that it is a fresh backup and initiates a full backup, printing each file name while copying:

```
[visheshkumar@vmachine ~]$ rsync -vr cpustat /tmp/
sending incremental file list
cpustat/
cpustat/19-07-23-11:32:26_io.sar
cpustat/20-07-23-11:15:36_io.sar
cpustat/20-07-23-11:21:13_io.sar
cpustat/20-07-23-11:22:21_io.sar
cpustat/20-07-23-11:25:31_io.sar
cpustat/20-07-23-11:30:00_io.sar
cpustat/20-07-23-11:48:34_io.sar

sent 10,599 bytes  received 153 bytes  21,504.00 bytes/sec
total size is 10,058  speedup is 0.94
```

Figure 16.1: *rsync command copying files recursively in verbose mode*

Now, compare the timestamps of the source and destination files. The files created at the destination will receive the current timestamp by default. If you want to preserve the timestamp among the source and destination files, use the **-t** option, which is used to preserve the modification timestamp.

Now, create a file named **abc** inside the source directory **cpustat**. Now, execute the **rsync** command given in *Figure 16.1* again. This time, only the newly added file is transferred, as other files do not have any changes made since the last backup. You will receive the output shown in *Figure 16.2*:

```
[visheshkumar@vmachine ~]$ rsync -vr cpustat /tmp/
sending incremental file list
cpustat/abc

sent 308 bytes  received 36 bytes  688.00 bytes/sec
total size is 10,058  speedup is 29.24
```

Figure 16.2: *rsync command taking incremental backup of given source directory*

To exclude some of the files from the source directory from being backed up, use the **`--exclude`** option, as shown in *Figure 16.3*:

```
[visheshkumar@vmachine ~]$ ls cpustat/
                                                                                abc
[visheshkumar@vmachine ~]$ rsync -vr --exclude={abc,19-07-23-11:32:26 io.sar} cpustat /tmp/
sending incremental file list
cpustat/
cpustat/20-07-23-11:15:36 io.sar
cpustat/20-07-23-11:21:13 io.sar
cpustat/20-07-23-11:22:21 io.sar
cpustat/20-07-23-11:25:31 io.sar
cpustat/20-07-23-11:30:00 io.sar
cpustat/20-07-23-11:48:34 io.sar

sent 8,226 bytes  received 134 bytes  16,720.00 bytes/sec
total size is 7,758  speedup is 0.93
```

Figure 16.3: *rsync command using exclude option to skip some files when performing backup*

Figure 16.3 lists the contents of our source directory and then transfers all the files excluding the specified files to the destination directory, **`/tmp`**. To take the backup of the whole system, you can specify the source path as **`/`** and exclude non-important directories from being backed up, as follows:

```
# rsync -vra --exclude ={/tmp/*,/media/*,/run/*,/var/run/*} / /backup
```

The preceding command takes a backup of the complete filesystem starting from root (**`/`**) while excluding non-important locations. The **`-a`** option in the preceding command preserves all the file attributes.

Do it yourself

Create a directory `dir1` in your home directory. Create a few files inside `dir1`, such as file1, `file2`, and `file3`. Use the chmod command to provide write permission to all the files to other users too. Note the attributes of the `dir1` directory and the containing files that you have just created using the `ls -l` command. Now, create another directory `dir2`, inside your home directory. The `dir2` directory would act as a destination for rsync. Use rsync to copy contents of the `dir1` directory to the `dir2` directory recursively, including the `dir1` directory, preserving permissions, access, and modification timestamp. Note the attributes of files and directories just copied under the `dir2` directory. Do the destination files receive the same attributes, such as permissions and timestamp.

tar

`tar` takes the backup of multiple files by archiving them. Using **`tar`**, many files are stored in a single file, known as **archives**. Traditionally, **`tar`** is used to take backups of drives or certain directories to store the generated archives onto the tape. That is why it is named **`tar` (tape archive**). But an archive can be a regular file as well, which usually takes the **`.tar`** extension. You can later use these archives to restore all the files or some of the files included in the archive. To restore the files from the archives, you must extract the archive at some location.

`tar` is also a popular choice when you need to send multiple files at the same time to the destination. You can simply collect all the required files into the tar archive and send the generated tar file to the destination machine using **scp** or other tools. Users can later use this **tar** file to extract the files from it and restore them to the desired place.

You can add more files to an already existing **tar** at any time. You can also upgrade the files included in the **tar**. Tar supports both full and incremental backups. Let us understand **tar** by creating an archive first. The usage of the **tar** command to create archives is as follows:

```
tar -cvf <archivename> source
```

Many options are used in the preceding usage syntax; let us understand each of them:

- **-c**: The **-c** option specifies that the user wants to **create** an archive of the given source files.
- **-v**: This is a verbose option used to list the files on the terminal that will be included in the archive.
- **-f < path and name of the archive file>**: The **-f** option specifies the name of the archive file to create.
- **source**: **source** is the source location or directory using which the archive is created.

Let us copy the contents of the home directory to the **/backup** location. Go to your home directory and type the following command:

```
#tar -cvf /backup/home_vishesh.tar .
```

In the preceding command, the destination archive name will be **home_vishesh.tar**, which will be created under **/backup**. Archive files usually take **.tar** as an extension. The source directory is the current directory, as a dot (**.**) is specified in the given command line.

Thus, the given command creates an archive named **home_vishesh.tar** under the **/backup** directory using all the files in the current directory. The **-v** option produces a list of all the files on the terminal that are being packed into the archive file.

Archives also store the metadata of the source directory. Directory structure and other file attributes are maintained in archives on its creation and later during restoration.

To list the files included in the archive, use the **-t** option as follows:

```
#tar -tvf home_vishesh.tar |less
```

Now, the previous command is self-explanatory. **-t** is used to list the contents of archive file, **-v** is used for verbose output, and **-f** is used to specify the name of the archive file. You can use less pager in the pipe if you have too many files included in the given archive.

You can use the **tar** file to restore the files to the source location when any loss occurs. Tar files can be transferred easily from one machine to another to create a replica of the source machine or to restore the files on another machine. You can use **scp** or any other tool to transfer the **tar** files to a remote location. The **-x** option is used to restore files from archives. Let us understand the restoration process locally. Go to the location where you want to restore the archives and execute the following command:

```
# tar -xvf /backup/home_vishesh.tar
```

In the preceding command, the **-x** option specifies extracting the files from the specified tar file and restoring them to the current directory. You can also use the **-C** option to specify the destination where you want to restore files from the **tar** archive. Use it as follows:

```
# tar -xvf somefiles.tar -C /backup/
```

It copies all the files from the archive named **somefile.tar** to **/backup/** directory. Suppose you want to restore only one of the files included in the archive file. Specify the name of the desired file as an argument when executing the restoration command, as follows:

```
# tar -xvf somefiles.tar -C /backup io.sar
```

The preceding command will restore only a single file, named **io.sar**, to the **/backup** location from the specified source **tar** file.

The size of the archive file depends on the total size of all the files it includes. For larger datasets, it may consume too much disk space. To conserve space, you can use compression-related options while creating archives. To compress the archive, you can use the **-z** option as follows:

```
# tar -cvzf home.tar.gz .
```

The preceding command uses the **-z** option, which compresses the created **tar** file using the **gzip** utility. To restore the **home.tar.gz** file which is just created, the tar file must first be decompressed using the **gunzip** utility, or you can use the **-z** option when restoring it, as follows:

```
# tar -xvzf home.tar.gz
```

The preceding command decompresses the tar file before restoring it to the current location. The **-Z** option compresses the tar file using the **compress** utility. You can also transfer files from multiple locations to a single archive as follows:

```
# tar -cvf all_files.tar . /book
```

The previous command creates the archive named **all_files.tar** using all the files from the current directory as well as the **/book** directory.

Other options that you can use with the **tar** command are listed as follows:

- **-A**: Appends the contents of the specified archive to another archive
- **--delete**: Removes the specified file from the given **tar** file
- **-r**: Adds the specified file to an already existing **tar** file
- **-u**: Appends files only if the file is newer than the copy in archive

- **-C <dir path>**: Used to specify a directory when creating archives or accessing them
- **--exclude=<pattern>:** Excludes files matching the given pattern
- **--remove-files**: Removes files after adding them to the archive

Following is one of the usages of the **tar** command:

```
# tar -A -f book.tar somefile.tar
```

The preceding command appends the contents of **somefiles.tar** to **book.tar**; it appends one **tar** file to another.

```
tar --delete backup -f home_vishess.tar
```

The preceding command removes the file named **backup** from the given **tar** file **home_vishesh.tar**. The following command adds a new file named **newfile** to an already existing **tar** file:

```
tar -r newfile -f home_vishesh.tar
```

To verify the addition of a new file, list the archival contents. The following command removes the source files after being added to the archive:

```
tar --remove-files -cvf somefile.tar io.out iostat.out
```

The preceding command creates an archive named **somefile.tar** using **io.out** and **iostat.out** from the current location. After adding them to archives, they are removed from the source location.

Restoring lost files

You could lose many important files mistakenly while working on a Linux system. File deletion using the **rm** command is permanent; you cannot undo this. If you are working in gnome and have deleted a file mistakenly, you can always restore it from trash, but deletion using **rm** cannot be undone. You will not find the files deleted using **rm** in trash. If you have a proper backup system in place, you can always restore your files immediately without much data loss. You can use any of the tools mentioned in the previous section to restore important files. If your filesystem is corrupted, you can use the **xfs_repair** utility to repair the **xfs** filesystem or the **e2fsck** utility to repair the **ext2** , **ext3** or **ext4** filesystem. These tools have already been discussed in *Chapter 2, Linux FileSystem and Administration*.

Whenever a file is deleted from the system, it is not deleted immediately from the disk. There is still a hope of recovering the lost file if the area where the file's data was stored does not get overwritten. If you act immediately, you can get your lost files back. As an immediate action, you can unmount the disk or stop all the writing on the disk and use tools like **TestDisk** for the recovery of permanently deleted files. The use of this tool is outside the scope of this book.

Troubleshooting using LogFiles

Log files play an important role for system administrators for the purpose of troubleshooting and debugging. They serve as a record of events, actions, and errors that occurred in the system. So, it is important to protect them for future analysis. In this section, we will discuss how to protect and retain the log files such that they can be read and analyzed when any troubleshooting is required.

Reading logs

In the earlier chapters, we discussed where to find log files and how to view log files. **systemd-journald** is the default log collector and log manager in RHEL 9. Let us revisit commands to view the logs that are collected in the **systemd journal**. The **journalctl** utility is used to fetch the whole logs or selected logs from the journal.

Simply typing the **journalctl** command on the terminal shows all the collected journal entries. To view the logs related to an executable file, say **/usr/sbin/sshd**, type the following:

```
journalctl /usr/sbin/sshd
```

To view the logs related to a device file, say **/dev/sda1**, type the following:

```
journalctl /dev/sda1
```

To view the logs for the current boot, use the **-b** option as follows:

```
journalctl -b
```

To view the logs from the previous boot, type the following:

```
Journalctl -b -1
```

To retrieve only the kernel messages, use the following:

```
journalctl -k
```

To view the logs related to a **systemd** unit, say **sshd.service**, use the **-u** option as follows:

```
journalctl -u sshd.service
```

To view the logs related to crond service, type the following:

```
journalctl -u crond.service
```

There are many more options that **journalctl** supports, which will be of great help for system administrators for analyzing logs. They are as follows:

- **-g <pattern>**: Show entries that match the given pattern
- **-p <level>**: Show entries with the specified priority or higher
- **--facility=<facility>**: Show entries with the specified facility

- **`-S <date>`**: Show entries not older than the specified date
- **`-U <date>`**: Show entries not newer than the specified date

You can explore more on **`journalctl`** using **`man`** pages.

Retaining and rotating log files

Logs are our life savers. Reading and analyzing available logs is the first task that is performed by system administrators when they want to know what causes the problem in the system. Log files are not only used to keep system-generated logs but can also be used by developers to store application-related information, such as what the application is doing, what causes errors in the application, and what messages it has generated. This data is important when the need arises to troubleshoot application-related issues. Since logs are constantly recoding the system and user-generated logs, they keep growing, consuming a lot of disk space. It becomes cumbersome to open and review larger log files So, it is important to switch to a new log file whenever the log file size reaches a specified threshold. Older log files can be kept in archive form at a safer location, to be retrieved when the need arises to analyze them. Each application knows the name of the log file to write to. To start writing to a new log file, older log files can be renamed or moved to a safer location, and the new file must receive the older log file's name so that the system keeps writing in that file. The system is doing all this behind the scenes for you, using a service unit known as **logrotate service**. Logrotate automatically creates a new file when it passes the specified criteria. Older logs are just rotated to create new ones. To rotate a logfile, the current log file is renamed just by adding a suffix of the current timestamp, and a new logfile having the original log file name is created.

By default, log files are rotated at a specified time interval, say daily, weekly, monthly, and so on. You can also configure logrotate to rotate the log file when they grow large or when they reach a specified size. Before delving into the configuration of logrotate, let us explore the **`/var/log`** directory, which houses important system logs. This directory also keeps rotated logs, as shown in *Figure 16.4*. You will find many log files numbered according to the time they are rotated. Type **`ls`** to view how the files inside **`/var/log`** are rotated.

```
[root@vmachine log]# ls
                   boot.log-20230727  cron-20230726                       lastlog            messages-20230709                     spooler                  vmware-network.2.log  vmware-network.log
                   boot.log-20230728  cron-20230730    hawkey.log                            messages-20230716                     spooler-20230709         vmware-network.3.log  vmware-vgauthsvc.log.0
boot.log           btmp                                hawkey.log-20230709  maillog          messages-20230726  secure             spooler-20230716         vmware-network.4.log  vmware-vmsvc-root.log
boot.log-20230505  btmp-20230701      dnf.librepo.log  hawkey.log-20230716  maillog-20230709 messages-20230730  secure-20230709    spooler-20230726         vmware-network.5.log  vmware-vmtoolsd-root.log
boot.log-20230526                     dnf.log          hawkey.log-20230726  maillog-20230716                    secure-20230716    spooler-20230730         vmware-network.6.log  wtmp
boot.log-20230601  cron               dnf.log.1        hawkey.log-20230730  maillog-20230726                    secure-20230726                             vmware-network.7.log
boot.log-20230613  cron-20230709      dnf.rpm.log                           maillog-20230730 README             secure-20230730    tallylog                 vmware-network.8.log
boot.log-20230614  cron-20230716      firewalld        kdump.log            messages                                               vmware-network.1.log     vmware-network.9.log
```

***Figure 16.4**: Contents of /var/log directory*

Let us understand the rotation of **`/var/log/messages`**, which stores important system messages. When they are rotated, the older file is renamed using an added suffix in a specific format, **`YYYYmmdd`**. They are renamed, suffixing the date of rotation. You can easily guess which file may be appropriate for analysis purposes. If you want to view the system messages generated after July 9, 2023, then the file named **`messages-20230716`** is for you, as shown in the *Figure 16.4*. We can see that for some of the log files (including **`/var/log/`**

messages), only 4 older log files are kept. The number of log files to keep, the rotation schedule, rotation criteria, and more depend on the configuration of the logrotate. In the next section, we will understand how the logrotate works, where it is configured, how you can modify the settings related to various log files, and so on.

Understanding logrotate

logrotate is designed to ease the administration of logs. It allows automatic rotation, compression, removal, and archival of log files. They are archived so that they can be referred to later in case analysis is required.

The main configuration file for **logrotate** is **/etc/logrotate.conf**. Settings in this file determine the global settings that are applied to all the log files. To override the settings for any log file, place the related config file inside the **/etc/logrotae.d** directory. This directory is used to house application-specific log configuration files. Settings in application-specific configuration files override the same settings made in the main configuration file.

Note the contents of **/etc/logrotate.conf** by issuing the following command:

```
#grep -v '^$' logrotate.conf
# see "man logrotate" for details
# global options do not affect preceding include directives
# rotate log files weekly
weekly
# keep 4 weeks worth of backlogs
rotate 4
# create new (empty) log files after rotating old ones
create
# use date as a suffix of the rotated file
dateext
# uncomment this if you want your log files compressed
#compress
# packages drop log rotation information into this directory
include /etc/logrotate.d
# system-specific logs may be also be configured here.
```

Before understanding the meaning of each of the directives given in this file, let us review what is inside **/etc/logrotate.d**:

```
#ls /etc/logrotate.d
bootlog btmp chrony dnf firewalld iscsiuiolog kvm_stat psacct rsyslog samba
sssd subscription-manager wpa_supplicant wtmp
```

Each file in this directory stores the settings related to one or more logfiles. To read the content of the entire directory, you can use the following:

```
#cat *|less
```

The preceding command will make easier to find the lines about specific application-related files you are most interested in. Let us review the contents of config files named **rsyslog** and **bootlog** from the **/etc/logrotate.d** directory:

```
# cat rsyslog bootlog
/var/log/cron
/var/log/maillog
/var/log/messages
/var/log/secure
/var/log/spooler
{
  missingok
  sharedscripts
  postrotate
    /usr/bin/systemctl kill -s HUP rsyslog.service >/dev/null 2>&1 || true
  endscript
}
/var/log/boot.log
{
  missingok
  daily
  copytruncate
  rotate 7
  notifempty
}
```

The **/etc/logrotate.d/rsyslog** file stores the configuration settings for the **/var/log/cron**, **/var/log/maillog**, **/var/log/messages**, **/var/log/secure**, and **/var/log/spooler** log files as listed under a set of curly braces in the preceding output. The contents of **/etc/logrotate.d/bootlog** apply to the **/var/log/boot.log** file. Now, it is time to understand the meaning of important directives given in these configuration files:

- **hourly**: It is specified to rotate log file every hour.
- **daily**: It us specified to rotate log files every day; in the preceding output, */var/log/boot.log* is configured to rotate on daily basis.

- **`weekly [weekday]`:** It is specified to rotate log file once each weekday. **`<weekday>`** may accept 0 to 7. 0 means Sunday, 1 means Monday, ..., 6 means Saturday; 7 means each 7 days. It defaults to 0 if the weekday argument is not specified. In the preceding output, **`/etc/logrotate.conf`** is configured to rotate the log weekly, that is, every Sunday.
- **`monthly`:** Log files are rotated once on the first day of every month.
- **`yearly`**: Log files are rotated if the current year is not the same as the year of the last rotation.
- **`size <size>`**: Log files are rotated only if they grow bigger than the specified size bytes. This option is mutually exclusive to the time interval options.
- **`rotate <count>`:** It specifies how many rotated files to keep. If the count is 0, old versions are removed rather than rotated. **`/etc/logrotate.conf`** is configured to keep 4 rotated logs. For **`/var/log/boot.log`**, the rotate count is set to 7.
- **`create`:** It is specified to create **a** new log file immediately after rotation. The log file is created with the same name as the log file just rotated. This operation is performed just before the postrotate script is run.
- **`dateext`**: Old versions of log files are archived by renaming them using a date suffix in the format YYYYMMDD. The suffixed date is the date of rotation.
- **`compress`:** Logs are compressed after they are rotated. By default, this option is set to off in the main configuration file. You can uncomment this line if you want to enable compression globally. Log files are compressed with the gzip utility by default.
- **`include logrotate.d`**: The included directory contains the additional configuration for log files.
- **`postrotate`:** It specifies the commands to be executed after rotating each log file.
- **`endscript`**: It specifies the end of the command set to be executed as written under the **`postrotate-endscript`** section.
- **`sharedscripts`:** When multiple files are configured as in **`/etc/logrotate.d/rsyslog`**, the **`sharedscripts`** option prevents postscript from running for each rotated log. postrotate script will only be run once after all the configured logs in that block have been rotated and compressed (if set to on), not once for each log that is rotated.
- **`copytuncate`**: It creates a copy of the old log and then truncates the original log file to zero size in place. In the preceding output, we can see that this setting applies to **`/var/log/boot.log`**. This option is used with programs that cannot be made aware of new log files and keep writing to the previous log file forever.
- **`missingok`:** If the log file is missing, no error message is issued.
- **`nomissingok`:** If a log file does not exist, issue an error; this is the default.

- **ifempty:** Rotate the log file even if it is empty; this is the default.
- **notifempty:** Do not rotate the log if it is empty.

logrotate as a systemd service

logrotate runs as a systemd service called **logrotate.service**. To know **logrotate** as a **systemd** service, let us view its unit file, which resides under **/usr/lib/systemd/system**, as given in *Figure 16.5*. To view the contents of the unit file, you can either execute the **systemctl cat** command or directly view the contents of the unit file by issuing the **cat** command on it. View the **[Service]** section in the given figure. The **[Service]** section holds the information about the service, its type, binary, and so on. **logrotate** service is of the **oneshot** type, as the **Type** parameter suggests. The oneshot service type is a service that starts to take certain actions and exits immediately after performing its tasks. No processes are left running for this service. All the dependent processes start after the **oneshot** service finishes its execution. The related binary is **/usr/sbin/logrotate**, which runs using the **/etc/logrotate.conf** file. There is no **[Install]** section in this file, meaning this unit cannot be enabled or disabled. This unit is a static unit, meaning it cannot be controlled by the user and is controlled via other means. The **systemctl start** or **stop** command does not apply on static unit.

```
[root@vmachine ~]# systemctl cat logrotate.service

[Unit]
Description=Rotate log files
Documentation=man:logrotate(8) man:logrotate.conf(5)
RequiresMountsFor=/var/log
ConditionACPower=true

[Service]
Type=oneshot
ExecStart=/usr/sbin/logrotate /etc/logrotate.conf

# performance options
Nice=19
IOSchedulingClass=best-effort
IOSchedulingPriority=7

# hardening options
#  details: https://www.freedesktop.org/software/systemd/man/systemd.exec.html
#  no ProtectHome for userdir logs
#  no PrivateNetwork for mail deliviery
#  no NoNewPrivileges for third party rotate scripts
#  no RestrictSUIDSGID for creating setgid directories
LockPersonality=true
MemoryDenyWriteExecute=true
PrivateDevices=true
PrivateTmp=true
ProtectClock=true
ProtectControlGroups=true
ProtectHostname=true
ProtectKernelLogs=true
ProtectKernelModules=true
ProtectKernelTunables=true
ProtectSystem=full
RestrictNamespaces=true
RestrictRealtime=true
```

Figure 16.5: *Contents of systemd unit file:logrotate.service*

Now, the question that arises is, 'What triggers **logrotate** to start and perform its job?' By default, **logrotate** runs daily through a **systemd timer: logrotate.timer**. In *Chapter 15, Performance Monitoring and Tuning,* we used **cron**, which has been the default job scheduler in earlier versions of **RHEL**. Systemd itself provides a cron-like feature using its timer unit. Since the systemd has become the default system manager, **cron.service** is itself managed under systemd domain. In the earlier version, **logrotate** was installed as a service, but in the systemd version, logrotate runs as a systemd service and is scheduled by a **systemd** timer named **logrotate.timer**. A timer is a systemd unit that is responsible for executing a specific service at a fixed time interval. Here, **logrotate.timer** triggers **logrotate.service** at the fixed time interval.

Let us list unit files matching the pattern **logrotate**:

```
[root@vmachine ~]# systemctl list-unit-files logrotate*
UNIT FILE      STATE   VENDOR PRESET
logrotate.service static -
logrotate.timer  enabled enabled

2 unit files listed.
```

The preceding output shows two-unit files matching **logrotate**: **logrotate.service** and **logrotate.timer**. You can see that **logrotate.service** is a static unit, as it is a dependency of **logrotate.timer** and is controlled by it.

Let us list units matching **logrotate**:

```
# systemctl list-units --all|grep logrotate
 logrotate.service
loaded  inactive dead   Rotate log files
 logrotate.timer
                                            l      oaded  active  waiting
Daily rotation of log files
```

The previous output shows that **logrotate.timer** is active and is in waiting state, while **logrotate.service** is listed as inactive and dead. It is not running all the time, as **logrotate.service** runs only when **logrotate.timer** triggers it at its scheduled time. Since **logrotate.service** is of **oneshot** type, it becomes inactive after doing its job.

Now, it is time to understand a timer unit file. Each timer unit file has a unit specific **[Timer]** section, along with generic **[Unit]** and **[Install]** sections, as shown in *Figure 16.6*. The important directive in the **[Timer]** section is **OnCalender**. It specifies when to start this timer. In *Figure 16.6*, it is set to **Daily**. **logrotate.timer** runs daily with the elapse of 1 hour, as specified in **Accuracysec**. By default, the timer activates a service by the same name as the timer. Here, **logrotate.timer** activates **logrotate.service** daily, as specified in *Figure 16.6*. Since the prefix is common for timer and service unit, it is not specified in this unit file. If you want to specify a non-default service unit, use the **UNIT** option under the **[Timer]** section. Thus, **logrotate** runs daily by **logotate.timer**. The timer unit file also includes the **[Install]** section, unlike the respective service unit. **WantedBy** parameter allows creating **.wants** directory named **timers.target.wants** under **/etc/systemd/system** .

```
[root@vmachine ~]# systemctl cat logrotate.timer

[Unit]
Description=Daily rotation of log files
Documentation=man:logrotate(8) man:logrotate.conf(5)

[Timer]
OnCalendar=daily
AccuracySec=1h
Persistent=true

[Install]
WantedBy=timers.target
```

Figure 16.6: Contents of the logrotate.timer unit file

Let us issue the **systemctl status** command to view the status of **logrotate.timer** and **logrotate.service** unit. You will get the output shown in *Figure 16.7*:

```
[root@vmachine log]# systemctl status logrotate.service
○ logrotate.service - Rotate log files
     Loaded: loaded (/usr/lib/systemd/system/logrotate.service; static)
     Active: inactive (dead) since Mon 2023-07-31 15:16:00 IST; 6h ago
TriggeredBy: ● logrotate.timer
       Docs: man:logrotate(8)
             man:logrotate.conf(5)
    Process: 31228 ExecStart=/usr/sbin/logrotate /etc/logrotate.conf (code=exited, status=0/SUCCESS)
   Main PID: 31228 (code=exited, status=0/SUCCESS)
        CPU: 1.537s

Jul 31 15:15:58 vmachine.example.com systemd[1]: Starting Rotate log files...
Jul 31 15:16:00 vmachine.example.com systemd[1]: logrotate.service: Deactivated successfully.
Jul 31 15:16:00 vmachine.example.com systemd[1]: Finished Rotate log files.
Jul 31 15:16:00 vmachine.example.com systemd[1]: logrotate.service: Consumed 1.537s CPU time.
[root@vmachine log]# systemctl status logrotate.timer
● logrotate.timer - Daily rotation of log files
     Loaded: loaded (/usr/lib/systemd/system/logrotate.timer; enabled; vendor preset: enabled)
     Active: active (waiting) since Thu 2023-07-27 17:45:46 IST; 4 days ago
      Until: Thu 2023-07-27 17:45:46 IST; 4 days ago
    Trigger: Tue 2023-08-01 00:00:00 IST; 2h 35min left
   Triggers: ● logrotate.service
       Docs: man:logrotate(8)
             man:logrotate.conf(5)

Jul 27 17:45:46 vmachine.example.com systemd[1]: Started Daily rotation of log files.
```

Figure 16.7: Status of logrotate.service and logrotate.timer units

In *Figure 16.7*, the current state of **logrotate.service** is shown as inactive or dead. *Figure 16.7* also displays the time it was last activated. It last ran 6 hours ago. **logrotate.service** will be displayed as inactive from a specified time. The output also shows that it is a static unit. **logrotate.timer** is active and in waiting mode. *Figure 16.7* shows that it last ran 4 days ago. It also displays the time when it will trigger next and what service it will trigger.

Recovering system

This section lists the procedure that you can follow when your system does not boot. The following steps need to be performed with expert guidance.

If the system refuses to boot to the specified target, it requires troubleshooting. You can start by booting the system in a single user environment. You can boot to rescue mode, which provides a single-user environment for troubleshooting. In the rescue mode, the system attempts to mount all local filesystems and start certain important system services, but it does not activate network interfaces.

To enter the rescue mode, change the current target by issuing the following:

```
# systemctl rescue
```

or

```
# systemctl isolate rescue.target
```

You will see the console, as displayed in *Figure 16.8*. Enter the password for the root user when it prompts. To switch to your default target, say **graphical.target**, type the following:

```
systemctl isolate graphical.target
```

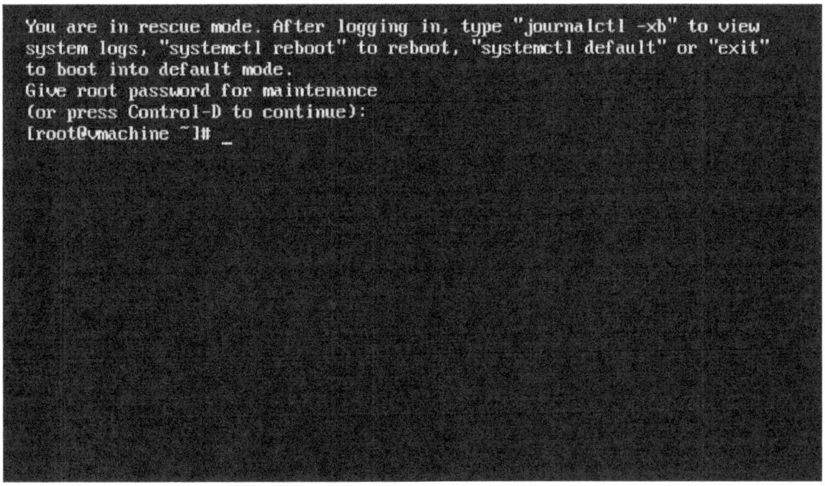

```
You are in rescue mode. After logging in, type "journalctl -xb" to view
system logs, "systemctl reboot" to reboot, "systemctl default" or "exit"
to boot into default mode.
Give root password for maintenance
(or press Control-D to continue):
[root@vmachine ~]# _
```

***Figure 16.8**: Booting into rescue mode*

If your system is unable to enter the rescue mode, you can boot to *emergency mode*, which provides a minimal environment. In emergency mode, the system mounts the root file system in read-only mode. It does not attempt to mount any other local file systems and only starts essential services.

As a system administrator, you can select a non-default target when booting to troubleshoot the boot process. Changing the target at boot time affects only a single boot. You can boot to *emergency mode*, which provides the most minimal environment possible. Follow the given steps to enter emergency mode:

1. Reboot the system and interrupt the boot loader menu countdown by pressing any key except the *Enter* key.
2. Move the cursor to the kernel entry that you want to start.
3. Press the **E** key to edit the current entry.
4. Move to the end of the line that starts with **linux** and press *Ctrl* + *E* to jump to the end of the line.
5. To choose an alternate boot target, append the **systemd.unit=** parameter to the end of the line that starts with **linux**, as follows:

   ```
   linux ($root)/vmlinuz-5.14.0-70.22.1.el9_0.x86_64 root=/dev/mapper/rhel-root ro crash\
   kernel=auto resume=/dev/mapper/rhel-swap rd.lvm.lv/swap rhgb quiet systemd.unit=<name>.target
   ```

6. Press *Ctrl* + *X* to boot with these settings.

When you are finished with your troubleshooting, try to reboot the machine.

Conclusion

Data loss can occur any time, and having a reliable backup strategy is crucial to safeguard your important files and information. Linux offers various efficient tools to take usable system backups. It supports tools for full and incremental backups.

rsync and tar utilities are popular backup tools these days. **rsync** takes a system backup by transferring files from one location to another. It can take a backup locally or remotely. Backups made with **rsync** can be used to restore lost files anytime. Tar utility packs multiple files into a tape archive, and they can then be transferred to a safer location. To restore files from a **tar** archive, you must first extract the required files from it. tar is a good tool when you want to transfer multiple files at a time to a remote location.

Log provides valuable information to system administrators and developers. It contains events on the system, informational messages and errors generated by the application, service-related messages, kernel messages, boot time messages, and more. It also logs successful and unsuccessful login attempts on the system. Logs are reviewed later, when the administrator needs to find the cause of the system error and when developers need to know what causes the application to generate errors. It is important to protect and retain logs in a safe place so that they can be accessed and read when analysis is required. **RHEL9** provides a **`logrotate systemd`** service that automatically rotates the log files at a specified time and then opens a new log file to write. **`logrotate`** service is triggered and controlled by the **`systemd`** timer unit: **`logrotate.timer`**. **`logrotate.timer`** triggers **`logrotate.service`** daily.

In the next chapter, we shall understand the creation and configuration of the web server and DB server, and learn how to create systemd service units.

References

https://access.redhat.com/documentation/en-us/red_hat_enterprise_linux/9/html/configuring_basic_system_settings/working-with-systemd-targets_configuring-basic-system-settings#troubleshooting-the-boot-process_configuring-basic-system-settings

Join our book's Discord space

Join the book's Discord Workspace for Latest updates, Offers, Tech happenings around the world, New Release and Sessions with the Authors:

https://discord.bpbonline.com

CHAPTER 17
Web Server and Database Server Setup in Linux

Introduction

When you use a web browser to access a website, you are accessing a web server located somewhere over the internet. The web server hosts web content to be delivered to the public online. Web contents are delivered to the clients via HTTP.

This chapter deals with one of the most widely used web servers: Apache HTTP server. **Apache HTTP server** is also known as **`httpd`**. This chapter covers the basic introduction of working with Apache web server and provides enough details to perform HTTP server installation, ensure its basic configuration, create a test website, and so on for web hosting.

Some web applications may also read/store some of the data from/to the database. The database management system is used to manage databases efficiently. MySQL, MariaDB, PostgreSQL, and Redis are some of the database management systems provided by RHEL9. This chapter discusses MySQL server installation and its configuration in RHEL9.0.

Structure

This chapter has the following structure:

- Defining a web server
- Apache HTTP server

- Understanding HTTPD log
- Name-based virtual host
- Securing HTTP communication
- Database server

Objectives

By the end of this chapter, you will be able to install the **httpd** server for web hosting purposes and configure the **httpd** server for multiple websites. You will also learn to manage the **httpd** server. You will be able to use the logging mechanism provided by the Apache web server efficiently.

This chapter lets you understand **httpd** access logs in detail so that you can efficiently identify unauthorized access requests made to the server. You will be able to successfully secure HTTP communication to the web server by using the SSL module. You will be able to install one of the database servers, the MySQL server, in Linux and perform basic MySQL configuration. You will also be able to harden the basic MySQL security and will also learn to execute basic SQL statements.

Defining a web server

A web server provides the foundation for delivering web content over the internet. Web content may be simple files, HTML or dynamic content, and other web pages. The web server accepts and processes incoming client requests and responds to them by sending the appropriate web pages. Thus, it works on a simple client-server model. Web clients are typically the web browser you usually use to access and read the contents of a website. Modern web servers can handle various tasks beyond serving static and dynamic content. They can manage user authentication, security protocols, load balancing, caching, SSL encryption, and more.

A web browser sends a request to the web server to access a resource using the URL in the following format:

```
protocol://<host address>/<filepath>
```

The previous URL format accepts the protocol used for the communication that needs to take place between the web client and the web server. The protocol and the host address are separated by `://`.

A host address is the fully qualified name of the web host serving the web content. If the file path is not specified, the default index page, known as the home page, will be delivered to the web client. If you want to fetch the web content from other locations, you can specify the file path. If the requested resource is static, the server retrieves the file from its storage and sends it directly to the client. If the resource is dynamic, the server generates the necessary content based on the request.

Let us take an example:

```
http://vmachine.example.com
```

The preceding URL is the one used to fetch the web page hosted on a machine named **vmachine.example.com**. It uses the HTTP protocol to fetch the web pages hosted on this machine. Since no file path is specified after the hostname, the default index page related to this website will be delivered to the client.

On receiving a request, the web server packages the response into an HTTP response before sending it back to the client. It also sends a status code that determines whether the request is successful and, if not, what kind of error condition exists.

Apache HTTP server, Nginx, and Microsoft IIS are some of the standard web server software. Apache HTTP server is the most popular among them as it provides many facilities like logging, security, authentication, and so on.

The next section discusses the Apache HTTP server.

Apache HTTP server

Apache HTTP server is a collaborative project supported by Apache Software Foundation. **Apache HTTP server is also known as httpd.** It is an open-source and cross-platform web server software used to host websites and serve web content to internet users. It is a widely popular web server as it can work among multiple platforms. The functionality provided by the Apache web server can be enhanced just by the addition of a module. This section discusses the installation of the **httpd** server and its configuration.

Installing httpd

RHEL 9.0 includes Apache HTTP Server, **httpd**. You can install it using the repository that we created earlier. Execute the following command to install **httpd**:

```
dnf install httpd
```

As we know, it will automatically resolve package dependencies and install **httpd** along with all the uninstalled dependencies, as shown in *Figure 17.1*:

```
[root@vmachine ~]# dnf install httpd
Updating Subscription Management repositories.
Last metadata expiration check: 7:06:54 ago on Thu 10 Aug 2023 00:33:10 IST.
Dependencies resolved.
================================================================================
 Package               Architecture   Version              Repository     Size
================================================================================
Installing:
 httpd                 x86_64         2.4.51-7.el9_0       appstreamiso   1.5 M
Installing dependencies:
 apr                   x86_64         1.7.0-11.el9         appstreamiso   127 k
 apr-util              x86_64         1.6.1-20.el9         appstreamiso    98 k
 apr-util-bdb          x86_64         1.6.1-20.el9         appstreamiso    15 k
 httpd-filesystem      noarch         2.4.51-7.el9_0       appstreamiso    17 k
 httpd-tools           x86_64         2.4.51-7.el9_0       appstreamiso    88 k
 redhat-logos-httpd    noarch         90.4-1.el9           appstreamiso    18 k
Installing weak dependencies:
 apr-util-openssl      x86_64         1.6.1-20.el9         appstreamiso    17 k
 mod_http2             x86_64         1.15.19-2.el9        appstreamiso   153 k
 mod_lua               x86_64         2.4.51-7.el9_0       appstreamiso    63 k

Transaction Summary
================================================================================
Install  10 Packages

Total size: 2.1 M
Installed size: 5.9 M
Is this ok [y/N]: y
```

***Figure 17.1**: dnf utility installing httpd*

Figure 17.1 shows that HTTP version 2.4.51 will be installed. After listing all the dependent packages, it will display the total size as well as the installed size that this installation will take. Pressing **`y`** when it prompts for confirmation will install the **`Apache httpd server`**.

To verify the installed **`httpd`** version, use the following command:

```
# httpd -v
Server version: Apache/2.4.51 (Red Hat Enterprise Linux)
Server built: Mar 21 2022 00:00:00
```

Configuring Apache

Apache HTTP Server (**`httpd`**) is configured by the sets of configuration files. You must edit the configuration files to change **`httpd's`** behavior, security settings, and more. The **`httpd`** server is configured using the following configuration files:

- **`/etc/httpd/conf/httpd.conf`**: This is the main configuration file and is used to configure global settings.
- **`/etc/httpd/conf.d/`**: After the main configuration file is read, all the files residing in this directory that ends with **`.con`***f* are read.
- **`/etc/httpd/conf.modules.d/`**: This auxiliary directory loads installed dynamic modules packaged in RedHat Enterprise Linux. By default, these configuration files are processed first.

Some of the important directives used in the main configuration files are mentioned as follows:

- **`ServerRoot:`** It specifies the server's root directory where the server hosts its configuration files and other important files, such as log files and more. This directory is used as a starting point for finding other configuration files, modules, log files, and other resources. By default, it is set to the following:

  ```
  ServerRoot "/etc/httpd"
  ```

- **Listen:** It binds the IP address and port to be used by the **httpd** server. By default, it is set to **Listen 80**, meaning that the **httpd** server listens on port **80** for incoming web requests for configured IPv4 or IPv6 addresses.
- **User:** It indicates the owner of **httpd** process.
- **Group:** It mentions the group owner of **httpd** process.
- **ServerAdmin:** It specifies the email address where problems with the server should be e-mailed.
- **ServerName** This directive is used to provide the name and the port that the server uses to identify itself. This is automatically set using the hostname of the server. If your server name is **vmachine.example.com**, it is set as follows:

  ```
  ServerName vmachine.example.com:80
  ```
- **DocumentRoot**: It specifies the directory from where this server serves the web documents. By default, this directive is set to **/var/www/html**, as follows:

  ```
  DocumentRoot "/var/www/html"
  ```
- **IncludeOptional** specifies other configuration files to load. The path given is relative to the current setting of **ServerRoot**. By default, it is set to the following:

  ```
  IncludeOptional conf.d/*.conf
  ```
- **ErrorLog**: It specifies the location where Apache **httpd** will record diagnostic information and errors that it encounters while processing requests. By default, it is set to the following:

  ```
  ErrorLog "logs/error_log"
  ```

  The given path is relative to the path set in the **ServerRoot** directive. Thus, by default, error logs are found under the **/etc/httpd/logs** directory.
- **CustomLog**: It specifies the path where the server access log is located. The server access log records all the requests processed by the server. By default, it is set to the following:

  ```
  CustomLog "logs/access_log" combined
  ```

  The given path is relative to the **ServerRoot** directory. So, the default path of the access log is **/etc/httpd/logs/access_log**. The last word of the directive, 'combined,' is just the nickname given to the log format that will be used to store logs in **httpd** access logs.
- **LogFormat**: It defines the format of log information stored in custom logs. The log format specifies what fields will be stored for each incoming log. By default, it is set to the following:

  ```
  LogFormat "%h %l %u %t \"%r\" %>s %b \"%{Referer}i\" \"%{User-Agent}
  i\"" combined
  LogFormat "%h %l %u %t \"%r\" %>s %b" common
  ```

The preceding two entries provide two types of log formats under the nicknames *combined* and *common*, the difference being that *combined* includes two extra fields: Referer information and User-agent. The **CustomLog** directive mentioned is a combined log format by default.

- **LogLevel**: This directive controls what level of logging messages will be logged in the error log. By default, it is set to the following:

  ```
  LogLevel warn
  ```

  After making changes in the configuration files, use the following command to check for possible errors:

  ```
  # apachectl configtest
  Syntax OK
  ```

After modifying the configuration files, you will need to restart or reload the Apache service for the changes to take effect. The next section discusses starting and stopping the **httpd** server and running your first web page.

Managing httpd server

After configuring the Apache HTTP server according to your needs, it is time to start the service. Use the following command to start the **httpd** server:

```
# systemctl start httpd
```

The **httpd** server is started now but is not enabled to start during boot. Execute the following command to start as well as enable it during boot:

```
# systemctl enable --now httpd
Created symlink /etc/systemd/system/multi-user.target.wants/httpd.service →
/usr/lib/systemd/system/httpd.service.
```

To stop **httpd** service, type the following:

```
# systemctl stop httpd
```

To restart running the **httpd** server, type the following:

```
systemctl restart httpd
```

To view the current status of the **httpd** service, you can use the following command:

```
systemctl status httpd
```

It will show you the output shown in *Figure 17.2*:

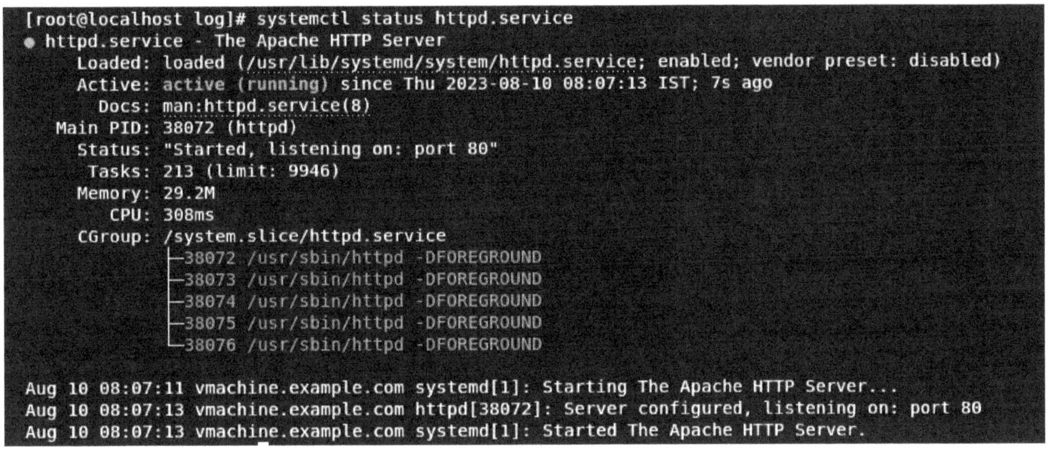

```
[root@localhost log]# systemctl status httpd.service
● httpd.service - The Apache HTTP Server
     Loaded: loaded (/usr/lib/systemd/system/httpd.service; enabled; vendor preset: disabled)
     Active: active (running) since Thu 2023-08-10 08:07:13 IST; 7s ago
       Docs: man:httpd.service(8)
   Main PID: 38072 (httpd)
     Status: "Started, listening on: port 80"
      Tasks: 213 (limit: 9946)
     Memory: 29.2M
        CPU: 308ms
     CGroup: /system.slice/httpd.service
             ├─38072 /usr/sbin/httpd -DFOREGROUND
             ├─38073 /usr/sbin/httpd -DFOREGROUND
             ├─38074 /usr/sbin/httpd -DFOREGROUND
             ├─38075 /usr/sbin/httpd -DFOREGROUND
             └─38076 /usr/sbin/httpd -DFOREGROUND

Aug 10 08:07:11 vmachine.example.com systemd[1]: Starting The Apache HTTP Server...
Aug 10 08:07:13 vmachine.example.com httpd[38072]: Server configured, listening on: port 80
Aug 10 08:07:13 vmachine.example.com systemd[1]: Started The Apache HTTP Server.
```

Figure 17.2: *httpd as a systemd service*

You can check whether **httpd** is running using port **80** by issuing the following command:

```
# ss -ntlp|grep http
```

```
LISTEN 0   511                   *:80                 *:*    users:(("http-
d",pid=38076,fd=4),("httpd",pid=38075,fd=4),("httpd",pid=38074,f-
d=4),("httpd",pid=38072,fd=4))
```

You can also verify whether the web server is running on port **80** by typing the following URL in your browser:

`http://<server host name or IP address>/`

For example, if you are a local machine, you can type the following:

`http://localhost`

If the server name is **vmachine.example.com**, you can type the following URL in your browser:

`http://vmachine.example.com`

If you get the RedHat Test Page as in *Figure 17.3*, it means that the Apache web server is successfully started and running on port **80** to serve the web contents to you. Usually, web content is kept inside the **DocumentRoot** directory. But by default, there is no web page inside this directory. So you receive the RedHat Test Page here. If the directory contains an **index.html** file, the contents of that file will be delivered, and that will be known as the home page of this web server. If **/var/www/html/** contains HTML files with a different name, say **example.html**, you can access them by entering the URL to that file, as follows:

`http://<server host name or IP address> /example.html`

You can specify the port number after the hostname, followed by the colon (`:`) character. This is usually required if the web server is running on a non-default port. To access the web server running on port **8080**, provide the URL as follows:

```
http://vmachine.example.com:8080
```

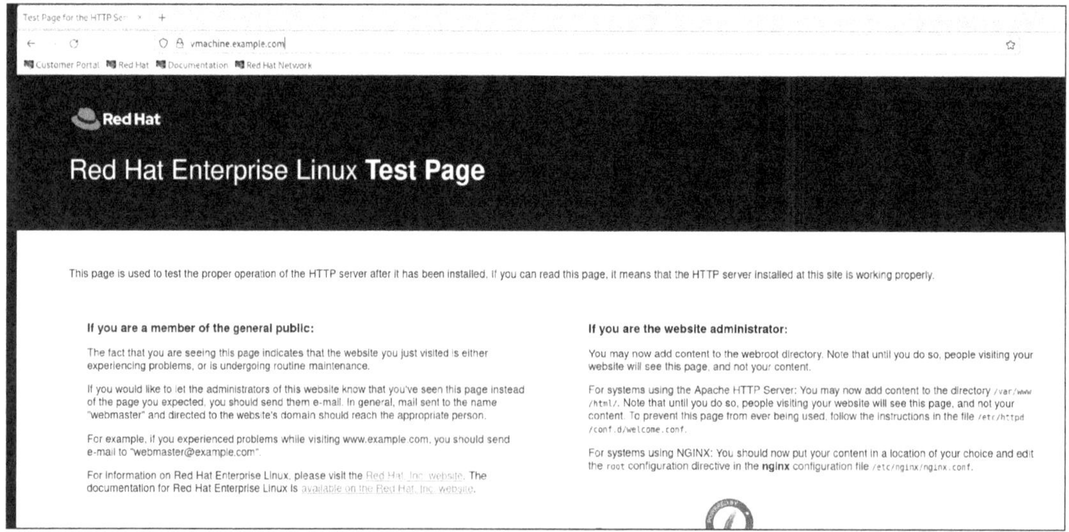

Figure 17.3: *Default Apache test page*

Creating your first web page

To access the web resources located on a web server, the server name has to be resolved first. To connect to a given server, the server name must be in DNS. If the server name is not in DNS, then it should be resolved by local naming method. Suppose we have a server named, vmachine.example.com running on local machine. To access this server, we must perform IP address mapping inside our **/etc/hosts** file by adding the following record:

```
127.0.0.1 vmachine.example.com
```

Local mapping of server names is usually required for testing purposes or when the server is not internet accessible. Let us understand the naming.

Here, **vmachine** is the name of the machine and **example.com** is the domain name. You may have seen the site names starting with **www** as **www.google.com**. Here, **www** is the web server name, and **google.com** is the domain name.

Now, it is time to create a web document to be accessible by our web server. The web server serves the document from the **DocumentRoot** directory. So, all the web documents must be placed inside the path under **DocumentRoot**. The files inside this directory must be readable and writable by the user who owns the **httpd** process.

Assuming that the **DocumentRoot** directive is set to **/var/www/html**, execute the following set of commands to create some documents to be viewed in the web browser:

```
cd /var/www/html
mkdir tasks
cd tasks
echo  "this is task 1">> task1
echo "this is task 2" >> task2
```

The previous set of commands creates a directory named **tasks** inside **/var/www/html** and two files, **task1** and **task2**, inside this directory. To fetch **task2** from the web server, we must specify the complete file path, as in the following URL:

```
http://vmachine.example.com/tasks/task2
```

If we just type **http://vmachine.example.com/tasks**, it will display a file list inside the specified path. Adding an index page inside the **/var/www/html/tasks** directory will show an index page when fetching a URL.

We still do not have any index page or home page for our website yet. Let us create it by using the following command:

```
echo "this is index page" >> /var/www/html/index.html
```

Now, type the following URL in the browser:

```
http://vmachine.example.com
```

This will serve the contents from our **index.html** that we have just added to our **DocumentRoot**.

If you have multiple websites using the same IP address, the mentioned procedure will provide the exact content for all those websites. If you want to provide different content for different websites, set up name-based virtual hosts. We will discuss name-based virtual hosts later in this chapter.

Let us edit the **/etc/hosts** file to provide more names to your web host:

```
127.0.0.1 one.example.com
127.0.0.1 two.example.com
```

Now, retrieving the contents hosted on the web server using any of the mentioned names will provide identical content to that of the original name: **http://vmachine.example.com**.

Understanding Httpd log

The Apache HTTP Server provides detailed and flexible logging facilities. The information in logs is organized in multiple fields. So, understanding the logs will help you analyze who is accessing what resources of the web server, the origin of the request, what generates an error, and more.

Let us understand the *error log*. Following is the sample error message:

```
[Thu Aug 10 14:38:37.195354 2023] [autoindex:error] [pid 38074:tid 38188]
[client fe80::20c:29ff:fe74:a45e%ens33:45582] AH01276: Cannot serve
directory /var/www/html/: No matching DirectoryIndex (index.html) found,
and server-generated directory index forbidden by Options directive
```

The preceding sample log contains many fields. The first item in the log entry is the date and time when the message is produced. The next is the module producing the message (autoindex, in this case) and the severity level of that message. The following field prints the process ID and, optionally, the thread ID of the process that faces the error condition. The following field is the client address that made the request. Finally, the detailed error message is printed.

Take the following sample entry from the *access log*:

```
127.0.0.1 - - [10/Aug/2023:23:40:54 +0530] "GET /favicon.ico HTTP/1.1" 404
196 "http://one.example.com/" "Mozilla/5.0 (X11; Linux x86_64; rv:91.0)
Gecko/20100101 Firefox/91.0"
```

The previous sample access log includes the combined format as set under the **LogFormat** directive in the default configuration. It has the following fields:

- **Host address:** This is the IP address of the client (remote host) that made the request to the server. It is represented by **%h** in the **LogFormat** directive. **127.0.0.1** is the host that made the current request in the mentioned sample.
- **Remote log name**: This is represented by **%l** in the **LogFormat** directive. Here, it is hyphenated (-), indicating that this information is not available.
- **Remote username**: This is the remote username who made the request. This is represented by **%u** in the **LogFormat** directive. In the previous example, this is again -, meaning that the information is not available.
- **Timestamp:** This is the local time when the request was received. This is represented by **'%t'**. In the preceding example, the time mentioned is [10/Aug/2023:23:40:54 +0530].
- **Request**: This is the request line received from the client. This is represented by **"%r"** (in double quotes " in the **LogFormat** directive. Here it is the following:

  ```
  GET /favicon.ico HTTP/1.1
  ```
- **Status code**: This is the status code that the server sends as a response to the client. This is represented by **"%>s"** in the **LogFormat** directive. Here, the status code is 404.

- **Response bytes:** This is the size of the response (in bytes) returned to the client, not including the response headers. This is represented by **`'%b'`** in the **`LogFormat`** directive. In the previous sample log, its value is 196.
- **Referer:** This is referrer information and implies the link from where the site has been referred. It is represented by **`\"%{Referer}i\"`** in the **`LogFormat`** directive. In the previous example, it is the following:

  ```
  "http://one.example.com/"
  ```

- **Useragent:** This is the information that the client browser reports about itself. It is represented by **`\"%{User-Agent}i\"`** in the **`LogFormat`** directive. In the previous example, the value received is as follows:

  ```
  "Mozilla/5.0 (X11; Linux x86_64; rv:91.0) Gecko/20100101 Firefox/91.0"
  ```

Name-based virtual host

Apache HTTP Server's virtual host facility allows you to host multiple websites on a single IP address. In the previous section, we configured many website names on the same physical hosts, but they deliver the same content. To host multiple websites on the same IP address, with each website delivering different content, we can use the feature of virtual hosting. Thus, a virtual host facility allows us to make efficient use of server resources by hosting multiple websites on the same physical server.

All the virtual hosts running on one physical server will point to the same IP address. Obviously, each website name must be properly configured in DNS so that those names can be mapped to an IP address associated with the server.

To run multiple websites on one physical machine, you must edit the configuration file to add an individual virtual host section for each website where each virtual host will have its separate configuration settings and website name. Each of the settings given outside the virtual host sections is a global setting that applies to all the virtual hosts. Any of the configuration directives given inside virtual host section will override the global setting. For example, you can keep the logs of each hosted website together under the directory mentioned in the global settings. This approach will make it difficult for you to identify a website-specific log. So, it is better to keep all the logs of all the hosted websites at separate locations by adding related configuration directives in each virtual host section.

Let us move on to creating different virtual hosts. Suppose you have two websites, namely **`one.example.com`** and **`two.example.com`**, to host on the same IP. Edit the **`/etc/httpd/conf/httpd.conf`** file. For two virtual hosts, we will configure two virtual host sections. Append the following virtual host section in this file:

```
<VirtualHost *:80>
  DocumentRoot "/var/www/one/"
  ServerName one.example.com
```

```
  CustomLog /var/log/httpd/one.example.com_access.log combined
  ErrorLog /var/log/httpd/one.example.com_error.log
</VirtualHost>

<VirtualHost *:80>
  DocumentRoot "/var/www/two/"
  ServerName two.example.com
  CustomLog /var/log/httpd/two.example.com_access.log combined
  ErrorLog /var/log/httpd/two.example.com_error.log
</VirtualHost>
```

Let us understand the meaning of each of the directives included in the preceding lines:

- **<VirtualHost *:80>**: It is the starting of the specific Virtual host definition.
- **DocumentRoot**: It specifies the path where web content for this virtual host is hosted.
- **ServerName**: It specifies the website name for which this virtual host serves the content.
- **CustomLog**: It defines the path of the access log of this virtual host. If this directive is not supplied, then access logs of this virtual host will be written into the access log available globally (that is, **/etc/httpd/logs/access_log**).
- **ErrorLog**: It defines the path of the error log of this virtual host. If this is not given here, then error logs related to this virtual host will get written into the error log available globally (that is, **/etc/httpd/logs/error_log**).
- **</VirtualHost>:** It is the end of this virtual host definition.

The directives that are not provided inside the virtual host section will be applied using the main configuration files, that is, global settings will still be applied to virtual hosts for the directives that are not provided under the virtual host section.

As a next step, create directories for **DocumentRoot**, as follows:

```
mkdir /var/www/one
mkdir /var/www/two
```

The given name in the virtual host definition must be resolved to the IP address of the web server. If the given name is not resolved by **Domain Name Server** (**DNS**), then you can make an entry for host resolution in the **/etc/hosts** file, as follows:

```
<ip address of the web server> one.example.com
<ip address of the web server>  two.example.com
```

Now, let us create some web content for both the web servers:

```
echo "hello one" > /var/www/one/index.html
echo "hello two" > /var/www/two/index.html
```

Restart the httpd server by executing the following:

```
systemctl restart httpd
```

Now, use your browser to access **one.example.com**. Virtual host sections will be searched in sequence for the given **ServerName**. When a match is found, it will use the settings from that section to deliver the appropriate web content. It should deliver you the newly added index page, as shown in *Figure 17.4*:

Figure 17.4: *Index page served by a virtual host*

In case the given website name does not match with any of the **ServerName** given in the **VirtualHost** sections, then the first virtual host definition is considered the default and is used to serve client requests.

Try to open the original website in your browser that you used earlier, as follows:

```
http://vmachine.example.com
```

What will you get? Refer to *Figure 17.5*. Here, you will get content delivered from the first virtual host entry, as no virtual host section matching the given website name is found.

Figure 17.5: *Web content using default virtual host*

Securing HTTP communication

Apache HTTP server provides the facility to secure the communication between web servers and web clients. It offers SSL/TLS encryption so that all the data exchanged between the server and the client remains secure. By default, Apache HTTP server uses an unencrypted HTTP connection to deliver the web content to the clients. Unsecured and unencrypted HTTP communication channels are more prone to cyberattacks. So, it becomes important to secure an HTTP connection. When a secured HTTP connection is established, it adds encryption and authentication to the communication between the client and server.

SSL is used to secure HTTP communication between the web client and the web server. The secured version is called **HTTPS** and uses the **https:// URL** scheme rather than **`http://`**. **`HTTPS`** runs on default **`server port: 443`**.

Securing HTTP connection requires a valid TLS/SSL certificate to be issued from a trusted Certificate Authority. This certificate must be installed on the web server. A TLS/SSL certificate identifies the server and ensures that data is coming from a trusted site. It also ensures that all the data that is exchanged between client and server will be encrypted. To get a valid certificate, you must raise and send a certificate request to a valid certificate authority such as Verisign and GoDaddy. A certificate includes the public key, the distinguished name of the entity, the signature of the trusted authority, the period of validity, and more.

To enable HTTPS, we are required to install the **`mod_ssl`** module that provides the **OpenSSL** library. Openssl is used to generate key pairs and certificate requests. Follow the given steps to create an HTTPS connection:

1. As a first step, execute the following:

   ```
   dnf install mod_ssl
   ```

   The preceding command will install the **`mod_ssl`** module. The installation of **`mod_ssl`** also creates config file named **`ssl.conf`** inside the **`/etc/httpd/conf.d/`** directory and provides access to the **`openssl`** library.

2. The next step is to obtain SSL certificate to install on web server. Here, we will not generate a certificate request and send it to CA to get it signed, but we will create a self-signed certificate for our demonstration here.

3. The next command will create key pairs and a self-signed certificate that must be known to the server. Choose a location where you want to store the key file and certificate. Here, we choose **`/opt/cert/example`**.

   ```
   mkdir -p /opt/cert/example
   cd /opt/cert/example
   ```

After you have created the required directories, move to that location and issue the following command to generate a self-signed certificate:

```
openssl req -new -x509 -nodes -out server.crt -keyout server.key
```

You will get output as shown in *Figure 17.6*:

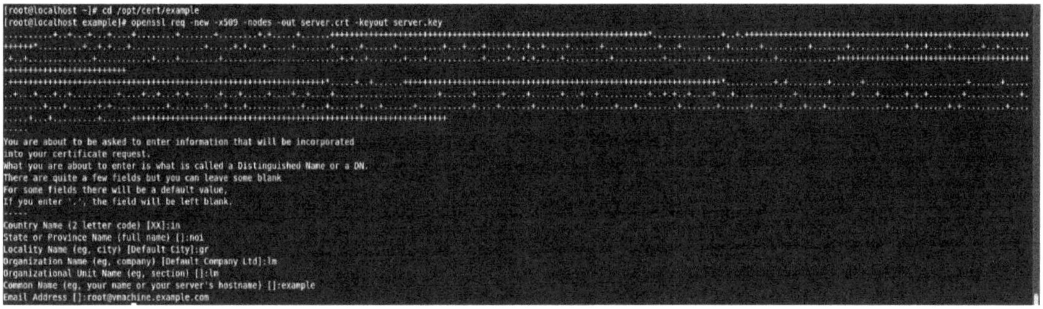

```
[root@localhost ~]# cd /opt/cert/example
[root@localhost example]# openssl req -new -x509 -nodes -out server.crt -keyout server.key
-----
You are about to be asked to enter information that will be incorporated
into your certificate request.
What you are about to enter is what is called a Distinguished Name or a DN.
There are quite a few fields but you can leave some blank
For some fields there will be a default value,
If you enter '.', the field will be left blank.
-----
Country Name (2 letter code) [XX]:in
State or Province Name (full name) []:noi
Locality Name (eg, city) [Default City]:gr
Organization Name (eg, company) [Default Company Ltd]:lm
Organizational Unit Name (eg, section) []:lm
Common Name (eg, your name or your server's hostname) []:example
Email Address []:root@vmachine.example.com
```

***Figure 17.6**: Process to generate a self-signed certificate*

-x509 is specified in the preceding command to create a self-signed certificate. This command asks you to provide the information that needs to be included in the certificate request. Enter the information asked, and on the basis of this information, it will generate a certificate file and a key file named **server.crt** and **server.key**, respectively, under **/opt/crt/example**.

4. Now, the server must be configured to make it aware of the certificate location to pass the certificate to the web client. Let us modify some of the parameters in the **ssl.conf** file:

   o **Listen:** When SSL is enabled, the server must also listen to https on port **443**. It should be set as follows:

   ```
   Listen 443 https
   ```

   o **SSLEngine:** To enable SSL, this must be turned on. This must be set as follows:

   ```
   SSLEngine on
   ```

   o **SSLCertificateFile**: It points to the server's certificate. Let us edit this entry as follows:

   ```
   SSLCertificateFile /opt/cert/example/server.crt
   ```

   o **SSLCertificateKeyFile**: It points to the server's private key. It should be edited as follows:

   ```
   SSLCertificateKeyFile /opt/cert/example/server.key
   ```

5. After editing the configuration file, you must restart the **httpd** service as follows:

```
systemctl restart httpd.service
```

6. Access the website using the https protocol as follows:

   ```
   https://vmachine.example.com
   ```

The browser will give a warning message for the potential risk. This is because the certificate is not trusted and we have placed this certificate just for testing purposes. You can ignore the message and proceed to the website. Click on **Advanced...** and then click **Accept the Risk and Continue**.

The demonstration shown here is just for testing purposes. For the production environment, you must attach a certificate to the website signed by a trusted CA such as GoDaddy, Verisign, etc. The process of issuing a CA certificate is beyond the scope of this book.

Database server

A database server is a program that is used to manage and store databases efficiently. It stores the data in an organized and structured way. It provides the infrastructure for efficiently storing, organizing, retrieving, and managing data for various applications and services scaling from small to large enterprises.

RHEL9 provides many database packages such as MySQL, MariaDB, and PostgreSQL. In this book, we will discuss the installation and configuration of MySQL server only.

Let us start by installing the MySQL server on your RHEL9 box. RHEL9 software provides a **mysql-server** package via its **`appstream`** repository. We have already created this repository in *Chapter 14, Package Installation*. In this section, we will discuss the installation and configuration of the MySQL server.

Installing MySQL server

To install **`mysql-server`**, type the following:

```
dnf install mysql-server
```

The preceding command installs **`mysql-server ver 8.0`**. along with all of its dependencies. It creates a system service named **`mysqld.service`**, which runs on the default port **`3306`**.

After installation, you must start it as follows:

```
systemctl start mysqld
```

You can check the current status of the **`mysqld`** service using the following command:

```
systemctl status mysqld
```

The **`mysqld`** is currently running but is not enabled to run during boot. To enable it during boot, type the following:

```
systemctl enable mysqld.service
```

The installation of the MySQL server also provides many utilities for you to manage and secure itself. One such utility is **`mysql_secure_installation`**, which is used to provide basic security to MySQL server. You should execute this utility after the installation of the **`msyqld`** service. Let us run the following command and provide answers for the questions it prompts:

```
$ mysql_secure_installation

mysql_secure_installation

Securing the MySQL server deployment.

Connecting to MySQL using a blank password.

VALIDATE PASSWORD COMPONENT can be used to test passwords
and improve security. It checks the strength of password
and allows the users to set only those passwords which are
secure enough. Would you like to setup VALIDATE PASSWORD component?

Press y|Y for Yes, any other key for No: y

There are three levels of password validation policy:

LOW  Length >= 8
MEDIUM Length >= 8, numeric, mixed case, and special characters
STRONG Length >= 8, numeric, mixed case, special characters and dictionary
file

Please enter 0 = LOW, 1 = MEDIUM and 2 = STRONG: 1
Please set the password for root here.

New password:

Re-enter new password:

Estimated strength of the password: 50
Do you wish to continue with the password provided?(Press y|Y for Yes, any
other key for No): y
... Failed! Error: Your password does not satisfy the current policy
requirements
```

```
New password:

Re-enter new password:

Estimated strength of the password: 100
Do you wish to continue with the password provided?(Press y|Y for Yes, any
other key for No): y
By default, a MySQL installation has an anonymous user,
allowing anyone to log into MySQL without having to have
a user account created for them. This is intended only for
testing, and to make the installation go a bit smoother.
You should remove them before moving into a production
environment.
New password:

Re-enter new password:

Estimated strength of the password: 100
Do you wish to continue with the password provided?(Press y|Y for Yes, any
other key for No): y
By default, a MySQL installation has an anonymous user,
allowing anyone to log into MySQL without having to have
a user account created for them. This is intended only for
testing, and to make the installation go a bit smoother.
You should remove them before moving into a production
environment.

Remove anonymous users? (Press y|Y for Yes, any other key for No): y
Success.

Normally, root should only be allowed to connect from
'localhost'. This ensures that someone cannot guess at
the root password from the network.

Disallow root login remotely? (Press y|Y for Yes, any other key for No): y
Success.

By default, MySQL comes with a database named 'test' that
```

```
anyone can access. This is also intended only for testing,
and should be removed before moving into a production
environment.

Remove test database and access to it? (Press y|Y for Yes, any other key
for No): y
 - Dropping test database...
Success.

 - Removing privileges on test database...
Success.

Reloading the privilege tables will ensure that all changes
made so far will take effect immediately.

Reload privilege tables now? (Press y|Y for Yes, any other key for No):
Success.

All done!
```

The preceding command executes an interactive script to add security on the database. It works in the following way:

1. At first, it asks whether you want to apply a password validation feature. You have the option to choose from a low to strong password policy.
2. Next, it asks you to set the password for MySQL root user. In MySQL, the root user is the database user who has the highest privileges and has complete control over the database. You have to set the password according to the specified password policy.
3. Next, it asks whether you want to remove an anonymous user. Anonymous users may log in from anywhere on the database without entering the password, which is not safe. So, you should remove this user.
4. MySQL root user must not be allowed to log in remotely. So, the next prompt in the script disables the remote login of the MySQL root user. In this setup, MySQL root users can log in only locally.
5. The next prompt asks you to remove the database named test, which comes by default with this installation.
6. At last, the script asks to reload the privilege table. The privilege table stores user permissions and passwords. A database named **`mysql`**, which comes by default

with installation, has many tables storing user access and permissions. Any changes that have been performed by this script must be reflected on privilege tables of **mysql** database so that new settings may take effect in the running MySQL server. So, this step reloads privilege tables onto memory.

Using database server

The installation of **mysql-server** also provides a MySQL client called **mysql** to access the MySQL server. In this section, we will learn to use **mysql** client to access and fetch data from the MySQL server.

Login to MySQL server

To login to the MySQL server, you must authenticate yourself to the server as a valid database user. To authenticate successfully to the server, a username and an associated password is required. Simply typing **mysql** on the command line will generate an error as no authentication information is supplied, as given in *Figure 17.7*. To log in to MySQL, the **-u** and **-p** options are used on the command line to supply the username and password, respectively. Type the following:

```
mysql -u root -p
```

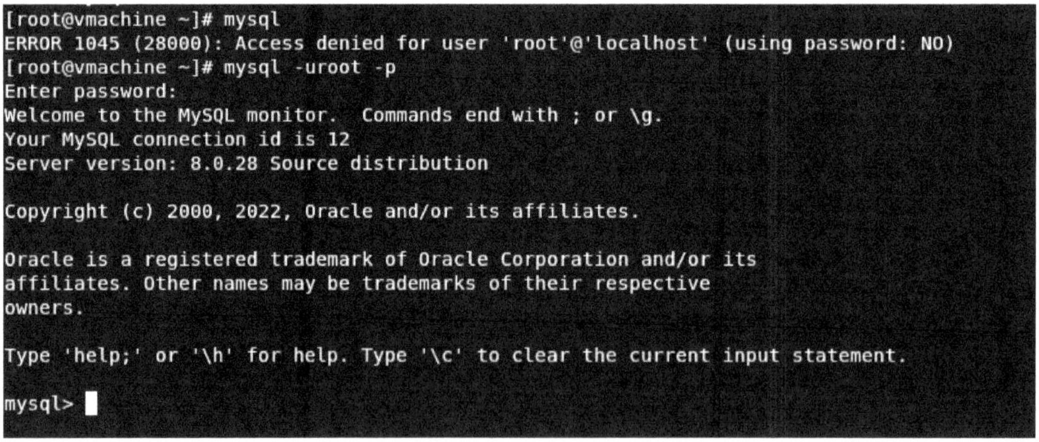

```
[root@vmachine ~]# mysql
ERROR 1045 (28000): Access denied for user 'root'@'localhost' (using password: NO)
[root@vmachine ~]# mysql -uroot -p
Enter password:
Welcome to the MySQL monitor.  Commands end with ; or \g.
Your MySQL connection id is 12
Server version: 8.0.28 Source distribution

Copyright (c) 2000, 2022, Oracle and/or its affiliates.

Oracle is a registered trademark of Oracle Corporation and/or its
affiliates. Other names may be trademarks of their respective
owners.

Type 'help;' or '\h' for help. Type '\c' to clear the current input statement.

mysql> ▌
```

Figure 17.7: *Login to MySQL Server*

The preceding command attempts to log in as root user. Pressing *Enter* will lead the program to ask you to enter the password for the root user. The server authenticates you using the information stored in the database. If the authentication is successful, the connection is established between the client and the server. Here, you will get a **mysql** prompt that will accept instructions from the user and send it to the server to execute them.

Querying database

Data is stored in MySQL in the form of tables. Each table has a predefined structure having a set of columns/fields and their data types. The structure of the table determines the definition of the table. Data is stored in the tables in the form of rows and columns.

MySQL server fetches the data from the database according to the given instructions. Instructions given to MySQL are called **SQL statements**. Besides fetching data from the database server, SQL statements are used to perform other operations on the database, such as **inserting, updating, indexing** and **deleting data**.

The **`mysql`** client also supports many commands that perform some action. In this section, we will learn to use some of the commands supported by the **`mysql`** client as well as basic SQL statements. Note that this chapter provides just a brief overview of MySQL; you must read the official documentation of MySQL for more knowledge.

SQL statements and the various clauses used with them are case-insensitive. The names of the objects created on the database are **case-sensitive**. As a good practice, SQL statements are written in CAPS, whereas table names, function names, and more are given in lowercase for better understanding of the written statements.

Now, it is time to view the first MySQL statement in action. Note that SQL statements always end with a semicolon (**`;`**). Type the following statement in the **`mysql`** prompt:

```
mysql > show databases;
```

It will give you the list of databases as given in *Figure 17.8*:

```
mysql>
mysql> show databases;
+--------------------+
| Database           |
+--------------------+
| information_schema |
| mysql              |
| performance_schema |
| sys                |
+--------------------+
4 rows in set (0.03 sec)
```

Figure 17.8: *SQL statement to fetch the list of stored databases on MySQL server*

Let us view what these databases contain:

- **`information_schema`:** It is used to store database-related metadata, like table name, structure, columns of each table, its definition, indexes available, and so on.
- **`mysql`:** **`mysql`** database contains user information, privileges granted to each, and so on.
- **`performance_schema`:** It is used to store execution statistics of various activities being performed on the MySQL server, which can be used to monitor the performance and diagnose any performance bottlenecks.
- **`sys`:** It organizes the data collected by **`performance_schema`** in a user-friendly way, which helps in analyzing performance-related problems.

The next statement displays the MySQL server version to which you are connected. Type the following command at the **mysql** prompt:

```
select version();
```

The output is given in *Figure 17.9*:

```
mysql> select version();
+-----------+
| version() |
+-----------+
| 8.0.28    |
+-----------+
1 row in set (0.00 sec)
```

Figure 17.9: *SQL statement displaying the version of the connected MySQL server*

Let us create your first non-default database as follows:

```
mysql> create database example ;
Query OK, 1 row affected (0.03 sec)
```

The preceding statement creates a database named **example**.

Now, you can use the newly created database to store your data by creating tables and inserting data into these tables. Execute the **use <dbname>** command to make **<dbname>** the current database, as follows:

```
mysql> use example;
Database changed
```

Now, an **example** is the current database. Any further SQL statement will be applied to the selected database.

The **CREATE TABLE** statement creates the table as shown in the following example:

```
mysql> create table tab1 (c1 int, c2 varchar(20));
Query OK, 0 rows affected (0.21 sec)
```

The preceding SQL statement creates the table named **tab1**, having two columns, namely, **c1** of **int** type and **c2** of **varchar** type. The number in parentheses is the maximum size of the data to be stored in a column.

If you want to view the definition of an existing table anytime, you can use the **SHOW CREATE TABLE** statement as follows:

```
mysql> show create table tab1;
+-------+-----------------------------------------------------------
-------------------------------------------------------------------
--------+
| Table | Create Table
```

```
|
+-------+-------------------------------------------------------------
----------------------------------------------------------------------
--------+
| tab1 | CREATE TABLE 'tab1' (
 'c1' int DEFAULT NULL,
 'c2' varchar(20) DEFAULT NULL
) ENGINE=InnoDB DEFAULT CHARSET=utf8mb4 COLLATE=utf8mb4_0900_ai_ci |
+-------+--------------------------------------
```

The previous command displays the structure of the table named **tab1**. To fetch the data from a table, say **tab1**, we use a **SELECT** statement. The **SELECT** statement is used to query data according to the given criteria or instructions. To fetch all the data from the table, type the following:

```
select * from tab1;
```

In the preceding command, * refers to all columns. The **SELECT** statement accepts the **FROM** clause to specify the table name from which you want to view data. Currently, our table, **tab1**, is empty, so the preceding command returns 0 rows.

Our table is empty. Let us fill some data into this by using the **INSERT** statement, as follows:

```
mysql> insert into tab1 values(12, 'abc');
Query OK, 1 row affected (0.01 sec)
```

In the preceding command, the **VALUES** clause is used to specify the values for the columns, which creates the first row of the table. Let us verify the row inserted using the **SELECT** statement:

```
mysql> select * from tab1;
+------+------+
| c1 | c2 |
+------+------+
| 12 | abc |
```

Similarly, you can execute the preceding **insert** statement to store more rows in a database:

```
insert into tab1 values(11,'xyz');
Query OK, 1 row affected (0.02 sec)
```

To verify row addition, execute the following:

```
mysql> select * from tab1;
+------+------+
| c1 | c2 |
```

```
+------+------+
| 12 | abc |
| 11 | xyz |
+------+------+
2 rows in set (0.00 sec)
```

You can also use a **SELECT** statement to fetch a set of columns only. Provide the comma-separated list of column names instead of *, as follows:

```
mysql> select c1 from tab1;
+------+
| c1 |
+------+
| 12 |
| 11 |
+------+
2 rows in set (0.01 sec)
```

The preceding command selects only a column named **c1** from the specified table.

By default, **select** brings all the rows from the table. The **SELECT** statement can also be used to filter the records from the table. You can view only the records that match a specific condition. To fetch only the records matching the specified criteria, the **WHERE** clause is used in the **SELECT** statement as follows:

```
mysql> select c1 from tab1 where c1=12;
+------+
| c1 |
+------+
| 12 |
+------+
1 row in set (0.00 sec)
```

The preceding command fetches only the records where **c1 = 12**. To fetch records matching a specific string, the string must be enclosed in single quotes, as follows:

```
mysql> select * from tab1 where c2='abc';
+------+------+
| c1 | c2 |
+------+------+
| 12 | abc |
+------+------+
```

```
1 row in set (0.00 sec)
```

The preceding command fetches only the records where **c2** equals **abc**. The following command does not return anything, as no records exist in the table for the specified condition:

```
mysql> select * from tab1 where c2='x';
Empty set (0.00 sec)
```

To exit **mysql** client, you can type the **exit** command at the **mysql** prompt:

```
mysql>exit
```

Configuring MySQL

Though the default configuration is sufficient to run and use the MySQL server, you should customize the default configuration settings of the MySQL server in a production environment. Proper customization of MySQL configuration is required according to the organization's need, and the type and size of data. MySQL server runs with many options and system variables that are set during its startup. If you want to make any changes to the default configuration, you can edit the main configuration file of the MySQL server, **/etc/my.cnf**. It also includes the files residing under **/etc/my.cnf.d**.

Some of the MySQL parameters modify the server's behavior, while others affect server performance. Any change in these parameters and server settings requires expertise and knowledge.

To change the settings related to the **msyqld** service, edit the parameters given under the **[mysqld]** section in the configuration file. To modify the default port of the **mysqld** service, edit the **port** parameter. To determine the IP address on which the server listens for client requests, modify the **bind-address** parameter. To listen to client requests over TCP/IP connections, the **skip-networking** parameter must be set to 0.

For details on various options and parameters using which **mysqld** runs, you can read the MySQL manual at **https://dev.mysql.com/doc/refman/8.0/en/server-configuration.html.**

Conclusion

A web server is used for web hosting. Usually, you use web browsers like Mozilla Firefox to view web content. These web browsers act like web clients. A web server serves web content at the request of web clients via HTTP/HTTPS. HTTPS uses SSL to secure all the communications between the web client and the web server. HTTP server, httpd, developed by Apache Software Foundation, is one of the most popular open-source web servers. Its flexibility and security-rich features have contributed to its popularity in hosting websites. Apache HTTP server also allows more than one website to run on the same physical server using the concept of virtual hosting. Websites may interact with database servers to store and access data.

This chapter discussed one of the popular open-source database servers, MySQL. MySQL clients interact with the MySQL server by giving instructions using SQL statements. SQL statements can be written to query the database for data retrieval, insert the data into the database, update the existing data, delete the existing data from the database, and more.

In the next chapter, we will discuss the miscellaneous topics that have not been discussed in any of the earlier chapters but are important for you to learn.

Join our book's Discord space

Join the book's Discord Workspace for Latest updates, Offers, Tech happenings around the world, New Release and Sessions with the Authors:

https://discord.bpbonline.com

CHAPTER 18
Miscellaneous

Introduction

This chapter includes many different topics, such as configuring email client on RHEL 9.0 and retrieving hardware information.

Structure

This chapter discusses the following topics:

- Configuring and using email client usage
- Fetching hardware information
- Udev rules
- Time synchronization
- Auditing log
- Changing kernel parameters

Objectives

By the end of this chapter, you will be capable of installing and configuring the email client **mutt**. You will be able to use various command-line utilities to fetch hardware information. You will possess the ability to perform data transfer over the web using the **curl** command line utility and also know how to write **udev** rules. You will be able to sync the machine's clock with the **ntp** server using the **chronyd** systemd service. You will gain proficiency in analyzing and understanding audit logs. Additionally, you will know how to change kernel parameters on a Linux system.

Configuring and using email client

In Linux, various services are required to notify the users about their status or errors they faced while executing. This notification is sent to the user via sending email. So, an email client must be installed at the user's end so that they can be notified about the received messages while accessing and reading these electronic messages anytime.

`mutt` is a powerful email client that is used to send and read emails using a command-line interface or text-based interface. **CLI** mode of **mutt** can also be used to send emails via scripts.

Type the following command to install the **mutt** email client:

```
dnf install mutt
```

Mutt also requires you to run **sendmail**. **Sendmail** is a mail transport agent used by **mutt** to send emails. You can install it by issuing the following:

```
dnf install sendmail
```

After **sendmail** installation, you must start it by issuing the following:

```
systemctl start sendmail
```

When you run the **mutt** command for the first time, it will ask you the following:

```
"/root/Mail does not exist. Create it? ([yes]/no):"
```

Press **yes** to create it.

Let us use **mutt** to send your first email to a user named **sam**, as follows:

```
echo "hello"|mutt -s "hello" sam
```

The previous command sends an email with the subject field set as **hello**. The **-s** option is used to provide subject to your email. The recipient name is the last argument in the command line. The output of the **echo** command is passed to the **mutt** command as the email body.

If you do not provide the body of the message on the **mutt** command line, then it will open an interface for you. Just type the following:

```
mutt -s "welcome to our organization" sam
```

Pressing the *Enter* key will open an interface with the following fields in sequence, allowing you to modify it:

- **To field**: This field displays the entries made by you. You can make any change here if you want to. Pressing *Enter* will open the next field.
- **Subject field**: This field displays the entries made in the subject field. You can edit this field if you want to.

Next, it will open the **vi** editor, where you can type the contents of the email. Press **:wq** to save the message and exit the editor.

Now, it will show you an interface where you can verify all the entries done by you. It also provides you with the option to modify any of the entries by pressing the correct key. The keystrokes that can be used here are given at the top of the interface. Pressing **y** will send the message.

A user's mailbox is stored under the **/var/spool/mail/** directory. This directory contains a mailbox file for each user, which is named the same as the username. For example, all the mails delivered to the user named **sam** will be stored in the **/var/spool/mail/sam** file.

To view the messages, open your mailbox by typing the following:

```
mutt
```

It opens the mailbox in an interactive mode. The console will display all the emails received, sorted by the time received, with the last read message highlighted in red. Press the down or up arrow keys to move between the messages. Press the *Enter* key to read the selected email. Press **q** to go back to the previous screen. Pressing **q** on the very first window will lead you to exit you from **mutt**.

Press **d** to delete the message. It will mark the message as deleted, but it will not delete the message permanently yet. You have the option to undo the delete by pressing **u**. When you press **q** to exit mutt, it will ask you to purge all the deleted messages. Pressing **y** will remove all the messages having delete marks permanently.

Other options that you can use with the **mutt** command are listed here:

- **-R**: Open the current user's mailbox in read only mode.
- **-a <list of files> --**: Specify the space-separated list of files to be attached to the message; note that the list of files must be terminated with the "**--**" sequence
- **-b <address>**: Specify a **Blind Carbon-Copy** (**BCC**) address
- **-c <address>**: Specify a **Carbon-Copy** (**CC**) address
- **-f <file>**: Specify which mailbox to read
- **-z**: Exit immediately if there are no messages in the mailbox

Following are a few usages of the **mutt** command:

```
echo "please review the attached file"|mutt -s "pfa" -a abc noc -- sam
```

The preceding command sends an email to the user **sam** with two files attached, namely, **abc** and **noc**. '--' is the termination character for the **-a** option.

If the root user wants to view another user's mailbox, the **-f** option can be used to specify the mailbox file to open, as follows:

```
mutt -f /var/spool/mail/visheshkumar
```

The preceding command opens the mailbox of the user named **visheshkumar**.

Fetching hardware information

We have used the **/proc** virtual filesystem to view the information about attached hardware. It provides information that is not easy to understand. So, we need to use some other utilities that help you gather detailed information about the hardware attached on your Linux system.

lsblk

The **lsblk** command displays a list of available block devices and detailed information of each device. It prints the device list in a tree-like structure. It reads information from **udev**, therefore this command can also be run by non-root users. To display a list of block devices, type the following at a shell prompt:

```
lsblk
```

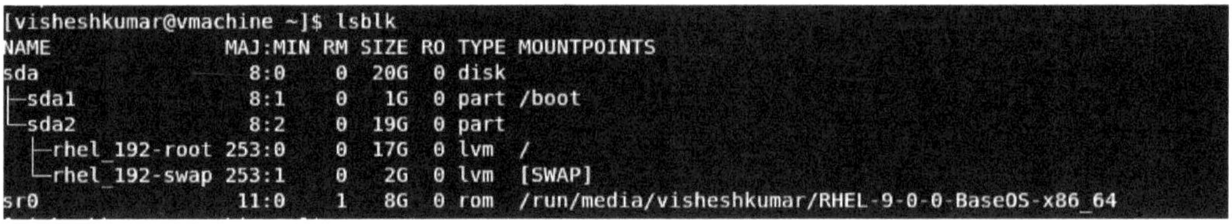

```
[visheshkumar@vmachine ~]$ lsblk
NAME              MAJ:MIN RM  SIZE RO TYPE MOUNTPOINTS
sda                 8:0    0   20G  0 disk
├─sda1              8:1    0    1G  0 part /boot
└─sda2              8:2    0   19G  0 part
  ├─rhel_192-root 253:0    0   17G  0 lvm  /
  └─rhel_192-swap 253:1    0    2G  0 lvm  [SWAP]
sr0                11:0    1    8G  0 rom  /run/media/visheshkumar/RHEL-9-0-0-BaseOS-x86_64
```

Figure 18.1: *lsblk command showing the list of block devices*

The output given in *Figure 18.1* shows the block devices list in a tree-like structure. It shows that the device named **sda** has been partitioned into **sda1** and **sda2**. **sda1** carries the boot filesystem, while root and swap volumes are part of the **sda2** device.

For each listed block device, the **lsblk** command displays information in the following fields:

- **NAME**: Device name
- **MAJ:MIN**: Major and minor device number
- **RM**: Determines if the device is removable
- **SIZE**: Mentions the size of block device

- **`RO`**: Determines if the device is read-only
- **`TYPE`**: Determines the device type
- **`MOUNTPOINTS`**: Specifies the mountpoints of the device

findmnt

The **`findmnt`** command displays a list of currently mounted filesystems in a tree-like format. Typing **`findmnt`** at the shell prompt will give you output as given in *Figure 18.2*:

Figure 18.2: *findmnt command displaying a list of mounted filesystems*

For each listed file system, the **`findmnt`** command displays the following fields:

- **`TARGET`**: The target mount point
- **`SOURCE`**: Source device
- **`FSTYPE`**: File system type
- **`OPTIONS`**: Mount options, using which the filesystem is mounted

To display the details of only the specified filesystem, say **`xfs`**, use the **`-t`** option, as follows:

```
findmnt -t xfs
```

lspci

The **`lspci`** command allows you to display information about PCI buses and devices that are attached to them. Typing **`lspci`** at the shell prompt lists all PCI devices that are in the system. You can also use the **`-v`** command-line option to display more verbose output.

lsusb

The **`lsusb`** command provides information about USB buses and devices that are attached to them. Typing **`lsusb`** would list all USB devices that are in the system.

lscpu

The **lscpu** command allows you to list the CPUs available on the system, along with detailed information of each CPU, including the number of cores, capabilities, architecture, vendor, family, model, CPU caches, and flags. Simply typing **lscpu** prints information about all the CPUs.

curl

curl is a command-line utility usually used to perform data transfer over the web. You can use **curl** to fetch web pages from the internet and display them on the terminal. It can also be used to upload the files to the server. It supports many protocols for data transfer, such as **HTTP, HTTPS, SCP, FTP**, and **SFTP**.

If you want to view content from a website, say **in.bpbonline.com** on the terminal, type the following:

```
curl https://in.bpbonline.com
```

It fetches the contents from the specified URL and prints it on the **stdout**. You can save the content to a disk file instead of displaying it on **stdout**. The **-o** option comes in handy here. The following command saves the downloaded contents to a web file named **bpbhomepage** in the current directory:

```
curl -o bpbhomepage https://in.bpbonline.com
```

To ignore the SSL certificate warning, you can use the **-k** option as follows:

```
curl -k https://in.bpbonline.com
```

You can also specify headers in the request in curl, as follows:

```
curl -H 'content-type: application/json' https://in.bpbonline.com
```

By default, **curl** assumes that a request is called using the **GET** method, but in case you call the web page using any other method, then you can specify the following:

```
curl -XPOST https://in.bpbonline.com
```

If you need to pass payload in the request, you can use the **-d** (data) option in the **curl** command and execute the **curl** command as follows:

```
curl -XPOST https://in.bpbonline.com -d '{"name": "test"}'
```

The **curl** is a Swiss army knife command as it very helpful in troubleshooting, scripts and automation work.

Udev rules

We know that the devices attached to the system are represented as files in the **/dev** directory. For example, if you attach a USB storage to a system running Linux, the device file appears in **/dev** as **/dev/ttyUSB0** or **/dev/ttyUSB1**, or something similar. This naming of the file in the **/dev** directory is dynamic, and it is not possible to predict what device name will be given to the attached device.

Sometimes, a user needs to refer to these disks with a specific name every time they are attached to the system. This is where udev daemon come into the picture. Udev daemon works on the basis of a set of specified rules. These rules determine how to identify the attached device. Red Hat Enterprise Linux already contains the default **udev** rules for the attached storage devices that create symbolic links in the **/dev/disk/** directory. The default rules are given in system rules files located under **/usr/lib/udev/rules.d**. For any new rules, one must not interfere with the system rules directory; new rules must be added under the **/etc/udev/rules.d** directory. New rules can be added in the **/etc/udev/rules.d** directory. Rule files carry the **.rules** file extension. Files with any other extension are ignored. When **udev** receives any device event, it reads all the rules files from all the directories mentioned earlier and executes instructions given in the matched rules. Instructions may provide additional device information to be stored in the **udev** database or create meaningful symbolic names. In this section, we will see how to write a new rule for the newly added storage device.

Let us create a rule file **usb.rules** under **/etc/udev/rules.d/**. Add the following rule to this file. This rule creates the persistent name for the USB device whose product ID is **7523** and vendor ID is **1a86**. This creates a symbolic link to this device named **meter1** under **/dev**.

```
SUBSYSTEM=="tty", ATTRS{idVendor}=="1a86", ATTRS{idProduct}=="7523",
KERNELS=="1-1.2", SYMLINK+="meter1"
```

To verify the creation of symbolic name, **meter1**, issue the following:

```
ls -l /dev/meter1

lrwxrwxrwx 1 root root 7 Aug 19 18:15 /dev/meter1 -> ttyUSB0
```

The following command queries the **udev** database for the given device's information:

```
udevadm info /dev/ttyUSB0

P: /devices/platform/soc/3f980000.usb/usb1/1-1/1-1.2/1-1.2:1.0/ttyUSB0/tty/
ttyUSB0

N: ttyUSB0

L: 0

S: serial/by-path/platform-3f980000.usb-usb-0:1.2:1.0-port0

S: serial/by-id/usb-1a86_USB2.0-Serial-if00-port0

S: meter1

E: DEVPATH=/devices/platform/soc/3f980000.usb/usb1/1-1/1-1.2/1-1.2:1.0/
ttyUSB0/tty/ttyUSB0

E: DEVNAME=/dev/ttyUSB0
```

```
E: MAJOR=188
E: MINOR=0
E: SUBSYSTEM=tty
E: USEC_INITIALIZED=12105514
E: ID_PATH=platform-3f980000.usb-usb-0:1.2:1.0
E: ID_PATH_TAG=platform-3f980000_usb-usb-0_1_2_1_0
E: ID_VENDOR=1a86
E: ID_VENDOR_ENC=1a86
E: ID_VENDOR_ID=1a86
E: ID_MODEL=USB2.0-Serial
E: ID_MODEL_ENC=USB2.0-Serial
E: ID_MODEL_ID=7523
E: ID_REVISION=0254
E: ID_SERIAL=1a86_USB2.0-Serial
E: ID_TYPE=generic
E: ID_BUS=usb
E: ID_USB_INTERFAC…
```

The previous output shows the information in various fields. The **S** field contains the symbolic name **meter1**. You can also check other information shown in the output against the command that we executed. For example, **ID_MODEL_ID=7523** and **ID_VENDOR=1a86**.

Time synchronization

Each computer in the organization needs to synchronize the system time with **NTP servers**. Accurate timestamping is required in system and application logs, and for many other reasons. Time synchronization is also very important in many applications in our daily life. RHEL9 uses the **chronyd systemd** service for system clock synchronization. Earlier versions of RHEL used ntpd for clock synchronization. Since RHEL8, **chronyd** replaced **ntpd**. *Chronyd* synchronizes the system clock with greater accuracy than **ntpd**.

Network Time Foundation provides many time servers to which your machine can connect to synchronize their time. Time servers are known as **NTP servers**. Client machines use the **Network Time Protocol** (NTP) protocol to sync system clock with **NTP servers**.

To synchronize the clock, the client machine should know the name of the **NTP servers** to connect. The name of the **NTP server** can be accessed through the following:

- Your organization if they are using it
- Your **Internet Service Provider** (ISP)

- From the **NTP** home page, you can find one or more public time servers in a hierarchy. There are **stratum1** and **startum2** time servers. Servers at stratum 1 can be called primary, which are directly synchronized to national time services via satellite, radio, and more. Servers at stratum 2 can be referred to as secondary servers, which synchronize themselves to stratum 1 servers, and the level further goes down in the hierarchy.
- You can join public servers from **pool.ntp.org.**

For clock synchronization, the **chronyd** service must always be running. View the current status of this service by typing the following:

```
systemctl status chronyd
```

Chronyd runs using a configuration file named **/etc/chrony.conf**. In the default configuration, the following entry specifies that that this client machine is synchronizing its time by using a pool of public servers:

```
pool 2.rhel.pool.ntp.org iburst
```

Here, **iburst** enables the aggressive mode, where the system will send multiple packets in case it detects **NTP** source unresponsive. If you made any changes to the configuration file, you must restart **chronyd** as follows:

```
systemctl restart chronyd
```

chronyd can also work as a server or a peer to provide time synchronization services to other computers in the network. **chronyc** is the command-line interface to monitor the working of **chronyd**. It can be used in interactive or non-interactive mode. When you simply type **chronyc** on the terminal, you are using it interactively. The following prompt appears in interactive mode, which is ready to accept many commands:

```
chronyc>
```

To use **chronyc** in non-interactive mode, execute it along with a command, as follows:

```
chronyc <command name>
```

The important command that is usually used is **sources.** Use it as follows, using the **-v** option that prints output in verbose mode:

```
chronyc sources -v
```

It will give you the output as shown in *Figure 18.3*. The output shows the list of **NTP servers** that is being polled by **chronyd**.

```
[visheshkumar@vmachine ~]$ chronyc sources -v

  .-- Source mode  '^' = server, '=' = peer, '#' = local clock.
 / .- Source state '*' = current best, '+' = combined, '-' = not combined,
| /             'x' = may be in error, '~' = too variable, '?' = unusable.
||                                                 .- xxxx [ yyyy ] +/- zzzz
||      Reachability register (octal) -.           |  xxxx = adjusted offset,
||      Log2(Polling interval) --.      |          |  yyyy = measured offset,
||                                \     |          |  zzzz = estimated error.
||                                 |    |           \
MS Name/IP address         Stratum Poll Reach LastRx Last sample
===============================================================================
^? time.cloudflare.com           0   6   377     -     +0ns[   +0ns] +/-    0ns
^? ntp5.mum-in.hosts.301-mo>     0   6   377     -     +0ns[   +0ns] +/-    0ns
^? time.cloudflare.com           0   6   377     -     +0ns[   +0ns] +/-    0ns
^? 144.24.146.96                 0   6   377     -     +0ns[   +0ns] +/-    0ns
[visheshkumar@vmachine ~]$ chronyc sources
MS Name/IP address         Stratum Poll Reach LastRx Last sample
===============================================================================
^? time.cloudflare.com           0   6   377     -     +0ns[   +0ns] +/-    0ns
^? ntp5.mum-in.hosts.301-mo>     0   6   377     -     +0ns[   +0ns] +/-    0ns
^? time.cloudflare.com           0   6   377     -     +0ns[   +0ns] +/-    0ns
^? 144.24.146.96                 0   6   377     -     +0ns[   +0ns] +/-    0ns
[visheshkumar@vmachine ~]$
```

Figure 18.3: *chronyc sources command printing the time sources*

Audit log

Linux Audit System is important to keep an eye on the security of the system and maintain it. It helps in keeping records of all the events that occurred in the system. It gathers vast amounts of information about events occurring in the system according to certain pre-defined rules known as **audit rules**. The collected information about events is recorded in text-based log files known as **audit logs**. The information written in the audit log is known as **audit trail**. Audit logs store who has done what operations on the system and who is responsible for generating what events. It does not play any role in enhancing the security of the system. Rather, it is used to track various user activities on the system; whether authorized or unauthorized, and all the events that occurred on the system. These audit logs are later reviewed by the system administrators to inform themselves of any security violations that occur. This information may be used to further enhance the security of the system.

Auditing the system is a requirement of security compliance like PCI-DSS, and more. Audit log keeps track of the following information:

- Date and time of the event occurring
- The identity of the user who triggered the event
- Any changes made to audit log file
- Any changes made to the audit config file

- Any unauthorized access attempt made to audit log file
- Addition of audit rule
- Any unauthorized access to system files
- Successful and unsuccessful attempts to log in to the system

Whenever an event is performed on the system, it is recorded in audit logs only if a related set of rules is found in the rule files. In the absence of rules related to specific events, no audit trails are generated. The amount of audit logs generated depends on the rules specified. Linux audit system is able to perform intensive logging. Too much auditing gives you more information but may impact performance in an adverse manner. So, one should choose what to audit and what not to audit. Audit rules must be written only for the system events that are important for you to log from a security perspective.

auditd is the daemon for the Linux Auditing System. It is responsible for writing audit records to the disk. It runs using the default configuration given in **/etc/audit/auditd.conf**, and the **argenrules** program reads the audit rules located in **/etc/audit/rules.d/** and compiles them into **/etc/audit/audit.rules**. Thus, the **/etc/audit/audit.rules** file is generated whenever the **auditd** service starts.

On the occurrence of any event in the system, **auditd** checks all the rules to match against the event that occurred. If any matching rule is found, it gathers more information about the event and creates an audit trail in the audit log file. The default audit log file where all the audit trails are stored is **/var/log/audit/audit.log**. Next, we will see how the default configuration of **auditd** can be customized.

Configuring Auditd

Audit logs are written to an audit file named **/var/log/audit/audit.log** whenever the rule against the current event is matched. If an audit log file cannot be written due to space issues or other reasons, you can choose whether to continue system operations. This may be configured in a configuration file named **/etc/audit/auditd.conf**. Let us view some of the important configuration options that are worth mentioning:

- **log_file**: It specifies the full path name of the log file where auditing events are stored. It defaults to **/var/log/audit/audit.log**.
- **max_log_file**: It specifies the maximum file size in megabytes. When this limit is reached, it will trigger an action set in **max_log_file_action**. It defaults to 8.
- **max_log_file_action**: This parameter tells the system what action to take when the audit log file has reached its maximum size as specified in **max_log_file**. Valid values that this parameter may take are **ignore**, **syslog**, **suspend**, **rotate** and **keep_logs**. It defaults to **ROTATE**.

- **num_logs:** It specifies the number of log files to keep if rotate is given in **max_log_file_action**. It defaults to 5.
- **space_left**: It specifies the amount of free space left in the filesystem containing the audit log file when the audit daemon takes the action specified by **space_left_action**. It defaults to 75.
- **space_left_action**: It specifies the action to take when the amount of free space reaches lower than the value specified in **space_left**. Valid values are **ignore**, **syslog**, **rotate**, **email**, **exec**, **suspend**, **single**, and **halt**. It defaults to **SYSLOG**. This is treated as a warning sign.
- **admin_space_left:** It specifies the amount of free space left on the filesystem (having audit log file) when the audit daemon must take the action specified in **admin_space_left_action**. The value of this parameter should be lower than the value set in **space_left**. It defaults to 50. This is the last chance for the administrator to do something before running out of disk space.
- **admin_space_left_action**: It specifies the action to take when the free space goes lower than the value specified in **admin_space_left**. Valid values are **ignore**, **syslog**, **rotate**, **email**, **exec**, **suspend**, **single**, and **halt**. It defaults to **SUSPEND**. **SUSPEND** means to stop writing audit records to the disk.
- **disk_full_action**: This parameter specifies what action to take when the partition where the audit log files are written has become full. Valid values are **ignore**, **syslog**, **rotate**, **exec**, **suspend**, **single**, and **halt**. It defaults to **SUSPEND**.
- **disk_error_action**: This parameter tells the system what action to take when there is an error condition on disk while writing audit events to disk or rotating logs. Valid values are **ignore**, **syslog**, **exec**, **suspend**, **single**, and **halt**. It defaults to **SUSPEND**.

Managing auditd

To turn on auditing, **auditd** must be running. We cannot use the **systemctl** command for every operation to manage **auditd**. The **systemctl** command can only be used to enable and start the **auditd** service and to view its running status. For the rest of the operations on **auditd**, we must use the **service** command as follows:

```
service auditd <action>
```

Where **<action>** can be stop, restart, reload, rotate, resume, and more.

For example, the following command stops **auditd** service:

```
service auditd stop
```

We also have **auditctl** utility to manage the **auditd** daemon and control its behavior. This tool is also used to control many settings and parameters of **auditd** in runtime. In the next section, we will see the usage of **auditctl** to create new audit rules.

Defining rules

Audit rule file is an important component of Audit system. By default, **auditd** runs with several pre-configured rules. **auditd** generates several audit trails in audit logs. Audit rules can be set either on the command line using the **auditctl** utility or in the rule file under the **/etc/audit/rules.d/** directory. In this section, we will discuss managing audit rules both ways.

Let us create a rule that will generate audit records whenever deletion of files under **/var/tmp** occurs on the system. We will use **auditctl** utility to do so, as follows:

```
auditctl -a always,exit -F dir=/var/tmp -F arch=b64 -S unlink -S rename -S
rmdir -k delete_vartmp
```

The previous rule is a **syscall** rule that creates audit log entry on the deletion of any files from the directory **/var/tmp**. Audit log entry is created when a file is deleted on the occurrence of a specified **syscall** event. The name of the **syscall** is mentioned using the **-S** option. The multiple **-S** option may be used to generate audit records on the occurrence of all the specified **syscalls**. **-k** is used to provide a key to the audit record. Key is just a random text string that you may want to be inserted along with the audit trail to help identify itself. **-F** is used to specify fields to match against. It accepts many fields in the form of **field_name=value**. Here, the **dir** field is used to provide the name of the directory to match against.

Rules configured using **auditctl** do not persist across reboots. To define audit rules that persist across reboots, they must be included in a rule file under the **/etc/audit/rules.d/** directory and use the **augenrules** program to read rule files from this directory. Only files having the extension **.rules** are read. To make the preceding rule permanent, append the following line at the end of the **/etc/audit/rules.d/audit.rules** file.

```
-a always,exit -F dir=/var/tmp -S unlink -S rename -S rmdir -k delete_
vartmp
```

For the testing purpose, create a directory named **todelete** under **/var/tmp**. Now, delete it using the **rmdir** command. This operation will generate the audit trail in the audit log file.

Let us execute the following command to view the audit trail produced during the execution of the **rmdir** command.

```
ausearch -k delete_vartmp
```

The preceding command searches and prints the audit logs that match the given key. The output produced the result in many fields. You must interpret the produced result properly to gain the most out of it. The next section discusses how to view and interpret audit trails.

Viewing audit log

Keeping audit records is of no use if it has not been reviewed and analyzed. Analyzing audit logs helps in further strengthening the security of the system. Monitoring audit records informs the administrator of any failed login attempts made to access the system. It also informs the administrator of any potential security breaches. So, it becomes very important to read and interpret the gathered audit logs. The audit logs are too big to read and analyze them using a text editor or a pager. Instead, you can use **ausearch** to search the audit logs according to a given criteria and **aureport** to generate summary reports out of the existing audit logs.

Retype the command that we used earlier:

```
ausearch -k delete_vartmp
```

The preceding command searches the audit log and fetches records where the key matches **'delete_vartmp'** and produces the output as given in *Figure 18.4*:

```
time->Mon Aug 28 16:40:43 2023
type=PROCTITLE msg=audit(1693221043.321:1960): proctitle=617564697463746C002D6100616C776179732C65786974002D4600646972002F7661722F746D70002D460061726368006236
4002D5300756E6C696E6B002D530072656E616D65002D5300726D646972002D6B0064656C6574655F766172746D70
type=SOCKADDR msg=audit(1693221043.321:1960): saddr=100000000000000000000000
type=SYSCALL msg=audit(1693221043.321:1960): arch=c000003e syscall=44 success=yes exit=1080 a0=4 a1=7ffc43d7c870 a2=438 a3=0 items=0 ppid=6116 pid=20267 auid=
1000 uid=0 gid=0 euid=0 suid=0 fsuid=0 egid=0 sgid=0 fsgid=0 tty=pts1 ses=2 comm="auditctl" exe="/usr/sbin/auditctl" subj=unconfined_u:unconfined_r:unconfined
_t:s0-s0:c0.c1023 key=(null)
type=CONFIG_CHANGE msg=audit(1693221043.321:1960): auid=1000 ses=2 subj=unconfined_u:unconfined_r:unconfined_t:s0-s0:c0.c1023 op=add_rule key="delete_vartmp"
list=4 res=1
----
time->Mon Aug 28 16:41:04 2023
type=PROCTITLE msg=audit(1693221064.049:1961): proctitle=726D646972006868
type=PATH msg=audit(1693221064.049:1961): item=1 name="hh" inode=34813599 dev=fd:00 mode=040755 ouid=0 ogid=0 rdev=00:00 obj=unconfined_u:object_r:user_tmp_t:
s0 nametype=DELETE cap_fp=0 cap_fi=0 cap_fe=0 cap_fver=0 cap_frootid=0
type=PATH msg=audit(1693221064.049:1961): item=0 name="/var/tmp" inode=16864055 dev=fd:00 mode=041777 ouid=0 ogid=0 rdev=00:00 obj=system_u:object_r:tmp_t:s0
nametype=PARENT cap_fp=0 cap_fi=0 cap_fe=0 cap_fver=0 cap_frootid=0
type=CWD msg=audit(1693221064.049:1961): cwd="/var/tmp"
type=SYSCALL msg=audit(1693221064.049:1961): arch=c000003e syscall=84 success=yes exit=0 a0=7ffd88677737 a1=1 a2=7f84a136dc80 a3=55b1a4f09340 items=2 ppid=239
4 pid=20270 auid=1000 uid=0 gid=0 euid=0 suid=0 fsuid=0 egid=0 sgid=0 fsgid=0 tty=pts0 ses=2 comm="rmdir" exe="/usr/bin/rmdir" subj=unconfined_u:unconfined_r:
unconfined_t:s0-s0:c0.c1023 key="delete_vartmp"
----
```

***Figure 18.4**: Audit trails filtered by ausearch utility*

Let us interpret the audit trail shown in *Figure 18.4*. Here, the audit entries generated due to two system events are logged. One event generated multiple audit trails. The audit trails related to each system event are separated by **----** (4 dashes). All the log entries belonging to one event carry the same timestamp and serial number. The first logged event has generated 4 log records, while the second event has generated 5 audit entries. The first audit event is produced when we add the audit rule using the given key. It is confirmed with the **op=add_rule** field given in the log entry of the first event listed in the given figure. The second set of audit trails is generated when **rmdir** syscall is issued on the system and our new rule matches this event.

Each audit record carries multiple fields. To understand the information collected in each audit record, the meaning of each field should be properly understood. To interpret the meaning of the given audit record, you can run **ausearch** using the **-i** option, which converts the numeric value given in some of the fields to a meaningful text or description.

Let us pass the preceding command to the interpreter, as follows:

```
ausearch -i -k delete_vartmp
```

And you will get output as shown in *Figure 18.5*, which is more understandable:

```
type=PROCTITLE msg=audit(28/08/23 16:40:43.321:1960) : proctitle=auditctl -a always,exit -F dir /var/tmp -F arch b64 -S unlink -S rename -S rmdir -k delete_va
rtmp
type=SOCKADDR msg=audit(28/08/23 16:40:43.321:1960) : saddr={ saddr fam=netlink nlnk-fam=16 nlnk-pid=0 }
type=SYSCALL msg=audit(28/08/23 16:40:43.321:1960) : arch=x86_64 syscall=sendto success=yes exit=1080 a0=0x4 a1=0x7ffc43d7c870 a2=0x438 a3=0x0 items=0 ppid=61
16 pid=20267 auid=visheshkumar uid=root gid=root euid=root suid=root fsuid=root egid=root sgid=root fsgid=root tty=pts1 ses=2 comm=auditctl exe=/usr/sbin/audi
tctl subj=unconfined_u:unconfined_r:unconfined_t:s0-s0:c0.c1023 key=(null)
type=CONFIG_CHANGE msg=audit(28/08/23 16:40:43.321:1960) : auid=visheshkumar ses=2 subj=unconfined_u:unconfined_r:unconfined_t:s0-s0:c0.c1023 op=add_rule key=
delete vartmp list=exit res=yes
----
type=PROCTITLE msg=audit(28/08/23 16:41:04.049:1961) : proctitle=rmdir hh
type=PATH msg=audit(28/08/23 16:41:04.049:1961) : item=1 name=hh inode=34813599 dev=fd:00 mode=dir,755 ouid=root ogid=root rdev=00:00 obj=unconfined_u:object_
r:user tmp t:s0 nametype=DELETE cap fp=none cap fi=none cap fe=0 cap fver=0 cap frootid=0
type=PATH msg=audit(28/08/23 16:41:04.049:1961) : item=0 name=/var/tmp inode=16864055 dev=fd:00 mode=dir,sticky,777 ouid=root ogid=root rdev=00:00 obj=system_
u:object_r:tmp_t:s0 nametype=PARENT cap_fp=none cap_fi=none cap_fe=0 cap_fver=0 cap_frootid=0
type=CWD msg=audit(28/08/23 16:41:04.049:1961) : cwd=/var/tmp
type=SYSCALL msg=audit(28/08/23 16:41:04.049:1961) : arch=x86_64 syscall=rmdir success=yes exit=0 a0=0x7ffd88677737 a1=0x1 a2=0x7f84a136dc80 a3=0x55b1a4f09340
 items=2 ppid=2394 pid=20270 auid=visheshkumar uid=root gid=root euid=root suid=root fsuid=root egid=root sgid=root fsgid=root tty=pts0 ses=2 comm=rmdir exe=/
usr/bin/rmdir subj=unconfined_u:unconfined_r:unconfined_t:s0-s0:c0.c1023 key=delete_vartmp
----
```

Figure 18.5: Audit trails produced using interpret option of ausearch

Each audit log entry starts with the **`type`** field, which stores the type of the audit record. Let us understand the meaning of a few important fields given in the previous figure:

- **`type=syscall`** specifies that the current audit record is triggered by a system call to the kernel.
- **`type=cwd`** records the current working directory when the system call was executed.
- **`type=PROCTITLE`** holds the full command line that triggered this audit event.
- **`proctitle`** field holds the command line that generated this audit event.
- **`msg`** field holds a time stamp and a unique event id of the record in the form audit (**`time_stamp:eventID`**). Multiple records can share the same time stamp and event id if they were generated as part of the same audit event.
- **`success`** field records whether the system call recorded in the particular event succeeded or failed.
- **`exit`** field contains a value that specifies the exit code returned by the system call.
- **`ppid`** and **`pid`** are the **`ppid`** and **`pid`** of the process, respectively, that triggered this event.
- **`auid`** is the id of the user who initiated this event.
- **`tty`** is the terminal from which the command is invoked.
- **`comm`** is the name of the command that writes this log event.
- **`exec`** records the path of the executable that caused this event.
- **`subj`** records the SELinux context.
- **`key`** specifies an identification string associated with this log event.

Using aureport

The **aureport** tool is used to generate a summary report for all the audit events. You can also use this tool to generate summary reports on specific events. Different options are used to generate different reports. Some of the options that can be used with the **aureport** tool are listed as follows:

- **--auth**: To report about authentication attempts
- **--comm**: To report about the commands run
- **--config**: To report about config changes
- **--host**: To report about hosts
- **--i**: To interpret numeric entities into text
- **-k**: To report about audit rule keys
- **--login**: To report about logins
- **-m**: To report about account modifications
- **-p**: To report about processes
- **-s**: To report about syscalls
- **-x**: To report about executables
- **-ts [start-date] [start-time]**: To search for events with time stamps equal to or after the given start time
- **-te [end-date] [end-time]**: To search for events with time stamps equal to or before the given end time

Using ausearch

Another tool of great interest is **ausearch**. This tool is used to filter the audit records based on certain criteria. You can execute **ausearch** using different options to filter the records. Options provide a way to specify the criteria for **ausearch**. Some of the important options are listed as follows:

- **-a <event_id>**: Search for an event based on the given event ID
- **--comm <comm-name>**: Search for an audit event based on the given command name
- **--exit <exit-code>**: Search for an audit event based on the given exit code
- **--host <host-name>**: Search for an event with the given hostname

- **-i**: Interpret numbers into meaningful text
- **-k <key-string>**: Search for an event based on the given key string
- **--message <message-type>**: Search for the event based on the given message type
- **-te [end-date] [end-time]**: Search for events with time stamps equal to or before the given end time
- **-ts [start-date] [start-time]**: Search for events with time stamps equal to or after the given start time
- **--success <success-value>**: Search for an event matching the given success value. Success-value can be **yes** and **no**

The following command searches audit logs on the basis of command name:

```
ausearch --comm rmdir
```

Changing kernel parameters

Kernel parameters control the behavior and configuration of the **Linux kernel**. The settings of **kernel parameters** can affect system performance, security, and functionality. We can adjust the value of **kernel parameters** according to the organization's needs. One should know the implications of changing any of the kernel parameters.

In RHEL9, **systemd-sysctl.service** is used to configure **kernel parameters**. It reads configuration files from the following directories in the given order to load settings from all system configuration files:

```
/etc/sysctl.d/*.conf
/run/sysctl.d/*.conf
/usr/local/lib/sysctl.d/*.conf
/usr/lib/sysctl.d/*.conf
/etc/sysctl.conf
```

Only files with the **.conf** extension are read. Once a file of a given filename is loaded, any file of the same name in subsequent directories is ignored.

To view the current settings of kernel parameters or change any of them, you can use either of the following:

- The `sysctl` command
- The virtual filesystem mounted on `/proc/sys`

Both the above ways would apply the changes immediately on the running system, but these changes are lost when system reboots. To view the list of all the **kernel parameters** and their current settings, type the following:

```
sysctl -a
```

Now, you will get output as shown in *Figure 18.6*:

```
dev.hpet.max-user-freq = 64
dev.raid.speed_limit_max = 200000
dev.raid.speed_limit_min = 1000
dev.scsi.logging_level = 0
dev.tty.ldisc_autoload = 1
fs.aio-max-nr = 65536
fs.aio-nr = 2661
fs.binfmt_misc.status = enabled
fs.dentry-state = 112661        87435   45      0       19873   0
fs.dir-notify-enable = 1
fs.epoll.max_user_watches = 2154674
fs.fanotify.max_queued_events = 16384
fs.fanotify.max_user_groups = 128
fs.fanotify.max_user_marks = 80450
fs.file-max = 9223372036854775807
fs.file-nr = 8288       0       9223372036854775807
fs.inode-nr = 93124     792
fs.inode-state = 93124  792     0       0       0       0       0
```

Figure 18.6: List of few kernel parameters

Figure 18.6 shows that the kernel parameter name is formed using many dots (**.**). Each dot can be said to signify a subdirectory inside **/proc/sys**. For example, take the **fs.aio-nr** parameter. Under **/proc/sys**, you will have a corresponding file **fs/aio-nr**. Take an example of another parameter, say **dev.scsi.logging_level**. Under **/proc/sys**, we will have the corresponding file **dev/scsi/logging_level**. Let us verify them using the **ls** command, as follows:

```
ls /proc/sys/dev/scsi
logging_level


ls -l /proc/sys/fs/aio-nr
-r--r--r--. 1 root root 0 Aug 29 10:38 /proc/sys/fs/aio-nr
```

To change the value of any kernel parameter, you can use the **sysctl** command as follows:

```
sysctl <parameter name> = <parameter value>
```

Now, change the kernel parameter **fs.nr_open**, which determines the maximum number of file handles a process can allocate. Let us view the current setting by providing the parameter name with the **sysctl** command, as follows:

```
sysctl fs.nr_open
fs.nr_open = 1073741816
```

You can also view the current setting using **/proc/sys**, as follows:

```
cat /proc/sys/fs/nr_open
1073741816
```

To change the value of this parameter to 1048576, type the following:

```
sysctl fs.nr_open=1048576
fs.nr_open = 1048576
```

To change the current parameter setting using **/proc/sys**, execute the following:

```
echo 1073741816 > /proc/sys/fs/nr_open
```

To verify the change, view the current value of the parameter, say **fs.nr_open**, by typing the following:

```
sysctl fs.nr_open
```

or,

```
cat /proc/sys/fs/nr_open
```

The previous methods make temporary changes in the **kernel parameters**. To persist changes in the **kernel** parameters, we must edit the **/etc/sysctl.conf** file. This file contains the settings in the form **parameter=value**. Add your settings in this file in the given format, as follows:

```
fs.nr_open = 1048576
```

To apply the changes made in the file on the current boot, issue the following:

```
sysctl -p /etc/sysctl.conf
```

Conclusion

At first, we learned about mutt, which is a very powerful text-based email client used to read and send electronic emails. It is also very simple to configure and use. Next, we talked about various command-line tools to fetch detailed information about the available hardware. We also learned how to write udev rules to provide persistent naming to devices.

This chapter also discussed the **auditd** daemon that reads audit rules file and matches the rules against the current system event to generate audit logs. Audit rules determines what is captured in the audit log file. Rules written under **/etc/audit/rules.d/** are read during the startup of auditd and are compiled in **/etc/audit/audit.rules**. These audit logs are later reviewed and analyzed by the system administrator to detect any suspicious activity. **Kernel parameter** determines the system behavior and performance. To temporarily change **kernel parameters** in the current session, use the **sysctl** command. To make the current value of the parameter permanent so that it remains available across reboots, edit the **/etc/sysctl.conf** file.

References

https://access.redhat.com/documentation/en-us/red_hat_enterprise_linux/6/html/deployment_guide/s1-sysinfo-filesystems#s2-sysinfo-filesystems-lsblk

Join our book's Discord space

Join the book's Discord Workspace for Latest updates, Offers, Tech happenings around the world, New Release and Sessions with the Authors:

https://discord.bpbonline.com

Index

M

R

T

U